Kaplan Publishing are constantly find ways to make a difference to your studies and our exciting online resources really different to students looking for exam success.

This book comes with free EN-gage online resources so that you can study anytime, anywhere.

Having purchased this book, you have access to the following online study materials:

CONTENT	ACCA (including FFA,FAB,FMA)		AAT		FIA (excluding FFA,FAB,FMA)	
	Text	Kit	Text	Kit	Text	Kit
iPaper version of the book	✓	✓	✓	✓	✓	✓
Interactive electronic version of the book	✓					
Fixed tests / progress tests with instant answers	✓		✓			
Mock assessments online			✓	✓		
Material updates	✓	✓	✓	✓	✓	✓
Latest official ACCA exam questions		✓				
Extra question assistance using the signpost icon*		✓				
Timed questions with an online tutor debrief using the clock icon*		✓				
Interim assessment including questions and answers		✓			✓	
Technical articles	✓	✓			✓	✓

* Excludes F1, F2, F3, FFA, FAB, FMA

How to access your online resources

Kaplan Financial students will already have a Kaplan EN-gage account and these extra resources will be available to you online. You do not need to register again, as this process was completed when you enrolled. If you are having problems accessing online materials, please ask your course administrator.

If you are already a registered Kaplan EN-gage user go to www.EN-gage.co.uk and log in. Select the 'add a book' feature and enter the ISBN number of this book and the unique pass key at the bottom of this card. Then click 'finished' or 'add another book'. You may add as many books as you have purchased from this screen.

If you purchased through Kaplan Flexible Learning or via the Kaplan Publishing website you will automatically receive an e-mail invitation to Kaplan EN·gage online. Please register your details using this email to gain access to your content. If you do not receive the e-mail or book content, please contact Kaplan Flexible Learning.

If you are a new Kaplan EN-gage user register at www.EN-gage.co.uk and click on the link contained in the email we sent you to activate your account. Then select the 'add a book' feature, enter the ISBN number of this book and the unique pass key at the bottom of this card. Then click 'finished' or 'add another book'.

Your Code and Information

This code can only be used once for the registration of one book online. This registration and your online content will expire when the final sittings for the examinations covered by this book have taken place. Please allow one hour from the time you submit your book details for us to process your request.

Please scratch the film to access your EN-gage code.

Please be aware that this code is case-sensitive and you will need to include the dashes within the passcode, but not when entering the ISBN. For further technical support, please visit www.EN-gage.co.uk

ACCA

Paper F6

Taxation

Complete Text

Finance Act 2012
for 2013 examination sittings

British library cataloguing-in-publication data

A catalogue record for this book is available from the British Library.

Published by:
Kaplan Publishing UK
Unit 2 The Business Centre
Molly Millars Lane
Wokingham
Berkshire
RG41 2QZ

ISBN 978-0-85732-661-4

Printed and bound in Great Britain.

Acknowledgements

We are grateful to the Association of Chartered Certified Accountants for permission to reproduce past examination questions. The answers have been prepared by Kaplan Publishing.

Contents

KAPLAN PUBLISHING

Paper Introduction

How to Use the Materials

These Kaplan Publishing learning materials have been carefully designed to make your learning experience as easy as possible and to give you the best chances of success in your examinations.

The product range contains a number of features to help you in the study process. They include:

(1) Detailed study guide and syllabus objectives

(2) Description of the examination

(3) Study skills and revision guidance

(4) Complete text or essential text

(5) Question practice

The sections on the study guide, the syllabus objectives, the examination and study skills should all be read before you commence your studies. They are designed to familiarise you with the nature and content of the examination and give you tips on how to best approach your learning.

The **complete text or essential text** comprises the main learning materials and gives guidance as to the importance of topics and where other related resources can be found. Each chapter includes:

- The **learning objectives**, which have been carefully mapped to the examining body's own syllabus learning objectives or outcomes. You should use these to check you have a clear understanding of all the topics on which you might be assessed in the examination.

- The **chapter diagram** which provides a visual reference for the content in the chapter, giving an overview of the topics and how they link together.

- The **content** for each topic area which commences with a brief explanation or definition to put the topic into context before covering the topic in detail. You should follow your studying of the content with a review of the example. These are worked examples which will help you to understand better how to apply the content for the topic.

- **Test your understanding** sections which provide an opportunity to assess your understanding of the key topics by applying what you have learned to short questions. Answers can be found at the back of each chapter.

KAPLAN PUBLISHING

- **Summary diagrams** at the end which show the important links between topics and the overall content of the paper. These diagrams should be used to check that you have covered and understood the core topics before moving on.

- **Questions to practice** are provided at the back of the text.

Icon Explanations

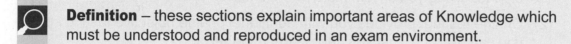 **Definition** – these sections explain important areas of Knowledge which must be understood and reproduced in an exam environment.

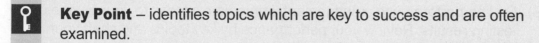 **Key Point** – identifies topics which are key to success and are often examined.

Expandable Text – within this complete text and in the online version expandable text provides a more detailed explanation of key terms. These sections are printed in the text, and appear hidden in the online version but can be shown on screen. They will help to provide a deeper understanding of core areas. Reference to this text is vital when self studying.

Test Your Understanding – following key points and definitions are exercises which give the opportunity to assess the understanding of these core areas. Within the text the answers to these sections are at the end of the chapter, within the online version the answers can be hidden or shown on screen to enable repetition of activities.

Example – to help develop an understanding of topics the illustrative examples can be used and the Test Your Understanding (TYU) exercises.

Exclamation Mark – this symbol signifies a topic which can be more difficult to understand. You may need to take extra time to carefully review these areas in detail.

On-line subscribers

Our on-line resources are designed to increase the flexibility of your learning materials and provide you with immediate feedback on how your studies are progressing.

If you are subscribed to our on-line resources you will find:

(1) On-line reference material: reproduces your Complete or Essential Text on-line, giving you anytime, anywhere access.

(2) On-line testing: provides you with additional on-line objective testing so you can practice what you have learned further.

(3) On-line performance management: immediate access to your on-line testing results. Review your performance by key topics and chart your achievement through the course relative to your peer group.

Ask your local customer services staff if you are not already a subscriber and wish to join.

KAPLAN PUBLISHING

Syllabus

Paper background

The aim of ACCA Paper F6, **Taxation**, is to develop knowledge and skills relating to the tax system as applicable to individuals, single companies and groups of companies.

Objectives of the syllabus

- Explain the operation and scope of the tax system.

- Explain and compute the income tax liabilities of individuals.

- Explain and compute the corporation tax liabilities of individual companies and groups of companies.

- Explain and compute the chargeable gains arising on companies and individuals.

- Explain and compute the inheritance tax liabilities of individuals.

- Explain and compute the effect of national insurance contributions on employees, employers and the self employed.

- Explain and compute the effects of value added tax on incorporated and unincorporated businesses.

- Identify and explain the obligations of tax payers and/or their agents and the implications of non-compliance.

Core areas of the syllabus

- The UK tax system

- Income tax liabilities

- Corporation tax liabilities

- Chargeable gains

- Inheritance tax

- National insurance contributions

- Value added tax

- The obligations of tax payers and/or their agents.

Syllabus objectives

We have reproduced the ACCA's syllabus below, showing where the objectives are explored within this book. Within the chapters, we have broken down the extensive information found in the syllabus into easily digestible and relevant sections, called Content Objectives. These correspond to the objectives at the beginning of each chapter.

Syllabus learning objective	Chapter reference

A   THE UK TAX SYSTEM

1   The overall function and purpose of taxation in a modern economy

(a) Describe the purpose (economic, social, etc) of taxation in a modern economy.[2]   1

2   Different types of taxes

(a) Identify the different types of capital and revenue tax.[1]   1

(b) Explain the difference between direct and indirect taxation.[2]   1

3   Principal sources of revenue law and practice

(a) Describe the overall structure of the UK tax system.[1]   1

(b) State the different sources of revenue law.[1]   1

(c) Appreciate the interaction of the UK tax system with that of other tax jurisdictions.[2]   1

4   Tax avoidance and tax evasion

(a) Explain the difference between tax avoidance and tax evasion.[1]   1

(b) Explain the need for an ethical and professional approach.[2]   1

Excluded topics:

- Anti-avoidance legislation.

KAPLAN PUBLISHING

B   INCOME TAX LIABILITIES

1   The scope of income tax

(a) Explain how the residence of an individual is determined.[1]   2

Excluded topics:

- The treatment of a person who comes to the UK to work or a person who leaves the UK to take up employment overseas.

- Foreign income, non-residents and double taxation relief.

- Income from trusts and settlements.

- Child benefit income tax charge.

2   Income from employment

(a) Recognise the factors that determine whether an engagement is treated as employment or self-employment. [2]   4

(b) Recognise the basis of assessment for employment income.[2]   4

(c) Compute the income assessable.[2]   4

(d) Recognise the allowable deductions, including travelling expenses.[2]   4

(e) Discuss the use of the statutory approved mileage allowances.[2]   4

(f) Explain the PAYE system.[1]   12

(g) Identify P11D employees.[1]   4

(h) Compute the amount of benefits assessable.[2]   4

(i) Explain the purpose of a dispensation from HM Revenue & Customs.[2]   4

(j) Explain how charitable giving can be made through a payroll deduction scheme.[1]   4

Excluded topics:

- The calculation of a car benefit where emission figures are not available.

- The exemption for zero emission company motor cars

- Share and share option incentive schemes for employees.

- Payments on the termination of employment, and other lump sums received by employees.

3   Income from self employment

(ii) Compute the assessable profits for each partner following a change in the profit-sharing ratio.[2]   8

(iii) Compute the assessable profits for each partner following a change in the membership of the partnership.[2]   8

(iv) Describe the alternative loss relief claims that are available to partners.[1]   9

(v) Explain the loss relief restriction that applies to the partners of a limited liability partnership.[1]   9

Excluded topics:

- The 100% allowance for expenditure on renovating business premises in disadvantaged areas, flats above shops and water technologies.

- Capital allowances for industrial buildings, agricultural buildings, patents, scientific research and know-how.

- Capital allowances for motor cars already owned at 6 April 2009 (1 April 2009 for companies).

- Apportionment in order to determine the rate of writing down allowance or the amount of annual investment allowance where a period of account spans 6 April 2012 (1 April 2012 for companies).

- Enterprise zones.

- Investment income of a partnership.

- The allocation of notional profits and losses for a partnership.

- Farmers averaging of profits.

- The averaging of profits for authors and creative artists.

- Loss relief for shares in unquoted trading companies.

4 Property and investment income

(a) Compute property business profits.[2]   3

(b) Explain the treatment of furnished holiday lettings.[1]   3

(c) Describe rent-a-room relief.[1]   3

(d) Compute the amount assessable when a premium is received for the grant of a short lease.[2]   3

(e) Understand how relief for a property business loss is given.[2]   3

(f) Compute the tax payable on savings income.[2]   2 & 3

(g) Compute the tax payable on dividend income.[2]   2 & 3

(h) Explain the treatment of individual savings accounts (ISAs) and other tax exempt investments.[1]   2 & 3

Excluded topics:

- The deduction for expenditure by landlords on energy-saving items.

- Premiums for granting subleases.

- Junior ISAs.

5 The comprehensive computation of taxable income and income tax liability

(a) Prepare a basic income tax computation involving different types of income.[2]   2 & 3

(b) Calculate the amount of personal allowance available generally, and for people aged 65 and above.[2]   2

(c) Compute the amount of income tax payable.[2]   2

(d) Explain the treatment of interest paid for a qualifying purpose.[2]   2

(e) Explain the treatment of gift aid donations.[1]   2

(f) Explain the treatment of property owned jointly by a married couple, or by a couple in a civil partnership.[1]   2

Excluded topics:

- The blind person's allowance and the married couple's allowance.

- Tax credits.

- Maintenance payments.

- The income of minor children.

6 The use of exemptions and reliefs in deferring and minimising income tax liabilities

(a) Explain and compute the relief given for contributions to personal pension schemes, using the rules applicable from 6 April 2011.[2]   10

(b) Describe the relief given for contributions to occupational pension schemes, using the rules applicable from 6 April 2011.[1]   10

(c) Explain how a married couple or couple in a civil partnership can minimise their tax liabilities.[2]   3

Excluded topics:

- The conditions that must be met in order for a pension scheme to obtain approval from HM Revenue & Customs.

- The enterprise investment scheme and the SEED enterprise investment scheme.

- Venture capital trusts.

- Tax reduction scheme for gifts of pre-eminent objects.

C CORPORATION TAX LIABILITIES

1 The scope of corporation tax

Excluded topics:

- Investment companies.

- Close companies.

- Companies in receivership or liquidation.

- Reorganisations.

- The purchase by a company of its own shares.

- Personal service companies.

2 Taxable total profits

- Controlled foreign companies.

- Foreign companies trading in the UK.

- Expense relief in respect of overseas tax.

- The set off of qualifying charitable donations and losses for the purposes of calculating double taxation relief.

- Transfer pricing transactions not involving an overseas company.

5   The use of exemptions and reliefs in deferring and minimising corporation tax liabilities.

The use of such exemptions and reliefs is implicit within all of the above sections 1 to 4 of part C of the syllabus, concerning corporation tax.

D   CHARGEABLE GAINS

1   The scope of the taxation of capital gains

   (a) Describe the scope of capital gains tax.[2]   13

   (b) Explain how the residence and ordinary residence of an individual is determined.[2]   13

   (c) List those assets which are exempt.[1]   13

Excluded topics:

- Assets situated overseas and double taxation relief.

- Partnership capital gains.

2   The basic principles of computing gains and losses.

   (a) Compute capital gains for both individuals and companies.[2]   13 & 20

   (b) Calculate the indexation allowance available to companies.[2]   20

   (c) Explain the treatment of capital losses for both individuals and companies.[1]   13 & 20

   (d) Explain the treatment of transfers between a husband and wife or between a couple in a civil partnership.[2]   14

(e) Compute the amount of allowable expenditure for a part disposal.[2]

14

(f) Explain the treatment where an asset is damaged, lost or destroyed, and the implications of receiving insurance proceeds and reinvesting such proceeds.[2]

14

Excluded topics:

- Small part disposals of land.

- Losses in the year of death.

- Relief for losses incurred on loans made to traders.

- Negligible value claims.

3 Gains and losses on the disposal of movable and immovable property

(a) Identify when chattels and wasting assets are exempt.[1]

14

(b) Compute the chargeable gain when a chattel is disposed of.[2]

14

(c) Calculate the chargeable gain when a wasting asset is disposed of.[2]

14

(d) Compute the exemption when a principal private residence is disposed of.[2]

16

(e) Calculate the chargeable gain when a principal private residence has been used for business purposes.[2]

16

(f) Identify the amount of letting relief available when a principal private residence has been let out.[2]

16

Excluded topics:

- The disposal of leases and the creation of sub-leases.

4 Gains and losses on the disposal of shares and securities

(a) Calculate the value of quoted shares where they are disposed of by way of a gift.[2]

15

(b) Explain and apply the identification rules as they apply to individuals and to companies, including the same day, nine day, and thirty day matching rules.[2]

15 & 20

(c) Explain the pooling provisions.[2]

15 & 20

KAPLAN PUBLISHING

(d) Explain the treatment of bonus issues, rights issues, takeovers and reorganisations.[2]　　　　　15 & 20

(e) Explain the exemption available for gilt-edged securities and qualifying corporate bonds [1]　　　　　15

Excluded topics:

- A detailed question on the pooling provisions for shares as they apply to limited companies.

- The small part disposal rules applicable to rights issues.

- Substantial shareholdings.

- Gilt-edged securities and qualifying corporate bonds other than the fact that they are exempt.

5   The computation of the capital gains tax payable by individuals

(a) Compute the amount of capital gains tax payable.[2]　　　　　13

6   The use of exemptions and reliefs in deferring and minimising tax liabilities arising on the disposal of capital assets

(a) Explain and apply Entrepreneurs' relief as it applies to individuals.[2]　　　　　16

(b) Explain and apply rollover relief as it applies to individuals and companies.[2]　　　　　16 & 20

(c) Explain and apply holdover relief for the gift of business assets.[2]　　　　　16

(d) Explain and apply the incorporation relief that is available upon the transfer of a business to a company.[2]　　　　　16

Excluded topics:

- Reinvestment relief.

- Entrepreneurs' relief for associated disposals.

E **INHERITANCE TAX**

1 The scope of inheritance tax

   (a) Describe the scope of inheritance tax.[2]   17

   (b) Identify and explain the persons chargeable.[2]   17

Excluded topics:

- Pre 18 March 1986 lifetime transfers.

- Transfers of value by close companies.

- Domicile, deemed domicile, and non-UK domiciled individuals.

- Trusts.

2 The basic principles of computing transfers of value

   (a) State, explain and apply the meaning of transfer of value, chargeable transfer and potentially exempt transfer.[2]   17

   (b) Demonstrate the diminution in value principle.[2]   17

   (c) Demonstrate the seven year accumulation principle taking into account changes in the level of the nil rate band.[2]   17

Excluded topics:

- Excluded property.

- Related property.

- The tax implications of the location of assets.

- Gifts with reservation of benefit.

- Associated operations.

3 The liabilities arising on chargeable lifetime transfers and on the death of an individual

   (a) Understand the tax implications of chargeable lifetime transfers and compute the relevant liabilities.[2]   17

   (b) Understand the tax implications of transfers within seven years of death and compute the relevant liabilities.[2]   17

   (c) Compute the tax liability on a death estate.[2]   17

   (d) Understand and apply the transfer of any unused nil rate band between spouses.[2]   17

KAPLAN PUBLISHING

Excluded topics:

- Specific rules for the valuation of assets (values will be provided).
- Business property relief.
- Agricultural relief.
- Relief for the fall in value of lifetime gifts.
- Quick succession relief.
- Double tax relief.
- Variation of wills and disclaimers of legacies.
- Grossing up on death.
- Post mortem reliefs.
- Double charges legislation.
- The reduced rate of inheritance tax payable on death when a proportion of a person's estate is bequeathed to charity.

4 The use of exemptions in deferring and minimising inheritance tax liabilities

   (a) Understand and apply the following exemptions:

      (i)   small gifts exemption[2]   17

      (ii) annual exemption[2]   17

      (iii) normal expenditure out of income[2]   17

      (iv) gifts in consideration of marriage[2]   17

      (v) gifts between spouses.[2]   17

Excluded topics:

- Gifts to charities.
- Gifts to political parties.
- Gifts for national purposes.

5 Payment of inheritance tax

   (a) Identify who is responsible for the payment of inheritance tax.[2]   17

   (b) Advise the due date for payment of inheritance tax.[2]   17

Excluded topics:

- Administration of inheritance tax other than listed above.
- The instalment option for the payment of tax.
- Interest and penalties.

KAPLAN PUBLISHING

3   The computation of VAT liabilities

    (a) Explain how VAT is accounted for and administered.[2]   26

    (b) Recognise the tax point when goods or services are supplied.[2]   25

    (c) List the information that must be given on a VAT invoice.[1]   26

    (d) Explain and apply the principles regarding the valuation of supplies.[2]   25

    (e) Recognise the circumstances in which input VAT is non-deductible.[2]   25

    (f) Compute the relief that is available for impairment losses on trade debts.[2]   25

    (g) Explain the circumstances in which the default surcharge, a penalty for an incorrect VAT return, and default interest will be applied.[1]   26

    (h) Explain the treatment of imports, exports and trade within the European Union.   26

Excluded topics:

- VAT periods where there is a change of VAT rate.

- Partial exemption.

- In respect of property and land: leases, do-it-yourself builders, and a landlord's option to tax.

- Penalties apart from those listed in the study guide.

4   The effect of special schemes

    (a) Describe the cash accounting scheme, and recognise when it will be advantageous to use the scheme.[2]   26

    (b) Describe the annual accounting scheme, and recognise when it will be advantageous to use the scheme.[2]   26

    (c) Describe the flat rate scheme, and recognise when it will be advantageous to use the scheme.[2]   26

Excluded topics:

- The second-hand goods scheme.

- The capital goods scheme.

- The special schemes for retailers.

H THE OBLIGATIONS OF TAX PAYERS AND/OR THEIR AGENTS

1 The systems for self-assessment and the making of returns

    (a) Explain and apply the features of the self-assessment system as it applies to individuals.[2]   12

    (b) Explain and apply the features of the self-assessment system as it applies to companies, including the use of iXBRL.[2]   24

2 The time limits for the submission of information, claims and payment of tax, including payments on account

    (a) Recognise the time limits that apply to the filing of returns and the making of claims.[2]   12 & 24

    (b) Recognise the due dates for the payment of tax under the self-assessment system.[2]   12

    (c) Compute payments on account and balancing payments/repayments for individuals.[2]   12

    (d) Explain how large companies are required to account for corporation tax on a quarterly basis.[2]   24

    (e) List the information and records that taxpayers need to retain for tax purposes.[1]   12 & 24

Excluded topics:

- The payment of CGT by annual instalments.

3 The procedures relating to compliance checks, appeals and disputes

    (a) Explain the circumstances in which HM Revenue & Customs can make a compliance check into a self-assessment tax return.[2]   12 & 24

    (b) Explain the procedures for dealing with appeals and disputes.[1]   12 & 24

4 Penalties for non-compliance

    (a) Calculate late payment interest.[2]   12 & 24

    (b) State the penalties that can be charged.[2]   12 & 24

KAPLAN PUBLISHING

The superscript numbers in square brackets indicate the intellectual depth at which the subject area could be assessed within the examination.

Level 1 (knowledge and comprehension) broadly equates with the Knowledge module.

Level 2 (application and analysis) with the Skills module.

Level 3 (synthesis and evaluation) to the Professional level.

However, lower level skills can continue to be assessed as you progress through each module and level.

The Examination

Examination format

The paper will be predominantly computational and will have five questions, all of which will be compulsory.

- Question 1 will focus on income tax and question 2 will focus on corporation tax.

- The two questions 1 and 2 will be for a total of 55 marks, with one of the questions being for 30 marks and the other for 25 marks.

- Question 3 will focus on chargeable gains (either personal or corporate or both), and will be for 15 marks.

- Questions 4 and 5 will be on any area of the syllabus, can cover more than one topic and will be for 15 marks.

There will always be a minimum of 10 marks on value added tax. These marks will normally be included within question 1 or 2, although there might be a separate question on value added tax.

There will always be between 5 and 15 marks on inheritance tax. Inheritance tax may be included within questions 3, 4 or 5.

National insurance contributions will not be examined as a separate question, but may be examined in any question involving income tax or corporation tax.

Groups and overseas aspects of corporation tax may be examined in Question 2, 4 or 5.

A small element of chargeable gains may be included in questions other than question 3.

Any of the five questions might include the consideration of issues relating to the minimisation or deferral of tax liabilities.

Total marks: 100

Total time allowed: 3 hours plus 15 minutes reading and planning time.

Paper based examination tips

Spend the reading time of the examination reading the paper carefully.

Divide the time you spend on questions in proportion to the marks on offer. One suggestion **for this examination** is to allocate 1.8 minutes to each mark available, so a 10 mark question should be completed in approximately 18 minutes.

Unless you know exactly how to answer the question, spend some time planning your answer. Stick to the question and tailor your answer to what you are asked. Pay particular attention to the verbs in the question.

Spend the last five minutes reading through your answers and making any additions or corrections.

If you **get completely stuck** with a question, leave space in your answer book and return to it later.

If you do not understand what a question is asking, state your assumptions. Even if you do not answer in precisely the way the examiner hoped, you should be given some credit, if your assumptions are reasonable.

You should do everything you can to make things easy for the marker. The marker will find it easier to identify the points you have made if your answers are legible.

Computations: It is essential to include all your workings in your answers. Many computational questions require the use of a standard format. Be sure you know these formats thoroughly before the exam and use the layouts that you see in the answers given in this book and in model answers.

Reports, memos and other documents: some questions ask you to present your answer in the form of a report or a memo or other document. So use the correct format – there are easy marks to gain here.

Study skills and revision guidance

This section aims to give guidance on how to study for your ACCA exams and to give ideas on how to improve your existing study techniques.

Preparing to study

Set your objectives

Before starting to study decide what you want to achieve – the type of pass you wish to obtain. This will decide the level of commitment and time you need to dedicate to your studies.

Devise a study plan

Determine which times of the week you will study.

Split these times into sessions of at least one hour for study of new material. Any shorter periods could be used for revision or practice.

Put the times you plan to study onto a study plan for the weeks from now until the exam and set yourself targets for each period of study - in your sessions make sure you cover the course, course assignments and revision.

If you are studying for more than one paper at a time, try to vary your subjects as this can help you to keep interested and see subjects as part of wider knowledge.

When working through your course, compare your progress with your plan and, if necessary, re-plan your work (perhaps including extra sessions) or, if you are ahead, do some extra revision/practice questions.

KAPLAN PUBLISHING

Effective studying

Active reading

You are not expected to learn the text by rote, rather, you must understand what you are reading and be able to use it to pass the exam and develop good practice. A good technique to use is SQ3Rs – Survey, Question, Read, Recall, Review:

(1) **Survey the chapter** – look at the headings and read the introduction, summary and objectives, so as to get an overview of what the chapter deals with.

(2) **Question** – whilst undertaking the survey, ask yourself the questions that you hope the chapter will answer for you.

(3) **Read** through the chapter thoroughly, answering the questions and making sure you can meet the objectives. Attempt the exercises and activities in the text, and work through all the examples.

(4) **Recall** – at the end of each section and at the end of the chapter, try to recall the main ideas of the section/chapter without referring to the text. This is best done after a short break of a couple of minutes after the reading stage.

(5) **Review** – check that your recall notes are correct.

You may also find it helpful to re-read the chapter to try to see the topic(s) it deals with as a whole.

Note taking

Taking notes is a useful way of learning, but do not simply copy out the text. The notes must:

- be in your own words
- be concise
- cover the key points
- be well organised
- be modified as you study further chapters in this text or in related ones.

Trying to summarise a chapter without referring to the text can be a useful way of determining which areas you know and which you don't.

Three ways of taking notes:

(1) **Summarise the key points of a chapter.**

(2) **Make linear notes** – a list of headings, divided up with subheadings listing the key points. If you use linear notes, you can use different colours to highlight key points and keep topic areas together. Use plenty of space to make your notes easy to use.

(3) **Try a diagrammatic form** – the most common of which is a mind map. To make a mind map, put the main heading in the centre of the paper and put a circle around it. Then draw short lines radiating from this to the main sub-headings, which again have circles around them. Then continue the process from the sub-headings to sub-sub-headings, advantages, disadvantages, etc.

Highlighting and underlining

You may find it useful to underline or highlight key points in your study text - but do be selective. You may also wish to make notes in the margins.

Revision

The best approach to revision is to revise the course as you work through it. Also try to leave four to six weeks before the exam for final revision. Make sure you cover the whole syllabus and pay special attention to those areas where your knowledge is weak. Here are some recommendations:

Read through the text and your notes again and condense your notes into key phrases. It may help to put key revision points onto index cards to look at when you have a few minutes to spare.

Review any assignments you have completed and look at where you lost marks – put more work into those areas where you were weak.

Practise exam standard questions under timed conditions. If you are short of time, list the points that you would cover in your answer and then read the model answer, but do try to complete at least a few questions under exam conditions.

Also practise producing answer plans and comparing them to the model answer.

If you are stuck on a topic find somebody (a tutor) to explain it to you.

Read good newspapers and professional journals, especially ACCA's Student Accountant – this can give you an advantage in the exam.

KAPLAN PUBLISHING

Ensure you **know the structure of the exam** – how many questions and of what type you will be expected to answer. During your revision attempt all the different styles of questions you may be asked.

Further reading

You can find further reading and technical articles under the student section of ACCA's website.

TAX RATES AND ALLOWANCES

Supplementary instructions given in the examination

1   Calculations and workings need only be made to the nearest £.
2   All apportionments should be made to the nearest month.
3   All workings should be shown.

	INCOME TAX	Normal rates	Dividend rates
		%	%
Basic rate	£1 – £34,370	20	10
Higher rate	£37,371 – £150,000	40	32.5
Additional rate	£150,001 and above	50	42.5

A starting rate of 10% applies to savings income where it falls within the first £2,710 of taxable income.

	Personal allowances	£
Personal allowance	Standard	8,105
Personal allowance	65 – 74	10,500
Personal allowance	75 and over	10,660
Income limit for age related allowances		25,400
Income limit for standard personal allowance		100,000

Car benefit percentage

The relevant base level of CO_2 emissions is 100 grams per kilometre.

The percentage rates applying to petrol cars with CO_2 emissions up to:

	%
75 grams per kilometre or less	5
76 to 99 grams per kilometre	10
100 grams per kilometre	11

Car fuel benefit

The base level figure for calculating car fuel benefit is £20,200.

Individual Savings Accounts (ISAs)

The overall investment limit is £11,280, of which £5,640 can be invested in a cash ISA

Pension scheme limits

Annual allowance   £50,000

The maximum contribution that can qualify for tax relief without any earnings is £3,600.

Authorised mileage rates: cars

Up to 10,000 miles	45p
Over 10,000 miles	25p

KAPLAN PUBLISHING

Capital allowances

Plant and machinery

	%
Main pool	18
Special rate pool	8

Motor cars

New cars with CO_2 emissions up to 110 grams per kilometre	100
CO_2 emissions between 111 and 160 grams per kilometre	18
CO_2 emissions above 160 grams per kilometre	8

Annual investment allowance

First £25,000 of expenditure	100

CORPORATION TAX

Financial Year	2010	2011	2012
Small profits rate	21%	20%	20%
Main rate	28%	26%	24%
Lower limit	£300,000	£300,000	£300,000
Upper limit	£1,500,000	£1,500,000	£1,500,000
Standard fraction	7/400	3/200	1/100

Marginal relief

Standard fraction × (U – A) × N/A

VALUE ADDED TAX

Standard rate	20%
Registration limit	£77,000
Deregistration limit	£75,000

INHERITANCE TAX
Rates

£1 – £325,000		Nil
Excess	– Death rate	40%
	– Lifetime rate	20%

Taper relief

Years before death	Percentage reduction %
Over 3 but less than 4 years	20
Over 4 but less than 5 years	40
Over 5 but less than 6 years	60
Over 6 but less than 7 years	80

CAPITAL GAINS TAX

Rate of tax	– Lower rate	18%
	– Higher rate	28%
Annual exempt amount		£10,600
Entrepreneurs' relief	– Lifetime limit	£10,000,000
	– Rate of tax	10%

NATIONAL INSURANCE CONTRIBUTIONS
(not contracted out rates)

		%
Class 1 Employee	£1 – £7,605 per year	Nil
	£7,606 – £42,475 per year	12.0
	£42,476 and above	2.0
Class 1 Employer	£1 – £7,488 per year	Nil
	£7,489 and above per year	13.8
Class 1A		13.8
Class 2	£2.65 per week	
	Small earnings exception limit	£5,595
Class 4	£1 – £7,605 per year	Nil
	£7,606 – £42,475 per year	9.0
	£42,476 and above per year	2.0

RATES OF INTEREST (assumed)

Official rate of interest:	4.0%
Rate of interest on underpaid tax	3.0%
Rate of interest on overpaid tax	0.5%

KAPLAN PUBLISHING

The UK tax system

Chapter learning objectives

Upon completion of this chapter you will be able to:

- describe the purpose (economic, social, etc.) of taxation in a modern economy

- identify the different types of capital and revenue tax

- explain the difference between direct and indirect taxation

- describe the overall structure of the UK tax system

- explain the different sources of tax law

- appreciate the interaction of the UK tax system with overseas tax systems

- define the terms tax avoidance and tax evasion and recognise the difference between them

- recognise the purpose of the professional and ethical framework in which the accountant operates.

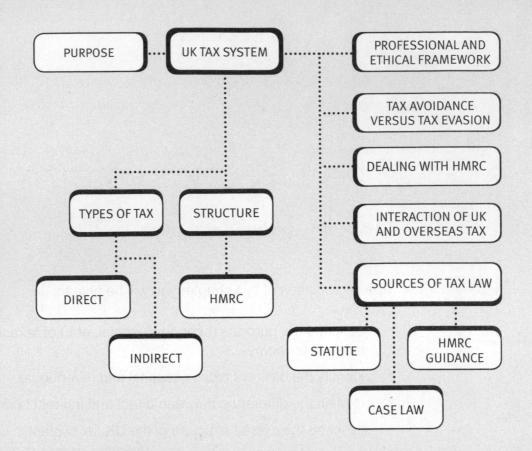

Purpose of taxation

Economic

- The system of taxation and spending by government impacts on the economy of a country as a whole.

- Taxation policies are used to influence many economic factors such as inflation, employment levels, imports/exports.

- They are also used to direct the behaviour of business and individuals.

The current UK tax system encourages:

(1) individual saving habits by offering tax incentives on savings accounts such as Individual Savings Accounts (ISAs)

(2) charitable donations by offering tax relief through Gift Aid

(3) entrepreneurs and investors by offering tax relief for investments in specified schemes

The current UK tax system discourages:

(1) motoring by imposing fuel duties

(2) smoking and drinking alcohol by imposing significant taxes on cigarettes and alcoholic drinks

(3) environmental pollution by imposing a variety of taxes such as landfill tax, climate change levy and linking CO_2 emissions to the taxation of company cars.

- As government objectives change, taxation policies are altered.

Social justice

The type of taxation structure imposed has a direct impact on the accumulation and redistribution of wealth within a country.

The main taxation principles are listed below. The arguments for and against each of these are often the matter of significant political debate.

Progressive taxation

- As income rises the proportion of taxation raised also rises.
  For example: 10% on £10,000 of income and 30% on £30,000 of income. Income tax is an example of a progressive tax.

Regressive taxation

- As income rises the proportion of taxation paid falls.
  For example, the tax on a litre of petrol is the same regardless of the level of income of the purchaser.
  This is a regressive tax as it represents a greater proportion of income for a low income earner than a high income earner.

Proportional taxation

- As income rises the proportion of tax remains constant.
  For example, 10% of all earnings regardless of the level.

Ad Valorem principle

- A tax calculated as a percentage of the value of the item.
  For example, 20% VAT on most goods sold in the UK.

1 Types of tax

The UK tax system, administered by HM Revenue and Customs (HMRC), comprises a number of different taxes. The following taxes are examinable.

Income tax

- Payable by individuals on their earnings (e.g. self-employment and employment) and investment income.

National insurance contributions (NICs)

- Payable by individuals who are either employed or self-employed on their earnings.
- Also payable by businesses (e.g. sole trader, company) in relation to their employees.

Capital gains tax

- Payable by individuals on the disposal of capital assets.
- Capital assets include land, buildings and shares, but could include smaller items, such as antiques.

Inheritance tax

- Payable by executors on the value of the estate of a deceased person.
- Also payable in respect of certain gifts during an individual's lifetime.

Corporation tax

- Payable by companies on their income and gains.

Value added tax (VAT)

- Payable on the supply of goods and services to the final consumer.

2 Direct versus indirect taxation

Direct taxation

- The taxpayer pays direct taxes directly to HMRC.
- They are based on income/profits and the more that is earned/received, the more tax is paid.
- Examples of direct taxes include income tax, corporation tax, capital gains tax and inheritance tax.

Indirect taxation

- An indirect tax is collected from the taxpayer via an intermediary such as a retail shop.

- The intermediary then pays over the tax collected to HMRC.

- An example of indirect taxation is VAT. The consumer pays VAT to the supplier, who then pays it to HMRC.

3 Structure of the UK tax system

HM Revenue and Customs

- HMRC is the government department that controls and administers all areas of UK tax law.

- Heading up HMRC are the Commissioners whose main duties are:
  - to implement statute law
  - to oversee the process of UK tax administration.

- HMRC is organised into four operational groups:
  - Personal tax
  - Benefits and credits
  - Business tax, and
  - Enforcement and compliance.

- HMRC have offices located throughout the UK.

- The organisation of HMRC is undergoing change.

- Staff who work for HMRC are known as Officers of Revenue and Customs.

HMRC offices

Different offices of HMRC are responsible for different aspects of work:

- Enquiry offices are open for taxpayer queries. A taxpayer can visit in person if they wish.

- Service offices deal with general checking and tax compliance work.

- District offices examine selected returns and accounts of individuals, businesses and companies and may have responsibility for other tax matters.

- Accounting and payment offices collect tax.

- Other offices deal with Pay As You Earn (PAYE) and any other tax matters.

4 Sources of tax law

The basic rules of the UK tax system have been established from the following main sources:

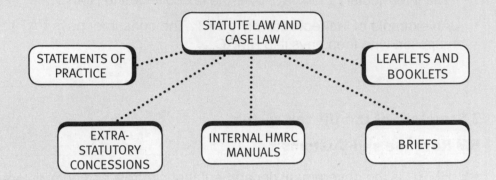

Sources of tax law

Tax legislation/statutes

- These are law and therefore adherence is mandatory.

- Tax legislation is normally updated each year by one annual Finance Act that follows from the proposals made by the Chancellor of the Exchequer in his annual Budget statement.

- Statutory instruments are issued where detailed notes are required on an area of tax legislation.

Case law

- Case law refers to the decisions made in tax cases brought before the courts.

- Often the case challenges current tax legislation or argues a certain interpretation of the tax law should be applied.

- These rulings are binding and therefore provide guidance on the interpretation of tax legislation.

HMRC guidance

- As the tax legislation can be complex to understand and open to misinterpretation, further guidance is issued by HMRC in order to:
  - explain how to implement the law
  - give their interpretation of the law.

- The main types of guidance are listed below.

KAPLAN PUBLISHING

Statements of Practice

- Provides HMRC's interpretation of tax law and often provides clarification or detail of how rules should be applied.

Extra statutory concessions

- Extra statutory concessions allow a relaxation of the strict letter of the law in certain circumstances. A concession is often given where undue hardship or anomalies would otherwise occur.

Internal guidance manuals

- HMRC's own manuals, produced for their staff, give guidance on the interpretation of the law. They are also available to the public.

Briefs

- Provide details of a specific tax issue that has arisen in the year.

Leaflets and booklets

- Aimed at the general public and provide explanations of various tax issues in non-technical language.

Interaction of UK and overseas tax systems

Due to the differing tax systems in overseas countries, it is possible that income is taxed under two different systems.

Double taxation relief (DTR)

Agreements between most countries have been established to decide how a particular individual/company should be taxed.

- These are known as bilateral double taxation treaties.
- Such treaties take precedence over domestic UK tax law and either:
  - exempt certain overseas income from tax in the UK, or
  - provide relief where tax is suffered in two countries on the same income.
- Where no such treaty exists, the UK system still allows for relief to be given where double tax is paid.

Further detail of the operation of the DTR system for companies is found in Chapter 23. DTR for individuals is not examinable.

Influence of the European Union (EU)

- One of the aims of the EU is to remove trade barriers and distortions due to different economic and political policies imposed in different member states.

- Although EU members do not have to align their tax systems, members can agree to jointly enact specific laws, known as Directives.

- To date the most important of these has been agreements regarding VAT. EU members have aligned their VAT **policies** according to European legislation. They have not however aligned their **rates** of VAT.

- Many cases have been brought before the European Court of Justice regarding the discrimination of non-tax residents by the UK tax system, some of which have resulted in changes to UK tax law.

5 Tax avoidance versus tax evasion

The difference between tax avoidance and evasion is important due to the legal implications.

Tax evasion

- The term tax evasion summarises any action taken to evade taxes by illegal means.

- The main forms of tax evasion are:
  - suppressing information
    (e.g. failing to declare taxable income to HMRC)

  - submitting false information
    (e.g. claiming expenses that have not been incurred).

- Tax evasion is an illegal activity; and carries a risk of criminal prosecution (fines and/or imprisonment).

Tax avoidance

- Tax avoidance is using the taxation regime to one's own advantage by arranging your affairs to minimise your tax liability.

- It is legal and does not entail misleading HMRC (e.g. making tax savings by investing in ISAs).

- The term is also used to describe tax schemes that utilise loopholes in the tax legislation.

- HMRC have now introduced disclosure obligations regarding tax schemes that involve declaring the details of such schemes to HMRC.

Test your understanding 1

State which of the following is tax evasion:

- Selling a capital asset in May 2012 instead of March 2012 to ensure that the gain is taxed in a later tax year.

- Altering a bill of £700 to read £7,000 on your tax return.

- Moving taxable interest into a tax free ISA account.

6 Professional and ethical guidance

The ACCA 'Professional Code of Ethics and Conduct' has already been covered in your earlier studies. A reminder of the key points is given in expandable text.

Fundamental principles

The ACCA expects its members to:

- adopt an ethical approach to work, employers and clients

- acknowledge your professional duty to society as a whole

- maintain an objective outlook, and

- provide professional, high standards of service, conduct and performance at all times.

To meet these expectations the ACCA 'Code of Ethics and Conduct' sets out five fundamental principles, which members should abide by:

- Objectivity

- Professional competence and due care

- Professional behaviour

- Integrity

- Confidentiality.

Remember: OPPIC

Objectivity (O)

* Members should not allow bias, conflicts of interest or the influence of others to override objectivity.

Professional competence and due care (P)

* Members have an ongoing duty to maintain professional knowledge and skills to ensure that a client/employer receives competent, professional service based on current developments.

* Members should be diligent and act in accordance with applicable technical and professional standards when providing professional services.

Professional behaviour (P)

* Members should refrain from any conduct that might bring discredit to the profession.

Integrity (I)

* Members should act in a straightforward and honest manner in all professional and business relationships.

Confidentiality (C)

* Members should respect the confidentiality of information acquired as a result of professional and business relationships and should not disclose any such information to third parties unless:
    - they have proper and specific authority, or
    - there is a legal or professional right or duty to disclose (e.g. Money laundering).

* Confidential information acquired as a result of professional and business relationships, should not be used for the personal advantage of members or third parties.

Advise on taxation issues

A person advising either a company or an individual on taxation issues has duties and responsibilities towards both his client, and HM Revenue and Customs.

KAPLAN PUBLISHING

Dealing with HMRC

It is important to ensure that information provided to HMRC is accurate and complete.

A member must not assist a client to plan or commit any offence.

If a member becomes aware that the client has committed a tax irregularity:

- they must discuss it with the client and ensure that proper disclosure is made.

Examples would include:

- not declaring income that is taxable
- claiming reliefs to which they are not entitled
- not notifying HMRC where they have made a mistake giving rise to an underpayment of tax, or an increased repayment.

Where a client has made an error:

- it will be necessary to decide whether it was a genuine error or a deliberate or fraudulent act.

Once an error (or similar) has been discovered:

- the member should explain to the client the requirement to notify HMRC as soon as possible, and the implications of their not doing so.

Should the client refuse to make a full and prompt disclosure to HMRC:

- the member must write and explain the potential consequences.

If the client still refuses to make a full disclosure, the member:

- should cease to act for the client.
- must then also write to HMRC informing them that they have ceased to act for the client, but without disclosing the reason why.
- must then consider their position under the Money Laundering Rules.

Money Laundering Regulations

Money Laundering is the term used for offences including benefiting from or concealing the proceeds of a crime.

An individual is engaged in money laundering if they:

(i) conceal, disguise, transfer or remove criminal property from the UK

(ii) enter into or become concerned in an arrangement that they know or suspect involves the acquisition of criminal property on behalf of another person

(iii) acquire or have possession of criminal property.

Criminal property includes the proceeds of tax evasion.

A member must therefore:

- arrange satisfactory evidence of a client's identity before agreeing to act for them

- ensure their staff are trained and up to date with the relevant regulations

- put in place an appropriate system for reporting suspicious transactions. This includes appointing a Money Laundering Reporting Officer (MLRO) within the firm.

The MLRO will decide whether a transaction should be reported to the Serious Organised Crime Agency (SOCA).

Where a report is made the client should not be informed as this may amount to 'tipping off', which is an offence.

A report to SOCA does not remove the requirement to disclose the information to HMRC.

Test your understanding 2

When you were checking a recent tax computation from HMRC you notice that they have made an error which has resulted in your client receiving a larger repayment than should have been made.

What actions should you take?

KAPLAN PUBLISHING

7 Chapter summary

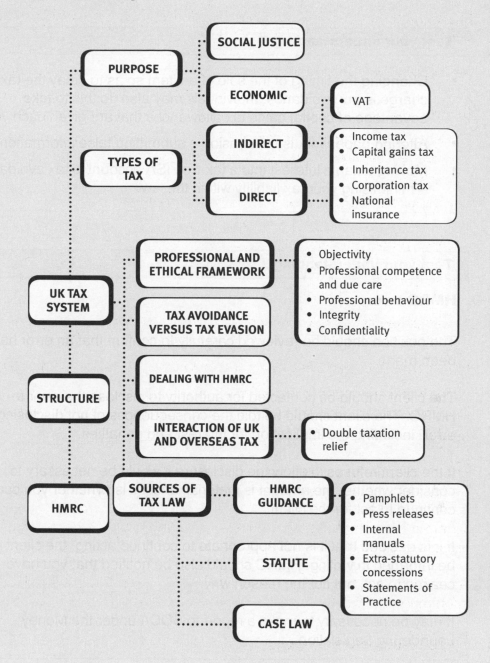

Test your understanding answers

Test your understanding 1

- Changing the timing of the sale of an item so as to delay the tax charge is tax avoidance. Individuals may also do this to take advantage of capital gains tax allowances that are given each year.

- Altering paperwork is tax evasion – submitting false information.

- Moving taxable interest into a tax-free ISA account is tax avoidance – minimising your tax liability within the law.

Test your understanding 2

HMRC error

The position should be reviewed carefully to confirm that an error has been made.

The client should be contacted for authority to disclose the error to HMRC. The client should be told the consequences of not disclosing the error, including the implication for interest and penalties.

If the client refuses to allow the disclosure it would be necessary to consider whether the amount is material, and if it is, whether you can continue to act for the client.

If it is decided that it is not appropriate to continue acting, the client must be informed in writing. HMRC should also be notified that you have ceased to act, but not the reason why.

It may be necessary to make a report to SOCA under the Money Laundering Legislation.

Basic income tax computation

Chapter learning objectives

Upon completion of this chapter you will be able to:

- identify the scope of income tax and those assessable

- explain how the residence of an individual is determined

- recognise the different types of taxable income for an individual

- select and calculate personal age allowances in a variety of situations

- calculate the income tax liability arising on different types of income

- distinguish between income tax liability and income tax payable

- recognise qualifying reliefs deductible from total income and explain the tax treatment

- explain the tax treatment of charitable donations.

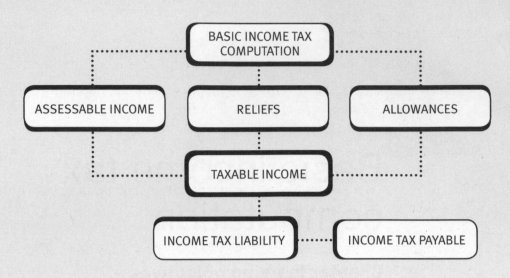

1 The principles of income tax

Introduction

This and the following eight chapters deal in detail with the way in which individuals, whether they are employed, self-employed or simply in receipt of investment income, are assessed to income tax.

Income tax is an important topic as it will be the focus of question one in the examination which will be for either 25 marks or 30 marks.

This chapter sets out the basis upon which individuals are assessed to income tax and how an individual's income tax liability is calculated.

Basis of assessment

Individuals are assessed to income tax on their income arising in a **tax year.**

- A tax year is the year ended on 5 April and is labelled by the calendar years it straddles.

- The year from 6 April 2012 to 5 April 2013, is referred to as the tax year 2012/13.

Personal allowances

Every taxpayer may be entitled to a basic personal allowance (PA).

- The PA is an amount of tax-free income that every taxpayer is entitled to each tax year.

- Personal allowances are dealt with in more detail in section 3.

Assessable persons

- All individuals, including children, are chargeable to income tax.
- Both spouses within a married couple are treated as separate individuals for the purposes of income tax.

Husband and wife

There are special rules governing the allocation of income between spouses where assets are jointly owned:

- Generally, income generated from assets jointly owned will be split 50:50 between spouses regardless of the actual percentage ownership.
- Election available:
  Where jointly owned assets are held other than in a 50:50 ratio, an election can be made to HM Revenue & Customs (HMRC) for the income to be taxed on the individual spouses according to their actual percentage ownership.

Civil partners (same-sex couples registered as a civil partnership) are treated in the same way as married couples.

Children

- A child under the age of 18 is a taxable person.
- However, their income typically falls short of their personal allowance in any tax year and therefore no tax liability actually arises on their income.

Tax status of an individual

- All persons resident, ordinarily resident and domiciled in the UK are assessed to UK tax on their worldwide income.

Definition of residence

Broadly, a person is deemed resident in the UK for a tax year if they are present in the UK for a period of six months (183 days) or more.

An individual is also UK resident if he or she has made frequent and substantial visits to the UK.

Visits of (in aggregate) three months (91 days) a year, on average, for four consecutive years are regarded as 'frequent and substantial'.

Definition of ordinary residence

An individual's ordinary residence is the place where he normally resides.

Ordinary residence implies residence with some degree of continuity, ignoring incidental or temporary absences.

Ordinary residence
An individual who has previously been resident and ordinarily resident in the UK may still be regarded as UK ordinarily resident for a year that he spends wholly overseas if it is their intention to return to the UK. An individual must be absent from the UK for at least three years before they will be regarded as having lost their ordinary residence status.

Definition of domicile

An individual's domicile is basically his permanent home.

You need to be aware of these definitions. However, in the F6 examination, for income tax, in computational questions the individual will always be:

- resident, ordinarily resident and domiciled in the UK, and

- therefore taxed on their worldwide income.

2 Taxable income

Basic pro forma

The first stage of the income tax computation is to prepare a short statement summarising all taxable income.

- All income is included **gross** in the computation.

- Any exempt income identified can be excluded, but should be noted as exempt in your exam answer.

Income tax computation – 2012/13

	£
Trading income	X
Employment income	X
Property income	X
	—
Other income	X
Savings income	
Building society interest (× 100/80)	X
Bank interest (× 100/80)	X
UK dividends (× 100/90)	X
	—
Total income	X
Less: Reliefs	(X)
	—
Net income	X
Less: Personal allowance (PA)	(X)
	—
Taxable income	X
	—

Classification of income

There are a number of different sources of income. For example:

- Income earned from employment and self-employment
- Income arising from the ownership of property
- Investment income (e.g. savings income and dividends)
- Income exempt from income tax.

It is important to classify each source of income correctly as the tax rules are different for each source.

It is also important to correctly classify each source as 'other income', 'savings income' and 'dividend income' as they are taxed at different rates.

All taxable income is included in the income tax computation **gross**.

- Some income, such as employment income and bank interest will have had some tax deducted at source.

- Where a net figure is given, the income must be grossed up before being included in the income tax computation.

Other income

Other income comprises earned income and property income.

Earned income can be generated in the following ways:

- The profit of a trade, profession or vocation of a self-employed individual is assessed as trading income (see Chapter 5).

- Earnings derived from an office or employment are assessed as employment income (see Chapter 4).

Property income is typically rental income, but also includes other items such as the income element of a premium on granting a short lease (see Chapter 3).

Investment income

Sources of investment income include:

- Savings income – usually bank and building society interest.
  This can be received either net (of 20% income tax) or gross.
  Either way, savings income is included in the tax computation gross (see Chapter 3 for more detail).

- Dividend income is received net of a 10% tax credit.
  The grossed up amount (amount received × 100/90) is included in the income tax computation (see Chapter 3 for more detail).

Exempt income

The types of exempt income which may be tested in the exam are:

- Interest from National Savings and Investments ('NS&I') Certificates
- Gaming, lottery and premium bonds winnings
- Income received from an Individual Savings Account (ISA)
- Some social security benefits.

Reliefs

Reliefs are deductible from an individual's total income.

They include certain payments that an individual makes and certain losses that may be incurred by an individual (see section 6 for more detail).

3 Personal allowances

Every taxpayer (including children) is entitled to a personal allowance (PA).

- The amount for 2012/13 is £8,105.
- The PA is deducted from the taxpayer's net income from the different sources of income in the following order:

  (1) Other income

  (2) Savings income

  (3) Dividend income

- Surplus personal allowances are lost, they cannot be set against capital gains nor can they be transferred to any other taxpayer.
- There is no restriction to the PA where the individual is only alive for part of the year (i.e. full allowance available in year of birth or death).

Reduction of personal allowance – high income individuals

- The PA is gradually reduced for individuals (regardless of age) with income in excess of £100,000.
- The reduction of the PA is based on the taxpayer's adjusted net income (ANI) which is calculated as follows:

	£
Net income	X
Less: Gross Gift Aid donations	(X)
Less: Gross personal pension contributions	(X)
Adjusted net income (ANI)	X

- Where the taxpayer's ANI exceeds £100,000, the PA is reduced by:
  - **50% × (ANI – £100,000)**
  - If necessary, the reduced PA is rounded up to the nearest pound.
- A taxpayer with ANI in excess of £116,210 will therefore be entitled to no PA at all, as the excess above £100,000 is twice the PA.
- The effective rate of tax on income between £100,000 and £116,210 is therefore 60%. This is made up of:
  - higher rate income tax = 40%
  - lost PA (½ × 40%) = 20%
- Taxpayers at or near this margin may therefore wish to consider making additional Gift Aid or personal pension contributions in order to reduce their ANI below £100,000.

Example 1 – Reduction of personal allowance

Ethan received trading income of £110,000 in 2012/13. He also made Gift Aid donations of £4,000 (gross).

Compute Ethan's taxable income for 2012/13.

Answer to Example 1

Income tax computation – 2012/13

	£
Trading income (Note)	110,000
Less: Adjusted PA (W)	(5,105)
Taxable income	104,895

Working: Adjusted PA

	£	£
Basic personal allowance		8,105
Net income (Note below)	110,000	
Less: Gross Gift Aid donation	(4,000)	
Adjusted net income	106,000	
Less: Income limit	(100,000)	
	6,000	
Reduction of PA (50% × £6,000)		(3,000)
Adjusted PA		5,105

Note: In this example, as there are no other sources of income and no reliefs; the trading income = total income = net income.

Test your understanding 1

Ellie received employment income of £125,000 in 2012/13. She also made Gift Aid donations of £16,000 (gross).

Compute Ellie's taxable income for 2012/13.

KAPLAN PUBLISHING

Age allowance

Taxpayers aged 65 and over **at any time** in the tax year, are entitled to a higher rate of personal allowance as follows (see tax tables):

- **Aged 65 – 74:** increased PA of £10,500 in 2012/13.
- **Aged 75 and over:** increased PA of £10,660 in 2012/13.
- The age of the taxpayer at the **end of the tax year** determines the higher personal age allowance (PAA).
- If the taxpayer dies before the end of the tax year, the age he or she would have been at the end of the tax year determines the PAA.
- The PAA is given to provide some protection for those on lower incomes.
- An income restriction therefore operates to reduce the PAA, where the taxpayer's adjusted net income (ANI) exceeds £25,400 for 2012/13.
- The definition of ANI is the same as that used for the reduction of the basic PA for high income individuals (above).
- Where the taxpayer's ANI exceeds £25,400, the PAA is reduced by:
  - **50% × (ANI – £25,400)**
  - If necessary, the reduced PAA is rounded up to the nearest pound.
- This formula gives a progressive reduction in the PAA. However, the age allowance can never fall below the basic PA of £8,105 for 2012/13.
- Remember that the basic PA may then be further reduced if the ANI of the individual exceeds £100,000, regardless of age.
- Therefore, an elderly taxpayer with income in excess of £100,000:
  - will not be entitled to the PAA as the level of income will reduce the PAA to the basic PA, and
  - the basic PA will then be further reduced as explained earlier.
- Always assume the taxpayer is aged under 65 in the examination unless the question says otherwise.

Example 2 – Personal age allowances

At the end of 2012/13:

- Dennis will be 71 and has adjusted net income of £26,250
- Nora will be 90 and has adjusted net income of £26,800
- Peter will be 80 and has adjusted net income of £32,300
- Juliet will be 74 and has adjusted net income of £105,000

Calculate the personal allowance available to each taxpayer.

Answer to example 2

	Dennis	Nora	Peter	Juliet
Age at the end of the tax year:	71	90	80	74
	£	£	£	£
Personal age allowance	10,500	10,660	10,660	8,105 (note)
Less: Restriction				
50% × (£26,250 – £25,400)	(425)			
50% × (£26,800 – £25,400)		(700)		
50% × (£32,300 – £25,400) = £3,450 but restricted			(2,555)	
50% × (£105,000 – £100,000)				(2,500)
Adjusted PAA	10,075	9,960	8,105	5,605

Note: Juliet's income exceeds £25,400 to such an extent that her PAA is reduced to the basic PA. It is then further reduced as her income exceeds £100,000.

Test your understanding 2

Taxpayer	Date of birth	Net income
Vera	4 June 1939	£19,000
Agatha	15 March 1936	£26,500
Henry	20 August 1926	£27,500
Leon	7 September 1944	£30,400
Charlotte	21 July 1935	£108,500

Calculate the personal allowance available to each taxpayer in 2012/13.

4 Income tax liability

The second stage of the income tax computation is to compute the income tax liability on the taxable income.

Different rates of tax apply dependent upon the type of income.

	£		£
Other income	X	@ 20/40/50%	X
Savings income	X	@ 20/40/50%	X
Dividend income	X	@10/32.5/42.5%	X
			—
Income tax liability			X
			—

The appropriate rate of tax depends on the level of taxable income.

Rates of income tax

The rates of income tax for 2012/13 for 'other income' and 'savings income' are as follows:

- a basic rate of 20% applies to the first £34,370 of taxable income

- a higher rate of 40% applies where taxable income falls between £34,370, and £150,000

- an additional rate of 50% applies to taxable income in excess of £150,000.

Special rates of tax apply to dividend income.

The income tax rates for all sources of income for 2012/13 are:

Level of income	Other income	Savings income	Dividend income
Basic rate band (first £34,370)	20%	20% (see note below)	10%
Higher rate (£34,371 – £150,000)	40%	40%	32.5%
Additional rate (excess over £150,000)	50%	50%	42.5%

These rates are supplied to you in the examination.

The income tax liability must be calculated in a strict order as follows:

(1) Other income

(2) Savings income

(3) Dividend income

Note: Special rates may apply to savings income if it falls within the first £2,710 of taxable income.

The special rates for savings and dividend income are considered in more detail in Chapter 3.

Approach to the income tax computation

(1) Calculate the individual's net income.

(2) If aged 65 or more, consider the availability of PAA and the reduction of the PAA if ANI exceeds £25,400.

(3) Regardless of age, consider the reduction of the basic PA if ANI exceeds £100,000.

(4) Deduct the appropriate amount of personal allowance to calculate the taxable income.

(5) Calculate the income tax liability bearing in mind the higher rate threshold of £34,370 and the additional rate threshold of £150,000 (see examples below).

Example 3 – Income tax liability

Tony has assessable trading income of £20,165 and employment income of £3,000 for 2012/13. He has no savings or dividend income.

Calculate Tony's income tax liability for 2012/13.

Answer to example 3	£
Trading income	20,165
Employment income	3,000
	–––––––
Total income	23,165
Less: PA	(8,105)
	–––––––
Taxable income	15,060
	–––––––
Income tax liability (£15,060 × 20%)	3,012
	–––––––

Example 4 – Income tax liability

Teresa has assessable trading income of £43,765 and employment income of £4,000 for 2012/13. She has no savings or dividend income.

Calculate Teresa's income tax liability for 2012/13.

Answer to example 4

		£
Trading income		43,765
Employment income		4,000
Total income		47,765
Less: PA		(8,105)
Taxable income		39,660

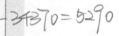

Income tax:	£		£
Basic rate	34,370	x 20%	6,874
Higher rate	5,290	x 40%	2,116
	39,660		
Income tax liability			8,990

Example 5 – Income tax liability

Thomas has assessable trading income of £135,000 and employment income of £33,680 for 2012/13. He does not have any savings income or dividend income.

Calculate Thomas' income tax liability for 2012/13.

Answer to example 5

	£
Trading income	135,000
Employment income	33,680
Total income	168,680
Less: Adjusted PA (Note)	(Nil)
Taxable income	168,680

Income tax:	£	£
Basic rate	34,370 × 20%	6,874
Higher rate	115,630 × 40%	46,252
Additional rate	18,680 × 50%	9,340
	——————	
	168,680	
	——————	
Income tax liability		62,466

Note: In this example, as total income = net income = ANI, and this exceeds £116,210 (£100,000 plus more than double the PA), the PA is reduced to £Nil.

Test your understanding 3

(1) Andrew has income from self-employment of £15,000 and employment income of £2,500.

(2) Alice has income from self-employment of £36,000 and employment income of £21,000.

(3) Anthony has income from self-employment of £238,780.

Assume that these taxpayers have no other income in 2012/13.

Calculate the income tax liabilities of Andrew, Alice and Anthony for 2012/13.

5 Income tax payable

Some income (such as savings, dividends and most employment income) is received **after** some income tax has been deducted at source.

In determining taxable income, all income must be included in the income tax computation **gross.**

The income tax liability is then calculated on the **gross taxable income.**

To avoid the double payment of tax, credit is then given for any income tax already deducted at source as the final adjustment in an income tax computation.

The final income tax payable computation therefore shows how much of the income tax liability is still outstanding as follows:

	£
Income tax liability	X
Less: Tax credits on dividends	(X)
Tax deducted from savings income	(X)
PAYE on employment income	(X)

Income tax payable	X

The income tax payable is the amount still outstanding and <u>due to be paid</u> by the taxpayer.

It will be collected via the self-assessment system (see Chapter 12).

In the event that the amount of tax already suffered/paid during the year is greater than the liability, a refund will be given via the self-assessment system.

In summary:

- **Income tax liability:**
  - The total income tax due on the taxpayer's total gross income, after deducting reliefs and personal allowances.

- **Income tax payable:**
  - The final tax bill to be paid via self-assessment after deducting credits for any tax already suffered/paid at source.

Example 6 – Income tax payable

Akram has assessable trading income of £41,535 and employment income of £9,000 (gross), for 2012/13. He does not have any savings income or dividend income. He suffered tax at source on his employment income (PAYE) of £179.

Calculate Akram's income tax payable for 2012/13.

Answer to example 6

Income tax computation – 2012/13

		£
Trading income		41,535
Employment income		9,000
Total income		50,535
Less: PA		(8,105)
Taxable income		42,430

Income tax:	£	£
Basic rate	34,370 x 20%	6,874
Higher rate	8,060 x 40%	3,224
	42,430	
Income tax liability		10,098
Less: PAYE		(179)
Income tax payable		9,919

Test your understanding 4

Waqar provides you with the following information for 2012/13:

Salary	£28,000
Trading income	£20,000

He has no other sources of income for the year, although he does notify you that he suffered £3,979 PAYE, during 2012/13.

Calculate Waqar's income tax payable for 2012/13.

KAPLAN PUBLISHING

6 Reliefs against total income

Tax relief is given for certain payments made by an individual and for trading losses.

- Relief is given by deducting the payments/losses from total income.

- The only payments deductible from total income which are examinable are certain qualifying interest payments.

- Losses are covered in detail in Chapter 9.

- In order to maximise the use of reliefs, qualifying interest payments should be deducted from total income in priority to losses incurred.

Qualifying interest payments

Relief is given for interest paid on loans incurred to finance expenditure for a qualifying purpose.

There are a number of qualifying purposes to which the loan must be applied. The only ones relevant to your examination are as follows:

- **Employees**
  - The purchase of plant or machinery by an employed person for use in his employment.

  - The purchase of shares in an employee-controlled trading company by a full time employee.

- **Partners**
  - The purchase of a share in a partnership, or the contribution to a partnership of capital or a loan. The borrower must be a partner in the partnership.

  - The purchase of plant or machinery for use in the partnership, by a partner.

Relief is given by deducting the amount of interest **paid** in a tax year from total income.

Example 7 – Reliefs against total income

Anwar and Barry each have total income of £50,000 none of which is savings or dividend income.

They made the following payments during 2012/13.

- Anwar made interest payments during the year totalling £2,000 on his mortgage for his principal private residence.

- Barry made interest payments of £2,000 on a loan to invest in a partnership in which he is a partner.

Calculate the income tax liability for Anwar and Barry for 2012/13.

Answer to example 7

Income tax computations – 2012/13

				Anwar	Barry
				£	£
Total income				50,000	50,000
Less: Reliefs – Qualifying interest paid					(2,000)
				─────	─────
Net income				50,000	48,000
Less: PA				(8,105)	(8,105)
				─────	─────
Taxable income				41,895	39,895
				─────	─────
Income tax:	£	£		£	£
Basic rate	34,370	34,370	x 20%	6,874	6,874
Higher rate	7,525	5,525	x 40%	3,010	2,210
	─────	─────			
	41,895	39,895			
	─────	─────			
Income tax liability				9,884	9,084
				─────	─────

Note: Mortgage interest paid for a principal private residence is not qualifying interest and therefore not deductible as a relief.

Test your understanding 5

Emmanuel provides the following information in respect of 2012/13:

Employment income	£29,600
Trading income	£19,000
Qualifying interest payment	£4,000

He notifies you that PAYE suffered was £4,299, for 2012/13.

Calculate Emmanuel's income tax payable for 2012/13.

KAPLAN PUBLISHING

7 Charitable giving

Tax relief is available for charitable giving in one of two ways:

- Donations under the Gift Aid scheme
- Payroll giving under the Payroll Deduction Scheme.

Donations under the Gift Aid scheme are covered below and the Payroll Deduction Scheme is covered in Chapter 4.

Donations under the Gift Aid scheme

Taxpayers who wish to make gifts of money to charity can obtain tax relief under the Gift Aid scheme as follows:

- Donations made under the scheme attract relief at the donor's highest rate of tax.
- There are no minimum or maximum contribution limits, and gifts can either be one-off or a series of donations.
- The payments are made with basic rate tax deducted at source. Effectively providing basic rate tax relief at the time of payment.
- The basic rate tax is claimed by the charity from HMRC.

Therefore, if an individual wants a charity to receive £100:

- the individual pays the charity £80, and
- the charity claims £20 from HMRC.

Basic rate taxpayers – obtain the tax relief at the time of payment, by only paying 80% of the amount due.

Higher and additional rate taxpayers – relief comes in two parts:

- 20% tax relief is granted at the time the payment is made, as above.
- Higher and additional rate relief is obtained by adding the gross amount of the donation to the basic and higher rate bands in the income tax liability calculation.

  The effect of extending the basic and higher rate bands is that:

  - income equivalent to the value of the gross donation is taxed at 20%, rather than 40%, and
  - if an additional rate taxpayer, at 40% rather than 50%.

This gives the further 20% tax relief that the higher rate taxpayer is entitled to, and a further 10% tax relief for the additional rate taxpayer (i.e. 30% in total).

Example 8 – Donations under Gift Aid scheme

Brenda earns £50,000 each year and makes a donation of £3,600 to the RSPB under the Gift Aid scheme.

Calculate Brenda's income tax liability for 2012/13.

Answer to example 8

Income tax computation – 2012/13

			£
Employment income			50,000
Less: PA			(8,105)
			―――
Taxable income			41,895
Income tax:	£		£
Extended basic rate band (W)	38,870	x 20%	7,774
Higher rate	3,025	x 40%	1,210
	―――		
	41,895		
	―――		
Income tax liability			8,984

Working: Extended basic rate band

	£
Basic rate band	34,370
Plus: Gross Gift Aid donation (£3,600 x 100/80)	4,500
	―――
Extended basic rate band	38,870
	―――

Note: Although the higher rate band is also extended by £4,500, this has no affect on Brenda's tax liability as she is not an additional rate taxpayer.

Test your understanding 6

Both Paul and Peter earn £46,995 a year. Peter makes a donation of £2,000 to a charity under the Gift Aid scheme.

Calculate the income tax payable for both Paul and Peter for 2012/13.

Test your understanding 7

Clare has assessable trading income of £156,000 and employment income of £12,000 for 2012/13. She does not have any savings income or dividend income. She makes Gift Aid donations to a charity of £47,000.

Calculate Clare's income tax liability for 2012/13.

8 Chapter summary

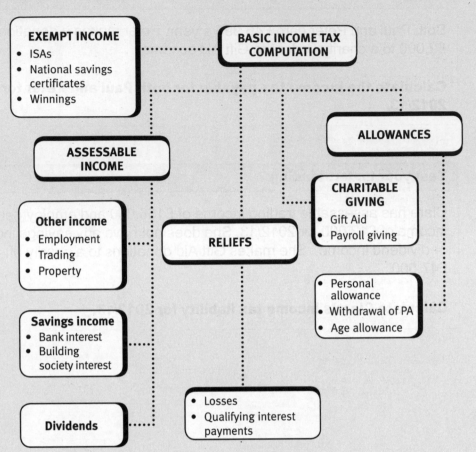

EXEMPT INCOME
- ISAs
- National savings certificates
- Winnings

BASIC INCOME TAX COMPUTATION

ALLOWANCES

ASSESSABLE INCOME

CHARITABLE GIVING
- Gift Aid
- Payroll giving

Other income
- Employment
- Trading
- Property

RELIEFS

Savings income
- Bank interest
- Building society interest

- Personal allowance
- Withdrawal of PA
- Age allowance

Dividends

- Losses
- Qualifying interest payments

Test your understanding answers

Test your understanding 1

Ellie
Income tax computation – 2012/13

	£
Employment income (Note)	125,000
Less: Adjusted PA (W)	(3,605)
Taxable income	121,395

Working: Adjusted PA

	£	£
Basic personal allowance		8,105
Net income (Note)	125,000	
Less: Gross Gift Aid donations	(16,000)	
Adjusted net income	109,000	
Less: Income limit	(100,000)	
	9,000	
Reduction of PA (50% × £9,000)		(4,500)
Adjusted PA		3,605

Note: In this question, as there are no other sources of income and no reliefs; the employment income = total income = net income.

Personal age allowances

	Vera	Agatha	Henry	Leon	Charlotte
Age at the end of the tax year:	73	77	86	68	77
	£	£	£	£	£
Personal age allowance	10,500	10,660	10,660	10,500	8,105 (note)
Less: Restriction					
No restriction required	Nil				
50% × (£26,500 – £25,400)		(550)			
50% × (£27,500 – £25,400)			(1,050)		
50% × (£30,400 – £25,400) = £2,500 but restricted				(2,395)	
50% × (£108,500 – £100,000)					(4,250)
Adjusted PAA	10,500	10,110	9,610	8,105	3,855

Note: Charlotte's income exceeds £25,400 to such an extent that her PAA is reduced to the basic PA. It is then further reduced as her income exceeds £100,000.

Andrew
Income tax computation – 2012/13

	£
Trading income	15,000
Employment income	2,500
Total income	17,500
Less: PA	(8,105)
Taxable income	9,395
Income tax liability (£9,395 x 20%)	1,879

Alice
Income tax computation – 2012/13

	£
Trading income	36,000
Employment income	21,000
Total income	57,000
Less: PA	(8,105)
Taxable income	48,895

	£	£
Income tax:	34,370 x 20%	6,874
Basic rate	14,525 x 40%	5,810
Higher rate		
	48,895	
Income tax liability		12,684

Anthony
Income tax computation – 2012/13

	£
Trading income	238,780
Less: Adjusted PA (Note)	(Nil)
Taxable income	238,780

	£	£
Income tax:		
Basic rate	34,370 × 20%	6,874
Higher rate	115,630 × 40%	46,252
Additional rate	88,780 × 50%	44,390
	238,780	
Income tax liability		97,516

Note: In this example, as there is no other source of income and no reliefs; trading income = total income = net income = ANI. As ANI exceeds £116,210 (£100,000 plus more than double the PA), the PA is reduced to £Nil.

Waqar
Income tax computation – 2012/13

		£
Trading income		20,000
Employment income		28,000
		———
Total income		48,000
Less: PA		(8,105)
		———
Taxable income		39,895
		———

Income tax:	£	£
Basic rate	34,370 x 20%	6,874
Higher rate	5,525 x 40%	2,210
	———	
	39,895	
	———	
Income tax liability		9,084
Less: PAYE		(3,979)
		———
Income tax payable		5,105
		———

KAPLAN PUBLISHING

Test your understanding 5

Emmanuel
Income tax computation – 2012/13

	£
Trading income	19,000
Employment income	29,600
Total income	48,600
Less: Reliefs – Qualifying interest	(4,000)
Net income	44,600
Less: PA	(8,105)
Taxable income	36,495

Income tax:	£		£
Basic rate	34,370	x 20%	6,874
Higher rate	2,125	x 40%	850
	36,495		
Income tax liability			7,724
Less: PAYE			(4,299)
Income tax payable			3,425

Test your understanding 6

Paul and Peter
Income tax computations – 2012/13

					Paul	Peter
					£	£
Income					46,995	46,995
Less: PA					(8,105)	(8,105)
Taxable income					38,890	38,890
Income tax:	£	£			£	£
	34,370	36,870	(W)	x 20%	6,874	7,374
	4,520	2,020		x 40%	1,808	808
	38,890	38,890				
Income tax liability					8,682	8,182

Despite having the same income, Peter's income tax liability is £500 lower than Paul's. This represents the additional 20% tax saving on the gross payment of £2,500 (£2,000 x 100/80) to the charity.

Working: Peter's extended basic rate band

	£
Basic rate band threshold	34,370
Gross Gift Aid donation (£2,000 x 100/80)	2,500
Extended basic rate band	36,870

KAPLAN PUBLISHING

Clare

Income tax computation – 2012/13

	£
Trading income	156,000
Employment income	12,000
Total income	168,000
Less: Adjusted PA (W1)	(3,480)
Taxable income	164,520

Income tax:	£	£
Basic rate (W2)	93,120 × 20%	18,624
Higher rate (W2)	71,400 × 40%	28,560
	164,520	
Income tax liability		47,184

Workings

(W1) Adjusted personal allowance

	£	£
Basic personal allowance		8,105
Net income	168,000	
Less: Gross Gift Aid donation		
(£47,000 × 100/80)	(58,750)	
Adjusted net income	109,250	
Less: Income limit	(100,000)	
	9,250	
Reduction of PA (50% × £9,250)		(4,625)
Adjusted PA		3,480

(W2) **Extended band thresholds**

	BR Band £	HR Band £
Current threshold	34,370	150,000
Plus: Gross Gift Aid donation	58,750	58,750
Revised threshold	93,120	208,750

Clare's taxable income falls above the basic rate band threshold but below the threshold where the additional rate applies.

Property and investment income

Chapter learning objectives

Upon completion of this chapter you will be able to:

- identify savings income

- calculate tax on savings income

- compute the tax payable on dividend income

- explain the basis for computing property business profits

- explain the rules for allowing expenses and identify the key deductions from property business profits

- demonstrate the reliefs available for a property business loss

- compute the amount assessable when a premium is received for the grant of a short lease

- define when a letting qualifies as furnished holiday lettings

- explain the differences between furnished holiday lettings and normal furnished lettings

- explain when rent a room relief applies

- explain the key features of an Individual Savings Account

- explain how a married couple or a couple in a civil partnership can minimise their tax liabilities.

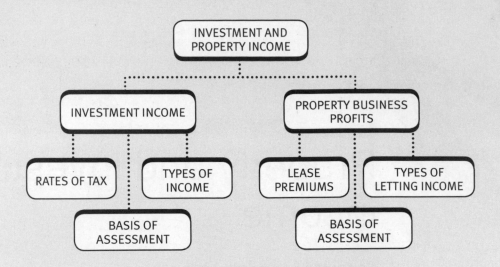

Introduction

The primary source of income for most taxpayers is derived from earnings, either from employment or self-employment. However, some taxpayers also have investment income.

This chapter covers the taxation of income from investments. The main sources are savings income, dividend income and property income.

1 Savings income

The main types of savings income are bank and building society interest.

Basis of assessment

Banks and building societies pay interest to individuals net of 20% tax.

Interest received from unquoted company loan stock is also received net of 20% tax.

An individual is taxed on the grossed up amount of the savings income **received in a tax year**.

- The gross amount of interest is calculated as:

$$\textbf{(interest received} \times \textbf{100/80)}$$

- The 20% tax is retained by the bank, building society or unquoted company and then paid direct to HMRC on behalf of the individual.

Where the tax suffered on interest exceeds the individual's tax liability, it is repaid via the self-assessment system (see Chapter 12).

KAPLAN PUBLISHING

Rates of tax on savings

- Savings income is normally taxed in the same way as 'other income' at the basic, higher and additional rates of tax (20%, 40% and 50%).

- However, a starting rate of tax of 10% will apply to savings income where it falls into the first £2,710 of taxable income.

- To determine the appropriate rate of tax to apply to savings income, it is treated as the next slice of a taxpayer's income **after** 'other income' has been taxed (i.e. savings income is taxed after employment income, trading income and property income).

Therefore, the rate of tax applicable to taxable savings income will depend on the level of taxable 'other income' as follows:

- No taxable 'other income'
  – the first £2,710 of taxable savings income is taxed at 10%.

- Taxable 'other income' below £2,710
  – savings income falling into the rest of the first £2,710 is taxed at 10%.

- Taxable 'other income' in excess of £2,710
  – the 10% rate is not applicable.

The remainder of savings income is then taxed at 20%/40%/50% according to the band in which the income falls:

- savings income falling into the remainder of the £34,370 (basic rate band) will be taxed at 20%

- the next £115,630 will be taxed at 40%, and

- the excess above £150,000 will be taxed at 50%.

As the taxpayer has 20% tax deducted at source on bank and building society interest and unquoted loan stock interest:

- if the recipient is a basic rate taxpayer, there is no additional tax liability to pay on this income. Whilst the income will be recorded gross in the tax computation, the tax paid at source will fully meet the liability.

- if the taxpayer only pays tax at the starting rate (10%) he or she will be entitled to a refund.

- for higher and additional rate taxpayers, an additional liability falls due.

Savings income received gross

The following interest is received gross (i.e. no tax is deducted at source).

- Interest from National Savings and Investments bank ('NS&I') accounts, including income from NS&I Easy Access Savings Accounts (EASA), NS&I Investment Accounts and NS&I Direct Saver Accounts.

- Interest from gilt-edged securities, or gilts, including Treasury stock, Government stock and Exchequer stock.

- Interest from quoted company loan stock.

Remember, income from NS&I Certificates is exempt.

Income tax computation

Where an individual has different sources of income, set up a computation (see below) using columns for each type of income to ensure that you:

- calculate the income tax liability on the different sources of income in the correct order, and

- apply the correct rates of income tax.

Income tax computation – 2012/13

	Total	Other income	Savings income	Dividends
	£	£	£	£
Employment income	X	X		
Trading profits	X	X		
Property income	X	X		
Interest (× 100/80)	X		X	
Dividends (× 100/90)	X			X
Total income	X	X	X	X
Less: Reliefs	(X)	(X)		
Net income	X	X	X	X
Less: PA	(X)	(X)		
Taxable income	X	X	X	X

Test your understanding 1

Jamie received bank interest of £1,600 during 2012/13.

Calculate Jamie's income tax payable assuming he also had employment income and PAYE deductions in 2012/13 of:

(a) £25,000 (PAYE £3,379)

(b) £45,000 (PAYE £7,884)

(c) £9,350 (PAYE £249)

Set off of reliefs and personal allowances

To give the highest tax saving, PAs and reliefs are deducted from income in the following order:

(1) Other income

(2) Savings income

(3) Dividend income.

This is because the basic rate of tax on other income and savings income (20%) is higher than the corresponding lower rate of tax on dividends (10%).

Example 1 – Set off of reliefs and personal allowances

Simon earned employment income of £8,900 and received building society interest of £6,000 (net) in 2012/13. He paid qualifying interest of £100 during the year.

PAYE of £159 was deducted from his employment income.

Calculate the income tax repayable to Simon.

Answer to example 1

Income tax computation – 2012/13

	Total	Other income	Savings income
	£	£	£
Employment income	8,900	8,900	–
Savings income (£6,000 × 100/80)	7,500	–	7,500
Total income	16,400	8,900	7,500
Less: Interest paid	(100)	(100)	
Net income	16,300	8,800	7,500
Less: PA	(8,105)	(8,105)	–
Taxable income	8,195	695	7,500

			£
Income tax:			£
Other income – basic rate	695	x 20%	139
Savings income – starting rate	2,015	x 10%	201
	2,710		
Rest of savings income – basic rate	5,485	x 20%	1,097
	8,195		
Income tax liability			1,437
Less: PAYE			(159)
Tax credit on savings income (£7,500 x 20%)			(1,500)
Income tax repayable			(222)

Note: The starting rate band of £2,710 for savings income is firstly
reduced by other income before being applied to savings income.
The savings income is partly taxed at the starting rate of 10%,
with the balance taxed at the basic rate of 20%.
Here, tax is repayable because the tax credits exceed the tax
liability.

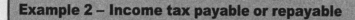

Example 2 – Income tax payable or repayable

Patrick has the following total income in 2012/13, which includes £1,600 (net) of savings income:

(a) £3,000

(b) £33,000

(c) £43,600

Patrick has no dividend income.

Calculate Patrick's income tax payable or repayable for the year.

Answer to example 2

(a) **Total income £3,000**

Income tax computation – 2012/13

	Total	Other income	Savings income
	£	£	£
Other income	1,000	1,000	
Savings income (£1,600 × 100/80)	2,000		2,000
Total income	3,000	1,000	2,000
Less: PA	(3,000)	(1,000)	(2,000)
Taxable income	Nil	Nil	Nil

	£
Income tax liability	Nil
Less: Tax credit on savings income (£2,000 × 20%)	(400)
Income tax repayable	(400)

(b) Total income £33,000

Income tax computation – 2012/13

	Total £	Other income £	Savings income £
Other income	31,000	31,000	
Savings income (£1,600 × 100/80)	2,000		2,000
Total income	33,000	31,000	2,000
Less: PA	(8,105)	(8,105)	–
Taxable income	24,895	22,895	2,000

Income tax:	£		£
Other income – basic rate	22,895 × 20%		4,579
Savings income – basic rate	2,000 × 20%		400
	24,895		
Income tax liability			4,979
Less: Tax credit on savings income (£2,000 × 20%)			(400)
Income tax payable			4,579

(c) Total income £43,600

Income tax computation – 2012/13

	Total £	Other income £	Savings income £
Other income	41,600	41,600	
Savings income (£1,600 × 100/80)	2,000		2,000
Total income	43,600	41,600	2,000
Less: PA	(8,105)	(8,105)	–
Taxable income	35,495	33,495	2,000

Income tax:	£	£
Other income – basic rate	33,495 x 20%	6,699
Savings income – basic rate	875 x 20%	175
	34,370	
Savings income – higher rate	1,125 x 40%	450
	35,495	
Income tax liability		7,324
Less: Tax credit on savings income (£2,000 × 20%)		(400)
Income tax payable		6,924

2 Dividend income

Dividends received from a company are charged to income tax in the tax year in which they are **received**.

The receipt date is taken as the date on the dividend voucher.

Tax treatment of dividends

As with savings income, dividends are received net. However for dividends, the process differs slightly:

- Dividends are deemed to be received net of a notional tax credit of 10%. Therefore, any dividends received must be grossed up by 100/90 prior to inclusion within the income tax computation as follows:

(Dividend received × 100/90)

- As with savings income, the tax credit is available to be set against the taxpayer's tax liability.

- However, as the tax credit is notional (i.e. the paying company does not actually make any payment to HMRC on the shareholder's behalf), it can only be used to reduce the taxpayer's income tax liability.

- It is not possible to reclaim this tax credit in cash should it exceed the tax liability for the year.

- Tax credits on dividends are set off, against a taxpayer's income tax liability, in priority to all other tax credits, including PAYE.

Rates of tax on dividends

The following rates of tax apply to dividend income:

Dividends falling into the:	Rate of tax
Basic rate band (first £34,370)	10%
Higher rate (£34,371 – £150,000)	32.5%
Additional rate (over £150,000)	42.5%

In calculating the income tax liability, dividends are treated as the top slice of income (i.e. taxed **after** 'other income' and 'savings income').

- If the recipient is a basic rate taxpayer, there is no additional liability to pay or refund to claim on any dividend income received. The tax credit will fully meet the liability.

- For higher rate and additional rate taxpayers, an additional liability falls due at 32.5% (higher rate) or 42.5% (additional rate), with a notional tax credit of 10% suffered at source.

Example 3 – Dividend income

Jeremy earned employment income of £14,000 and received dividends of £6,750 in 2012/13. PAYE of £1,179 was deducted in respect of the employment income.

Calculate Jeremy's income tax payable for 2012/13.

Answer to example 3

Income tax computation – 2012/13

	Total	Other income	Dividend income
	£	£	£
Employment income	14,000	14,000	
Dividends (£6,750 × 100/90) (Note 1)	7,500		7,500
Total income	21,500	14,000	7,500
Less: PA (Note 2)	(8,105)	(8,105)	
Taxable income	13,395	5,895	7,500

Income tax:	£	£
Other income	5,895 x 20%	1,179
Dividend income (Note 3)	7,500 x 10%	750
	13,395	
Income tax liability		1,929
Less: Tax credit on dividend (Note 4)		(750)
PAYE		(1,179)
Income tax payable		Nil

Notes:

(1) Remember that dividends are always deemed to have been received net of a 10% tax credit and must be grossed up by 100/90, before including in the tax computation.

(2) The PA is deducted from 'other income' as this results in the highest tax saving.

(3) The dividends are treated as the highest part of Jeremy's income and as he is only a basic rate taxpayer, all the dividends will be taxed at 10%.

(4) The dividend credit can never create a refund; at best it can reduce the income tax liability to £Nil. It is set off in priority to other tax credits and PAYE.

Example 4 – Dividend income

Jacob earned employment income of £27,900 and received dividends of £15,750 in 2012/13. PAYE of £3,959 was paid in respect of the employment income.

Calculate Jacob's income tax payable for 2012/13.

Answer to example 4

Income tax computation – 2012/13

	Total	Other income	Dividend income
	£	£	£
Employment income	27,900	27,900	
Dividends (£15,750 × 100/90) (Note)	17,500		17,500
Total income	45,400	27,900	17,500
Less: PA	(8,105)	(8,105)	
Taxable income	37,295	19,795	17,500

Income tax:		£		£
Other income – basic rate	19,795	x 20%		3,959
Dividend income – basic rate (Note)	14,575	x 10%		1,457
	34,370			
Dividend income – higher rate	2,925	x 32.5%		951
	37,295			

	£
Income tax liability	6,367
Less: Tax credit on dividend (£17,500 x 10%)	(1,750)
PAYE on employment income	(3,959)
Income tax payable	658

Note: The dividends are treated as the highest part of Jacob's income. The first £14,575 of the gross dividend falls into the basic rate band, and is taxed at the lower rate of 10%, the remaining £2,925 (£17,500 – £14,575) falls into the higher rate band, and is taxed at the higher rate of 32.5%.

Example 5 – Dividend income

Simone received dividends of £7,650 in 2012/13. She received no other income during the year.

Calculate Simone's income tax payable/repayable for 2012/13.

Answer to example 5

Income tax computation – 2012/13

	£
Dividends (£7,650 × 100/90)	8,500
Less: PA	(8,105)
	———
Taxable income	395
	———
Income tax liability (£395 x 10%)	39
Less: Tax credit on dividends (£395 x 10%) (Note)	(39)
	———
Income tax payable	Nil
	———

Note: The tax credit on the dividends in excess of the tax liability is not repayable and therefore lost.

Test your understanding 2

Emily has income in 2012/13 as follows:

Employment income (PAYE deducted in the year is £6,299)	£39,600
Bank interest received	£1,600
Dividends received	£2,700

Calculate Emily's income tax payable for the year.

Example 6 – Comprehensive scenarios

Gordon Lamont, a single man, received dividend income of £1,350 and bank interest of £300 (net), in 2012/13. He also has trading income. Assume his trading income in 2012/13 is as follows:

Situation:	£
A	3,970
B	8,600
C	45,745
D	149,875

Calculate the income tax payable/repayable for each situation.

Answer to example 6

Situation A: Income tax computation – 2012/13

	Total	Other income	Savings income	Dividend income
	£	£	£	£
Trading income	3,970	3,970		
Bank interest (£300 × 100/80)	375		375	
Dividends (£1,350 × 100/90)	1,500			1,500
Total income	5,845	3,970	375	1,500
Less: PA (restricted)	(8,105)	(3,970)	(375)	(1,500)
Taxable income	Nil	Nil	Nil	Nil

	£
Income tax	Nil
Less: Tax credit on dividend income (Note)	Nil
Tax credit on savings income (£375 x 20%)	(75)
Income tax repayable	(75)

Note: The tax credit on the dividend income is only available to reduce a liability; it cannot create a refund.

Situation B: Income tax computation – 2012/13

	Total	Other income	Savings income	Dividend income
	£	£	£	£
Trading income	8,600	8,600		
Savings (£300 × 100/80)	375		375	
Dividends (£1,350 × 100/90)	1,500			1,500
Total income	10,475	8,600	375	1,500
Less: PA	(8,105)	(8,105)		
Taxable income	2,370	495	375	1,500

Income tax:		£	£
Other income – basic rate	495	x 20%	99
Savings income – starting rate	375	x 10%	37
Dividend income – basic rate	1,500	x 10%	150
	2,370		

Income tax liability	286
Less: Tax credit on dividend income (£1,500 x 10%)	(150)
Tax credit on savings income (£375 x 20%)	(75)
Income tax payable	61

Situation C: Income tax computation – 2012/13

	Total £	Other income £	Savings income £	Dividend income £
Trading income	45,745	45,745		
Savings (£300 × 100/80)	375		375	
Dividends (£1,350 × 100/90)	1,500			1,500
Total income	47,620	45,745	375	1,500
Less: PA	(8,105)	(8,105)		
Taxable income	39,515	37,640	375	1,500

Income tax:	£	£
Other income – basic rate	34,370 x 20%	6,874
Other income – higher rate	3,270 x 40%	1,308
	37,640	
Savings income – higher rate	375 x 40%	150
Dividend income – higher rate	1,500 x 32.5%	487
	39,515	

	£
Income tax liability	8,819
Less: Tax credit on dividend income (£1,500 x 10%)	(150)
Tax credit on savings income (£375 x 20%)	(75)
Income tax payable	8,594

Situation D: Income tax computation – 2012/13

	Total	Other income	Savings income	Dividend income
	£	£	£	£
Trading income	149,875	149,875		
Savings (£300 × 100/80)	375		375	
Dividends (£1,350 × 100/90)	1,500			1,500
Total income	151,750	149,875	375	1,500
Less: Adjusted PA (Note)	(Nil)	(Nil)		
Total income	151,750	149,875	375	1,500

Income tax:	£		£
Other income – basic rate	34,370 × 20%		6,874
Other income – higher rate	115,505 × 40%		46,202
	149,875		
Savings income – higher rate	125 × 40%		50
	150,000		
Rest of savings income – additional rate	250 × 50%		125
Dividend income – additional rate	1,500 × 42.5%		637
	151,750		

Income tax liability	53,888
Less: Tax credit on dividend income (£1,500 x 10%)	(150)
Tax credit on savings income (£375 x 20%)	(75)
Income tax payable	53,663

Note: As total income exceeds £100,000 by more than double the personal allowance, the PA is reduced to £Nil.

Test your understanding 3

Susan has the following income and outgoings for 2012/13:

	£
Trading income	11,615
Employment income (gross)	13,000
Bank interest (amount received)	2,800
Dividend income (amount received)	1,800
Qualifying interest (amount paid)	1,000

PAYE of £979 was deducted from the employment income.

Calculate Susan's income tax payable for 2012/13.

Test your understanding 4

Alfie earned employment income of £187,450, and received bank interest of £15,000 and dividends of £13,500 in 2012/13.

PAYE of £71,851 was deducted from his employment income.

Calculate Alfie's income tax payable for 2012/13.

3 Property income

For the purposes of the examination, you are required to be able to deal with the following:

- Property business profits arising from the rental/lease of property.

- The premium received on the grant of a short lease.

- Profits arising from the commercial letting of furnished holiday accommodation.

- Rental income received from the rent-a-room scheme.

Property business profit – basis of assessment

The key assessment rules for property business profits are as follows:

- The assessable income from land and buildings for each tax year is computed as:

	£
Rental income	X
Less: Related expenses	(X)
Assessable income	X

- If the landlord lets more than one property, the assessable amount for each year is the aggregate of the profits and losses from all properties (except furnished holiday lettings – see later).
- The rental income and related expenses are assessable/deductible on an accruals basis. Accordingly, the due dates for payment of rent and actual payment dates are irrelevant.
- All calculations in the examination are made to the nearest month.

Example 7 – Property income

Hembery owns a property that was let for the first time on 1 July 2012. The rent of £5,000 p.a. is paid alternatively:

(a) quarterly in advance

(b) quarterly in arrears.

Hembery paid allowable expenses of £200 in December 2012 (related to redecoration following a burst pipe), and of £400 in May 2013 (related to repair work which was completed in March 2013).

Calculate Hembery's property business profit for 2012/13.

Answer to example 7

	£	£
Rent accrued (9/12 × £5,000) (Note 1)		3,750
Allowable expenses		
Redecoration	200	
Repairs (Note 2)	400	
		(600)
Property business profit		3,150

Notes:

(1) The rent under each alternative is the same – the accruals basis of assessment means the rents accrued between 6 April 2012 to 5 April 2013. The actual payment terms or payment dates are irrelevant.

(2) As the work was completed in March 2013 under the accruals basis the expenditure is deductible in 2012/13, the period in which the work was undertaken, and not when the expenditure is paid.

Property business profit – allowable deductions

The expenses allowable against the rental income are computed under the normal rules for the assessment of trading income. These are discussed more fully in Chapter 5.

The main rules are as follows:

- To be allowable, the expenses must have been incurred **wholly** and **exclusively** for the **purposes of the property business.**
  This covers items such as:
    - insurance
    - agents fees and other management expenses
    - repairs
    - interest on a loan to acquire or improve the property.

- Irrecoverable debts are allowable. If a tenant leaves without paying the outstanding rent, the amount owed can be deducted as an expense.

- Relief is available for any expenditure incurred before letting commenced, under the normal pre-trading expenditure rules (see Chapter 5).

- Capital expenditure is not normally an allowable deduction. The main distinction between capital and revenue expenditure is between improvements and repairs.
    - Repairs expenditure would normally be allowable.
    - Improvement expenditure is not allowable.

KAPLAN PUBLISHING

> ### Distinction between repairs and capital expenditure
>
> Caution is required where an item is in need of repair.
>
> For example, the replacement of kitchen units with similar standard units would normally be regarded as a repair. However, had the new units been state of the art new kitchen units, the expenditure would probably have been regarded as an improvement.

- Depreciation may be charged in accounts as a means of writing off the cost of capital expenditure over the life of an asset. Depreciation is not an allowable deduction.

- Normal capital allowances (see Chapter 6) cannot be claimed for expenditure on plant and machinery for use in a dwelling house. However, a form of capital allowances known as the 'renewals basis' can be claimed for furnished accommodation.

Renewals basis

- The renewals basis allows relief for the expense of renewing furniture to the same standard.

- The original cost and any improvement element in a replacement is disallowed.

- The detailed record keeping requirements of this method of relief normally discourage its use in practice.

Wear and tear allowance

The renewals basis of giving relief for capital expenditure is normally replaced by a 'wear and tear' allowance, which is calculated as 10% of the rent received, net of any council tax or water rates on the property paid by the landlord.

Wear and tear allowance

= 10% × (rents received – council tax – water rates)

Note: This formula is **not** provided in the exam.

Example 8 – Property income

Giles owns a cottage that he lets out furnished at an annual rent of £3,600, payable monthly in advance.

During 2012/13, he incurs the following expenditure:

May 2012	Replacement of one broken kitchen unit with a unit of similar standard	£275
June 2012	Insurance for year from 5 July (previous year £420)	£480
November 2012	Drain clearance	£380
May 2013	Redecoration (work completed in March 2013)	£750

The tenant had vacated the property during June 2012, without having paid the rent due for June. Giles was unable to trace the defaulting tenant, but managed to let the property to new tenants from 1 July 2012.

Calculate the property business profit for 2012/13, assuming Giles claims the 10% wear and tear allowance.

Answer to example 8

Property business profit – 2012/13

	£	£
Rent accrued		3,600
Expenses		
Repair to kitchen units (Note 1)	275	
Irrecoverable debt – June 2012 rent (1/12 × £3,600)	300	
Insurance (3/12 × £420 + 9/12 × £480)	465	
Drain clearance	380	
Redecoration	750	
Wear and tear = 10% × rent received (Note 2)		
10% × (£3,600 – £300)	330	
		(2,500)
Property business profit		1,100

Notes:

(1) The replacement of a kitchen unit with one of a similar standard would normally be treated as an allowable repair.

(2) The wear and tear allowance is based on rents **received** = (rents accrued less irrecoverable debt).

KAPLAN PUBLISHING

Test your understanding 5

Eastleigh acquired two properties on 1 June 2012, that were first let on 1 July 2012.

Property A is let unfurnished for an annual rent of £4,000, payable quarterly in advance. Eastleigh incurred the following expenditure in respect of this property.

20.6.12	Repairs to roof following a storm on 15 June	£1,600
29.6.12	Insurance for year ended 31.5.13	£420
1.2.13	Repainting exterior	£810

Property B is let furnished for an annual rent of £5,000, payable quarterly in arrears. The tenants were late in paying the amount due on 31 March 2013 – this was not received until 15 April 2013.

Eastleigh incurred the following expenditure in respect of this property in 2012/13.

4.6.12	Letting expenses paid to agent	£40
29.6.12	Insurance for year ended 31.5.13	£585

Assuming Eastleigh claims the wear and tear allowance where applicable, calculate his property business profit for 2012/13.

Property business losses

If rental income is less than the allowable expenditure, a loss arises.

- If the landlord owns more than one property, the profits and losses on all the properties are aggregated to calculate the assessable income for the year. This effectively provides instant loss relief.

- If there is an overall loss on all properties, the property income assessment for the year will be £Nil.

- Any unrelieved loss is carried forward indefinitely and offset against the first available future property business profits.

Example 9 – Property losses

Sheila owns three properties that were rented out. Her assessable income and allowable expenses for the two years to 5 April 2013 were:

Property	1	2	3
	£	£	£
Income			
2011/12	1,200	450	3,150
2012/13	800	1,750	2,550
Expenses			
2011/12	1,850	600	2,800
2012/13	900	950	2,700

Calculate Sheila's property business profit/(loss) for 2011/12 and 2012/13.

Answer to example 9

Property	1	2	3	Total
	£	£	£	£
2011/12				
Income	1,200	450	3,150	4,800
Less: Expenses	(1,850)	(600)	(2,800)	(5,250)
Profit/(loss)	(650)	(150)	350	(450)
Property business profit				Nil
Loss carried forward				450
2012/13				
Income	800	1,750	2,550	5,100
Less: Expenses	(900)	(950)	(2,700)	(4,550)
Profit/(loss)	(100)	800	(150)	550
Less: Loss brought forward				(450)
Property business profit				100

Note: There is no need to calculate the profit/(loss) on each property separately. One computation amalgamating all income and expenses is all that is required.

KAPLAN PUBLISHING

Example 10 – Property income and losses

For many years Tom Jones has owned six houses in Upland Avenue that are available for letting unfurnished. The following details have been provided by the client:

Property number	21	23	25	38	40	67
	£	£	£	£	£	£
Rent due for y/e 5.4.13	2,080	1,820	2,340	1,300	1,300	2,080
Insurance due for y/e 5.4.13	280	220	340	150	150	140

Tom employs a gardener to look after all the properties, and pays him £1,200 a year. There are also accountancy charges of £480 a year; both of these costs are allocated equally to each property.

Numbers 23 and 40, had new tenancies in the year. The cost of advertising for tenants was £50, in respect of number 23 and £100 for number 40. The new tenant at number 23 took over immediately the old tenant moved out. Unfortunately, the old tenant at Number 40 defaulted on rent of £350, due before the new tenant moved in.

During the year Tom had to replace the boiler in number 40, at a cost of £800. During the year he also had to replace the water tank at number 21, at a cost of £100 and a replacement roof for number 25, cost him £5,000.

Tom has loans outstanding on each of the six properties and pays interest of £500 per year on each loan.

(a) **Explain how relief for a property business loss can be obtained.**

(b) **Calculate Tom's property business loss for 2012/13.**

Answer to example 10

(a) **Relief for property business losses**

Where a taxpayer owns numerous properties, accounts will normally be prepared for each property for each tax year, resulting in either a profit or loss in each case. These are automatically offset against each other for the tax year to ascertain the property business profit or loss for the year.

However, it is not necessary to consider profits and losses on each property separately. For tax purposes the computation is drawn up to show the total rents, expenses, etc. for all the properties, instead of property by property, thereby giving automatic loss relief.

Where the aggregated total is a loss, this is carried forward indefinitely, to be offset against the first available future aggregate property business profits.

(b) **Property business loss – 2012/13**

	£	£
Rents accrued		
(£2,080 + £1,820 + £2,340 + £1,300 + £1,300 + £2,080)		10,920
Less: Expenses payable		
Insurance		
(£280 + £220 + £340 + £150 + £150 + £140)	1,280	
Gardener	1,200	
Accountancy	480	
Advertising (£50 + £100)	150	
Repairs (£100 + £5,000 + £800) (Note)	5,900	
Irrecoverable debt	350	
Interest (£500 × 6)	3,000	
		(12,360)
Property loss		(1,440)
Assessable property income		Nil

Note:

The replacement of the boiler, water tank and roof are taken to be necessary replacements with assets of a similar kind and will therefore normally be treated as allowable revenue expenditure. Had there been an element of improvement in the expenditure, some or all may be disallowed as capital in nature.

4 Premiums received on the grant of a short lease

Definitions

A **premium** is a lump sum payment made by the tenant to the landlord in consideration for the granting of a lease.

The **grant** of a lease is where the owner of a property gives the tenant the exclusive right to use the property for a fixed period of time.

A **short lease** is a lease for a period of less than or equal to 50 years.

Income tax treatment

- Part of the premium received in respect of the **granting** of a **short lease** is assessed on the landlord as property business income in the year the lease is granted.

- The amount assessable as property business income is:

	£
Premium	X
Less: Premium × 2% × (n – 1)	(X)
	——
Property business income	X
	——

Where:

n = Length of lease = number of **complete** years (ignore part of a year).

Alternative calculation:

Property business income = Premium x (51 – n) / 50

Note: These formulae are **not** provided in the exam.

Example 11 – Premiums received on the grant of a short lease

Rodney granted a 21-year lease to Charles on 1 July 2012, for a premium of £10,500.

Calculate the amount assessable on Rodney as property business income in 2012/13.

Answer to example 11

	£
Premium	10,500
Less: £10,500 × 2% × (21 − 1)	(4,200)
Property business income	6,300

Alternative calculation:
Property business income = £10,500 × (51 − 21) / 50 = £6,300

Test your understanding 6

Albert grants an 18-year lease to Derek for £26,000, on 6 May 2012.

Calculate the amount assessable on Albert as property business income for 2012/13.

---

5 Furnished holiday lettings

Profits arising from the commercial letting of furnished holiday accommodation (FHA) is still assessable as property business income but it is treated as though the profits arose from a single and separate trade.

As a result, separate records regarding these properties have to be kept because there are specific rules and reliefs that apply to such properties.

Qualifying conditions

The letting will only be treated as FHA if it meets the following conditions:

- The property is let **furnished**.

- The letting is on a **commercial basis** with a view to the realisation of profits.

- It is **available** for commercial letting, to the public generally, as holiday accommodation for not less than **210 days** a year.

- The accommodation is **actually let** for at least **105 days** a year (excluding periods of 'long-term occupation' – see below).
    - Where a taxpayer owns more than one property, the 105 days test is satisfied if the average number of days for which the properties are let in the year is at least 105.

- The property must not be let for periods of 'long-term occupation' in excess of 155 days in a year.

Long-term occupation is defined as a period of more than 31 consecutive days when the property is let to the same person.

It is possible for the property to be let to the same person for more than 31 days, however, when aggregating all such periods of longer term occupation (which could be a few periods of letting to different persons), the total must not exceed 155 days.

Tax treatment of furnished holiday lettings

Any profits from commercially let FHA remain assessable as property income. However, the profits are treated as arising from a separate trade carried on by the landlord, and are not pooled with other rental property.

The following advantages and reliefs are available:

- The profits are treated as relevant earnings for the purposes of relief for personal pension scheme contributions (see Chapter 10).

- Normal capital allowances will be available in respect of plant and machinery including furniture and furnishings. This will usually be more beneficial than the wear and tear allowance or the renewals basis.

- Capital gains tax roll-over relief and Entrepreneurs' relief is available (see Chapter 16).

- Any losses made in a qualifying UK FHA business may only be set against income from the same UK FHA business.

6 Rent-a-room relief

If an individual lets furnished accommodation in their main residence, and the income is liable to tax as property income, a special exemption applies.

Gross annual rental receipts are £4,250 or less

- The income is exempt from tax.

  Note that the rent-a-room relief limit is **not** given in the tax tables in the examination.

- The individual's limit of £4,250 is reduced by half to £2,125 if, during a particular tax year, any other person(s) also received income from letting accommodation in the property while the property was the first person's main residence.

This rule allows a married couple taking in lodgers to either have all the rent paid to one spouse (who will then have the full limit of £4,250), or to have the rent divided between the spouses (and each spouse will then have a limit of £2,125).

- An individual may elect to ignore the exemption for a particular year, for example, if a loss is incurred when taking account of expenses.

Gross annual rental receipts are more than £4,250

- The individual may choose between:
  - paying tax on the excess gross rent over £4,250
  - being taxed in the normal way on rental income.

In summary, assess the lower of:

Method 1 – Normal assessment		Method 2 – Rent-a-room relief	
	£		£
Rental income	X	Rental income	X
Less: Expenses	(X)	Less: Rent-a-room relief	(4,250)
Less: Wear and tear allowance	(X)		
	—		—
Profit	X	Profit	X
	—		—

In deciding whether to elect for rent-a-room relief, the key question will therefore be whether or not expenses (including the wear and tear allowance) exceed £4,250.

7 Individual savings accounts

The objective of Individual savings accounts (ISAs) is to enable the taxpayer to invest in an account that will create tax efficient income streams.

ISA annual subscription limits

For the tax year 2012/13, there is an annual subscription limit of £11,280, of which a maximum of £5,640 may go into a cash ISA.

The balance of the annual total limit not invested in a cash ISA may be invested in a stocks ISA.

Note that spouses and civil partners each have their own limits.

The ISA limits will be provided in the tax rates and allowance tables in the examination.

Individual savings accounts

ISAs are the most common form of tax efficient investment. They can be opened by any individual aged 16 or over who is resident and ordinarily resident in the UK. However an individual must be aged 18 or over to open a stocks and shares ISA.

An ISA offers the following tax reliefs:

- Income (interest and dividends) is received free of income tax.

- Disposals of investments within an ISA are free of capital gains tax.

There is no minimum holding period, so withdrawals can be made from the account at any time.

There are two types of ISAs:

Cash ISAs

This includes bank and building society accounts, as well as those National Savings products where the income is not exempt from tax.

Stocks and shares ISAs

Investment is allowed in shares and securities listed on a stock exchange anywhere in the world.

8 Husband and wife planning

Spouses have their own personal allowances and income tax rate bands.

A married couple can transfer income generating assets between them, at no tax cost, to minimise their joint tax liability.

These rules also apply to partners within a Civil Partnership.

Example 13 – Husband and wife planning

Margaret is married to Alfred. She is aged 45 and has employment income of £50,000 p.a. She has various bank accounts from which she receives interest of £4,500 each year.

Alfred, aged 52, earns £20,000 trading profits from self-employment each year. He has no other income.

Calculate the couple's income tax liability for 2012/13 and advise how they could have saved tax by reorganising their investments.

Answer to example 13

Margaret – Income tax computation – 2012/13

	Total	Other income	Savings income
	£	£	£
Employment income	50,000	50,000	
Bank interest (£4,500 × 100/80)	5,625		5,625
Total income	55,625	50,000	5,625
Less: PA	(8,105)	(8,105)	
Taxable income	47,520	41,895	5,625

Income tax:	£		£
Other income – basic rate	34,370	x 20%	6,874
Other income – higher rate	7,525	x 40%	3,010
	41,895		
Savings income – higher rate	5,625	x 40%	2,250
	47,520		
Income tax liability			12,134

Alfred – Income tax computation – 2012/13

	£
Trading income	20,000
Less: PA	(8,105)
Taxable income	11,895
Income tax liability (£11,895 x 20%)	2,379

Tax saving advice

Margaret is a higher rate taxpayer paying tax on her investment income at 40% in 2012/13. Alfred, however, is a basic rate taxpayer.

If the bank accounts were in Alfred's name he would have paid tax on the interest at 20% thus saving the couple tax of £1,125 (£5,625 × 20%).

Alternatively Margaret could take advantage of an ISA and invest £5,640. The interest would be tax free. If some of the bank account is in Alfred's name he could also transfer £5,640 into an ISA.

9 Chapter summary

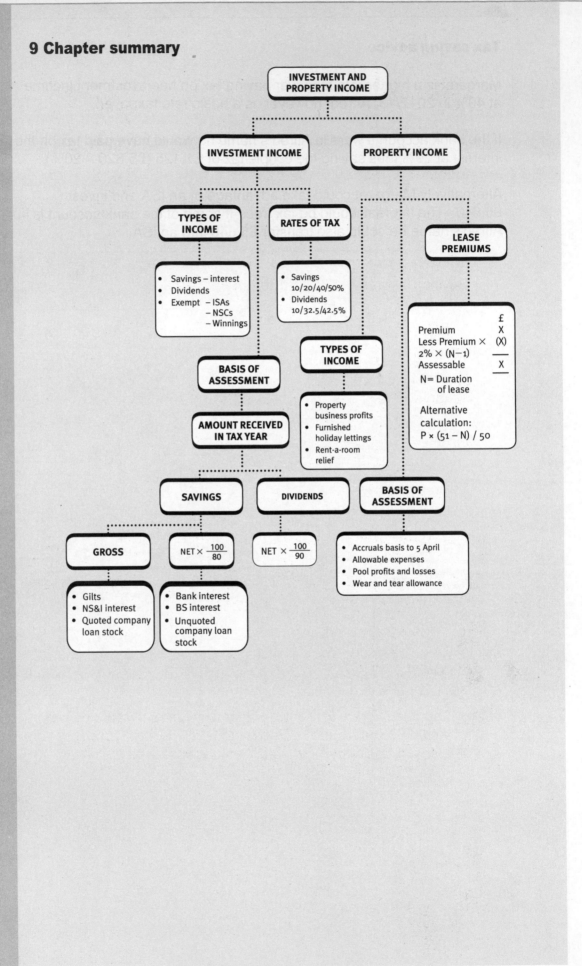

Test your understanding answers

Test your understanding 1

Jamie

(a) **Income tax computation – 2012/13**

	Total	Other income	Savings income
	£	£	£
Employment income	25,000	25,000	
Savings income (£1,600 × 100/80)	2,000		2,000
Total income	27,000	25,000	2,000
Less: PA	(8,105)	(8,105)	
Taxable income	18,895	16,895	2,000

Income tax:		£	£
Other income – basic rate	16,895	x 20%	3,379
Savings income – basic rate	2,000	x 20%	400
	18,895		

Income tax liability		3,779
Less: Tax credit on savings income (£2,000 × 20%)		(400)
PAYE		(3,379)
Income tax payable		Nil

Note: The starting rate for savings income is not applicable as 'other income' exceeds the £2,710 band limit. Savings income, to the extent it falls in the basic rate band, is assessed at 20%.

(b) **Income tax computation – 2012/13**

	Total	Other income	Savings income
	£	£	£
Employment income	45,000	45,000	
Savings income (£1,600 × 100/80)	2,000		2,000
	———	———	———
Total income	47,000	45,000	2,000
Less: PA	(8,105)	(8,105)	
	———	———	———
Taxable income	38,895	36,895	2,000
	———	———	———

Income tax:	£		£
Other income – basic rate	34,370 x 20%		6,874
Other income – higher rate	2,525 x 40%		1,010
	———		
	36,895		
Savings income – higher rate	2,000 x 40%		800
	———		
	38,895		
	———		
Income tax liability			8,684
Less: Tax credit on savings income (£2,000 × 20%)			(400)
PAYE			(7,884)
			———
Income tax payable			400
			———

Note: In this situation, the starting rate for savings income is not applicable and all of the savings income falls in the higher rate band. It is therefore assessed at 40%. The deduction for the amount already paid is given, and the additional liability of £400 is settled via the self-assessment process.

(c) Income tax computation – 2012/13

	Total	Other income	Savings income
	£	£	£
Employment income	9,350	9,350	
Savings income (£1,600 × 100/80)	2,000		2,000
Total income	11,350	9,350	2,000
Less: PA	(8,105)	(8,105)	
Taxable income	3,245	1,245	2,000

Income tax:		£		£
Other income – basic rate	1,245	x 20%		249
Savings income – starting rate	1,465	x 10%		146
	2,710			
Rest of savings income – basic rate	535	x 20%		107
	3,245			
Income tax liability				502
Less: Tax credit on savings income (£2,000 × 20%)				(400)
PAYE				(249)
Income tax repayable				(147)

Note: The starting rate band of £2,710 for savings income is firstly reduced by taxable other income before being applied to savings income.

The savings income is partly taxed at the starting rate of 10%, with the balance taxed at the basic rate of 20%.

Here, tax is repayable because the tax credits exceed the tax liability.

Test your understanding 2

Emily
Income tax computation – 2012/13

	Total	Other income	Savings income	Dividend income
	£	£	£	£
Employment income	39,600	39,600		
Savings (£1,600 × 100/80)	2,000		2,000	
Dividends (£2,700 × 100/90)	3,000			3,000
Total income	44,600	39,600	2,000	3,000
Less: PA	(8,105)	(8,105)		
Taxable income	36,495	31,495	2,000	3,000

Income tax:		£	£
Other income – basic rate	31,495	x 20%	6,299
Savings income – basic rate	2,000	x 20%	400
Dividend income – basic rate	875	x 10%	87
	34,370		
Dividend income – higher rate	2,125	x 32.5%	691
	36,495		

Income tax liability		7,477
Less: Tax credit on dividend income (£3,000 x 10%)		(300)
PAYE on employment income		(6,299)
Tax credit on interest (£2,000 x 20%)		(400)
Income tax payable		478

Test your understanding 3

Susan
Income tax computation – 2012/13

	Total £	Other income £	Savings income £	Dividend income £
Trading income	11,615	11,615		
Employment income	13,000	13,000		
Savings (£2,800 × 100/80)	3,500		3,500	
Dividends (£1,800 × 100/90)	2,000			2,000
Total income	30,115	24,615	3,500	2,000
Less Reliefs: Interest paid	(1,000)	(1,000)		
Net income	29,115	23,615	3,500	2,000
Less: PA	(8,105)	(8,105)		
Taxable income	21,010	15,510	3,500	2,000

Income tax:		£		£
Other income – basic rate		15,510 x 20%		3,102
Savings income – basic rate		3,500 x 20%		700
Dividend income – basic rate		2,000 x 10%		200
		21,010		

	£
Income tax liability	4,002
Less: Tax credit on dividend income (£2,000 x 10%)	(200)
PAYE on employment income	(979)
Tax credit on interest (£3,500 x 20%)	(700)
Income tax payable	2,123

Whilst the presentation above is the one that you have become used to, the columnar approach takes longer, time that may be valuable in the exam. It is possible to complete the computation with a single column and then separate the income, in the liability calculation at the foot of the computation.

Only use this approach however if you are totally comfortable that you will be able to correctly identify the different sources of income and apply the correct tax rates.

Susan: Income tax computation – 2012/13

	£
Trading income	11,615
Employment income	13,000
	———
	24,615
Savings income (£2,800 × 100/80)	3,500
Dividend income (£1,800 × 100/90)	2,000
	———
Total income	30,115
Less: Reliefs – interest paid	(1,000)
	———
Net income	29,115
Less: PA	(8,105)
	———
Taxable income	21,010
	———

Analysis of income:	£
Other income (£21,010 – £3,500 – £2,000)	15,510
Savings	3,500
Dividends	2,000

Income tax liability computation = as before

Test your understanding 4

Alfie
Income tax computation – 2012/13

	Total	Other income	Savings income	Dividend income
	£	£	£	£
Employment income	187,450	187,450		
Savings (£15,000 × 100/80)	18,750		18,750	
Dividends (£13,500 × 100/90)	15,000			15,000
Total income	221,200	187,450	18,750	15,000
Less: Adjusted PA (Note)	(Nil)	(Nil)		
Taxable income	221,200	187,450	18,750	15,000

Income tax:		£		£
Other income – basic rate		34,370 × 20%		6,874
Other income – higher rate		115,630 × 40%		46,252
Other income – additional rate		37,450 × 50%		18,725
		187,450		
Savings income – additional rate		18,750 × 50%		9,375
Dividend income – additional rate		15,000 × 42.5%		6,375
		221,200		

	£
Income tax liability	87,601
Less: Tax credit on dividend income (£15,000 x 10%)	(1,500)
Tax credit on savings income (£18,750 x 20%)	(3,750)
PAYE	(71,851)
Income tax payable	10,500

Note: As total income exceeds £100,000 by more than double the PA, the PA is reduced to £Nil.

Test your understanding 5

Eastleigh
Property business income – 2012/13

	£	£
Property A		
Rent (9/12 × £4,000)		3,000
Less: Insurance (10/12 × £420)	350	
Repainting exterior	810	
Roof repairs (pre-trading expenditure)	1,600	
		(2,760)
Profit		240
Property B		
Rent (9/12 × £5,000)		3,750
Less: Insurance (10/12 × £585)	488	
Letting expenses	40	
		(528)
		3,222
Wear and tear allowance (10% × £3,750)		(375)
Profit		2,847
Property business profit (£240 + £2,847)		3,087

Test your understanding 6

Albert
Property business income – 2012/13

	£
Premium	26,000
Less: £26,000 × 2% × (18 – 1)	(8,840)
Property business income	17,160

Alternative calculation = £26,000 × (51 – 18) / 50 = £17,160

Employment income

Chapter learning objectives

Upon completion of this chapter you will be able to:

- recognise the factors that determine whether an engagement is treated as employment or self-employment

- state the basis of assessment for income from employment

- list the statutory allowable employment income deductions, including an explanation of how charitable giving can be made through a payroll deduction scheme

- determine when travel expenses are allowable

- explain the basis for other allowable employment income expenses

- determine when the statutory approved mileage allowance is due and calculate it

- explain the purpose of a dispensation from HM Revenue and Customs

- recognise the general principles in calculating benefits

- recognise the exempt benefits

- calculate the benefits assessable on all employees

- explain the basis of determining whether an individual is a P11D employee and state the effect

- calculate the benefits arising on an employer-provided vehicle

- identify the circumstances when the provision of a loan will result in an employee benefit and calculate the loan interest benefit

- calculate the employee benefit where an asset is provided for private use

- calculate the benefit when an asset is transferred to an employee

- calculate the benefit(s) when accommodation is provided to an employee

- given details of a remuneration package calculate the employment income assessable.

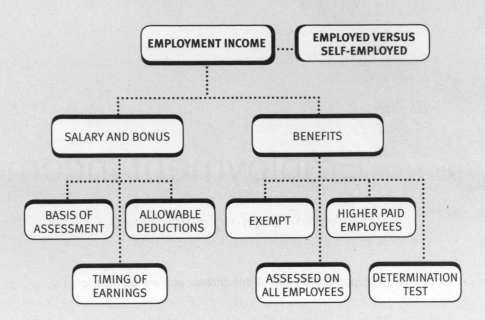

1 The scope of employment income

Employment or self-employment?

The distinction between employment and self-employment is fundamental:

- an employee is taxable under the employment income provisions

- a self-employed person is assessed on the profits derived from his trade, profession or vocation, under the trading income provisions.

The following principles, laid down by statute and case law decisions, are important matters to be taken into account in deciding whether a person is employed or self-employed.

The primary test of an employment is the nature of the contract that exists:

Nature of contract	Status
'of service'	employment
'for services'	self-employment

However, even in the absence of a written contract of service any of the following matters would corroborate the existence of such a contract, and, therefore, employment:

- an obligation by the employer to offer work and an obligation by the employee to undertake the work offered. An employee would not normally be in a position to decline work when offered

- the employer controls the manner and method of the work

- the individual is entitled to benefits normally provided to employees such as sick pay and holiday pay

- the individual is committed to work a specified number of hours at certain fixed times, and is paid by the hour, week or month
- the engagement is for a long period of time
- the individual does not provide his own equipment
- the individual is obliged to work personally and exclusively for the employer, and cannot hire his own helpers
- the work performed by the individual is an integral part of the business of the employer, and not merely an accessory to it
- the economic reality of self-employment is missing – namely the financial risk arising from not being paid an agreed, regular amount
- the individual cannot profit from sound management.

There is much case law on this area. However, note that an important case concerning a vision mixer who was engaged under a series of short-term contracts in the film industry, established the following fundamental points:

- it is necessary to look at the overall picture and to decide by examining a number of criteria, and
- no one factor is conclusive.

In this particular case, like many persons engaged in a profession or specialised vocation, he did not have all the trappings of a business, and did not supply his own equipment. However, the 'number of separate engagements' was held to be a key factor in the decision to treat him as self-employed.

2 Basis of assessment

Assessable earnings

- All directors and employees are assessed on the amount of earnings received in the tax year (the **receipts basis**).
- The term 'earnings' includes not only cash wages or salary, but also bonuses, commission, round sum allowances and benefits made available to the employee by the employer.

The date earnings are received

The date of receipt is the **earlier** of the following:

- Actual payment of, or on account of, earnings.
- Becoming entitled to such a payment.

In the case of directors, who are in a position to manipulate the timing of payments, there are extra rules.

They are deemed to receive earnings on the **earliest** of four dates; the two general rules set out above, and the following two rules:

- when sums on account of earnings are credited in the accounts
- where earnings are determined:
    - before the end of a period of account = the end of that period
    - after the end of a period of account = date the earnings are determined.

3 Deductibility of expenses from employment income

General rule

Expenditure will only be deductible if it is incurred **wholly**, **exclusively** and **necessarily** in the **performance of duties**.

General rule for employment income expenses

- In the performance of the duties

    This aspect of the test means that there is no deduction for expenditure incurred beforehand, to gain the requisite knowledge or experience to do the work. So, for example, the cost of attending evening classes by a schoolteacher has been disallowed.

- Necessarily

    For expenditure to comply with this test, it must be an inherent requirement of the job, not something imposed by the employee's circumstances. Thus an employee with poor eyesight was unable to deduct the cost of spectacles. In other words, to be necessary expenditure, each and every person undertaking the duties would have to incur it.

- Wholly and exclusively

    To be deemed wholly and exclusively incurred, such expenditure must be made with the sole objective of performing the duties of the employment.

Two examples show this distinction:

- If an employee is required to wear clothes of a high standard for his employment and so purchases them, the expenditure is not deductible. The employee's clothes satisfy both professional and personal needs.

- Expenditure on a home telephone can be partly deductible. Business calls are made 'wholly and exclusively' and so are deductible. But, for the same reason applied to the clothes, no part of the line rental for a home phone may be deducted.

Expenditure allowed by statute

A deduction for certain types of expenditure is specifically permitted by statute as follows:

- contributions to registered occupational pension schemes (within certain limits) (see Chapter 10)

- fees and subscriptions to professional bodies and learned societies, provided that the recipient is approved for the purpose by HMRC, and its activities are relevant to the individual's employment

- payments to charity made under a payroll deduction scheme, operated by an employer

- expenditure on travel and other expenditure is deductible to the extent that it complies with very stringent rules

- capital allowances are available for plant and machinery necessarily provided by an employee for use in his or her duties.

Capital allowances – example

Capital allowances will be available where an employee uses his own computer for business use. Allowances will be restricted to the proportion of business use (see Chapter 6).

Payroll deduction scheme

- Under the payroll deduction scheme an employee authorises his employer to make deductions from his salary and pay the amounts over to specified charities.

- There is no limit on the amount of donations that an employee can make under the scheme.

- The donations are deducted from the employee's gross pay before tax (PAYE) is applied to his taxable pay.

Travel expenditure

Travel expenses may be deducted only where they:

- are incurred necessarily in the performance of the duties of the employment; or

- are attributable to the necessary attendance at any place by the employee in the performance of their duties.

Relief is not given for the cost of journeys that are ordinary commuting or for the cost of private travel.

- Ordinary commuting is the journey made each day between home and a permanent workplace, or to a place which is essentially the same as their workplace (i.e. situated nearby).

- Private travel is a journey between home and any other place that is not for the purposes of work.

Travel expenditure

- Relief is available for travelling expenditure where an employee travels to visit a client. Where such travel is integral to the performance of the duties, it is allowable. This will include travel undertaken by commercial travellers and service engineers who move from place to place during the day.

- No relief is given for travelling between two separate employments. However, if an employee has more than one place where duties have to be performed for the same employer, then travelling expenses between them are allowable.

In addition, the following rules apply for travel to a temporary workplace:

- Relief is given where an employee travels directly from home to a temporary place of work.

- A temporary workplace is defined as one where an employee goes to perform a task of limited duration, or for a temporary purpose.

- A place of work will not be classed as a temporary workplace where an employee works there continuously for a period which lasts, or is expected to last, more than 24 months.

- Where an employee passes their normal permanent workplace on the way to a temporary workplace, relief will still be available provided the employee does not stop at the normal workplace, or any stop is incidental (e.g. to pick up some papers).

4 Approved mileage allowance payments

Allowable rates

Employees who use their own motor cars for business purposes are normally paid a mileage allowance by their employer.

HMRC approved mileage rates which are tax allowable are as follows:

First 10,000 miles p.a.	45p
Over 10,000 miles p.a.	25p

- Details of the approved mileage allowance payment (AMAP) will be given in the tax rates and allowances provided in the examination.

- If the mileage allowance paid by the employer = the AMAP:
  No benefit arises

- Where payments made to the employee > the AMAP:
  Excess = assessed on the employee as a benefit

- Where the payment to the employee < the AMAP:
  Difference = allowable deduction from employee's employment income

Example 1 – Approved mileage allowance payments

An employee uses her own 1,800 cc motor car for business travel. During 2012/13, she drove 13,000 miles on business. Her employer paid her 30p per mile. £3900

Calculate the expense claim for 2012/13 that can be made against taxable employment income.

Answer to example 1

The mileage allowance of £3,900 (13,000 at 30p) will be tax free, but in addition, the employee can make an expense claim as follows:

	£
10,000 miles at 45p	4,500
3,000 miles at 25p	750
	———
Allowable amount	5,250
Less: Mileage allowance received	(3,900)
	———
Expense claim	1,350
	———

The £1,350 can be deducted in arriving at the individual's assessable employment income for 2012/13.

Test your understanding 1

John has travelled 12,000 business miles in 2012/13, in his own car. His employer pays him 42p per mile for each business mile.

(a) **Calculate how much of the mileage allowance is taxable.**

(b) **Explain how your answer would differ, if John's employer paid 35p per mile.**

Test your understanding 2

Underwood is employed as an insurance salesman at a monthly salary of £950. In addition to his basic salary, he receives a bonus that is paid in May each year, and relates to the sales he achieved in the year to the previous 31 October.

His bonuses are as follows:

Bonus for year to:	Paid during:	£
31 October 2010	May 2011	1,920
31 October 2011	May 2012	1,260
31 October 2012	May 2013	2,700

Underwood made the following payments in respect of his employment in 2012/13.

	£
Contribution to occupational pension scheme	342
Subscription to Chartered Insurance Institute	100
Payroll deduction scheme (in favour of Oxfam)	200

Compute Underwood's assessable income from employment for 2012/13.

P11D Dispensations

Where an employee is reimbursed with business related expenses (e.g. for rail fares for business trips), the employer should report the expenses to HMRC on the employee's P11D.

The reimbursed expenses are treated as taxable employment income and the employee must then make a claim for a deduction against his employment income for the business related expenses in his tax return.

An employer can reduce the administrative burden associated with reporting and recording business related expenses paid to employees, by getting approval in advance that specified expenses do not need to be reported to HMRC. This process is referred to as obtaining a dispensation from HMRC.

The effect of obtaining a dispensation is that it permits:

- the employer to omit information from forms such as the P11D, which would otherwise require reporting, and

- it saves employees claiming a deduction in their tax returns for expenses incurred wholly, exclusively and necessarily, in the performance of their duties, that have been reimbursed by their employer.

The employer is required to apply in advance for permission to make such payments and, upon receiving approval from HMRC, can continue to apply the dispensation until further notice.

5 Employment benefits

In addition to salary, the term 'earnings' within the scope of income tax also covers benefits received by the employee.

There are three main types of benefits:

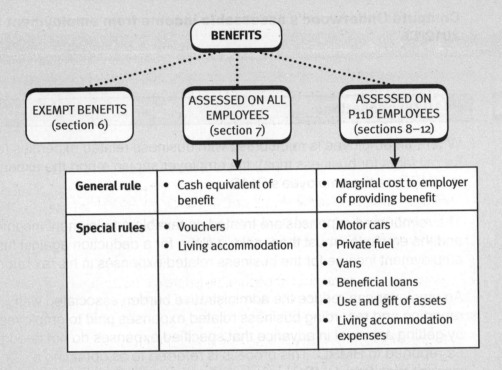

General rules in relation to benefits

There are two general rules which can be applied in relation to **all** taxable benefits. The taxable benefit will be:

- **reduced** by any contributions made by the employee towards the cost of the benefit (however, see exception in relation to private fuel).

- **pro-rated** if it was only available for part of the year.

6 Exempt benefits

There are a significant number of benefits that the employer can provide to the employee, that do not attract a tax charge.

Of these the most commonly examined include:

- An employer's contribution to a registered pension scheme.

- The use of subsidised on-site restaurant or canteen facilities, provided they are available for all employees.

- Luncheon vouchers up to a value of 15p per working day.

- The provision of a car parking space provided at or near the place of work, including the reimbursement of the cost of such a parking place.

- The provision of one mobile telephone (including smart phones) for private use by an employee.

- Certain benefits aimed at encouraging employees to travel to work other than by private car. This exemption includes work buses, subsidies to public bus services, and the provision of bicycles and cycling safety equipment, provided they are available to employees generally.

- Christmas parties, annual dinner dances, etc. for staff generally, provided they are of modest cost (up to £150 p.a. per head).

- Workplace nurseries for child care.

- Certain payments to an approved child carer.

  The limit is £55 per week for a basic rate taxpayer, £28 per week for a higher rate taxpayer and £22 per week for an additional rate taxpayer. These limits mean that all taxpayers receive exactly the same amount of tax relief from the childcare exemption.

  However, the provision of cash allowances or vouchers to meet the expense of child care with non-approved carers is taxable.

- Relocation and removal expenses up to £8,000.

- Expenses incurred by employees whilst away overnight on the employer's business, such as telephone calls home, laundry, etc. up to a maximum of UK £5 per night, overseas £10 per night.

- Home worker's additional household expenses of up to £4 per week or £18 per month can be paid tax-free without the need for any supporting evidence.

- Loans with a beneficial interest rate, provided the loan is ≤ £5,000 throughout the tax year (see later).

- Provision of job related accommodation (see later).

Further exempt benefits

- Home worker's additional household expenses:
  For higher amounts than £4 per week or £18 per month to be exempt, it is necessary to have supporting evidence that the payments are wholly in respect of **additional** household expenses incurred by the employee, in carrying out his duties at home.

- Entertainment provided for an employee, by reason of his or her employment, by a genuine third party (e.g. a ticket or seat at a sporting or cultural event provided by a business contact or client, to generate goodwill).

- Gifts received, by reason of his or her employment, from genuine third parties, provided the cost from any one source does not exceed £250 in a tax year.

- Long service awards in kind (e.g. gold watches) are exempt up to a cost of £50 for each year of service of 20 years or more.

- Provision of travel, accommodation and subsistence during public transport disruption caused by industrial action.

- Employer funded training. Where the expenses of training are paid for by the employer, no taxable benefit arises on the employee.

- Medical insurance for treatment and medical services where the need for treatment arises while abroad in the performance of employment duties.

- Security assets and services. Where a security asset or security service is provided by reason of employment, or where reimbursement is made for the cost of such measures.

- Recreational or sporting facilities available to employees generally and not to the general public, whether provided directly or by a voucher.

- Welfare counselling for employees provided the service is available to employees generally.

- Pension's advice for employees. The advice must cost no more than £150 per employee per year and must be available to all employees.

- Employee liability insurance. Liability insurance is aimed at protecting an employee from a work-related liability.

- Provision by employers of eye care tests and/or corrective glasses for VDU use by their employees, provided they are made available to all employees.

- Awards for up to £25 under a staff suggestion scheme, which is available to all employees, for suggestions outside their duties. Higher awards may be justified if they reflect the financial importance of the suggestion to the business.

This is an extremely comprehensive list.

In reality, the examiner is likely to refer to one or two within a question that you will be expected to identify as exempt.

Relocation and removal expenses

No assessable benefit arises on payment or reimbursement of removal expenses and benefits, provided that the following criteria are met:

- The expenses are incurred in connection with either:
  - a totally new employment
  - a new role with the existing employer; or
  - a change in the location at which the employee's duties are carried out.

- It is necessary to acquire a new residence as commuting would not be viable.

- The costs met or reimbursed must be qualifying expenses. These include costs of selling the first house, travel and subsistence when looking for a new house, removal expenses and interest on a bridging loan whilst the employee owns both homes.

- The expenditure must be incurred by the end of the tax year following the one in which the employment change occurred.

7 Benefits assessable on all employees

The general rule is that the assessable amount of the benefit received by a non-P11D employee (see section 8) is:

- the **cash equivalent value** on disposal to a third party
- unless there are specific statutory rules for valuing a benefit.

Specific rules have been established for certain benefits that are assessable on all employees:

- vouchers and credit tokens
- living accommodation.

Vouchers and credit tokens

Vouchers are broadly documents with which an individual can obtain goods and services.

The provision of vouchers is assessed as follows:

Cash vouchers	• Subject to income tax through the PAYE system when given to employee • No further benefit arises
Non-cash vouchers	• Benefit = cost of providing voucher • Exception = vouchers to provide exempt benefits (e.g. luncheon vouchers up to 15p per day, child care vouchers up to relevant limits) • Excess over exempt limit = benefit
Credit token (e.g. company credit card)	• Benefit = value of goods and services bought for private use

No assessable benefit arises where the employee can show that the use of vouchers or credit tokens was wholly, exclusively and necessarily in the performance of the duties of their employment.

For example, where a voucher for travel for business purposes is provided, no benefit arises.

Living accommodation

Where an employee is provided with living accommodation as a result of his employment, the benefit is assessed as follows:

	Benefit arising
Basic charge	Higher of: • **Annual value of the property**, and • Rent paid by the employer, if any (only applicable if the property is rented on behalf of the employee).
Additional charge for expensive accommodation	(Cost of providing the accommodation – £75,000) × the appropriate percentage Note that this is charged in addition to the basic charge and the formula is not provided in the exam.

Annual value

The annual value is assumed to be the rateable value of the property. This figure will always be given to you in the examination.

Expensive living accommodation

An additional benefit arises where the 'cost of the accommodation' provided exceeds £75,000.

- The 'cost of providing the accommodation' is calculated as:

	£
Original cost (or market value – see below)	X
Add: Capital improvements prior to the start of the current tax year	X

Cost of providing accommodation	X

- The appropriate percentage is the official rate of interest (ORI) in force at the start of the tax year.

  For 2012/13, the ORI is 4% and will be provided in the tax rates and allowances in the examination.

- Where the employer acquired the accommodation more than **six years** before first providing it to the employee:

  Use the property's **market value when first provided** to the employee, rather than the original cost.

- Note that regardless of the market value, this additional benefit is only imposed if the 'cost of providing the accommodation' exceeds £75,000.

The total living accommodation benefits can be reduced to the extent that the accommodation is used wholly, exclusively and necessarily for business purposes.

Job-related accommodation

No benefit arises if the property is job-related accommodation (JRA).

To qualify as JRA, the property must be provided:

- where it is necessary for the proper performance of the employee's duties (e.g. a caretaker), or

- where it will enable the better performance of the employee's duties and, for that type of employment, it is customary for employers to provide living accommodation (e.g. hotel-worker), or

- where there is a special threat to the employee's security and he resides in the accommodation as part of special security arrangements (e.g. prime minister).

Exception for directors

A director can only claim one of the first two exemptions if:

- they have no material interest in the company (i.e. hold no more than 5% of the company's ordinary share capital), and

- they are a full-time working director or the company is a non-profit making organisation.

Example 2 – Living accommodation

Jack was provided with a house to live in by his employer in July 2011. It cost them £200,000 in June 2008 and has an annual value of £3,000 p.a. Assume the official rate of interest is 4%.

Calculate the assessable benefit for 2012/13 assuming the accommodation is not job-related.

Answer to example 2

	£	£
Basic charge:		
Higher of		
(i) annual value	3,000	
(ii) rent paid by employer	Nil	
		3,000
Expensive living accommodation charge		
(£200,000 – £75,000) × 4%		5,000
Taxable benefit		8,000

Note: The official rate of interest will not normally be given in the question as it is given in the tax tables.

Example 3 – Living accommodation

Sachin lives in a house provided by his employer which cost £90,000, when it was acquired in June 2007.

Since this time the following improvements have taken place:

Date of expenditure:	Type of expenditure:	£
February 2008	Conservatory	15,000
August 2010	Redecoration	2,000
July 2012	Garage extension	10,000

The house has an annual value of £1,700.
The market value of the house was as follows:

April 2012	£200,000
June 2012	£165,000

The accommodation is not job-related and Sachin pays a rent of £100 per month to his employer.

(a) **Calculate the amount assessable for 2012/13 in the following situations:**

    (i) **Sachin moved in during June 2012.**

    (ii) **Sachin moved in during June 2012, but the property was actually acquired by his employer in June 2004.**

(b) **For each of the scenarios above and assuming Sachin remains in the property, with no further improvements than the ones referred to above, what will be the 'cost of providing the accommodation' for calculating the expensive accommodation charge for 2013/14?**

Answer to example 3

(a) **Assessable benefits for accommodation – 2012/13**

    (i) **Property acquired – June 2007**

	£	£
Basic charge:		
Higher of		
(i) annual value	1,700	
(ii) rent paid by employer	Nil	
		1,700
Expensive living accommodation charge (W1)		
(£105,000 – £75,000) × 4%		1,200
		2,900
Restriction for part-year occupation		
(June 2012 – March 2013) (10/12 × £2,900)		2,417
Less: Contributions paid by employee		
(10 months × £100)		(1,000)
Taxable benefit		1,417

    (ii) **Property acquired – June 2004**

	£	£
Basic charge:		
Higher of		
(i) annual value	1,700	
(ii) rent paid by employer	Nil	
		1,700
Expensive living accommodation charge (W2)		
(£165,000 – £75,000) × 4%		3,600
		5,300
Restriction for part-year occupation		
(10/12 × £5,300)		4,417
Less: Contributions paid by employee		
(10 months × £100)		(1,000)
Taxable benefit		3,417

(b) Cost of providing accommodation – 2013/14

	Scenario (a)(i) £	Scenario (a)(ii) £
Original cost + improvements (W1)	105,000	
Market value (W2)		165,000
Garage extension (July 2012)	10,000	10,000
	115,000	175,000

Workings

(W1) Cost of providing accommodation – 2012/13

	£
Cost (June 2007)	90,000
Improvements:	
Conservatory (Feb 2008)	15,000
Redecoration (Aug 2010) (Note 1)	Nil
Garage extension (July 2012) (Note 2)	Nil
Cost of providing accommodation	105,000

(W2) Market value

As Sachin has moved in more than 6 years after the employer acquired the property, the market value at the date the property was made available to Sachin (i.e. £165,000) is substituted for cost. The cost of the conservatory is already accounted for in the market value as at June 2012.

As in scenario (a)(i) the improvements that take place in 2012/13 do not come into the calculation until the following year.

Notes:

(1) The redecoration does not represent capital expenditure and therefore is not included in the calculation.

(2) Only those improvements up to the start of the tax year are included. As the garage extension does not take place until July 2012, it will not be included in the calculation until 2013/14.

8 Benefits assessable on P11D employees and directors

Principles of assessment

Special provisions apply to:

- employees earning at a rate of £8,500 p.a. or more, and
- directors.

These are sometimes referred to as 'P11D employees'.

General rule

The general rule is that the assessable amount of the benefit is:

- the **cost of providing** the benefit
- unless there are specific statutory rules for valuing a benefit.

Under case law, the 'cost of providing' the benefit has been held to mean the **additional or marginal cost** incurred by the employer – not a proportion of the total cost.

This principle is particularly relevant where employers provide in-house benefits, such as free tickets for employees of a bus company, or airline, reduced fees for children of school teachers in a public school.

Specific rules

Specific rules have been established for the following benefits that are assessable on P11D employees:

- Motor cars and vans (section 9).

- Private fuel (section 9).

- Beneficial loans (section 10).

- Use and gift of assets (section 11).

- Living accommodation expenses (section 12).

Note that:

- An employee is deemed to be provided with a benefit, not only when it is provided to him directly, but also when it is provided to a member of his family or household.

- To be taxed under these principles, a benefit must be provided to the employee by reason of his employment.

P11D employees

The benefits provided to employees earning at a rate of £8,500 p.a. or more, are reported to HMRC on form P11D. The term 'P11D employee' is therefore sometimes used to denote an employee earning at a rate of £8,500 p.a. The term 'higher-paid' employee can also be used.

Directors are automatically subject to the benefits regime for those earning at a rate of over £8,500 p.a. unless:

- they earn less than £8,500 p.a., and

- do not have a material interest in the company (i.e. they own less than 5% of ordinary share capital), **and**

- they are a full-time working director of the company.

The threshold income level

The calculation to ascertain whether a person reaches the threshold income level of £8,500 p.a. is as follows:

	£
Cash earnings (e.g. salary. bonuses and other cash remuneration, including reimbursed expenses)	X
Benefits assessable on all employees	X
Benefits assessable only on P11D employees	X
	X
Less: Contributions to employer's pension scheme	(X)
Donations to charity under payroll deduction scheme	(X)
Total earnings (for £8,500 test purposes)	X

Note that:

- There is no reduction in this calculation for any expenses incurred, apart from contributions to registered pension funds and charitable donations, under an approved payroll deduction scheme.

- In reality, it is likely that the vast majority of employees receiving benefits would fall within the category of being a P11D employee. An employee working full time on the minimum wage would earn more than £8,500 p.a. It is only possible for a part time employee to earn less than this amount. However, the examiner retains the right to test this area of the law to determine whether the £8,500 limit is exceeded.

9 Motor cars, vans and private fuel

Motor cars

Where a company car is available to the employee for private use a taxable benefit arises, calculated as follows:

	£
(List price when new) × appropriate %	X
Less: Employee contributions for the private use of the car	(X)
Assessable benefit	X

List price

The list price of a car is the **price when the car is first registered.**

- The price (including taxes) is the price appropriate for the car on the assumption that it is sold in the UK, as an individual sale in the retail market, on the day before the car's first registration.

  Note that the actual price paid for the car is not relevant. Consequently employees of large companies cannot benefit from bulk discounts their employer might negotiate with car dealers.

- **Include** the value of **all accessories** and extras fitted at the time of issue, plus the cost of any added subsequently.

- **Reduced by** any **capital contributions** made by the employee towards the original purchase of the car, subject to a **maximum of £5,000.**

Note that capital contributions by an employee, which reduce the list price of the car, should not be confused with employee contributions towards the running costs for the private use of the car, which are deducted from the taxable car benefit.

Appropriate percentage

The appropriate percentage depends on the CO_2 emissions of the car.

CO_2 emissions per km	Petrol car %	Diesel car %
75 grams or less	5	8
76 – 99 grams	10	13
100 grams or more	11	14
Each complete additional 5 grams emission above 100 grams	An additional 1% is added to the 11% or 14% up to a maximum % of 35%	

Note that the maximum % that can be applied to any car is 35%.

Additional points to note

- Where an employee changes their car during the year:
  - a separate calculation needs to be performed in respect of each car, with appropriate time apportionments.

- Where the car is unavailable for a period during the tax year (but was available both before and after, e.g. if it was under repair after a crash:
    - the benefit charge is proportionately reduced, however, the reduction applies only if the car was unavailable for a continuous period of at least 30 days.

- The car benefit takes into account all of the running expenses of the vehicle, so there is no additional benefit when the employer pays for insurance, road fund licence, maintenance etc.

- If a chauffeur is provided with the car:
    - this service constitutes an additional benefit.

- A separate benefit charge is made for private car fuel (see below).

- When more than one car is made available simultaneously to an employee:
    - the benefit in respect of the second car is computed in exactly the same way as set out above.

Example 4 – Company car

Boris is provided with a company car with CO_2 emissions of 190 g/km.

Identify the % to be used in calculating the assessable benefit arising on the provision of the company car.

Explain the difference if the car provided had a diesel engine.

Answer to example 4

	%
Basic % for petrol car	11
Plus: (190 − 100) = 90 ÷ 5	18
Appropriate %	29

If the car had a diesel engine, the % would be increased by 3% to 32%.

Note that if the CO_2 emissions of the car were 194 g/km the starting point of the calculation would still be 190 g/km as you always round down the g/km to the nearest full number divisible by 5.

Test your understanding 4

Louis is provided with a company car by his employer.
It has a carbon dioxide emission rate of:

(1) 152 g/km.

(2) 88 g/km.

(3) 217 g/km.

(4) 60 g/km.

Calculate the appropriate percentage assuming the car runs on petrol or diesel.

Pool cars

There is no assessable benefit if the car provided is a pool car.

To qualify as a pool car, **all** of the following conditions must be met during the tax year in question:

- The car must be used by more than one employee (and not usually by one employee to the exclusion of the others).

- It must not normally be kept overnight at or near the residence of any of the employees making use of it.

- Any private use by an employee must be merely incidental to his or her business use of it.

Example 5 – Company cars

During 2012/13 Fashionable plc provided the following employees with company motor cars:

(1) Amanda was provided with a new diesel powered company car on 6 August 2012. The motor car has a list price of £13,500 and an official CO_2 emission rate of 117 g/km.

(2) Betty was provided with a new petrol powered car throughout 2012/13. The motor car has a list price of £16,400 and an official CO_2 emission rate of 177 g/km.

(3) Charles was provided with a new petrol powered car throughout 2012/13. Fashionable plc purchased the car for £21,000 and Charles was required to contribute £3,000 towards the purchase cost. The motor car has a list price of £22,600 and an official CO_2 emission rate of 239 g/km. Charles paid the company £1,200 during 2012/13 for the private use of the motor car.

(4) Derek was provided with a new petrol powered car throughout 2012/13. The car has a list price of £60,000 and an official CO_2 emission rate of 55 grams per kilometre. Fashionable plc also paid for the road tax, insurance and maintenance on the car, which cost £1,600 during 2012/13.

Calculate the car benefit assessable on each of the above employees of Fashionable plc in 2012/13.

Answer to example 5

	£
Amanda	
Benefit: (£13,500 × 17%) (W1)	2,295
Less: Reduction for non-availability (W2)	(765)
Assessable benefit	1,530
Betty	
Benefit: (£16,400 × 26%) (W3)	4,264
Charles	
Benefit: (£19,600 × 35%) (W4)	6,860
Less: Payment for use of car (W5)	(1,200)
Assessable benefit	5,660
Derek	
Benefit: (£60,000 × 5%) (W6)	3,000

Workings

(W1) Appropriate percentage

	%
Basic % for diesel car	14
Plus: (115 – 100) = 15 ÷ 5	3
	17

The CO_2 emissions figure of 117 is rounded down to 115 so that it is divisible by 5. The minimum percentage of 14% is increased in 1% steps for each 5 g/km above the base level.

(W2) Reduction for non-availability

The motor car was not available for four months of 2012/13, so the benefit is reduced by £765 (£2,295 × 4/12).

Alternatively, the benefit can be time apportioned and calculated more quickly for the 8 months the car was available as follows:

(£13,500 x 17% x 8/12) = £1,530

(W3) Appropriate percentage

	%
Basic % for petrol car	11
Plus: (175 – 100) = 75 ÷ 5	15
	26

The CO_2 emissions figure of 177 is rounded down to 175 so that it is divisible by 5. The minimum percentage of 11% is increased in 1% steps for each 5 g/km above the base level.

(W4)
The car benefit is based on the list price of the car. The price paid for the car by the company is not relevant.

Charles has contributed £3,000 towards the purchase price of the car. As this is less than £5,000, the capital contribution of £3,000 is deducted from the list price of the car upon which the benefit is calculated. The price on which the car benefit is calculated is £19,600 (£22,600 – £3,000).

The CO_2 emissions are above the base level of 100 g/km.

	%
Basic % for petrol car	11
Plus: (235 – 100) = 135 ÷ 5	27
	——
	38
	——
Restricted to	35
	——

(W5) The contributions by Charles for the private use of the car reduce the assessable benefit.

(W6) CO_2 emissions are 55 g/km, therefore the 5% rate applies. The benefit above covers the road tax, insurance and maintenance of the vehicle.

Test your understanding 5

Sue is provided with a 2,000cc petrol driven car by her employer. The emission rate shown on the registration document is 186 grams of carbon dioxide per kilometre and the list price of the car when new was £16,000. During 2012/13, Sue drove 3,000 business miles and paid her employer £2,000 in respect of her private use of the car.

Paul is provided with a 2,300cc diesel powered car by his employer. The list price of the car when new was £36,000. Paul contributed £6,000 towards the cost of the car. During 2012/13, Paul drove 28,000 business miles. The emission rating of the car is 222 g/km.

Calculate the benefit taxable on Sue and Paul for 2012/13.

Private fuel

In addition to the provision of the motor car, some employees also have all (or part) of their fuel for private mileage paid for by their employer.

This is an entirely separate benefit from the provision of the car, and the rules are as follows:

- The benefit where car fuel is provided for private motoring in a car provided by reason of a person's employment is also based on the CO_2 emissions of the car.

- The fuel benefit is calculated as:

  (Base figure) x appropriate percentage

  - The base figure for 2012/13 is £20,200.
  - This is given in the tax rates and allowances in the examination.

- The CO_2 percentage used in the calculation of the car benefit is also used to calculate the fuel benefit charge.
  - The percentage will therefore range from 10% to 35% (5% or 8% for cars with emissions below 75 g/km).

Fuel provided for part of the tax year

It is not possible to opt in and out of the fuel benefit charge.

If, for example, fuel is provided from 6 April to 30 September 2012, then the fuel benefit for 2012/13 will only be charged for six months as the provision of fuel has permanently ceased.

If fuel is provided from 6 April to 30 September 2012, and then again from 1 January to 5 April 2013, the fuel benefit will not be reduced since the cessation was only temporary.

- No reduction is made to the fuel benefit for payments made by the employee
  - **unless** they pay for **all fuel** used for private motoring.
  - in that case there would be no fuel benefit.

  This is the exception to the general rule that applies to all other benefits.

- The fuel benefit only applies to vehicles for which there is a car benefit charge. It does not therefore apply to pool cars.

Example 6 – Private fuel

Continuing with the situations set out in Example 5 Fashionable plc.

Amanda was provided with fuel for private use between 6 August 2012 and 5 April 2013.

Betty was provided with fuel for private use between 6 April and 31 December 2012.

Charles was provided with fuel for private use between 6 April 2012 and 5 April 2013. He paid Fashionable plc £600 during 2012/13, towards the cost of private fuel, although the actual cost of this fuel was £1,000.

Derek was provided with fuel for private use throughout 2012/13.

Calculate the car fuel benefit assessable on each of the above employees of Fashionable plc in 2012/13.

Answer to example 6

	£
Amanda	
Benefit: (£20,200 × 17%)	3,434
Less: Reduction for non-availability (W1)	(1,145)
Assessable benefit	2,289
Betty	
Benefit: (£20,200 × 26%)	5,252
Less: Reduction for non-availability (W2)	(1,313)
Assessable benefit	3,939
Charles	
Benefit: (£20,200 × 35%) (W3)	7,070
Derek	
Benefit: (£20,200 × 5%)	1,010

Workings

(W1) Reduction for non-availability:

The motor car was not available for four months of 2012/13, so the benefit is reduced by £1,145 (£3,434 × 4/12).

Alternatively the benefit can be time apportioned and calculated more quickly for the 8 months fuel was provided:

£20,200 x 17% x 8/12 = £2,289

(W2) Reduction for non-availability:

Fuel was not available for three months of 2012/13, so the benefit is reduced by £1,313 (£5,252 × 3/12).
Alternatively the benefit is calculated as:
(£20,200 x 26% x 9/12) = £3,939

(W3) There is no reduction for the contribution paid by Charles towards the cost of private fuel, since he did not reimburse the full cost of the private fuel.

Test your understanding 6

Charles took up employment with Weavers Ltd on 1 July 2012. His remuneration package included a 5 year-old 2,500cc petrol-driven car with a list price of £24,000. He took delivery of the car on 1 August 2012. The car has CO_2 emissions of 205 g/km. As a condition of the car being made available to him for private motoring, Charles paid £100 per month for the car and £50 per month for petrol.

Weavers Ltd incurred the following expenses in connection with Charles's car:

Servicing	£450
Insurance	£980
Fuel (of which £1,150 was for business purposes)	£3,500
Maintenance	£640

Calculate Charles's assessable benefits for 2012/13 in connection with his private use of the car.

Test your understanding 7

Joan was employed as sales manager of Wilt Ltd from 1 August 2012 at a salary of £60,000 p.a. From 1 November 2012, the company provided her with a 1,800cc car, the list price of which was £15,000 and the emission rate was 149 g/km. Up to 5 April 2013, she drove 6,000 miles of which 4,500 were for private purposes. The company paid for all running expenses.

Between 1 November 2012 and 31 January 2013, the company paid for all petrol usage including private use. Joan made a contribution to her employer of £15 per month towards the provision of the petrol for her private use. From 1 February 2013 her employer only paid for business use petrol.

Calculate Joan's taxable earnings for 2012/13.

Vans

The benefit rules for vans are different from those for the motor car.

- The benefit for the private use of a van for 2012/13 is a flat rate scale charge of **£3,000 p.a.**

- No benefit arises where the private use of a van is **insignificant**.

  When determining the level of private use, journeys between home and work are ignored. This is not the case for cars.

- Proportionate reductions are made where the van is unavailable.

  Use the same definition for 'unavailable' as for cars.

- Where employees share the private use of the van, the scale charge is divided between the employees on a just and reasonable basis (e.g. by reference to the amount of private use).

- In addition a benefit of **£550 p.a.** arises where fuel is provided for private mileage.

- The benefit figures in respect of vans are not provided in the tax rates and allowances in the examination.

10 Beneficial loans

Beneficial loans are those made to an employee at a rate below the **official rate** of interest (ORI).

The examiner will assume that the ORI is 4% throughout 2012/13.

Employees are liable to a benefit charge on:

	£
Interest that would be payable on the loan (had interest been charged at the official rate)	X
Less: Interest actually paid in respect of the tax year	(X)
Assessable benefit	X

- There are two methods of calculating the benefit:
  - **The average (or simple) method** – this uses the average balance of the loan outstanding during the year.

    (Bal. outstanding at start of tax year + Bal. outstanding at end of tax year) x 1/2

    If the loan was taken out or repaid during the tax year:

    - that date is used instead of the beginning or end of the tax year, and

    - the resulting benefit is time apportioned for the number of months it was available during the tax year.

  - **The precise (or accurate) method** – this calculates the benefit day by day on the balance actually outstanding.

    However, calculations in the exam should be on a monthly basis.

  Either the taxpayer or HMRC can decide that the precise method should be used.

- An exemption applies for small loans where the total of all of an employee's cheap or interest free loans (excluding loans which qualify for tax relief) is no more than £5,000, at any point in the tax year:
  - no benefit arises.

- If an interest free or cheap loan is used for a purpose that fully qualifies for tax relief (e.g. loan to buy plant used wholly for employment):
  - no benefit arises.

- If all or part of a loan to an employee (whether or not made on low-interest or interest-free terms) is written off:
  - the amount written off is treated as an assessable benefit and charged to income tax.

Example 7 – Beneficial loans

Daniel was granted a loan of £35,000 by his employer on 31 March 2012, to help finance the purchase of a yacht. Interest is payable on the loan at 3% p.a.

On 1 June 2012, Daniel repaid £5,000 and on 1 December 2012, he repaid a further £15,000. The remaining £15,000 was still outstanding on 5 April 2013. Daniel earns £30,000 p.a.

Calculate the assessable benefit for 2012/13 using:

(a) **the average method**

(b) **the precise method.**

Answer to example 7

(a) Average method

	£	£
(£35,000 + £15,000) x 1/2 × 4%		1,000
Less: Interest paid		
6.4.12 – 31.5.12: (£35,000 × 3% × 2/12)	175	
1.6.12 – 30.11.12: (£30,000 × 3% × 6/12)	450	
1.12.12 – 5.4.13: (£15,000 × 3% × 4/12)	150	
	——	(775)
Benefit		225

(b) Precise method

	£
6.4.12 – 31.5.12: (£35,000 × 4% × 2/12)	233
1.6.12 – 30.11.12: (£30,000 × 4% × 6/12)	600
1.12.12 – 5.4.13: (£15,000 × 4% × 4/12)	200
	1,033
Less: Interest paid (as above)	(775)
Benefit	258

In this situation HMRC could opt for the precise method, although they would probably accept £225 as the difference of £33 (£258 – £225) is not significant.

Test your understanding 8

Bob is loaned £10,000, interest free, by his employer on 6 August 2011. He repaid £2,000 on 6 September 2012.

Calculate the amount taxable on Bob in 2012/13.

Exemption for commercial loans

There is an exemption for loans made to employees on commercial terms by employers who lend to the general public (e.g. banks).

The exemption will apply where:

- the loans are made by an employer whose business includes the lending of money

- loans are made to employees on the same terms and conditions as are available to members of the public

- a substantial number of loans on these terms are made to public customers.

11 Assets provided to employees

Private use of an asset provided by the employer

The general rule that applies to the provision of assets (other than cars and vans) is that an employee is taxed on an annual benefit of:

20% of an asset's market value at the time it is first provided

- Where the employer rents the asset made available to the employee instead of buying it, the employee is taxed on the **higher** of:
    - the rental paid by the employer, or
    - 20% of market value

- The provision of one mobile phone to an employee is an exempt benefit. The above rules however, will apply to any additional mobile phones provided.

- These rules do not apply to cars, vans and living accommodation. As we have already seen special rules apply to the provision of these assets.

Example 8 – Use of assets

Helen is provided with a computer by her employer for private use, which cost £800.

(a) **Compute the benefit arising on the employee.**
(b) **What if the employer rents the computer for £200 p.a.?**

Answer to example 8

(a) The benefit taxed as employment income is £160 (£800 × 20%).

The benefit is assessed for **each** tax year in which it is provided (not just the one in which it was first made available).

(b) The rent paid of £200 will be assessed on the employee as this is higher than the general rule calculation.

Gifts of assets

If an employer purchases a new asset and gives it to an employee immediately, the employee is taxed on the cost to the employer.

Private use followed by gift of the asset

Where an asset is used by an employee and then subsequently given to that employee, the employee is taxed on the higher of:

	£	£
Asset market value (MV) when gifted		X
		—
Asset MV when **first made available** to the employee	X	
Less: The benefits assessed on the employee during the time they had the use of it, but did not own it	(X)	
	—	X
		—

The purpose of the special rule for gifts of used assets is to prevent employees gaining from gifts of assets that depreciate in value rapidly once they are used.

Where the asset being given to an employee is a used car, van or bicycle provided for journeys to work, the above rules do not apply. Instead, the benefit is the market value at the date of transfer.

Example 9 – Use of assets

Brian's employer, X Ltd, purchased a dishwasher for his use on 1 June 2011, costing £600. On 6 April 2012, X Ltd gave the dishwasher to Brian (its market value then being £150).

(a) **Calculate the benefit assessable on Brian for the gift of the dishwasher.**

(b) **What would the benefit be if Brian had paid X Ltd £100 for the dishwasher?**

Answer to example 9

(a) **Gift of dishwasher**

	£
Market value when first made available to Brian	600
Less: Benefit already assessed 2011/12:	
(£600 × 20% × 10/12) (Note)	(100)
	———
Taxable benefit on gift: 2012/13	500
	———

The benefit is £500 since this is greater than the dishwasher's market value when given to Brian (£150).

(b) **Sale of dishwasher to Brian for £100**

	£
Benefit as calculated in (a) above	500
Less: Price paid	(100)
	———
Taxable benefit on gift: 2012/13	400
	———

Note: Where the benefit is provided for only part of a tax year, the benefit is reduced proportionately.

Test your understanding 9

A suit costing £300 was purchased for Bill's use by his employer on 6 April 2011. On 6 August 2012, the suit is purchased by Bill for £20, when the market value was £30. Bill earns £30,000 p.a.

Calculate the amounts taxable on Bill for each of the tax years affected by the information above.

KAPLAN PUBLISHING

12 Expenses connected with living accommodation

In addition to the benefit charges outlined in section 7 (which apply to living accommodation provided to all employees):

- expenses connected with living accommodation (such as lighting and heating) are also taxable on higher paid employees where the cost is met by his employer.

Job-related accommodation

Where the employee's accommodation is job-related, there is a limit on this additional living accommodation expenses benefit.

The limit applies to the following types of expense:

- heating, lighting and cleaning
- repairing, maintaining or decorating the premises
- furniture and other goods normal for domestic occupation.

The assessable benefit for the expenses is limited to 10% of net earnings (i.e. employment income excluding this benefit for living accommodation).

Example 10 – Expenses connected with living accommodation

Amy is a hotel manager and is provided with accommodation. Her salary is £25,000. She has other employment benefits of £500 and makes payments into her employer's registered occupational pension scheme of £2,000 p.a.

The accommodation has an annual value of £1,500 and cost her employer £90,000 four years ago. The accommodation contains furniture which cost the employer £10,000 four years ago (when she first occupied the accommodation). The employer pays all of her household bills totalling £1,000.

(a) **Calculate the taxable benefit for 2012/13, assuming the accommodation is not job-related.**

(b) **Explain how the taxable benefit will differ if the accommodation is job-related. You are not required to calculate the benefit.**

Answer to example 10

(a) Taxable benefit – not job-related accommodation

	£
Basic charge – Annual value	1,500
Expensive accommodation charge	
(£90,000 – £75,000) × 4%	600
Provision of services – furniture (20% × £10,000)	2,000
– household bills	1,000
	———
Total benefit	5,100
	———

Note: Be careful when calculating the accommodation benefit. Before starting to calculate consider all the factors that can impact the calculation (e.g. is it job related, does it cost more than £75,000, is it owned or rented by the employer?)

(b) Job related accommodation

If the accommodation is job related, there will be:

– No basic charge.

– No expensive accommodation charge.

– The provision of services benefit will be restricted to 10% of Amy's net earnings.

13 Comprehensive examples

Example 11 – Employment benefits

Mr Darcy, managing director of the Pemberley Trading Co Ltd, is paid an annual salary of £36,000 and also bonuses based on the company's performance. Pemberley Trading Co Ltd's accounting year ends on 31 December each year and the bonuses are normally determined and paid on 31 May thereafter. In recent years bonuses have been:

	£
Year to 31 December 2010	4,000
Year to 31 December 2011	8,000
Year to 31 December 2012	4,000

KAPLAN PUBLISHING

Mr Darcy has the use of a company car (3,500cc) for private purposes. It was purchased in 2006, at its list price of £20,000. Running expenses, including diesel paid by the company, were £2,600 in the year. The car has CO_2 emissions of 210 g/km.

Compute Mr Darcy's income tax liability for 2012/13.

Briefly give reasons for your treatment of items included or excluded, in arriving at his taxable income.

Answer to example 11

Mr Darcy – Income tax computation – 2012/13

	£
Salary	36,000
Bonus (Note 1)	8,000
	44,000
Car benefit (£20,000 × 35%) (W)	7,000
Car fuel benefit (£20,200 × 35%) (Note 2)	7,070
Total income	58,070
Less: PA	(8,105)
Taxable income	49,965

Income tax:

	£		£
Basic rate	34,370 x 20%		6,874
Higher rate	15,595 x 40%		6,238
	49,965		
Income tax liability			13,112

Notes: Explanation of treatment

(1) Under the receipts basis for directors the bonus is treated as received, and therefore taxed, when it is determined. Thus the bonus determined in May 2012, is taxable in 2012/13.

(2) A fuel benefit will arise as Mr Darcy is provided with fuel for private motoring.

Working: Car benefit percentage

	%
Basic % for diesel car	14
Plus: $(210 - 100) = 110 \div 5$	22
	36 Restricted to 35%

Test your understanding 10

Mrs Cornell is a senior executive with Berkeley plc. Her salary is £20,000 p.a. In the tax year 2012/13 her employers will make the following benefits available to her:

(1) A Ford Granada 2,300cc motor car from 6 October 2012. Its list price will be £20,000 in October 2012 and its CO_2 emissions will be 174 g/km. The company will pay all running expenses including private diesel.

(2) She will continue to have the use of a stereo system owned by the company which cost £2,000 two years ago and which is kept at her home.

(3) Berkeley plc has provided Mrs Cornell with a television for her personal use since 6 April 2010 when it cost £1,200. On 6 April 2012 the television was sold to Mrs Cornell for £225 when its market value was £375.

(4) Berkeley plc provided Mrs Cornell with an interest-free loan of £30,000 on 1 January 2012. She will repay £10,000 of the loan on 30 June 2012. The loan is not used for a qualifying purpose.

In addition she has been offered the choice of luncheon vouchers of £2 per day (for 200 working days) or free meals worth £3 per day in the company's canteen (for 200 working days). Meals are available free of charge to all other employees.

After making the most tax efficient choice in respect of the lunch facilities, calculate the total value for taxation purposes of the benefits Mrs Cornell will receive for the tax year 2012/13.

Test your understanding 11

Basil Ransom is managing director of Boston plc. He is also a substantial shareholder in the company.

The company's accounts show the following information:

Years ended 30 April:	2011	2012	2013
	£	£	£
Salary, as managing director	13,620	43,560	44,100
Performance bonus	10,000	15,000	18,000

The performance bonus is determined and paid in the July following the accounting year end.

Mr Ransom has the use of a 2,800cc Porsche motor car with a list price of £34,000. The CO_2 emissions were 227g/km. All petrol and expenses were paid by the company. Mr Ransom drove a total of 18,000 miles in 2012/13, of which 10,000 were for private purposes.

He reimbursed the company £50 in respect of private petrol.

Mr Ransom also has had the use of a company house since 6 April 2012, whose annual value is £1,200 and which is provided rent free. The house had cost £90,000 in 2004 and its market value in April 2012 was £135,000.

The company pays private medical insurance for all its employees. Mr Ransom's share of the group premium was £320 for 2012/13. In June 2012 he needed to have treatment following a motor accident and the cost to the insurance company was £1,720.

In 2012/13 Mr Ransom was reimbursed £1,500 in respect of business travelling in the UK.

Calculate Mr Ransom's employment income for 2012/13.

14 Chapter summary

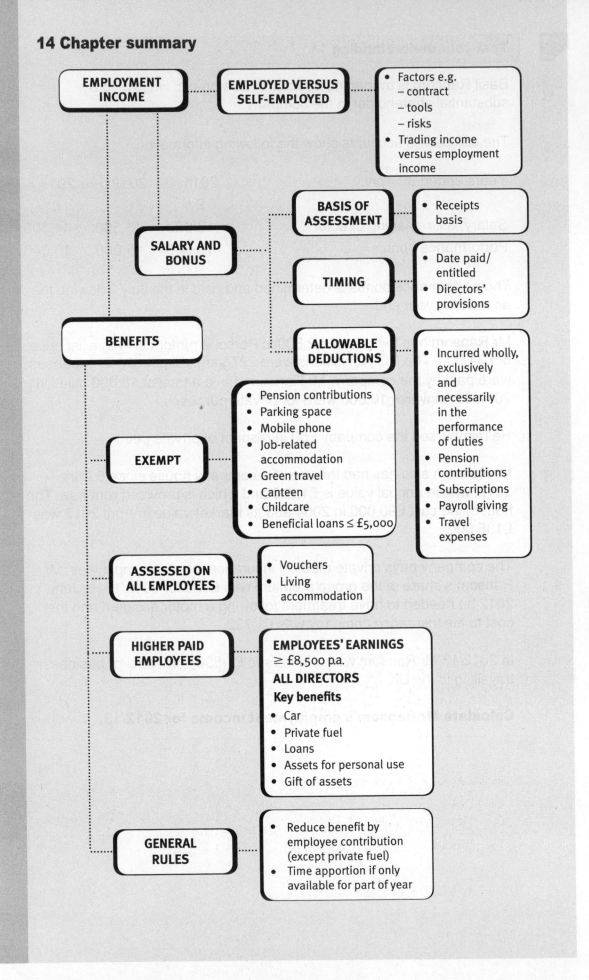

EMPLOYMENT INCOME

EMPLOYED VERSUS SELF-EMPLOYED
- Factors e.g.
  - contract
  - tools
  - risks
- Trading income versus employment income

SALARY AND BONUS

BASIS OF ASSESSMENT
- Receipts basis

TIMING
- Date paid/ entitled
- Directors' provisions

ALLOWABLE DEDUCTIONS
- Incurred wholly, exclusively and necessarily in the performance of duties
- Pension contributions
- Subscriptions
- Payroll giving
- Travel expenses

BENEFITS

EXEMPT
- Pension contributions
- Parking space
- Mobile phone
- Job-related accommodation
- Green travel
- Canteen
- Childcare
- Beneficial loans ≤ £5,000

ASSESSED ON ALL EMPLOYEES
- Vouchers
- Living accommodation

HIGHER PAID EMPLOYEES

EMPLOYEES' EARNINGS ≥ £8,500 p.a.
ALL DIRECTORS
Key benefits
- Car
- Private fuel
- Loans
- Assets for personal use
- Gift of assets

GENERAL RULES
- Reduce benefit by employee contribution (except private fuel)
- Time apportion if only available for part of year

Test your understanding answers

Test your understanding 1

John

(a) **Taxable amount**

	£	£
Income (12,000 × 42p)		5,040
Less: Allowable expenses		
10,000 × 45p	4,500	
2,000 × 25p	500	
	———	(5,000)
		———
Taxable amount		40
		———

(b) **If employer paid 35p**

If John's employer paid 35p per mile, the total income paid to John would be 12,000 × 35p = £4,200.

John could deduct the shortfall of £800 (£5,000 – £4,200) from his employment income, as an allowable expense.

Test your understanding 2

Underwood

	£
Basic salary (£950 × 12)	11,400
Bonus paid in May 2012 (receipts basis)	1,260
	———
	12,660
Less: Allowable expenses	
Subscription	(100)
Pension contribution	(342)
Payroll deduction scheme	(200)
	———
Taxable employment income	12,018
	———

Test your understanding 3

Paolo
Assessable benefit for accommodation – 2012/13

	£
Basic charge – annual value (no rent paid by employer)	2,500
Expensive living accommodation charge	
(£105,000 – £75,000) × 4%	1,200
	3,700
Less: Contribution by employee (£110 × 12)	(1,320)
Taxable benefit	2,380

Test your understanding 4

Louis

CO_2 emissions		Petrol %	Diesel %
152 g/km	Basic %	11	14
	Plus: (150 – 100) x 1/5	10	10
		21	24
88 g/km	Basic %	10	13
217 g/km	Basic %	11	14
	Plus: (215 – 100) x 1/5	23	23
		34	37
	Restricted to maximum		35
60 g/km	Basic % – Less than 75 g/km	5	8

Test your understanding 5

Sue

	£
£16,000 × 28% (W)	4,480
Less: Contribution	(2,000)
	_____
Benefit	2,480
	_____

Working: Appropriate %	%
Basic % for petrol car	11
Plus: (185 – 100) = 85 ÷ 5	17
	___
	28
	___

Paul

Benefit (£31,000 × 35% (W))	£10,850
	_____

Working: Appropriate %	%
Basic % for diesel car	14
Plus: (220 – 100) = 120 ÷ 5	24
	___
	38 Restricted to 35%
	___

Note that the amount of business mileage driven is not relevant to the calculation.

List price = (£36,000 – £5,000 maximum capital deduction) = £31,000

Test your understanding 6

Charles

	£
Car benefit: (£24,000 × 32% (W1) x 8/12 (W2))	5,120
Less: Employee contribution (£100 × 8 months)	(800)
	4,320
Fuel benefit: (£20,200 × 32% (W3) x 8/12 (W2))	4,309
Total assessable benefits	8,629

Workings

	%
(W1) Appropriate %	
Basic % for petrol car	11
Plus: (205 – 100) = 105 ÷ 5	21
	32

(W2) Reduction for non-availability of car

Car first made available on 1 August 2012, therefore it has been available for 8 months.

(W3) Car fuel

The fuel benefit is calculated using the same percentage as the car benefit.

Charles cannot deduct the £50 per month paid towards his private petrol and does not qualify for a reduction of the fuel scale charge, because he does not pay for all fuel used for private motoring.

KAPLAN PUBLISHING

Test your understanding 7

Joan

	£
Salary (£60,000 × 8/12)	40,000
Car benefit (£15,000 × 20% (W1) x 5/12)	1,250
Fuel benefit (£20,200 × 20% × 3/12 (W2))	1,010
Taxable earnings	42,260

Workings

(W1) Appropriate %

	%
Basic % for petrol	11
Plus: (145 – 100) = 45 ÷ 5	9
	20

The car has only been available for 5 months.

(W2) The petrol was only provided for 3 months in 2012/13. The contribution towards the cost of private petrol does not reduce the fuel benefit, as the cost was not reimbursed in full.

Test your understanding 8

Bob

(a) Average method

	£
4% × ½ × (£10,000 + £8,000)	360
Less: Interest paid by employee	(Nil)
	——
Taxable benefit	360
	——

(b) Precise method

6.4.12 – 5.9.12: (£10,000 × 4% × 5/12)	167
6.9.12 – 5.4.13: (£8,000 × 4% × 7/12)	187
	——
	354
	——

In this situation, whilst Bob can opt for the precise method it is likely he will accept an assessment of £360, as the difference is only £6 (£360 – £354).

Test your understanding 9

Bill

	£	£
2011/12		
Annual value (20% × £300)		60
		——
2012/13		
Annual value (20% × £300) × 4/12		20
Assessment upon gift, greater of:		
Suit's current market value	30	
	——	
Suit's original market value	300	
Less: Taxed in respect of use to date:		
2011/12	(60)	
2012/13	(20)	
	——	
	220	
	——	
Higher of above:	220	
Less: Price paid by employer	(20)	
	——	
	200	200
	——	——
Amount assessable in 2012/13		220
		——

Note: Essentially, Bill has received a £300 suit for £20 and been
assessed on taxable income of £280 (£60 + £220).

Mrs Cornell
Taxable benefits – 2012/13

	£
Car (W1)	2,800
Fuel (W1)	2,828
Stereo system (20% × £2,000)	400
Television (W2)	495
Beneficial loan (W3)	900
Lunch facility (W4)	Nil
	———
Taxable benefits	7,423
	———

Workings

(W1) **Car and fuel benefit**

	%
Base % for diesel car	14
Plus: (170 – 100) = 70 ÷ 5	14
	———
	28
	———

Car benefit = (28% × £20,000) = £5,600 for 12 months

The car was only available from 6 October 2012:
(£5,600 × 6/12) = £2,800

Fuel benefit = (28% × £20,200 × 6/12) = £2,828

(W2) **Television**

Greater of:	
(1) Original cost less benefits assessed	
£1,200 – (£240 + £240)	£720
(2) Current market value	£375

	£
Original cost less benefits assessed	720
Less: Amount paid to employer	(225)
	———
Assessable benefit	495

(W3) **Beneficial loan**

Average value	£
(£30,000 + £20,000) × ½ × 4%	1,000

Precise method
£30,000 × 3/12 (April/May/June) × 4% | 300
£20,000 × 9/12 (July to March) × 4% | 600
| 900

Therefore Mrs Cornell should elect for the precise method.

(W4) **Lunch facilities**

Luncheon vouchers
200 days × (£2 – 15p) | £370

Canteen (200 days × £3/day) | Exempt

Basil Ransom

Employment income – 2012/13

	£
Salary (1/12 × £43,560 + 11/12 × £44,100)	44,055
Performance bonus (received in July 2012)	15,000
Benefits:	
Car benefit (35% × £34,000) (W1)	11,900
Fuel benefit (35% × £20,200) (W1)	7,070
Living accommodation:	
Annual value	1,200
Expensive accommodation charge	
(£135,000 – £75,000) × 4% (W2)	2,400
Private medical insurance	320
Reimbursed expenses	1,500
	———
	83,445
Less: Deduction from employment income claim	(1,500)
	———
Employment income	81,945
	———

Workings

(W1) Car and fuel percentage

	%
Basic % for petrol car	11
Plus: (225 – 100) = 125 ÷ 5	25
	——
	36 Restricted to 35%
	——

There is no deduction for the reimbursement of part of the cost of the private petrol provided.

(W2) Expensive living accommodation charge

The house was acquired by the employer more than six years before it was made available to the employee, therefore the market value at the date it was provided to Mr Ransom is used instead of the cost.

5

Income from self-employment

Chapter learning objectives

Upon completion of this chapter you will be able to:

- state the basis of assessment for income from self-employment

- describe and apply the badges of trade

- calculate the tax adjusted trading profit/loss

- recognise the relief that can be obtained for pre-trading expenditure.

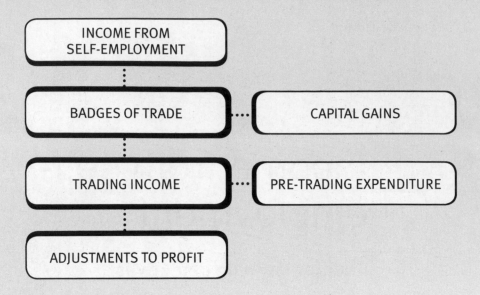

1 Trading income

The profits of an unincorporated trader arising from a trade, profession or vocation are assessed as trading income.

Individuals with an unincorporated business are usually referred to as 'self-employed' or 'sole traders'.

Basis of assessment

The profits of an unincorporated business are assessed on a **current year basis (CYB)**.

This means the profits assessed in a tax year are those of the **twelve month accounting period ending in that tax year**.

Test your understanding 1

A sole trader prepares his accounts for the year ended 31 December 2012.

In which tax year will the profits be assessed?

The detailed basis of assessment rules are covered in more detail in Chapter 7.

2 Badges of trade

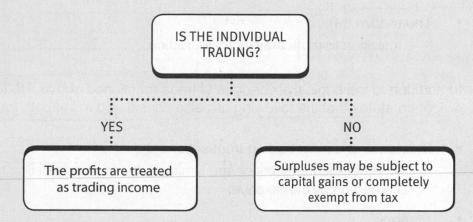

To determine whether an individual is trading, a number of tests, known as the 'badges of trade', are considered.

Nature of trade

'Trade includes any venture in the nature of trade.'

Although the above is the statutory definition of a trade, in practice it is not a very helpful one. What constitutes a trade has been reviewed numerous times by the Courts and criteria have been developed and are set out by a Royal Commission. These criteria which should be considered are known as the 'badges of trade'.

The badges of trade which are used to determine if an activity is in the nature of a trade are as follows (and can be remembered by using the mnemonic 'SOFIRM'):

- The subject matter of the transaction (S).
    - are the goods of a type normally used for trading?

- The length of the period of ownership (O).
    - short period of ownership is more likely to indicate trading.

- The frequency of similar transactions by the same person (F).
    - frequent transactions indicate trading.

- Supplementary work, improvements and marketing (I).
    - work performed on goods to make them more marketable indicates trading.

- The circumstances/reason for the sale (R).
    - forced sale to raise cash indicates not trading.
- The motive (M).
    - intention to profit may indicate trading.

In addition to the original six badges of trade mentioned above, HMRC guidance states that the following are also considered to indicate trading:

- Existence of similar trading transactions
    - whether the transactions are similar to those of an existing trade carried on by the taxpayer
- Finance
    - whether the taxpayer took out a loan to buy the asset which they expect to repay from the proceeds of sale
- Method of acquisition
    - whether the taxpayer acquired the asset by way of purchase rather than receiving it as a gift or by inheritance.

It is vital to appreciate that no one badge is decisive. In any set of circumstances some badges may indicate trading whilst others may not.

It is the overall impression, taking into account all relevant factors, that is important.

Badges of trade

Subject matter of the transaction (S)

An asset is said to have been acquired for one of three reasons:

- an investment – capital in nature and not subject to income tax
- goods for private use of the individual (or family) – not subject to tax
- trade inventory – a trading transaction and subject to income tax.

Normally, to be considered an investment, goods must either be income producing (e.g. land or shares), or liable to be held for aesthetic reasons (e.g. works of art).

When an individual acquired 1,000,000 rolls of toilet paper and resold them at a profit, he was held not to have acquired them for private use, or as an investment and consequently was judged to have made a trading profit.

The length of the period of ownership (O)

As a general rule, the longer the period between acquisition and disposal, the more likely the transaction will not be treated as trading.

Care must be taken in applying this principle and in particular the nature of the asset has to be taken into account.

For instance, it would be necessary to hold land for far longer than quoted shares to obtain the benefit of this rule, since normally the market in land operates much more slowly than that in shares.

The frequency of similar transactions by the same person (F)

As in the toilet rolls case above, a single transaction may be regarded as trading. However, usually the more often similar transactions are entered into, the more likely they will be regarded as trading activities.

Again the nature of the assets involved is important:

- A taxpayer was held to be trading on the evidence of over 200 Stock Exchange sales and purchases over a period of three years.

- A taxpayer was engaged in buying the shares of mill-owning companies and then selling the assets of the companies (asset stripping). One transaction of this kind might have been regarded as capital, but when he had done the same thing four times, he was held to be trading.

Supplementary work, improvements and marketing (I)

For example, the purchase of brandy in bulk and subsequent blending and re-casking before resale was held to be a trade.

The circumstances/reason for the sale (R)

An individual who deliberately purchases goods is more likely to be regarded as trading than one who acquires them accidentally, for example, by inheritance or by gift.

The motive (M)

The more obvious an individual's intention to profit from a transaction the more likely it is that it will be viewed as trading.

For example, an individual purchased a large quantity of silver bullion as a hedge against the devaluation of sterling. The profit resulting from its resale was regarded as a trading profit, on the basis that the motive for the transaction was to make a profit in sterling terms.

It is important to appreciate, however, that the absence of a profit motive does not of itself preclude the transaction from being treated as trade.

Existence of similar trading transactions

Where an individual undertakes a transaction that is related to his existing trade it is more difficult to argue that this is not a trading transaction than if the transaction was not so related.

Thus it is harder for a property developer to argue that a property was acquired for investment and not trading purposes than a butcher.

Finance

Where it is necessary to take out a loan to fund the purchase of an asset and it is expected that the loan will only be repaid when the asset is sold this is an indication of trading.

An individual who took out a loan to acquire silver bullion at a high interest rate and in circumstances where it was clear that he would need to sell the asset in the short term to repay the loan was held to be trading.

Method acquisition

It is much harder to argue that a trade exists where an asset is acquired by gift or inheritance than if the taxpayer purchases it.

In such cases HMRC must demonstrate that before the sale of the asset the taxpayer had a change of intention such that the asset had become trading stock (e.g. where land is developed for sale).

3 Adjusting the accounting profit

The net profit per the financial accounts and the taxable trading profit figure are rarely the same figure.

The main reason for this is that tax law does not allow a tax deduction for all accounting expenses.

Therefore, a number of adjustments need to be made to the accounting profit for tax purposes in order to calculate the taxable trading profit (known as the **tax adjusted trading profit**).

Adjustments

There are four types of adjustment that need to be made to move from accounting profit to the tax adjusted trading profit as follows:

Reason for adjusting profits	Adjustment required
Expenditure which tax law prevents from being an allowable deduction may be charged in the 'statement of profit or loss'.	**Add** to accounting profit.
Taxable trading income may not be included in the 'statement of profit or loss'.	**Add** to accounting profit.
Expenditure that is deductible for tax purposes may not be charged in the 'statement of profit or loss'.	**Deduct** from accounting profit.
Income may be included in the 'statement of profit or loss' that is not taxable as trading income.	**Deduct** from accounting profit.

Remember that as you are starting from the accounting profit, you are adjusting for items which have already been accounted for, and are reversing what went through the 'statement of profit or loss'.

Therefore, expenses already charged in the accounts are **added back** to the accounting profit.

Pro forma – Tax adjusted trading profit

	£	£
Net profit per accounts	X	
Add: Expenditure not allowed for taxation purposes	X	
Expenditure allowable for taxation purposes	0	
Taxable trading profit not credited in the accounts	X	
Less: Expenditure not charged in the accounts but allowable for taxation purposes		X
Income included in the accounts that is not taxable as trading profit		X
Capital allowances (see Chapter 6)		X
	X	Y
	(Y)	
Tax adjusted trading profit	X	

The examiner requires answers to be presented as above in order to obtain full marks in these questions.

The question requirement will specify the net profit figure to start from. Adjustments are to be listed in the order the items appear in the question.

However, in addition to the adjustments required, it is important to also show **all** items of expenditure which do **not** require any adjustment in your proforma answer, and indicate by the use of a 0 that these items are allowable.

It is not necessary to add any explanatory notes to your answer, unless notes are specifically requested by the question.

Before considering the adjustments in detail, two important points need to be emphasised:

- We are only calculating the **taxable trading profit** here. The fact that an item of income (such as rental income) is excluded in calculating the tax adjusted trading profit, does not mean that it is not taxable. It just means that it is not taxable as trading income.

  As we saw in Chapter 3, rental income is taxable as property business income and comes into the income tax computation as a separate source of income.

- In deciding whether or not an adjustment is necessary, the principles of normal commercial accountancy will apply unless overridden by tax law (i.e. if an item is allowed for accounting; it is allowed for tax **unless** there is a provision in tax law requiring an adjustment).

4 Disallowable expenditure

Disallowable expenditure is the most common adjustment. The following are the main examples that you can expect to see in the examination.

Expenditure not incurred wholly and exclusively for trading purposes

The general rule to follow in deciding whether expenditure is an allowable deduction from trading profits is that only expenditure incurred **wholly and exclusively for the purposes of the trade** is allowable.

Expenditure may be disallowed because:

- it is too remote from the purposes of the trade – the remoteness test
- it has more than one purpose and one of them is not trading – the duality principle.

Remoteness test and duality principle

Remoteness test

Expenditure is regarded as being too remote from the trade when it is incurred in some other capacity than that of trading. For example, normal accountancy and compliance taxation fees are allowable, but the cost of any personal tax advice work is not.

Duality principle

- The duality principle is best illustrated by decided cases:
  - A self-employed trader was unable to eat lunch at home and claimed the extra cost of eating out as a tax allowable expense. It was held that the expenditure was not allowable. The duality of purpose lay in the fact that the taxpayer needed to eat to live, not just to work.

  - A self-employed barrister was refused a tax allowable expense for her expenditure on the black clothing necessary for court appearances. It was held that the expenditure had been for her personal as well as professional needs.

- Where expenditure has been incurred for both trading and non-trading purposes, a deduction can be claimed for the business use proportion, provided it can be separately identified. This is particularly relevant to expenditure on motor cars, where business and private mileage can be identified.

Appropriations

Appropriations are the withdrawal of funds from a business (i.e. profit extraction rather than expenses incurred in earning them) and, as such, are disallowed expenses. The most common examples are:

- interest paid to the owner on capital invested in the business.

- salary/drawings taken by a sole trader or partner.

- any private element of expenditure relating to the owner's motor car, telephone etc.

Example 1 – Motor expenses

Jim is a self-employed solicitor. During the year ended 31 December 2012, Jim drove a total of 20,000 miles and his motor expenses amounted to £10,800.

Each working day Jim drives from his home to his office, which is ten miles away. He works five days a week and 50 weeks a year.

Jim drove 1,500 miles on a holiday in August 2012, but for the rest of the year his wife's car was used for private journeys. Jim's wife owns her own car, and is not involved in Jim's business.

Calculate the amount of Jim's motor expenses that are allowable.

Answer to example 1

Jim's motor expenses will be apportioned according to his proportion of business mileage to total mileage for the year.

Travel from home to work and back is classed as private mileage, so Jim's total private mileage is 6,500 miles ((10 miles × 5 days × 50 weeks × 2 journeys a day) + 1,500 holiday). His business mileage is therefore 13,500 miles (20,000 − 6,500).

Of the motor expenses, £7,290 (£10,800 × 13,500/20,000) is allowable and £3,510 (£10,800 × 6,500/20,000) is disallowed.

Excessive salary paid to a sole trader's family

- Business owners (especially sole traders) often employ their spouses or members of their families in their business.

- Any salary paid to the family of the owner of an unincorporated business will be allowable provided it is not excessive. In other words, it must be remuneration at the commercial rate for the work performed.
  Any excessive salary payments are disallowed.

Test your understanding 2

Sheila is in business running her own advertising agency. Her husband Richard has given up work to look after their daughter who was born three years ago.

Until 2012 Sheila employed a part-time typist, who was paid £4,500 p.a. but the typist then left and Sheila could not find a suitable replacement. Richard therefore agreed to do Sheila's typing at home.

During the year ended 5 April 2013, Sheila paid Richard a salary of £10,000.

Explain the probable adjustment in calculating the tax adjusted trading profit for the year ended 5 April 2013.

Interest payable

- Interest on borrowings such as business account overdrafts, credit cards or hire purchase contracts, is an allowable trading expense calculated on an accruals basis.

- For unincorporated businesses, late payment interest in respect of income tax or capital gains tax is never allowable and likewise repayment interest is not taxable.

Capital expenditure

- Expenditure on capital assets is not an allowable trading expense.

- Any expense in the form of depreciation, loss on sale of non-current assets or the amortisation of a lease is also disallowed.

- The distinction between revenue expenditure (allowable) and capital expenditure (disallowable) is not always clear-cut. This is especially the case when deciding if expenditure is in respect of a repair to an asset (revenue expenditure) or is an improvement (capital expenditure).

Repair v Improvement

Whilst you are not required to know the legal cases from which the following decisions were reached, it is important to understand the legal principles behind case decisions regarding capital expenditure as this will help with exam questions:

- The cost of initial repairs in order to make an asset usable is disallowable.

  For example, a taxpayer failed to obtain a deduction for repair work on a newly bought ship, in order to make the ship seaworthy.

- The cost of initial repairs is allowable if the asset can be put into use before any repairs are carried out.

  For example, a taxpayer obtained a deduction for the cost of renovating newly acquired cinemas. The work was to make good normal wear and tear and the purchase price was not reduced to take account of the necessary repair work.

- The treatment of restoration costs is another disputed area. To be allowable, it needs to be proven that the restoration renews a subsidiary part of an asset, rather than replacing the entire asset.

For example, the replacement of a factory chimney was held to be a repair to the factory.

Where it is deemed as the renewal / replacement of a separate asset it is treated as disallowed capital expenditure.

For example, the replacement of an old stand with a new one at a football club, was held to be expenditure on a new asset and thus capital expenditure.

- Capital expenditure on plant and machinery is disallowed but may qualify for capital allowances.

  These are effectively a form of depreciation allowance for tax purposes. Capital allowances are covered in detail in Chapter 6.

Car leasing

- Rental and lease charges payable in respect of leased motor cars are allowable where the CO_2 emissions of the car are 160 g/km or less.
- Where CO_2 emissions exceed 160 g/km, 15% of the rental/lease charges are disallowed.

Example 2 – Car leasing

Roger enters into a leasing contract for a motor car with CO_2 emissions of 168 g/km, paying £8,000 p.a. in rental charges.

Calculate the amount of the rental charge that is disallowed.

Answer to example 2

Disallowable rental charge = (15% × £8,000) = £1,200

Subscriptions and donations

- Trade or professional subscriptions are normally deductible since they will be made wholly and exclusively for the purposes of the trade.
- A charitable donation must meet three tests to be allowable.

It must be:

- wholly and exclusively for trading purposes (for example, promoting the business name)
- local and reasonable in size in relation to the business making the donation, and
- made to an educational, religious, cultural, recreational or benevolent organisation.

- If the donation is disallowed but the payment was made to a charity, the taxpayer can instead claim relief under the Gift Aid provisions.
- Subscriptions and donations to political parties are disallowed.
- Non-charitable gifts are not allowable, except as set out below.

Entertaining and gifts

- Entertainment expenditure is disallowed.
- The only exception is for expenditure relating to employees, provided it is not incidental to the entertainment of others.

Gifts to employees

- Gifts to employees are normally treated as allowable for the employer.
- Care must be taken, however, as the gift may fall within the benefit rules and be assessed on the employee as employment income.

Gifts to customers

- Gifts to customers are only allowable if:
  - they cost less than £50 per recipient per year; and
  - the gift is not of food, drink, tobacco or vouchers exchangeable for goods; and
  - the gift carries a conspicuous advertisement of the business making the gift.
- The cost of a gift that does not meet these conditions is disallowed.
- If the total of gifts in the tax year exceeds £50, it is the full cost of the item that is disallowable, not just the excess.
- Gifts of business samples to the public to advertise the goods are allowable.

Legal and professional charges

In order to determine whether legal and professional charges are allowable, it is important to review the reasons for the business incurring the costs.

As a general principle, where expenditure is incurred for the purposes of the trade, the expenditure is allowable. Examples include:

- legal fees chasing trading debts
- charges incurred in defending the title to non-current assets.

Where expenditure is of a capital nature, it is disallowable. For example:

- fees associated with acquiring new non-current assets.
- There are the following exceptions:
  - Fees and other costs of obtaining long-term debt finance are allowable for a sole trader.
  - The cost of registering patents is allowable.
  - The expense of renewing a short lease (i.e. less than 50 years) is allowable, although the legal expenses incurred on the initial granting of the lease are not.

Impaired debts and allowances for trade receivables

The following are allowable items:

- The write-off of a trade debt

  Note that the recovery of a trade debt previously written-off is taxable.

- An allowance for the irrecoverability or impairment of trade receivables, provided it is calculated in accordance with UK generally accepted accounting practice (UK GAAP) or International accounting standards (IAS).

  Note that the reduction in an allowance for trade receivables is taxable income.

The following items are disallowable:

- The write-off of a non-trade debt (e.g. a loan to a customer or a former employee).

Example 3 – Impaired debts and allowances for receivables

Mary's statement of profit or loss for the year ended 30 June 2012 includes a figure for impaired debts of £300. This is made up as follows:

	£	£
Trade debts written-off		520
Loan to former staff written-off		280
Allowance for impaired receivables		
As at 1 July 2011	900	
As at 30 June 2012	700	
	———	(200)
Trade debts recovered		(400)
Loan to supplier written-off		250
Loan to a customer recovered		(150)
		———
		300
		———

The loan to supplier written-off relates to a loan to a supplier with cash flow problems. The loan to the customer recovered is in respect of a loan written-off two years ago.

Calculate the adjustment required in preparing Mary's tax adjusted trading profit.

Answer to example 3

	£	£
Trade debts written-off	0	
Loan to former staff written-off	280	
Loan to supplier written-off	250	
Movement in allowance for impaired receivables		0
Trade debts recovered		0
Loan to customer recovered		150
	———	———
	530	150
	(150)	———
	———	
Amount to add back to profit	380	
	———	

To be allowed, debt write-offs must be in respect of normal trade debts. The recovery of such debts already written-off is taxable.

The write-off of other debts is not allowable when computing trading profit. Their recovery, after being written-off, is not taxable and will therefore not be included in the tax adjusted trading profit.

Amounts charged (or credited to) the statement of profit or loss in respect of allowances for trade receivables are allowable deductions against (or taxable for) trading profits.

Other items

Set out below is a list of some other items you may encounter and a brief description of how to treat each.

Type of expenditure	Treatment	Notes
Provisions for future costs, (e.g. provision for future warranty costs)	Allow	Provided they are calculated in accordance with UK GAAP or IAS and their estimation is sufficiently accurate
Compensation for loss of office paid to an employee	Allow	Only if for benefit of trade
Redundancy pay in excess of the statutory amount	Allow	On the cessation of trading the limit is 3 × the statutory amount
Counselling services for redundant employees	Allow	
Damages paid	Allow	Only if paid in connection with trade matter and is not a fine for breaking the law (see below)
Defalcations (e.g. theft/ fraud)	Allow	Only if by employee, not the business owner/director
Educational courses	Allow	Only if for trade purposes
Fines	Disallow	Unless parking fines incurred on business by employee, but not business owner/director
Payment that constitutes a criminal offence	Disallow	
Pension contributions to registered pension scheme	Allow	Provided paid (not accrued) by the year end

KAPLAN PUBLISHING

Premiums for insurance against an employee's death or illness	Allow	
Removal expenses	Allow	Provided not an expansionary move
Salaries accrued at year end	Allow	Provided paid not more than 9 months after year end

Test your understanding 3

For each item of expenditure state whether you need to adjust for tax purposes by adding an amount to the accounting profit.

Item of expenditure	Add back?
Drawings of the proprietor	
£45,000 salary paid to the proprietor's spouse. Typical market rate is estimated at £15,000	
Subscription to golf club where sole trader may meet/entertain clients	
Legal fees to acquire a short lease (7 years)	
Trade related NVQ training course for apprentice employee	

5 Other adjustments

Taxable trading income not included in the statement of profit or loss

This adjustment is normally only needed when a trader removes goods from the business for their own use.

- The trader is treated as making a sale to himself based on the selling price of the goods concerned.

- Note that this rule does not apply to the supply of services.

The adjustment required depends on the treatment in the accounts:

- if the trader has accounted for the removal of the goods, he will have adjusted for the cost element, therefore for tax purposes:
  - the profit element of the transaction needs to be added in the adjustment of profits computation

- if the trader has not accounted for the removal of the goods:
  - the full selling price must be added in the adjustment of profits computation.

Example 4 – Goods for own use

A car dealer removes a vehicle from the business for his own personal use. It had originally cost the business £10,000 and has a market value of £12,500. No entries have been made in the accounts to reflect this transaction, other than the original purchase.

Explain the adjustment, if any, that should be made to the accounts, for tax purposes, to reflect the above transaction.

Answer to example 4

The tax adjusted trading profit must reflect the transaction as if the owner has sold the vehicle to himself based on the selling price of the goods.

In determining the adjustment required, it is important to identify the entries made in the accounts to date. In this example, only the original cost has been recorded, therefore the adjustment is to add the market value £12,500 to the accounting profit.

If the removal of the vehicle had been accounted for, only the profit element of £2,500 would need to be added to the accounting profit.

Example 5 – Goods for own use

A toy seller takes items with a cost price of £480 from inventory. No adjustment has been made in the accounts.

Explain the adjustment required if:

(a) **the normal mark-up on goods is 25%**

(b) **the profit margin is 25%**

Answer to example 5

(a) The full selling price of £600 (£480 × 1.25) must be added back in the tax computation.

(b) The full selling price of £640 (£480 × 100/75) must be added back in the tax computation.

Note that 25% mark-up means that the profit is 25% of cost, whereas 25% profit margin means that profit is 25% of the selling price. It is important to distinguish between these to calculate the correct sales revenue figure.

Deductible expenditure not charged in the statement of profit or loss

- The most important item of deductible expenditure not charged in the statement of profit or loss is the figure for capital allowances. These are deductible as if they were a trading expense.

  Capital allowances are covered in detail in Chapter 6.

- In addition to this, other examples include:
  - allowable trading element of lease premiums paid on short leases
  - where a business owner uses their private residence partly for business purposes
    (e.g. uses a room in their private house as an office, the business portion of running expenses is allowable).
  - business calls from the private telephone of the sole trader
  - expenses that are wholly and exclusively for the trade that have been met from the private funds of the owner.

Short lease premiums

- When a landlord receives a premium for the grant of a short lease a proportion of the lease premium is charged to income tax as property income (see Chapter 3).

- Where a business pays a premium for a short lease, for premises used in the business, a proportion of the amount assessable on the landlord can be deducted in calculating the taxable trading profit.

  This will not be reflected in the accounts. However, the cost of the lease will be charged in the accounts in an annual amortisation charge.

The adjustments required for the lease are therefore as follows:

- Add back: the amortisation charged in the statement of profit or loss (disallowable as capital).

- Deduct: allowable proportion of the lease premium.

The allowable deduction for the trader is the property income element of the premium (see Chapter 3) spread evenly over the period of the lease.

Remember that the property income assessable on the landlord is calculated as:

P less (P × 2% × (n − 1))   or   P × (51 − n) / 50

Where: P = total premium
        n = duration of lease in years

Example 6 – Lease premium

Lawrie prepares accounts to 31 March. On 1 April 2012 he paid a premium of £25,200 for the grant of a 21-year lease on business premises.

Calculate the allowable deduction Lawrie can claim in his tax adjusted trading profit.

Answer to example 6

	£
Premium	25,200
Less (£25,200 × 2% × (21 – 1))	(10,080)
Amount assessed on landlord	15,120

Alternative calculation: (£25,200 x ((51 – 21)/50)) = £15,120

The annual allowable trading deduction for Lawrie is therefore £720 (£15,120 × 1/21) each year.

If the premium had not been paid at the start of the accounting period, this deduction would be time apportioned for the y/e 31 March 2013.

Example 7 – Use of home for business

Sam is in business as a central heating engineer. She uses one room of her five-room house as an office, and no adjustment has been made in her accounts for the year ended 5 April 2013, in respect of this.

Her household expenses relating to the year ended 5 April 2013, are:

	£
Electricity	400
Gas	250
Rates	450
Television repairs	50
Groceries	600
Video rental	200
Mortgage interest on £20,000 mortgage	900

Calculate the amount Sam can claim as an allowable deduction for her use of an office at home.

> ### Answer to example 7
>
> As Sam uses one room out of five as an office, it is appropriate to allow one fifth of her expenses that relate to running the home.
>
> Sam's television repairs, groceries and video rental are all of a private nature and are therefore not deductible.
>
> The total of the remaining items is £2,000 (£400 + £250 + £450 + £900).
>
> Therefore, Sam's allowable deduction for the use of the office is £400 (£2,000 × 1/5).

Income included in the statement of profit or loss that is not taxable trading income

There are three categories of income which need to be adjusted for:

- Capital receipts
  (which may be treated as chargeable gains – see Chapter 13).

  In addition, any profit on the sale of a capital asset should also be deducted in calculating the tax adjusted trading profit.

- Other forms of income (such as savings income or dividends) must be deducted in arriving at the taxable trading profit.

  However, they may be subject to income tax by being included elsewhere in an individual's income tax computation.

- Income that is exempt from tax
  (such as interest received on overpaid income tax).

6 Relief for pre-trading expenditure

Any revenue expenditure, incurred in the **seven years** before a business commences to trade, is treated as an expense on the day that the business starts trading.

Example 8 – Relief for pre-trading expenditure

Able commenced trading on 1 April 2012. He had spent £6,000 in the previous six months advertising that he was about to start trading.

Explain how the expenditure of £6,000 on advertising is treated for tax purposes.

Answer to example 8

The £6,000 advertising expenditure is treated as a trading expense as if it had been incurred on 1 April 2012.

7 Comprehensive example

Test your understanding 4

On 1 June 2012 William Wise, aged 38, commenced in self-employment running a retail clothing shop.

William's statement of profit or loss for the year ended 31 May 2013:

	£	£
Gross profit		139,880
Administration expenses:		
Depreciation	4,760	
Light and heat (Note 1)	1,525	
Motor expenses (Note 2)	4,720	
Repairs and renewals (Note 3)	5,660	
Rent and rates (Note 1)	3,900	
Professional fees (Note 4)	2,300	
Wages and salaries (Note 5)	83,825	
		(106,690)
Other operating expenses (Note 6)		(2,990)
Net profit		30,200

Notes:

(1) Private accommodation

William and his wife live in a flat that is situated above the clothing shop. Of the expenditure included in the statement of profit or loss for light, heat, rent and rates, 40% relates to the flat.

(2) Motor expenses

During the year ended 31 May 2013, William drove a total of 12,000 miles, of which 9,000 were for private journeys.

(3) Repairs and renewals

The figure of £5,660 for repairs and renewals includes £2,200 for decorating the clothing shop during May 2012, and £1,050 for decorating the private flat during June 2012. The building was in a usable state when it was purchased.

(4) Professional fees

	£
Accountancy	700
Legal fees in connection with the purchase of the shop	1,200
Debt collection	400
	2,300

Included in the figure for accountancy is £250 in respect of capital gains tax work.

(5) Wages and salaries

The figure of £83,825 for wages and salaries includes the annual salary of £15,500 paid to William's wife. She works in the clothing shop as a sales assistant. The other sales assistants doing the same job are paid an annual salary of £11,000.

(6) Other operating expenses

The figure of £2,990 for other operating expenses, includes £640 for gifts to customers of food hampers costing £40 each, £320 for gifts to customers of pens carrying an advertisement for the clothing shop costing £1.60 each, £100 for a donation to a national charity, and £40 for a donation to a local charity's fête. The fête's programme carried a free advertisement for the clothing shop.

(7) Goods for own use

During the year ended 31 May 2013, William took clothes out of the shop for his personal use without paying for them. The cost of these clothes was £460, and they had a selling price of £650. He has not made any adjustment in the accounts in respect of this.

(8) Plant and machinery

The capital allowances available for the year ended 31 May 2013 are £13,060.

Calculate William's tax adjusted trading profit for the year ended 31 May 2013.

Your computation should commence with the net profit figure of £30,200 and should list all the items referred to in notes 1 to 8, indicating by the use of a zero (0) any items that do not require adjustment.

8 Chapter summary

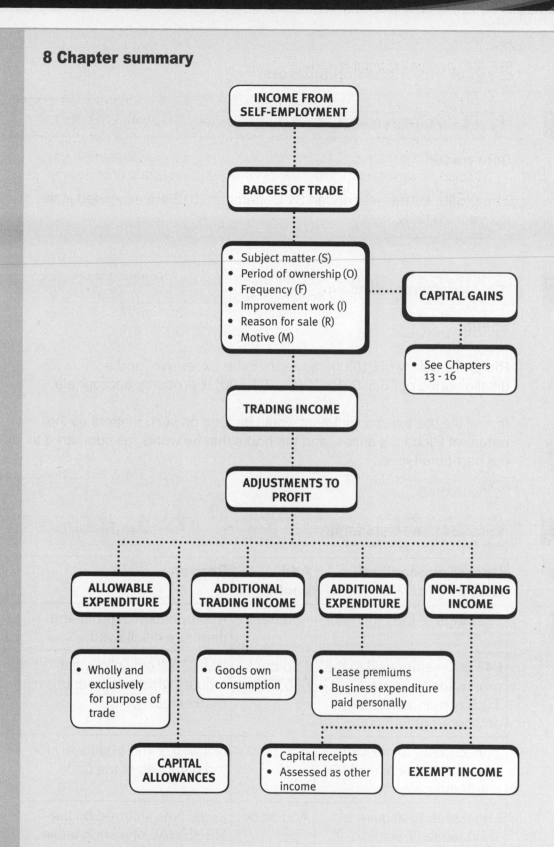

Test your understanding answers

Test your understanding 1

Sole trader

The profits for the year ended 31 December 2012 are assessed in the tax year 2012/13.

Test your understanding 2

Sheila

Richard's salary of £10,000 appears to be excessive, and a disallowance of £5,500 (£10,000 – £4,500) is probably appropriate.

In real life the exact adjustment would depend on such matters as the nature of Richard's duties, and the hours that he works, as compared to the part-time typist.

Test your understanding 3

Item of expenditure	Add back?	Reason
Drawings of the proprietor	Add back	Appropriation of profit and therefore disallowed
£45,000 salary paid to the proprietor's spouse. Typical market rate is estimated at £15,000	Add back £30,000	HMRC will only allow that amount which represents a market rate
Subscription to golf club where sole trader might meet/entertain clients	Add back	Not wholly and exclusively for the purposes of the trade
Legal fees to acquire a short lease (7 years)	Add back	Legal fees incurred on the RENEWAL of a short lease only are allowed
Trade related NVQ training course for apprentice employee	No adjustment	Provided the course is for the purpose of the trade it will be allowable

Test your understanding 4

William Wise

Tax adjusted trading profit – year ended 31 May 2013

	£	£
Net profit as per accounts	30,200	
Add: Depreciation	4,760	
Light and heat (40% × £1,525)	610	
Motor expenses (9,000/12,000 × £4,720)	3,540	
Decorating clothing shop	0	
Decorating private flat	1,050	
Rent and rates (40% x £3,900)	1,560	
Accountancy	0	
Capital gains tax work	250	
Legal fees re purchase of new shop	1,200	
Debt collection	0	
Excessive remuneration to WIlliam's wife (£15,500 – £11,000)	4,500	
Gift of food hampers	640	
Gift of pens	0	
Donation to national charity	100	
Donation to local charity	0	
Goods own consumption	650	
Less: Capital allowances		13,060
	49,060	13,060
	(13,060)	
Tax adjusted trading profit	36,000	

Capital allowances: Plant and machinery

Chapter learning objectives

Upon completion of this chapter you will be able to:

- define plant and machinery for capital allowance purposes
- compute writing down allowances (WDAs) for an accounting period
- compute First Year allowances (FYAs) available
- compute the Annual Investment Allowance (AIA) available for certain types of expenditure
- compute capital allowances for motor cars
- compute balancing allowances and balancing charges
- recognise the impact of private use of an asset on capital allowances
- recognise when the small pool WDA is available
- explain the treatment of short life assets
- explain the treatment of assets included in the special rate pool.

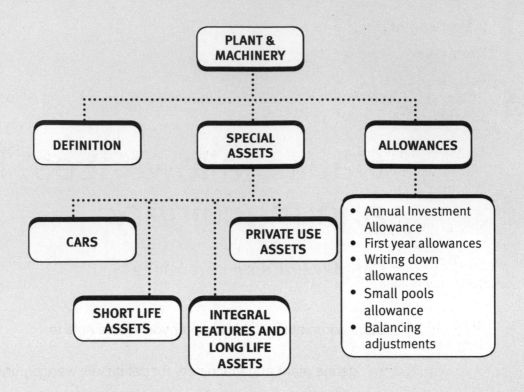

1 Capital allowances

Purpose of capital allowances

Capital allowances are provided to give a business tax relief for capital expenditure on qualifying assets.

Remember that depreciation charged in the accounts is not allowable in computing taxable trading profits; capital allowances are given instead.

Who may claim capital allowances?

Capital allowances are available to persons who buy **qualifying assets** for use in a trade or profession.

Qualifying expenditure

Capital allowances are given on the original cost of a capital asset and all subsequent qualifying expenditure of a capital nature, (e.g. improvements).

Relief for capital allowances

Capital allowances are:

* an allowable deduction in calculating the tax adjusted trading profit

* calculated for a trader's period of account (i.e. the period for which they prepare accounts).

2 Meaning of plant and machinery

Definition

'Machinery' has a commonly understood meaning. It includes all machines, computers, office equipment, etc.

The term 'plant' however, is not clearly defined in the tax legislation. HMRC has however codified some rules based on decided Court cases and has specifically deemed certain types of expenditure to be plant and machinery.

Key principles

The key principles to apply in deciding the appropriate treatment of a capital purchase is to consider the function that the asset performs for the business:

Does the asset perform:	This means that the asset is:	Plant and machinery?
An active function	Apparatus **with which** the business is carried on	Yes
A passive function	The setting **in which** the business is carried on	No

Assets deemed to be plant

There are certain types of expenditure that, although not plant using the above key principles, are to be treated as plant by specific legislation.

These include:

- the cost of alterations to buildings needed for the installation of plant
- expenditure on acquiring computer software.

Assets deemed not to be plant

Statute also makes it clear that land, buildings and structures cannot be plant for capital allowance purposes.

Summary

Determining what is and what is not plant can be difficult in practice.

In the exam the most common examples of plant and machinery are:

- computers and software
- machinery
- cars and lorries
- office furniture
- moveable partitions
- air-conditioning
- alterations of buildings needed to install plant and machinery.

Definition of plant and machinery

The original interpretation of plant and machinery was provided in the case of Yarmouth v France (1887). Plant was said to include:

'Whatever apparatus is used by a businessman for carrying on his business – not his stock-in-trade that he buys or makes for sale – but all goods and chattels, fixed or moveable, live or dead, which he keeps for permanent employment in his business.'

This is obviously a very far-reaching definition. It includes not only the obvious items of plant and machinery, but also such items as moveable partitions, office furniture and carpets, heating systems, motor vehicles, computers, lifts and any expenditure incurred to enable the proper functioning of the item, such as reinforced floors or air conditioning systems for computers.

The Courts' interpretation of 'plant'

The original definition of plant has been subsequently refined by the Courts.

In particular, the key test that has been applied is a functional one. If the item is part of the setting or premises it is not plant, and thus no capital allowances are available, but if it fulfils a function it is plant.

The dividing line here is not always clear. Examples below show how the Courts have reacted to claims for capital allowances:

- A canopy covering petrol pumps at a petrol station was held to be part of the setting and not plant and machinery (it did not assist in serving petrol to customers).

- False ceilings in a restaurant were held not to be plant (all they did was hide unsightly pipes).

- Swimming pools at a caravan park were held to be plant and machinery (the caravan park as a whole was the setting but the pool and its associated pumping and filtering equipment had an active role of providing leisure apparatus).

Buildings cannot be plant

Statutory provisions give detailed lists of items associated with buildings that are part of the building, and are deemed not to be plant, such as:

- walls, floors, ceilings, doors, windows and stairs

- mains services and systems of water, electricity and gas.

However the following may fall within the definition of a building but will still normally qualify as plant:

- electrical, cold water and gas systems provided mainly to meet the particular requirements of the trade, or to serve particular machinery used for the purposes of the trade

- space or water heating systems, systems of ventilation and air cooling, and any ceiling or floor comprised in such systems

- manufacturing or processing equipment, storage equipment, display equipment, counters, check outs and similar equipment

- cookers, washing machines, dishwashers, refrigerators and similar equipment

- wash basins, sinks, baths, showers, sanitary ware and similar equipment

- furniture and furnishings

- lifts, escalators and moving walkways

- sprinkler equipment and fire alarm systems

- movable partition walls

- decorative assets provided for the enjoyment of the public in a hotel, restaurant or similar trade

- advertising hoardings, signs and similar displays.

3 Calculating the allowances

The general pool (or main pool)

Generally expenditure on plant and machinery becomes part of a pool of expenditure upon which capital allowances are claimed. Normally capital allowances are not calculated on individual assets.

- Most items of plant and machinery purchased are included within the general pool (also known as the main pool).

- Some motor cars are also included in the general pool, namely:
  - New or second hand cars with CO_2 emissions between 111 g/km and 160 g/km

  - Second hand cars with CO_2 emissions of 110g/km or below

  The detailed rules relating to all types of cars are in section 6.

- When an asset is acquired, the purchase price increases the value of the pool.

- When an asset is disposed of, the pool value is reduced by the sale proceeds.

Certain items are not included in the general pool.

For unincorporated businesses, these are:

- new motor cars with CO_2 emissions of 110 g/km and below or in excess of 160 g/km

- assets that are used partly for private purposes by the owner of the business

- expenditure incurred on short life assets where an election to de-pool is made

- expenditure incurred on items that form part of the 'special rate pool'.

These exceptional treatments are dealt with later in this chapter.

The next few sections go through the different elements, and detailed rules, for calculating the allowances on different types of capital assets. A step-by-step approach is explained, building up to a full capital allowances proforma which appears in section 11 of this Chapter.

In all of the examples and Test Your Understandings, a standard layout is adopted to build the bigger picture. It is very important that this standard layout is used for capital allowance computations in the examination.

The Annual Investment Allowance (AIA)

The Annual Investment Allowance (AIA) is a 100% allowance for the first £25,000 of expenditure incurred by a business on plant and machinery.

The key rules for the allowance are as follows:

- available to **all** businesses regardless of size;

- available on acquisitions of general plant and machinery and acquisitions of 'special rate pool' items (see later);

- **not** available on any cars;

- limited to a maximum of £25,000 expenditure incurred in each accounting period of 12 months in length;

- for long and short accounting periods the allowance is pro-rated;

- not available in the accounting period in which the trade ceases.

Where a business spends more than £25,000 in a 12 month accounting period on assets qualifying for the AIA:

- the expenditure above the £25,000 limit will qualify for writing down allowances (WDA) (see below).

Note also that:

- the taxpayer does not have to claim all / any of the AIA if he does not want to

- any unused AIA cannot be carried forward or carried back, the benefit of the allowance is just lost.

Example 1 – AIA

Matthew commenced trading on 6 April 2012. In his first year of trading he made the following purchases:

Plant and machinery	£65,000
Office furniture and equipment	£15,000
A new car with CO_2 emissions of 138 g/km for his manager	£11,000

(a) **Calculate Matthew's AIA for the year ended 5 April 2013 and the balance on the general pool after deducting the AIA.**

(b) **What if Matthew did not purchase the plant and machinery?**

Answer to example 1

(a) **Year ended 5 April 2013**

	£	General pool £
Additions:		
Not qualifying for AIA:		
Car (CO_2 emissions < 160 g/km)		11,000
Qualifying for AIA:		
Plant and machinery	65,000	
Office furniture and equipment	15,000	
	80,000	
Less: AIA (Maximum)	(25,000)	
		55,000
Balance after AIA (Note 1)		66,000

(b) **If Matthew did not purchase the plant and machinery**

	£	General pool £
Additions:		
Not qualifying for AIA:		
Car (CO_2 emissions < 160 g/km)		11,000
Qualifying for AIA:		
Office furniture and equipment	15,000	
Less: AIA (Note 2)	(15,000)	
		Nil
Balance after AIA (Note 1)		11,000

Notes:

(1) The balance after AIA on the general pool is eligible for a writing down allowance (WDA)(see below).

(2) The unused AIA of £10,000 (£25,000 – £15,000) is lost.

First year allowances (FYA) – low emission cars

The AIA is not available on cars, however a 100% first year allowance (FYA) is available on the purchase of **new low emission cars.**

A low emission car emits 110 or less grams per kilometre of carbon dioxide (i.e. CO_2 emissions ≤ 110 g/km).

The 100% FYA is given as follows:

- In the period of acquisition, a 100% FYA is given instead of the WDA, (i.e. cannot have both FYA and WDA on that expense in the first year).

- Unlike the AIA and WDA, the FYA is never pro-rated for accounting periods of greater or less than 12 months.

- The taxpayer does not have to claim all/any of the FYA.

- If the FYA is not fully claimed the balance of cost goes into the general pool but is not entitled to any other allowance in that year.

- FYAs are not given in the final period of trading (see section 5).

- If the low emission car is not new (i.e. secondhand) it is treated in the same way as a car with CO_2 emissions of between 111 – 160 g/km.

See section 6 for more detail on other types of cars.

Writing down allowances (WDA)

- An annual WDA of 18% is given on a reducing balance basis in the general pool.

- It is given on:
  - the unrelieved expenditure in the general pool brought forward at the beginning of the period of account (i.e. tax written down value) (TWDV), plus
  - any additions on which the AIA or FYA is not available, plus
  - any additions not covered by the AIA (i.e. exceeding the limit)
  - after taking account of disposals.

- The TWDV brought forward includes all prior expenditure, less allowances already claimed.

Computations

In the F6 exam you will normally do computations for one accounting period only. However, for tutorial purposes, the examples in this chapter may cover multiple accounting periods to enable you to practise the technique.

In all questions you should assume that the 2012/13 rules apply throughout.

Example 2 – Writing down allowances

Calculate the total capital allowances available to Matthew in Example 1 part (a).

Answer to example 2

y/e 6 April 2013	£	General pool £	Allowances £
Additions:			
Not qualifying for AIA or FYA:			
New Car (CO$_2$ between 111 – 160 g/km)		11,000	
Qualifying for AIA and FYA:			
Plant and machinery	65,000		
Office furniture	15,000		
	———		
	80,000		
Less: AIA	(25,000)		25,000
	———	55,000	
		———	
		66,000	
Less: WDA (18% x £66,000)		(11,880)	11,880
		———	
TWDV c/f		54,120	
		———	
Total allowances			36,880
			———

Example 3 – Writing down allowances

Grace commenced trading on 1 April 2012. Her trading profits, adjusted for tax purposes but before capital allowances, are as follows:

Year ended 31 March 2013	£45,770
Year ended 31 March 2014	£30,995

On 9 May 2012, she bought plant and machinery for £35,000, a secondhand motor car with CO$_2$ emissions of 131 g/km for £6,500 and a new motor car with CO$_2$ emissions of 107 g/km for £13,600.

Calculate Grace's tax adjusted trading profit for both years.

Assume the 2012/13 rules apply throughout.

KAPLAN PUBLISHING

Answer to example 3

Tax adjusted trading profit

	Adjusted trading profit £	Capital allowances (W) £	Tax adjusted trading profit £
y/e 31 March 2013	45,770	(41,570)	4,200
y/e 31 March 2014	30,995	(2,435)	28,560

Working: Capital allowances computation

		General pool	Allowances
y/e 31 March 2013	£	£	£
Additions:			
Not qualifying for AIA or FYA:			
Car (CO$_2$ between 111 – 160 g/km)		6,500	
Qualifying for AIA:			
Plant and machinery	35,000		
Less: AIA	(25,000)		25,000
		10,000	
		16,500	
Less: WDA (18% x £16,500)		(2,970)	2,970
Additions qualifying for FYA:			
New low emission car (CO$_2$ ≤ 110 g/km)	13,600		
Less: FYA (100%)	(13,600)		13,600
		Nil	
TWDV c/f		13,530	
Total allowances			41,570
y/e 31 March 2014			
Less: WDA (18% x £13,530)		(2,435)	2,435
TWDV c/f		11,095	
Total allowances			2,435

Test your understanding 1

Gayle commenced trading on 6 April 2012. Her trading profits, adjusted for tax purposes but before capital allowances, are as follows:

Year ended 5 April 2013	£45,740
Year ended 5 April 2014	£53,850

On 1 May 2012, Gayle acquired plant and machinery for £28,000, a new motor car with CO_2 emissions of 156 g/km for £10,000 and a new motor car with CO_2 emissions of 94 g/km for £11,100.

Calculate Gayle's tax adjusted trading profit for both years.

Assume the 2012/13 rules apply throughout.

Short or long periods of account

- The AIA and WDAs are given for periods of account (i.e. the period for which a trader prepares accounts). The £25,000 AIA and the percentage of 18% is based on a period of account of 12 months.

- Shorter or longer periods of account result in the allowances being pro-rated.

- If the period of account exceeds 18 months; it must be split into a 12-month period and a second period to deal with the remaining months.

- The most common occasion for a business having a non 12-month period of account is at the start of trading.

- Remember that FYAs are never pro-rated.

Example 4 – WDA: Long period of account

Giles commenced trading on 1 April 2012. He prepares accounts for the 14 month period ended 31 May 2013 and the year ended 31 May 2014.

On 1 June 2012, he bought plant and machinery for £28,000, a new motor car with CO_2 emissions of 149 g/km for £9,800 and a new motor car with CO_2 emissions of 100 g/km for £13,000.

Calculate his capital allowances for each of the periods of trading.

Assume the 2012/13 rules apply throughout.

Answer to example 4

Capital allowances computation

	General pool	Allowances
14 m/e 31 May 2013	£	£	£
Additions:			
Not qualifying for AIA or FYA:			
Car (CO_2 between 111 – 160 g/km)		9,800	
Qualifying for AIA:			
Plant and machinery	28,000		
Less: AIA (Note)	(28,000)		28,000
		Nil	
Less: WDA (18% × £9,800 × 14/12)		(2,058)	2,058
Additions qualifying for FYA:			
New low emission car (CO_2 ≤ 110 g/km)	13,000		
Less: FYA (100%)	(13,000)		
		Nil	13,000
TWDV c/f		7,742	
Total allowances			43,058
y/e 31 May 2014			
Less: WDA (18% × £7,742)		(1,394)	1,394
TWDV c/f		6,348	
Total allowances			1,394

Note: The AIA is pro-rated to £29,167 (£25,000 x 14/12) and therefore all of the £28,000 expenditure is eligible for the allowance in the 14 months ended 31 May 2013. The unused allowance is lost.

Both the AIA and the WDA are pro-rated to reflect the 14 month period.

Test your understanding 2

Graham commenced trading on 1 May 2012. He prepares accounts for the 4 month period ended 31 August 2012 and then the year ended 31 August 2013.

On 1 May 2012, he bought plant and machinery for £10,000, a used motor car with CO_2 emissions of 109 g/km for £11,500 and a new motor car with CO_2 emissions of 104 g/km for £16,500.

Calculate the capital allowances for each period of trading.

Assume the 2012/13 rules apply throughout.

Length of ownership in the period of account

It is important to distinguish between the length of the period of account and the date of acquisition of the asset during the period:

- The WDA is pro-rated according to the length of the period of account.
- The WDA is never restricted by reference to the length of ownership of an asset in the period of account.
- If a business prepares accounts for the year ended 31 March 2013, the same WDA is given whether an asset is purchased on 10 April 2012 or on 31 March 2013.

  The WDA is available provided the asset is owned on the last day of the period of account. The actual length of ownership of the asset during the accounting period is not relevant.

4 Sale of plant machinery

At the point an asset is sold or scrapped the following steps are taken:

- The disposal value (sale proceeds) is deducted from the total of:
  - the TWDV brought forward on the pool plus
  - Additions to the general pool
    - additions not qualifying for either the AIA or FYA, and
    - additions qualifying for but not covered by AIA.
- The WDA for the year is then calculated on the remaining figure.

- If sale proceeds exceed the original cost of the asset:
  - the sale proceeds deducted from the pool are restricted to the original cost of the asset
  - note that any excess of sale proceeds over original cost may then be taxed as a chargeable gain (see later).
- Therefore, on a disposal, always deduct from the pool the lower of:
  - the sale proceeds, and
  - the original cost.

Example 5 – Sale of plant and machinery

Glyn prepares accounts to 31 March. In the year to 31 March 2013, the following transactions took place:

5 June 2012	Plant sold for £1,200 (purchased for £8,000)
3 September 2012	Plant purchased for £29,000

Compute the capital allowances for the year ended 31 March 2013, assuming that the TWDV on 1 April 2012 was £10,000.

Answer to example 5

Glyn – Capital allowances computation – y/e 31 March 2013

	General pool	Allowances
	£	£	£
TWDV b/f		10,000	
Additions qualifying for AIA:			
Plant and machinery	29,000		
Less: AIA	(25,000)		25,000
	———	4,000	
Disposal (lower of cost and SP)		(1,200)	
		———	
		12,800	
Less: WDA (18% x £12,800)		(2,304)	2,304
		———	
TWDV c/f		10,496	
		———	———
Total allowances			27,304
			———

Test your understanding 3

Gloria has owned and run her own business for many years. She prepares accounts to 31 March each year. During the year ended 31 March 2013, the following transactions took place:

21 July 2012	Purchased a motor car with CO_2 emissions of 145 g/km for £11,000.
14 October 2012	Sold a piece of plant for £2,400. She had paid £15,000 for this when she acquired it.
31 December 2012	Sold a van for £700. She had paid £600 for this when she acquired it.
31 March 2013	Purchased plant for £19,500.

The TWDV at 1 April 2012 was £21,000.

Compute the capital allowances for the y/e 31 March 2013.

Balancing charges

The basic idea underlying capital allowances is that the business will over time obtain relief for the actual net cost of an asset to the business (i.e. cost less sale proceeds (if any)).

Initially the asset is put into the pool at its original cost. If, on disposal of an asset in the pool, sale proceeds exceed the balance brought forward:

- the pool balance will become negative because too many allowances have been claimed in the past

- the negative amount = the excess allowances previously given

- these will be recovered and charged to tax by means of a balancing charge (BC)

- the BC reduces the capital allowances claim for the period

- if there is an overall net BC, it is added to the tax adjusted trading profit.

KAPLAN PUBLISHING

Test your understanding 4

Gavin has traded for many years in his ice cream manufacturing business. He prepares account to 31 March and during the year ended 31 March 2013 he made the following transactions:

14 June 2012	Sold some machinery for £12,100 which originally cost £26,000.
30 November 2012	Purchased a new car with CO_2 emissions of 109 g/km for £14,000.
16 March 2013	Purchased some equipment for £23,500.

The TWDV at 1 April 2012 was £11,000.

(a) **Calculate Gavin's capital allowances for the y/e 31 March 2013.**

(b) **Explain what would have happened had Gavin made no additions in the year.**

5 Cessation of trade

When the business is **permanently discontinued**, a normal capital allowance computation is not calculated in the final period to the cessation of trade. Instead the following steps should be followed:

(1) Add in any additions made in the final period.

(2) Do not calculate any AIAs, WDAs or FYAs.

(3) Deduct any disposals made in the final period and any sale proceeds on the ultimate disposal of plant and machinery.

(4) Calculate a **balancing charge** (BC) (as above) or **balancing allowance** (BA) (see below) as appropriate.

(5) There should not be any balances carried forward at the end of trade.

Balancing allowances

At cessation, if there is still a balance of unrelieved expenditure in the pool, a business can claim relief for the unrelieved balance by way of a balancing allowance (BA).

- This is the only time a BA will arise in the general pool.

- A BA is computed by reference to the excess of the pool balance at the end of the final period of account over the sale proceeds received on the ultimate disposal of plant and machinery.

Test your understanding 5

Gene has previously prepared accounts to 31 March. He decided to cease to trade on 31 December 2013, after a period of ill health.

The following transactions have recently taken place:

21.2.13   Plant sold for £320 (originally purchased for £2,000)
10.9.13   Plant purchased for £4,000

On the completion of the sale of his business, Gene received £5,400 for his plant and machinery. No item was sold for more than its original cost.

The TWDV on 1 April 2012, was £9,000.

Compute the capital allowances for the year ended 31 March 2013, and the period ended 31 December 2013.

Assume the 2012/13 rules apply throughout.

6 Motor cars

The treatment of motor cars depends on its CO_2 emissions as follows:

CO_2 emissions	Description	Treatment in capital allowances computation:
≤ 110 g/km	Low emission	If purchased new: eligible for 100% FYA (see section 3) If secondhand: treat as a standard emission car
111 – 160 g/km	Standard emission	Included in general pool as an addition not qualifying for AIA or FYA
> 160 g/km	High emission	Include in the 'special rate pool' as an addition not qualifying for AIA or FYA (see section 8)

Note however that:

- Motor cars with an element of private use, regardless of their level of emissions, are treated separately (see section 7).

Remember that the AIA is not available on any type of car.

Example 6 – Motor cars

Glenda prepares accounts to 31 March. At 1 April 2012, the TWDV of the general pool was £21,200. The following transactions took place during the two years ended 31 March 2014:

25.04.12	Purchased a motor car with CO_2 emissions of 153 g/km for £10,600
11.06.13	Purchased plant and machinery for £36,000
15.08.13	Sold some equipment for £9,400 (originally purchased for £15,000)

Calculate the capital allowances for the two years to 31 March 2014. Assume the 2012/13 rules apply throughout.

Answer to example 6

Capital allowances computations

	General pool	Allowances
y/e 31 March 2013	£	£
TWDV b/f	21,200	
Additions: Not qualifying for AIA or FYA:		
Car (CO_2 between 111 – 160 g/km)	10,600	
	31,800	
Less: WDA (18% x £31,800)	(5,724)	5,724
TWDV c/f	26,076	
Total allowances		5,724

y/e 31 March 2014			
Additions: Qualifying for AIA:			
Plant and machinery	36,000		
Less: AIA	(25,000)		25,000
		11,000	
Disposal (lower of cost and SP)		(9,400)	
		27,676	
Less: WDA (18% x £27,676)		(4,982)	4,982
TWDV c/f		22,694	
Total allowances			29,982

Test your understanding 6

Glen prepares accounts to 31 March. At 1 April 2012, the TWDV of the general pool was £48,100.

Transactions during the year ended 31 March 2013 were:

10.5.12	Purchased plant for £28,300
25.6.12	Purchased two new cars, one with CO_2 emissions of 147 g/km for £10,600 and one with CO_2 emissions of 101 g/km for £13,000
18.1.13	Sold plant £4,600 (originally purchased for £9,500)

Calculate the capital allowances for the year to 31 March 2013.

7 Assets with private use by the owner of the business

Where an asset is **used by the owner of the business**, partly for business and partly for private purposes:

- only the business proportion of the available capital allowances are available as a tax deduction.

The following rules must be followed when computing the allowances:

- The cost of the privately used asset is not brought into the general pool, but must be the subject of a separate computation.

- The AIA, FYA or WDA on the asset is based on its full cost
  - but only the business proportion of any allowance is actually deductible in computing the taxable trading profit.

- Note that if applicable, the business can choose the expenditure against which the AIA is allocated.

- It will therefore be most beneficial for the AIA to be allocated against the general pool expenditure rather than any private use asset as only the business proportion of any AIA available can be claimed.

- However note that in examinations the assets most commonly used for private purposes are cars, which are not eligible for the AIA.

- Motor cars with private use are always treated separately – regardless of their CO_2 emissions.

- On disposal of the asset, a balancing adjustment is computed by comparing sale proceeds (SP) with the TWDV.

There is a balancing charge (BC) if SP exceeds the TWDV, and a balancing allowance (BA) if SP are less than the TWDV.

- Having computed the balancing adjustment, the amount assessed or allowed is then reduced to the business proportion.

Note that these rules only apply if there is **private use by the owner** of the business.

Private use of an asset by an employee has no effect on the business's entitlement to capital allowances.

Example 7 – Assets with private use by the owner of the business

George runs a business and prepares his accounts to 5 April. As at 6 April 2012, the TWDV in the general pool was £11,700.

The following transactions took place in the year ended 5 April 2013:

- Purchased plant for £43,500
- Purchased a motor car with CO_2 emissions of 158 g/km for £16,000
- Sold some machinery for £5,500 (originally purchased for £18,000)
- Purchased a motor car with CO_2 emissions of 136 g/km for £9,400 (used 45% for private purposes by George)

Calculate the capital allowances for the year to 5 April 2013.

Answer to example 7

Capital allowances computation – y/e 5 April 2013

	General pool	Private use car	Business use	Allowances
	£	£	%	£
TWDV b/f	11,700			
Additions: Not qualifying for AIA:				
Car (CO$_2$ between 111 – 160 g/km)	16,000			
Private use car		9,400		
Additions: Qualifying for AIA:				
Plant and machinery	43,500			
Less: AIA	(25,000)			25,000
	18,500			
Disposal (lower of Cost and SP)	(5,500)			
	40,700	9,400		
Less: WDA (18% x £40,700)	(7,326)			7,326
WDA (18% x £9,400)		(1,692)	× 55%	931
TWDV c/f	33,374	7,708		
Total allowances				33,257

Test your understanding 7

Georgina runs a small business and prepares accounts to 31 March. At 1 April 2012, the TWDV in the general pool was £21,200. The following transactions took place during the y/e 31 March 2013:

10.5.12   Purchased plant for £6,600

25.6.12   Purchased a motor car with CO$_2$ emissions of 134 g/km for £17,000

15.2.13   Sold some machinery for £9,400 (originally purchased for £12,000)

16.2.13   Purchased a motor car with CO$_2$ emissions of 116 g/km for £10,600 (used 40% for private purposes by Georgina)

14.3.13   Purchased a new motor car with CO$_2$ emissions of 107 g/km for £11,750

Calculate the capital allowances for the year to 31 March 2013.

8 Special rate pool

The 'special rate pool' is a pool of qualifying expenditure that operates in the same way as the general pool except that:

* the WDA is 8% for a 12 month period (rather than 18%).

Qualifying expenditure

The 'special rate pool' groups together expenditure incurred on the following type of assets:

* long-life assets
* 'integral features' of a building or structure
* thermal insulation of a building
* high emission cars (with CO_2 emissions of > 160g/km)

Long-life assets

Long-life assets are defined as plant and machinery with:

* an expected working life of 25 years or more.
    - Examples of long-life assets might include aircraft used by an airline and agricultural equipment used by a farm.
    - The 25 year working life is from the time that the asset is first brought into use, to the time that it ceases to be capable of being used. It is not sufficient to just look at the expected life in the hands of the current owner.
* a total cost of at least £100,000 (for a 12-month period).

Where the business spends less than £100,000 p.a. on long-life assets, they are treated as normal additions to either the general or special rate pool, depending on the type of expenditure.

The following can never be classed as long-life assets:

* Motor cars
* Plant and machinery situated in a building that is used as a retail shop, showroom, hotel or office.

Integral features of a building or structure and thermal insulation

'Integral features of a building or structure' include expenditure incurred on:

- electrical (including lighting) systems;
- cold water systems;
- space or water heating systems;
- powered systems of ventilation, air cooling or air purification;
- lifts, escalators and moving walkways.

Thermal insulation in all business buildings (except residential buildings in a property business) is also included in the special rate pool.

High emission cars

Note that where a high emission car is privately used by the owner of the business, it will be included in a separate column like other private use cars, but only receive a WDA of 8%.

The AIA in the special rate pool

- the AIA is available against all expenditure in this pool (except high emission cars), and
- the business can choose the expenditure against which the AIA is allocated.

It will therefore be most beneficial for the AIA to be allocated against expenditure in the following order:

(1) the 'special rate pool' (as assets in the 'special rate pool' are only eligible for 8% WDA, whereas general plant and machinery is eligible for 18% WDA).

(2) the general pool

(3) short life assets (see later)

(4) private use assets.

KAPLAN PUBLISHING

Example 8 – Long-life assets

Apple runs a manufacturing business and prepares her accounts to 31 March each year. As at 1 April 2012, the tax written down value in the general pool was £103,000.

In the year ended 31 March 2013 Apple incurred the following expenditure:

- Spent £105,000 on a new air-conditioning system for the factory which is expected to last 30 years.

- Purchased a new computer and related software for £25,000 and £5,000 respectively.

- Spent £15,000 on a new packing machine. Apple also incurred £4,000 on alterations to the factory in order to accommodate the new machine.

- Purchased a new car with CO_2 emissions of 168 g/km for £28,000.

In addition she sold old machinery for £10,000 (original cost £60,000).

Calculate the capital allowances available to Apple for the year ended 31 March 2013.

Answer to example 8

Capital allowances computation – y/e 31 March 2013

		General pool £	Special rate pool £	Allow- ances £
TWDV b/f		103,000	Nil	
Additions:				
Not qualifying for AIA or FYA:				
Car (CO_2 > 160 g/km)			28,000	
Qualifying for AIA:				
Long life asset (Note 1)	105,000			
Less: AIA (Max) (Note 2)	(25,000)			25,000
			80,000	
Computer and software	30,000			
Machine (Note 3)	19,000			
	49,000			
Less: AIA (Note 2)	(Nil)			
		49,000		
Disposal (lower of Cost and SP)		(10,000)		
		142.000	108,000	
Less: WDA (18% x £142,000)		(25,560)		25,560
WDA (8% x £108,000)			(8,640)	8,640
TWDV c/f		116,440	99,360	
Total allowances				59,200

Notes:

(1) The air-conditioning unit has an expected life of more than 25 years and is therefore a long-life asset. As Apple has incurred more than £100,000 on such assets in the year the air-conditioning unit is included in the 'special rate pool' and WDAs are restricted to 8%.

(2) The AIA is allocated to the additions in the 'special rate pool' in priority to the additions in the general pool. The maximum £25,000 is therefore all allocated to the special rate pool expenditure and there is no AIA available for the general pool expenditure.

(3) Software and the cost of altering buildings to accommodate plant are specifically deemed by statute to be items of general plant and machinery.

9 The small pool WDA

Where the balance immediately before the calculation of the WDA:

- on the general and/or 'special rate' pool
- is £1,000 or less (see below)

the balance can be claimed as a WDA and written off in that year.

Note that the **£1,000 limit** is for a **12 month accounting period**, it is therefore pro-rated for long and short accounting periods.

The claim is optional. However, the taxpayer will normally want to claim the maximum available and reduce the balance on the pool to £Nil.

Test your understanding 8

Angelina is in business as a sole trader and prepares accounts to 31 March each year.

During the year ending 31 March 2013 she purchased the following:

15 June 2012	Purchased new office furniture for £18,800.
2 July 2012	Purchased a new car (with CO_2 emissions of 187 g/km) for £10,000 which Angelina will use 20% of the time for private purposes.
10 July 2012	Installed a new water heating system in her business premises at a cost of £7,000 and a new lighting system at a cost of £8,000.

In addition on 1 July 2012 she sold office equipment for £18,700 (original cost £28,000).

As at 1 April 2012 the TWDV on her general pool was £10,800, and on the special rate pool was £16,600.

Calculate Angelina's capital allowances for the y/e March 2013.

10 Short life assets

The short life asset election exists to enable businesses to accelerate capital allowances on certain qualifying expenditure.

Qualifying expenditure

For the purposes of the examination, qualifying expenditure is:

*   all plant and machinery (with the exception of motor cars) which would normally go in the general pool
*   where it is the intention to sell or scrap the item **within eight years** of the end of the period of account in which the asset is acquired.

Process for computation

If the election is made, the following steps must be taken:

*   Each short life asset is the subject of a separate column within the capital allowances computation.
*   On disposal within eight years of the end of the period of account in which the asset was acquired:
    *   a separate balancing allowance or balancing charge is calculated.
*   The election (written application to HMRC) must be made to enable assets to be treated separately in the capital allowances computation as short life assets. This is known as de-pooling.
*   This election must be made by the first anniversary of 31 January following the end of the tax year in which the trading period of expenditure ends.
*   If no disposal has taken place within eight years of the end of the period of account in which the acquisition took place:
    *   the unrelieved balance is transferred to the general pool
    *   the transfer takes place in the first period of account following the eight-year anniversary.
*   Note that the AIA is available against short life assets and the business can choose the expenditure against which the AIA is matched. However, if eligible for the AIA, there will be no expenditure left to 'de-pool' and the short life asset election will not be made.

    If there is expenditure in excess of the maximum £25,000 of expenditure eligible for the AIA, it may be advantageous for the AIA to be allocated against the general pool expenditure rather than a short life asset and for the short life asset election to be made.

Expenditure in excess of the AIA that is de-pooled is eligible for WDAs.

- It will be advantageous to make the election if it is anticipated that a balancing allowance will arise within the following eight accounting periods.

Example 9 – Short life assets

Gina has traded for many years preparing accounts to 31 March each year. The TWDV on the general pool was £15,000 on 1 April 2012.

In May 2012, she acquired a new machine costing £10,000. She anticipated that the machine would last two years and she eventually sold it on 30 June 2014, for £1,750.

In August 2012, she acquired general plant and machinery for £27,000.

Calculate the allowances available for each year, illustrating whether or not an election to treat the new machine as a short life asset would be beneficial.

Assume the 2012/13 rules apply throughout.

Answer to example 9

Gina – Capital allowances computation
– without making a short life asset election

	£	General pool £	Allowances £
y/e 31 March 2013			
TWDV b/f		15,000	
Additions: Qualifying for AIA:			
Plant and machinery (£27,000 + £10,000)	37,000		
Less: AIA	(25,000)		25,000
	———	12,000	
		———	
		27,000	
Less: WDA (18% x £27,000)		(4,860)	4,860
		———	
TWDV c/f		22,140	
		———	
Total allowances			29,860
			———

y/e 31 March 2014

Less: WDA (18% x £22,140)	(3,985)	3,985
	————	
TWDV c/f	18,155	
Total allowances		3,985

y/e 31 March 2015

Disposal (lower of Cost and SP)	(1,750)	
	————	
	16,405	
Less: WDA (18% x £16,405)	(2,953)	2,953
	————	
TWDV c/f	13,452	
Total allowances		2,953

Gina – Capital allowances computation
– with a short life asset election

	General pool	Short life asset	Allowances
	£	£	£
y/e 31 March 2013			
TWDV b/f	15,000		
Additions: Qualifying for AIA:			
Plant and machinery	27,000	10,000	
Less: AIA	(25,000)	(Nil)	25,000
	———		
	2,000		
	———		
	17,000	10,000	
Less: WDA (18% x £17,000/£10,000)	(3,060)	(1,800)	4,860
	———	———	
TWDV c/f	13,940	8,200	
Total allowances			29,860
y/e 31 March 2014			
Less: WDA			
(18% x £13,940 / £8,200)	(2,509)	(1,476)	3,985
	———	———	
TWDV c/f	11,431	6,724	
Total allowances			3,985

y/e 31 March 2015

Disposal (lower of cost and SP)		(1,750)	
		_____	_____
	11,431	4,974	
Balancing allowance		(4,974)	4,974
		_____	
Less: WDA (18% x £11,431)	(2,058)		2,058
	_____		
TWDV c/f	9,373		
	_____		_____
Total allowances			7,032
			_____

The total allowances claimed without making the election are £36,798 (£29,860 + £3,985 + £2,953). In the event Gina makes the election, the allowances available for the three years are £40,877 (£29,860 + £3,985 + £7,032).

Note that the election just accelerates the allowances available and only changes the timing of the allowances. The total allowances available will eventually be the same, however, without the election, it will take considerably longer to get the relief.

Therefore, if not covered by the AIA, it is recommended that the short life treatment is taken but only if it is expected that a balancing allowance can be accelerated. It is not advantageous to accelerate a balancing charge.

11 Summary of computational technique

- Capital allowances are an important element of the syllabus and are certain to appear in the exam, within at least one of the questions.

- To be successful answering these questions, it is vital to use a methodical approach to work through the information in the question.

- Always follow the approach to computational questions outlined below and always ensure that you answer the question using the following proforma amended to reflect the particular circumstances of the question.

Approach to computational questions

(1) Read the information in the question and decide how many columns / pools you will require.

(2) Draft the layout and insert the TWDV b/f (does not apply in a new trade).

(3) Insert additions not eligible for the AIA or FYAs into the appropriate column taking particular care to allocate cars into the correct column according to CO_2 emissions.

(4) Insert additions eligible for the AIA in the first column, then allocate the AIA to the additions

– remember to time apportion if the accounting period is not 12 months

– allocate the AIA to 'special rate pool' additions in priority to additions in the general or single asset columns.

(5) Any 'special rate pool' additions in excess of the AIA are added to the 'special rate pool' to increase the balance available for 8% WDA.

Any general pool expenditure in excess of the AIA should be added to the general pool to increase the balance qualifying for 18% WDA.

The same approach is taken for additions to single asset columns.

(6) Deal with any disposal by deducting the lower of cost or sale proceeds.

(7) Work out any balancing charge / balancing allowance for assets in individual pools.

Remember to adjust for any private use.

(8) Consider if the small pools WDA applies to the general pool and / or the 'special rate pool'.

(9) Calculate the WDA on each of the pools at the appropriate rate (either 18% or 8%).
Remember to:

– time apportion if the accounting period is not 12 months

– adjust for any private use if an unincorporated business

(10) Insert additions eligible for FYAs (i.e. any new cars with emissions of 110 g/km or less) which will get 100% FYA.

Remember the FYA is never time-apportioned.

(11) Calculate the TWDV to carry forward to the next accounting period and total the allowances column.

(12) Deduct the total allowances from the tax adjusted trading profits.

KAPLAN PUBLISHING

Proforma capital allowances computation

The following proforma computation should be used for unincorporated businesses:

Pro forma capital allowances computation – unincorporated businesses

	Notes	£	General pool £	Special rate pool £	Short life asset £	Private use asset (Note 2) £	Allowances £
TWDV b/f			X	X	X		
Additions:							
Not qualifying for AIA or FYA:	(1)						
Second hand cars (up to 110 g/km)			X				
Cars (111 – 160 g/km)			X				
Cars (over 160 g/km)				X			
Car with private use						X	
Qualifying for AIA:							
Special rate pool expenditure	(3)	X					
Less: AIA (Max £25,000 in total)		(X)					X
Transfer balance to special rate pool				X			
Plant and machinery		X					
Less: AIA (Max £25,000 in total)		(X)					X
Transfer balance to general pool			X				
Disposals (lower of original cost or sale proceeds)	(4)		(X)	(X)	(X)	X	
			X	X	X / (X)		
BA / (BC)							x / (X)
Small pools WDA	(5)			(X)			
WDA at 18%			(X)				X
WDA at 8%							X
WDA at 8%/18% (depending on emissions)						(X) × BU%	X
Additions qualifying for FYAs:							
New low emission cars (up to 110 g/km)		X					
Less: FYA at 100%		(X)	Nil				X
TWDV c/f			X	X		X	
Total allowances							X

Notes to the pro forma capital allowances computation

(1) Cars are pooled according to their CO_2 emissions into either the 'general' or 'special rate' pool.
New low emission cars receive 100% FYA.

(2) Cars with private use are de-pooled regardless of their CO_2 emissions, and only the business proportion of allowances can be claimed. However, the CO_2 emissions are important in determining the rate of WDA available.

(3) Allocate the AIA to the 'special rate' pool expenditure in priority to general pool plant and machinery assets as a WDA of only 8% is available on the 'special rate' pool as opposed to 18% available on 'general' pool items.

(4) Expenditure qualifying for AIA in the general pool which exceeds the level of AIA available, is eligible for a WDA of 18%.

(5) Small pools WDA: can claim up to a maximum WDA of £1,000 but on the general pool and/or 'special rate pool' only.

(6) The taxpayer does not have to claim all or any of the AIA or WDA.

12 Comprehensive example

Example 10 – Comprehensive example

Ashley runs a manufacturing business and prepares accounts to 31 March each year. During the year ending 31 March 2013 Ashley incurred the following expenditure:

1 May 2012   Spent £170,000 on a new air-conditioning system for the factory which is expected to last 30 years.

1 June 2012   Purchased new machinery for £40,000.

3 June 2012   Purchased a new car with CO_2 emissions of 109 g/km for £17,000.

15 July 2012   Purchased a new car with CO_2 emissions of 146 g/km for £18,000.

In addition on 1 July 2012 Ashley sold an old machine for £10,000 (original cost £15,000).

As at 1 April 2012 the tax written down value on the general pool was £64,000.

Calculate Ashley's capital allowances for the y/e 31 March 2013.

Answer to example 10

Capital allowances computation – y/e 31 March 2013

	General pool £	Special rate pool £	Allow-ances £
TWDV b/f	64,000	Nil	
Additions:			
Not qualifying for AIA or FYA:			
Car (CO_2 emissions 146 g/km)	18,000		
Qualifying for AIA:			
Integral features	170,000		
Less: AIA (Max)	(25,000)		25,000
		145,000	
Plant and machinery	40,000		
Less: AIA (Max used)	(Nil)		
	40,000		
Disposal (lower of Cost and SP)	(10,000)		
	112,000	145,000	
Balancing allowance			
Less: WDA (18% x £112,000)	(20,160)		20,160
WDA (8% x £145,000)		(11,600)	11,600
Car (CO_2 < 110 g/km)	17,000		
Less: FYA (100%)	(17,000)		17,000
		Nil	
TWDV c/f	91,840	133,400	
Total allowances			73,760

Note: The AIA is allocated to the additions in the 'special rate pool' (WDA 8%) in priority to the additions in the general pool (WDA 18%).

Test your understanding 9

On 1 January 2013, Gordon commenced in self-employment running a music-recording studio. He prepared his first set of accounts for the three months to 31 March 2013.

The following information relates to the three months to 31 March 2013:

(1) The tax adjusted trading profit for the period is £30,590. This figure is before taking account of capital allowances.

(2) Gordon purchased the following assets:

		£
1 January 2013	Recording equipment	34,125
15 January 2013	Motor car with CO_2 emissions of 162 g/km (used by Gordon – 60% business use)	15,800
20 February 2013	Motor car with CO_2 emissions of 156 g/km (used by employee – 20% private use)	10,400
4 March 2013	Recording equipment (expected to be scrapped in 2 years)	3,250

Calculate Gordon's tax adjusted trading profit for the period ended 31 March 2013.

13 Chapter summary

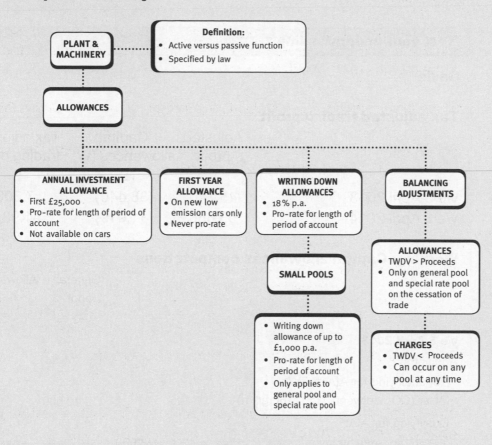

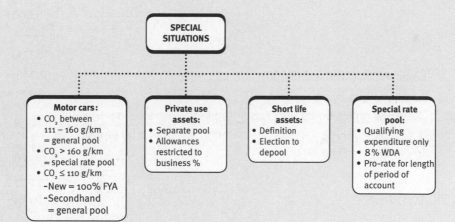

Test your understanding answers

Test your understanding 1

Gayle

Tax adjusted trading profit

	Adjusted profit £	Capital allowances (W) £	Tax adjusted trading profit £
y/e 5 April 2013	45,740	(38,440)	7,300
y/e 5 April 2014	53,850	(1,919)	51,931

Working: Capital allowances computations

		General pool £	Allowances £
	£		
y/e 5 April 2013			
Additions:			
Not qualifying for AIA or FYA:			
Car (CO_2 between 111 – 160 g/km)		10,000	
Qualifying for AIA:			
Plant and machinery	28,000		
Less: AIA	(25,000)		25,000
	———	3,000	
		———	
		13,000	
Less: WDA (18% x £13,000)		(2,340)	2,340
Additions qualifying for FYA:			
New low emission car ($CO_2 \leq 110$ g/km)	11,100		
Less: FYA (100%)	(11,100)		11,100
	———	Nil	
		———	
TWDV c/f		10,660	
			———
Total allowances			38,440
			———
y/e 5 April 2014			
Less: WDA (18% x £10,660)		(1,919)	1,919
		———	
TWDV c/f		8,741	
		———	———
Total allowances			1,919
			———

Test your understanding 2

Graham
Capital allowances computations

		General pool	Allowances
4 m/e 31 August 2012	£	£	£
Additions:			
Not qualifying for AIA or FYA:			
Secondhand low emission car		11,500	
Qualifying for AIA:			
Plant and machinery	10,000		
Less: AIA (Note)	(8,333)		8,333
		1,667	
		13,167	
Less: WDA (18% × £13,167 × 4/12)		(790)	790
Additions qualifying for FYA:			
New low emission car ($CO_2 \leq 110$ g/km)	16,500		
Less: FYA (100%)	(16,500)		16,500
		Nil	
TWDV c/f		12,377	
Total allowances			25,623
y/e 31 August 2013			
Less: WDA (18% × £12,377)		(2,228)	2,228
TWDV c/f		10,149	
Total allowances			2,228

Note: The maximum AIA is pro-rated to £8,333 (£25,000 x 4/12).
The AIA and the WDA are pro-rated for the 4 month period.

Test your understanding 3

Gloria
Capital allowances computation – 31 March 2013

	General pool	Total allowances
	£	£	£
TWDV b/f		21,000	
Additions:			
Not qualifying for AIA or FYA:			
Car (111 – 160 g/km)		11,000	
Qualifying for AIA:			
Plant and machinery	19,500		
Less AIA	(19,500)		19,500
	———	Nil	
		———	
		32,000	
Disposals (lower of cost or sale proceeds)			
Plant		(2,400)	
Van		(600)	
		———	
		29,000	
Less: WDA (18% × £29,000)		(5,220)	5,220
		———	
TWDV c/f		23,780	
		———	———
Total allowances			24,720
			———

Test your understanding 3

Test your understanding 4

(a) **Gavin**

Capital allowances – year ended 31 March 2013

	General pool	Allowances
	£	£	£
TWDV b/f		11,000	
Additions qualifying for AIA:			
Plant and machinery	23,500		
Less: AIA	(23,500)		23,500
	————	Nil	
Disposals			
(lower of SP and Cost)		(12,100)	
		————	
Balancing charge (Note)		(1,100)	
		1,100	(1,100)
Less: WDA		————	
Additions qualifying for FYA:		Nil	
Low emission car	14,000		
Less: FYA	(14,000)		14,000
	————	Nil	
		————	————
			36,400
			————

Note: A BC reduces the capital allowances claim in the period.

(b) **If Gavin had made no additions in the year**

No AIA or FYA would have been available and therefore a net balancing charge of £1,100 would arise.

This would be added to Gavin's tax adjusted trading profits for the year.

Test your understanding 5

Gene
Capital allowances computations

	General pool £	Total allowances £
Year ended 31 March 2013		
TWDV b/f	9,000	
Disposals (lower of cost or sale proceeds)	(320)	
	8,680	
WDA (18% x £8,680)	(1,562)	1,562
TWDV c/f	7,118	
Total allowances		1,562
Period ended 31 December 2013		
Additions:		
Not qualifying for AIA or FYA (Note 1)		
Plant and machinery	4,000	
	11,118	
Disposals (lower of cost or sale proceeds)	(5,400)	
	5,718	
Balancing allowance (Note 2)	(5,718)	5,718
Total allowances		5,718

Notes:

(1) There is no AIA, FYA or WDA available in the final period of account.

(2) A balancing allowance is treated as normal capital allowances, and is therefore deducted from the tax adjusted trading profits.

Test your understanding 6

Glen
Capital allowances computation – y/e 31 March 2013

	£	General pool £	Allowances £
TWDV b/f		48,100	
Additions:			
Not qualifying for AIA or FYA:			
Car (CO_2 between 111 – 160 g/km)		10,600	
Qualifying for AIA:			
Plant and machinery	28,300		
Less: AIA	(25,000)		25,000
		3,300	
Disposal (lower of cost and SP)		(4,600)	
		57,400	
Less: WDA (18% x £57,400)		(10,332)	10,332
Additions qualifying for FYA:			
Low emission car (CO_2 ≤ 110 g/km)	13,000		
Less: FYA (100%)	(13,000)		13,000
		Nil	
TWDV c/f		47,068	
Total allowances			48,332

Test your understanding 7

Georgina
Capital allowances computation – y/e 31 March 2013

	General pool	Private use car (BU 60%)	Business use	Allowances
	£	£	£	%	£
TWDV b/f		21,200		
Additions:				
Not qualifying for AIA or FYA:				
Car (CO_2 between 111 – 160 g/km)		17,000		
Private use car			10,600	
Qualifying for AIA:				
Plant and machinery	6,600			
Less: AIA	(6,600)			6,600
	———	Nil		
Disposal (lower of Cost and SP)		(9,400)		
	———	———		
	28,800	10,600		
Less: WDA (18% x £28,800)	(5,184)			5,184
WDA (18% x £10,600)		(1,908)	× 60%	1,145
Additions: Qualifying for FYA				
New car (CO_2 < 110 g/km)	11,750			
Less: FYA (100%)	(11,750)			11,750
	———	Nil		
	———	———		
TWDV c/f	23,616	8,692		
	———	———		———
Total allowances				24,679
				———

KAPLAN PUBLISHING

Test your understanding 8

Angelina
Capital allowances computation – 31 March 2013

		General pool	Special rate pool	Private use car (BU 80%)	Business use	Allow-ances
	£	£	£	£	%	£
TWDV b/f			10,800	16,600		
Additions:						
Not qualifying for AIA or FYA:						
Private use car – high emission					10,000	
Qualifying for AIA:						
Integral features		15,000				
Less: AIA (Note)		(15,000)				15,000
		———	Nil			
Qualifying for AIA:						
Plant and machinery		18,800				
Less: AIA (£25,000 – £15,000)		(10,000)				10,000
		———	8,800			
Disposal (lower of Cost and SP)		(18,700)				
		———	———	———		
		900	16,600	10,000		
Less: Small pool WDA		(900)				900
Less: WDA (8% x £16,600)			(1,328)			1,328
WDA (8% x £10,000)				(800)	× 80%	640
		———	———	———		
TWDV c/f		Nil	15,272	9,200		
		———	———	———		———
Total allowances						27,868
						———

Note: The AIA is allocated to the additions in the 'special rate pool' (WDA 8%) in priority to the additions in the general pool (WDA 18%).

Test your understanding 9

Gordon
Period ended 31 March 2013

	£
Adjusted profit	30,590
Less: Capital allowances (W1)	(8,308)
Tax adjusted trading profit	22,282

(W1) Capital allowances computation – p/e 31 March 2013

	General pool £	Short life asset £	Private use car £	Business use %	Allow-ances £
Additions:					
Not qualifying for AIA or FYA:					
Car (CO$_2$ 156 g/km) (Note 1)	10,400				
Private use car			15,800		
Qualifying for AIA:					
Equipment	34,125	3,250			
Less: AIA (Max) (Note 2)	(6,250)	(Nil)			6,250
	—— 27,875				
	38,275	3,250	15,800		
Less: WDA (18% × 3/12)	(1,722)	(146)			1,868
WDA (8% × 3/12) (CO$_2$ > 160 g/km)			(316)	× 60%	190
TWDV c/f	36,553	3,104	15,484		
Total allowances					8,308

Notes:

(1)   Private use by an employee is not relevant. A separate private use asset column is only required where there is private use by the owner of the business.

(2)   The AIA is pro-rated for the three month period. The maximum allowance is therefore £6,250 (£25,000 x 3/12). The AIA is allocated to the general plant and machinery in priority to the short life asset.

7

Sole traders: Basis of assessment

Chapter learning objectives

Upon completion of this chapter you will be able to:

- Explain the basis of assessment for income from self-employment

- Compute the assessable trading profits for a new business

- Compute the assessable trading profits on cessation of a business

- Recognise the factors that will influence the choice of accounting date for a new business

- State the conditions that must be met for a change of accounting date to be valid

- Compute the assessable profits on a change of accounting date

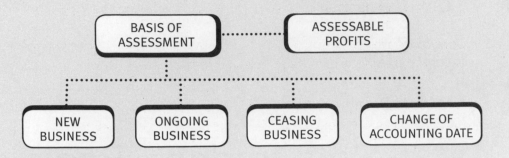

1 Introduction

Once the tax adjusted trading profit has been calculated for a period of account, it is important to identify in which tax year it will be assessed.

- Income tax is charged for a tax year or year of assessment which runs from 6 April to the following 5 April.

- Since traders do not necessarily prepare their accounts to coincide with the tax year, there needs to be a system for attributing profits earned in a period of account to a particular tax year.

The profit-earning (or loss-making) period of account that is attributed to a particular tax year is known as the 'basis period' for that tax year.

- In the examination, where the apportionment of tax adjusted trading profits into different tax years is required, the apportionment should be performed on a monthly basis as shown in all the illustrations below.

2 Ongoing year rules

The basic rule is:

- The profits for a year of assessment are the tax adjusted trading profits for the **12 month period of account ending in that year**.

- This is sometimes referred to as the **current year basis** of assessment (or CYB for short).

> ### Test your understanding 1
>
> A sole trader prepares his accounts to 31 December each year. He has been operating for several years.
>
> **State which profits will be assessed in 2012/13.**

Test your understanding 2

Jerry prepares accounts to 30 September annually. His recent tax adjusted trading profits have been as follows:

	£
Year to 30 September 2011	20,000
Year to 30 September 2012	22,000

State in which tax years these profits will be assessed.

3 Opening year rules

Assuming a business starts to trade on 1 January 2012 and prepares accounts for calendar years, the first tax year it is trading in is 2011/12.

However, the first accounting period will not end until 31 December 2012 and using the principle above this period will not be taxed until 2012/13.

In order to ensure that there is an assessment for each tax year that a business is trading, the following special provisions apply:

Year of assessment	Basis of assessment
First tax year (tax year in which trade starts)	From: Date of commencement To: following 5 April ('Actual basis')
Second tax year The accounting period ending in the tax year is:	
(i) 12 months	That period of account (CYB)
(ii) less than 12 months	The first 12 months of trade
(iii) more than 12 months	12 months to the accounting date ending in the second tax year (i.e. the last 12 months of the long period of account)
There is no accounting period ending in the second tax year	Actual profits in the second tax year: From: 6 April To: 5 April

Third tax year	12 months to the accounting date ending in the third tax year – normally CYB – if a long period of account = last 12 months of the long period
Fourth tax year onwards	Normal current year basis

Note that whichever scenario applies, from year 2 onwards the basis period will always be exactly 12 months long.

Example 1 – Opening year rules

Jenny commenced trading on 1 January 2012 and prepared her first set of accounts to 31 December that year. Her tax adjusted trading profits were £12,000 for the y/e 31 December 2012.

Explain which profits will be assessed in Jenny's first two tax years of trading.

Answer to example 1

First tax year – 2011/12

The profits assessed for 2011/12 will be the actual profits falling in the first tax year on a pro rata basis.

Tax year	Basis period	Calculation	Assessable profits
2011/12	01.01.12 – 05.04.12	(3/12 × £12,000)	£3,000

Second tax year – 2012/13

In the second tax year there is a 12 month period of account ending in the tax year. The current year basis can therefore be applied.

Tax year	Basis period		Assessable profits
2012/13	CYB (y/e 31 December 2012)		£12,000

You will notice that in the two years above, the profits for the period 1 January to 5 April (£3,000) have been assessed twice.

These are referred to as **overlap profits**.

Overlap profits

- Profits that are assessed in more than one tax year are known as the overlap profits.

- Overlap profits arise in every scenario at commencement of trade other than when the trader opts to take a 31 March year-end.

- The overlap profits are carried forward and are normally deducted from the assessment for the period in which the business ceases.

- Whilst the trader will get relief for overlap profits, relief may not be obtained for many years if the business continues for a long while.

- Overlap profits may also be relieved when a business changes its accounting date (see section 6).

Test your understanding 3

Rob started to trade on 1 September 2011 and prepared his first accounts for the year ended 31 August 2012. His tax adjusted trading profits were £18,000 in that year.

Calculate his assessable profits for 2011/12 and 2012/13.

Identify the months that have been taxed more than once and the overlap profits arising.

Summary of opening year rules

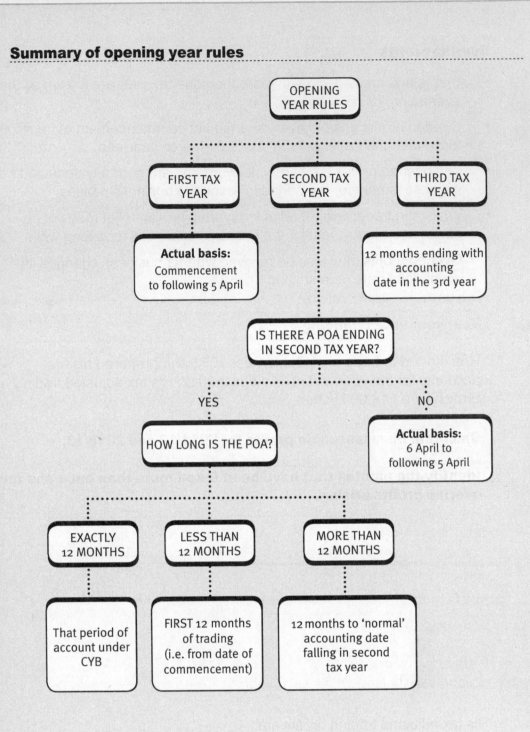

Example 2 – Opening year rules

Arthur commenced trading on 1 May 2010. He prepares accounts to 30 June each year. His tax adjusted trading profits were as follows:

Period ended 30.6.11	£28,000
Year ended 30.6.12	£30,000

Calculate Arthur's trading profit assessments for his first three tax years and his overlap profits.

Answer to example 2

Tax year	Basis period	Calculation	Assessable profits
			£
2010/11	1.5.10 – 5.4.11 (actual basis)	11/14 x £28,000	22,000
2011/12	year to 30.6.11 (Note)	12/14 x £28,000	24,000
2012/13	y/e 30.6.12 – CYB		30,000

Note: As the period of account ending in 2011/12 is 14 months long, the basis period is the 12 months to the normal accounting date (i.e. 30 June).

The overlap profits are for the period 1 July 2010 to 5 April 2011:
= (£28,000 × 9/14) = £18,000

Test your understanding 4

George commenced trade on 1 October 2009 and decided to prepare accounts to 31 December each year.

His tax adjusted trading profits are:

	£
Period to 31 December 2010	30,000
Year ended 31 December 2011	36,000
Year ended 31 December 2012	40,000

Calculate the trading profits assessed on George for all relevant tax years. State the overlap profits arising.

Example 3 – Opening year rules

Pattie commenced trading on 1 September 2010. She prepared accounts to 30 June 2011 and annually thereafter.

Her tax adjusted trading profits for the first two periods were as follows:

Period ended 30 June 2011	£30,000
Year ended 30 June 2012	£48,000

Calculate Pattie's trading profit assessments for her first three tax years and her overlap profits.

Answer to example 3

Tax year	Basis period	Calculation	Assessable profits £
2010/11	1.9.10 – 5.4.11	(£30,000 × 7/10) (actual)	21,000
2011/12	1.9.10 – 31.8.11	£30,000 + (2/12 × £48,000) (Note)	38,000
2012/13	y/e 30.6.12 – CYB		48,000

Note: Because the accounting date ending in the second year of assessment is less than 12 months after the commencement of trading, the basis of assessment is the first 12 months of trading.

Overlap profits = £29,000: £21,000 (1.9.10 to 5.4.11) and £8,000 (1.7.11 to 31.8.11: 2/12 × £48,000).

Test your understanding 5

Fred commenced a new trade on 1 June 2009 and decided that his normal accounting date would be 30 April each year.

Given below are the tax adjusted trading profits since commencement:

Period to 30 April 2010	£11,000
Year ended 30 April 2011	£18,000
Year ended 30 April 2012	£22,000

Calculate the trading profits assessable on Fred for all relevant tax years and his overlap profits.

Example 4 – Opening year rules

Cordelia commenced trading on 1 July 2010. She prepared accounts to 30 April 2012 and annually thereafter. Her tax adjusted trading profits for the first two periods were as follows:

Period ended 30.04.12	£55,000
Year ended 30.04.13	£32,000

Calculate Cordelia's trading profit assessments for her first three tax years and her overlap profits.

Answer to example 4

Tax year	Basis period	Calculation	Assessable profits £
2010/11	(01.07.10 – 05.04.11)	£55,000 × 9/22 (actual)	22,500
2011/12	(06.04.11 – 05.04.12)	£55,000 × 12/22 (Note 1)	30,000
2012/13	(Year to 30.04.12)	£55,000 × 12/22 (Note 2)	30,000
2013/14	(Year to 30.04.13)	CYB	32,000

Notes:

(1) Because there is no accounting date ending in the second year of assessment, the basis of assessment is the actual basis for the period from 6.4.11 to 5.4.12.
(2) In year three, the basis period is the profits of the 12 months ending with the accounting date in that year.

Overlap profits: £27,500 (01.05.11 to 05.04.12 = 11/22 × £55,000)

Test your understanding 6

Maria commenced business on 1 January 2009 and prepared her first accounts for the period to 30 June 2010, and thereafter to 30 June in each year.

Her tax adjusted trading profits have been:

Period to 30 June 2010	£27,000
Year ended 30 June 2011	£30,000
Year ended 30 June 2012	£40,000

Calculate the trading profits assessed on Maria for all relevant tax years. State the overlap profits.

4 Closing year rules

- The objective in the final year of assessment is to ensure that any profits not previously assessed are assessed here.

- Any overlap profits from commencement are deducted from the assessment for the final year.

- To identify the basis period for the final tax year:

  - Identify the tax year in which the trade ceases. This is the last year that profits must be assessed.

  - For the immediately preceding tax year, identify the assessment under normal CYB rules.

  - All profits after this period of account will not have been assessed and so fall into the assessment for the final tax year of trade.

  - Remember to deduct overlap profits in this final assessment.

Example 5 – Closing year rules

Michael ceased trading on 31 March 2013. His tax adjusted trading profits for the final three periods of trading are as follows:

Year ended 30.4.11	£40,000
Year ended 30.4.12	£42,000
Period ended 31.3.13	£38,000

He has unrelieved overlap profits of £27,000.

Calculate Michael's final two trading profit assessments.

Answer to example 5

The final year of assessment is 2012/13, the year in which trade ceases.

		£
2011/12	Penultimate year: CYB (Year to 30.4.11)	40,000
2012/13	Final year: all profits not yet assessed (23 months from 1.5.11 – 31.3.13) (£42,000 + £38,000)	80,000
	Less: Overlap profits	(27,000)
	Final assessable amount	53,000

Test your understanding 7

Major, who has been trading for many years, decides to cease trading on 31 December 2012. Major regularly prepared accounts to 30 June in each year.

The recent tax adjusted trading profits have been:

	£
Period to 31 December 2012	6,000
Year ended 30 June 2012	12,000
Year ended 30 June 2011	15,000
Year ended 30 June 2010	20,000
Year ended 30 June 2009	18,000

The overlap profits on commencement were £7,500.

Calculate the trading profits that will be assessed on Major for all tax years affected by the above accounts.

Test your understanding 8

Benny commenced to trade on 1 July 2007 and prepared his first accounts to 31 August 2008 and thereafter to 31 August annually. Benny ceased to trade on 31 December 2012.

Given below are the tax adjusted trading profits for all the relevant periods:

	£
Period ended 31 August 2008	10,500
Year ended 31 August 2009	18,000
Year ended 31 August 2010	22,500
Year ended 31 August 2011	31,500
Year ended 31 August 2012	27,000
Period ended 31 December 2012	8,400
	117,900

Compute the trading profits that will have been assessed on Benny for each tax year.

5 Choice of accounting date

There are various factors to consider in identifying the accounting date that a business adopts:

- An accounting date of just after, rather than just before, 5 April (such as 30 April) will ensure the maximum interval between earning profits and having to pay the related tax liability.

- However, an accounting date just after 5 April will result in increased overlap profits upon the commencement of trading.

  Although there is relief for overlap profits, there may be a long delay before relief is obtained.

- Alternatively an accounting date of just before 5 April, such as 31 March, will give the shortest interval between earning profits and having to pay the related tax liability. However, there will be no overlap profits.

6 Change of accounting date

Conditions

Provided certain conditions are met, an unincorporated business is allowed to change its accounting date. There may be tax advantages in doing so, or the change may be made for commercial reasons. For example, it may be easier to perform an inventory check at certain times of the year.

The detailed conditions and consequences of failing to meet the conditions are covered in expandable text.

Conditions to be met for a valid change

- The change of accounting date must be notified to HMRC on/before 31 January following the tax year in which the change is to be made.

- The first accounts to the new accounting date must not exceed 18 months in length.

- If the period between the old accounting date and the proposed new accounting date is longer than 18 months, then two sets of accounts will have to be prepared.

- There must be no other change of accounting date during the previous five tax years, unless HMRC accept that the present change is made for genuine commercial reasons.

Failure to meet the conditions

If the conditions are not met, the old accounting date will continue to apply. If accounts are prepared to the new accounting date, then the figures will have to be apportioned accordingly.

If the conditions are met, then the period of account for the tax year in which the change of accounting date is made, will either be less than or more than 12 months in length.

Change of accounting date – calculations

A trader has previously prepared accounts to 30 June. If he changes his accounting date to 30 September, the next set of accounts are going to be for either 3 or 15 months.

However, all basis of assessments other than for the first and final tax years must be of 12 months in duration.

As the period of account in which the accounting date changed will not be 12 months, the assessment in the tax year of change will either be:

- made up to 12 months, by creating further overlap profits, or
- reduced back to 12 months by relieving earlier overlap profits.

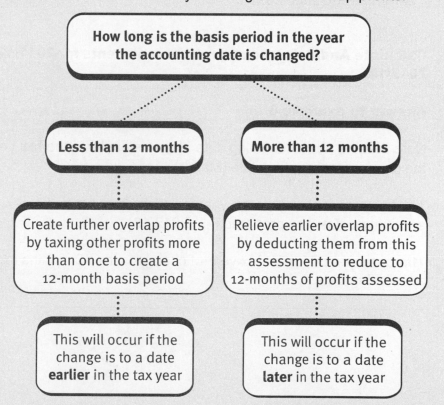

New date is earlier in the tax year

Where the new accounting date is earlier in the tax year than the old one, the basis period for the tax year of change will be the **12 month period ending with the new accounting date**.

This will result in some profits being assessed more than once. Overlap profits will therefore arise, which are treated in exactly the same way as overlap profits arising on the commencement of trade.

It is possible to have either a long or short period of account ending on the new date.

Example 6 – New date earlier – short period

Andrea, a sole trader, has always prepared her accounts to 31 March. She decides to change her accounting date to 30 June by preparing accounts for the three-month period to 30 June 2012.

Andrea's tax adjusted trading profits are as follows:

	£
Year ended 31 March 2012	60,000
Three months to 30 June 2012	20,000
Year ended 30 June 2013	85,000

Calculate Andrea's trading profit assessments for 2011/12 to 2013/14.

Answer to example 6

Note that the new accounting date (June) is earlier in the **tax year** than the previous accounting date (March).

The tax year of change is the year in which accounts to the new accounting date are prepared (i.e. 2012/13).

The basis period for the tax year of change is the 12 months to the new accounting date.

The trading profits assessable will be as follows:

Tax year	Basis period	Assessable profits £
2011/12	Year to 31.3.12 (Normal CYB)	60,000
2012/13	12-month period to new accounting date of 30.6.12	
	Year to 31.3.12: (£60,000 × 9/12)	45,000
	Period to 30.6.12	20,000
		65,000
2013/14	Year to 30.6.13 (CYB)	85,000

Note: The change in accounting date has created further overlap profits of £45,000, as the 9 months to 31 March 2012 are assessed in both 2011/12 and 2012/13. The overlap profits will be offset in the final year of assessment.

As well as moving to an earlier date in the tax year with a short accounting period, it is possible to do this with a long accounting period.

Example 7 – New date earlier – long period

If Andrea had instead prepared accounts for the 15-month period to 30 June 2013, then the result would have been virtually the same. Assume the tax adjusted profit for the 15-month period ended 30 June 2013 is £105,000.

Calculate Andrea's trading profit assessments for 2011/12 to 2013/14.

Answer to example 7

The tax year in which the change takes place is still 2012/13 as Andrea does not adopt her normal 31 March year-end here.

Because all the criteria are met, she is allowed to adopt the new accounting date in this year, and the profits assessed are those for the 12 months to the new accounting date – 30 June.

Tax year	Basis period	Assessable profits
		£
2011/12	Year to 31.3.12 (Normal CYB)	60,000
2012/13	12-month period to new accounting date of 30.6.12	
	Year to 31.3.12: (£60,000 × 9/12)	45,000
	Period to 30.6.13: (£105,000 × 3/15)	21,000
		66,000
2013/14	Year to 30.6.13: (£105,000 × 12/15)	84,000

Overlap profits still arise in respect of the nine months to 31 March 2012, as before = £45,000.

New date is later in the tax year

Where the new accounting date is later in the tax year than the old one the basis period for the tax year of change will be the period ending with the new accounting date.

As the resulting basis period may be more than 12 months, a corresponding proportion of any overlap profits that arose upon the commencement of trading are offset against the assessable profits.

Again, it is possible to have either a short accounting period creating the new date, or a long period.

Example 8 – New date later – long period

Peter, a sole trader, commenced trading on 1 July 2009, and has always prepared his accounts to 30 June. He has now decided to change his accounting date to 30 September by preparing accounts for the 15-month period to 30 September 2012.

Peter's tax adjusted trading profits are as follows:

	£
Year ended 30 June 2010	18,000
Year ended 30 June 2011	24,000
Period ended 30 September 2012	30,000
Year ended 30 September 2013	36,000

Calculate Peter's trading profit assessments for 2009/10 to 2013/14.

Answer to example 8

The tax year of change is the tax year in which accounts are prepared to the new accounting date (i.e. 2012/13).

As the new accounting date is later in the tax year, the basis period is the period ending with the new accounting date.

Tax year	Basis period	Assessable profits £
2009/10	1.7.09 to 5.4.10: Actual (£18,000 × 9/12)	13,500
2010/11	Year to 30.6.10: CYB	18,000
2011/12	Year to 30.6.11: CYB	24,000
2012/13	15 months period to 30.9.12	30,000
	Less: Overlap profits (£13,500 × 3/9)	(4,500)
		25,500
2013/14	Year to 30.9.13: CYB	36,000

The overlap profits on commencement of trade are £13,500, representing the 9 months (1.7.09 to 5.4.10) that have been taxed twice.

In 2012/13 the period of account is 15 months. No assessment can be for more than 12 months and in this case, Peter is allowed to offset three months' worth of his overlap profits.

The remaining 6 months of overlap profits are carried forward as normal and available for relief, either on a further change in accounting date, or on the cessation of trade.

7 Chapter summary

BASIS OF ASSESSMENT

NEW BUSINESS

- Year 1 = actual basis
- Year 2 = options
  - CYB
  - If accounts < 12 months: First 12 months of trading
  - If accounts > 12 months: 12 months to accounting date
  - No accounts: actual basis
- Year 3 = 12 months ending with accounting date in 3rd tax year
- Year 4 and thereafter = CYB

CHANGE OF ACCOUNTING DATE

- Conditions must be met
- New date earlier in tax year = 12 months to new accounting date. More overlap profits
- New date later in tax year = profits of period of account ending with new accounting date. Relieve overlap profits

ONGOING BUSINESS

CYB

Profits assessed in a particular tax year are those of the 12-month period of account ending in that tax year

ASSESSABLE PROFITS

- Tax-adjusted trading profit

CEASING BUSINESS

Final year assessment

	£
All profits not previously assessed	X
Less: Overlap profits	(X)
	X

Test your understanding answers

Test your understanding 1

Ongoing years

His assessable profits for the 2012/13 tax year will be based on the tax adjusted trading profits for the accounting year to 31 December 2012.

Test your understanding 2

Jerry

Tax year	Basis period	Assessable profits
		£
2011/12	Year to 30.9.11	20,000
2012/13	Year to 30.9.12	22,000

Test your understanding 3

Rob

Tax year	Basis period	Assessable profits
		£
2011/12	01.09.11 – 05.04.12: Actual (£18,000 x 7/12)	10,500
2012/13	y/e 31 August 2012: CYB	18,000

The profits between 1 September 2011 and 5 April 2012 (7 months) are taxed in both tax years.

Overlap profits are therefore £10,500 (7/12 × £18,000).

Test your understanding 4

George

Tax year	Basis period	Assessable profits £
2009/10	01.10.09 – 05.04.10: Actual (6/15 × £30,000)	12,000
2010/11	01.01.10 – 31.12.10: 12 months ending on accounting date (12/15 × £30,000)	24,000
2011/12	y/e 31.12.11: CYB	36,000
2012/13	y/e 31.12.12: CYB	40,000

Overlap profits: 01.01.10 to 05.04.10 = (3/15 × £30,000) = £6,000

Test your understanding 5

Fred

Tax year	Basis period	Assessable profits £
2009/10	01.06.09 – 05.04.10: Actual (10/11 × £11,000)	10,000
2010/11	01.06.09 – 31.05.10: First 12 months £11,000 + (1/12 × £18,000)	12,500
2011/12	y/e 30.04.11: CYB	18,000
2012/13	y/e 30.04.12: CYB	22,000

As the period of account ending in the second year is less than 12 months long, the basis period is the first 12 months of trading.

Overlap profits = £11,500
i.e. 01.06.09 to 05.04.10 (£10,000) and 01.05.10 to 31.05.10 (1/12 × £18,000).

Test your understanding 6

Maria

Tax year	Basis period	Assessable profits £
2008/09	01.01.09 – 05.04.09: Actual (3/18 × £27,000)	4,500
2009/10	06.04.09 – 05.04.10: Actual (12/18 × £27,000) (Note)	18,000
2010/11	01.07.09 – 30.06.10: 12m to the accounting date (12/18 × £27,000)	18,000
2011/12	y/e 30.06.11: CYB	30,000
2012/13	y/e 30.06.12: CYB	40,000

Note: There is no period of account ending in the second year. The profits are therefore assessed on the actual basis.

Overlap profits: 01.07.09 – 05.04.10
= (9/18 × £27,000) = £13,500

Test your understanding 7

Major

Tax year	Basis period	Assessable profits £
2009/10	y/e 30.06.09: CYB	18,000
2010/11	y/e 30.06.10: CYB	20,000
2011/12	y/e 30.06.11: CYB	15,000
2012/13	01.07.11 – 31.12.12: Final – anything not yet taxed (£12,000 + £6,000 – £7,500)	10,500

The final year of assessment is 2012/13, the year in which trade ceases.

Test your understanding 8

Benny

Tax year	Basis period	Assessable profits £
2007/08	01.07.07 – 05.04.08: Actual (9/14 × £10,500)	6,750
2008/09	01.09.07 – 31.08.08: 12m to accounting date (12/14 × £10,500)	9,000
2009/10	y/e 31.08.09: CYB	18,000
2010/11	y/e 31.08.10: CYB	22,500
2011/12	y/e 31.08.11: CYB	31,500
2012/13	01.09.11 – 31.12.12: Final – anything not yet taxed (£27,000 + £8,400 – £5,250)	30,150
		117,900

Overlap profits: 01.09.07 to 05.04.08 = (7/14 × £10,500) = £5,250

Note that over the life of the business the total profits of £117,900 have been assessed to tax.

Partnerships

Chapter learning objectives

Upon completion of this chapter you will be able to:

- explain how a partnership is assessed to tax

- show the allocation of profits/losses between partners for the period of account

- show the allocation of profits/losses between partners for the period of account following a change in the profit-sharing ratio

- calculate the assessable profit for ongoing/new and ceasing partners.

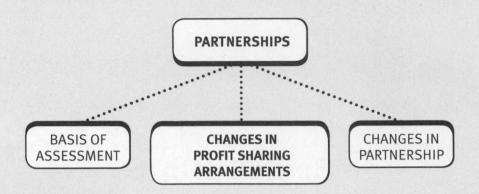

1 Introduction

Definition

- A partnership is a body of persons carrying on business together with a view to profit.

Basis of assessment

- Each partner is taxed individually, despite the partnership being a single trading entity.

- Each partner is assessed on his share of the partnership profits as if he were a sole trader.

- To determine a partner's assessable profits:
  - firstly, the trading profits per the partnership accounts are adjusted for tax purposes as for a sole trader (see Chapter 5).

  - secondly, the tax adjusted trading profits of the partnership are allocated to the individual partners.

  - finally, the basis of assessment rules are applied to determine each partner's assessable profits in a tax year (see Chapter 7).

2 The allocation of profits and losses

The computation of partnership profits and losses

- The principles of computation of a partnership's total tax adjusted trading profits are the same as those for a sole trader.

- Partners' salaries and interest on capital are not deductible expenses in the adjustment of profits computation, since these are merely an allocation of profit.

  They will not be assessed as employment or savings income in the income tax computation; they are all assessed as that partners' share of the trading income.

The allocation of the profit or loss

- The tax adjusted trading profit or loss is allocated (divided) between the partners according to their profit-sharing arrangements for that period of account.

- Partners may be entitled to salaries (a fixed allocation of profit) and interest on capital.

- The balance of profits remaining after the allocation of any salaries or interest will be allocated in the profit-sharing ratio (PSR).

- Whether it is described as salary, interest on capital or profit share, the total allocated to a partner is assessable as trading profit.

Example 1 – The allocation of profits and losses

Phil and Dan have been in partnership for a number of years. The partnership agreement provides that each should take a salary of £25,000, 5% interest on capital balances at the start of the accounting period and then split the profit remaining 60:40 in Phil's favour.

Calculate the trading income assessable for each partner for 2012/13, if the tax adjusted trading profits for the year ended 30 September 2012, were £74,000.

Their respective capital balances at 1 October 2011, were

Phil	£75,000
Dan	£60,000

Answer to example 1

Year ended 30 September 2012	Total £	Phil £	Dan £
Salary	50,000	25,000	25,000
Interest on capital (£75,000/£60,000 × 5%)	6,750	3,750	3,000
	56,750	28,750	28,000
Balance (£74,000 – £56,750) (60:40)	17,250	10,350	6,900
Total allocation of partnership profits	74,000	39,100	34,900

The allocated profit represents each partner's share of their profits for this period of account.

Each partner's allocated share of the profit is then assessed to tax on the individual partners as trading profit using the basis of assessment rules for a sole trader.

Trading profit assessment – 2012/13
(CYB = Year ended 30 September 2012)

Phil	£39,100
Dan	£34,900

Test your understanding 1

Paul and Art have been in partnership for many years preparing accounts to 31 December each year.

The partnership agreement provides Paul with a salary of £3,000 and Art is entitled to 15% interest on his capital balance at the start of the period. His capital balance was £27,000 on 1 January 2012. Paul and Art agreed to split any remaining profits equally.

Calculate the trading income assessments for each partner for 2012/13, if in the year ended 31 December 2012, the tax adjusted trading profits were £30,000.

Partnership capital allowances

Capital allowances are calculated in the same way as for a sole trader:

- Capital allowances are deducted as an expense in calculating the tax adjusted trading profit or loss of the partnership. The profit allocated between the partners is therefore after deducting capital allowances.

- Individual partners cannot claim capital allowances on their own behalf.

- If assets are owned privately (such as motor cars), then the business proportion of such assets must be included in the partnership's capital allowances computation. The total capital allowances are then deducted as an expense.

KAPLAN PUBLISHING

3 Changes in profit-sharing ratio

The profit-sharing ratio may change for a number of reasons:

- The existing partners decide to allocate profits in a different way. This may be as a result of a change in duties, seniority or simply by agreement of the parties concerned.

- The membership of a partnership may change as the result of the admission, death or retirement of a partner.

- Provided that there is at least one partner common to the business before and after the change, the partnership will automatically continue.

- Where there is a change in membership, the commencement or cessation basis of assessment rules will apply to the individual partner who is joining or leaving the partnership only.

4 The effect of a change in the profit-sharing ratio

- If a partnership changes its basis of profit-sharing during a period of account, then the accounting period is split, with a different allocation of profits in the different parts.

Example 2 – The effect of a change in the profit-sharing ratio

David and Peter are in partnership. Their tax adjusted trading profit for the year ended 30 September 2012, was £16,500.

Up to 30 June 2012, profits were shared between David and Peter 3:2, after paying annual salaries of £3,000 and £2,000 respectively.

From 1 July 2012, profits are shared 2:1 after paying annual salaries of £6,000 and £4,000.

Show the trading profit assessments for David and Peter for 2012/13.

Answer to example 2

	Total £	David £	Peter £
1.10.11 – 30.6.12			
Salaries (9/12)	3,750	2,250	1,500
Balance (3:2)	8,625	5,175	3,450
(Profits £16,500 × 9/12 = £12,375)	12,375		
1.7.12 – 30.9.12			
Salaries (3/12)	2,500	1,500	1,000
Balance (2:1)	1,625	1,083	542
(Profits £16,500 × 3/12 = £4,125)	4,125		
Total allocation of partnership profits	16,500	10,008	6,492

Trading income assessments – 2012/13
(CYB = Year ended 30 September 2012):

David	£10,008
Peter	£6,492

Test your understanding 2

John and Major have been in partnership for many years preparing accounts to 31 December.

Their original profit-sharing arrangement provides for salaries of £4,500 and £3,000 p.a. for John and Major respectively and the balance in the ratio of 3:2 in John's favour.

From 1 July 2012, John will receive a salary of £9,000 p.a. and Major a salary of £6,000 p.a., with the balance in the ratio 2:1 in John's favour.

Their recent tax adjusted trading profits for the accounting year ended 31 December 2012, are £24,800.

Show the division of profits for the year ended 31 December 2012 and the trading income assessment to be raised on each partner for 2012/13.

5 Commencement and cessation

Changes in membership

- The normal opening year and closing year basis of assessment rules apply upon commencement and cessation of a partnership.

- A change in the membership of the partnership part way through will normally affect only the partner joining or leaving. The continuing partners are assessed on a CYB basis.

Commencement – New partner

The steps taken are:

- Identify the start date of the new partner.
- Allocate the profits between the old and new partner(s):
  - If the new start date is part way through the period of account, the allocation of profits will need to be split between the two periods concerned.
  - If the new partner joins at the start of a new period of account, profits in the period will be allocated throughout using the new PSR.
- Determine the assessable trading profits for the tax year:
  - For those partners common to the old and new partnership, there will be no change in the method of calculating their assessable trading income and the normal CYB approach applies.
  - For the partner joining, they must apply the opening year rules, as for the sole trader in Chapter 7. A partner will be treated as commencing when he or she joins the partnership.
  - Each partner has his or her own overlap profits, available for overlap relief.

Example 3 – Commencement and cessation

Alex, Arsene and Jose have been in partnership for a number of years. Their recent results have been as follows:

	£
Year ended 30 September 2011	103,500
Year ended 30 September 2012	128,000

The relationship is often fractious and there have been a number of disputes over the years. In an attempt to improve the dynamics, on 1 January 2012, Rafa was admitted to the partnership.

Profits had been shared equally, after allocating salaries and interest on capital, prior to the admission of Rafa.

Partner	Salary £	Capital balance £	Interest on capital
Alex	15,000	100,000	5%
Arsene	12,000	80,000	5%
Jose	10,000	40,000	5%

Rafa's admission changed the profit-sharing arrangements as follows:

Partner	Salary £	Capital balance £	Interest on capital	Profit share
Alex	20,000	100,000	5%	35%
Arsene	18,000	80,000	5%	30%
Jose	15,000	40,000	5%	25%
Rafa	10,000	Nil	n/a	10%

The projected result for year ended 30 September 2013, is a profit of £140,000.

Calculate the assessable trading profit for each of the partners from 2011/12 to 2013/14.

Answer to example 3

Step 1: Allocate the tax adjusted trading profits for each accounting period between the partners

	Total £	Alex £	Arsene £	Jose £	Rafa £
Y/e 30.9.11					
Salary	37,000	15,000	12,000	10,000	
Interest at 5% on capital	11,000	5,000	4,000	2,000	
PSR	55,500	18,500	18,500	18,500	
Total	**103,500**	**38,500**	**34,500**	**30,500**	
Y/e 30.9.12					
1.10.11 – 31.12.11					
Salary (3/12)	9,250	3,750	3,000	2,500	
Interest at 5% (× 3/12)	2,750	1,250	1,000	500	
PSR	20,000	6,667	6,667	6,666	
(Profits £128,000 × 3/12 = £32,000)	32,000				
1.1.12 – 30.9.12					
Salary (9/12)	47,250	15,000	13,500	11,250	7,500
Interest at 5% (× 9/12)	8,250	3,750	3,000	1,500	Nil
PSR (35:30:25:10)	40,500	14,175	12,150	10,125	4,050
(Profits £128,000 × 9/12 = £96,000)	96,000				
Total	**128,000**	**44,592**	**39,317**	**32,541**	**11,550**
Y/e 30.9.13					
Salary	63,000	20,000	18,000	15,000	10,000
Interest at 5% on capital	11,000	5,000	4,000	2,000	Nil
PSR (35:30:25:10)	66,000	23,100	19,800	16,500	6,600
Total	**140,000**	**48,100**	**41,800**	**33,500**	**16,600**

Step 2: Compute each partner's assessable trading profits.

Alex, Arsene and Jose: will be assessed on a CYB for each tax year.

Tax year	Basis period	Alex £	Arsene £	Jose £
2011/12	year ended 30.9.11	38,500	34,500	30,500
2012/13	year ended 30.9.12	44,592	39,317	32,541
2013/14	year ended 30.9.13	48,100	41,800	33,500

Rafa: will be treated as commencing on 1 January 2012.

Tax year	Basis period	Assessable profits £
2011/12	1 January 2012 to 5 April 2012 (£11,550 × 3/9)	3,850
2012/13	First 12 months (£11,550 + (£16,600 × 3/12))	15,700
2013/14	Year ended 30 September 2013	16,600

He will carry forward overlap profits of £8,000 (£3,850 + £4,150).

Note: This question tests knowledge of a wide range of issues in relation to partnerships. It is unlikely that such a wide range of issues would be tested in a single question in the examination.

Test your understanding 3

Able and Bertie have been in partnership since 1 July 2010 preparing their accounts to 30 June each year. On 1 July 2012, Carol joins the partnership. Profits are shared equally.

The partnership's tax adjusted trading profits are as follows:

	£
Year ended 30 June 2011	10,000
Year ended 30 June 2012	13,500
Year ended 30 June 2013	18,000

Show the amounts assessed on the individual partners for 2010/11 to 2013/14.

Cessation – Partner leaving

The steps taken are:

- Identify the partner ceasing to be a member.

- Allocate the profits, remembering that if this is part-way through the period of account it will affect the profit-sharing ratio for that period of account and this will need to be calculated in two parts.

- For the partners continuing, use the normal CYB basis of assessment.

- For the partner ceasing, use the closing year rules and deduct any overlap profits they have available.

Example 4 – Commencement and cessation

Ball, Sphere, Globe and Bauble have been in partnership for a number of years, preparing accounts to 30 September each year.

The profit sharing arrangements have been as follows:

Partner	Annual salary £	Capital balance £	Interest on capital	Profit share
Ball	20,000	100,000	5%	35%
Sphere	18,000	80,000	5%	30%
Globe	15,000	40,000	5%	25%
Bauble	10,000	Nil	n.a.	10%

Ball has decided to resign as a partner at the end of March 2013.

The existing salary and interest arrangements will remain in place, but the balance of the profit will then be split equally between the three remaining partners.

Profits for the year end 30 September 2012 and 2013 are expected to be £180,000 and £210,000 respectively.

Calculate the assessable trading profits of each partner for 2012/13 and 2013/14. Ball informs you he had £15,000 of overlap profits from commencement.

Answer to example 4

Allocation of profits

	Total £	Ball £	Sphere £	Globe £	Bauble £
Y/e 30.9.12					
Salary	63,000	20,000	18,000	15,000	10,000
Interest at 5% on capital	11,000	5,000	4,000	2,000	Nil
PSR (35:30:25:10)	106,000	37,100	31,800	26,500	10,600
Total	**180,000**	**62,100**	**53,800**	**43,500**	**20,600**
Y/e 30.9.13					
1.10.12 – 31.3.13					
Salary (6/12)	31,500	10,000	9,000	7,500	5,000
Interest at 5% (× 6/12)	5,500	2,500	2,000	1,000	Nil
PSR (35:30:25:10)	68,000	23,800	20,400	17,000	6,800
(Profits £210,000 × 6/12 = £105,000)	105,000				
1.4.13 – 30.9.13					
Salary (6/12)	21,500	Nil	9,000	7,500	5,000
Interest at 5% (6/12)	3,000	Nil	2,000	1,000	Nil
PSR (1:1:1)	80,500	Nil	26,834	26,833	26,833
(Profits £210,000 × 6/12 = £105,000)	105,000				
Total	**210,000**	**36,300**	**69,234**	**60,833**	**43,633**

Assessable trading profit
Sphere, Globe and Bauble will continue to be assessed on CYB:

Tax year	Basis period	Sphere £	Globe £	Bauble £
2012/13	year ended 30.9.12	53,800	43,500	20,600
2013/14	year ended 30.9.13	69,234	60,833	43,633

KAPLAN PUBLISHING

Ball will be treated as ceasing to trade on 31 March 2013 as follows:

Tax year	Basis period	Assessable profits
		£
2012/13	Year ended 30 September 2012	62,100
	Period ended 31 March 2013	36,300
		98,400
	Less: Overlap relief	(15,000)
	Assessable trading profit	83,400

Test your understanding 4

Continuing the TYU 3 above with Able, Bertie and Carol.

After suffering a period of ill health, Bertie plans to retire on 31 December 2013.

Profits for year ended 30 June 2014, are expected to be £24,000.

The profit-sharing ratio will remain unchanged until Bertie retires. Thereafter it will be split 65:35 in Able's favour.

Calculate Bertie's revised trading income assessment for 2013/14 as a result of his retirement and Able and Carol's assessable trading income for 2014/15.

6 Chapter summary

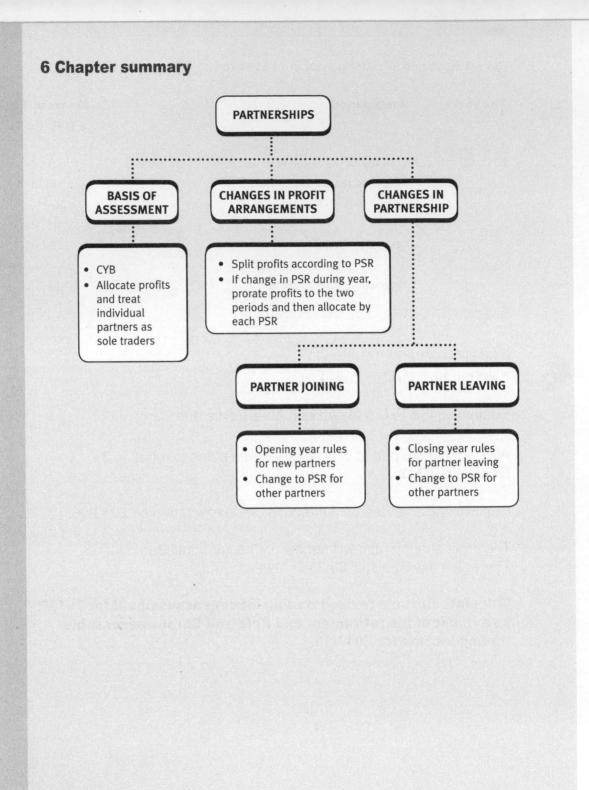

Test your understanding answers

Test your understanding 1

Paul and Art

Year ended 31 December 2012	Total	Paul	Art
	£	£	£
Salary	3,000	3,000	
Interest on capital (£27,000 × 15%)	4,050		4,050
	7,050		
Balance (£30,000 – £7,050) (50:50)	22,950	11,475	11,475
Allocation of partnership profits	30,000	14,475	15,525

Trading profit assessment for 2012/13
(CYB, Year ended 31 December 2012)

Paul	£14,475
Art	£15,525

Test your understanding 2

John and Major

	Total £	John £	Major £
1.1.12 – 30.6.12			
Salaries (6/12)	3,750	2,250	1,500
Balance (3:2)	8,650	5,190	3,460
(Profits £24,800 × 6/12 = £12,400)	12,400		
1.7.12 – 31.12.12			
Salaries (6/12)	7,500	4,500	3,000
Balance (2:1)	4,900	3,267	1,633
(Profits £24,800 × 6/12 = £12,400)	12,400		
Total allocation of partnership profits	24,800	15,207	9,593

Trading income assessments for 2012/13
(CYB Year ended 31 December 2012):

John	£15,207
Major	£9,593

KAPLAN PUBLISHING

Able and Bert

Step 1: Allocation of the tax adjusted trading profits

	Total £	Able £	Bertie £	Carol £
Y/e 30.6.11	10,000	5,000	5,000	
Y/e 30.6.12	13,500	6,750	6,750	
Y/e 30.6.13	18,000	6,000	6,000	6,000

Step 2: Compute each partner's assessable trading profits

Able and Bertie will both be assessed as follows, based upon a commencement on 1 July 2010:

Tax year	Basis period	Assessable profits £
2010/11	1 July 2010 to 5 April 2011 (£5,000 × 9/12)	3,750
2011/12	Year ended 30 June 2011	5,000
2012/13	Year ended 30 June 2012	6,750
2013/14	Year ended 30 June 2013	6,000

They will each carry forward overlap profits of £3,750 in respect of the period 1 July 2010 to 5 April 2011.

Carol will be treated as commencing on 1 July 2012, and will be assessed on her share of the partnership profits as follows:

Tax year	Basis period	Assessable profits £
2012/13	1 July 2012 to 5 April 2013 (£6,000 × 9/12)	4,500
2013/14	Year ended 30 June 2013	6,000

She will carry forward overlap profits of £4,500 in respect of the period 1 July 2012 to 5 April 2013.

Test your understanding 4

Able, Bertie and Carol

Allocation of profits:

	Total £	Able £	Bertie £	Carol £
Y/e 30 June 2014:				
1.7.13 – 31.12.13				
£24,000 × 6/12 (1/3:1/3:1/3)	12,000	4,000	4,000	4,000
1.1.14 – 30.6.14				
£24,000 × 6/12 (65:35)	12,000	7,800	Nil	4,200
Total	24,000	11,800	4,000	8,200

Assessable trading profit:

Able and Carol will both be assessed on the current year basis:

Tax year	Basis period	Able £	Carol £
2014/15	Year ended 30 June 2014	11,800	8,200

Bertie will be treated as ceasing to trade on 31 December 2013.
His final tax year of trade is 2013/14.

Tax year	Basis period	Assessable profits £
2013/14	Year ended 30 June 2013 (see TYU 3)	6,000
	Period ended 31 December 2013	4,000
		10,000
	Less: Overlap relief (see TYU 3)	(3,750)
	Assessable trading profit	6,250

KAPLAN PUBLISHING

Trading losses for individuals

Chapter learning objectives

Upon completion of this chapter you will be able to:

- understand how to calculate a trading loss for a tax year

- explain how trading losses can be carried forward for an ongoing business

- demonstrate when a trading loss can be used against total income and chargeable gains

- explain how a trading loss can be relieved in the early years of a trade

- calculate a terminal loss

- explain how a terminal loss can be relieved

- demonstrate the optimum use of trading loss reliefs

- describe the alternative loss relief claims that are available to partners

- explain the loss relief restriction to the partners of a limited liability partnership

- identify the circumstances when trading losses can be carried forward and used on the incorporation of a business.

1 Introduction

Identifying a trading loss

A trading loss arises when the normal tax adjusted trading profit computation gives a negative result.

A trading loss can occur in two situations, as follows:

	£	£
Tax adjusted trading profit / (loss) before capital allowances	X	(X)
Less: Capital allowances	(X)	(X)
Trading loss	(X)	(X)

Note that capital allowances:

- are taken into account in calculating the amount of the trading loss available for relief;

- can increase a tax adjusted trading loss; and

- can turn a tax adjusted trading profit into a trading loss.

Where a trading loss occurs:

- the individual's trading income assessment will be £Nil

- a number of loss relief options are available to obtain relief for the loss.

Tax year of loss

The 'tax year of the loss' is the tax year in which the loss making period ends.

For example: a loss for the year ended 31 December 2012 arises in the tax year 2012/13. Therefore, the 'tax year of the loss' is 2012/13.

KAPLAN PUBLISHING

Loss relief options

The main reliefs available for a trading loss are as follows:

- Carry forward against future trading profits (section 3)
- Relief against total income (section 4)
- Opening year loss relief against total income (section 6)
- Terminal loss relief against previous trading profits (section 7)

2 Loss relief options in ongoing years

If an individual makes a trading loss in the ongoing years, they initially have to decide whether to claim relief against total income or carry forward all of the loss.

The choices can be summarised as follows:

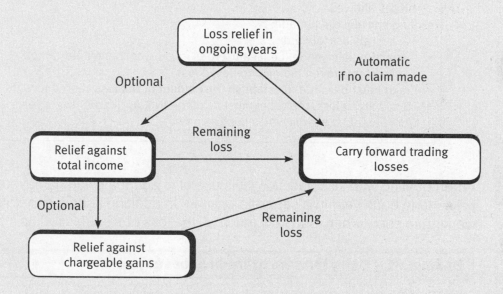

Where a claim against total income is made:

- any remaining loss is automatically carried forward

unless the individual then makes a claim to:

- set the loss against chargeable gains.

Note that a claim against gains can only be made after a claim against total income has been made.

3 Carry forward of trading losses

Principles of the relief

The key rules are as follows:

```
┌─────────────────────────────────┐
│   Carry forward trading losses  │
└─────────────────────────────────┘
```

- **Automatic relief**
- **Carry forward** against
  - **First available**
  - **Trading profits**
  - Of the **same trade**
- Can carry forward indefinitely
- But **must set off maximum amount** possible each year, no partial offset allowed
- If no specific claim made:
  - carry all loss forward
- If specific claim made (i.e. against total income or chargeable gains):
  - carry forward remaining unrelieved loss
- Claim must be made to **establish the amount of the loss** carried forward
- For a 2012/13 loss, the claim must be made by **5 April 2017** (i.e 4 years from end of tax year in which the loss arose)

When dealing with loss questions it is useful to adopt a columnar layout, presenting each year in a separate column. In addition keep a separate working to show when, and how much of, the loss has been used up.

Example 1 – Carry forward of trading losses

Edward has had the following recent tax adjusted trading results:

		£
Year to 31 December 2010	Loss	(5,000)
Year to 31 December 2011	Profit	3,000
Year to 31 December 2012	Profit	10,000

Assuming that Edward wishes to carry the loss forward, calculate his assessable trading profits for 2010/11 to 2012/13 inclusive.

KAPLAN PUBLISHING

Answer to example 1

	2010/11	2011/12	2012/13
	£	£	£
Trading income (Note)	Nil	3,000	10,000
Less: Loss relief b/f (W)	Nil	(3,000)	(2,000)
Net trading income	Nil	Nil	8,000

Working – Loss memorandum

	£
Trading loss – year to 31 December 2010	5,000
Less: Used in 2011/12	(3,000)
Less: Used in 2012/13	(2,000)
Loss carried forward to 2013/14	Nil

Note: The trading income assessment in the tax year of the loss (2010/11) is £Nil.
In the examination **never** put the loss in the income tax computation, **always** show trading income assessment as £Nil. In addition, always show the amount of the loss in a separate loss working.

Test your understanding 1

Michael has been trading for many years as a retailer. His recent tax adjusted trading results are as follows:

		£
Year to 31 August 2010	Loss	(9,000)
Year to 31 August 2011	Profit	6,000
Year to 31 August 2012	Profit	19,000

Michael has had no other sources of income.

Calculate Michael's assessable trading income for 2010/11 to 2012/13, assuming he carries the loss forward.

Carry forward loss relief is useful as:

- the taxpayer gets the potential of an unrestricted period over which to utilise the available loss
  - providing that he continues to trade, and
  - makes subsequent future profits from the same trade.

However, there are a number of disadvantages to carrying losses forward:

- In a prolonged difficult period for a business, relief may take a long time to materialise.
- Obtaining relief in a later period is less advantageous from the perspective of cash flow and time value of money.
- There is no certainty about the levels of future trading profits and whether it will be possible to utilise the loss.

Consequently taxpayers are likely to consider the alternative loss reliefs available.

4 Loss relief against total income

A taxpayer making a loss in 2012/13 has the option to make:

- a claim against **total income**.

Then, if any loss remains, they can make:

- a separate claim against **chargeable gains**.

However, note that the latter option is only possible after a claim against total income has been made.

Relief against total income is **optional** but if claimed it permits the taxpayer to relieve trading losses against the **total income** of the:

- 'tax year of the loss', **and/or**
- previous tax year.

A claim may be made in:

- either year in isolation, or
- both years, in any order.

For example: A loss for the year ended 31 December 2012 arises in the tax year 2012/13.

Therefore, the 'tax year of the loss' is 2012/13 and the loss can be set against total income in:

- 2012/13, and/or
- 2011/12.

Example 2 – Loss relief against total income

Graham's recent tax adjusted results are as follows:

		£
Year to 31 December 2011	Profit	10,000
Year to 31 December 2012	Loss	(6,000)
Year to 31 December 2013	Profit	12,000

Explain how Graham can utilise the loss arising in y/e 31 December 2012 assuming he claims to offset it against his total income.

Answer to example 2

The loss of £6,000 arises in the tax year 2012/13.

Loss relief is available against total income in 2012/13 and/or 2011/12.

Obtaining relief for the loss

Due to the wording 'and/or', and the fact that a claim can be made in any order, the taxpayer has five key options to consider:

(1) set against total income of the year of the loss, then set against total income of the previous year; or

(2) set against total income of the previous year, then set against total income of the current year; or

(3) set against total income of the year of the loss only

(4) set against total income of the previous year only

(5) make no claim and carry all of the loss forward.

In the case of the first four options, any unrelieved loss will be carried forward automatically.

However, a key point to note is that if relief against total income is claimed, the taxpayer must set off the **maximum amount possible** for a given year; a partial claim is not allowed.

Other points to note:

*   Qualifying interest payments (see Chapter 2) are also deducted from total income. In order not to waste the relief for interest payments, these should be deducted from total income in priority to losses.

*   Personal allowances are deducted from net income (i.e. total income after deducting reliefs). Therefore, a claim for loss relief against total income may result in personal allowances being wasted.

*   The two years available for potential claims are treated separately and thus a claim is required for each year.

*   A written claim must be made within one year of 31 January following the end of the tax year of loss.

    For a 2012/13 loss the claim must be made by 31 January 2015.

*   A taxpayer may have losses for two consecutive tax years and wish to relieve both against total income.

    In these circumstances the total income of a year is relieved by the loss of that year, in priority to the loss carried back from the following year.

Example 3 – Loss against total income

Derek's recent tax adjusted trading results are as follows:

		£
Year ended 31 July 2010	Profit	18,000
Year ended 31 July 2011	Loss	(43,200)
Year ended 31 July 2012	Profit	13,000
Year ended 31 July 2013	Profit	15,000

Derek's other income each year is £12,000 (gross).

Show Derek's net income for all tax years affected assuming:

(a) **No claim is made against total income for the trading loss.**

(b) **Claims against total income are to be made to obtain relief for the loss as early as possible.**

Answer to example 3

(a) **No relief against total income** – If no claim is made against total income, the trading loss of 2011/12 is carried forward against future trading profits.

	2010/11 £	2011/12 £	2012/13 £	2013/14 £
Trading profits	18,000	Nil	13,000	15,000
Less: Loss relief b/f	–	–	(13,000)	(15,000)
	18,000	Nil	Nil	Nil
Other income	12,000	12,000	12,000	12,000
Net income	30,000	12,000	12,000	12,000

Working – Loss memorandum

	£
Loss in y/e 31 July 2011	43,200
Less: Used in 2012/13	(13,000)
Less: Used in 2013/14	(15,000)
Loss relief carry forward to 2014/15	15,200

(b) **Claims against total income** – Claims against total income can only be made for 2010/11 and/or 2011/12 and any balance is carried forward.

	2010/11 £	2011/12 £	2012/13 £	2013/14 £
Trading income	18,000	Nil	13,000	15,000
Less: Loss relief b/f	–	–	(1,200)	–
	18,000	Nil	11,800	15,000
Other income	12,000	12,000	12,000	12,000
Total income	30,000	12,000	23,800	27,000
Less: Loss relief	(30,000)	(12,000)	–	–
Net income	Nil	Nil	23,800	27,000

> **Working – Loss memorandum**
>
> | | £ |
> | --- | --- |
> | Loss in y/e 31 July 2011 | 43,200 |
> | Less: Used in 2010/11 | (30,000) |
> | Less: Used in 2011/12 | (12,000) |
> | | |
> | Loss to carry forward | 1,200 |
> | Less: Used in 2012/13 | (1,200) |
> | | |
> | Loss to carry forward | Nil |

Test your understanding 2

Adrian's recent results have been:

		£
Year ended 31 December 2011	Profit	34,000
Year ended 31 December 2012	Loss	(48,000)
Year ended 31 December 2013	Profit	6,800

In 2011/12, Adrian has other income of £5,000. In 2012/13, he had other income of £6,000 and he paid qualifying interest of £2,500. In 2013/14 he had other income of £9,000.

Show how relief for the loss would be given against total income, assuming that Adrian makes claims to the extent that they are beneficial. State the amount of the remaining loss, if any.

Assume the 2012/13 tax rates and allowances continue in the future.

5 Relief of trading losses against chargeable gains

If any loss remains after a claim against total income, a taxpayer can make a claim against chargeable gains.

Relief against chargeable gains is **optional** but if claimed it permits the taxpayer to relieve trading losses against the **chargeable gains** in the same years as a claim against total income, i.e. in the:

- 'tax year of the loss', and/or
- previous tax year.

A claim may be made in:

- either year in isolation, or
- both years, in any order.

The relief operates as follows:

- A trader is permitted to set unrelieved trading losses against chargeable gains, provided the total income of the tax year in question has been reduced to zero.

- There is no need to make a claim against total income for the previous year but relief against chargeable gains is only granted if total income has been reduced to nil in the same tax year.

- If claimed, the unrelieved trading loss, is treated as a current year capital loss (see Chapter 13).

- The loss is deducted before both the CGT annual exempt amount and any capital losses brought forward as follows:

	£
Chargeable gains in year	X
Less: Capital losses in year	(X)
	——
	X
Less: Trading loss relief (subject to the maximum amount)	(X)
Less: Capital losses b/f	(X)
	——
Net chargeable gains before annual exempt amount	X
	——

A key point to note is that if a claim is made against chargeable gains, the taxpayer must set off the **maximum amount** possible for a given year; a partial claim is not allowed.

The maximum amount of loss relief under these rules is the **lower** of:

- the remaining loss, or
- chargeable gains in the year **after** the deduction of current year capital losses **and** brought forward capital losses.

Other points to note:

- The annual exempt amount is deducted after this relief, therefore a claim may result in wasting the annual exempt amount.

- The two years available for potential claims are treated separately and thus a claim is required for each year.

- A written claim is required in the same time period as for a claim against total income (i.e. within one year of 31 January following the end of the tax year of loss).

  For a 2012/13 loss the claim must be made by 31 January 2015.

- Relief against chargeable gains saves tax at 10%, 18% or 28% (see Chapters 13 and 16).

Test your understanding 3

Charles made a trading profit of £3,000 in the year ended 31 December 2012 and a trading loss of £14,000 the following year.

He has other income of £4,500 (gross) in 2012/13 and also realised chargeable gains of £16,000 and capital losses of £5,000 in that tax year.

Calculate the amounts that remain in charge to tax for 2012/13, assuming that Charles claims loss relief against both total income and chargeable gains for that year, but makes no claims in respect of any other year.

The procedure for dealing with questions involving losses

As seen in the previous examples and test your understandings, the following procedure should be adopted when answering questions:

(1) Determine the tax adjusted profits and losses after capital allowances for each accounting period.

(2) Determine when losses arise and therefore when loss relief is available (i.e. in which tax years).

(3) Set up a pro forma income tax computation for each tax year side by side and leave spaces for the loss set off to be inserted later.

(4) Set up a loss memo working for each loss to show how it is utilised.

(5) If more than one loss – consider in chronological order.

(6) Consider each option – be prepared to explain the options, the consequences of making a claim, the advantages and disadvantages.

(7) Set off losses according to the requirements of the question, or in the most beneficial way if it is a tax planning question.

KAPLAN PUBLISHING

6 Relief for trading losses in the opening years

The options available in the opening years of trade are exactly the same as those available to an ongoing business, with one extra option to carry back losses three years against total income.

The choices can be summarised as follows:

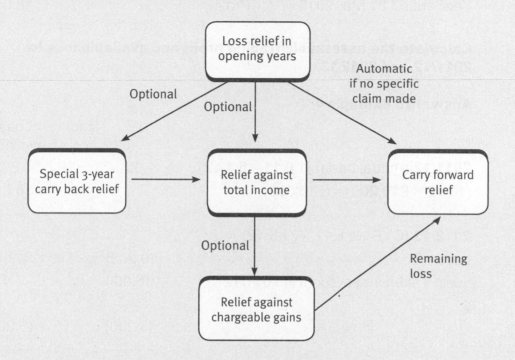

If an individual makes a trading loss in the opening years, they have to initially decide whether to claim normal relief against total income, special opening year loss relief or carry forward the loss.

However before a particular loss relief can be claimed it is necessary to determine the loss arising in each tax year.

Calculation of loss in opening years

The normal opening year basis of assessment rules apply regardless of whether the individual makes a profit or loss.

However in calculating a loss in the opening years note that:

- It is vital to remember that a loss may only be relieved once.

- There is no such thing as overlap losses.

- If a loss is included in the computation in more than one tax year, then the amount taken into account in the first tax year cannot also be included in the second tax year.

Example 4 – Loss relief against total income in opening years

Geraldine starts trading on 1 June 2011. Her results, as adjusted for tax purposes, are:

		£
Year ended 31 May 2012	Loss	(19,200)
Year ended 31 May 2013	Profit	48,000

Calculate the assessable trading profit and available loss for 2011/12 and 2012/13.

Answer to example 4

		Trading income	Loss available
	£	£	£
2011/12 (Actual basis) (1.6.11 – 5.4.12)			
(10/12 × £19,200) = (£16,000)		Nil	16,000
2012/13 (CYB) (1.6.11 – 31.5.12)			
Loss	(19,200)		
Less: Taken into account in 2011/12	16,000		
	(3,200)		(3,200)

Test your understanding 4

Georgina started trading on 1 May 2011. The results of her initial periods of trading were as follows:

		£
Year ended 30 April 2012	Loss	(36,000)
Year ended 30 April 2013	Profit	30,000
Year ended 30 April 2014	Profit	35,000

Calculate Georgina's assessable trading profit and available loss for each year affected by the above results.

Special opening year loss relief

As an alternative to, or in addition to, a claim against total income the taxpayer can make a special opening year loss relief claim.

The relief operates as follows:

> **Special opening year relief against total income**

- Optional claim
- Applies to loss arising in any of **first 4 tax years** of trading
- If claimed, set loss against
  - **total income**
  - **in 3 tax years** before tax year of loss
  - on a FIFO basis (i.e. earliest year first)
- There is no need for the trade to have been carried on in the earlier years
- **One claim** covers all 3 years
- For example:
  Loss in y/e 31.12.12 (2012/13) will be set off in:
  1. 2009/10
  2. 2010/11
  3. 2011/12
- If claimed
  - Must set off **maximum amount possible**
  - Cannot restrict set-off to preserve the personal allowance
  - Therefore, the benefit of the personal allowance may be wasted if a claim is made
- Relief must be claimed in writing
- For 2012/13 loss, the claim must be made by 31 January 2015

Example 5 – Relief for trading losses in opening years

Caroline started her business on 1 July 2011. Her trading results, as adjusted for tax purposes, for the first two years are as follows:

		£
Year ended 30 June 2012	Loss	(12,000)
Year ended 30 June 2013	Profit	4,130

Before becoming self-employed, Caroline had been employed as a dressmaker. Her remuneration from this employment, which ceased on 30 September 2010, for recent years, was:

2010/11	£7,300
2009/10	£13,490
2008/09	£12,960

Caroline has other income of £4,500 (gross) p.a.

Calculate the taxable income for all years after claiming special opening year loss relief.

Assume the 2012/13 tax rates and allowances apply throughout.

Answer to example 5

Taxable income computations

	2008/09	2009/10	2010/11	2011/12
	£	£	£	£
Employment income	12,960	13,490	7,300	Nil
Other income	4,500	4,500	4,500	4,500
Total income	17,460	17,990	11,800	4,500
Less: Loss relief (W)	(9,000)	(3,000)	–	–
Net income	8,460	14,990	11,800	4,500
Less: PA	(8,105)	(8,105)	(8,105)	(8,105)
Taxable income	355	6,885	3,695	Nil

	2012/13	2013/14
	£	£
Trading profit (W)	Nil	4,130
Other income		4,500	4,500
Total income	4,500	8,630
Less: PA	(8,105)	(8,105)
Taxable income	Nil	525

Notes

(1) When there is a loss in consecutive years, deal with the loss of the first tax year first.

(2) Under the special opening year loss relief rules, the loss of 2011/12 of £9,000 is set initially against total income of 2008/09. Any loss remaining would have been set automatically against total income of 2009/10 and finally against total income of 2010/11.

(3) The loss of 2012/13 of £3,000 is set initially against total income of 2009/10 before relieving 2010/11 and 2011/12 (had any loss remained).

(4) There is no requirement that the trade be carried on in the earlier year for which a claim is made.

Workings: New business – assessments/available loss

Tax year	Basis period	Available loss £	Assessable profits £
2011/12	1.7.11 – 5.4.12 (9/12 × £12,000)	9,000	Nil
2012/13	y/e 30.6.12 (£12,000 – £9,000)	3,000	Nil
2013/14	y/e 30.6.13		4,130

Test your understanding 5

Knight started a business on 1 May 2010. His taxable trade profits are:

		£
Year ended 30 April 2011	Profit	6,120
Year ended 30 April 2012	Loss	(28,480)
Year ended 30 April 2013	Profit	7,630

Prior to commencing in business Knight had been employed.

His employment earnings for 2008/09 and 2009/10 were £9,400 and £13,660 respectively. In addition he has savings income amounting to £1,700 (gross) each year.

Show how Knight will obtain relief for the loss if he makes a claim for special opening year loss relief.

7 Terminal loss relief

The options available in the closing years of trade are exactly the same as those available to an ongoing business, except that:

- the option to carry forward losses is not available as there will be no further trading profits once the trade ceases

- an extra option for terminal loss relief is available

- an additional option for incorporation relief is available if the business is ceasing because it is being incorporated (i.e. transferred to a company).

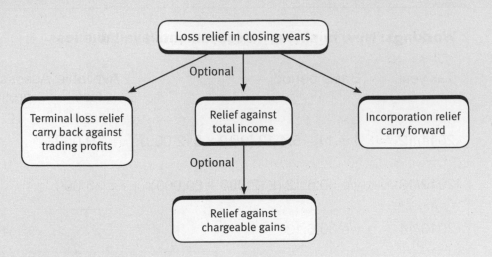

If an individual makes a trading loss in the closing years, they have to decide whether to claim relief against total income (and then possibly offset against gains) or claim terminal loss relief against trading profits.

Terminal loss relief

The relief operates as follows:

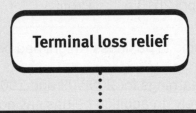

- **Optional** claim
  - however will normally be claimed
  - otherwise the benefit of the loss may be lost
- The relief is to set the **'terminal loss'** against **'trading profit'**
  - of the **last tax year** (if any), and then
  - **carry back three tax years**
  - on a **LIFO basis**
- The terminal loss is the **loss of the last 12 months** (see below)
- The relief must be **claimed in writing**
- For 2012/13 loss, the claim must be made by **5 April 2017** (i.e. within 4 years of the end of the last tax year of trading)

The terminal loss is the loss of the **last 12 months of trading** and is calculated as follows:

	£
6 April before cessation to the date of cessation	
(1) Actual trading loss in this period (ignore if a profit)	X
(2) Overlap profits not yet relieved	X
12 months before cessation to 5 April before cessation	
(3) Actual trading loss in this period (ignore if a profit)	X
	___
Terminal loss	X
	___

Note that in the closing years, it is not compulsory to make a claim against total income before claiming terminal loss relief.

However, where losses included in the above terminal loss calculation have already been relieved under another claim (i.e. against total income or chargeable gains), the amount of the terminal loss must be reduced.

Test your understanding 6

Yves ceased trading on 30 June 2012. His final period of trade was the nine months to 30 June 2012 and beforehand he prepared accounts annually to 30 September.

His tax adjusted trading results are as follows:

		£
Nine months to 30.6.12	Loss	(7,200)
Year to 30.9.11	Profit	100
Year to 30.9.10	Profit	7,300
Year to 30.9.09	Profit	7,500

There was overlap profits of £1,800 brought forward.

Yves had no other sources of income.

Calculate the terminal loss available to Yves and show how relief may be obtained for it.

8 Choice of loss reliefs

Utilising loss relief

When planning relief for trading losses, careful consideration needs to be given to the personal circumstances of the individual.

Tax advice should aim to satisfy the following goals of a taxpayer:

- Obtain tax relief at the highest marginal rate of tax.

- Obtain relief as soon as possible.

- Ensure the taxpayer's PA is not wasted, if possible.

It may not be possible to satisfy all of these aims, for example:

- in order to get a higher rate of relief, the taxpayer may have to waste their PA

- carrying losses forward may give a higher rate of relief, but the cash flow implications of claiming relief now rather than waiting for relief, may be more important to the taxpayer.

The specific circumstances faced by the taxpayer will help to determine which of these is most important.

Factors to consider

In understanding the position of the taxpayer, it is important to understand the comparative features of the various reliefs.

Income relieved	Timing of relief	Flexibility
Total income – normal claim (possibly also chargeable gains relief)	Current and/or previous tax year	Either, neither or both tax years (in either order). All or nothing.
Total income – special opening years claim	Preceding three tax years on a FIFO basis	Only in opening years. All or nothing. Can be used with a normal claim against total income.
Future trading profit	As soon as possible in future	None

Trading profit – terminal loss claim	Current and then preceding three tax years on a LIFO basis	Only on cessation.
		All or nothing.
		Can be used with a normal claim against total income.

Choice of loss relief

Although the reliefs against total income (normal relief and special opening year relief) obtain relief more quickly than relief by carry forward, they frequently involve loss of personal allowances.

However, for a large loss that will eliminate several years' modest trading profits, there is no point in choosing to carry forward a loss if there is no non-trading income in those future years to obtain relief for personal allowances. All that will have happened is that future personal allowances rather than current ones will be wasted.

The taxpayer can choose when to claim relief against total income, that is, in the tax year of the loss; or the preceding year, as the legislation does not dictate that either takes priority.

If neither a current nor a previous year claim against total income appears appropriate, look at the chargeable gains position.

Where the taxpayer has made a large chargeable gain, a claim against it may be appropriate. Since the claim can only be made once total income for the year is reduced to zero, it will generally involve wasting at least one year's personal allowance.

However, at all times be mindful of the rate of tax relief available as the taxpayer's primary aim is usually to save as much tax as possible.

9 Partnership losses

The allocation of trading losses

Trading losses are allocated between partners in exactly the same way as trading profits.

Loss relief claims available

Claims available to partners are the same as those for sole traders.

- A partner joining a partnership may be entitled to claim opening year loss relief, where a loss is incurred in the first four tax years of his membership of the partnership.
  This relief would not be available to the existing partners.

- A partner leaving the partnership may be entitled to claim for terminal loss relief.
  Again, this relief would not be available to the partners remaining in the partnership.

Test your understanding 7

Diane, Lynne and John are in partnership preparing their accounts to 5 April. During 2012/13, John left the partnership and Rose joined in his place.

For the year ended 5 April 2013, the partnership made a tax adjusted loss of £40,000.

State the loss relief claims that will be available to the partners.

Example 6 – Partnership loss

Jake and Milo have been in partnership together since 1999, but ceased trading on 30 September 2012. Profits and losses have always been shared 40% to Jake and 60% to Milo.

The tax adjusted trading profits and losses for the final four years before allocation between the partners are as follows:

		£
2009/10	Profit – y/e 30.9.09	16,200
2010/11	Profit – y/e 30.9.10	15,200
2011/12	Profit – y/e 30.9.11	14,100
2012/13	Loss – y/e 30.9.12	(34,700)

Jake is single and had no other income or outgoings.

Milo is single and also has no other income or outgoings apart from bank interest of £4,350 (gross) received on 1 December 2012 from investing a recent inheritance. He has a chargeable gain of £23,900 for 2012/13 in respect of the disposal of an asset on 18 July 2012.

Assume that the 2012/13 rates and allowances apply to all years.

Ignore overlap relief.

(a) **Advise the partners of the possible ways of relieving the partnership loss for 2012/13.**

(b) **Advise the partners as to which loss relief claims would be the most beneficial.**

(c) **After taking into account the advice in (b), calculate the partners' taxable income for 2009/10 to 2012/13. Show Milo's tax saving under each of the options considered in part (b).**

Answer to example 6

(a) **Options for relieving loss**

There are two possible ways to relieve the partnership loss:

(1) A claim can be made against total income for 2012/13 and/or 2011/12.

Subject to this claim being made, it would then be possible to claim against chargeable gains of the same year.

(2) Terminal loss relief can be claimed.

The tax adjusted trading profits and loss will be split between the partners:

	Jake 40%	Milo 60%
	£	£
2009/10	6,480	9,720
2010/11	6,080	9,120
2011/12	5,640	8,460
2012/13	(13,880)	(20,820)

(b) Most beneficial relief

The most beneficial loss relief claim available to Jake would appear to be a terminal loss claim, as he has no other income or gains.

Milo could also make a terminal loss claim, but this would waste most of his personal allowances for several years.

He would be advised to make a claim against his total income of £4,350 for 2012/13, which wastes his personal allowance in that year, but then allows a claim against his chargeable gain of £23,900 for 2012/13.

(c) Jake – Taxable income

	2009/10	2010/11	2011/12	2012/13
	£	£	£	£
Trading profit	6,480	6,080	5,640	Nil
Less: Terminal loss (Note)	(2,160)	(6,080)	(5,640)	(Nil)
Net income	4,320	Nil	Nil	Nil
Less: PA (restricted)	(4,320)	–	–	–
Taxable income	Nil	Nil	Nil	Nil

Note: In this instance there is no need to do a separate terminal loss calculation as there are no overlap profits and the final accounts have been prepared for the final 12 months of trading.

Milo – Taxable income

	2009/10	2010/11	2011/12	2012/13
	£	£	£	£
Trading profit	9,720	9,120	8,460	Nil
Bank interest	–	–	–	4,350
Total income	9,720	9,120	8,460	4,350
Less: Loss relief	–	–	–	(4,350)
Net income	9,720	9,120	8,460	Nil
Less: PA	(8,105)	(8,105)	(8,105)	–
Taxable income	1,615	1,015	355	Nil

Assuming that 2012/13 rates apply throughout, claiming terminal loss relief would save income tax of:

(£1,615 + £1,015 + £355) = £2,985 × 20% = £597.

Claiming relief against total income and then chargeable gains in 2012/13 would save:

	£
Income tax – income would be covered by PA	Nil
Capital gains tax (£13,300 (W) × 18%)	2,394
Total tax saving	2,394

Working: Taxable gain without loss relief

	£
Chargeable gain	23,900
Less: Annual exempt amount	(10,600)
Taxable gain	13,300

Loss relief available is £16,470 (£20,820 – £4,350 used against total income).

The loss is offset before the deduction of the annual exempt amount (AEA). Thus the remaining loss of £16,470 is fully utilised, part of the AEA is wasted, and tax is saved on taxable gains of £13,300.

For further information regarding the calculation of tax on chargeable gains see Chapter 13.

Limited liability partnerships (LLP)

An LLP is a special type of partnership where the amount that each partner contributes towards the partnership losses, debts and liabilities is limited by agreement.

The taxation implications of an LLP are as follows:

- It is generally taxed in the same way as all other partnerships.

- The normal loss reliefs are available.

- However, the losses that may be set against income **not** deriving from the partnership is limited to the amount of capital that the partner has contributed to the partnership.

Test your understanding 8

Rob and Linda are partners in a limited liability partnership (LLP) to which they contributed capital of £45,000 and £15,000 respectively. The LLP prepares its accounts to 31 March each year and Rob and Linda share profits and losses 2:1. For the year to 31 March 2013, the LLP made a trading loss of £60,000.

State the amount of the loss available to Rob and Linda to set against total income in 2012/13.

10 Businesses transferred to companies

When an unincorporated business ceases, the individual will seek to obtain relief for any losses as soon as possible. Normally they will consider relief against total income and then chargeable gains first, then claim terminal loss relief, and any unrelieved losses remaining is lost.

However, where the business is ceasing because it is being incorporated, these unrelieved losses can be set against future income from the company.

The key rules relating to the relief are as follows:

> **Incorporation relief against future income from the company**

- Incorporation relief is available where an unincorporated business
  - is **transferred to a company**
  - **'wholly or mainly'** in exchange **for shares**
- 'Wholly or mainly' is usually taken to mean that **at least 80%** of the consideration received for the business from the company is in the form of shares
- The relief is to **carry the losses forward**
  - indefinitely
  - provided the owner retains the shares throughout the whole tax year in which the loss relief is given, and
  - provided the company continues to carry on the trade of the former unincorporated business
- Losses are **set against**
  - the **first available income** the individual derives **from the company** (e.g. salary, interest, dividends)
  - can set off against types of income from the company in any order
  - most beneficial order will be from employment income first, then savings income, then dividends
- Note that the losses cannot be set against the future profits of the company

11 Chapter summary

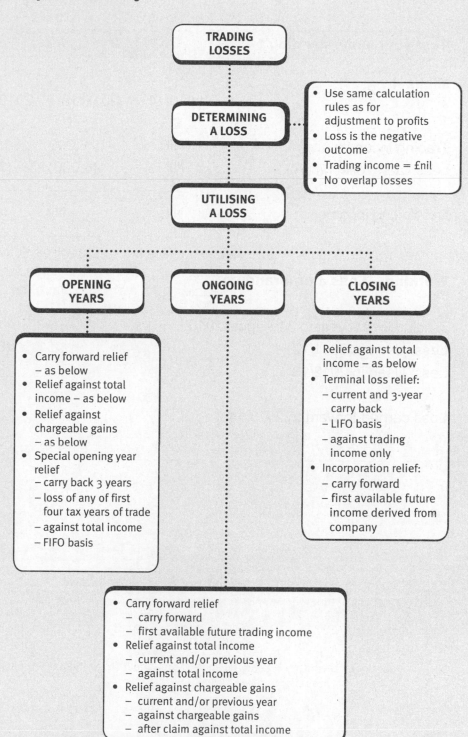

Test your understanding answers

Test your understanding 1

Michael

	2010/11	2011/12	2012/13
	£	£	£
Trading income	Nil	6,000	19,000
Less: Loss relief b/f (W)	Nil	(6,000)	(3,000)
Net trading income	Nil	Nil	16,000

Working – Loss memorandum

	£
Trading loss – year to 31 August 2010	9,000
Less: Used in 2011/12	(6,000)
Less: Used in 2012/13	(3,000)
Loss carried forward to 2013/14	Nil

Test your understanding 2

Adrian

Year of the loss = 2012/13

Relief against total income in: 2012/13 and /or 2011/12.

	2011/12	2012/13	2013/14
	£	£	£
Trading income	34,000	Nil	6,800
Less: Loss relief b/f (W)	–	–	(6,800)
	34,000	Nil	Nil
Other income	5,000	6,000	9,000
Total income	39,000	6,000	9,000
Less: Qualifying interest paid	Nil	(2,500)	Nil
	39,000	3,500	9,000
Less: Loss relief (W)	(39,000)	–	–
Net income	Nil	3,500	9,000
Less: PA (Note)	–	(3,500)	(8,105)
Taxable income	Nil	Nil	895

Working – Loss memorandum

	£
2012/13 – loss of y/e 31.12.12	48,000
Less: Used in 2011/12	(39,000)
Loss carried forward	9,000
Less: Used in 2013/14	(6,800)
Loss carried forward to 2014/15	2,200

Note: A claim for relief against total income in 2012/13 is not beneficial as the income is already covered by the PA. Therefore if a claim is made in this year it would needlessly utilise the loss, waste the PA for that year and save no tax.

However, a claim in 2011/12 will achieve a tax saving and will obtain relief for the loss as soon as possible. The PA in that year is wasted, however relief sooner rather than later and at a higher rate of tax is preferable to carrying forward a loss and waiting for the relief.

The best course of action will depend on the personal circumstances of each case but as a general principle there is no point in claiming relief against total income where personal allowances already cover all or most of the total income.

Test your understanding 3

Charles
Income tax computation – 2012/13

	£
Trading income (y/e 31.12.12)	3,000
Other income	4,500
	———
Total income	7,500
Less: Loss relief	(7,500)
	———
Net income	Nil
	———

Chargeable gains computation – 2012/13

Chargeable gains	16,000
Less: Capital losses – current year	(5,000)
	———
Net chargeable gains	11,000
Less: Trading loss relief (W)	(6,500)
	———
Net chargeable gains before annual exempt amount	4,500
	———

Note: As a result of the claims, Charles' personal allowance and part of the annual exempt amount are wasted.

KAPLAN PUBLISHING

Working – Loss memorandum

	£
Loss for year ending 31 December 2013	14,000
Less: Used in 2012/13 against total income	(7,500)
	6,500
Less: Used in 2012/13 against chargeable gains	(6,500)
Loss carried forward	Nil

Test your understanding 4

Georgina

		Trading income	Loss available
		£	£
2011/12 (Actual basis)			
1.5.11 – 5.4.12			
11/12 × (£36,000) = (£33,000)		Nil	33,000
	£		
2012/13 (CYB)			
Year ended 30 April 2012	36,000		
Less: Used in 2011/12 (Note)	(33,000)		
	(3,000)	Nil	3,000
2013/14 (CYB)			
Year ended 30 April 2013		30,000	Nil
2014/15 (CYB)			
Year ended 30 April 2014		35,000	Nil

Note: The loss allocated to 2011/12 cannot also be treated as a loss in 2012/13.

Test your understanding 5

Knight

	Loss available £	Trading profit £
2010/11 (1 May 2010 – 5 April 2011) (£6,120 × 11/12)		5,610
2011/12 (Year ended 30 April 2011)		6,120
2012/13 (Year ended 30 April 2012)	28,480	Nil
2013/14 (Year ended 30 April 2013)		7,630

Note: 2012/13 is the 'tax year of the loss'. Therefore, the loss of £28,480 is set off against total income of 2009/10 first, then 2010/11, and finally 2011/12.

	2009/10 £	2010/11 £	2011/12 £
Trading income	Nil	5,610	6,120
Employment income	13,660	Nil	Nil
Savings income	1,700	1,700	1,700
Total income	15,360	7,310	7,820
Less: Loss relief	(15,360)	(7,310)	(5,810)
Net income	Nil	Nil	2,010

Working – Loss memorandum

	£
Trading loss	28,480
Less: Used in 2009/10	(15,360)
Less: Used in 2010/11	(7,310)
Less: Used in 2011/12	(5,810)
	Nil

Test your understanding 5

Test your understanding 6

Yves

	2009/10 £	2010/11 £	2011/12 £	2012/13 £
Trading profit	7,500	7,300	100	Nil
Less: TLR (W2)	(iii) (1,575)	(ii) (7,300)	(i) (100)	Nil
Revised trading profit	5,925	Nil	Nil	Nil

Workings

(W1) Calculation of terminal loss

	£
6.4.12 to 30.6.12: Actual loss (3/9 × £7,200)	2,400
1.7.11 to 5.4.12: Actual loss	
(6/9 × £7,200) – (3/12 × £100)	4,775
Overlap profits	1,800
Terminal loss	8,975

(W2) Terminal loss relief (TLR)

The terminal loss is then relieved on a LIFO basis in the final year of assessment and the previous three years, against the trading profits.

Test your understanding 7

Diane, Lynne and John

All the partners will be entitled to relief against total income, as well as the option to extend the relief against chargeable gains.

All the partners except John will be entitled to carry forward loss relief.

John will be entitled to terminal loss relief since he has ceased trading.

Rose will be entitled to claim special opening years relief since she has commenced trading.

Diane and Lynne will not be entitled to terminal loss relief or special opening year loss relief.

Test your understanding 8

Rob and Linda

Rob will be entitled to £40,000 (£60,000 × 2/3) of the loss arising in the year ended 31 March 2013. This figure is less than the capital that he has contributed of £45,000 and the full amount of the loss (£40,000) is therefore available to be offset against Rob's non-partnership income for 2012/13.

Linda will be entitled to £20,000 (£60,000 × 1/3) of the loss arising in the year ended 31 March 2013.

The amount of the loss, which may be set against income not deriving from the partnership in 2012/13, is however limited to £15,000, being the amount of capital that she has contributed to the LLP.

The balance of the loss, £5,000 (£20,000 – £15,000), can only be claimed against partnership income, for example by carry forward.

Pensions

Chapter learning objectives

Upon completion of this chapter you will be able to:

- explain the basis for calculating the maximum annual contributions to a registered pension scheme for an individual

- calculate the tax relief available and explain how relief for pension contributions is given

- calculate whether pension contributions have exceeded the available annual allowance and calculate any annual allowance charge.

- explain the concept of the lifetime allowance and the implications of the allowance being exceeded.

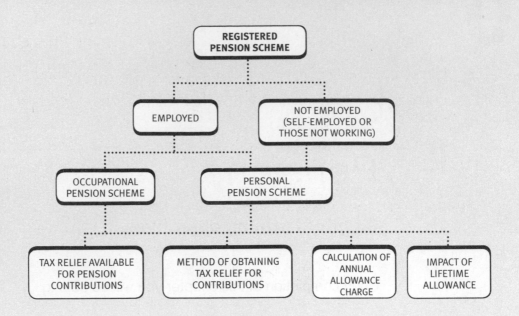

1 Types of registered pension schemes

An individual can set up an investment of funds to provide an income during his retirement in a tax-efficient way by making payments into a registered pension scheme.

A pension scheme is a savings plan for retirement that enjoys special tax privileges, but only if the scheme is registered with HMRC.

Investing in a registered pension scheme is a long-term investment and is very tax efficient for the following reasons:

- The individual obtains tax relief on the contributions made into the scheme.

- Where an employer contributes into the scheme, tax relief for the employer contributions is available without there being a taxable benefit for the employee.

- Registered pension scheme funds can grow tax-free as the scheme is exempt from income tax and capital gains tax.

- On retirement, some funds can be withdrawn as a tax-free lump sum.

The two main types of registered pension schemes available are:

- Occupational pension schemes

- Personal pension schemes.

If self-employed or unemployed, the individual can only set up a personal pension scheme.

If employed, the individual may:

- join an occupational pension scheme provided by his employer, or
- choose not to join the employer's scheme and set up a personal pension scheme, or
- contribute into both his employer's occupational scheme and set up a personal pension scheme.

Occupational pension schemes

An occupational pension scheme is a scheme set up by an employer for the benefit of his employees.

Employers may use the National Employment Savings Trust (NEST) or an insurance company to provide a pension scheme for its employees, or it may set up its own self-administered pension fund.

Contributions into occupational schemes may be made by the employer, and the employee.

Types of occupational pension schemes

Defined benefit scheme:

- the benefits obtained on retirement are linked to the level of earnings of the employee.

Money purchase scheme (or 'defined contribution' scheme):

- the benefits obtained depend upon the performance of the investments held by the pension fund.

Personal pension schemes

Personal pension schemes can be established by **any** individual:

- the employed
- the self-employed
- those not working (including children).

Contributions into personal pension schemes may be made by:

- the individual, and
- any third party on behalf of the individual (for example the employer, a spouse, parent or grandparent).

Personal pension schemes are usually 'money purchase' schemes administered by financial institutions on behalf of the individual.

Overview of the tax relief rules for registered pension schemes

- The **amount** of tax relief available for pension contributions is the same regardless of whether the scheme is an occupational or personal pension scheme.
- The **method** of obtaining tax relief for the contributions is different depending on the scheme.
- Once the funds are invested in the scheme, all registered pension schemes are governed by the same rules.

2 Tax relief for pension contributions

The relief for contributions made by individuals

Tax relief is available for pension contributions if both:

- the pension scheme is a registered scheme
- the individual is resident in the UK and aged under 75.

Regardless of the level of earnings, an individual may make pension contributions of **any amount** into either:

- a pension scheme, or
- a number of different pension schemes.

However, **tax relief** is only available for up to a **maximum annual amount** each tax year.

The tax relief given to an individual is therefore the **lower** of:

(1) Total gross pension contributions paid
(2) Maximum annual amount = **higher** of:
  - £3,600
  - 100% of the individual's 'relevant earnings', chargeable to income tax in the tax year.

Relevant earnings includes taxable trading profits, employment income and furnished holiday lettings but not investment income.

- The above maximum amount applies to the total gross contributions made into all schemes where:
  - an employee contributes to both an occupational and a personal pension scheme, or
  - an individual contributes into more than one personal pension scheme.

- An individual with no relevant earnings can still obtain tax relief on gross contributions of up to £3,600 p.a. This figure is provided in the tax rates and allowances in the exam.

Example 1 – Maximum tax relief for individuals

The following individuals made gross pension contributions into a personal pension scheme in 2012/13:

	Pension contributions (gross)	Relevant earnings
	£	£
Amy	2,500	Nil
Brenda	6,000	Nil
Caroline	36,000	75,000
Deborah	45,000	38,000

Explain the maximum amount of pension contribution for which tax relief is available for each individual in 2012/13.

Answer to example 1

	Tax relief	Explanation
Amy	£2,500	Relief = contributions made as they are below the maximum annual amount of £3,600 (higher of £3,600 and £Nil).
Brenda	£3,600	Contributions (£6,000) exceed the maximum annual amount (higher of £3,600 and £Nil). Relief = restricted to maximum annual amount of £3,600.

| Caroline | £36,000 | Relief = contributions made (£36,000) as they are below the maximum annual amount of £75,000 (higher of £3,600 and £75,000). |
| Deborah | £38,000 | Contributions (£45,000) exceed the maximum annual amount (higher of £3,600 and £38,000). Relief = restricted to the annual maximum amount of £38,000. |

Summary

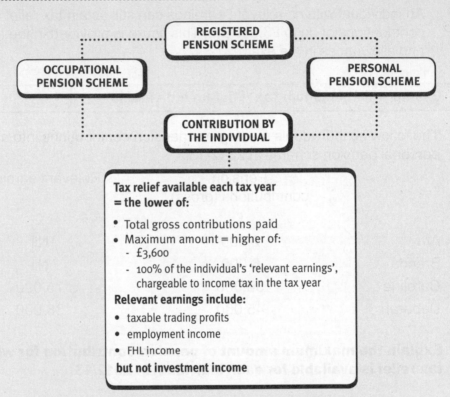

3 The method of obtaining relief for pension contributions

Personal pension schemes

The method of obtaining tax relief for contributions into a personal pension scheme (PPCs) is the same whether they are made by an employee, a self-employed individual or an individual who is not working.

Relief is given as follows:

Basic rate tax relief

*   Basic rate tax relief is automatically given by deduction at source when contributions are paid, as an individual makes contributions net of the basic rate of income tax (20%).

KAPLAN PUBLISHING

- Contributions into a personal pension scheme benefit from basic rate tax relief, even if the taxpayer is paying tax at the starting rate, higher rate or not paying tax at all.

- HMRC pay the 20% tax relief to the personal pension scheme.

Higher and additional rate tax relief

Relief is obtained in two parts:

- basic rate relief of 20% is given at source (as above)

- further higher and additional rate relief is given by extending the basic and higher rate tax bands by the gross amount of pension payments paid in the tax year (as for Gift Aid donations, see Chapter 2).

- This means that an amount of income equal to the gross pension contributions is removed from the charge to higher rate tax and is taxed at the basic rate instead, and the same amount is removed from the charge to additional rate tax and is taxed at the higher rate instead.

- For example, if an individual pays a contribution of £8,000 (net), this is equivalent to a gross contribution of £10,000 (£8,000 × 100/80).

- The individual's higher and additional rate thresholds are extended to £44,370 (£34,370 + £10,000), and £160,000 (£150,000 + £10,000).

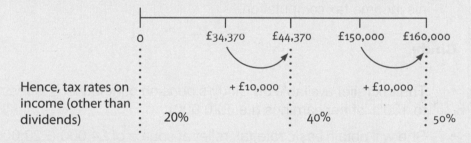

Example 2 – The method of obtaining relief for PPCs

The following individuals made gross pension contributions into a personal pension scheme in 2012/13.

	Pension contributions (gross)	Trading profits
	£	£
Andy	5,000	Nil
Brad	5,000	20,000
Cindy	25,000	20,000
Don	40,000	85,000
Ed	60,000	48,000
Fran	30,000	195,000

Explain how tax relief for the pension contributions will be given in 2012/13 for each individual and calculate the income tax liability of Don, Ed and Fran for 2012/13.

Answer to example 2

Andy

- As Andy has no earnings he will obtain tax relief on a maximum gross amount of £3,600.

- He will obtain basic rate tax relief at source of £720 (£3,600 × 20%) and pay £4,280 (£5,000 – £720) to the pension scheme.

Brad

- Brad's pension contributions are less than his earnings for the year and he will therefore receive tax relief on the full amount of the contribution.

- He will obtain basic rate tax relief at source of £1,000 (£5,000 × 20%) and pay £4,000 (£5,000 – £1,000) to the pension scheme.

- As Brad is not a higher rate taxpayer no adjustment is required in his income tax computation.

Cindy

- The tax relief available on Cindy's pension contributions is restricted to 100% of her earnings (i.e. £20,000).

- She will obtain basic rate tax relief at source of £4,000 (£20,000 × 20%) and pay £21,000 (£25,000 – £4,000) to the pension scheme.

- As Cindy is not a higher rate taxpayer no adjustment is required in her income tax computation.

Don

- Don's pension contributions are less than his earnings; he will therefore receive tax relief on the full amount of the contribution.

- He will obtain basic rate tax relief at source of £8,000 (£40,000 × 20%) and pay £32,000 (£40,000 – £8,000) to the pension scheme.

- Higher rate tax relief will be given by extending the basic rate band by £40,000 from £34,370 to £74,370.

Don's income tax computation for 2012/13 will be:

	£	£
Trading profit		85,000
Less: PA		(8,105)
Taxable income		76,895
Basic rate	74,370 @ 20%	14,874
Higher rate	2,525 @ 40%	1,010
	76,895	
Income tax liability		15,884

Ed

- The tax relief available on Ed's pension contributions is restricted to 100% of his earnings (i.e. £48,000).

- He will obtain basic rate tax relief at source of £9,600 (£48,000 × 20%) and pay £50,400 (£60,000 – £9,600) to the scheme.

- Higher rate tax relief will be given by extending the basic rate band by £48,000 from £34,370 to £82,370.

Ed's income tax computation for 2012/13 will be:

	£
Trading profit	48,000
Less: PA	(8,105)
Taxable income	39,895
Income tax (£39,895 × 20%)	7,979

Fran

- Fran's pension contributions are less than her earnings; she will therefore receive tax relief on the full amount of the contribution.

- She will obtain basic rate tax relief at source of £6,000 (£30,000 × 20%) and pay £24,000 (£30,000 – £6,000) to the pension scheme.

- Higher rate tax relief will be given by extending the basic rate band by £30,000 from £34,370 to £64,370.

- Additional rate tax relief will be given by extending the higher rate band by £30,000 from £150,000 to £180,000.

Fran's income tax computation for 2012/13 will be:

		£
Trading profit		195,000
Less: Adjusted PA (Note)		(Nil)
Taxable income		195,000

Income tax:	£	£
Basic rate	64,370 × 20%	12,874
Higher rate	115,630 × 40%	46,252
	180,000	
Additional rate	15,000 × 50%	7,500
	195,000	
Income tax liability		66,626

Note: In this example, trading income = total income = net income. ANI is net income less gross pension contributions (i.e. £195,000 – £30,000 = £165,000). As this exceeds £116,210 (more than double the PA), the PA is reduced to £Nil.

Occupational pension schemes

Where employees make pension contributions into an occupational pension scheme, payments are made gross and tax relief is given at source by the employer through the PAYE system, as an allowable deduction against employment income.

Tax relief is given at basic, higher and additional rates of tax depending on the individual's level of income as follows:

- The employer will deduct the pension contribution from the individual's earned income, before calculating income tax under the PAYE system.

- Tax relief is therefore automatically given at both the basic, higher and additional rates at source.

KAPLAN PUBLISHING

Henry is employed by Lloyd Ltd on an annual salary of £80,000 p.a. He is a member of the company's occupational pension scheme.

Henry pays 3% and Lloyd Ltd pays 5% of his salary into the scheme each year. He has no other income.

Calculate Henry's income tax liability for 2012/13, showing how tax relief is obtained for his pension contributions.

Contributions made by employers into registered pension schemes

Contributions paid by an employer into a registered pension scheme are:

- tax deductible in calculating the employer's taxable trading profits, provided the contributions are paid for the purposes of the trade, and

- an exempt employment benefit for the employee, and
- added to the pension contributions paid by the employee on which tax relief is given to determine whether the annual allowance has been exceeded and an income tax charge levied.

Employer contributions – trading deduction

The deduction against the employer's trading profits for pension contributions is given in the accounting period in which the contribution is actually **paid**; the accounting treatment is not followed.

Therefore, in the adjustment to profit computation:

- **add back** any **amount charged** in the income statement, and
- **deduct** the **amount paid** in the accounting period.

Annual allowance

There is no limit on the amount that may be paid into pension schemes by an individual, his employer or any other party.

However, as we have seen, tax relief for pension contributions made by an individual is restricted to the **maximum annual amount**.

In addition, if the total of all contributions on which tax relief has been obtained (by the individual, their employer and third parties) exceeds the **annual allowance (AA)**, a tax charge is levied on the individual.

- The AA for 2012/13 is £50,000, but this can be increased by **bringing forward** any unused annual allowances from the **previous three tax years**.

- The AA can only be carried forward if the individual was a member of a registered pension scheme for that tax year, otherwise it is lost.

- The AA for the **current year is used first**, then the AA from earlier years, **starting with the earliest tax year** (i.e. on a FIFO basis).

- The unused AA for the three years prior to 2012/13 is calculated using a limit of £50,000 each year as follows:

  For 2009/10 and 2010/11 a notional AA limit of £50,000 was used. If contributions exceeded £50,000 in 2009/10 and 2010/11, there is no unused AA and no impact on the unused AA for other years.

  For 2011/12 the AA limit was £50,000. If contributions exceeded £50,000 in 2011/12, the excess would have been matched against 2011/12 first, then the earlier three years on a FIFO basis (i.e. 2008/09, 2009/10 and then 2010/11).

Example 3 – Calculation of annual allowance

Steve and Mike made gross personal pension contributions as follows:

	Steve £	Mike £
2009/10	52,000	Nil
2010/11	35,000	5,000
2011/12	17,000	6,000

Steve has been a member of a registered pension scheme since 2004/05. Mike joined a registered pension scheme in 2010/11. Both have relevant earnings of £200,000 per annum.

State the maximum gross contribution that Steve and Mike could make in 2012/13 without incurring an annual allowance tax charge.

Answer to example 3

Steve

	£
Unused allowances	
2009/10 Contributions in excess of £50,000	Nil
2010/11 (£50,000 – £35,000)	15,000
2011/12 (£50,000 – £17,000)	33,000
	——
Total unused allowances b/f	48,000
Add: Allowance for 2012/13	50,000
	——
Maximum gross contribution for 2012/13 to avoid charge	98,000
	——

Mike

	£
Unused allowances	
2009/10 Not member of registered pension scheme	Nil
2010/11 (£50,000 – £5,000)	45,000
2011/12 (£50,000 – £6,000)	44,000
	——
Total unused allowances b/f	89,000
Add: Allowance for 2012/13	50,000
	——
Maximum gross contribution for 2012/13 to avoid charge	139,000
	——

Test your understanding 2

Ahmed has made the following gross contributions to his personal pension:

	£
2009/10	22,000
2010/11	36,000
2011/12	43,000
2012/13	68,000

State the amount of unused annual allowances to carry forward to 2013/14.

Calculation of annual allowance charge

Where the total of all contributions on which relief has been obtained exceeds the AA (including brought forward annual allowances) there is a tax charge on the excess.

The tax charge is calculated as if the excess is the individual's top slice of income (i.e. taxed last after all sources of income, including dividends).

For simplicity, the excess is included as 'other income' in the individual's income tax computation.

The AA charge becomes part of the individual's total liability and is either paid through the self assessment system or, in some cases, may be taken from the individual's pension fund.

Example 4 – Contributions in excess of the annual allowance

Julie has been a self-employed interior designer for a number of years. In the year to 31 March 2013 she made tax adjusted trading profits of £296,000. Julie made a gross contribution of £90,000 into her personal pension scheme in 2012/13.

Julie does not have any unused annual allowance brought forward.

Explain how tax relief will be obtained for the pension contribution made by Julie and calculate her income tax liability for 2012/13.

Answer to example 4

Julie can obtain tax relief for a pension contribution up a maximum of 100% of her earnings (i.e. £296,000 in 2012/13). She will therefore obtain relief on the gross contribution of £90,000.

Julie will have paid the pension contribution net of basic rate tax of £18,000 (£90,000 x 20%) and paid £72,000 (£90,000 – £18,000) into the pension scheme.

Higher rate relief is obtained by extending the basic rate band by £90,000 from £34,370 to £124,370. Additional rate relief is obtained by extending the higher rate band by £90,000 from £150,000 to £240,000.

However Julie's gross contributions of £90,000 have exceeded the AA of £50,000. She will therefore be taxed on an additional £40,000 (£90,000 – £50,000) at her highest marginal rates of tax as though the AA was taxed after all of her income.

Julie's income tax computation for 2012/13 will be:

	£
Trading income	296,000
Annual allowance charge	40,000
	336,000
Less: Personal allowance (Note)	(Nil)
Taxable income	336,000

Income tax liability	£	
Basic rate	124,370 @ 20%	24,874
Higher rate	115,630 @ 40%	46,252
	240,000	
Additional rate	96,000 @ 50%	48,000
	336,000	
Income tax liability		119,126

Note: Julie's ANI is £246,000 (£336,000 – £90,000). Since this exceeds £116,210, her PA will be reduced to £Nil.

Test your understanding 3

Marcus has been employed for many years.

In 2012/13 Marcus earned £302,500 and made a gross contribution of £126,000 into his personal pension scheme.

Marcus' pension contributions for the last 3 years have been:

	£
2009/10	37,000
2010/11	70,000
2011/12	44,000

Calculate Marcus' income tax liability for 2012/13.

Test your understanding 4

Hugh is a self-employed builder, who prepares accounts to September each year. His recent tax adjusted trading profits have been:

	£
Year ended 30 September 2011	140,000
Year ended 30 September 2012	150,000

Hugh's wife, Holly, has employment income from a part-time job of £3,500 p.a.

They also have a joint bank account on which they earned interest of £5,000 (gross) and Holly receives interest from a building society account of £20,000 (gross) in 2012/13.

During the year to 5 April 2013, Hugh paid £79,400 into his registered personal pension scheme. Hugh has contributed £35,000 into his personal pension each year for the last 3 years.

Holly paid £2,600 into her employer's registered occupational pension scheme and Holly's employer contributed a further £4,500.

Calculate how much of the pension contributions made by Hugh, Holly and Holly's employer in 2012/13 will obtain tax relief and explain how the tax relief will be obtained.

Summary

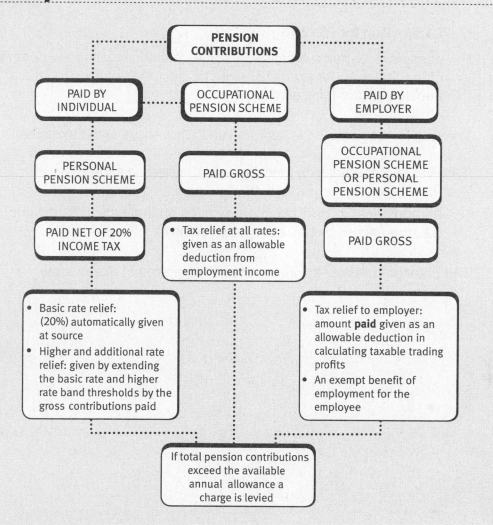

4 The lifetime allowance

There is no restriction on the **total** contribution that an individual may make into a registered pension scheme. There is only a limit upon the annual contributions upon which **tax relief** will be available.

Once invested, funds in a registered pension scheme each year will be accumulated and can grow in value, tax free, as the scheme is:

- exempt from income tax in respect of any income earned from the assets invested

- exempt from capital gains tax in respect of any capital disposals made by the trustees over the life of the scheme.

However, there is a maximum limit to the amount that an individual can accumulate in a pension scheme tax-free, known as the 'lifetime allowance'.

The lifetime allowance is:

- £1.5 million for 2012/13
- considered when a member becomes entitled to withdraw benefits out of the scheme (for example, when he becomes entitled to take a pension and/or lump sum payment).

The limit is not given in the tax rates and allowances in the examination.

If the value of the pension fund exceeds the lifetime allowance:

- an additional income tax charge arises on the excess fund value (i.e. the excess value above £1.5 million).

The detailed rules for the income tax charge are not examinable.

5 Chapter summary

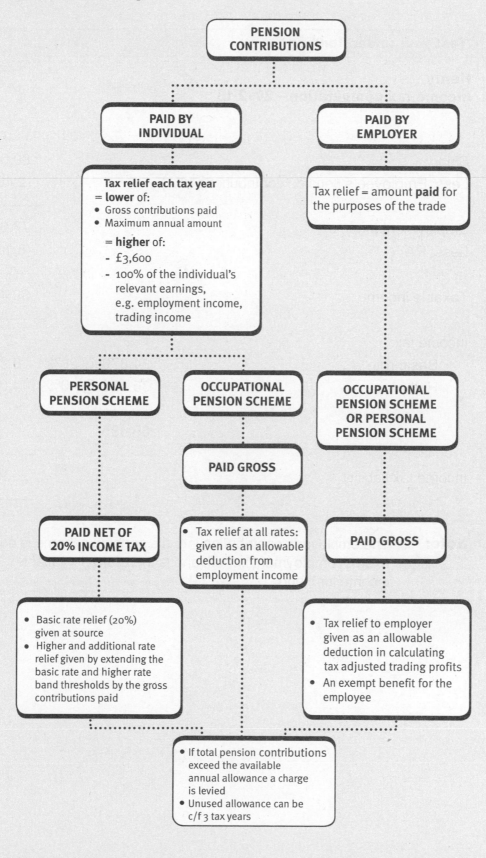

PENSION CONTRIBUTIONS

PAID BY INDIVIDUAL

PAID BY EMPLOYER

Tax relief each tax year
= **lower** of:
- Gross contributions paid
- Maximum annual amount

= **higher** of:
- £3,600
- 100% of the individual's relevant earnings, e.g. employment income, trading income

Tax relief = amount **paid** for the purposes of the trade

PERSONAL PENSION SCHEME

OCCUPATIONAL PENSION SCHEME

OCCUPATIONAL PENSION SCHEME OR PERSONAL PENSION SCHEME

PAID GROSS

PAID NET OF 20% INCOME TAX

- Tax relief at all rates: given as an allowable deduction from employment income

PAID GROSS

- Basic rate relief (20%) given at source
- Higher and additional rate relief given by extending the basic rate and higher rate band thresholds by the gross contributions paid

- Tax relief to employer given as an allowable deduction in calculating tax adjusted trading profits
- An exempt benefit for the employee

- If total pension contributions exceed the available annual allowance a charge is levied
- Unused allowance can be c/f 3 tax years

Test your understanding answers

Test your understanding 1

Henry
Income tax computation – 2012/13

	£
Salary	80,000
Less: Employee's pension contributions (3%)	(2,400)
Employment income	77,600
Less: PA	(8,105)
Taxable income	69,495

Income tax:	£	£
Basic rate	34,370 @ 20%	6,874
Higher rate	35,125 @ 40%	14,050
	69,495	
Income tax liability		20,924

Note: The employer's contribution into his pension scheme is an exempt employment benefit and is therefore not taxable income for Henry.

Test your understanding 2

Ahmed

	Allowance available £	Used 2012/13 £	Carried forward £
Allowance for 2012/13	50,000	(50,000)	Nil
Unused allowance b/f			
2009/10 (£50,000 – £22,000)	28,000	(18,000)	N/A
2010/11 (£50,000 – £36,000)	14,000		14,000
2011/12 (£50,000 – £43,000)	7,000		7,000
	99,000	(68,000)	21,000

Note: The allowance for the current tax year must be used first, then the unused allowance brought forward from the previous three years, starting with the earliest tax year.

The remaining allowance from 2009/10 of £10,000 (£28,000 – £18,000) cannot be carried forward to 2013/14 as it is more than three years ago.

Test your understanding 3

Marcus

- Marcus can obtain tax relief for a gross pension contribution of up to a maximum of 100% of his earnings (i.e. £302,500 in 2012/13).

- However, he only made a gross contribution of £126,000. Tax relief is therefore available on the full contribution of £126,000.

- Marcus will have paid the pension contribution net of basic rate tax of £25,200 (£126,000 x 20%) and paid £100,800 (£126,000 x 80%) into the pension scheme.

- Higher rate relief is obtained by extending the basic rate band threshold by £126,000 from £34,370 to £160,370. Additional rate relief is obtained by extending the higher rate band by £126,000 from £150,000 to £276,000.

- Marcus' unused annual allowances brought forward are as follows:

		£
2009/10	(£50,000 – £37,000)	13,000
2010/11	Contributions in excess of £50,000	Nil
2011/12	(£50,000 – £44,000)	6,000
		19,000

- However the gross contributions paid into the scheme on which tax relief has been given in 2012/13 of £126,000 exceeds the annual allowance available of £69,000 (£50,000 + £19,000 brought forward).

- Marcus will therefore be taxed on an additional £57,000 (£126,000 – £69,000) at his highest marginal rates of tax.

Marcus' income tax computation for 2012/13 will be:

			£
Employment income			302,500
Excess pension contributions (AA charge)			57,000
			359,500
Less: Personal allowance			(Nil)
Taxable income			359,500

Income tax:	£		
Basic rate	160,370	@ 20%	32,074
Higher rate	115,630	@ 40%	46,252
	276,000		
Additional rate	83,500	@ 50%	41,750
	359,500		
Income tax liability			120,076

Note: Marcus' ANI is £233,500 (£359,500 – £126,000). Since this exceeds £116,210, his personal allowance will be reduced to £Nil.

KAPLAN PUBLISHING

Test your understanding 4

Hugh

- Hugh can obtain tax relief for a pension contribution of up to a maximum of 100% of his earnings in 2012/13.

- His earnings are his assessable trading profits for 2012/13 (i.e. £150,000 for the year ended 30 September 2012).

- Unearned income such as bank interest is not included.

- Hugh will have paid the pension contribution net of basic rate tax of £19,850 (£79,400 × 20/80).

- The gross pension contribution is £99,250 (£79,400 × 100/80).

- As a higher rate taxpayer, higher rate tax relief is obtained by extending the basic rate band by £99,250 from £34,370 to £133,620.

- As Hugh's taxable income exceeds £150,000, additional rate relief is obtained by extending the higher rate band by £99,250 from £150,000 to £249,250. Hugh will therefore not have to pay any additional rate tax.

- Hugh's available annual allowance is £50,000 plus £45,000 brought forward (£50,000 – £35,000 = £15,000 p.a. x 3). The total annual allowance is therefore £95,000. His contributions exceed this by £4,250 (£99,250 – £95,000) and this amount will be added to his income and then subjected to tax at 40% (Hugh's highest rate of tax). Therefore, an additional £1,700 of tax will be payable.

- Hugh's PA is still available in full as his ANI is £57,500 (Net income = £150,000 + £2,500 + £4,250 = £156,750 less gross PPCs of £99,250), which is less than £100,000.

Holly

- Holly can obtain tax relief for a gross pension contribution of up to a maximum of the higher of £3,600 or 100% of her employment earnings in 2012/13 (i.e. £3,500).

- Her gross pension contribution of £2,600 is less than £3,600, therefore she can obtain tax relief for all £2,600 contributions paid.

- Holly's employer will deduct the gross contribution of £2,600 from her employment income before calculating her income tax liability under PAYE.

- Holly's employer's contributions of £4,500 are a tax free benefit.

Holly's employer

- Holly's employer will obtain tax relief for all of the £4,500 contribution made into the occupational pension scheme.

- Relief is given as an allowable deduction in the calculation of the employer's tax adjusted trading profits.

KAPLAN PUBLISHING

National insurance

Chapter learning objectives

Upon completion of this chapter you will be able to:

- identify the different types of National Insurance Contributions (NICs) and the persons who are liable

- define earnings for the purposes of Class 1 NICs

- calculate the Class 1 NIC primary and secondary liabilities on earnings

- state how and when Class 1 NICs are collected

- explain the basis of the Class 1A NIC charge and calculate the amount of Class 1A NICs payable

- state how and when Class 1A NICs are payable

- calculate Class 2 NICs for relevant self-employed persons

- explain how Class 2 NICs are collected

- identify the relevant earnings for Class 4 NICs and calculate the liability

- explain how and when Class 4 NICs are payable

- calculate the total NIC liability for a self-employed person.

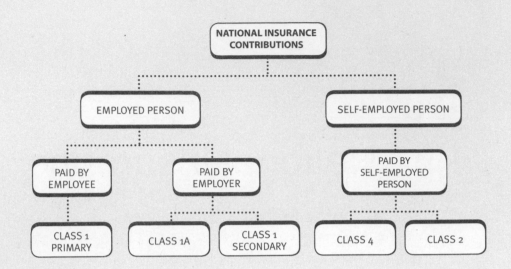

1 Classes of National Insurance Contributions

The amount of National Insurance Contribution (NIC) a person pays and the payment of contributions depend on the class of contribution.

The main classes and persons who are liable are as follows:

Class of contribution	Basis of assessment	Person liable
Class 1 primary	A percentage-based contribution levied on employee earnings in excess of the earnings threshold for 2012/13 (£7,605 for primary and £7,488 for secondary)	Employee
Class 1 secondary		Employer
Class 1A	A percentage-based contribution levied on assessable benefits provided to employees	Employer
Class 2	A flat rate weekly contribution	Self-employed
Class 4	A percentage-based contribution levied on tax adjusted trading profits in excess of the lower profits limit of £7,605 for 2012/13	Self-employed

Example 1 – Classes of NICs

Nicholas has been self-employed for many years. He employs a full-time salesman and six part-time employees. Nicholas' tax adjusted trading profits for 2012/13 are £86,000.

The salesman earns a salary of £14,000 p.a. and is provided with a company car. The remaining members of staff earn £3,000 p.a.

Explain which classes of NICs are payable by Nicholas.

Answer to example 1

Nicholas will pay:

(1) Flat rate Class 2 contributions in respect of his self-employed business.

(2) Class 4 contributions in respect of his self-employed business based on his tax adjusted trading profits as they are in excess of £7,605.

(3) Class 1 secondary contributions as Nicholas is an employer. The contributions will be based on the salesman's salary of £14,000 as his earnings are in excess of £7,488.

(4) Class 1A contributions based on the assessable employment benefit arising from the provision of a company car to the salesman.

Notes:

(1) No NICs are payable in respect of the remaining six part-time staff members as they each earn less than £7,488 p.a.

(2) The salesman is liable to pay Class 1 primary contributions based on his salary of £14,000.

Example 2 – Classes of NICs

Stephen works for Camberley Cars Ltd on a part-time basis earning a salary of £19,000 p.a. He is provided with a company car; petrol for both business and private mileage; and a place is provided for his daughter at the company's workplace nursery while he is working for them.

Stephen also runs a small bed and breakfast business from his home. In the year to 31 March 2013 his tax adjusted trading profit from the business is £10,300.

Explain which classes of NICs are payable by Stephen and Camberley Cars Ltd in respect of 2012/13.

Answer to example 2

Stephen will pay:

(1) Class 1 primary contributions based on his salary from Camberley Cars Ltd of £19,000 as his earnings are in excess of £7,605.

(2) Flat rate Class 2 contributions in respect of his bed and breakfast business.

(3) Class 4 contributions in respect of his bed and breakfast business based on his tax adjusted trading profits as they are in excess of £7,605.

Camberley Cars Ltd will pay:

(1) Class 1 secondary contributions based on Stephen's salary of £19,000 as his earnings are in excess of £7,488.

(2) Class 1A contributions based on the assessable employment benefit arising from the provision of a company car and private petrol to Stephen.

Note: Class 1A contributions are not required in respect of the provision of a nursery place as it is an exempt benefit.

2 NICs payable in respect of employees

The following NICs are payable in respect of employees:

- Class 1 primary contributions
- Class 1 secondary contributions
- Class 1A contributions.

Class 1 primary and secondary NICs

Both the primary Class 1 contribution paid by the employee and the secondary contribution paid by the employer are a percentage-based contribution levied on the 'gross earnings' of the employee in excess of the earnings thresholds.

For 2012/13, the earnings thresholds are:

Primary   £7,605
Secondary   £7,488

The definition of earnings for Class 1 NIC purposes

'Earnings' for the purpose of Class 1 NICs consists of:

- **any** remuneration derived from the employment, and
- paid in **cash** or assets which are readily convertible into cash.

The calculation of Class 1 NICs is based on:

gross earnings with **no allowable deductions**

(i.e. earnings before deductions that are allowable for income tax purposes, such as employee occupational pension scheme contributions and subscriptions to professional bodies).

Gross earnings **includes**:

- wages, salary, overtime pay, commission or bonus
- sick pay, including statutory sick pay
- tips and gratuities paid or allocated by the employer
- payment of the cost of travel between home and work
- vouchers (exchangeable for cash or non-cash items, such as goods).

'Gross earnings' **does not include**:

- exempt employment benefits (e.g. employer contributions into a pension scheme, a mobile phone, etc.) (see Chapter 4)
- most taxable **non-cash benefits** except remuneration received in the form of financial instruments, readily convertible assets and non-cash vouchers (see above)
- tips directly received from customers
- mileage allowance received from the employer provided it does not exceed the HMRC approved allowance mileage rate of 45p per mile
- business expenses paid for or reimbursed by the employer, including reasonable travel and subsistence expenses.

Note that dividends are not subject to NICs, even if they are drawn by a director/shareholder in place of a monthly salary.

Example 3 – Definition of Class 1 earnings

Janet and John are employed by Garden Gnomes Ltd and both pay into the company's occupational pension scheme. Their remuneration for 2012/13 is as follows:

	Janet £	John £
Salary	30,000	55,000
Bonus	Nil	4,000
Car benefit	Nil	3,950
Employer's pension contribution	2,300	4,575
Employee's pension contribution	1,650	3,800

Calculate Janet and John's 'gross earnings' for Class 1 NIC purposes.

Answer to example 3

	Janet £	John £
Salary	30,000	55,000
Bonuses	Nil	4,000
Gross earnings for Class 1 NICs	30,000	59,000

Notes:

(1) The employer's pension contributions are excluded as they are an exempt benefit.

(2) The employee's pension contributions are ignored as these are not deductible in calculating earnings for NIC purposes.

(3) The car benefit is excluded as it is a non-cash benefit which will be assessed to Class 1A NICs, not Class 1.

Eligible employees

Class 1 contributions are payable where the individual:

- is employed in the UK, and
- is aged 16 or over, and
- has earnings in excess of the earnings thresholds (£7,605 for primary contributions and £7,488 for secondary contributions for 2012/13).

Class 1 primary contributions

Class 1 primary contributions are payable by employees:

- aged 16 or over until
- attaining state pension age (see below).

The employer is responsible for calculating the amount of Class 1 primary NICs due and deducting the contributions from the employee's wages.

Note that Class 1 primary contributions:

- are not an allowable deduction for the purposes of calculating the individual employee's personal income tax liability
- do not represent a cost to the business of the employer, as they are ultimately paid by the employee. Therefore, they are not a deductible expense when calculating the employer's tax adjusted trading profits.

State pension age

Up to 5 April 2010 the state pension age was 65 for men and 60 for women.

Between 2010 and 2018 the retirement age for women will gradually increase to 65 and from 2018 onwards the retirement ages for both men and women are further increasing.

Knowledge of the detailed rules over this transitional period is not required.

Calculating Class 1 primary contributions

Primary contributions are normally calculated by reference to an employee's earnings period:

- if paid weekly, the contributions are calculated on a weekly basis
- if paid monthly, the contributions are calculated on a monthly basis.

In the examination, the Class 1 NIC limits are usually shown on an annual basis and Class 1 NIC calculations should therefore be performed on an annual basis unless you are clearly told otherwise.

The primary contributions payable are calculated as:

- 12% on gross earnings between £7,605 and £42,475
- 2% on gross earnings in excess of £42,475.

> **Earnings period**
>
> The annual earnings thresholds can be used to calculate the rate of Class 1 NICs payable where the employee's wages or salary does not fluctuate during the year.
>
> However, where an employee's salary fluctuates during the year:
>
> - the calculations must be performed on an earnings period basis
> - the annual limits are divided into weekly or monthly thresholds.
>
> The apportioned lower limit is £146 per week (£7,605 × 1/52) or £634 per month (£7,605 × 1/12); and the upper limit is £817 a week (£42,475 × 1/52) or £3,540 a month (£42,475 × 1/12).

Class 1 secondary contributions

Class 1 secondary contributions are payable by employers in respect of employees:

- aged 16 or over
- until the employee ceases employment.

There is no upper age limit for employer contributions, the employer is liable in full even if the employee is above state pension age.

Secondary contributions are an additional cost of employment and are a deductible expense when calculating the employer's tax adjusted trading profits.

Calculating Class 1 secondary contributions

Secondary contributions are calculated by reference to an employee's earnings period.

In the examination, Class 1 NIC calculations should be performed on an annual basis unless you are clearly told otherwise.

Secondary contributions are calculated as:

- 13.8% on all gross earnings above £7,488.

Note that there is:

- no upper earnings limit
- no change in the rate of NICs payable for employer contributions.

Example 4 – Class 1 NICs

Millie is employed by Blue Forge Ltd and is paid an annual salary of £43,000. Millie is also provided with the following taxable benefits:

	£
Company car	5,000
Vouchers for the local gym	2,000

Calculate the employee's and the employer's Class 1 NIC liability due for 2012/13.

Answer to example 4

Class 1 NICs are due on annual earnings of £45,000 (salary £43,000 and vouchers £2,000). The company car is a non-cash benefit and is therefore not subject to Class 1 NICs.

	£
Employee's Class 1 NICs	
(£42,475 – £7,605 @ 12%	4,184
(£45,000 – £42,475) @ 2%	50
	———
	4,234
	———
Employer's Class 1 NICs	
(£45,000 – £7,488) × 13.8%	5,177
	———

Test your understanding 1

Alex is paid £7,950 per year and Betty is paid £44,440 per year.

Calculate the employee's and the employer's Class 1 NIC liability due for 2012/13.

Company directors

Special rules apply to company directors to prevent the avoidance of NICs by paying low weekly or monthly salaries, and then taking a large bonus in a single week or month.

Therefore, when an employee is a company director, his Class 1 NICs are calculated as if he had an annual earnings period.

Payment of Class 1 contributions

The administration and payment of Class 1 NICs is carried out by the employer as follows:

- The employer is responsible for calculating the amount of Class 1 primary and secondary contributions at each pay date.

- Primary contributions are deducted from the employee's wages or salary by the employer and paid to HMRC on the employee's behalf.

- The total primary and secondary contributions are payable by the employer to HMRC, along with income tax deducted from the employees under PAYE.

- The payment is normally due on the 19th of each month, (i.e. due not later than 14 days after the end of each PAYE month).

- The specific payment rules for very small employers and those paying electronically are covered in detail in Chapter 12.

Class 1A NICs

Employers are required to pay Class 1A contributions on 'taxable benefits' provided to employees earning at a rate of £8,500 p.a. and directors, (i.e. higher paid employees).

No Class 1A contributions are payable in respect of:

- exempt benefits

- benefits already treated as earnings and assessed to Class 1 NICs, such as remuneration received in the form of non-cash vouchers (see above).

The contributions are calculated as:

- 13.8% on the value of the taxable benefits.

Class 1A contributions are an additional cost of employment and are a deductible expense when calculating the employer's tax adjusted trading profits.

Example 5 – Class 1A NICs

Simon is employed by Dutton Ltd at an annual salary of £52,000.

He was provided with a company car throughout 2012/13 that had a list price of £15,000. The car has CO_2 emissions of 178 g/km. Petrol for both business and private mileage is provided by his employer.

Calculate the employee's and the employer's Class 1 and Class 1A NIC liabilities due for 2012/13.

Answer to example 5

(a) **Class 1 NICs**

	£
Employee's Class 1 NICs	
(£42,475 – £7,605) x 12% (maximum)	4,184
(£52,000 – £42,475) x 2%	190
	4,374
Employer's Class 1 NICs	
(£52,000 – £7,488) x 13.8%	6,143

(b) **Class 1A NICs**

Simon's taxable benefits for Class 1A purposes are as follows:

	£
Company motor car	
11% + ((175 – 100) x 1/5) = 26% × £15,000	3,900
Private fuel provided by company (26% × £20,200)	5,252
Taxable benefits for Class 1A	9,152
Employer's Class 1A NICs (£9,152 at 13.8%)	1,263

Test your understanding 2

Sally is paid £25,000 per year and had taxable benefits for 2012/13 of:

	£
Company motor car	5,250
Private fuel provided by company	4,200
Beneficial loan	2,600
Vouchers to be used at the local department store	250

The company also provided Sally with a mobile phone, which cost £135.

Contributions into her personal pension scheme were as follows:

Employer's contribution	£2,540
Employee's contribution	£1,380

Calculate the employee's and the employer's Class 1 and Class 1A NIC liabilities due for 2012/13.

Payment of Class 1A contributions

Class 1A contributions are payable to HMRC by 19 July following the end of the tax year (i.e. by 19 July 2013 for 2012/13).

Summary

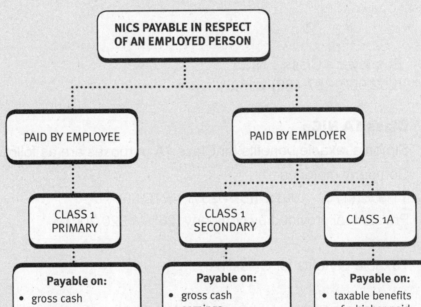

NICS PAYABLE IN RESPECT OF AN EMPLOYED PERSON

PAID BY EMPLOYEE

PAID BY EMPLOYER

CLASS 1 PRIMARY

Payable on:
- gross cash earnings
  - no allowable deductions
  - includes vouchers

Payable when:
- aged 16 - state pension age

Rate:
- 12% on earnings between £7,605 and £42,475
- 2% thereafter

Due date:
- payable under PAYE by 19th of each month

CLASS 1 SECONDARY

Payable on:
- gross cash earnings
  - no allowable deductions
  - includes vouchers

Payable when:
- aged 16 or over

Rate:
- 13.8% on earnings above £7,488

Due date:
- payable under PAYE by 19th of each month

CLASS 1A

Payable on:
- taxable benefits of a higher-paid employee
  - excludes exempt benefits and vouchers

Payable when:
- aged 16 or over

Rate:
- 13.8% on the value of taxable benefits

Due date:
- payable by 19th July following the end of the tax year

3 NICs payable in respect of self-employed individuals

The following NICs are payable by self-employed individuals:

- Class 2 contributions
- Class 4 contributions.

Class 2 contributions

Class 2 contributions are payable where the individual:

- is aged 16 or over
- until attaining state pension age (see section 2 above)
- if the accounting profits of the business in the tax year exceed the small earnings exception of £5,595.

Amount payable

Class 2 contributions are a flat rate payment of £2.65 per week.

The maximum total Class 2 NICs payable for 2012/13 is therefore £138 (£2.65 × 52 weeks).

Note that Class 2 contributions:

- are not an allowable deduction for the purposes of calculating the individual's income tax liability
- are not a deductible expense when calculating the business' tax adjusted trading profits.

Payment of Class 2 contributions

Class 2 NICs are due in two instalments:

- 31 January in the tax year
- 31 July following the end of the tax year.

Payments can be made in a variety of ways, including direct debit on a six monthly basis.

For businesses set up before 2011/12, if the taxpayer prefers, they can continue to pay under their existing monthly direct debit payment system.

Class 4 contributions

In addition to Class 2 NICs, a self-employed individual may also be liable to Class 4 NICs.

Class 4 contributions are payable by self-employed individuals who:

- at the start of the tax year, are aged 16 or over.

They continue to pay **until**:

- the end of the tax year in which they attain state pension age.

Class 4 NICs are a percentage-based contribution levied on the 'profits' of the individual in excess of £7,605 for 2012/13.

Note that Class 4 contributions:

- are not an allowable deduction for the purposes of calculating the individual's income tax liability
- are not a deductible expense when calculating the business' tax adjusted trading profits.

The definition of Class 4 profits

'Profits' for the purposes of Class 4 NICs consists of:

- the tax adjusted trading profits of the individual that are assessed for income tax after deducting trading losses (if any).

Note that 'profits' for Class 4 NICs are **before** deducting the individual's personal allowance that is available for income tax purposes.

If the individual has more than one business, the aggregate of all profits from all self-employed occupations are used to calculate the Class 4 NIC liability.

Calculating Class 4 NICs

The contributions payable are calculated as:

- 9% on profits between £7,605 and £42,475
- 2% on profits in excess of £42,475.

KAPLAN PUBLISHING

Example 6 – Class 4 NICs

James has been trading as a self-employed painter and decorator since 1998. His tax adjusted trading profits for 2012/13 are £56,000 and he has trading losses brought forward of £10,000.

His wife, Poppy, is a part-time mobile hairdresser. Her tax adjusted trading profits for 2012/13 are £8,560.

Calculate the Class 4 NICs payable by James and Poppy for 2012/13.

Answer to example 6

James	£
Tax adjusted trading profits	56,000
Less: Trading losses brought forward	(10,000)
Profits for Class 4 purposes	46,000

Class 4 NICs	£
(£42,475 – £7,605) × 9% (maximum)	3,138
(£46,000 – £42,475) × 2%	70
	3,208

Poppy – Class 4 NICs	
(£8,560 – £7,605) × 9%	86

Test your understanding 3

Jack is a self-employed builder who has been in business for many years and prepares accounts to 31 March each year.

His tax adjusted trading profit for the year ended 31 March 2013 is £46,850.

Calculate Jack's Class 2 and Class 4 NICs liability for 2012/13.

Payment of Class 4 contributions

Class 4 contributions are paid to HMRC at the same time as the individual's Class 2 NIC and income tax payments.

Unlike Class 2 NICs however, income tax and Class 4 NICs due are paid under self assessment, as follows:

Payment	Due date	Amount
Payments on account	• 31 January in the tax year (i.e. 31.1.2013 for 2012/13) • 31 July following the end of the tax year (i.e. 31.7.2013 for 2012/13)	Two equal instalments of: • 50% of the amount paid by self assessment in the preceding year
Balancing payment	• 31 January following the end of the tax year (i.e. 31.1.2014 for 2012/13)	Under or overpayment for the year

The detailed administration and payment rules are covered in Chapter 12.

Summary

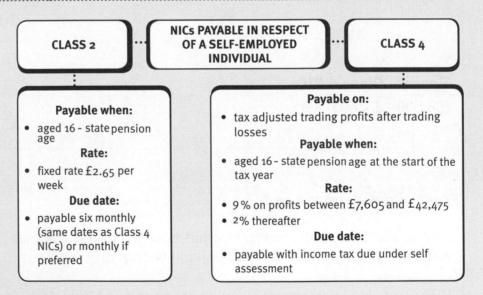

NICs PAYABLE IN RESPECT OF A SELF-EMPLOYED INDIVIDUAL

CLASS 2

Payable when:
• aged 16 - state pension age

Rate:
• fixed rate £2.65 per week

Due date:
• payable six monthly (same dates as Class 4 NICs) or monthly if preferred

CLASS 4

Payable on:
• tax adjusted trading profits after trading losses

Payable when:
• aged 16 - state pension age at the start of the tax year

Rate:
• 9% on profits between £7,605 and £42,475
• 2% thereafter

Due date:
• payable with income tax due under self assessment

4 Total NICs payable by a self-employed individual

A self-employed individual pays both Class 2 and Class 4 NICs in respect of his tax adjusted trading profits.

In addition, if the self-employed individual employs staff, he will be required to account for:

- Class 2 and Class 4 NICs in respect of his trading profits
- Class 1 primary, Class 1 secondary and Class 1A NICs in respect of earnings and benefits provided to employees.

Test your understanding 4

Diane has been a self-employed computer consultant for many years. Her tax adjusted trading profits for 2012/13 are £50,000.

Diane employs a full-time personal assistant at a salary of £15,800 p.a. She also provides the assistant with a diesel-engined company car, which has a list price of £13,500 and CO_2 emissions of 146 g/km. Diane pays for the assistant's private and business fuel.

Calculate the total NICs that Diane must account for to HMRC in respect of 2012/13.

5 Chapter summary

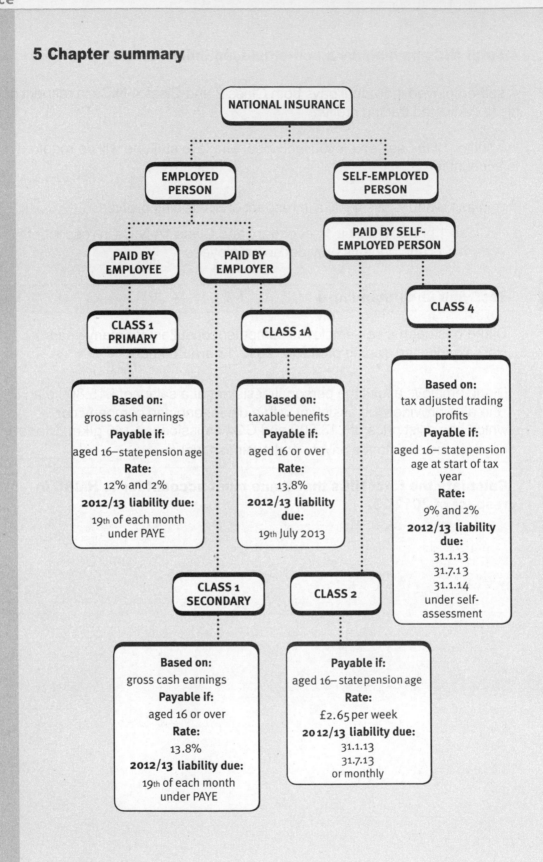

NATIONAL INSURANCE

EMPLOYED PERSON

SELF-EMPLOYED PERSON

PAID BY EMPLOYEE

PAID BY EMPLOYER

PAID BY SELF-EMPLOYED PERSON

CLASS 1 PRIMARY

CLASS 1A

CLASS 4

Based on:
gross cash earnings
Payable if:
aged 16 – state pension age
Rate:
12% and 2%
2012/13 liability due:
19th of each month under PAYE

Based on:
taxable benefits
Payable if:
aged 16 or over
Rate:
13.8%
2012/13 liability due:
19th July 2013

Based on:
tax adjusted trading profits
Payable if:
aged 16 – state pension age at start of tax year
Rate:
9% and 2%
2012/13 liability due:
31.1.13
31.7.13
31.1.14
under self-assessment

CLASS 1 SECONDARY

CLASS 2

Based on:
gross cash earnings
Payable if:
aged 16 or over
Rate:
13.8%
2012/13 liability due:
19th of each month under PAYE

Payable if:
aged 16 – state pension age
Rate:
£2.65 per week
2012/13 liability due:
31.1.13
31.7.13
or monthly

Test your understanding answers

Test your understanding 1

Alex	£
Employee's Class 1 NICs (£7,950 – £7,605) x 12%	41
	___
Employer's Class 1 NICs (£7,950 – £7,488) x 13.8%	64
	___

Betty	
Employee's Class 1 NICs	
(£42,475 – £7,605) x 12% (maximum)	4,184
(£44,440 – £42,475) x 2%	39
	___
	4,223
Employer's Class 1 NICs (£44,440 – £7,488) x 13.8%	5,099
	___

Test your understanding 2

Sally
Class 1 NICs

	£
Salary	25,000
Vouchers	250
	___
Cash earnings for Class 1 NICs	25,250
	___
Employee's Class 1 NICs (£25,250 – £7,605) x 12%	2,117
	___
Employer's Class 1 NICs (£25,250 – £7,488) x 13.8%	2,451
	___

Notes

(1) The provision of one mobile phone per employee, and employer pension contributions, are excluded as they are exempt benefits.

(2) The employee pension contributions are not allowable deductions in calculating earnings for NIC purposes.

(3) The car, fuel and beneficial loan benefits are excluded as they are non-cash benefits which are assessed to Class 1A NICs, not Class 1.

Class 1A NICs	£
Company motor car	5,250
Private fuel provided by company	4,200
Beneficial loan	2,600
	———
Taxable benefits for Class 1A	12,050
	———
Employer's Class 1A NICs (£12,050 at 13.8%)	1,663
	———

Test your understanding 3

Jack

Class 2 NICs (£2.65 × 52 weeks)	£138
	———

Class 4 NICs	£
(£42,475 – £7,605) × 9% (maximum)	3,138
(£46,850 – £42,475) × 2%	87
	———
	3,225
	———

Test your understanding 4

Diane

(1) Flat rate Class 2 contributions in respect of the business.

Class 2 NICs

(£2.65 × 52 weeks)   £138

(2) Class 4 contributions in respect of the business based on tax adjusted trading profits as they are in excess of £7,605.

Class 4 NICs	£
(£42,475 – £7,605) × 9% (maximum)	3,138
(£50,000 – £42,475) × 2%	150
	3,288

(3) Class 1 secondary contributions as Diane is an employer, based on her personal assistant's salary of £15,800.

Employer's Class 1 NICs

(£15,800 – £7,488) x 13.8%   £1,147

(4) Class 1A contributions based on the benefit arising from the provision of a company car to the personal assistant.

Company motor car	£
14% + ((145 – 100) × 1/ 5) = 23% × £13,500	3,105
Private fuel provided (23% × £20,200)	4,646
Taxable benefits for Class 1A	7,751

Employer's Class 1A NICs

(£7,751 at 13.8%)   1,070

(5) Class 1 primary contributions are levied on the personal assistant. However, it is Diane's responsibility to deduct the NICs from the assistant's salary and pay them to HMRC along with the Class 1 secondary contributions on the 19th of each month.

Employee's Class 1 NICs

(£15,800 – £7,605) x 12%   £983

Summary	£
Class 2	138
Class 4	3,288
Class 1 secondary	1,147
Class 1A	1,070
Diane's total liability	5,643
Class 1 primary	983
Total amount Diane must account for to HMRC	6,626

Tax administration for individuals

Chapter learning objectives

Upon completion of this chapter you will be able to:

- explain the self-assessment system as it applies to individuals
- state the time limits for notifying a liability and filing a return
- state the penalties for late submission of returns and notifying HMRC of liability
- list the information and records that the taxpayer needs to retain for tax purposes together with the retention period
- state the due dates for payment of tax under self-assessment
- compute payments on account and balancing payments / repayments
- state the effect of making a late payment on account / balancing payment
- calculate late payment interest
- state the penalties that can be charged on a late payment of tax
- determine the time limits for key claims
- explain the circumstances in which HMRC can enquire into a self-assessment tax return
- describe the procedures for dealing with appeals and disputes
- explain the PAYE system
- list the key PAYE forms and explain their purpose.

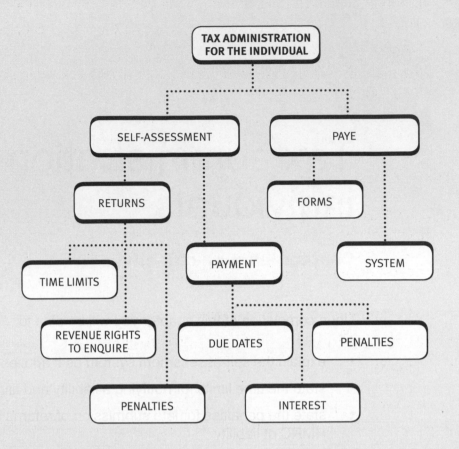

1 Personal tax administration

The collection of income tax

Income tax may be collected by deduction from the income at source (e.g. interest on building society deposit accounts is paid net of 20% income tax, employment income is received net of income tax under the PAYE system).

However, there are occasions which require the completion of a tax return and these include where:

- deduction at source does not satisfy a taxpayer's higher rate liability

- a taxpayer has income that is not taxed at source.

Self-assessment is the system for the collection of tax which is not deducted at source.

Self assessment

Under the self-assessment system for individuals, the onus is placed on the taxpayer to provide the information to calculate their own tax liability:

- The taxpayer will be sent a self-assessment tax return annually which must be completed and filed – either on paper or online.

- Different deadlines exist for filing paper and electronic (online) returns.

- The tax return covers income tax, Class 4 NIC and CGT liabilities for the tax year.

- Payment of the tax must be made by 31 January following the end of the tax year to which it relates.

- Interim payments on account may be required on 31 January in the tax year and 31 July following the tax year for certain taxpayers.

The self-assessment tax return

The deadline for submitting the 2012/13 self-assessment tax return depends on how the return is filed.

The deadline for submitting the return is the **later** of:

- 31 October 2013 for a paper return

- 31 January 2014 for an electronic (online) return

- three months after the issue of the return.

The 31 January following the end of the tax year is known as the **'filing date'**, regardless of whether the return is filed on paper or electronically.

This must be distinguished from the date on which the return is actually filed / submitted, which is the 'actual file date'.

Content of tax return

The return comes in two parts.

- In the first part, the taxpayer needs to provide all the information required to calculate his tax liability for the year.

  This will be some or all of:
  - taxable income from all sources
  - any capital gains for the tax year concerned
  - reliefs and allowances.

  Self-employed people: The return includes a section for standardised accounts information.

  Employees: Generally pay their tax liability under PAYE and often a self-assessment tax return will not be required as there is no further tax liability.

> **Partnerships:** Although partners are dealt with individually, a partnership return is required to aid self-assessment on the individual partners. This gives details of the partners, includes a partnership statement detailing the partnership's tax adjusted trading profit and shows how this is allocated between the partners.
>
> - The second part of the return concerns the calculation of the tax due. Whilst technically it is the taxpayer's responsibility to calculate (or 'self-assess') his or her own tax liability, in practice HMRC will normally calculate the tax on the taxpayer's behalf provided the return is submitted by the appropriate deadline.

- Where a return is filed electronically:
    - a calculation of the tax liability is automatically provided as part of the online filing process.

- Where a paper return is submitted:
    - HMRC will calculate the tax liability on behalf of the taxpayer, provided the return is submitted by the 31 October deadline. The taxpayer has the option of calculating the tax himself.
    - the calculation by HMRC is treated as a self-assessment on behalf of the taxpayer.

- Where HMRC calculates the tax it makes no judgement of the accuracy of the figures included in the return, but merely calculates the tax liability based on the information submitted.

- HMRC normally communicate with the taxpayer by issuing a statement of account.

    The statement of account sets out:

    - the tax charges
    - any charges of interest or penalties (see later)
    - any payments already made by the taxpayer.

    The statement is not a notice to pay but merely a reminder of the taxpayer's indebtedness.

Amendments to the return

Either party may amend the return:

- HMRC may correct any obvious errors or mistakes within **nine months** of the date that the return is filed with them.

  These would include arithmetical errors or errors of principle. However, this does not mean that HMRC has necessarily accepted the return as accurate.

- The taxpayer can amend the return within **12 months** of the 31 January filing date. For 2012/13, amendments must therefore be made by 31 January 2015.

  Note that the deadline is the same regardless of whether the return is filed on paper or electronically.

If an error is discovered at a later date then the taxpayer can make a claim for overpayment relief (see later) to recover any tax overpaid.

Notification of chargeability

Self-assessment places the onus on the taxpayers, therefore:

- Taxpayers who do not receive a return are required to notify HMRC if they have income or chargeable gains on which tax is due.

- The time limit for notifying HMRC of chargeability is six months from the end of the tax year in which the liability arises (i.e. 5 October 2013 for 2012/13).

- Notification is not necessary if there is no actual tax liability. For example, if the income or capital gain is covered by allowances or exemptions.

- A standard penalty may arise for failure to notify chargeability (see section 7).

Penalty for failure to submit a return

HMRC can impose fixed penalties and tax geared penalties for the failure to submit a return, depending on the length of the delay.

See section 7 for the detail on the penalties that can be imposed.

Determination of tax due if no return is filed

Where a self-assessment tax return is not filed by the filing date, HMRC may determine the amount of tax due. The impact of this is:

- The determination is treated as a self-assessment by the taxpayer.

- The determination can only be replaced by the actual self-assessment when it is submitted by the taxpayer (i.e. the submission of a tax return).

- There is no appeal against a determination, which therefore encourages the taxpayer to displace it with the actual self-assessment.

A determination can be made at any time within **three years** of the filing date (i.e. by 31 January 2017 for 2012/13 tax return).

Records

Taxpayers are required to keep and preserve records necessary to make a correct and complete return.

Taxpayers with a business

For a business (including the letting of property), the records that must be kept include:

- all receipts and expenses

- all goods purchased and sold

- all supporting documents relating to the transactions of the business, such as accounts, books, contracts, vouchers and receipts.

These taxpayers (i.e. the self-employed), must keep all their records (not just those relating to the business) until five years after the 31 January filing date.

For 2012/13 records must therefore be retained until 31 January 2019.

Other taxpayers

For other taxpayers, they are likely to have fewer records, but should keep evidence of income received such as dividend vouchers, P60s, copies of P11Ds and bank statements.

The records for these taxpayers must be retained until the **later** of:

- 12 months after the 31 January filing date (31 January 2015 for 2012/13)
- the date on which an enquiry into the return is completed
- the date on which it becomes impossible for an enquiry to be started.

Penalty for not keeping records

A penalty may be charged for failure to keep or retain adequate records.

The maximum penalty is only likely to be imposed in the most serious cases such as where a taxpayer deliberately destroys his records in order to obstruct an HMRC enquiry.

See section 7 for the detail on penalties which can be imposed.

2 Payment of tax

A taxpayer is required to settle liabilities by 31 January following the end of the tax year for:

- income tax
- Class 4 national insurance
- capital gains.

For 2012/13 this is by 31 January 2014.

Payments on account

For certain taxpayers, payments on account (POAs) may also be required.

If the taxpayer had an income tax liability in the previous year in excess of any tax deducted at source, a POA is normally required for the following year.

The exceptions to this are if:

- the relevant amount for the previous year is less than £1,000, or
- more than 80% of the income tax liability for the previous year was met by deduction of tax at source.

The impact of these provisions is that most employed people will not have to make POAs, since at least 80% of their tax liability is paid through PAYE.

Due dates

For those taxpayers who are required to make POAs, the payment dates for 2012/13 are:

- first POA – 31 January 2013
- second POA – 31 July 2013.

Any remaining liability is then settled on the 31 January 2014 due date.

POAs are only required for:

- income tax
- Class 4 National Insurance Contributions (NICs).

No POAs are ever required for capital gains tax.

In 2012/13 the payment dates for Class 2 NICs are aligned with the self assessment POAs but they are paid separately and are not part of the POA self assessment payment system.

Calculation of POAs

POAs are calculated using the previous year's 'relevant amount'. Therefore the POAs for 2012/13 are based on the 'relevant amount' for 2011/12.

The 'relevant amount' is calculated as:

	£
Total tax liability for the year (income tax and Class 4 NICs)	X
Less: Amounts paid at source	
(e.g. PAYE, tax on bank and building society interest, dividend tax credits)	(X)
Relevant amount	X

Note: No POAs are required if there is no 'relevant amount' in the previous year. Therefore, for example, a taxpayer who commences self-employment on 1 May 2012 will not have to make POAs for 2012/13, since he or she will not have a 'relevant amount' for 2011/12.

Example 1 – Payment of tax

Roderick, who is 47, is required to make payments on account of his 2012/13 tax liability. His income tax payable for 2011/12 was £5,100. Of this, £1,250 was collected via PAYE.

Calculate Roderick's POAs for 2012/13.

Answer to example 1

The relevant amount for the previous year is £3,850 (£5,100 – £1,250).

As this is exceeds £1,000 and exceeds 20% of the total tax liability (20% × £5,100 = £1,020), POAs are required.

The amounts payable as POAs are based on an **equal** division of the 'relevant amount' for the previous year's tax payable, hence (£3,850 × 1/2) = £1,925.

Roderick is required to make two POAs of £1,925 on 31 January 2013 and 31 July 2013.

Test your understanding 1

Ahmed's tax liability for 2011/12 was as follows:

	£
Income tax	9,400
Less: Tax deducted at source	(2,100)
	7,300
Class 4 NIC	700
CGT	3,500
	11,500
Total tax liability	11,500

Calculate Ahmed's POAs for 2012/13.

Claims to reduce POAs

- A taxpayer can claim to reduce POAs, at any time before 31 January following the tax year, if he expects the actual income tax and Class 4 NIC liability (net of tax deducted at source) for 2012/13 to be lower than 2011/12.

- The claim must state the grounds for making the claim.

Following a claim:

- The POAs will be reduced.

- Each POA will be for half the reduced amount, unless the taxpayer claims that there is no tax liability at all.

- If POAs are paid before the claim, then HMRC will refund the overpayment.

Incorrect claims to reduce POAs

A taxpayer should only claim to reduce POAs if the tax liability (net of tax deducted at source) for the current year is expected to be less than the POAs based on the previous year's 'relevant amount'.

In the event that the claim is incorrect and the actual tax liability for the current year turns out to be higher than the reduced POAs, then the following consequences arise:

- Interest will be charged on the tax underpaid.

- A penalty may be charged if a taxpayer fraudulently or negligently claims to reduce POAs. See section 7 for the detail on penalties which can be imposed.

- A penalty will not be sought in cases of innocent error. The aim is to penalise taxpayers who claim large reductions in payments on account without any foundation to the claim.

Balancing payments

The balancing payment is due on 31 January following the tax year.

For 2012/13 this will be 31 January 2014.

The balancing payment is calculated as:

	£	£
Total tax liability for the year		X
(Income tax, Class 4 NIC and CGT)		
Less: Amounts deducted at source	X	
Less: POAs	X	
	—	(X)
		—
Balancing payment		X
		—

- It is possible that a balancing repayment will be due, in which case HMRC will repay the amount of tax overpaid.

- Where the amount of tax due changes as a result of an amendment to the self-assessment (by either the taxpayer or HMRC), any additional tax due must be paid within 30 days of the notice of amendment if this is later than the normal due date.

Example 2 – Payment of tax

Continuing the example of Roderick from above. You now learn that his final liability for 2012/13 is £7,629. Of this amount £1,635 has been collected via the PAYE system.

State the total amount payable by Roderick on 31 January 2014 and what the payment relates to.

Answer to example 2

The payment made on 31 January 2014 will comprise two parts:

- the balancing payment for 2012/13

- the first POA for 2013/14.

The balancing payment for 2012/13 will be based on the final liability for 2012/13 less amounts collected at source and the POAs already made.

	£
2012/13 – IT liability	7,629
Less: PAYE	(1,635)
Less: POAs	(3,850)
	———
Balancing payment	2,144
	———

The first POA for 2013/14 will be 50% of the 'relevant amount' using the 2012/13 position.

	£
2012/13 – IT liability	7,629
Less: PAYE	(1,635)
Relevant amount	5,994

The first POA is (£5,994 × 1/2) = £2,997

Summary:	£
Balancing payment – 2012/13	2,144
First POA – 2013/14	2,997
Total payable by 31 January 2014	5,141

Test your understanding 2

Peter's tax payable for 2012/13 is as follows:

	£
Income tax	10,800
Less: Tax deducted at source (PAYE)	(2,500)
	8,300
Class 4 NIC	800
CGT	4,600
Total tax payable	13,700

He made POAs of £8,000 in respect of 2012/13.

Identify the balancing payment to be made for 2012/13, the first POA for 2013/14 and state the due date for payment of both.

3 Interest and penalties

There are two key types of interest:

- Late payment interest
  - calculated at 3% p.a.
- Repayment interest
  - calculated at 0.5% p.a.

The interest rates will be provided in the Tax Rates and Allowances section of the exam.

Late payment interest

Interest will automatically be charged if **any** tax is paid late.

Interest can arise in respect of:

- payments on account
- balancing payments
- any tax payable following an amendment to a self-assessment
- any tax payable following a discovery assessment.

All interest is charged

- from: the date the tax was due to be paid
- to: the date of payment.

The interest payable is calculated on a daily basis and is due for the period up to and including the day before the actual payment date (but not for the day of payment itself as the tax is not outstanding on that day).

> ### Example 3 – Interest
>
> A taxpayer pays his 2012/13 POAs on 15 March 2013 and 10 August 2013. The balancing payment is paid on 15 April 2014.
>
> **Identify the payments that will attract interest and state the period for which interest will be charged.**

Answer to example 3

Interest will be charged as follows:

- first POA: from 31 January 2013 to 14 March 2013
- second POA: from 31 July 2013 to 9 August 2013
- balancing payment: from 31 January 2014 to 14 April 2014.

Test your understanding 3

Rodney was due to make the following payments of tax for 2012/13.

Due Date	Payment	Actual date of payment
31 January 2013	£2,100	28 February 2013
31 July 2013	£2,100	31 August 2013
31 January 2014	£1,000	31 March 2014

Identify the periods for which interest will be charged.

Calculate to the nearest penny, the amount of interest payable on a daily basis assuming a 3% interest rate.

In examinations, if required, calculations are performed to the nearest month and £ unless indicated otherwise in the question.

Interest on incorrect claims to reduce POAs

- Interest will be charged where an excessive claim is made to reduce POAs.
- The charge is based on the difference between the amounts actually paid and the amounts that should have been paid.

  The amount that should have been paid is the lower of:

  - the original POAs based on the 'relevant amount' for the previous year
  - 50% of the final tax liability (excluding CGT, and net of tax deducted at source) for the current year.

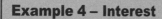

Example 4 – Interest

A taxpayer's relevant amount for 2011/12 is £5,000 (POAs for 2012/13 are therefore £2,500), but a claim is made to reduce the POAs to £1,000 each. These payments are made on time.

Subsequently the taxpayer identifies the actual tax liability (net of tax deducted at source) for 2012/13 to be £4,500. The correct balancing payment (i.e. £4,500 – £2,000 = £2,500) is paid on 31 January 2014.

Identify the amounts on which interest is to be charged and state the period(s) for which interest will be charged.

Answer to example 4

POAs should have been reduced to £2,250 (£4,500 × 1/2) rather than £1,000. Interest will therefore be charged as follows:

- on £1,250 from 31 January 2013 to 30 January 2014
- on £1,250 from 31 July 2013 to 30 January 2014.

Example 5 – Interest

Herbert's POAs for 2012/13 based on his income tax liability for 2011/12 were £4,500 each. However, Herbert made a claim to reduce these amounts to £3,500.

He made his interim POAs for 2012/13 as follows:

Payment	£	Date
First POA	3,500	29 January 2013
Second POA	3,500	12 August 2013

Herbert's eventual liability for 2012/13 was agreed as follows:

Income tax liability (net of tax deducted at source)	£10,000
Capital gains tax	£2,500

Herbert paid the balance of the tax due £5,500 on 19 February 2014.

Identify the amounts on which interest is to be charged and state the period(s) for which interest will be charged.

Answer to example 5

POAs should not have been reduced, therefore the amounts that should have been paid, on each of the due dates was £4,500.

First POA:

£3,500 is paid on time.

Interest charge therefore only levied on £1,000 that should also have been paid.

Levied for the period 31 January 2013 to 18 February 2014.

Second POA:

£3,500, as well as being the wrong amount, was also paid late.

On £3,500, interest charged 31 July 2013 to 11 August 2013.

On the additional £1,000 not paid, interest levied for the period 31 July 2013 to 18 February 2014.

On balancing payment:

Income tax of £9,000 (£4,500 × 2) has been dealt with above, so it is only the remaining £1,000 that will incur an interest charge, from 31 January 2014 to 18 February 2014.

Capital gains tax of £2,500 incurs interest from 31 January 2014 to 18 February 2014.

Repayment interest

Interest may be paid by HMRC on any overpayment of tax.

If applicable, interest runs:

- from: the later of:
    - the date the tax was due, or
    - the date HMRC actually received the tax
- to: the date of repayment.

Where interest is paid, it is only paid on the amount of tax that should have been paid (i.e. deliberate overpayments will not attract interest).

Penalties for late payments

Late payment interest is not a penalty, since it merely aims to compensate for the advantage of paying late.

Therefore, to further encourage compliance, penalties can also be imposed by HMRC where income tax, Class 4 NIC or CGT is paid late.

Penalties do not apply to POAs.

Penalties are calculated as follows:

Tax paid (Note)	Penalty (% of tax due)
More than 1 month late	5%
More than 6 months late	Additional 5%
More than 12 months late	Additional 5%

Technically the penalties apply if tax is paid more than 30 days late, 5 months and 30 days late and 11 months and 30 days late, but the examiner's article gives these time limits to the nearest month.

HMRC have the discretion to reduce a penalty in special circumstances, for example if they consider that the penalty would be inappropriate or disproportionate. However, the inability to pay will not be classified as special circumstances.

For details of other penalties relating to self assessment, see section 7.

Example 6 – Interest and penalties

A taxpayer's balancing payment due for 2012/13 is £5,000. Only £1,200 of this was paid on 31 January 2014.

Set out the interest and penalties that will be payable and state the implication of continued non-payment of the liability.

Answer to example 6

Interest

Interest will be charged on £3,800 from 31 January 2014 to the date of payment.

Penalties

A penalty of £190 (£3,800 at 5%) will be due if the tax of £3,800 is not paid by 1 March 2014.

A further penalty of £190 will be due if the tax is not paid by 31 July 2014, and again if the tax is not paid by 31 January 2015.

Test your understanding 4

Rowena's tax payable (after credits but before POAs) for 2012/13 is:

Income tax	£6,000
Capital gains tax	£3,000

POAs of £4,000 in total were made on the relevant dates. The balance of the tax due was paid as follows:

Income tax	1 March 2014
Capital gains tax	1 April 2014

Calculate the interest and penalties due.

Assume the rate of late payment interest is 3% p.a. and calculate on a monthly basis.

4 Claims

- A claim for a relief, allowance or repayment can be made to HMRC, usually via the tax return.

- The amount of the claim must be quantified at the time that the claim is made. For example, if loss relief is claimed, then the amount of the loss must be stated.

- Wherever possible the taxpayer must include claims in his or her self-assessment tax return.

KAPLAN PUBLISHING

Claims for earlier years

Certain claims will relate to earlier years. The most obvious example of this is the claiming of loss relief for earlier years.

The basic rule is that such a claim is:

- established in the later year
- calculated based on the tax liability of the earlier year.

The tax liability for the earlier year is not adjusted. Instead, the tax reduction resulting from the claim will be set off against the tax liability for the later year. The logic is that it avoids re-opening assessments for earlier years.

Alternatively if a separate claim is made HMRC will refund the tax due.

As the claim is only quantified by reference to the earlier year, POAs that are based on the relevant amount for the earlier year, will not change.

Example 7 – Claims for earlier years

A taxpayer's relevant amount for 2011/12 is £4,400. In 2012/13 the taxpayer makes a trading loss of £1,000, and makes a claim to offset this against his total income of 2011/12.

Explain how the taxpayer will receive the tax refund arising as a result of the relief for the loss arising in 2012/13.

Answer to example 7

The taxpayer's POAs for 2012/13 are £2,200 (£4,400 × 1/2), and these will not change as a result of the loss relief claim.

The tax refund due will be calculated at the taxpayer's marginal income tax rate(s) for 2011/12.

The tax refund due will either be set off against the 2012/13 tax liability, thereby affecting the balancing payment on 31 January 2014, or if there is insufficient tax left owing, HMRC will make a refund.

Claims for overpayment relief

Where an assessment is excessive due to an error or mistake in a return, the taxpayer can claim relief. The claim must be made within four years of the end of the tax year concerned.

For 2012/13 the claim must be made by 5 April 2017.

A claim can be made in respect of errors made, and mistakes arising from not understanding the law.

5 Compliance checks

HMRC's right of enquiry

HMRC have the right to enquire into the completeness and accuracy of any self-assessment tax return under their compliance check powers.

The enquiry may be made as a result of any of the following:

- a suspicion that income is undeclared

- deductions being incorrectly claimed

- other information in HMRC's possession

- being part of a random review process.

Additional points:

- HMRC do not have to state a reason for the enquiry and are unlikely to do so.

- An enquiry can be made even if HMRC calculated the taxpayer's tax liability.

- HMRC must give written notice before commencing an enquiry.

- The written notice must be issued within 12 months of the date the return is filed with HMRC. Once this deadline is passed, the taxpayer can normally consider the self-assessment for that year as final.

Enquiry procedures

HMRC can demand that the taxpayer produces any or all of the following:

- documents
- accounts
- other written particulars
- full answers to specific questions.

The information requested by HMRC should be limited to that connected with the return.

An appeal can be made against the request.

The enquiry ends when HMRC gives written notice that it has been completed. The notice will state the outcome of the enquiry.

The closure notice must include either:

- confirmation that no amendments are required
- HMRC's amendments to the self-assessment.

The taxpayer has 30 days to appeal against any amendments by HMRC. The appeal must be in writing.

Discovery assessment

HMRC must normally begin enquiries into a self-assessment return within 12 months of the date the return is filed, however a discovery assessment can be raised at a later date to prevent the loss of tax.

The use of a discovery assessment is restricted where a self assessment has already been made:

- Unless the loss of tax was brought about carelessly or deliberately by the taxpayer, a discovery assessment cannot be raised where full disclosure was made in the return, even if this is found to be incorrect.
- HMRC will only accept that full disclosure has been made if any contentious items have been clearly brought to their attention – perhaps in a covering letter or in the 'white space' on the tax return.

- Information lying in the attached accounts will not constitute full disclosure if its significance is not emphasised.

- Only a taxpayer who makes full disclosure in the tax return has absolute finality 12 months after the date the return is filed.

The time limit for issuing a discovery assessment is:

	Time from end of tax year	For 2012/13
Basic time limit	Four years	5 April 2017
Careless error	Six years	5 April 2019
Deliberate error	Twenty years	5 April 2033

A discovery assessment may be appealed against.

Information and inspection powers

- HMRC has one set of powers to inspect business records, assets and premises.

- The regime covers income tax, capital gains tax, corporation tax, VAT and PAYE.

- HMRC also have a single approach across all taxes to asking taxpayers for supplementary information, based on written formal information notices with a right of appeal.

  They can also request information from third parties provided either the taxpayer or the new First-tier Tax Tribunal agrees (section 6).

  Collection of data from third party bulk data gatherers (e.g. banks, building societies and stockbrokers) are included in these powers.

6 Appeals

A taxpayer can appeal against a decision made by HMRC, but they must do so within 30 days of the disputed decision.

Most appeals are then settled amicably by discussion between the taxpayer and HMRC.

However, if the taxpayer is not satisfied with the outcome of the discussions, they can proceed in one of two ways:

- request that their case is reviewed by another HMRC officer, or
- have their case referred to an independent Tax Tribunal.

If the taxpayer opts to have their case reviewed but disagrees with the outcome, they can still send their appeal to the Tax Tribunal.

The taxpayer must also apply to postpone all or part of the tax charged. Otherwise they will have to pay the disputed amount.

Tax Tribunals

The Tax Tribunal is an independent body administered by the Tribunals Service of the Ministry of Justice. Cases are heard by independently appointed tax judges and/or panel members. Each panel is appointed according to the needs of the case.

There are two tiers (layers) of the Tax Tribunal system:

- First-tier Tribunal, and
- Upper Tribunal.

First-tier Tribunal

The First-tier will be the first tribunal for most issues. They deal with:

- *Default paper cases:* simple appeals, (e.g. against a fixed penalty) – will usually be disposed of without a hearing provided both sides agree.
- *Basic cases:* straightforward appeals involving a minimal exchange of paperwork in advance of a short hearing.
- *Standard cases:* appeals involving more detailed consideration of issues and a more formal hearing.
- *Complex cases:* some complex appeals may be heard by the First-tier however they will usually be heard by the Upper Tribunal.

If the dispute is not resolved at the First-tier level then the appeal can go to the Upper Tribunal.

Upper Tribunal

The Upper Tribunal will mainly, but not exclusively, review and decide appeals from the First-tier Tribunal on a point of law.

In addition, they will also deal with:

- Complex cases requiring detailed specialist knowledge and a formal hearing – cases involving long and complicated issues, points of principle and large financial amounts which do not go through the First-tier Tribunal stage.

- Judicial review work delegated from the High Court and Court of Session.

- The enforcement of decisions, directions and orders made by Tribunals.

Hearings are held in public and decisions are published.

A decision of the Upper Tribunal may be appealed to the Court of Appeal. However, the grounds of appeal must always relate to a point of law.

The overriding objective of the tribunal rules is to allow cases to be dealt with fairly and justly. The tribunal system aims to avoid delays and unnecessary expense.

7 Penalties

Standard penalties

HMRC has standardised penalties across taxes for different offences.

The standard penalty applies to two key areas:

- submission of incorrect returns – all taxes
- failure to notify liability to tax – income tax, CGT, corporation tax, VAT and NIC.

The penalty is calculated as a percentage of 'potential lost revenue' which is generally the tax unpaid as a result of the error or failure to notify.

Taxpayer behaviour	Maximum penalty (% of revenue lost)
Genuine mistake (for incorrect returns)	No Penalty
Careless / Failure to take reasonable care	30%
Deliberate but no concealment	70%
Deliberate with concealment	100%

An incorrect return:

- must result in an understatement of the taxpayer's liability, and
- no reasonable steps have been taken to notify HMRC of the error.
- Includes:
  - deliberately supplying false information
  - deliberately withholding information
  - failure to supply a return
  - inflating a loss and / or claims for allowances and reliefs
  - inflating a tax repayment claim
  - submitting incorrect accounts in relation to a liability.

If there is more than one error in a return, a separate penalty can be charged for each error.

Failure to notify liability to tax applies where:

- the taxpayer has a liability to tax, and notification is required
- but notification of chargeability is not made to HMRC.

The maximum penalties can be reduced where:

- the taxpayer informs HMRC of the error (i.e. makes a disclosure), and
- co-operates with HMRC to establish the amount of tax unpaid
- with larger reductions given for unprompted disclosure.

An unprompted disclosure is where a taxpayer:

- makes a disclosure
- when they have no reason to believe that HMRC have, or are about to, discover the error.

A taxpayer can appeal to the First Tier of the Tax Tribunal against:

- a penalty being charged, and
- the amount of the penalty.

Penalties for late filing of returns

Standardised penalties are also being introduced for the late filing of tax returns in phases. However, for F6, in the 2013 sittings, these rules apply for individuals only.

Date return is filed	Penalty
– within 3 months of due date	– £100 fixed penalty
– between 3 – 6 months of due date	– Daily penalties of £10 per day (maximum 90 days)
– between 6 – 12 months of due date	– Additional 5% of tax due (minimum £300)
– more than 12 months after due date where withholding information was:	
– not deliberate	– Additional 5% of tax due (minimum £300)
– deliberate but no concealment	– 70% of tax due (minimum £300)
– deliberate with concealment	– 100% of tax due (minimum £300)

These penalties for submitting a return more than 12 months late can be reduced by prompted / unprompted disclosure.

Penalties for late payment of tax

Covered in section 3 of this chapter.

Other penalties

Offence	Penalty	
Penalty for fraud or negligence on claiming reduced payments on account		£
	POAs actually paid	X
	Less: POAs if claims not made	(X)
		X
Failure to keep and retain required records	Up to £3,000 per year of assessment	

8 The PAYE system

Pay as you earn (PAYE) is the system used for collecting income tax and national insurance at source from the earnings paid to employees:

- All payments of earnings assessable as employment income are subject to deduction of tax under the PAYE system.

- In many cases, the PAYE system removes the need to file a formal self-assessment tax return since the correct amount of tax will have been deducted from earnings.

- All employers making payments of earnings are required to deduct the appropriate amount of tax from each payment (or repay over-deductions) by reference to PAYE tax tables.

- The aim of the tax tables is for the tax deducted from payments to date to correspond with the correct proportion to date of the total tax liability (after allowances and reliefs) of the employee for the year.

Coding notice

To enable the employer to match the tax collected with the particular tax affairs of the individual taxpayer, HMRC issues a tax coding.

The system enables different amounts of tax to be collected from different taxpayers according to their personal circumstances.

Coding notice

- From the information supplied in his or her tax return, each employee is sent a coding notice that sets out the total reliefs and allowances available to him for the year.

- The last digit is removed to arrive at the code number shown. Thus, allowances of £8,105 become 810.

- The employer is also notified of the code number.

- Using this code number and a set of tax tables, the employer can calculate the correct amount of tax each week or month.

- Most code numbers issued to the employer carry a suffix of which the most usual is L. The letter L denotes that just the ordinary personal allowance of £8,105 has been given

- These letters are added in order to simplify the revision of codes, e.g. when the personal allowance is increased from one tax year to the next, all code numbers with the suffix L can easily be increased by the employer, so that PAYE can continue to operate effectively.

- Some code numbers carry a K prefix. This indicates that the deductions, such as benefits, to be made from allowances actually exceed the allowances. The code number is effectively 'negative'.

- Where an employee has not been allocated a code number (perhaps because the individual was previously self-employed), the employer must deduct tax under PAYE in accordance with an emergency code that reflects only the personal allowance (i.e. Code 810L). This code is applied until the correct code number is supplied by HMRC.

Tax code calculation

Allowances	£	Deductions	£
Personal allowance	X	Benefits	X
Allowable expenses	X	Adjustment for underpaid tax (must be less that £3,000)	X
Adjustment for overpaid tax	X	Other income	X
	—		—
Total allowances	X	Total deductions	X
	—		—

The tax code is:

(Total allowances less total deductions) × 1/10

The answer is then rounded down to the nearest whole number.

Calculation of deductions

PAYE is calculated on a tax deductions working sheet (P11), using tax tables provided by HMRC.

The tax tables are as follows.

Pay adjustment tables:	Based on an employee's tax code, this set of tables shows the cumulative amount of tax-free pay to which an employee is entitled for each week or month of the year.
Taxable pay tables:	Deducting tax-free pay from pay gives a figure for taxable pay. The taxable pay tables can then be used to calculate the amount of income tax due.

The tax is calculated for any given pay week or month on a cumulative basis (i.e. the tax for, say month five, is the difference between the cumulative total tax due at the end of month five compared with the cumulative total due at the end of month four).

Payments to HMRC

Employers are generally required to make monthly payments of income tax and NIC to HMRC as follows:

- The income tax and NIC that the employer deducts during each tax month is due for payment to HMRC not later than 14 days after the tax month ends.

- A tax month runs from the sixth of a month to the 5th of the following month.

- Therefore the payment due date is the 19th of each month.

- Employers whose average monthly payments of PAYE and NICs are less than £1,500 in total are allowed to make quarterly, rather than monthly, payments. Payments are due by the 19th of the month following the quarters ending 5 July, 5 October, 5 January and 5 April.

- Employers with 250 or more employees must make their monthly PAYE payments electronically on the 22nd of each month.

- Other employers who voluntarily pay their PAYE deductions electronically also get an extension to the 22nd of the month.

9 Key PAYE forms

To standardise the correspondence with HMRC, specific forms are issued for use in certain circumstances. This ensures all appropriate information is gathered and simplifies the process.

They key forms that you are required to know are:

Form	Purpose of use	Timing
P45	When employee leaves	Ongoing with staffing changes
P46	When new employee joins without P45	Ongoing with new starters
P35	Year end summary	Annually following end of tax year
P14 – P60	Year end summary	Annually following end of tax year
P11D	Summary of benefits	Provided by 6 July following tax year

Procedures on leaving or joining

Procedure to be adopted when an employee leaves

When an employee leaves an employment the PAYE system is interrupted. Forms P45 must be completed for each employee immediately after they leave employment in order that either:

- a new employer can carry on making PAYE deductions using the appropriate code and cumulative totals from the last employment

- the employee can claim a tax repayment.

Procedure to be adopted when an employee joins

The operation of the PAYE system depends upon having a tax code for each employee. The form P45 details his or her tax code, pay to date and tax to date and will allow the new employer to operate PAYE for the employee's pay.

Where form P45 cannot be produced the employee has to complete form P46 to identify the individual's circumstances so that the appropriate amount of tax can be deducted.

Most employers must file P45s and P46s online.

End-of-year procedure

The P35 and P14 returns will need to be completed at the end of each tax year.

Most employers must file their end of year returns online.

P35 employer's annual statement, declaration and certificate

This has to be submitted by 19 May, and performs the role of:

- an overall summary of tax and NIC deducted by the employer for the year

- a questionnaire to ensure compliance with PAYE arrangements

- a declaration and certificate to be signed by the employer confirming that all year-end returns have been completed.

P14 – P60 certificate of pay and tax deducted

Not later than 19 May the employer must send the first two copies of the form (P14) to HMRC, showing for each employee:

- Employee's National Insurance number
- Employer's name and address
- Personal details
- Total earnings for the year
- Final PAYE code
- Total income tax deducted for the year
- Total NIC for the year.

The third part of the form (P60) is given to the employee by 31 May in order to complete the employment pages of his self-assessment return.

10 Chapter summary

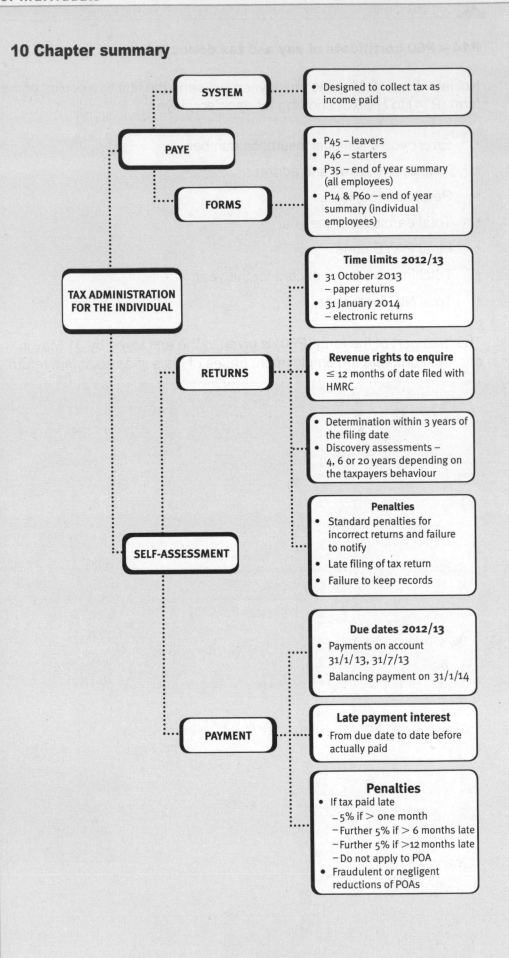

SYSTEM
- Designed to collect tax as income paid

PAYE

FORMS
- P45 – leavers
- P46 – starters
- P35 – end of year summary (all employees)
- P14 & P60 – end of year summary (individual employees)

TAX ADMINISTRATION FOR THE INDIVIDUAL

RETURNS

Time limits 2012/13
- 31 October 2013 – paper returns
- 31 January 2014 – electronic returns

Revenue rights to enquire
- ≤ 12 months of date filed with HMRC

- Determination within 3 years of the filing date
- Discovery assessments – 4, 6 or 20 years depending on the taxpayers behaviour

SELF-ASSESSMENT

Penalties
- Standard penalties for incorrect returns and failure to notify
- Late filing of tax return
- Failure to keep records

PAYMENT

Due dates 2012/13
- Payments on account 31/1/13, 31/7/13
- Balancing payment on 31/1/14

Late payment interest
- From due date to date before actually paid

Penalties
- If tax paid late
  - 5% if > one month
  - Further 5% if > 6 months late
  - Further 5% if >12 months late
  - Do not apply to POA
- Fraudulent or negligent reductions of POAs

Test your understanding answers

Test your understanding 1

Ahmed

The relevant amount is £8,000 (£7,300 + £700).

As this exceeds £1,000 and exceeds 20% of the total tax liability (20% × (£9,400 + £700) = £2,020)), POAs are required.

POAs will be due for 2012/13 as follows:

31 January 2013 (£7,300 + £700 = £8,000 × 1/2)	£4,000
31 July 2013	£4,000

Note: No POAs of capital gains tax are ever required and it is ignored in the calculations.

Test your understanding 2

Peter

	£
Total tax payable	13,700
Less: POAs	(8,000)
Balancing payment	5,700

The balancing payment comprises:

	£
Income tax and National Insurance (£8,300 + £800 − £8,000)	1,100
CGT	4,600
Balancing payment	5,700

The first POA for 2013/14 will be 50% of the 'relevant amount' using the 2012/13 position.

	£
2012/13 – IT payable (after deducting PAYE)	8,300
Class 4 NIC	800
Relevant amount	9,100

The first POA is (£9,100 × 1/2) = £4,550

Summary:

	£
Balancing payment – 2012/13	5,700
First POA – 2013/14	4,550
Total payable by 31 January 2014	10,250

Test your understanding 3

Rodney

Periods on which interest is charged:

On first POA	31 January 2013 – 27 February 2013	28 days
On second POA	31 July 2013 – 30 August 2013	31 days
On final payment	31 January 2014 – 30 March 2014	59 days

Interest payable:

On first POA	(£2,100 × 3% × 28/365) = £4.83
On second POA	(£2,100 × 3% × 31/365) = £5.35
On final payment	(£1,000 × 3% × 59/365) = £4.85

Test your understanding 4

Rowena

The relevant date for balancing payments is 31 January 2014.

No POAs are ever required for CGT.

The amounts due were therefore as follows:

| 31 January 2014 | Income tax (£6,000 – £4,000) | £2,000 |
| | Capital gains tax | £3,000 |

Interest will run as follows:

| Income tax | £2,000 from 31 January 2014 to 28 February 2014, (1/12 × 3% × £2,000) = £5 |
| CGT | £3,000 from 31 January 2014 to 31 March 2014, (2/12 × 3% × £3,000) = £15 |

In addition a penalty is due on the CGT (as it was more than one month late) of 5% of £3,000 = £150.

There is no penalty in respect of the late payment of income tax as it was paid within one month.

Total interest and penalties payable = (£5 + £15 + £150) = £170.

The penalty may be reduced if HMRC accept there were special circumstances.

Computation of gains and tax payable

Chapter learning objectives

Upon completion of this chapter you will be able to:

- identify the persons and the transactions that are liable to UK tax on capital gains
- define 'residence' and 'ordinary residence' for an individual and state its relevance for capital gains tax
- identify which assets are exempt
- understand how to calculate the gain on the disposal of an asset
- calculate the chargeable gain on the disposal of an asset for an individual
- demonstrate how capital losses can be relieved against gains for an individual
- calculate the net chargeable gains on assets after losses
- compute the amount of capital gains tax payable.

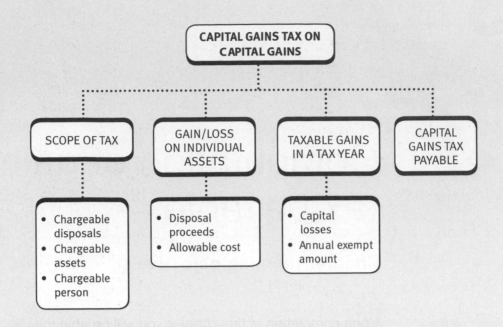

Introduction

This and the following three chapters deal with the way in which **individuals** are subject to tax on their capital gains.

The taxation of capital gains is an important topic as it will be the focus of question three, for **15 marks**, in the examination. Questions one and two may also contain an element of capital gains.

1 Scope of capital gains tax

Capital gains tax (CGT) is charged on gains arising on **chargeable disposals** of **chargeable assets** by **chargeable persons**.

Chargeable persons

Chargeable persons include individuals and companies.

In these CGT chapters we are concerned with disposals by individuals.

- Only individuals who are either:
  - UK resident or
  - UK ordinarily resident

  in the tax year in which the disposal takes place are subject to capital gains tax on their gains.

- Chargeable individuals are subject to CGT on all disposals of chargeable assets, regardless of where in the world the assets are situated.

- An individual who is neither UK resident nor UK ordinarily resident does not pay UK CGT on any assets, not even those situated in the UK.

Definition of residence and ordinary residence

The definition of residence and ordinary residence for CGT is the same as for income tax purposes (see Chapter 2).

Broadly, an individual will be a UK resident in a tax year if he is physically present in the UK for a period of six months or more.

An individual's ordinary residence is the place where the individual normally resides as opposed to his place of occasional residence.

Chargeable disposal

Chargeable disposal	Exempt disposal

The following are treated as chargeable disposals:
 	
(i) sale or gift of the whole or part of an asset
 	
(ii) exchange of an asset
 	
(iii) loss or total destruction of an asset
 	
(iv) receipts of a capital sum derived from an asset, for example:
 	
   • compensation received for damage to an asset
 	
   • receipts for the surrender of rights to an asset.
	Exempt disposals include:
	
	(i) disposals as a result of the death of an individual
	
	(ii) gifts to charities.

Chargeable assets

Chargeable assets	Exempt assets
All forms of capital assets, wherever situated, are chargeable assets. Common examples include: • Freehold land and buildings • Goodwill • Some types of leases • Unquoted shares • Quoted shares • Certain types of chattels – Chapter 14 Note: Chattels are tangible moveable assets (e.g. furniture, plant and machinery)	Exempt assets include: • Motor vehicles (including vintage cars) • Main residence • Cash • Certain types of chattels – Chapter 14 • Investments held within an ISA • Qualifying corporate bonds (QCBs) • Gilt-edged securities • National Savings Certificates • Foreign currency for private use • Receivables • Trading inventory • Prizes and betting winnings.

Note that exempt assets are outside the scope of CGT and therefore:

• gains are not taxable

• losses are not allowable.

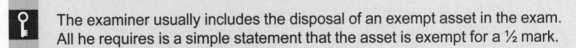

The examiner usually includes the disposal of an exempt asset in the exam. All he requires is a simple statement that the asset is exempt for a ½ mark.

Therefore, make sure you have learnt the key exempt assets, make the statement when you spot one, and do not be tempted in the exam to waste time doing unnecessary calculations on these assets.

Test your understanding 1

Which of the following disposals may give rise to a capital gain?

- Sale of shares in an unquoted trading company.

- Gift of antique painting.

- Sale of 13% Treasury stock 2018.

- Exchange, with a friend, of a house, which was not his main residence, for an apartment.

- Sale of a motor car to brother at less than market value.

- Gift of a London flat by an individual who is neither resident nor ordinarily resident in the UK.

2 Calculation of capital gain/loss on individual disposals

An individual is subject to CGT on the total **taxable gains** arising on the disposal of all assets in a tax year.

The following steps should be carried out to compute the chargeable gains tax payable by an individual for a tax year:

Step 1 Calculate the chargeable gains/allowable loss arising on the disposal of each chargeable asset separately

Step 2 Calculate the net chargeable gains arising in the tax year = (chargeable gains less allowable losses)

Step 3 Deduct capital losses brought forward

Step 4 Deduct the annual exempt amount = taxable gains

Step 5 Calculate the CGT payable for the tax year.

Pro forma – individual

Step 1: For each disposal by an individual calculate the chargeable gain/allowable loss as follows:

	£	£
Disposal proceeds		X
Less: Allowable selling costs		(X)
		—
Net disposal proceeds		X
Less: Allowable expenditure		
Cost of acquisition	X	
Incidental costs of acquisition	X	
Additional (capital) enhancement expenditure	X	
	—	(X)
		—
Chargeable gain/(allowable loss)		X/(X)
		—

Net disposal proceeds

- The disposal proceeds used in the computation is normally the sale proceeds received.

- Incidental costs arising on disposal are deducted from the gross proceeds (e.g. auctioneer's fees, estate agent fees).

- However, market value is substituted for actual gross proceeds received where:
    - the deal was not made at arm's length (e.g. a gift)
    - the law assumes that it was not made at arm's length (e.g. transfers between connected parties – see below).

Connected persons

- An individual is connected with family members, business partners and any company that he controls. For this purpose family members are:
    - ancestors, lineal descendants and their spouses/civil partners
    - brothers, sisters and their spouses/civil partners
    - his or her spouse/civil partner
    - the relatives (as above) of his or her spouse/civil partner.

KAPLAN PUBLISHING

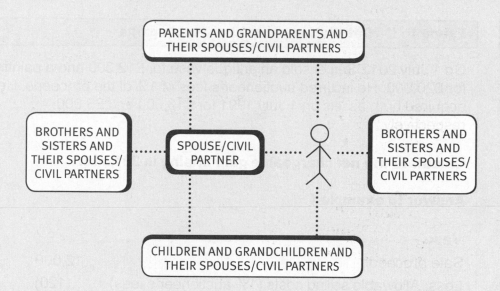

Allowable expenditure

The types of expenditure that rank as allowable deductions are:

- cost of acquisition (e.g. purchase cost)

- expenditure on enhancing the value of the asset (improvement expenditure)

- expenditure incurred to establish, preserve or defend the taxpayer's title to the asset

- incidental costs arising on the acquisition of the asset.

Where an individual acquires an asset as a gift (or from a sale for less than market value):

- the cost of acquisition = market value of the asset at the date of the gift (or sale at undervaluation).

Where an individual inherits an asset on death:

- the cost of acquisition = market value of the asset at the date of the death (i.e. probate value).

Example 1 – Calculation of net chargeable gains

On 1 July 2012 Sergei sold an antique vase for £12,000 and a painting for £20,000. He incurred auctioneer's fees of 1% of the proceeds. He acquired both assets on 1 July 1991 for £13,000 and £5,000, respectively.

Calculate the net chargeable gain arising in 2012/13.

Answer to example 1

Vase	£	£
Sale proceeds	12,000	
Less: Allowable selling costs (1% auctioneer's fees)	(120)	
	———	
Net sale proceeds	11,880	
Less: Allowable expenditure		
Cost of acquisition	(13,000)	
	———	
Allowable loss		(1,120)
Painting		
Sale proceeds	20,000	
Less: Allowable selling costs (1% auctioneer's fees)	(200)	
	———	
Net sale proceeds	19,800	
Less: Allowable expenditure		
Cost of acquisition	(5,000)	
	———	
Chargeable gain		14,800
		———
Net chargeable gain		13,680
		———

Test your understanding 2

On 1 August 2012, Margaret sold a holiday villa to her sister for £25,000. Its market value at that date was £100,000.

Margaret had acquired the villa on 1 June 1998 for £20,000 and had paid legal fees on acquisition of £500. On 1 May 2003, she had added a conservatory at a cost of £10,000.

Calculate the chargeable gain arising on the sale of the villa.

Test your understanding 3

Amanda sold a holiday cottage for £75,000 on 13 August 2012. It cost £53,500 in May 2000 and was extended in September 2004 at a cost of £16,000. The estate agent and solicitor fees for the purchase totalled £2,300 and for the sale totalled £5,400.

She also sold her grandmother's engagement ring for £12,000. She had inherited the ring on the death of her grandmother in August 2006 when the ring was valued at £9,000.

Calculate the net chargeable gain arising in 2012/13.

3 Calculation of CGT payable

An individual is subject to capital gains tax on the total taxable gains arising on the disposal of all assets in a tax year.

The following pro forma covers Steps 3 to 5 in the procedure to calculate the CGT payable by an individual.

Pro forma capital gains tax payable computation – 2012/13

	£
Net chargeable gains for the tax year	X
Less: Capital losses brought forward (see later)	(X)
	X
Less: Annual exempt amount (2012/13)	(10,600)
	X
Taxable gains	X
CGT payable (Taxable gains x 18% or 28%)	X

Annual exempt amount

Every individual is entitled to an annual exempt amount (AEA) for each tax year.

- For 2012/13, the AEA is £10,600.

- If an individual's net chargeable gains after capital losses for the tax year are:
  - £10,600 or less; they are not chargeable to tax
  - in excess of £10,600; they are chargeable to tax on the excess

- If the AEA is not utilised in any particular tax year, then it is wasted. It cannot be carried forward or backward to another tax year.

For the purpose of the examination, **taxable gain** means the **chargeable gains after deducting capital losses and the annual exempt amount**.

Capital losses

Current year capital losses

Capital losses arising on assets in the current tax year are set off:

- against chargeable gains arising in the same tax year
- to the maximum possible extent, (i.e. they cannot be restricted to avoid wasting all or part of the AEA).

Any unrelieved/unused capital losses are carried forward to offset against net chargeable gains in future years.

Brought forward capital losses

The maximum amount of brought forward losses that can be set off against gains in any tax year is restricted to the amount required to reduce the total net chargeable gains in the tax year to the level of the AEA.

Example 2 – Calculation of taxable gains in the tax year

Tom and Jerry made capital gains and allowable losses for the years 2011/12 and 2012/13 as set out below.

	Tom £	Jerry £
2011/12		
Chargeable gains	12,000	4,000
Allowable losses	8,000	7,000
2012/13		
Chargeable gains	13,000	12,300
Allowable losses	2,000	1,000

Calculate the taxable gains for Tom and Jerry for both 2011/12 and 2012/13 and the amount of any losses carried forward.

Answer to example 2

Tom – 2011/12

	£
Chargeable gains	12,000
Less: Allowable losses – current year	(8,000)
Net chargeable gains	4,000

Net chargeable gains are covered by the AEA. There are no losses to carry forward to 2012/13.

Tom – 2012/13

	£
Chargeable gains	13,000
Less: Allowable losses – current year	(2,000)
Net chargeable gains	11,000
Less: AEA	(10,600)
Taxable gains	400

Tom is taxed on gains of £400 in 2012/13.

Jerry – 2011/12

	£
Chargeable gains	4,000
Less: Allowable losses – current year	(4,000)
Net chargeable gains	Nil

Jerry is unable to use his 2011/12 AEA since his gains are all covered by current year losses. He has losses of £3,000 (£7,000 – £4,000) to carry forward to 2012/13.

Jerry – 2012/13

	£
Chargeable gains	12,300
Less: Allowable losses – current year	(1,000)
Net chargeable gains in the tax year	11,300
Less: Losses brought forward (2011/12)	(700)
	10,600
Less: AEA	(10,600)
Taxable gains	Nil

Jerry used £700 of his losses brought forward, to reduce his chargeable gains to the level of the AEA. He still has losses of £2,300 (£3,000 – £700) to carry forward to 2013/14.

Test your understanding 4

Fred and Barney made chargeable gains and allowable losses for the years 2011/12 and 2012/13 as set out below.

	Fred £	Barney £
2011/12		
Chargeable gains	15,000	5,000
Allowable losses	10,000	9,000
2012/13		
Chargeable gains	21,900	13,300
Allowable losses	11,000	2,500

Calculate the taxable gains for Fred and Barney for both 2011/12 and 2012/13 and the amount of any losses carried forward at the end of 2012/13.

Assume the 2012/13 rates and allowances apply throughout.

Computation of CGT payable

CGT is payable on the taxable gains arising in a tax year as follows:

- The rate of CGT is dependent upon the amount of a taxpayer's total taxable income.

- Taxable gains are taxed **after** taxable income (i.e. as the top slice).

- Where taxable gains fall into the basic rate band; CGT will be at 18%.

- To the extent that any gains (or any part of gains) exceed the basic rate band; they will be taxed at 28%.

- If the basic rate band is extended due to Gift Aid donations or personal pension contributions, the extended basic rate band will also be used to establish the rate of CGT.

- Any unused income tax personal allowance cannot be used to reduce taxable gains.

4 Payment of CGT

CGT is due as follows:

- On 31 January following the tax year (i.e. for 2012/13 payment must be made by 31 January 2014).

- No payments on account are ever made.

Test your understanding 5

Jade sold an investment property on 1 July 2012 for £650,000. She had acquired the building for £80,000 in June 1996 and had extended it at a cost of £30,000 in June 1998.

Jade also disposed of a painting on 1 September 2012 for £20,000, incurring auctioneer's fees of 1%. She had acquired the painting for £35,000 in April 1998.

Jade had capital losses brought forward of £16,000.

Jade's taxable income for 2012/13 is £25,000.

Calculate Jade's capital gains tax payable for 2012/13 and state the due date for payment.

5 Chapter summary

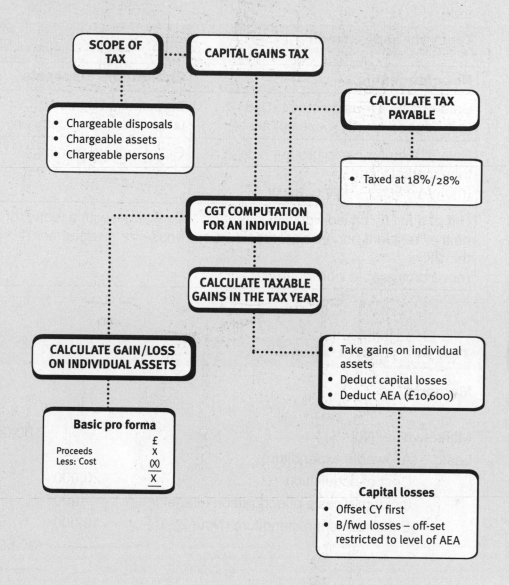

Test your understanding answers

Test your understanding 1

Not chargeable	Chargeable disposals
Sale of 13% Treasury stock 2018 (gilt-edged security – exempt asset)	Sale of shares in an unquoted trading company
Sale of a motor car to brother at less than market value (motor vehicle – exempt asset)	Gift of antique painting
Gift of a flat by an individual who is neither resident nor ordinarily resident in the UK (not a chargeable individual)	Exchange, with a friend, of a house for an apartment

Test your understanding 2

Margaret

	£	£
Market value (Note 1)		100,000
Less: Allowable expenditure		
Cost of acquisition	20,000	
Incidental costs of acquisition – legal fees	500	
Enhancement expenditure (Note 2)	10,000	
	———	(30,500)
		———
Chargeable gain		69,500
		———

Notes

(1) Market value is substituted for actual proceeds as the sale was to a connected person (Margaret's sister) and is therefore deemed to not be an 'arm's length transaction'.

(2) The conservatory is allowable expenditure as it enhanced the value of the villa.

Test your understanding 3

Amanda

Cottage

	£	£
Sale proceeds	75,000	
Less: Allowable selling costs	(5,400)	
	———	
Net sale proceeds	69,600	
Less: Allowable expenditure		
Cost of acquisition	(53,500)	
Incidental costs of acquisition	(2,300)	
Extension	(16,000)	
	———	
Allowable loss		(2,200)

Ring

	£	£
Sale proceeds	12,000	
Less: Probate value	(9,000)	
	———	
Chargeable gain		3,000
		———
Net chargeable gain		800
		———

Test your understanding 4

Fred
2011/12

	£
Chargeable gains	15,000
Less: Allowable losses – current year	(10,000)
	———
Net chargeable gains	5,000
	———

Net chargeable gains are covered by the AEA. There are no losses to carry forward to 2012/13.

2012/13	£
Chargeable gains	21,900
Less: Allowable losses – current year	(11,000)
Net chargeable gains	10,900
Less: AEA	(10,600)
Taxable gains	300

Fred is taxed on gains of £300 in 2012/13.

Barney

2011/12	£
Chargeable gains	5,000
Less: Allowable losses – current year	(5,000)
Net chargeable gains	Nil

Barney is unable to use his 2011/12 AEA since his gains are all covered by current year losses. He has losses of £4,000 (£9,000 – £5,000) to carry forward to 2012/13.

2012/13	£
Chargeable gains	13,300
Less: Allowable losses – current year	(2,500)
Net chargeable gains for year	10,800
Less: Losses brought forward (2011/12)	(200)
	10,600
Less: AEA	(10,600)
Taxable gains	Nil

Barney used £200 of his losses brought forward, to reduce his chargeable gains to the level of the AEA. He still has losses of £3,800 (£4,000 – £200) to carry forward to 2013/14.

Test your understanding 5

Jade
Capital gains tax computation – 2012/13

	£	£
Investment property		
Sale proceeds	650,000	
Less: Allowable expenditure		
Cost of acquisition	(80,000)	
Enhancement expenditure	(30,000)	
	‾‾‾‾‾‾	
Chargeable gain		540,000
Painting		
Sale proceeds	20,000	
Less: Allowable selling costs	(200)	
	‾‾‾‾‾‾	
Net sale proceeds	19,800	
Less: Allowable expenditure		
Cost of acquisition	(35,000)	
	‾‾‾‾‾‾	
Allowable loss		(15,200)
		‾‾‾‾‾‾
Net chargeable gains arising in the tax year		524,800
Less: Capital losses brought forward		(16,000)
		‾‾‾‾‾‾
Net chargeable gains		508,800
Less: AEA		(10,600)
		‾‾‾‾‾‾
Taxable gains		498,200
£		‾‾‾‾‾‾
9,370 × 18% (W)		1,687
488,830 × 28%		136,872
‾‾‾‾‾‾		
498,200		
‾‾‾‾‾‾		
Capital gains tax payable		138,559
		‾‾‾‾‾‾
Due date of payment		31 January 2014

Working:

Basic rate band remaining = (£34,370 – £25,000) = £9,370

Computation of gains: Special rules

Chapter learning objectives

Upon completion of this chapter you will be able to:

- show the tax treatment of a capital asset when the transfer is between spouses or registered civil partners

- calculate the chargeable gain when there is a part disposal of an asset

- define a wasting and non-wasting chattel

- identify when chattels and wasting assets are exempt

- compute the chargeable gain/allowable loss when a chattel is disposed of

- calculate the chargeable gain/allowable loss when a chargeable wasting asset is disposed of

- explain why the disposal of plant and machinery does not create a capital loss

- identify the tax treatment where an asset is lost/destroyed

- identify the tax treatment where an asset is damaged.

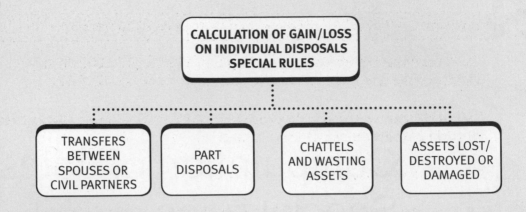

Introduction

The basic pro forma for calculating gains on the disposal of assets is adapted by special rules in the following circumstances:

- transfers between spouses or civil partners
- part disposals
- chattels and wasting assets
- assets lost or destroyed
- damaged assets.

1 Transfers between spouses or civil partners

Where an asset is transferred between spouses or civil partners:

- no gain or loss arises on the transfer
- any actual proceeds are ignored
- the transferor is deemed to dispose of the asset at its acquisition cost
- the deemed proceeds of the transferor are treated as the deemed acquisition cost of the transferee (i.e. the recipient spouse acquires the asset at its original acquisition cost).

However note that these rules only apply whilst the spouses or civil partners are living together (i.e. not separated).

Example 1 – Transfers between spouses and civil partners

David purchased some jewellery in August 1995 for £50,000. In July 2012 he gave it to his wife Victoria when it was worth £200,000.

Calculate the deemed sale proceeds of David's disposal and state Victoria's deemed acquisition cost.

Answer to example 1

David is deemed to have transferred the asset at its acquisition cost so that no gain or loss arises on the transfer.

The deemed proceeds are therefore £50,000 and Victoria's deemed acquisition cost is the same as David's deemed proceeds (i.e. £50,000).

Subsequent disposal by transferee

On a subsequent disposal of the transferred asset by the transferee, the deemed acquisition cost (often referred to as the base cost of the asset) is the original acquisition cost by the first spouse.

Example 2 – Subsequent disposal

Jack acquired a holiday cottage for £29,175 on 1 September 1987 and transferred it to his wife, Jill, on 31 August 2008. Jill sold the cottage to a third party on 31 January 2013 for £42,000.

Compute the chargeable gain on Jill's disposal in January 2013.

Answer to example 2

	£
Sale proceeds	42,000
Less: Deemed acquisition cost (Base cost)	(29,175)
Chargeable gain	12,825

Test your understanding 1

John acquired a warehouse for £100,000 on 1 September 1994. On 1 May 2008 he gave the warehouse to his wife, Tania, when it was worth £300,000. Tania sold the warehouse for £350,000 on 1 July 2012.

Tania had no other capital disposals in 2012/13, but has capital losses brought forward of £11,300. Her taxable income for 2012/13 is £45,000.

Calculate Tania's capital gains tax payable in 2012/13.

Planning opportunities

Married couples and civil partners can transfer assets between them at no tax cost (i.e. the assets are transferred at no gain/no loss). This provides opportunities to minimise their total capital gains tax liability.

They can transfer assets between them to maximise the use of:

- each individual's annual exempt amount
- each individual's basic rate band, and
- capital losses.

Example 3 – Planning opportunities

Adam, who is married to Kerry, made three chargeable disposals in the tax year 2012/13, as follows:

Asset 1	Chargeable gain	£10,500
Asset 2	Chargeable gain	£22,000
Asset 3	Chargeable gain	£46,000

Adam's taxable income for the year is £32,600, whilst Kerry has no taxable income.

(a) **Calculate Adam's CGT payable for 2012/13.**

(b) **Advise how tax savings could have been made by the couple, and calculate the revised CGT payable by the couple assuming they had taken your advice.**

Answer to example 3

(a) **Adam's CGT payable – 2012/13**

	£
Asset 1	10,500
Asset 2	22,000
Asset 3	46,000
Total chargeable gains	78,500
Less: AEA	(10,600)
Taxable gains	67,900

	£		£
Basic rate (£34,370 – £32,600)	1,770	x 18%	319
Higher rate	66,130	x 28%	18,516
	67,900		
Capital gains tax payable			18,835

(b) **Advice**

As a married couple, Kerry and Adam can transfer assets between themselves at nil gain/nil loss (i.e. at no tax cost).

Accordingly, they should transfer assets between themselves to ensure that they both use their AEAs and basic rate bands.

If Adam had transferred Asset 3 to Kerry, then the gain on the asset would be reduced by her AEA of £10,600 and taxed largely at 18%.

Adam's revised CGT payable for the year is as follows:

	£
Asset 1	10,500
Asset 2	22,000
	32,500
Less: AEA	(10,600)
Taxable gain	21,900

	£		
Basic rate (£34,370 – £32,600)	1,770	x 18%	319
Higher rate	20,130	x 28%	5,636
	21,900		
Capital gains tax liability			5,955

Kerry's CGT payable would be:

	£
Asset 3	46,000
Less: AEA	(10,600)
Taxable gain	35,400

	£		£
Basic rate	34,370	x 18%	6,187
Higher rate	1,030	x 28%	288
	35,400		
Capital gains tax liability			6,475

Total CGT payable (£5,955 + £6,475)	12,430
Tax saving (£18,835 – £12,430)	6,405

Alternative calculation:

Use of Kerry's AEA (£10,600 × 28%)	2,968
Use of Kerry's basic rate band (£34,370 × (28% – 18%))	3,437
	6,405

2 Part disposals

When there is a part disposal of an asset, we need to identify how much of the original cost of the asset relates to the part of the asset disposed of.

- The allowable expenditure of the part of the asset disposed of is calculated using the following formula:

    Cost x A / (A + B)

    Where: A = Value of the part disposed of
    B = Market value of the remainder at the time of the part disposal.

- The allowable expenditure, calculated using the formula, is then used in the basic capital gains tax computation as normal.

Example 4 – Part disposal

Yayha acquired 20 acres of land in March 1998 for £6,000. On 1 August 2012, he disposed of 8 acres for £8,000. The value of the remaining 12 acres at this date was £15,000.

On 1 September 2012, Yayha sold the remainder of the land for £18,000.

Calculate the chargeable gains arising on the disposals of land in 2012/13.

Answer to example 4

1 August 2012 disposal

	£
Sale proceeds	8,000
Less: Deemed cost of part disposed of £6,000 × £8,000/(£8,000 + £15,000)	(2,087)
Chargeable gain	5,913

Note that the number of acres owned and sold is irrelevant in calculating the cost of the land disposed of.

Always use the (A/A + B) formula, which uses the **value** of the asset disposed of and retained.

1 September 2012 disposal

	£
Sale proceeds	18,000
Less: Deemed cost of the remainder (£6,000 – £2,087 (above))	(3,913)
Chargeable gain	14,087

Test your understanding 2

Jacob bought 10 acres of land for £8,000 in August 2002. He sold 3 acres of the land for £20,000 in January 2013. At that time the remaining land was worth £60,000.

In March 2013 Jacob sold the remaining acres for £75,000.

Jacob's taxable income for 2012/13 is £15,000.

Calculate the capital gains tax payable for 2012/13 and state the due date of payment.

Test your understanding 3

Gemma bought an investment property in May 2000 for £50,000. On 1 July 2006 she disposed of part of the land attached to the property for £40,000. The value of the property and the remaining land at this date was £100,000.

On 1 August 2012 Gemma sold the property and remaining land for £200,000.

Gemma's taxable income for 2012/13 is £50,000.

Calculate the capital gains tax payable for 2012/13.

3 Chattels and wasting assets

It is important to be able to identify a chattel and a wasting asset as there are special rules for calculating the gain or loss arising on them.

Chattels

Chattels are defined as tangible moveable property (e.g. a picture or table).

Note that the asset must be:

- moveable – therefore a building is not a chattel
- tangible – therefore shares are not chattels.

Wasting assets

A wasting asset is an asset with a predictable life not exceeding 50 years.

Chattels may be wasting or non-wasting as follows.

	Wasting chattels	Non-wasting chattels
Expected life	Not exceeding 50 years	More than 50 years
Examples	Greyhound Boat Plant and machinery Racehorse	Antiques Jewellery Paintings

Plant and machinery is deemed to have a useful life of less than 50 years and is therefore **always** a wasting chattel (but see below).

Chattels – exempt disposals

Certain disposals of chattels are exempt from capital gains tax as follows.

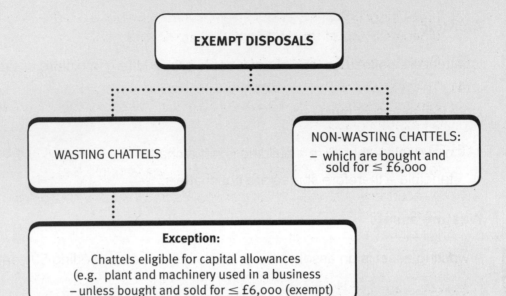

EXEMPT DISPOSALS

WASTING CHATTELS

NON-WASTING CHATTELS:
– which are bought and sold for ≤ £6,000

Exception:
Chattels eligible for capital allowances
(e.g. plant and machinery used in a business
– unless bought and sold for ≤ £6,000 (exempt)

Example 5 – Chattels

Mr Windsor has made the following disposals in 2012/13.

(1) A painting was sold in July 2012 for £5,600. He originally bought it in February 1990 for £3,500.

(2) A piece of land, which he bought in April 2005 for £2,000 (an investment property), was sold in September 2012 for £5,000.

(3) He sold a vintage car for £25,000 in November 2012 that had originally cost him £5,500 in June 1999.

(4) He bought a moveable crane for £20,000 in August 1992, which he used in his haulage business. He sold the crane for £10,000 in January 2013.

(5) An antique vase was sold in August 2012 for £10,000. It originally cost £8,000 in April 2000.

(6) In October 2012 he sold his half share in a racehorse for £5,000, which he had acquired in June 2001 for £4,000.

For each of the above transactions, state whether they are chattels (wasting or non-wasting) and whether they will be subject to capital gains tax.

KAPLAN PUBLISHING

Answer to example 5

(1) The painting is a non-wasting chattel which was bought and sold for less than £6,000. This is therefore an exempt disposal.

(2) Land is not moveable property and is therefore not a chattel. The disposal is therefore chargeable to capital gains tax.

(3) Cars are always exempt assets for capital gains tax purposes.

(4) The crane is a wasting chattel which is eligible for capital allowances as it is used in a business. The disposal is therefore **not** an exempt disposal.

(5) The antique vase is a non-wasting chattel. As it was bought and sold for more than £6,000 it is chargeable to capital gains tax.

(6) A racehorse is a wasting chattel and is therefore exempt from capital gains tax.

Test your understanding 4

Which of the following disposals are exempt from, and which are chargeable to, capital gains tax?

(1) Gift of a necklace which was bought for £4,000. Its market value at the date of the gift was £7,000.

(2) Sale of shares in a quoted trading company for £2,000 which were bought for £1,000.

(3) Sale of a motor car, for £5,000, which was used for business purposes. It was acquired for £6,000.

(4) Sale of a boat for £20,000, which was acquired for £15,000.

(5) Sale of a painting for £5,000, which was acquired for £1,000.

(6) Sale of a greyhound for £10,000, which was acquired for £5,000.

Non-wasting chattels

When a non-wasting chattel is disposed of the following rules apply:

(1) asset bought **and** sold for £6,000 or less = exempt

(2) asset bought and sold for more than £6,000
= the chargeable gain is computed in the normal way

(3) asset either bought or sold for £6,000 or less
= special rules apply:

- **Sold at a gain**

  Calculate the chargeable gain as normal but the gain cannot exceed a maximum of:

  5/3 × (gross disposal consideration – £6,000)

- **Sold at a loss**

  Sale proceeds are deemed to be £6,000.

The above rules are referred to as **the £6,000 rule** and can be summarised in the table below.

	Cost	
	£6,000 or less	**More than 6,000**
Sale proceeds: **£6,000 or less**	Exempt	Allowable loss but proceeds are deemed = £6,000
More than £6,000	Taxed on lower of: • Normal calculation. • 5/3 × (gross proceeds – £6,000)	Normal CGT computation

Example 6 – Non-wasting chattel

Andrew sold a picture on 1 February 2013 for £6,600. He had acquired it on 1 March 2004 for £3,200.

Calculate the chargeable gain arising on the disposal.

Answer to example 6

As the picture is a non-wasting chattel, that was sold for more than £6,000, the disposal is not an exempt disposal.

	£
Sale proceeds	6,600
Less: Cost	(3,200)
Chargeable gain	3,400

Gain cannot exceed: 5/3 × (£6,600 – £6,000) = £1,000

Example 7 – Non-wasting chattel

Brian bought an antique table for £6,500 in September 2001 and sold it for £5,600 in December 2012. He incurred £250 to advertise it for sale.

Calculate the allowable loss arising, if any.

Answer to example 7

This is a disposal of a non-wasting chattel that cost more than £6,000 but which was sold for less than £6,000. The disposal is not an exempt disposal but the allowable loss is restricted as follows:

	£
Deemed sale proceeds	6,000
Less: Expenses of sale	(250)
Cost	(6,500)
	———
Allowable loss	(750)
	———

Test your understanding 5

Marjory bought two antique tables in March 1985 each for £1,000. She sold them both in October 2012 for £6,400 and £13,600 respectively.

Calculate the chargeable gains arising on the disposal of the two antique tables.

Test your understanding 6

Brian bought a picture in April 1983 for £10,000 plus purchase costs of £500. The market for the artist's work slumped and Brian sold the picture on 27 June 2012 for £500, less disposal costs of £50.

Calculate the allowable loss on disposal of the picture.

Test your understanding 7

During January 2013, Sally sold four paintings, which she had acquired in May 2001. Details were as follows.

Painting	Cost	Proceeds
	£	£
1	2,000	7,000
2	8,000	4,500
3	3,000	5,500
4	7,000	9,500

Calculate Sally's net chargeable gains for 2012/13.

Chattels – summary

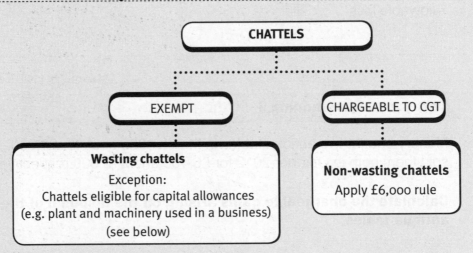

Wasting assets

Wasting assets (i.e. predictable life of less than 50 years) can be split into the following categories:

- Chattels not eligible for capital allowances = exempt from CGT.

- Chattels eligible for capital allowances.

- Other wasting assets.

KAPLAN PUBLISHING

Chattels eligible for capital allowances

For example, plant and machinery that has been used for the purposes of a trade.

Where capital allowances have been claimed on an asset, in the gain/loss computation we must take into account the tax relief already given for the net cost of the asset in the capital allowances computation.

Accordingly the following rules apply:

- **Sold at a gain**

  Calculate the gain as normal, applying the £6,000 rule if applicable.

- **Sold at a loss**

  The capital loss is restricted as relief for the loss has already been given through the capital allowances system.

  In the capital loss computation, the net capital allowances (i.e. net of balancing charges on disposal) are deducted from the allowable expenditure.

  Accordingly, plant and machinery which is eligible for capital allowances and sold at a loss, results in a no gain/no loss situation for CGT purposes.

Example 8 – Plant and machinery – Sarah

Sarah bought a machine for use in her trade for £35,000 in May 2006. In October 2012 she decided to replace it and sold the old machine for £40,000.

Calculate the chargeable gain arising on the disposal in October 2012.

Answer to example 8

The asset was sold at a gain. The capital gain is therefore calculated as normal.

	£
Sale proceeds	40,000
Less: Cost	(35,000)
Chargeable gain	5,000

Example 9 – Plant and machinery – Fred

Fred bought a machine for use in his trade for £35,000 in April 2002. In October 2012 he decided to replace it and sold the old machine for £26,500.

Calculate the chargeable gain or allowable loss arising.

Answer to example 9

Fred has sold the machine for a real loss of £8,500 (£35,000 – £26,500). He is compensated for this loss through the capital allowances system (i.e. he receives net capital allowances of £8,500 during his period of ownership of the machine).

The capital loss computation is therefore adjusted to reflect the relief for the loss already given through capital allowances as follows:

	£	£
Sale proceeds		26,500
Less: Cost	35,000	
Less: Net capital allowances	(8,500)	
		(26,500)
Allowable loss		Nil

KAPLAN PUBLISHING

Other wasting assets

This category covers wasting assets that are not chattels as they are not tangible and/or not moveable (e.g. a copyright). The allowable expenditure on these assets is deemed to waste away over the life of the asset on a straight line basis.

Consequently, when a disposal is made:

- the allowable expenditure is restricted to take account of the asset's natural fall in value
- the asset's fall in value is deemed to occur on a straight line basis over its predictable useful life
- the allowable cost is calculated as:

$$\text{Cost} \times \frac{\text{Remaining life at disposal}}{\text{Estimated useful life}}$$

Example 10 – Other wasting assets – Ian

On 1 February 2003 Ian bought a wasting asset at a cost of £24,000. It had an estimated useful life of 30 years. He sold the asset for £38,000 on 1 February 2013.

Calculate the chargeable gain or allowable loss arising.

Answer to example 10

	£
Sale proceeds	38,000
Less: Allowable element of acquisition cost (W)	(16,000)
Chargeable gain	22,000

Working: Allowable element of acquisition cost

Remaining life at disposal = 20 years
Estimated useful life = 30 years

Allowable cost = £24,000 × 20/30 = £16,000

Example 11 – Other wasting assets – Jan

On 1 March 2008 Jan bought a wasting asset at a cost of £19,000. It had an estimated useful life of 40 years. She sold the asset for £30,000 on 1 March 2013.

Calculate the chargeable gain or allowable loss arising.

Answer to example 11

	£
Sale proceeds	30,000
Allowable element of acquisition cost (W)	(16,625)
Chargeable gain	13,375

Working: Allowable element of acquisition cost

Remaining life at disposal = 35 years
Estimated useful life = 40 years

Allowable cost = £19,000 × 35/40 = £16,625

Wasting assets – summary

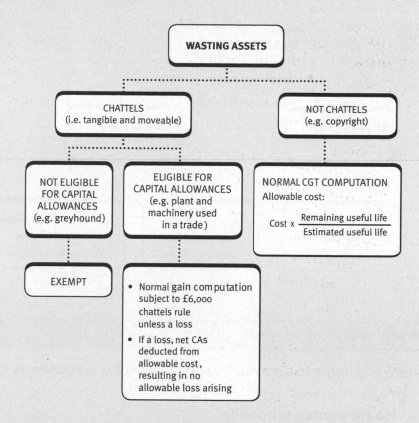

4 Assets lost or destroyed or damaged

A capital transaction usually has two parties, a buyer and a seller.

However, when an asset is damaged, destroyed or lost and the asset's owner receives compensation (either from the perpetrator or an insurance company) the position is different. The owner has received a capital sum without disposing of the asset and the payer has received nothing in return. Consequently, a special set of rules is required.

The rules vary according to whether:

*   the asset has been completely lost/destroyed or merely damaged
*   the owner has replaced or restored the asset.

Asset lost or destroyed

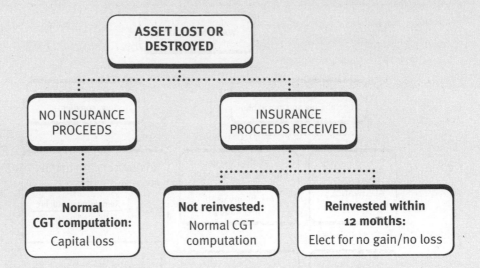

Assets lost or destroyed

There is a deemed disposal for capital gains tax purposes as follows:

(a) **No insurance proceeds**

Compute a capital loss using the normal CGT computation:

- Disposal proceeds will be £Nil.
- Deduction of the allowable expenditure will create a loss.

(b) **Insurance proceeds received – no replacement of asset**

Chargeable gain/loss is computed using the normal CGT computation pro forma.

(c) **Insurance proceeds received – asset replaced within 12 months**

The taxpayer can claim that the destruction/loss of the asset is treated as a no gain/no loss disposal (as for husband and wife transfers).

If the insurance proceeds are greater than the deemed disposal proceeds under the no gain/no loss computation, the excess is deducted from the replacement asset's allowable cost.

The date of disposal is the date that the insurance proceeds are received, not when the destruction or loss of the asset occurred.

Example 12 – Assets lost or destroyed – Nadir

Nadir purchased a business asset for £15,000 on 1 April 1990, which was destroyed by fire on 31 July 2012. The asset was not insured.

Calculate the allowable loss arising in 2012/13.

Answer to example 12

	£
Proceeds	Nil
Less: Cost	(15,000)
Allowable loss	(15,000)

Example 13 – Assets lost or destroyed – Padma

Padma purchased an antique table for £35,000 on 1 May 1992, which was destroyed by fire on 30 June 2012. She received insurance proceeds of £50,000 on 1 September 2012. She did not replace the table.

Calculate the chargeable gain arising in 2012/13.

Answer to example 13

	£
Insurance proceeds	50,000
Less: Cost	(35,000)
Chargeable gain	15,000

Example 14 – Assets lost or destroyed – Silvio

Silvio purchased a painting for £57,000 on 1 June 1993, which was destroyed in a fire on 31 July 2012. He received insurance proceeds of £50,000 on 1 September 2012. He did not replace the painting.

Calculate the allowable loss arising in 2012/13.

Answer to example 14

	£
Insurance proceeds	50,000
Less: Cost	(57,000)
Allowable loss	(7,000)

Example 15 – Assets lost or destroyed – Bill

Bill purchased an asset for £25,000 on 1 October 1990, which was destroyed by fire on 30 September 2012. He received compensation of £35,000 from his insurance company on 1 January 2013. He purchased a replacement asset for £40,000 on 1 February 2013.

Assuming that Bill claims the loss by fire to be a no gain/no loss disposal, calculate the allowable expenditure (base cost) of the replacement asset.

Answer to example 15

	£	£
Cost of replacement asset		40,000
Less: Compensation	35,000	
Less: Deemed disposal proceeds of old asset (W)	(25,000)	
		(10,000)
Replacement asset base cost		30,000

Working – deemed disposal proceeds

Since the disposal of the old asset is assumed to be on a no gain/no loss basis. The disposal proceeds are the allowable cost of the asset.

Allowable cost = Deemed disposal proceeds	£25,000

Example 16 – Assets lost or destroyed – Belinda

Belinda purchased an antique necklace for £21,140 on 1 October 1996, which she lost on 30 June 2008. She received compensation of £45,000 from her insurance company on 1 October 2008 and purchased a replacement necklace for £50,000 on 1 November 2008.

She sold the replacement necklace for £65,000 on 1 March 2013.

Assuming that Belinda claims the loss of the necklace to be a no gain/no loss disposal, calculate the chargeable gain arising on the sale of the replacement necklace on 1 March 2013.

Answer to example 16

	£
Sale proceeds	65,000
Less: Cost (W)	(26,140)
Chargeable gain	38,860

Working – Replacement asset base cost

	£	£
Cost of replacement necklace		50,000
Less: Insurance proceeds	45,000	
Less: Deemed disposal proceeds of lost necklace		
= Base cost	(21,140)	
		(23,860)
Replacement asset base cost		26,140

Asset damaged

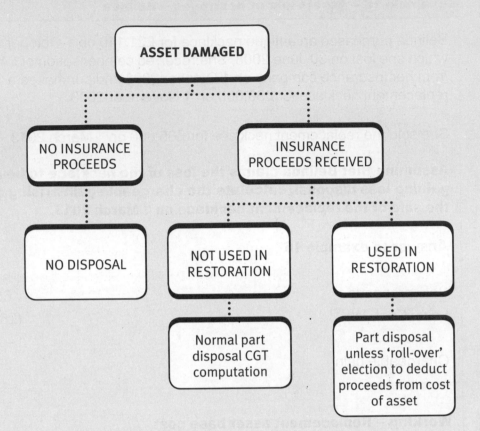

Asset damaged

There are no implications for capital gains tax purposes unless compensation (e.g. insurance proceeds) is received.

Where an asset is damaged and compensation is received there is a part disposal for capital gains tax purposes.

The allowable cost is calculated using the normal part disposal formula:

Cost × A / A + B

Where: A = Compensation received
        B = Market value of the remainder at the time of the part disposal (i.e. value in its damaged condition).

The computation is varied depending on how the insurance proceeds are applied.

(a) Proceeds not used in restoration work

Normal part disposal capital gains computation is used. The value of the part retained is the value of the asset in its damaged condition.

(b) Proceeds fully used in restoration work

Where all of the insurance proceeds are used in restoring the asset the taxpayer may claim to deduct the proceeds from the cost of the asset rather than be treated as having made a part disposal of the asset.

This is a form of 'roll-over relief' (see Chapter 16).

Example 17 – Asset damaged – Sasha

Sasha purchased a painting on 1 April 2000 for £10,000. The painting was damaged on 1 May 2012 when it was worth £50,000. After the damage the painting was worth £25,000. On 1 July 2012 insurance proceeds of £30,000 were received, which were not used to restore the painting.

Calculate the chargeable gain arising in respect of the painting.

Answer to example 17

	£
Insurance proceeds	30,000
Less: Deemed cost £10,000 × £30,000/(£30,000 + £25,000)	(5,455)
Chargeable gain	24,545

Example 18 – Asset damaged – Amy

Amy purchased a painting on 1 April 2000 for £10,000. The painting was damaged on 1 May 2012 when it was worth £50,000. After the damage the painting was worth £40,000. On 1 July 2012 insurance proceeds of £8,000 were received. All of the proceeds were used immediately to restore the painting.

Assuming Amy elects for the insurance proceeds to be rolled over against the cost of the painting, calculate the revised base cost for CGT purposes of the painting after it has been restored.

Answer to example 18

There is no part disposal and the revised base cost of the painting is:

	£
Original cost	10,000
Less: Insurance proceeds	(8,000)
Revised base cost	2,000

Example 19 – Asset damaged – Sari

Sari purchased an investment property on 1 May 2002 for £200,000. In June 2012 it was damaged by fire. On 1 August 2012 insurance proceeds of £100,000 were received which were used to restore the property. After the restoration the property was worth £500,000.

Assuming Sari elects for the insurance proceeds to be rolled over against the cost of the property calculate the revised base cost for CGT purposes of the property after it has been restored.

Answer to example 19

As the proceeds are fully used in restoration and the 'roll over' election is made, there is no part disposal and the revised base cost is:

	£
Original cost	200,000
Less: Insurance proceeds	(100,000)
Revised base cost	100,000

5 Chapter summary

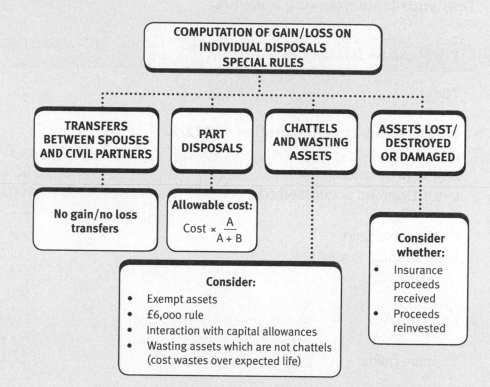

COMPUTATION OF GAIN/LOSS ON
INDIVIDUAL DISPOSALS
SPECIAL RULES

TRANSFERS
BETWEEN SPOUSES
AND CIVIL PARTNERS

PART
DISPOSALS

CHATTELS
AND WASTING
ASSETS

ASSETS LOST/
DESTROYED
OR DAMAGED

No gain/no loss
transfers

Allowable cost:

$$\text{Cost} \times \frac{A}{A + B}$$

Consider:
- Exempt assets
- £6,000 rule
- Interaction with capital allowances
- Wasting assets which are not chattels (cost wastes over expected life)

Consider whether:
- Insurance proceeds received
- Proceeds reinvested

Test your understanding answers

Test your understanding 1

Tania

Capital gains tax computation – 2012/13

	£
Disposal proceeds	350,000
Less: Deemed acquisition cost	(100,000)
Chargeable gain	250,000
Less: Capital losses b/f	(11,300)
	238,700
Less: AEA	(10,600)
Taxable gains	228,100
Capital gains tax payable (£228,100 x 28%)	63,868

Notes: Tania's deemed acquisition cost is equal to the deemed proceeds on the transfer from her husband, John. This is equal to his acquisition cost.

Since Tania's taxable income exceeds the basic rate band she will be taxed on all her gains at 28%.

KAPLAN PUBLISHING

Test your understanding 2

Jacob

Disposal in January 2013	£	£
Sale proceeds		20,000
Less: Deemed cost of part disposed of		
£8,000 × £20,000/(£20,000 + £60,000)		(2,000)
		────
		18,000

Disposal in March 2013		
Sales proceeds	75,000	
Less: Deemed cost of remainder		
(£8,000 – £2,000)	(6,000)	
	────	69,000
		────
Total chargeable gains		87,000
Less: AEA		(10,600)
		────
Taxable gains		76,400
		────

	£	
Basic rate (£34,370 – £15,000)	19,370 × 18%	3,487
Higher rate	57,030 × 28%	15,968
	────	
	76,400	
	────	────
Capital gains tax liability		19,455
		────

Due date	31.1.2014

Test your understanding 3

Gemma

Disposal of the remainder – 2012/13

	£
Sale proceeds	200,000
Less: Deemed cost of remainder (£50,000 – £14,286) (W)	(35,714)
Chargeable gain	164,286
Less: AEA	(10,600)
Taxable gain	153,686
Capital gains tax (£153,686 × 28%) (Note)	43,032

Note: Gemma has no basic rate band remaining, therefore the gains are taxed at 28%.

Working – Allowable expenditure

The allowable expenditure in relation to the part disposal of the land on 1 July 2006 was:

£50,000 × £40,000/(£40,000 + £100,000) = £14,286

Test your understanding 4

Exempt disposals	Chargeable disposals
(3) Motor car – exempt asset	(1) Necklace (deemed proceeds £7,000). Non-wasting chattel not sold and bought for ≤ £6,000
(4) Boat – wasting chattel	(2) Shares – not chattels (not tangible property)
(5) Painting – non wasting chattel bought and sold for ≤ £6,000	
(6) Greyhound – wasting chattel	

Test your understanding 5

Marjory

	Table A £	Table B £
Sale proceeds	6,400	13,600
Less: Cost	(1,000)	(1,000)
Chargeable gains	5,400	12,600
Gains cannot exceed:		
5/3 × (sale proceeds – £6,000)	667	12,667
Decision = take the lower gain	667	12,600

Note: Both tables are chattels and were bought for less than £6,000 and sold for more than £6,000; therefore the 5/3 rule needs to be considered.

Test your understanding 6

Brian

	£
Deemed sale proceeds	6,000
Less: Selling costs	(50)
Net sale proceeds	5,950
Less: Cost (including acquisition expenses)	(10,500)
Allowable loss	(4,550)

Note: It is the **gross** sale proceeds **before** deducting selling costs that are deemed to be £6,000. The £500 actual sale proceeds received are ignored.

Test your understanding 7

Sally

Net chargeable gains – 2012/13

Painting	1	2	4
	£	£	£
Sale proceeds	7,000		9,500
Deemed proceeds		6,000	
Less: Cost	(2,000)	(8,000)	(7,000)
Chargeable gain/(allowable loss)	5,000	(2,000)	2,500
Gain cannot exceed			
5/3 × (£7,000 – £6,000)	1,667		

Net chargeable gains (£1,667 – £2,000 + £2,500) = £2,167

Note: Painting 3 is exempt as the cost and proceeds are both less than £6,000.

KAPLAN PUBLISHING

CGT: Shares and securities for individuals

Chapter learning objectives

Upon completion of this chapter you will be able to:

- identify the exemption for government securities and qualifying corporate bonds

- calculate the value of quoted shares where they are disposed of by way of a gift

- understand why identification rules are required when acquiring and disposing of shares

- apply the correct matching rules on a disposal of shares by an individual

- explain the pooling principle

- calculate a gain on the disposal of shares by an individual

- identify the treatment of a bonus issue

- identify the treatment of a rights issue

- explain the tax treatment on a takeover or reorganisation of a shareholding in exchange for other shares

- explain the treatment on a takeover where there is cash and shares consideration

- calculate the chargeable gain on the cash element on a takeover.

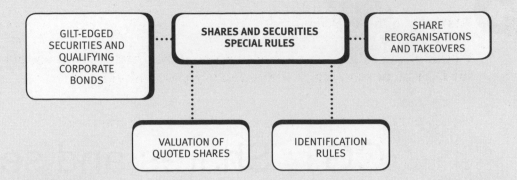

Introduction

The basic chargeable gain computation is used as normal on a disposal of shares or securities. However, because shares are indistinguishable from each other there are special rules to identify the allowable cost.

This chapter covers the rules as they apply to disposals by an individual.

1 Government securities and qualifying corporate bonds

All shares and securities disposed of by an individual are subject to capital gains tax except for the following, which are exempt:

- listed government securities (gilt-edged securities or gilts)

- qualifying corporate bonds (e.g. company loan notes)

- shares held in an Individual Savings Account (ISA).

Definition of a qualifying corporate bond

A qualifying corporate bond (QCB) is one that:

(a) represents a normal commercial loan;

(b) is expressed in sterling and has no provision for either conversion into, or redemption in, any other currency; and

(c) was issued after 13 March 1984 or was acquired by the disposer after that date (whenever it was issued).

KAPLAN PUBLISHING

Test your understanding 1

Which of the following shares and securities are exempt assets for CGT purposes when disposed of by an individual?

(1) £1 ordinary shares in the unquoted property development company, Sealand Ltd.

(2) 10½% Exchequer Stock 2019.

(3) 10% preference shares in the quoted trading company, Ace plc.

(4) 6% loan note issued by Amble plc in 2009.

2 Valuation of quoted shares

On a sale of shares between unconnected parties, the actual proceeds are used in the capital gains computation.

However, it is necessary to identify the market value of quoted shares when shares are either:

- gifted

- transferred to a connected party.

Their market value is taken from prices quoted in the Stock Exchange Daily Official List and is the **lower** of:

- the value using the '¼ up method'
  i.e. lower quoted price + ¼ (higher price – lower price)

- the average of the highest and lowest recorded bargains.

Example 1 – Valuation of quoted shares

Shares in XYZ plc are quoted in the Stock Exchange Daily Official List at 230p to 270p. On the same day the highest and lowest recorded bargains were 224p and 276p.

If a disposal of XYZ plc shares were made on that day to a connected party, what would their value be for CGT purposes?

Answer to example 1

The value of XYZ plc shares is 240p, being the lower of:

(a) ¼ up rule:

Lower price	230p
Add: (270p – 230p) × ¼	10p
	240p

(b) Average of highest and lowest recorded bargains

(276p + 224p) × ½	250p

Test your understanding 2

Shares in Sawyer plc are quoted in the Stock Exchange Daily Official List at 460p to 540p.

On the same day the recorded bargains were 552p, 470p and 448p.

If a gift of Sawyer plc shares were made on that day, what would their value be for CGT purposes?

KAPLAN PUBLISHING

3 Identification rules

It is necessary to have identification (or matching) rules to determine which shares have been disposed of as:

- Shares and securities that are bought in a particular company of the same class are not distinguishable from one another.
- Each time shares are bought in any quoted company the price paid may be different.
- They enable you to decide which shares have been sold and to work out the allowable cost to use in the capital gains computation.

Identification rules for disposals by individuals

When shares are disposed of they are matched against shares acquired of the same class in the following order:

- Same day as the date of disposal.
- Within **following** 30 days.
- The share pool (shares acquired before the date of disposal are pooled together).

Shares acquired within the following 30 days

It may appear strange that a disposal is matched with acquisitions following the date of sale. The reason for this is to counter a practice known as 'bed and breakfasting'.

Without this 30-day matching rule, shares could be sold at the close of business one day and then bought back at the opening of business the next day. A gain or loss would be established without making a genuine disposal of the shares.

This was useful for an individual to establish:

- a capital loss (e.g. in the same tax year that he or she has chargeable gains), or
- a capital gain to use his or her AEA, if it had not been used already, and effectively reacquire the same shares with a higher base cost for future disposals.

The 30-day matching rule makes the practice of 'bed and breakfasting' much more difficult, since the subsequent re-acquisition of shares cannot take place within 30 days.

Example 2 – Identification rules

Frederic had the following transactions in the shares of DEF plc, a quoted company.

			£
1 June 1996	Bought	4,000 shares for	8,000
30 July 2000	Bought	1,800 shares for	9,750
30 April 2005	Bought	500 shares for	4,000
20 May 2010	Bought	1,000 shares for	8,500
15 March 2013	Sold	3,500 shares for	36,000
28 March 2013	Bought	800 shares for	6,400

Identify with which acquisitions the shares sold on 15 March 2013 will be matched.

Answer to example 2

		Number of shares
Shares sold		3,500
(1)	Shares acquired on same day	(Nil)
(2)	Shares acquired in following 30 days	
	28 March 2013	(800)
		————
		2,700

(3)	Share pool		
	(Shares pre 15 March 2013))		
	1 June 1996	4,000	
	30 July 2000	1,800	
	30 April 2005	500	
	20 May 2010	1,000	
		————	
		7,300	
		————	
	The disposal from the share pool is therefore 2,700 out of 7,300 shares		(2,700)
			————
			Nil
			————

The share pool

The share pool is sometimes referred to as the 's104 pool' or the 'FA 1985 pool'.

For an individual, the share pool contains shares in the same company, of the same class purchased before the date of disposal.

- The share pool simply keeps a record of the number of shares acquired and sold and the cost of those shares.

- When shares are disposed of out of the share pool, the appropriate proportion of the cost which relates to the shares disposed of is calculated. The shares are disposed of at their average cost.

  Thus if there are 6,000 shares in the pool with a cost of £8,000 and 2,000 shares are disposed of:

  - the cost of the shares removed is £2,667 ((2,000/6,000) × £8,000).

4 Calculating the gain/loss on the disposal of shares

Once the identification rules have been used to identify which shares have been disposed of, the cost of those shares is used in the normal chargeable gains computation.

Example 3 – Calculating the gain/loss on the disposal of shares

Frances sold 11,000 ordinary shares in Hastings Co plc, a quoted company, on 18 December 2012 for £50,000. She had bought ordinary shares in the company on the following dates.

	Number of shares	Cost
		£
6 April 1998	8,000	7,450
12 December 2006	4,000	5,500
10 January 2013	2,000	6,000

Calculate the chargeable gain arising on the disposal of shares.

Assume that Hastings Co plc is not Frances' personal trading company.

Answer to example 3

Capital gains computation – 2012/13

Stage 1   **Use the identification rules to identify the shares disposed of.**

			Number
Shares sold			11,000
(1)	Shares acquired on same day		(Nil)
(2)	Shares acquired in following 30 days		
	10 January 2013		(2,000)
			9,000
(3)	Share pool (9,000 out of 12,000 shares)		(9,000)
			Nil

Stage 2   **Calculate the chargeable gain arising on each of the individual parcels of shares disposed of.**

(a) **Shares acquired on 10 January 2013**

	£
Sale proceeds (2,000/11,000 × £50,000)	9,091
Less: Acquisition cost	(6,000)
Chargeable gain	3,091

(b) **Shares in the share pool**

	£
Sale proceeds (9,000/11,000 × £50,000)	40,409
Less: Acquisition cost (W)	(9,713)
Chargeable gain	30,696
Total chargeable gains	**33,787**

Working: share pool

	Number	Cost £
Acquisition – 6 April 1998	8,000	7,450
Acquisition – 12 December 2006	4,000	5,500
	12,000	12,950
Disposal – 18 December 2012 (9,000/12,000) × £12,950 (Note)	(9,000)	(9,713)
Balance carried forward	3,000	3,237

Note: The 'average cost' method is used to calculate the cost removed from the share pool on the disposal.

If the individual disposes of shares in his personal trading company and is also an employee of that company, Entrepreneurs' relief is available. This relief is covered in detail in Chapter 16.

Test your understanding 3

Zoe purchased 2,000 shares in XYZ Ltd on 16 April 1995 for £10,000.

In addition she acquired 1,500 shares in the company on 30 April 2009 for £18,000, and 500 shares on 31 May 2009 for £7,000. On 10 February 2013, Zoe bought a further 200 shares in XYZ Ltd for £3,600.

Zoe sold 3,500 shares in XYZ Ltd on 31 January 2013 for £70,000.

Calculate Zoe's chargeable gain on the disposal of shares.

Assume that XYZ Ltd is not Zoe's personal trading company.

5 Bonus issues and rights issues

Bonus issues

A bonus issue is the distribution of free shares to shareholders based on their existing shareholding.

For capital gains tax purposes they are treated as follows:

- For the purposes of the share identification rules the bonus shares acquired will be included in the share pool.

- The bonus shares are not treated as a separate holding of shares.

- The number of shares are included in the pool, but at Nil cost.

Example 4 – Bonus issues

Blackburn had the following transactions in the shares of Gray Ltd:

January 2009	Purchased 3,500 shares for £7,350
May 2009	Purchased 500 shares for £1,750
June 2010	Bonus issue of one for five
September 2012	Sold 2,600 shares for £10,400

Calculate the chargeable gain arising on the disposal.

Assume that Gray Ltd is not Blackburn's personal trading company.

Answer to example 4

	£
Sale proceeds	10,400
Less: Cost (Working)	(4,929)
Chargeable gain	5,471

Working: Share pool

		Number	Cost £
Jan 2009	Purchase	3,500	7,350
May 2009	Purchase	500	1,750
		4,000	9,100
June 2010	Bonus issue (1:5)	800	Nil
		4,800	9,100
September 2012	Sale	(2,600)	(4,929)
Balance c/f		2,200	4,171

Test your understanding 4

Kieran had the following transactions in Black plc shares:

January 2005	Purchased 3,000 shares for £6,000
May 2009	Bonus issue of one for three
June 2010	Purchased 500 shares for £1,500
February 2013	Sold 3,000 shares for £12,000

Calculate the chargeable gain arising on the disposal.

Assume that Black plc is not Kieran's personal trading company.

Rights issues

A rights issue is the offer of new shares to existing shareholders only, in proportion to their existing shareholding, usually at a price below the current market price.

Rights issues are similar in concept to bonus issues, however because money is paid for the new shares there are additional factors to consider:

- As for bonus issues, for the purposes of the share identification rules the rights shares acquired will be included in the share pool.

- The rights shares are not treated as a separate holding of shares.

- The number of shares are included in the pool, and the cost, in the same way as a normal purchase.

Example 5 – Rights issue

Carmichael had the following transactions in Rudderham Ltd shares:

January 2008	Purchased 2,700 shares for £5,400
May 2009	Purchased 600 shares for £1,500
June 2010	Took up 1 for 3 rights issue at £2.30 per share
August 2012	Sold 4,000 shares for £14,000

Calculate the chargeable gain on the disposal.

Assume that Rudderham Ltd is not Carmichael's personal trading company.

Answer to example 5

	£
Sale proceeds	14,000
Less: Cost (Working)	(8,573)
Chargeable gain	5,427

Working: Share pool

		Number	Cost £
Jan 2008	Purchase	2,700	5,400
May 2009	Purchase	600	1,500
		3,300	6,900
June 2010	Rights issue (1:3) @ £2.30 per share	1,100	2,530
		4,400	9,430
August 2012	Sale	(4,000)	(8,573)
Balance c/f		400	857

Example 5 – Rights issue

Test your understanding 5

Victor had the following transactions in the ordinary shares of Victorious Vulcanising plc, a quoted company:

April 2000	Purchased 1,000 shares for £11,000
September 2009	Rights issue of 1 for 2 at £6 each
August 2012	Sold 1,200 shares for £46,000

Calculate Victor's chargeable gain for 2012/13.

Assume that Victorious Vulcanising plc is not Victor's personal trading company.

6 Reorganisations and takeovers

Definitions

A reorganisation involves the exchange of existing shares in a company for other shares of another class in the same company.

A takeover occurs when one company acquires the shares in another company either in exchange for shares in itself, cash or a mixture of both.

Consideration: shares for shares

Where the consideration for the reorganisation or takeover only involves the issue of shares in the acquiring company, the tax consequences are:

* **No CGT** is charged at the time of the reorganisation/ takeover.

* The cost of the original shares becomes the cost of the new shares.

* Where the shareholder receives more than one type of share in exchange for the original shares, the cost of the original shares is allocated to the new shares by reference to the market values of the various new shares on the first day of dealing in them.

This treatment is **automatic**.

However, the shareholder can elect for the event to be treated as a disposal for CGT purposes.

If the election is made, Entrepreneurs' relief may be available against the gain. This relief is considered in detail in Chapter 16.

Example 6 – Reorganisations and takeovers

Major purchased 2,000 ordinary shares in Blue plc for £5,000 in June 2002. In July 2010, Blue plc underwent a reorganisation and Major received two 'A' ordinary shares in exchange for each of his ordinary shares.

In December 2012, Major sold all his holding of 'A' ordinary shares for £8,000.

Calculate the chargeable gain arising on the disposal.

Assume that Blue plc is not Major's personal trading company.

Answer to example 6

	£
Sale proceeds	8,000
Less: Cost (Note)	(5,000)
	———
Chargeable gain	3,000
	———

Note: The cost of the original ordinary shares (£5,000) becomes the cost of the new 'A' ordinary shares.

Example 7 – Reorganisations and takeovers

In July 2012, Craig sold his entire holding of ordinary shares in Corus plc for £75,000. Craig had originally purchased 20,000 £1 ordinary shares in BNB plc at a cost of £20,000 in April 2001.

In July 2004, BNB plc was taken over by Corus plc. Craig received one ordinary 50p share and one 50p 6% preference share in Corus plc for each ordinary share he held in BNB plc.

Immediately after the takeover the values of these new shares were quoted as:

50p ordinary share	£1.80 each
50p preference shares	£0.80 each

Compute the chargeable gain arising on the disposal.

Assume that Craig has never worked for Corus plc or BNB plc.

KAPLAN PUBLISHING

Answer to example 7

	£
Sale proceeds	75,000
Less: Allocated acquisition cost (W)	(13,846)
Chargeable gain	61,154

Working: Acquisition cost

Following the takeover in July 2004 of BNB plc by Corus plc, Craig now owns the following shares in Corus plc as per the terms of the takeover:

	Total M.V. £	Original cost £
20,000 50p ordinary shares @ £1.80	36,000	13,846
20,000 50p preference shares @ £0.80	16,000	6,154
	52,000	20,000

Allocate the original cost incurred in April 2001 to the shares now owned in July 2004, using the normal average cost method.

(£36,000/£52,000) × £20,000 = £13,846
(£16,000/£52,000) × £20,000 = £6,154

Test your understanding 6

In June 2009, Marie purchased 2,000 ordinary shares in Black Ltd for £5,000. In July 2010 Black Ltd was taken over by Red plc, and Marie received 2 ordinary shares and 1 preference share in Red plc for each ordinary share in Black Ltd.

Immediately after the takeover the ordinary shares in Red plc were valued at £2 and the preference shares in Red plc were valued at £1.

In December 2012, Marie sold all her holding of ordinary shares in Red plc for £11,000.

Calculate the chargeable gain arising on the disposal.

Assume that Marie has never worked for Red plc or Black Ltd.

Takeovers: consideration in cash and shares

If the consideration for the takeover includes a cash element:

*   there is a part disposal of the original shares
*   a gain arises on the cash element of the consideration on the date the cash is received.

Cash proceeds – part disposal computation

In these circumstances the part of the cost of the original holding apportioned to the cash is calculated as:

$$\frac{\text{Cash received}}{\text{Cash received} + \text{M.V. of new shares}} \times \text{Cost of original shares}$$

Example 8 – Reorganisations and takeovers

Patrick bought 10,000 shares in Target plc in May 2004 for £20,000. On 3 November 2012, the entire share capital of Target plc was acquired by Bidder plc. Target plc shareholders received 2 Bidder plc shares and £0.50 cash for each share held. Bidder plc shares were quoted at £1.25.

Calculate the chargeable gain as a result of the takeover in November 2012.

Assume that Patrick has not worked for Target plc or Bidder plc.

Answer to example 8

The total consideration provided by Bidder plc is:

	MV £	Cost £
Shares (10,000 × 2 × £1.25)	25,000	16,667
Cash (10,000 × 1 × £0.50)	5,000	3,333
	30,000	20,000

KAPLAN PUBLISHING

As Patrick has received part of the consideration in cash he has made a part disposal of the original shares.

	£
Disposal proceeds (cash)	5,000
Less: Deemed cost (£5,000/£30,000) × £20,000	(3,333)
Chargeable gain	1,667

Patrick's allowable cost on the future disposal of his shares in Bidder plc will be £16,667 (£20,000 − £3,333).

Test your understanding 7

Paula bought 25,000 shares in Tiny plc in May 2005 for £20,000. On 3 October 2012 the entire share capital of Tiny plc was acquired by Big plc. Tiny plc shareholders received 2 Big plc shares and £1.20 cash for each share held. Big plc shares were quoted at £1.75.

Calculate the chargeable gain as a result of the takeover in October 2012 and state the allowable cost of Paula's shares in Big plc.

Assume that Paula has not worked for either Tiny plc or Big plc.

7 Chapter summary

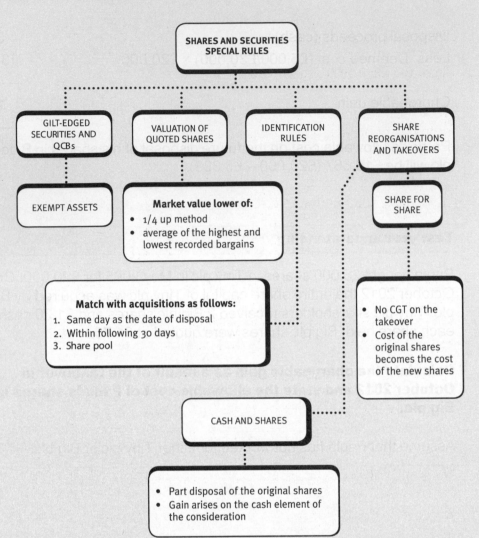

Test your understanding answers

Test your understanding 1

Exempt shares and securities

10½% Exchequer Stock 2019 is a government security and the 6% loan note is a qualifying corporate bond.

Test your understanding 2

Sawyer plc

The value of the shares in Sawyer plc would be the lower of:

(1) ¼ up rule: 460p + ¼ (540p – 460p) = 480p

(2) Average of the highest and lowest bargains
      = (552p + 448p) x ½ = 500p

The value is therefore 480p or £4.80 per share.

Test your understanding 3

Zoe

(a) **Match with acquisitions within following 30 days**
     (10 February 2013) (200 shares)

	£
Sale proceeds (£70,000 × 200/3,500)	4,000
Less: Purchase price	(3,600)
Chargeable gain	400

(b) **Match with acquisitions in the share pool
(balance of 3,300 shares)**

	£
Sale proceeds (£70,000 × 3,300/3,500)	66,000
Less: Purchase price (W)	(28,875)
Chargeable gain	37,125
Total chargeable gains (£400 + £37,125)	37,525

Working – Share pool

	Number	Cost £
Acquisitions		
16/4/95	2,000	10,000
30/4/09	1,500	18,000
31/5/09	500	7,000
	4,000	35,000
Sale 31/1/13 (£35,000 x (3,300/4,000))	(3,300)	(28,875)
Balance carried forward	700	6,125

Test your understanding 4

Kieran

	£
Sale proceeds	12,000
Less: Cost (Working)	(5,000)
Chargeable gain	7,000

KAPLAN PUBLISHING

Working: Share pool

		Number	Cost £
Jan 2005	Purchase	3,000	6,000
May 2009	Bonus issue (1:3)	1,000	Nil
June 2010	Purchase	500	1,500
		4,500	7,500
February 2013	Sale	(3,000)	(5,000)
Balance c/f		1,500	2,500

Test your understanding 5

Victor

	£
Sale proceeds	46,000
Less: Cost (Working)	(11,200)
Chargeable gain	34,800

Working:

Share pool

		Number	Cost £
April 2000	Purchase	1,000	11,000
Sept 2009	Rights issue (1:2) @ £6 per share	500	3,000
		1,500	14,000
August 2012	Sale	(1,200)	(11,200)
Balance c/f		300	2,800

Test your understanding 6

Marie

Capital gains computation – 2012/13

	£
Sale proceeds	11,000
Less: Cost (W)	(4,000)
Chargeable gain	7,000

Working – Cost of ordinary shares in Red plc

	MV £	Cost £
Marie received		
4,000 ordinary shares, valued at (4,000 x £2)	8,000	4,000
2,000 preference shares, valued at (2,000 × £1)	2,000	1,000
Cost attributable to the ordinary shares is thus: (£8,000/£10,000 × £5,000) = £4,000	10,000	5,000

Note: The cost of the preference shares is carried forward until those shares are disposed.

Test your understanding 7

Paula

The total consideration provided by Big plc is:

	MV £	Cost £
Shares (25,000 × 2 × £1.75)	87,500	14,894
Cash (25,000 × 1 × £1.20)	30,000	5,106
	117,500	20,000

Paula has made a part disposal on 3 October 2012 in relation to the cash consideration.

	£
Disposal proceeds (cash)	30,000
Less: Original cost (£30,000/£117,500 × £20,000)	(5,106)
Chargeable gain	24,894

Paula's allowable cost on the future disposal of her shares in Big plc will be £14,894 (£20,000 – £5,106).

chapter

16

CGT: Reliefs for individuals

Chapter learning objectives

Upon completion of this chapter you will be able to:

- define 'principal private residence'
- calculate the relief on disposal of a principal private residence
- calculate the gain when a principal private residence has been used partly for business purposes
- identify when letting relief is available on a principal private residence and calculate the relief
- explain and apply Entrepreneurs' relief
- explain and apply roll-over relief as it applies to individuals
- explain and apply hold-over relief for the gift of business assets
- explain when incorporation relief is available upon the transfer of a business to a company
- apply incorporation relief.

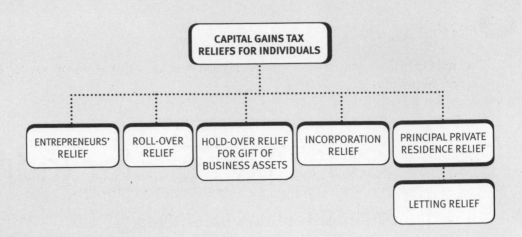

Introduction

In certain situations the tax payable on the disposal of an asset may be reduced or a gain may be delayed by claiming capital gains tax reliefs.

The main reliefs available to individuals are as follows.

	Relief	**Available on the:**
Non-business assets	Principal private residence relief	disposal of an individual's private residence
	Letting relief	disposal of private residence after letting
Business assets	Entrepreneurs' relief	disposal of certain business assets
	Roll-over relief	sale of and reinvestment in certain new business assets
	Hold-over relief	gift of certain business assets
	Incorporation relief	incorporation of a business

1 Principal private residence (PPR) relief

PPR relief applies when an individual disposes of:

- a dwelling house (including normally up to half a hectare of adjoining land)
- which has at some time during his ownership been his only or main private residence.

The relief

The relief applies where the PPR has been occupied for either the whole or part of the period of ownership.

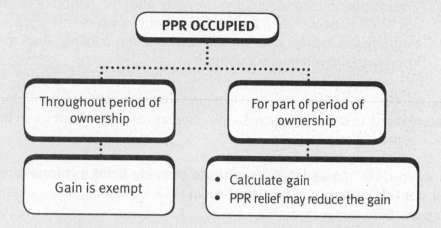

Calculating the relief

Where there has been a period of absence from the PPR the procedure is:

- Calculate the gain on the disposal of the property.
- Compute the total period of ownership.
- Calculate the periods of occupation (see below).
- Calculate the PPR relief as follows:

Gain × (Periods of occupation / Total period of ownership)

- Deduct the PPR relief from the gain on the property.

Periods of occupation

The period of occupation includes periods of both actual occupation and deemed occupation.

Periods of deemed occupation are:

(a) the last 3 years of ownership (always exempt, unconditionally)

(b) up to 3 years of absence for any reason

(c) any period spent employed abroad

(d) up to 4 years of absence while working elsewhere in the UK (employed or self employed) or self employed abroad.

Note that:

- The absences in (b) to (d) must be preceded and followed by a period of actual occupation.

- The condition to reoccupy the property after the period of absence does not need to be satisfied for (c) and (d) above where an employer requires the individual to work elsewhere immediately, thus making it impossible to resume occupation.

Usually, the examiner does not like students to provide explanatory notes to calculations in the exam, unless they are specifically asked for in the requirement.

However, he has said that you **should provide brief explanatory notes** for periods of **deemed occupation** in PPR questions, and that such explanations will earn marks.

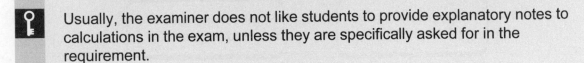

Further points

Ownership of more than one residence

Where an individual has more than one residence he is entitled to nominate which of them is to be treated as his principal residence for capital gains purposes by notifying HMRC in writing.

The election must be made within two years of acquiring an additional residence otherwise it is open to HMRC, as a question of fact, to decide which residence is the main residence.

Married couples/civil partners

Provided that they are not separated or divorced, a married couple (or civil partnership) is entitled to only one residence between them for the purposes of the PPR relief.

Example 1 – Principal private residence relief

On 1 May 1985 Mr Flint purchased a house in Southampton for £25,000, which he lived in until he moved to a rented flat on 1 July 1986.

He remained in the flat until 1 October 1988, when he accepted a year's secondment to his firm's New York office.

He returned to the UK on 1 October 1989 and moved into a relative's house, until he returned to his own home on 31 January 1990.

On 1 July 2003 he changed jobs and rented a flat near his new employer's offices in Newcastle. Here he remained until he sold his Southampton house on 1 February 2013 for £95,000.

Calculate the chargeable gain after reliefs, if any, arising on the disposal of the house on 1 February 2013.

Answer to example 1

	£
Sale proceeds	95,000
Less: Cost	(25,000)
	70,000
Less: PPR relief (W)	(53,393)
Chargeable gain after reliefs	16,607

Working – Chargeable and exempt periods of ownership

	Total	Exempt	Chargeable
May 1985 – June 1986	14		
(actual occupation)		14	–
July 1986 – September 1988	27		
(absent – any reason)		27	–
October 1988 – September 1989	12		
(absent – employed abroad)		12	–
October 1989 – January 1990	4		
(absent – any reason)		4	–
Feb 1990 – June 2003	161		
(actual occupation)		161	–
July 2003 – January 2010	79		
(absent – see note)		–	79
February 2010 – January 2013	36		
(final 36 months)		36	–
	333	254	79

Total period of ownership (79 + 254) = 333 months.

Exempt element of gain = (£70,000 x 254/333) = £53,393.

Notes

(1) After Mr Flint left his residence to work in Newcastle he never returned. Consequently the exemption for working away from home in the UK is not available as there is not actual occupation both before and after the period of absence.

(2) The remaining 5 months (36 months – 27 months – 4 months) for 'any reason' is also not available for exemption as Mr Flint never reoccupied the property after leaving for Newcastle.

(3) In contrast, the final 36 months of ownership is always exempt unconditionally, there is no such restriction.

Test your understanding 1

Arthur bought a house on 1 January 1991 and sold it on 30 September 2012 making a gain of £189,000.

He occupied the house as follows:

1 January 1991 – 31 December 1992	Lived in house
1 January 1993 – 30 June 1999	Employed overseas
1 July 1999 – 31 December 2004	Travels the world
1 January 2005 – 30 September 2012	Lived in house

Calculate the chargeable gain after reliefs, if any, arising on the disposal of the house on 30 September 2012.

Business use

Where a house, or part of it, is used wholly and exclusively for business purposes, this part loses its PPR relief and becomes taxable.

It should be noted that:

- The taxpayer cannot benefit from the rules of deemed occupation for any part of the property used for business purposes.

- However where part of the property was used for business purposes but was also at any time used as the taxpayer's main residence, the exemption for the last 36 months applies to the whole property.

- The 36 month exemption does not however apply to any part of the property used for business purposes **throughout** the whole period of ownership.

KAPLAN PUBLISHING

Example 2 – Principal private residence relief

On 30 June 2012 Alex sold his house for £125,000, resulting in a capital gain of £70,000. The house had been purchased on 1 July 1998, and one of the five rooms has always been used for business purposes.

Calculate the chargeable gain after reliefs arising on the disposal of the house.

Answer to example 2

Alex owned the house for 168 months and used 1/5th of the house (one of the five rooms) for business purposes. The 36 month exemption does not apply to the part of the property used for business purposes as it has never been used at any time for private purposes.

The chargeable gain is therefore: (£70,000 × 1/5) = £14,000

Alternative approach:

	£
Chargeable gain before reliefs	70,000
Less: PPR relief (£70,000 x 4/5)	(56,000)
Chargeable gain after reliefs	14,000

Test your understanding 2

On 30 September 2012 Todd sold his house for £150,000, resulting in a chargeable gain before reliefs of £60,000. The house had been purchased on 1 October 2003, and one of the seven rooms had always been used for business purposes.

Calculate the chargeable gain after reliefs arising on the disposal of the house.

Letting relief

Letting relief is available where an individual's PPR is let out for residential use. It applies when:

- the owner is absent from the property and lets the house out, or

- the owner lets part of the property whilst still occupying the remainder.

It does not apply to let property which is not the owner's PPR (e.g. buy-to-let properties).

Letting relief is the lowest of:

- £40,000

- the amount of the gain exempted by the normal PPR rules

- the part of the gain (still in charge) attributable to the letting period.

Example 3 – Letting relief

Mr Hill bought a house in Luton on 1 June 1986. He occupied the house as follows:

1 June 1986 – 31 May 1987	Lived in as PPR.
1 June 1987 – 30 November 2002	Travelled the world
	Let the house from 1 June 1991 to 31 March 2001.
1 December 2002 – 1 July 2012	Lived in as PPR.

He sold the house on 1 July 2012 realising a chargeable gain of £209,730.

Calculate the chargeable gain after reliefs arising on the sale of the house.

Answer to example 3

	£
Chargeable gain before reliefs	209,730
Less: PPR relief (W1)	(109,220)
	100,510
Less: Letting relief (W2)	(40,000)
Chargeable gain after reliefs	60,510

KAPLAN PUBLISHING

Workings

(1) PPR relief

Total period of ownership/occupation:

1 June 1986 – 1 July 2012 = 26 years 1 month (313 months)

	Total	Exempt	Chargeable
1.6.86 – 31.05.87	12		
Actual occupation		12	
1.6.87 – 30.11.02	186		
3 years – any reason		36	
Rest of period – chargeable			150
1.12.02 – 1.7.12	115		
Last 3 years		36	
Rest of period – actual occupation		79	
Number of months	313	163	150

PPR relief = (£209,730 × 163/313) = £109,220

Letting relief

The house was let from 1.6.91 to 31.3.01 and therefore, letting relief is available for this period of 118 months.

Letting relief = lowest of:

1 Maximum = £40,000
2 PPR = £109,220
3 Gain on letting (£209,730 × 118/313) = £79,067   £40,000

Test your understanding 3

On 30 September 2012, Jane Smith made a gift of a house to her grandson Norman. The house had been bought by Jane on 1 September 1999 for £45,000, and was extended at a cost of £10,600 during June 2000. A market value of £140,000 at 30 September 2012 had been agreed by HMRC.

Jane occupied the house as her main residence until 30 September 2003 when she went to live with her sister. The house was rented out from 1 October 2004 to the date of the deemed sale.

Calculate the chargeable gain after reliefs arising on the gift.

Summary

```
                    ┌───────────────────────┐
                    │  PRINCIPAL PRIVATE     │
                    │  RESIDENCE RELIEF      │
                    └───────────────────────┘
```

OCCUPIED THROUGHOUT OWNERSHIP

OCCUPIED FOR PART OF PERIOD OF OWNERSHIP

GAIN EXEMPT

BUSINESS USE

LETTING RELIEF

PPR exemption:

$$\text{Gain} \times \frac{\text{Occupation}}{\text{Period of ownership}}$$

Part used wholly for business is not covered by the PPR exemption

Lower of:
- £40,000
- PPR exemption
- chargeable gain attributable to letting period

Periods of occupation
- Actual occupation
- Deemed occupation
  - Last 3 years
  - 3 years any reason
  - Any period employed abroad
  - Up to 4 years, working elsewhere in UK (employed or self employed) or self employed abroad

- Deemed occupation must be preceded and followed by a period of actual occupation

2 Entrepreneurs' relief

Entrepreneurs' relief reduces the rate of CGT payable on certain qualifying business disposals to 10%.

The relief operates as follows:

- The first £10 million of gains on 'qualifying business disposals' will be taxed at 10%, regardless of the level of the taxpayer's income.

- Any gains above the £10 million limit are taxed in full at the 18% or 28% rate depending on the individual's taxable income.

- Gains qualifying for Entrepreneurs' relief are set against any unused basic rate band before non-qualifying gains.

- The 10% CGT rate is calculated after the deduction of:
  - allowable losses, and
  - the AEA.

- However, the taxpayer can choose to set losses (other than any losses on assets that are part of the disposal of the business) and the AEA against non-qualifying gains first, in order to maximise the relief.

- It is therefore helpful to keep gains which qualify for Entrepreneurs' relief separate from those which do not qualify.

The relief must be claimed within 12 months of the 31 January following the end of the tax year in which the disposal is made.

For 2012/13 disposals, the relief must be claimed by 31 January 2015.

The £10 million limit is a lifetime limit which is diminished each time a claim for the relief is made.

Qualifying business disposals

The relief applies to the disposal of:

- the whole or part of a business carried on by the individual either alone or in partnership

- assets of the individual's or partnership's trading business that has **now ceased**

- shares **provided**:
  - the shares are in the individual's 'personal trading company', **and**
  - the individual is an employee of the company (part time or full time).

An individual's 'personal trading company' is one in which the individual:

- owns at least 5% of the ordinary shares
- which carry at least 5% of the voting rights.

Note that:

- the disposal of an individual business asset used for the purposes of a continuing trade does not qualify. There must be a disposal of the whole or part of the trading business. The sale of an asset in isolation will not qualify.
- "Part of a business" is likely to be interpreted as meaning a "substantial part" which is "capable of independent operation".
- Where the disposal is a disposal of assets (i.e. not shares), relief is not available on gains arising from the disposal of those assets held for investment purposes.
- There is no requirement to restrict the gain qualifying for relief on shares by reference to any non-business assets held by the company.
- There are no minimum working hours for an employee to qualify.

Qualifying ownership period

The asset(s) being disposed of must have been owned by the individual making the disposal in the 12 months prior to the disposal.

Where the disposal is an asset of the individual's or partnership's trading business that has now ceased the disposal must also take place within three years of the cessation of trade.

Example 4 – Entrepreneurs' relief

In 2012/13, Katie sold her trading business which she set up in 2001 and realised the following gains and losses:

	£
Factory	275,000
Goodwill	330,000
Warehouse	(100,000)
Investment property	200,000

All of the assets have been owned for many years.

Katie also sold her shares in an unquoted trading company and realised a gain of £600,000. She owned 25% of the ordinary shares of the company which she purchased ten years ago. She has worked for the company on a part time basis for the last three years.

Katie has not made any other capital disposals in 2012/13 but she has capital losses brought forward of £9,000. She has never claimed any Entrepreneurs' relief in the past.

She has taxable income of £30,000.

Calculate Katie's capital gains tax payable for 2012/13.

Answer to example 4

	£	£
Not qualifying for Entrepreneurs' relief		
Sale of investment property (Note 1)	200,000	
Qualifying for Entrepreneurs' relief		
Sale of trading business:		
Factory		275,000
Goodwill		330,000
Warehouse (Note 2):		(100,000)
		————
		505,000
Sale of trading company shares		600,000
	————	————
	200,000	1,105,000
Less: Capital losses b/f (Note 3)	(9,000)	(Nil)
Less: AEA (Note 3)	(10,600)	(Nil)
	————	————
Taxable gains	180,400	1,105,000
	————	————
Capital gains tax:		
Qualifying gains (£1,105,000 x 10%)		110,500
Non-qualifying gains (£180,400 x 28%) (Note 4)		50,512
		————
		161,012
		————

Notes:

(1) Despite being part of the sale of the whole business, the gain on the investment property does not qualify for Entrepreneurs' relief (ER).

(2) The net chargeable gains on the disposal of an unincorporated business qualify for ER (i.e. the gains after netting off all losses arising on the disposal of the business, but excluding investment assets).

(3) Capital losses and annual exempt amount are first set against gains not qualifying for ER.

(4) The gains qualifying for ER are deemed to utilise the basic rate band (BRB) first. Therefore the BRB remaining of £4,370 (£34,370 – £30,000) is set against the gains qualifying for ER. The remaining gains are taxed at 28%.

Example 5 – Entrepreneurs' relief

Kevin disposed of a business in November 2012, realising chargeable gains of £6.6 million. He had started the business in January 2005 and has used all the chargeable assets for business use throughout the period of ownership.

He has previously claimed Entrepreneurs' relief for qualifying gains of £4 million.

He also disposed of a holiday home in February 2013, realising a chargeable gain of £20,000. The home had never been his principal private residence.

Kevin had taxable income of £40,000 in 2012/13.

Calculate Kevin's capital gains tax payable for 2012/13.

Answer to example 5

Kevin – 2012/13

	£	£
Not qualifying for Entrepreneurs' relief		
Sale of holiday home	20,000	
Qualifying for Entrepreneurs' relief		
Sale of trading business		6,600,000
Less: AEA (Note 1)	(10,600)	Nil
Taxable gains	9,400	6,600,000

Capital gains tax:

Qualifying gains (£6,000,000 x 10%) (W)	600,000
(£600,000 x 28%) (Note 2 and 3)	168,000
Non-qualifying gains (£9,400 x 28%) (Note 3)	2,632
	770,632

Working: Qualifying gains in 2012/13

	£
Lifetime limit	10,000,000
Claims prior to 2012/13	(4,000,000)
Qualifying gains in 2012/13	6,000,000

Notes:

(1) The AEA is set against gains not qualifying for ER.

(2) Kevin has a lifetime limit of £10 million. He has already claimed relief for £4 million therefore he has £6 million limit remaining. After the first £6 million of gains qualifying for ER have been taxed at 10%, any remaining qualifying gains are taxed at the appropriate rate depending on the taxpayer's level of income.

(3) Kevin's taxable income is £40,000, therefore the basic rate band is no longer available. All other gains are therefore taxed at 28%.

Test your understanding 4

In 2012/13 Paul sold shares in Dual Ltd, an unquoted trading company, and realised a gain of £430,000. Paul has worked for Dual Ltd for many years and has owned 10% of the ordinary shares of the company for the last five years.

Paul set up a trading business in 2006 and in 2012/13 he sold a warehouse used in the business, realising a gain of £245,000.

Paul's taxable income was £28,000 in 2012/13.

In 2013/14 Paul sold the rest of the business and realised gains of:

Factory	£6,495,000
Goodwill	£130,000

All of the assets in the business have been owned for many years.

Paul also sold an antique table and realised a gain of £5,325.

His taxable income in 2013/14 was £38,000, and prior to 2012/13 Paul has claimed Entrepreneurs' relief of £3.5 million.

Calculate Paul's CGT payable for 2012/13 and 2013/14.

Assume that the AEA and rates for 2012/13 continue in the future.

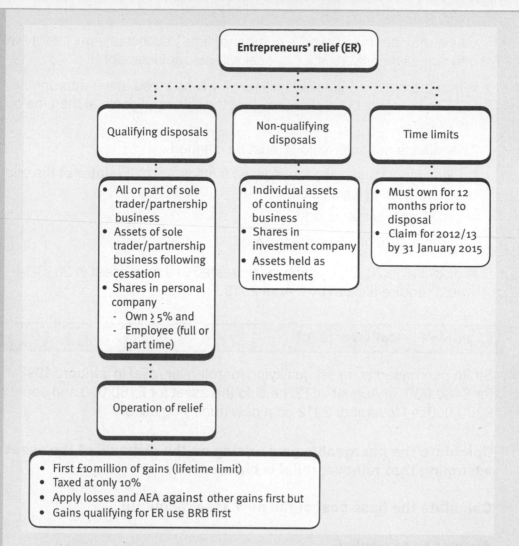

3 Replacement of business asset relief (Roll-over relief)

Roll-over relief (ROR) allows the gain arising on the disposal of a qualifying business asset to be rolled over (i.e. deferred) when the sale proceeds are reinvested in a new qualifying business asset.

The relief is available to both individuals and companies.

The relief

The relief operates as follows:

- The gain arising on the disposal of the qualifying business asset is deducted from (rolled over against) the acquisition cost of the new asset.

- Provided the proceeds are fully reinvested, no tax is payable at the time of the disposal.

- ROR effectively increases the gain arising on the disposal of the replacement asset, as its base cost has been reduced by the amount of deferred gain.

- Gains may be 'rolled over' a number of times such that a tax liability will only arise when there is a disposal without replacement.

- When the deferred gain crystallises, it will be taxed at the appropriate CGT rate applicable at that time (not the rate applicable at the time of the deferral).

- The relief is not automatic, it must be claimed.

- An individual must claim the relief within 4 years of the **later of** the end of the tax year in which the:
  – disposal is made, and
  – replacement asset is acquired.

- A disposal in 2012/13 which is reinvested in a new asset in 2013/14 would require a claim by 5 April 2018.

Example 6 – Roll-over relief

Smith purchased an asset qualifying for roll-over relief in January 1997 for £160,000. In August 2012, he sold the asset for £180,000 and spent £200,000 in November 2012 on a new qualifying asset.

Calculate the chargeable gain arising on the disposal of the asset assuming that roll-over relief is claimed.

Calculate the base cost of the new asset acquired.

Answer to example 6

Gain on disposal of asset	£
Sale proceeds	180,000
Less: Cost	(160,000)
	20,000
Less: ROR (Roll-over relief) (deferred gain)	(20,000)
Chargeable gain	Nil

Base cost of new asset	£
Acquisition cost	200,000
Less: ROR (deferred gain)	(20,000)
Revised base cost	180,000

Conditions

Where a **qualifying business asset** is sold at a gain, the taxpayer may roll over the gain provided the proceeds are reinvested in a replacement qualifying business asset within the **qualifying time period**.

Qualifying business assets

The main categories of assets qualifying for roll-over relief on a disposal by an individual are:

- goodwill
- land and buildings
- fixed plant and machinery (i.e. not moveable).

Both the old and the replacement assets must be qualifying business assets and have been used in a trade.

Qualifying time period

The replacement assets must be acquired within a period:

- beginning **one** year before, and
- ending **three** years after the date of sale of the old asset.

Example 7 – Rollover relief

Jones purchased a warehouse in February 2003 for £170,000. In July 2012, he sold the warehouse for £300,000. He used the warehouse for the purposes of his trade throughout the period of ownership.

In December 2014 Jones bought a new warehouse for £360,000 for the purposes of his trade. He plans to sell the warehouse in January 2016 for £550,000.

Calculate the chargeable gains arising on the two sales.

Answer to example 7

First warehouse – July 2012 – 2012/13

	£
Sale proceeds	300,000
Less: Cost	(170,000)
	130,000
Less: ROR (Note)	(130,000)
Chargeable gain	Nil

Note: The full gain of £130,000 can be rolled over (i.e. deferred) as:

- the asset disposed of is a qualifying business asset

- the replacement asset is a qualifying business asset

- the reinvestment has been made in December 2014 (i.e. within the qualifying period of July 2011 to July 2015)

- the amount reinvested exceeds the sale proceeds received (i.e. purchase price of new warehouse of £360,000 exceeds the sale proceeds of £300,000).

Second warehouse – January 2016 – 2015/16

	£	£
Sale proceeds		550,000
Less: Base Cost		
Cost	360,000	
Less: ROR	(130,000)	
		(230,000)
Chargeable gain		320,000

Note: This gain can also be rolled-over (i.e. deferred) if a qualifying replacement asset is purchased in the qualifying time period.

However, assuming the gain is not deferred and the rates of CGT remain unchanged, the gain in 2015/16 will be taxed at 18% or 28% depending on the level of taxable income in that tax year.

The gain will not be taxed at 10% as it does not qualify for ER. This is because the disposal of an individual asset used for the purposes of a continuing trade does not qualify. The trade itself is not being disposed of.

Test your understanding 5

Chris acquired a freehold building in April 1995. In May 1998 he sold the building for £100,000 and realised a gain of £56,360. In August 1999, another freehold building was bought for £140,000 and this was sold in November 2012 for £380,000.

All of the buildings were used for the purposes of a trade by Chris.

Calculate the chargeable gain arising on the disposal of the second building in 2012/13.

Partial reinvestment of proceeds

Full roll-over relief is only available when all of the proceeds from the sale of the old asset are reinvested.

Where there is partial reinvestment of the proceeds, part of the gain is chargeable at the time of the disposal.

The gain which is **chargeable** (cannot be rolled over) is the **lower** of:

- the amount of the proceeds **not** reinvested
- the full gain.

Test your understanding 6

Jarvis bought a factory in September 1997 and in December 2012, wishing to move to a more convenient location, he sold the factory for £750,000. The cost of the factory was £635,000.

Jarvis moved into a rented factory until March 2013 when he purchased and moved into a new factory.

Calculate the amount of the gain which is chargeable, if any, on the sale of the original factory and calculate the base cost of the new factory assuming the new factory was purchased for

(a) £700,000, or
(b) £550,000?

Non-business use

Full roll-over relief is only available where the old asset being replaced was used entirely for trade purposes throughout the trader's period of ownership.

Where this condition is not met, roll-over relief is still available but it is scaled down in proportion to the non-trade use.

Example 8 – Roll-over relief

Robert acquired a freehold building in April 1995 for £65,500. He only used 60% of the freehold building for the purposes of his trade. The building was sold in November 2012 for £162,000.

A replacement building was acquired in January 2012 for £180,000 and this was used 100% for trade purposes by Robert.

The replacement building was sold for £250,000 in May 2013.

Calculate the gain rolled over and the chargeable gains arising on the disposals in November 2012 and May 2013.

Answer to example 8

First building – November 2012 – 2012/13

	£
Sale proceeds	162,000
Less: Cost	(65,500)
Chargeable gain before reliefs	96,500

Note: The asset disposed of is a qualifying business asset for ROR purposes, but as only 60% of the building has been used for trade purposes, the gain eligible for ROR must be restricted to 60%.

	Business portion	Non-business portion
	£	£
Split of chargeable gain (60%:40%)	57,900	38,600
Less: ROR (Note)	(57,900)	(n/a)
Chargeable gain	Nil	38,600

Note:
- the replacement asset is a qualifying business asset, used 100% for the purposes of the trade

- the reinvestment has been made in January 2012 (i.e. within the qualifying period of November 2011 to November 2015).

- the amount reinvested for the purposes of the trade (i.e. purchase price of new warehouse of £180,000) exceeds the sale proceeds received on the first building relating to the trade use of the building (i.e. £162,000 x 60% = £97,200).

- therefore ROR is available on all of the business portion of the gain.

Sale of replacement building – May 2013 – 2013/14

	£	£
Sale proceeds		250,000
Less: Base Cost		
Cost	180,000	
Less: ROR	(57,900)	
		(122,100)
Chargeable gain		127,900

Note: Assuming there is no replacement of this asset and the rates of CGT remain unchanged, the gains in 2012/13 and 2013/14 will be taxed at 18% or 28% depending on the level of taxable income in those years.

They will not be taxed at 10% as the gains do not qualify for ER. This is because the disposal of an individual asset used for the purposes of a continuing trade does not qualify.

Test your understanding 7

Hadley purchased a factory in November 1988 and not needing all the space, he let out 15% of it.

In August 2012 he sold the factory for £560,000 and realised a capital gain of £45,000.

In October 2012 Hadley bought another factory which he used 100% for business purposes for £500,000 claiming roll-over relief.

(a) **Calculate the chargeable gain arising on the disposal in August 2012.**

(b) **Calculate the base cost of the new factory.**

Depreciating assets

Roll-over relief is modified where the new asset is a depreciating asset:

- If the replacement asset acquired is a depreciating asset, the gain cannot be rolled over, instead it is deferred until the earliest of the following three events:

    - Disposal of replacement asset.

    - The depreciating asset ceases to be used for the purposes of the trade.

    - Ten years from the date of acquisition of the replacement asset.

- The deferred gain is not deducted from the cost of the new asset.

- The deferred gain is just 'frozen' and becomes chargeable on the earliest of the three events above.

- When the deferred gain crystallises, it will be taxed at the appropriate CGT rate applicable at that time (not the rate applicable at the time of the deferral).

A depreciating asset is a wasting asset (i.e. with a predictable life of 50 years or less), or an asset that will become a wasting asset within ten years (e.g. fixed plant and machinery or leasehold property with ≤ 60 years remaining on the lease).

- If prior to the deferred gain crystallising, a non-depreciating asset is bought, then the original deferred gain can now be rolled over.

Example 9 – Depreciating assets

Cooper purchased a freehold factory in June 1985 for £250,000. In May 2011 he sold it for £420,000 and in June 2011 bought fixed plant and machinery for £450,000. In March 2013, Cooper sold the fixed plant and machinery for £475,000.

Calculate the chargeable gains arising in 2011/12 and 2012/13 assuming Cooper claims to roll over the gains where possible.

Answer to example 9

Freehold factory – May 2011 – 2011/12

	£
Sale proceeds	420,000
Less: Cost	(250,000)
	170,000
Less: Deferred gain (see Note)	(170,000)
Chargeable gain	Nil

Note:
- the asset disposed of is a qualifying business asset
- the replacement asset is a qualifying business asset, but is a depreciating asset (fixed plant and machinery)
- the reinvestment has been made in June 2011 (i.e. within the qualifying period of May 2010 to May 2014)
- the amount reinvested (i.e. purchase price of new plant and machinery of £450,000) exceeds the sale proceeds received on the factory of £420,000.
- therefore all of the gain can be deferred, but the deferred gain is not deducted from the base cost of the plant and machinery
- the gain of £170,000 is frozen and becomes chargeable on the earliest of:
  - the sale of the fixed plant and machinery (March 2013)
  - the date the plant and machinery ceases to be used in the trade (presumably March 2013)
  - ten years from the acquisition of the plant and machinery (June 2021)

Sale of plant and machinery – March 2013 – 2012/13

	£
Sale proceeds	475,000
Less: Cost	(450,000)
Capital gain on plant and machinery	25,000
Deferred gain becomes chargeable	170,000
Chargeable gains	195,000

Note: Assuming there is no replacement of this asset and the rates of CGT remain unchanged, the gains in 2012/13 will be taxed at 18% or 28% depending on the level of taxable income in that year.

They will not be taxed at 10% as the gains do not qualify for ER. This is because the disposal of an individual asset used for the purposes of a continuing trade does not qualify.

Test your understanding 8

Amir purchased a freehold factory in May 1987 and in May 2000 he sold it for £350,000 realising a capital gain of £150,000. In July 2002 Amir bought fixed plant and machinery for £400,000. In March 2014 Amir sold the fixed plant and machinery for £500,000.

Calculate the chargeable gains arising in respect of the sale of the freehold factory and the fixed plant and machinery, assuming Amir claims to roll over the gains where possible.

Clearly identify in which tax year the gains arise.

KAPLAN PUBLISHING

Summary

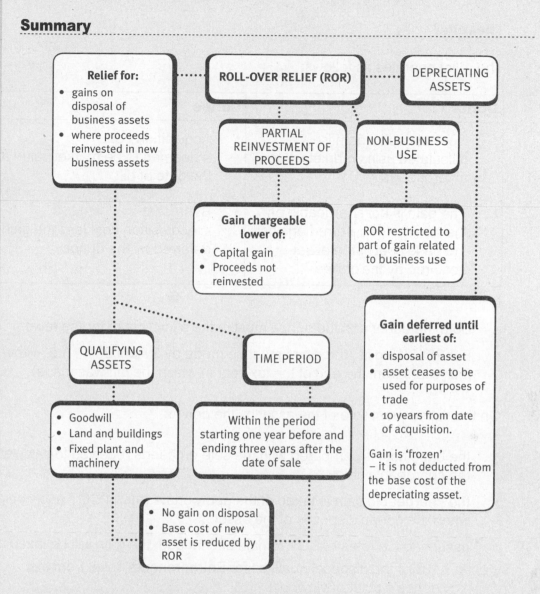

4 Gift of business assets – hold-over relief

The gift of an asset is a chargeable disposal which gives rise to a capital gains tax liability for the donor, however the donor has not received any funds with which to pay the tax.

Gift relief allows the gain arising on the gift of qualifying business assets to be held over (i.e. deferred) until the asset is eventually sold by the donee.

The relief however is only available for:

* qualifying business assets
* gifted by individuals.

The relief

The relief operates as follows:

Donor	Donee
• Normal capital gain is calculated using market value as proceeds • The gain is not chargeable on the donor; it is deferred against the base cost of the asset acquired by the donee	• Acquisition cost = deemed to be market value at the date of gift • Base cost = Acquisition cost less the gain deferred by the donor

- Both the donor and the donee must make a joint claim for the relief.

- For 2012/13 gifts, the claim must be made by 5 April 2017, (i.e. within four years from the end of the tax year in which the gift was made).

On the subsequent sale of the asset by the donee:

- the base cost is compared with the sale proceeds received to calculate the chargeable gain.

- the chargeable gain is taxed at the appropriate rate of CGT applicable when the donee disposes of the asset.

- assuming the rates of CGT remain unchanged, the gain will be taxed at:
  - 10% if the disposal qualifies for Entrepreneurs' relief from the donee's point of view, or
  - 18% or 28% depending on the level of the donee's taxable income in the year of disposal.

Example 10 – Gift of business assets – hold-over relief

Jones bought a business asset for £25,000 in August 2004. In August 2012 he gave it to Smith, when its market value was £40,000. Jones and Smith have made an election to hold over any gain arising.

Show Jones's capital gains tax position on the gift to Smith and calculate Smith's base cost in the asset.

Answer to example 10

Jones's CGT position
Gift to Smith – August 2012

	£
Market value of asset	40,000
Less: Cost	(25,000)
	———
	15,000
Less: Gift relief for business assets	(15,000)
	———
Chargeable gain	Nil
	———

Smith's base cost
Smith has allowable expenditure to set against a future disposal, calculated as follows:

	£
Market value of asset acquired	40,000
Less: Gift relief (Jones's held over gain)	(15,000)
	———
Base cost	25,000
	———

Qualifying assets

The relief is only available where there is a gift of a qualifying asset.

The following are the main categories of qualifying asset.

- Assets used in the trade of:
    - the donor (i.e. where he is a sole trader)
    - the donor's personal company (this extends the relief to assets owned by the individual but used in the company owned by him directly for trading purposes).

- Unquoted shares and securities of any trading company.

- Quoted shares or securities of the individual donor's personal trading company.

A company qualifies as an individual's personal trading company if at least 5% of the voting rights are owned by the individual.

However, unlike Entrepreneurs' relief, there is no minimum holding period and no requirement for the individual to work for the company to quality for gift relief.

Rate of CGT – tax planning

The outright gift of a qualifying asset results in:

- no chargeable gain arising on the donor at the time of the gift

- a higher gain arising on the donee on the subsequent disposal of the asset by the donee

- which is taxed at 0%, 10%, 18% or 28% depending on:
  - the availability of the donee's annual exempt amount,
  - the availability of Entrepreneurs' relief from the donee's point of view or, if not available,
  - the level of the donee's taxable income in that tax year.

However, claiming gift relief is optional, and if it is not claimed:

- the gain arising at the time of the gift is assessed on the donor

- which is taxed at 0%, 10%, 18% or 28% depending on the same factors from the donor's perspective.

Consequently:

- the donor may **choose not to claim** gift relief in order to:
  - crystallise a gain and utilise their AEA, and/or
  - claim Entrepreneurs' relief
  - so that the gain is taxed at 0% or 10% now rather than potentially at a higher rate later.

This may be advantageous if:

- the donor qualifies for Entrepreneurs' relief now but the donee will not qualify for the relief when they subsequently dispose of the asset (for example if they would not satisfy the one-year ownership rule)

- the donor has no other gains and therefore AEA available, and/or is a basic rate taxpayer whereas the donee is likely to be a higher rate taxpayer when the asset is disposed of.

Note that the donor and donee are independent persons and thus in the above two situations the donor may be more concerned about his tax liability on the gift than the donee's liability on the ultimate disposal.

KAPLAN PUBLISHING

However, a gift relief claim must be signed by both the donor and donee and so the tax position of both parties must be considered.

Note also that if gift relief is claimed, all of the gain must be deferred; partial claims are not possible.

Sales at an undervalue

The relief applies not just to outright gifts but also to sales for less than market value (i.e. where there is an element of gift).

For sales at an undervalue the relief is modified as follows:

- Any proceeds received which exceed the **original cost** of the asset gifted are chargeable to CGT on the donor at the date of the gift.

- The rest of the gain may be deferred (held over).

The chargeable gain arising on the donor will be taxed at 0%, 10%, 18% or 28% depending on the same factors mentioned above.

Example 11 – Gift of business assets – hold-over relief

Ronald bought a business asset on 4 July 2002 for £20,000. He gave this asset to his son, Regan, on 1 September 2004 when the market value was £52,000. Ronald and Regan made a joint election to hold over any gain arising. Regan sold the asset on 18 December 2012 for £95,000.

(a) **Calculate the gain 'held over' and the chargeable gain arising on the eventual disposal by Regan in 2012/13.**

(b) **Calculate the gain eligible for gift relief and the base cost for Regan, assuming the same facts as above, but Regan pays his father on 1 September 2004:**

    (i)   **£28,000 or**

    (ii) **£18,000.**

Answer to example 11

(a) **Ronald – Capital gains computation – 2004/05**

	£
Deemed disposal proceeds (MV at date of gift)	52,000
Less: Acquisition cost	(20,000)
	32,000
Less: Gift relief	(32,000)
Chargeable gain	Nil

As Ronald and Regan have made a joint election, all of the gain of £32,000 can be 'held over' (i.e. deferred) from Ronald to Regan.

Therefore there would be no chargeable gain on Ronald in 2004/05.

Regan – Capital gains computation – 2012/13

	£	£
Sale proceeds		95,000
Less Base cost:		
MV at date of gift	52,000	
Less: Gain held over from Ronald	(32,000)	
		(20,000)
Chargeable gain		75,000

Note: This gain will be taxed at 18% or 28% depending on the level of Regan's taxable income in that year. It is not taxed at 10% as the gain does not qualify for ER. This is because this is the gift of an individual asset, not the disposal of a whole or substantial part of a business.

KAPLAN PUBLISHING

(b) Sale at undervaluation

(i)   Ronald – Capital gains computation – 2004/05

	£	£
Deemed disposal proceeds (MV at date of gift)		52,000
Less: Acquisition cost		(20,000)
		———
Potential gain (as before)		32,000
Actual proceeds	28,000	
Less: Original cost	(20,000)	
	———	
Excess proceeds over cost chargeable now	8,000	
Less: Gain eligible to be held over		(24,000)
		———
Chargeable gain		8,000
		———

This gain was taxed on Ronald at the rate of CGT applicable in 2004/05.

Regan – Base cost (for future disposal)

	£
Deemed acquisition cost (MV at date of gift)	52,000
Less: Gain held over from Ronald	(24,000)
	———
Base cost	28,000
	———

(ii) Ronald – Capital gains computation – 2004/05

	£
Deemed disposal proceeds (MV at date of gift)	52,000
Less: Acquisition cost	(20,000)
	———
Potential gain (as before)	32,000

Actual proceeds of £18,000 are less than original cost of £20,000 therefore the entire gain is eligible for gift relief.

	£
Less: Gain eligible to be held over	(32,000)
	———
Chargeable gain	Nil
	———

Regan – Base cost (for future disposal)	
	£
Deemed acquisition cost	52,000
Less: Gain held over from Ronald	(32,000)
Base cost	20,000

Test your understanding 9

Alice bought a business asset in May 2006 for £120,000. She gave this asset to her brother, Adam, on 29 June 2011 when the market value was £150,000. Alice and Adam made a joint election to hold over any gain arising. Adam sold the asset on 1 May 2012 for £180,000.

(a) **Calculate the gain 'held over' and the chargeable gain arising on the chargeable disposal by Adam in 2012/13.**

(b) **Calculate the gain eligible for gift of business assets relief and the base cost of Adam if, instead of giving the asset to Adam, Alice had sold it to him for £130,000.**

Assets not used wholly for trade purposes

The relief is restricted where either:

- only part of an asset is used for trading purposes
- an asset is used for trading purposes for only part of the donor's period of ownership.

Assets apart from shares

Only the gain relating to the period that the asset was used in the trade or the part of the asset used for trading purposes is eligible for gift relief.

The restriction to the relief operates in the same way as roll-over relief where assets have not been wholly used in the trade.

KAPLAN PUBLISHING

Example 12 – Gift of business assets – hold-over relief

David acquired a freehold building in May 2005 for £160,000. He used 60% of the freehold building in his trade for business purposes.

In September 2012 he gave the building to his son, Ben, when its market value was £250,000. David and Ben signed an election to hold over the gain arising on the gift.

Calculate the gain held over and the chargeable gain arising on the gift of the building in September 2012.

Answer to example 12

David – Capital gains computation – 2012/13

	£
Market value at date of gift	250,000
Less: Acquisition cost	(160,000)
	————
Potential gain	90,000

As only 60% of the building has been used for the purposes of a trade, the gain eligible to be held over must also be restricted by the same %.

	£
Less: Gain eligible to be held over (60% × £90,000)	(54,000)
	————
Chargeable gain (40% of £90,000)	36,000
	————

Note: This gain is taxed at 18% or 28% depending on the level of David's taxable income in 2012/13. It will not be taxed at 10% as the gain does not qualify for ER. This is because this is the gift of an individual asset, not the disposal of a whole or substantial part of a business.

Shares in a personal trading company

Where the assets being gifted are shares; the gain eligible to be held over is restricted if:

- the shares are in the donor's personal company
  (i.e. at least 5% of the voting rights are owned by the donor)
  – whether quoted or unquoted; and

- the company owns chargeable non-business assets.

In this situation the gain eligible for gift relief is:

$$\text{Total gain} \times \frac{\text{M.V. of chargeable business assets (CBA)}}{\text{M.V. of chargeable assets (CA)}}$$

Note that where the donor holds less than 5% of the voting rights:

- for unquoted shares
  – the restriction does not apply; full relief is available

- for quoted shares – gift relief is not available at all.

Chargeable assets (CA)

A chargeable asset is one that, if sold, would give rise to a chargeable gain or an allowable loss (i.e. capital assets that are chargeable).

Exempt assets such as motor cars are therefore excluded.

Inventory, receivables, cash, etc. are also excluded as they are not capital assets and therefore not chargeable.

Chargeable business assets (CBA)

These are defined as chargeable assets (as defined above) that are used for the purposes of a trade.

Chargeable business assets therefore **exclude** shares, securities or other assets owned by the business but held for investment purposes.

Consequences of restricting gift relief

Note that if the individual disposes of shares in a personal trading company:

- gift relief is available:
  - subject to the (CBA / CA) restriction above
  - regardless of whether or not the individual works for the company

- a chargeable gain will therefore arise at the time of the gift on the donor as not all of the gain can be deferred

KAPLAN PUBLISHING

- the chargeable gain will be taxed on the donor at 0%, 10%, 18% or 28% depending on:
  - the availability of the donor's annual exempt amount,
  - the availability of Entrepreneurs' relief from the donor's point of view and, if not available,
  - the level of the donor's taxable income in that tax year.
- Entrepreneurs' relief is available if:
  - the donor works for the company, and
  - it has been the donor's personal trading company
  - for the 12 months prior to the disposal.

Example 13 – Gift of business assets – hold-over relief

Jin Ming has been a full-time working director of Porcelain Products Ltd since 1 December 1994 and has owned 10% of the company's ordinary shares since 1 December 1998.

He resigned from the company in 2005 but kept the shares until 1 December 2012 when he gave his 10% shareholding, valued at £950,000, to his daughter Jun Ying.

The agreed capital gain on the disposal of the shares was £700,000. Jin and Jun signed an election to hold over the gain on the gift.

The market values of the assets held by the company at 1 December 2012 were:

	£
Land and buildings	550,000
Motor cars	80,000
Cash	45,000
Receivables	35,000
Inventory	50,000
Shares held as investments	60,000

Calculate Jin Ming's chargeable gain in 2012/13; and the base cost of the shares acquired by Jun Ying.

Answer to example 13

Jin Ming – Capital gains computation – 2012/13

	£
Total gain on disposal of shares	700,000
Less: Gift relief (W) £700,000 × (£550,000 / £610,000)	(631,148)
Chargeable gain	68,852

Working:

MV of CA = (£550,000 + £60,000) = £610,000
MV of CBA = £550,000

Note: The gain will be taxed at 18% or 28% depending on the level of Jin Ming's taxable income in 2012/13. It will not be taxed at 10% as the gain does not qualify for ER.

This is because Jim Ming did not work for the company in the 12 months before the disposal.

Base cost for Jun Ying	£
MV at date of gift	950,000
Less: Gift relief (held over gain)	(631,148)
Base cost	318,852

Test your understanding 10

Fred owned 100% of the shares in Fred Ltd and worked for his company until he became unwell in October 2008. His son stepped in and ran the company for Fred.

On 20 February 2013, Fred made a gift of his shares to his son, and this resulted in a chargeable gain of £420,000.

At the time of the gift the market value of the assets owned by Fred Ltd were as follows:

	£
Freehold trading premises	400,000
Investments – Shares in UK companies	100,000
Inventory and work in progress	130,000
Receivables	100,000
Cash	30,000
	760,000

Calculate the amount of Fred's chargeable gain and the amount that can be held over as a gift of business assets.

Summary

GIFT OF BUSINESS ASSETS RELIEF

EFFECT OF THE RELIEF

QUALIFYING ASSETS

SALES AT AN UNDERVALUE

Donor:
- Proceeds = Market value
- No gain

Donee:
- Donor's gain deducted from base cost of donee gifted asset

- Assets used in trade of donor or donor's personal company
- Shares in unquoted trading company or in donor's personal trading company

Proceeds in excess of the original cost are chargeable at the date of gift

NON-BUSINESS USE

Joint election required for disposals in 2012/13 by 5 April 2017

ASSETS OTHER THAN SHARES

SHARES

Relief restricted to part of gain related to business use

If shares are in donor's personal company the gain held over is:

$$\text{Total gain} \times \frac{\text{MV of CBA}}{\text{MV of CA}}$$

5 Incorporation relief

Where an individual transfers their business to a company, for capital gains tax purposes:

- the individual assets of the business are deemed to have been disposed of
- at market value.

Incorporation relief is a form of roll-over relief to allow the gains arising on incorporation to be deferred until the shares in the newly formed company are disposed of.

The conditions

Incorporation relief is available where the following conditions apply:

- The unincorporated business is transferred as a going concern.
- All of the assets of the business (other than cash) are transferred.
- The consideration for the transfer of the business must be wholly or partly in the form of shares in the company.

The relief

Incorporation relief operates as follows:

- The net chargeable gains arising on the deemed disposal of the individual assets are rolled over (i.e. deferred) against the acquisition cost of the shares in the new company.
- The rolled over gain is deducted from the base cost of the shares.
- Where the consideration for the transfer of the business to the company is wholly shares, the full gain is rolled over.
- Where part of the consideration for the transfer of the business is not shares (e.g. cash or loan notes), the gain eligible for relief is:

$$\text{Net chargeable gains} \times \frac{\text{Value of shares issued}}{\text{Total consideration}}$$

- The relief is automatic provided the conditions above are met.
- An individual can elect for incorporation relief not to apply (i.e. disapply the relief).

Note that a chargeable gain arises at the time of incorporation where:

- part of the consideration is in the form of cash, or
- incorporation relief is disapplied.

This gain will usually be taxed at 10% as the gain relates to the disposal of an unincorporated business and the business is likely to have been owned for at least 12 months before incorporation, and therefore Entrepreneurs' relief would apply.

Rate of CGT – tax planning

It is important to note that:

- The subsequent disposal of the shares acquired at the time of incorporation should normally qualify for Entrepreneurs' relief and any gain arising will be taxed at 10% provided the conditions are satisfied.

- However, if this in unlikely (e.g. if the individual plans to dispose of the shares within one year and will fail the one-year ownership rule on the disposal), the individual may:

  - **choose to disapply** incorporation relief in order to crystallise a gain on incorporation, so that they can

  - claim Entrepreneurs' relief, and

  - the gains are taxed at 10% on incorporation.

Example 14 – Incorporation relief

Sarah incorporated her sewing business on 25 June 2012. The assets transferred to the new company, Sarah Ltd, are set out below. In exchange for the transfer of the business she received 100,000 £1 ordinary shares, worth £240,000.

Assets transferred	MV at 25.6.12	Original cost
	£	£
Freehold premises – acquired May 2000	150,000	70,000
Furniture and fittings	5,000	10,000
Plant and machinery	5,500	15,000
Inventory	25,500	25,000
Goodwill	54,000	–
	240,000	120,000

All items of plant and machinery and furniture and fittings were bought and sold for less than £6,000.

Calculate the net chargeable gain arising, if any, on the incorporation of Sarah's business and state Sarah's base cost in the shares in Sarah Ltd.

Answer to example 14

	£	£
Freehold premises		
MV on incorporation	150,000	
Less: Acquisition cost	(70,000)	
	———	80,000
Goodwill		
MV on incorporation	54,000	
Less: Acquisition cost	(Nil)	
	———	54,000
Total capital gains		134,000
Less: Incorporation relief (Note)		(134,000)
		———
Chargeable gain		Nil
		———
Base cost of shares in Sarah Ltd		
Market value of shares		240,000
Less: Incorporation relief		(134,000)
		———
Base cost		106,000
		———

Note: As the consideration is wholly in shares the gains arising on incorporation can be rolled over in full.

Test your understanding 11

On 8 March 2013 Chandra incorporated a wholesale business that she had run as a sole trader since 1 May 2006. The market value of the business on 8 March 2013 was £250,000.

All of the business assets were transferred to a new limited company, with the consideration consisting of 200,000 £1 ordinary shares valued at £200,000 and £50,000 in cash.

The only chargeable asset of the business was goodwill and this was valued at £100,000 on 8 March 2013. The goodwill has a nil cost.

Calculate the chargeable gains arising from Chandra's disposals during 2012/13, and state the base cost of the shares in the new company.

Example 15 – Incorporation relief

Sam started a retail business in 1985 which has been very successful. Sam is a higher rate taxpayer.

On 1 October 2012 he transferred his business to a company, Sam Ltd. The assets transferred are set out below. In exchange he received 4,000 £1 ordinary shares, valued at £80,000 and £20,000 cash.

Assets transferred	M.V. at 1.10.12	Gain
	£	£
Freehold premises	35,000	25,000
Furniture and fittings	8,000	–
Plant and machinery	14,000	–
Inventory	25,000	–
Goodwill	18,000	18,000
	100,000	43,000

On 1 February 2013 Sam sold his entire holding in Sam Ltd for £150,000.

Calculate Sam's chargeable gains for 2012/13 and consider any tax advice you may wish to give Sam. Assume that Sam has no CGT annual exempt amount available.

Answer to example 15

Capital gain on transfer of business – October 2012

	£
Total gains	43,000
Less: Incorporation relief	
(£43,000 × £80,000/(£80,000 + £20,000))	(34,400)
Chargeable gain	8,600

This gain is taxed at 10% as it qualifies for Entrepreneurs' relief.

Assuming there is no AEA available, the CGT will therefore be £860.

Disposal of shares – February 2013

	£	£
Sale proceeds		150,000
Less Base cost:		
Market value of shares	80,000	
Less: Incorporation relief	(34,400)	
		(45,600)
Chargeable gain (Note)		104,400

This gain is taxed at 28% as Sam is a higher rate taxpayer. It is not taxed at 10% as the gain does not qualify for ER. This is because Sam has owned the shares for less than 12 months.

Assuming there is no AEA available the CGT will be £29,232 (£104,400 × 28%).

The total tax will be £30,092 (£860 + £29,232).

Tax advice

In these circumstances it would be advantageous to disapply incorporation relief and claim Entrepreneurs' relief so that:

- the whole gain of £43,000 arising at the date of incorporation is taxed at 10% (i.e. £4,300)

- the gain on the shares will be £70,000 (£150,000 – £80,000 (MV of shares acquired on incorporation))

- this gain is taxed at 28% (i.e. £70,000 × 28% = £19,600).

The total tax will be £23,900 (£4,300 + £19,600).

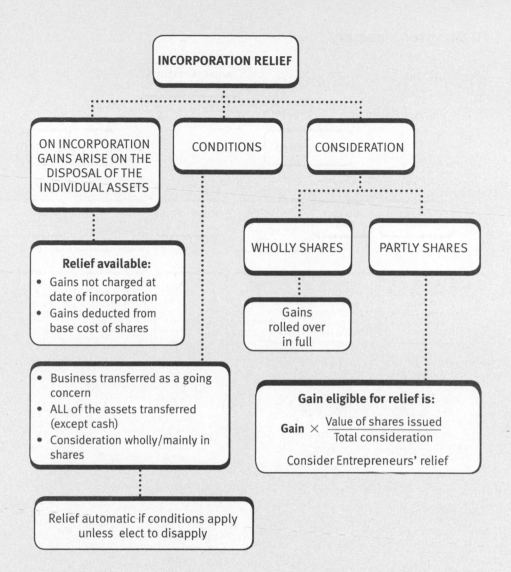

INCORPORATION RELIEF

ON INCORPORATION GAINS ARISE ON THE DISPOSAL OF THE INDIVIDUAL ASSETS

CONDITIONS

CONSIDERATION

WHOLLY SHARES

PARTLY SHARES

Relief available:
- Gains not charged at date of incorporation
- Gains deducted from base cost of shares

Gains rolled over in full

- Business transferred as a going concern
- ALL of the assets transferred (except cash)
- Consideration wholly/mainly in shares

Gain eligible for relief is:

$$\text{Gain} \times \frac{\text{Value of shares issued}}{\text{Total consideration}}$$

Consider Entrepreneurs' relief

Relief automatic if conditions apply unless elect to disapply

6 Chapter summary

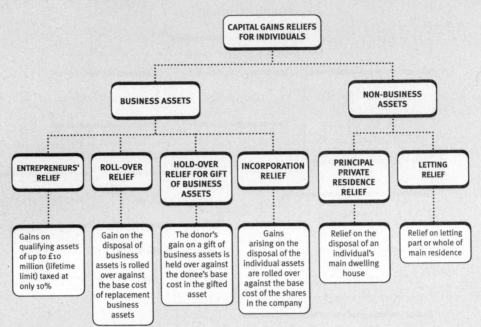

Test your understanding answers

Test your understanding 1

Arthur

Step 1   Calculate gain before reliefs (given) = £189,000

Step 2   Identify – periods of ownership, actual occupation, and deemed occupation.

	Total	Exempt	Chargeable
1.1.91 – 31.12.92	24		
Actual occupation		24	
1.1.93 – 30.6.99	78		
Employed overseas (any period exempt)		78	
1.7.99 – 31.12.04	66		
Travelling (3 years exempt for any reason)		36	
Rest of period chargeable			30
1.1.05 – 30.9.12	93		
Actual occupation		93	
Number of months	261	231	30

The periods of occupation before and after deemed occupation do **not** need to be **immediately** before and after (for example the employment overseas ended on 30 June 1999 and is followed by actual occupation which did not start until 1 January 2005).

Step 3   Deduct PPR relief.

	£
Gain before reliefs	189,000
Less: PPR (£189,000 x 231/261)	(167,276)
Chargeable gain after reliefs	21,724

Test your understanding 2

Todd

Todd owned the house for nine years and used 1/7th of the house (one of the seven rooms) for business purposes.

The last 36 months exemption does not apply to the business element of the gain as this part of the house has never been used for private purposes.

The chargeable gain after reliefs = (£60,000 × 1/7) = £8,571.

Test your understanding 3

Jane Smith

	£
Market value	140,000
Less: Cost	(45,000)
Enhancement expenditure	(10,600)
Chargeable gain before reliefs	84,400
Less: PPR relief (£84,400 × 85/157) (W1)	(45,694)
	38,706
Less: Letting relief = lowest of:	
(a) Maximum = £40,000	
(b) PPR relief = £45,694	
(c) Letting gain = £84,400 × 60/157	(32,255)
Chargeable gain after reliefs	6,451

Working: PPR and letting relief

	Total	Exempt	Chargeable after PPR	Letting relief
1.9.99 –30.9.03	49			
Actual occupation		49		
1.10.03 – 30.9.04	12			
Empty – chargeable			12	
1.10.04 – 30.9.12	96			
Last 3 years		36		
Rest of period – chargeable but let (Note)			60	60
	——	——	——	——
Number of months	157	85	72	60
	——	——	——	——

Note: The property was let from 1.10.04 to 30.9.12 (96 months) however the last 3 years are exempt under the PPR rules. Therefore letting relief is available but only for the remaining 60 months in that period.

Test your understanding 4

Paul

	£	£
2012/13		
Not qualifying for Entrepreneurs' relief		
Sale of warehouse (Note 1)	245,000	
Qualifying for Entrepreneurs' relief		
Sale of company shares		430,000
Less: AEA (Note 2)	(10,600)	(Nil)
	————	————
Taxable gains	234,400	430,000
	————	————
Capital gains tax:		
Qualifying gains (£430,000 × 10%)		43,000
Non qualifying gains (£234,400 × 28%) (Note 3)		65,632
		————
		108,632
		————

2013/14	£	£
Not qualifying for Entrepreneurs' relief		
Sale of antique table	5,325	
Qualifying for Entrepreneurs' relief		
Sales of trading business:		
Factory		6,495,000
Goodwill		130,000
		————
	5,325	6,625,000
Less: AEA	(5,325)	(5,275)
	————	————
Taxable gains	Nil	6,619,725
	————	————

Capital gains tax:		
Qualifying gains	(£6,070,000 × 10%) (Note 4) (W)	607,000
	(£549,725 × 28%) (Note 5)	153,923
Non-qualifying gains	(£Nil × 28%)	Nil
		————
		760,923
		————

Working: Qualifying gains in 2013/14

	£
Lifetime limit	10,000,000
Claims prior to 2012/13	(3,500,000)
Claim in 2012/13	(430,000)
	————
Qualifying gains in 2013/14	6,070,000
	————

Notes:

(1) The disposal of the warehouse in 2012/13 is the disposal of an individual business asset used for the purposes of a continuing trade. To qualify for ER, there must be a disposal of the whole or part of the trading business. The sale of an asset in isolation will not qualify.

(2) The AEA is set against gains not qualifying for ER, and any remaining AEA is then set against gains qualifying for ER.

(3) The gains qualifying for ER are deemed to utilise the basic rate (BRB) band first. Therefore the remaining BRB in 2012/13 of £6,370 (£34,370 – £28,000) is set against the gains qualifying for ER leaving the remaining gains to be taxed at 28%.

KAPLAN PUBLISHING

(4) After the first £10 million of gains qualifying for ER have been taxed at 10%, any remaining qualifying gains are taxed at the appropriate rate depending on the taxpayer's level of income.

(5) There is no BRB band remaining in 2013/14 as Paul's taxable income exceeds £34,370 and even if there were, the remaining amount is set against gains qualifying for ER leaving remaining gains to be taxed at 28%.

Test your understanding 5

Chris

Second building – November 2012 – 2012/13	£	£
Sale proceeds		380,000
Less: Base cost		
Cost	140,000	
Less: ROR (Note)	(56,360)	
	———	(83,640)
		———
Chargeable gain		296,360
		———

The chargeable gain arising in 2012/13 will be taxed at 18% or 28% depending on the level of taxable income.

It will not be taxed at 10% as the disposal of an individual asset used for the purposes of a continuing trade does not qualify for ER. The trade itself is not being disposed of.

Notes:

(1) The full gain arising in May 1998 of £56,360 can be rolled over (i.e. deferred) as:

   – the asset disposed of is a qualifying business asset

   – the replacement asset is a qualifying business asset

   – the reinvestment has been made in August 1999 (i.e. within the qualifying period of May 1997 to May 2001)

   – the amount reinvested exceeds the sale proceeds received (i.e. purchase price of new warehouse of £140,000 exceeds the sale proceeds of £100,000).

(2) The gain arising in 2012/13 of £296,360 can also be deferred, provided a qualifying business asset is purchased within the qualifying period (i.e. Nov 2011 to Nov 2015).

Test your understanding 6

Jarvis

	(a)	(b)
	£700,000	**£550,000**
New factory purchased for		
	£	£
Sale proceeds	750,000	750,000
Less: Cost	(635,000)	(635,000)
Gain before relief	115,000	115,000
Less: ROR (balancing figure)		
(£115,000 – £50,000)	(65,000)	
(£115,000 – £115,000)		(Nil)
Chargeable gain (W)	50,000	115,000

Working

	£	£
Chargeable gain now = Lower of:		
(i) Sale proceeds not reinvested		
(£750,000 – £700,000)	50,000	
(£750,000 – £550,000)		200,000
(ii) Gain on disposal of original factory before relief	115,000	115,000
Therefore chargeable gain in 2012/13	**50,000**	**115,000**

Base cost of new replacement factory

Cost	700,000	550,000
Less: ROR	(65,000)	(Nil)
	635,000	550,000

Note: The chargeable gain arising in 2012/13 will be taxed at 18% or 28% depending on the level of taxable income.

It will not be taxed at 10% as the gain does not qualify for ER. This is because the disposal of an individual asset used for the purposes of a continuing trade does not qualify. The trade itself is not being disposed of.

Test your understanding 7

Hadley

Disposal of factory – August 2012 – 2012/13

The asset disposed of is a qualifying business asset, but as only 85% of the building has been used for trade purposes, the gain must be split and only 85% is eligible for ROR.

	Business portion £	Non-business portion £
Split of capital gain (85% : 15%)	38,250	6,750
Less: ROR (Note)	(38,250)	(n/a)
Chargeable gain	Nil	6,750

Notes:
- the replacement asset is a qualifying business asset, used 100% for the purposes of the trade

- the reinvestment has been made in October 2012 (i.e. within the qualifying period of August 2011 to August 2015)

- the amount reinvested for the purposes of the trade (i.e. purchase price of new warehouse of £500,000) exceeds the sale proceeds received on the first building relating to the trade use of the building (i.e. £560,000 × 85% = £476,000)

- therefore ROR is available on all of the business portion of the gain.

- the chargeable gain is taxed at 18% or 28% depending on the level of taxable income. It is not taxed at 10% as the gain does not qualify for ER. This is because the chargeable gain is arising on an investment asset.

Base cost of replacement factory – October 2012

	£
Cost	500,000
Less: ROR	(38,250)
	461,750

Amir

Freehold factory – May 2000 – 2000/01

	£
Capital gain	150,000
Less: Deferred gain (Held over gain) (see Note)	(150,000)
Chargeable gain	Nil

Note:

- the asset disposed of is a qualifying business asset

- the replacement asset is a qualifying business asset, but is a depreciating asset (fixed plant and machinery)

- the reinvestment has been made in July 2002 (i.e. within the qualifying period of May 1999 to May 2003)

- the amount reinvested (i.e. purchase price of new plant and machinery of £400,000) exceeds the sale proceeds received on the factory of £350,000

- therefore all of the gain can be deferred, but the deferred gain is not deducted from the base cost of the plant and machinery

- the gain of £150,000 is frozen and becomes chargeable on the earliest of:

  - the sale of the fixed plant and machinery (March 2014)

  - the date the plant and machinery ceases to be used in the trade (presumably March 2014)

  - ten years from the acquisition of the plant and machinery (July 2012)

Chargeable event – earliest date = July 2012 – 2011/12

Deferred gain (Held over gain) becomes chargeable	£150,000

This gain is taxable at 18% or 28% depending on the level of taxable income. It is not taxable at 10% as the gain does not qualify for ER.

This is because it is the disposal of an individual asset used for the purposes of a continuing trade.

Sale of plant and machinery – March 2014

	£
Sale proceeds	500,000
Less: Cost	(400,000)
Chargeable gain – 2013/14	100,000

Assuming that this asset is not replaced and the rates of CGT remain unchanged, this gain will be taxable at 18% or 28% depending on the level of taxable income. It is not taxable at 10% as the gain does not qualify for ER. This is because it is the disposal of an individual asset used for the purposes of a continuing trade.

Test your understanding 9

Alice

(a) **Alice – Capital gains computation – 2011/12**

	£
MV at date of gift	150,000
Less: Acquisition cost	(120,000)
Chargeable gain	30,000
Less: Gift relief	(30,000)
Chargeable gain	Nil

As Alice and Adam made a joint election this gain of £30,000 can be 'held over' from Alice to Adam (under the 'gift relief' provisions).

Therefore there would be no chargeable gain on Alice in 2011/12.

Adam – Capital gains computation – 2012/13

	£	£
Sale proceeds		180,000
Less: Base cost		
MV at date of gift	150,000	
Less: Gain held over	(30,000)	
		(120,000)
Chargeable gain		60,000

Note: Assuming the rates of CGT remain unchanged, this gain will be taxable at 18% or 28% depending on the level of taxable income. It is not taxable at 10% as the gain does not qualify for ER. This is because it is the gift of an individual asset, not the disposal of a whole or substantial part of a business.

(b) **Alice – Capital gains computation – 2011/12**

	£	£
MV at date of gift		150,000
Less: Acquisition cost		(120,000)
Potential gain (as above)		30,000
Actual proceeds	130,000	
Less: Original cost	(120,000)	
Excess proceeds over cost	10,000	
Less: Gain eligible to be held over		(20,000)
Chargeable gain		10,000

This gain is taxable at 18% or 28% depending on the level of taxable income. It is not taxable at 10% as the gain does not qualify for ER. This is because it is the disposal of an individual asset used for the purposes of a continuing trade, not the disposal of a whole or substantial part of a business.

Adam – Base cost (for future disposal)

	£
Deemed acquisition cost (MV at date of gift)	150,000
Less: Gain held over from Alice	(20,000)
Base cost	130,000

Test your understanding 10

Fred

Fred Ltd's chargeable business assets total £400,000 (premises), whilst the chargeable assets total £500,000 (premises and shares held as investments).

Therefore £336,000 (£420,000 × £400,000/£500,000) of the capital gain can be held over.

Fred's chargeable gain in 2012/13 is therefore £84,000 (£420,000 – £336,000).

Note: This gain is taxable at 18% or 28% depending on the level of taxable income. It is not taxable at 10% as the gain does not qualify for ER. This is because Fred did not work for the company in the 12 months before he disposed of the shares.

Test your understanding 11

Chandra

Capital gains computation – 2012/13

	£
Goodwill	
MV on incorporation	100,000
Less: Acquisition cost	(Nil)
	100,000
Less: Incorporation relief	
£100,000 × £200,000/£250,000 (Note 1)	(80,000)
Chargeable gain	20,000

Note: The question only requires the calculation of the chargeable gain. However, if asked for the CGT liability, the gain not covered by the AEA is taxed at 10% as the gain would qualify for ER. This is because it is the disposal of an unincorporated business which has been owned for more than 12 months.

Base cost of the shares

	£
Market value	200,000
Less: Incorporation relief	(80,000)
Base cost	120,000

Inheritance tax

Chapter learning objectives

Upon completion of this chapter you will be able to:

- outline the principal events for IHT

- explain the concept of 'transfer of value'

- state which persons are chargeable to IHT

- recognise and explain the different types of lifetime gifts

- calculate the transfer of value for IHT

- identify when exemptions are available to reduce a lifetime transfer of value and apply them in the most beneficial way

- explain the annual exemption and demonstrate how it reduces the transfer of value

- explain the procedure and calculate the charge to IHT on a chargeable lifetime transfer during lifetime

- demonstrate the seven year cumulation period

- explain the procedure and calculate the charge to IHT on all lifetime transfers within 7 years of death

- recognise when taper relief is available to reduce the IHT charge

- prepare a death estate computation for IHT and calculate the IHT liability

- advise on the due date for payment of inheritance tax

- identify methods of inheritance tax planning to minimise inheritance tax liabilities.

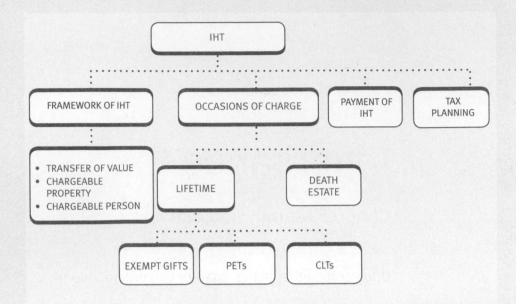

Introduction

Most inheritance tax (IHT) is collected on the death of an individual based on the value of their death estate. However, if IHT only applied on death, it would be an easy tax to avoid by giving away assets immediately before death. Therefore, there are IHT implications arising on some lifetime gifts as well as on death.

The chapter covers the principles that underpin IHT, deals with the way in which an individual is liable to IHT and considers the IHT payable on lifetime gifts and on the death estate. The detailed death estate computation is then covered, along with payment dates and some basic IHT planning.

1 The charge to Inheritance Tax (IHT)

Inheritance tax is charged on:

- a **transfer of value**
- of **chargeable property**
- by a **chargeable person**.

A charge to inheritance tax (IHT) arises:

- on the death of an individual
- on lifetime gifts where the donor dies within 7 years of the date of a gift
- on some lifetime gifts which are taxed immediately.

The donor is the person who makes the transfer of the asset, and the recipient is known as the donee.

Transfer of value

A transfer of value is **a gift of any capital asset** which results in a reduction in the value of the donor's estate.

To be treated as a transfer of value the transfer must be a 'gratuitous disposition'. This basically means a gift.

A bad business deal will therefore not be liable to inheritance tax, even though there is a fall in value of the estate, as it was not the donor's intention to give anything away.

To calculate the transfer of value for IHT purposes, the **loss to donor** principle is used (also referred to as the **diminution in value** concept).

The loss to the donor, is the difference between the value of the donor's estate before and after the gift, and is the starting point for IHT calculations:

	£
Value of estate before gift	X
Less: Value of estate after gift	(X)
	—
Diminution in value or Transfer of value	X
	—

The loss to the donor is usually the **open market value** of the asset gifted.

However, in some circumstances, the transfer of value from the donor's point of view is not necessarily the same as the value of the asset received from the donee's point of view.

This is most common with unquoted shares, where a controlling shareholding has a higher value per share than a minority shareholding.

站在the Donor的
角度上看transfer
的8 amount

Test your understanding 1

Linda owns 6,000 shares which represents a 60% holding in Loot Ltd. On 31 December 2012 she gave a 20% holding in the company to her friend, Bob.

The values of shareholdings in Loot Ltd on 31 December 2012 have been agreed for IHT purposes as follows:

Holding	Value per share
Up to 25%	£9
26% to 50%	£15
51% to 74%	£26
75% or more	£45

Calculate the transfer of value relating to the gift of unquoted shares for IHT purposes.

Chargeable property

Note that **all property to which a person is beneficially entitled** is deemed to form part of their estate.

Therefore, a gift of **any asset** is a transfer of value. There is no such thing as an exempt asset for IHT purposes.

Chargeable persons

A chargeable person for the purposes of the F6 examination will always be an individual.

Individuals

All individuals are potentially liable to IHT.

An individual who is domiciled in the UK will be liable to inheritance tax on their worldwide assets.

If not UK domiciled, they are liable on UK assets only.

However, for the purposes of the F6 examination, all individuals will be UK domiciled.

Note that a husband and wife and partners in a registered civil partnership are chargeable to IHT separately.

2 Occasions of charge

The main charge to IHT arises on the death of an individual as they become liable on the following:

- the value of all of the net assets in their estate at the date of death
- any lifetime gifts made in the seven years before their death, provided they are not exempt gifts.

3 Lifetime gifts

There are three categories of lifetime gifts that can be made by an individual and are treated for IHT purposes as follows:

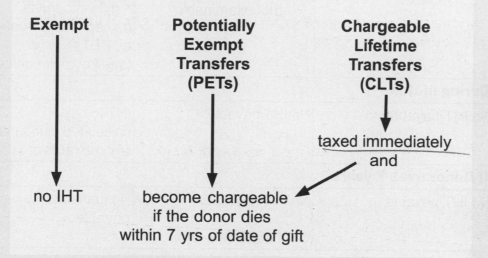

Types of lifetime gifts

The definition of each type of gift and an overview of the way in which they are taxed is summarised in the table below:

Exempt transfers	Potentially Exempt Transfers (PETs)	Chargeable lifetime transfers (CLTs)
Definition		
A gift that is specifically deemed to be exempt from IHT (see below)	A gift by an individual • to another individual • into a <u>disabled trust</u> • into certain <u>old trusts</u> (not examinable)	No definition = residual category (i.e. a gift which is not exempt nor a PET) Main example: = gifts into trusts (except those treated as PETs) (see key point below)
During lifetime		
No IHT payable	No IHT payable	IHT to pay calculated using the lifetime rates of tax
If Donor lives 7 years		
No IHT payable	No IHT payable Gift becomes exempt	No further IHT payable
If Donor dies within 7 years		
No IHT payable	The PET becomes chargeable on death for the first time	Possibly extra IHT, calculated using the death rates of tax

It is important to note that in practice, the majority of lifetime transfers made by individuals are either:

• exempt transfers, or

• transfers from one individual to another (i.e. a PET).

Gifts into trusts are a complicated area in practice, but for the F6 examination, **all gifts into trusts** will be treated as **CLTs**.

Chargeable lifetime transfers (CLTs)

A CLT is a gift which is not exempt and not a PET. They are not common in practice, but appear in examination questions because they are chargeable to IHT at the time of the gift.

The main example of a CLT made by an individual during their lifetime is a gift into a trust.

Trusts

A trust is an arrangement where property (known as the trust assets or settled property) is transferred by a person (known as the settlor) to the trustees, to be held for the benefit of one or more specified persons (known as the beneficiaries) on specified terms in the trust deed.

The most common example of a trust is where parents wish to give assets to their children, but not until they are adults. They therefore put the assets into a trust with the children as beneficiaries, and the assets are controlled by the trustees until the children reach a specified age.

It is not necessary to understand the workings of trusts for the F6 examination, only to learn that gifts into trusts are CLTs.

Potentially exempt transfers (PETs)

PETs have derived their name from the fact that if the donor lives for more than seven years after making the gift, then the transfer is exempt (i.e. free from IHT). Therefore, at the time of such transfer, it has the potential to be exempt.

However, if the donor dies within seven years of making the gift, then IHT may become chargeable on these gifts.

Note that transfers on death can never be PETs.

4 Exemptions and reliefs for IHT

The following table summarises the exemptions and reliefs available for IHT that are examinable in F6.

Exemptions and reliefs available against:	
Lifetime gifts only	Lifetime gifts and death estate
• Small gifts exemption	• Inter spouse exemption
• Marriage exemption	
• Normal expenditure out of income	
• Annual exemption	

5 Exemptions available for lifetime gifts only

The following exemptions are available to reduce lifetime transfers only. They do not apply to the death estate.

Note that the rules and limits for these exemptions are **not** given in the examination, and must be learnt.

Small gifts exemption

Lifetime gifts are exempt if they are:

• an outright gift of no more than £250

• per recipient

• per tax year.

The small gift exemption does not apply if the gift is in excess of £250.

Therefore, a gift of £300 will not qualify. Similarly, if an individual makes a gift of £240 to a person followed by another gift of £100 to the same person in the same tax year, neither gift will be exempt.

However, the donor can make gifts of up to £250 to any number of different recipients and they will all be exempt.

Marriage exemption

A lifetime transfer made "in consideration of a marriage" (or registration of a civil partnership) is exempt up to the following maximum limits:

- £5,000 by a parent
- £2,500 by a grandparent or remoter ancestor
- £2,500 by a party to the marriage or civil partnership (e.g. from the groom to the bride)
- £1,000 by anyone else.

The exemption is conditional on the marriage taking place.

Normal expenditure out of income

IHT is levied on transfers of capital wealth.

Therefore, a lifetime transfer will be exempt if it can be shown that the gift:

- is made as part of a person's normal expenditure out of income, and
- does not affect the donor's standard of living.

To be treated as 'normal', gifts must be habitual (i.e. there is a regular pattern of giving). For example, payment of school fees for a grandchild or annual payments into a life insurance policy for the benefit of a child are usually exempted under this rule.

The annual exemption

The annual exemption (AE) is an exemption available against **lifetime** transfers and operates as follows:

- The AE:
  - exempts the **first £3,000** of lifetime transfers in any one tax year
  - is applied chronologically to the first gift in the tax year, then (if there is any left) the second gift and so on
  - must be applied to the first gift each year, even if the first gift is a PET and never becomes chargeable.

- Any unused AE:
  - may be carried forward to the next year
  - however, it can be carried forward for one year only, and
  - can only be used after the current year's AE.
- The maximum AE in any one year is therefore £6,000 (£3,000 × 2).
- If other exemptions are available they are given before the AE.

Test your understanding 2

Julie made the following lifetime gifts:

(a) 31 August 2010, £600, to her son

(b) 31 October 2010, £800, to a trust

(c) 31 May 2011, £2,100, to trust

(d) 30 November 2011, £1,100, to a trust

(e) 30 April 2012, £5,000, to her daughter.

Calculate the chargeable amount for each of the gifts.

---

6 Exemptions available for lifetime transfers and the death estate

Inter spouse exemption

Transfers between spouses are exempt:

- regardless of the value of the transfer, and
- whether they are made during the individual's lifetime or on death.

The same rule applies to partners in a registered civil partnership.

Test your understanding 3

Maggie made the following lifetime transfers:

(i) Unquoted shares worth £525,000 in the family company to her husband on 1 June 2012.

(ii) £15,000 to her son on 6 July 2012 as a wedding present.

(iii) £20,000 to her nephew on 27 September 2012.

(iv) £235 to a friend for her 40th birthday on 4 November 2012.

(v) £270,000 into a trust on 24 December 2012.

Calculate the chargeable amount for each of Maggie's lifetime gifts.

7 IHT payable during an individual's lifetime on CLTs

Lifetime IHT is payable when an individual makes a gift into a trust.

The procedure to calculate the lifetime IHT on a CLT

The lifetime tax should be calculated on each gift separately, in chronological order, as follows:

(1) Calculate the chargeable amount of the gift:

	£
Value of estate before transfer	X
Less: Value of estate after transfer	(X)
Transfer of value	X
Less: Specific exemptions	
(i.e. spouse/ civil partner)	(X)
Marriage exemption	(X)
Annual exemptions	(X)
Chargeable amount	X

(2) Calculate the amount of nil rate band available after deducting gross chargeable transfers in the previous 7 years (see below).

(3) Calculate the tax on the excess at either 20 or 25% depending on who has agreed to pay the tax; the donor or the donee (see below).

(4) Calculate the gross amount of the gift to carry forward for future computations.

(5) If required by the examination question, state the due date of payment of the IHT (see below).

The nil rate band

All individuals are entitled to a nil rate band (NRB) and are taxed on the value of gifts in excess of the NRB at different rates depending on who has agreed to pay the lifetime tax.

The NRB identifies the maximum value of lifetime and death gifts, which can be gifted without incurring any IHT liability.

The NRB has steadily increased each tax year in the past, although it has remained the same for the last four years.

For lifetime calculations, the appropriate NRB applicable at the **time of the gift** should be used.

The current NRB of £325,000 will be included in the tax rates and allowances in the examination.

However, where NRBs are required for previous years, these will be provided in the actual examination question to which they relate.

The appropriate rate of tax

The appropriate rate of tax to apply to lifetime gifts depends on who has agreed to pay the tax due.

Transferee pays the tax

If the **trustees** of the trust (i.e. the donee) agree to **pay** the tax:

- the gift is referred to as a **gross gift**, and
- the appropriate rate of tax is 20%.

KAPLAN PUBLISHING

Transferor pays the tax

If the **donor** agrees to **pay** the tax:

- The gift is referred to as a **net gift**.
- As a result of the gift, their estate is being reduced by:
  - the value of the gift, **and**
  - the associated tax payable on the gift.
- Accordingly the amount of the gift needs to be 'grossed up' to include the tax that the donor has to pay
- The appropriate rate of tax is therefore 25% (i.e. 20/80ths of the net gift)
- The gross transfer to carry forward is the net chargeable amount plus any IHT paid by the donor.

In summary, the rate of tax on the value of CLTs in excess of the NRB is:

Payer:		Appropriate rate
Trustees of the trust	Gross gift	20%
Donor	Net gift	25% (or 20/80)

Note that the tax due on a CLT is primarily the responsibility of the donor.

Therefore, where an examination question does not specify who has agreed to pay the tax:

- **always** assume that the **donor will pay** and that the gift is therefore a net gift.

The normal due date of payment of lifetime IHT

The date of payment of lifetime IHT depends on the date of the gift:

Date of CLT	Due date of payment
6 April to 30 September	30 April in the following year
1 October to 5 April	Six months after the end of the month of the CLT

Test your understanding 4

Charlotte makes a gift into a trust on 13 June 2012 of £366,000.

She has made no previous lifetime gifts.

Calculate the amount of lifetime IHT due on the gift into the trust and state the gross chargeable amount of the gift to carry forward for future computations, assuming:

(a) **the trustees of the trust have agreed to pay any IHT due.**

(b) **Charlotte has agreed to pay any IHT due.**

State the due date for payment of tax in both cases.

The seven year cumulation period

In the TYU above, the individual had made no previous lifetime gifts and therefore all of the NRB was available to calculate the tax. However, the NRB is available for a 'seven year cumulation period'.

Each time a CLT is made, in order to calculate the IHT liability, it is necessary to look back seven years and calculate how much NRB is available to match against that particular gift.

For lifetime calculations, to calculate the NRB available at any point in time, it is necessary to take account of the total of the **gross** amounts of all other **CLTs** made within the **previous seven years**.

- These CLTs in the seven year cumulation period are deemed to have utilised the NRB first.

- There will therefore only be NRB available to match against this latest gift if the total of the CLTs in the previous seven years is less than the NRB at the time of the gift.

- Note that although PETs may use the AE during the donor's lifetime, they do not affect the NRB available as they are not yet chargeable.

Test your understanding 5

During his lifetime Alex had made the following gifts:

03/04   02/03.
-3000 -3000 = 164,000

- 30 June 2003, £170,000 to a trust
- 12 June 2007, £150,000 to his daughter *07/08. 06/07 = 144,000*
- 30 June 2008, £191,000 to a trust. *08/0f   188. 000*
- 15 December 2012, £256,000 to a trust *12/13   250,000*
  11/12

The trustees of the first two trusts paid the IHT liabilities. Alex paid the tax on the last gift.

The nil rate bands for earlier years are as follows:

2003/04	£255,000
2007/08	£300,000
2008/09	£312,000

Calculate the IHT arising as a result of Alex's lifetime transfers.

State who will pay the tax, the due date for payment and the gross chargeable amount of each gift to carry forward to future computations.

Test your understanding 6

During his lifetime Sidney had made the following cash gifts:

- 21 April 2002, £98,000 to a trust (trustees to pay tax)
- 15 April 2007, £140,000 to his son
- 19 March 2008, £221,000 to a trust (Sidney to pay tax)
- 9 May 2012, £395,000 to a trust (trustees to pay tax)

The nil rate bands for earlier years are as follows:

2002/03	£250,000
2007/08	£300,000

Calculate the IHT arising as a result of Sidney's lifetime transfers.

Summary of lifetime calculations

Remember to:

- only calculate IHT on CLTs

- consider the IHT position for each CLT separately and in chronological order

- use the NRB applicable for the tax year of the gift

- tax is due at 20% if the trustees pay, and 25% if the donor pays.

Also remember that PETs are not chargeable at this stage, but may use the annual exemptions.

8 IHT payable on lifetime gifts as a result of death

On the death of an individual, an IHT charge could arise in relation to lifetime gifts **within seven years of death** as follows:

- PETs become chargeable for the first time.

- Additional tax may be due on a CLT.

The IHT payable on lifetime gifts as a result of death is **always** paid by the recipient of the gift:

Type of gift:	Paid by:
CLT	Trustees of the trust
PET	Donee

Calculating the death IHT on lifetime gifts

The death tax should be calculated on each gift separately, in chronological order, as follows:

(1) Identify all gifts within seven years of death.

(2) Calculate the **gross chargeable amount** of each gift and any **lifetime tax paid**.

(3) Calculate the amount of NRB available after deducting **gross chargeable transfers** in the 7 years before the gift:

- use the NRB for the year of **death** (rather than the year of the gift)

- **include PETs** which have become chargeable (but not those that have become completely exempt).

(4) Calculate the **death tax** on the excess at **40%**.

(5) Calculate and deduct any **taper relief** available (see below).

(6) For CLTs, deduct any **lifetime IHT paid**.

(7) If required by the question, state who will pay the tax and the due date of payment (see below).

Further points regarding death tax calculations on lifetime gifts

Chargeable amount

- The **gross** chargeable amount of each gift is taxed on death.

- The gross amount of CLTs will have already been calculated in the lifetime IHT calculations.

- Remember to use the grossed up value of any CLTs where the tax is paid by the donor.

- The chargeable amount of a PET is calculated using the values at the time of the gift and PETs may use up the AEs, even though they only become chargeable if the donor dies within 7 years.

The nil rate band

- The NRB for the year of the gift is first used against the lifetime calculations as seen above.

- The NRB for the year of death is then used to calculate the death tax but this time it is matched against **all** chargeable gifts (i.e. CLTs and PETs) in chronological order.

The seven year cumulation period

The seven year cumulation period for the NRB applies in a similar way as for the lifetime calculations.

However, note that:

- it is necessary to take into account the total of the **gross** amounts of **all chargeable gifts** made within the **previous seven years** (not just CLTs)

- therefore, to calculate the death IHT on each gift, it is necessary to look back seven years from the **date of each gift** and include the gross amount of:
  - all CLTs, **and**
  - PETs which have become chargeable due to the death of the individual.

This means that a CLT made more than 7 years before death may still affect the NRB when calculating death tax on lifetime gifts.

However, ignore any PETs made more than 7 years ago as they are not taxable.

The death rate of tax

The death rate of IHT is 40% on the excess over the NRB available.

Taper relief

Where IHT is chargeable on **any** lifetime transfer due to death, the amount of IHT payable on death will be reduced by taper relief:

- where more than 3 years have elapsed since date of gift
- by a percentage reduction according to the length of time between
  - the date of the gift, and
  - the date of the donor's death.

Note that the relief applies to both CLTs and PETs.

The rates of taper relief are given in the tax rates and allowances in the examination, and are as follows:

Years between date of gift and date of death:

More than	Not more than	Taper relief %
0	3	Nil
3	4	20
4	5	40
5	6	60
6	7	80
7		100

Deduction of lifetime IHT paid

For CLTs, any lifetime IHT already paid can be deducted from the liability calculated on death.

However, no refund is made if the tax already paid is higher than the amount now due on death.

At best, the deduction of lifetime tax paid will bring the liability on death down to £Nil.

The normal due date of payment of IHT on death

IHT as a result of death is due **six months** after the **end of the month of death**.

Example 1 – Death tax payable on lifetime gifts

Fred had made the following lifetime transfers:

- 31 July 2003, £80,000, to his son
- 30 November 2006, £110,000, to his daughter
- 30 April 2007, £235,000, to his son.

He died on 30 June 2012.

The nil rate bands for earlier years are as follows:
2003/04   £255,000
2006/07   £285,000
2007/08   £300,000

Calculate the IHT arising as a result of Fred's death on 30 June 2012. State who will pay the tax and the due date of payment.

Answer to example 1

PET – 31 July 2003

- The PET made on 31 July 2003 to his son is more than seven years before 30 June 2012.

- It is therefore completely exempt. No IHT is payable during his lifetime and no IHT is due as a result of his death.

- The gift is ignored and is not accumulated for future calculations.

PETs – 30 November 2006 and 30 April 2007

The two gifts on 30 November 2006 and 30 April 2007 are PETs. Therefore no lifetime IHT is payable. However, both gifts will become chargeable as a result of Fred's death within seven years.

Answer to example 1

IHT payable during lifetime

	PET 31.7.2003		PET 30.11.2006		PET 30.4.2007	
		£		£		£
Transfer of value		80,000		110,000		235,000
Annual exemption						
– Current year	2003/04	(3,000)	2006/07	(3,000)	2007/08	(3,000)
– Previous year	2002/03 b/f	(3,000)	2005/06 b/f	(3,000)	2006/07 b/f	(Nil)
Chargeable amount		74,000		104,000		232,000
IHT payable (as all PETs)		Nil		Nil		Nil
Gross chargeable amount c/f		74,000		104,000		232,000

All gifts are PETs, therefore there is no lifetime tax to pay. However the gross chargeable amount of the PETs must be established at the time of the gift.

Note: The earlier NRBs given in the question are not required, as they are only required if there is lifetime tax to pay.

IHT payable on death

Date of death: 30 June 2012
7 years before: 30 June 2005

PET on 31.7.2003 is more than 7 years before death – therefore no IHT payable on death

	PET 30.11.2006		PET 30.4.2007	
	£	£	£	£
Gross chargeable amount b/f (as above)		104,000		232,000
NRB @ date of death – 2012/13	325,000		325,000	
Less: GCTs < 7 years before gift				
(30.11.1999 – 30.11.2006)				
(ignore 31.7.2003 PET as completely exempt)	(Nil)			
(30.4.2000 – 30.4.2007)				
(ignore 31.7.2003 PET as completely exempt, but include 30.11.2006 PET as became chargeable)			(104,000)	
NRB available		(325,000)		(221,000)
Taxable amount		Nil		11,000
IHT payable @ 40%		Nil		4,400
Less: Taper relief				
(30.4.2007 – 30.6.2012) (5 – 6 years before death)		(Nil)	(60%)	(2,640)
				(Nil)
Less: IHT paid in lifetime		Nil		(Nil)
IHT payable on death		Nil		1,760
Paid by (always the donee)				Son
Due date of payment (six months after end of month of death)				31.12.2012

Example 2 – Death tax payable on lifetime gifts

On 15 July 2006 Zoe made a transfer of £365,000 into a trust. She has made no other lifetime transfers. The IHT due in respect of this gift was paid by Zoe.

Zoe died on 30 September 2012.

The nil rate band for 2006/07 is £285,000.

Calculate the IHT arising on Zoe's lifetime gift, and the additional IHT arising as a result of her death.

State who will pay the tax and the due date of payment.

Answer to example 2

Lifetime IHT

15 July 2006 – CLT (2006/07)	£	£
Transfer of value		365,000
Less: AE – 2006/07		(3,000)
– 2005/06 b/f		(3,000)
		———
Net chargeable amount		359,000
NRB at date of gift (2006/07)	285,000	
Less: GCTs in 7 yrs pre-gift (15.7.99 to 15.7.06)	(Nil)	
	———	
NRB available		(285,000)
		———
Taxable amount		74,000
		———
Lifetime IHT due (£74,000 × 25%) (= net gift as Zoe paying the tax)		18,500
		———
Payable by		Zoe
Due date (gift in first half of tax year)		30.4.07
Gross amount to carry forward for future computations (£359,000 + £18,500)		377,500
		———

KAPLAN PUBLISHING

IHT payable on death

15 July 2006 – CLT	£	£
Gross chargeable amount (above)		377,500
NRB at death	325,000	
Less: GCTs in 7 yrs pre-gift (15.7.99 to 15.7.06)	(Nil)	
NRB available		(325,000)
Taxable amount		52,500
IHT due on death (£52,500 × 40%)		21,000
Less: Taper relief		
(15.07.06 to 30.09.12) (6 – 7 yrs) (80%)		(16,800)
Chargeable (20%)		4,200
Less: IHT paid in lifetime (CLT)		(18,500)
IHT payable on death		Nil

There is no repayment of lifetime IHT.

Example 3 – IHT payable on lifetime gifts as a result of death

Matthew has made the following lifetime gifts:

	Nil rate band
1 September 2002, £95,000, to a trust.	£250,000
1 May 2006, £275,000, to his son Alexander.	£285,000
1 June 2007, £236,000, to a trust.	£300,000
1 July 2009, £21,000, to his daughter Jayne.	£325,000
1 August 2010, £93,000, to a trust.	£325,000

Matthew has agreed to pay any IHT due on CLTs.

Matthew died on 1 December 2012.

Calculate the IHT payable on the lifetime transfers during Matthew's lifetime and on his death.

State who will pay the tax and the due date of payment.

Answer to example 3

IHT payable during lifetime

	CLT 1.9.2002	PET 1.5.2006	CLT 1.6.2007	PET 1.7.2009	CLT 1.8.2010
	£	£	£	£	£
Transfer of value	95,000	275,000	236,000	21,000	93,000
Annual exemption					
– Current year	(3,000) 2002/03	(3,000) 2006/07	(3,000) 2007/08	(3,000) 2009/10	(3,000) 2010/11
– Previous year	(3,000) 2001/02 b/f	(3,000) 2005/06 b/f	(Nil) 2006/07 b/f	(3,000) 2008/09 b/f	(Nil) 2009/10 b/f
Chargeable amount	89,000	269,000	233,000	15,000	90,000
NRB @ date of gift	Net £	Net £	Net £	Net £	Net £
– 2002/03	250,000				
– 2007/08			300,000		
– 2010/11					325,000
Less: GCTs < 7 years before gift	(Nil)				
(1.9.1995 – 1.9.2002)					
(1.6.2000 – 1.6.2007) (ignore PET)			(89,000)		
(1.8.2003 – 1.8.2010) (ignore both PETs and gift on 1.9.2002 drops out as too old)					(238,500)
NRB available	(250,000)		(211,000)		(86,500)
Taxable amount	Nil	Nil	22,000	Nil	3,500
IHT payable	Nil	Nil	5,500 @ 25%	Nil	875 @ 25%
Paid by			Matthew		Matthew
Due date of payment			30.4.2008		30.4.2011
Gross chargeable amount	89,000 (£89,000 net + £Nil tax)	269,000	238,500 (£233,000 net + £5,500 tax)	15,000	90,875 (£90,000 net + £875 tax)

IHT payable on death

| Date of death: | 1 December 2012 |
| 7 years before: | 1 December 2005 |

CLT on 1.9.2002 is more than 7 years before death – therefore no IHT payable on death

	PET 1.5.2006		CLT 1.6.2007		PET 1.7.2009		CLT 1.8.2010	
	£	£	£	£	£	£	£	£
Gross chargeable amount b/f (as above)		269,000		238,500		15,000		90,875
NRB @ date of death – 2012/13	325,000		325,000		325,000		325,000	
Less: GCTs < 7 years before gift								
(1.5.1999 – 1.5.2006) (always include CLTs) (£89,000 + £269,000)	(89,000)							
(1.6.2000 – 1.6.2007) (include 1.5.2006 PET as it became chargeable)			(358,000)					
(1.7.2002 – 1.7.2009) (£358,000 + £238,500) (include 1.5.2006 PET as it became chargeable)					(596,500)			
(1.8.2003 – 1.8.2010) (£269,000 + £238,500 + £15,000) (earliest CLT on 1.9.2002 drops out, include both PETs)							(522,500)	
NRB available	(236,000)		(Nil)		(Nil)		(Nil)	
Taxable amount		33,000		238,500		15,000		90,875
IHT payable @ 40%		13,200		95,400		6,000		36,350
Less: Taper relief								
(1.5.2006 – 1.12.2012) (6 – 7 years before death)	(80%)	(10,560)						
(1.6.2007 – 1.12.2012) (5 – 6 years before death)			(60%)	(57,240)				
(1.7.2009 – 1.12.2012) (3 – 4 years before death)					(20%)	(1,200)		
(1.8.2010 – 1.12.2012) (< 3 years before death)								—
Less: IHT paid in lifetime		(Nil)		(5,500)		(Nil)		(875)
IHT payable on death		2,640		32,660		4,800		35,475
Paid by (always the donee)		Alexander		Trustees		Jayne		Trustees
Due date of payment		30.6.2013		30.6.2013		30.6.2013		30.6.2013

Test your understanding 7

Mr Rice makes the following lifetime gifts:

1 May 2004	£182,000 to a trust; Mr Rice paid the IHT.
30 June 2005	£60,000 to his niece on her 21st birthday.
11 June 2006	£169,000 to his nephew on his wedding day.
11 November 2008	£146,000 to a trust; trustees paid the IHT.

The nil rate bands for earlier years are as follows:

2004/05	£263,000
2005/06	£275,000
2006/07	£285,000
2008/09	£312,000

(a) **Calculate the IHT liabilities arising as a result of the lifetime gifts.**

(b) **Assuming Mr Rice dies on 14 February 2013, calculate the additional IHT on the lifetime gifts as a result of Mr Rice's death.**

(c) **Calculate the nil rate band left to set against the death estate.**

9 IHT payable on the death estate

On the death of an individual, an inheritance tax charge arises on the value of their estate at the date of death.

The death estate includes all assets held at the date of death.

The value of assets brought into an individual's estate computation is normally the **open market value (OMV)** of the asset at the date of death (known as the probate value).

The values to use will always be provided in the examination.

The death estate computation

The gross chargeable value of an individual's estate is calculated using the following pro forma:

Pro forma death estate computation

	£	£
Freehold property		x
Less: Repayment mortgage (Note)		(x)
		x
Business owned by sole trader/partnership		x
Stocks and shares (including ISAs)		x
Government securities		x
Insurance policy proceeds (Note)		x
Death in service policy		x
Leasehold property		x
Motor cars		x
Personal chattels		x
Debts due to the deceased		x
Interest and rent due to the deceased		x
Cash at bank and on deposit (including ISAs)		x
		x
Less: Debts due by the deceased	(x)	
Outstanding taxes (e.g. IT, CGT due)	(x)	
Funeral expenses	(x)	
		(x)
		x
Less: Exempt legacies (i.e. to spouse or civil partner)		(x)
Gross chargeable estate		x

Note:

- Endowment mortgages are not deductible from the property value as these are automatically repaid on the owner's death.

- When the deceased has a life insurance policy on their own life, the proceeds of that policy are included in the death estate, rather than the market value of the policy at the date of their death.

Allowable deductions in the death estate computation

Funeral expenses

The costs of the individual's funeral are allowable providing they are reasonable, even though the cost is incurred after the date of death.

Reasonable costs of mourning clothes for the family and the cost of a tombstone are also allowable.

Costs of administering the estate

The cost of administering the estate by the executors / personal representatives is not an allowable deduction as it is for professional services carried out after the death.

Other allowable deductions

Debts are deductible if they:

- were outstanding at the date of death, and
- had been incurred for valuable consideration, or were imposed by law (i.e. legally enforceable debts).

This will include all outstanding taxes such as income tax, NICs and CGT, although not the IHT due on death itself.

Note that a 'promise' to pay a friend, for example, is not legally enforceable and therefore not deductible.

If a debt is secured against specific property it is deducted from the value of that property. This will be the case with a repayment mortgage secured against freehold property.

Note that endowment mortgages are not deducted from the value of the property as the endowment element of the policy should cover the repayment of the mortgage.

Exempt legacies

The only exempt legacies that are allowable in the death estate and examinable at F6 are gifts to the spouse or civil partner (see section 6).

KAPLAN PUBLISHING

The procedure to calculate the IHT on the death estate

The procedure to calculate the IHT on the death estate is as follows.

(1) Deal with the IHT on lifetime gifts within seven years of the date of death first **before** looking at the estate computation.

(2) Calculate the gross chargeable estate value.

(3) Calculate the amount of NRB available after deducting GCTs in the previous 7 years (i.e. CLTs and PETs).

(4) Calculate the tax on the excess at 40%.

(5) If required by the question, state who will pay the tax and the due date of payment (see below).

Further points regarding IHT payable on the death estate

The nil rate band

The NRB available to an individual on death of £325,000 is first used to calculate the death tax on lifetime gifts, then the estate after the lifetime gifts have been dealt with.

The seven year cumulation period

The seven year accumulation period applies in a similar way to the death calculations on lifetime gifts as follows:

- it is necessary to take into account the total of the gross amounts of all **chargeable gifts** made within the **previous seven years**

- therefore, look back seven years from the date of death and accumulate the gross amounts of:
  - **all** CLTs, **and**
  - **all** PETs (because all PETs within 7 years of death will have become chargeable on death).

The death rate of tax

The death rate of IHT is 40% on the excess over the NRB available.

The normal due date of payment of IHT on death estate

IHT as a result of death is due on the earlier of:

* **six months** after the end of the month of death, or
* on delivery of the account of the estate assets to HMRC.

Example 4 – IHT payable on the death estate

Sara died on 15 June 2012 leaving a gross chargeable estate valued at £427,000 which was bequeathed to her brother.

(a) **Calculate the IHT liability arising on Sara's estate assuming she made no lifetime transfers**

(b) **What if Sara had gross chargeable transfers of £147,000 in the seven years prior to her death?**

Answer to example 4

(a) **No lifetime transfers**

	£	£
Gross chargeable estate value		427,000
NRB at death	325,000	
Less: GCTs in 7 yrs pre death	(Nil)	
NRB available		(325,000)
Taxable amount		102,000
IHT due on death (£102,000 × 40%)		40,800

(b) **Lifetime transfers = £147,000**

	£	£
Gross chargeable estate value		427,000
NRB at death	325,000	
Less: GCTs in 7 yrs pre-death	(147,000)	
NRB available		(178,000)
Taxable amount		249,000
IHT due on death (£249,000 × 40%)		99,600

Test your understanding 8

Timothy died on 23 April 2012 leaving a gross chargeable estate valued at £627,560 which was bequeathed to his girlfriend.

Timothy had made the following lifetime gifts:

	Nil rate band
1 June 2002, £180,000, to a trust	£250,000
16 March 2007, £228,000, to his cousin	£285,000

Calculate the IHT liability arising on Timothy's estate and state the due date of payment.

Test your understanding 9

Tom dies on 30 June 2012 and leaves the following assets:

	£
House	200,000
Cottage	250,000
Bank account	75,000
Quoted shares	100,000
Car	15,000

At the date of Tom's death he owes £2,000 on his credit card, and owes £3,000 of income tax and CGT.

In Tom's will he leaves

- the house and shares to his wife
- the cottage to his son
- the residue to his daughter.

Tom made a lifetime gift of £115,000 in cash to his son in August 2008 (nil rate band is £312,000).

Compute the IHT payable on Tom's death.

Payment of inheritance tax on the death estate

IHT on the death estate is initially paid by the executors (personal representatives).

The tax is paid from the estate, and so it is effectively borne by the person who inherits the residue of the assets (known as the residual legatee) after the specific legacies have been paid,

A summary of the payment of tax is shown below:

Recipient / asset	Paid by	Suffered by
Spouse	N/A – exempt	N/A – exempt
Specific UK assets	Executors	Residual legatee
Residue of estate	Executors	Residual legatee

KAPLAN PUBLISHING

Summary

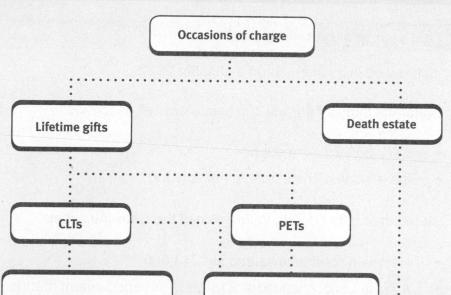

Occasions of charge

Lifetime gifts

Death estate

CLTs

PETs

First computation
= Lifetime IHT:
1. Calculate the chargeable amount of the gift
   - use diminution in value principle if necessary
   - consider exemptions:
     - spouse
     - small gifts
     - normal expenditure from income
     - ME, AE
2. Calculate the lifetime IHT at 20% or 25% after taking account of:
   - whether a gross or net gift
   - the NRB available during lifetime
   - gross CLTs in the 7-year cumulation period
3. Calculate the gross amount to carry forward for future computations

Second computation
= Death IHT on lifetime gifts:
1. Calculate the gross chargeable amount of gifts in the seven years before death
2. Calculate the tax at 40% after taking account of
   - the NRB available on death
   - gross CLTs and PETs which have become chargeable in the 7-year cumulation period
3. Calculate and deduct taper relief
4. For CLTs, deduct lifetime IHT paid

Last computation = Death IHT on estate value:
1. Calculate the gross chargeable estate value
   - allowable deductions - funeral expenses, outstanding debts, including tax bills
   - legacies to spouse / civil partner are exempt
2. Calculate the tax at 40% after taking account of
   - the NRB available on death
   - gross CLTs and PETs in the 7 years before death

10 Comprehensive example – death estate

Test your understanding 10

Wilma died in a car crash on 4 October 2012.

Under the terms of her will, the estate was left as follows:

- £170,000 to her husband
- the residue of the estate to her son Joe.

At the date of her death, Wilma owned the following assets.

- Her main residence valued at £243,000.
- A flat in London valued at £150,000. An endowment mortgage of £70,000 was secured on this property.
- Four shops valued at a total of £231,250.
- A holiday cottage situated in Cornwall worth £20,000.
- 20,000 shares in ZAM plc. The shares were valued at 200p each.
- 8,000 units in the CBA unit trust, valued at 130p each.
- Bank balances of £57,850.
- Wilma has a life insurance policy which was valued at £100,000 on her death. The insurance proceeds paid to the executors of her estate were £260,000.

Wilma's outstanding income tax liability was £7,500, and her funeral expenses amounted to £2,000. She had made no lifetime gifts.

(a) **Calculate the IHT that will be payable as a result of Wilma's death.**

(b) **Show who will pay and who will suffer the IHT liability and how the estate is distributed between the beneficiaries.**

11 Payment of IHT

Summary of normal dates of payment

IHT is payable as follows:

Transfer	Due Date
CLTs between 6 April and 30 September	30 April in the following year
CLTs between 1 October and 5 April	6 months after the end of the month in which the transfer is made
PETs chargeable as a result of death	6 months after the end of the month of death
Additional tax due on CLTs within 7 years before the death	6 months after the end of the month of death
Estate at death	On delivery of the estate accounts to HMRC. Interest runs from 6 months after the end of the month of death.

12 IHT Planning

It is important for an individual to plan their lifetime gifts to be tax efficient and to make a will so that their estate is distributed in a tax efficient way.

There are a number of tax planning measures that can reduce an individual's liability to IHT, for the F6 examination you should be aware of:

- lifetime tax planning
- husband and wife planning (and civil partners).

The overall objectives of all IHT tax planning measures are:

- to minimise the amount of tax payable
- to maximise the inheritance of the next generation.

Lifetime tax planning

IHT planning during an individual's lifetime involves making gifts of wealth as early as possible, as there are many advantages to making lifetime gifts

Advantages of lifetime giving

- Lifetime giving reduces the IHT payable on death as the assets gifted will not be included in the donor's chargeable estate on death.

- IHT on lifetime gifts is likely to be less than the IHT payable on the death estate because:
  - If the gift is a PET, no IHT will be payable if the donor survives seven years.
  - If the gift is a CLT, the tax is calculated at 20% and no additional IHT will be payable on death if the donor survives 7 years.
  - If the donor does not survive seven years, taper relief will be available after three years.
  - A lifetime gift is valued at the time of the gift and the value is 'frozen'. This locks in the value of an appreciating asset, so any increase in value up to the date of death will not be taxed.
  - Exemptions such as normal gifts out of income, small gifts, marriage and AEs may reduce or eliminate the value of a lifetime gift.

However, it is not necessarily advantageous to gift all assets pre-death, as:

- The donor will want to continue to enjoy a comfortable life in their old age, and
- IHT is not the only tax that needs to be considered in respect of lifetime gifts.

Disadvantages of lifetime giving

- The donor loses the use of the asset and any income that can be derived from the asset once given away.

- Capital gains tax:
  - may be payable on lifetime gifts of chargeable assets (either immediately or later if deferred with a gift relief claim)
  - but is not payable on assets held at the date of death.

- Therefore, individual's should be advised not to gift assets during their lifetime that give rise to large CGT liabilities.

KAPLAN PUBLISHING

Husband and wife

Inter spouse gifts during lifetime and on death are exempt. Accordingly, it used to be good tax advice to make sure a couple utilised this exemption during their lifetime to equalise their estates and ensure that they each fully utilised their nil rate bands on death.

However, it is now possible to transfer unused nil rate bands between spouses and therefore such advice is no longer necessary.

Transfer of unused nil rate band

Any amount of NRB that has not been utilised at the time of a person's death can be transferred to their spouse or civil partner.

As a result, each spouse or civil partner can leave the whole of their estate to the surviving spouse or civil partner with no adverse IHT consequences.

- The surviving spouse or civil partner will have the benefit of
  - their own NRB, **and**
  - any unused proportion of their spouse's or civil partner's NRB.

- The amount of the NRB that can be claimed is based on the **proportion that was unused** by the first spouse to die.

- The unused proportion is applied to the NRB available on the **second spouse's death**.

- The executors of the surviving spouse or civil partner must claim the transferred NRB by submitting the IHT return within
  - 2 years of the second death, or
  - 3 months of the executor starting to act.

Example 5 – Transfer of unused nil rate band

Winston died on 15 August 2003. Under the terms of his will £102,000 was left to his children, and the remainder of his estate to his wife, Florence.

Florence died on 24 February 2013.

The nil rate band in 2003/04 was £255,000.

Calculate the amount of nil rate band available against Florence's death estate.

Answer to example 5

On Winston's death the NRB available was £255,000 of which £102,000 was utilised. The remainder of the estate which was left to his wife was exempt.

The unused amount of £153,000 represented 60% of his NRB on death.

The NRB available on Florence's death is therefore:

	£
Florence's NRB on her death	325,000
Winston's unused band transferred (£325,000 × 60%)	195,000
	520,000

Test your understanding 11

Joan is 67 years old, and was widowed on the death of her husband Neil on 21 June 2004 (Nil rate band £263,000).

Neil had a chargeable estate valued at £800,000, and this was left entirely to Joan.

Joan died on 23 May 2012 leaving an estate valued at £1 million, to her two children.

Joan has made no lifetime transfers.

Calculate the IHT liability due as a result of Joan's death assuming:

(a) **Neil made no lifetime transfers**

(b) **Neil gave £176,950 to his son on 16 March 2004.**

13 Chapter summary

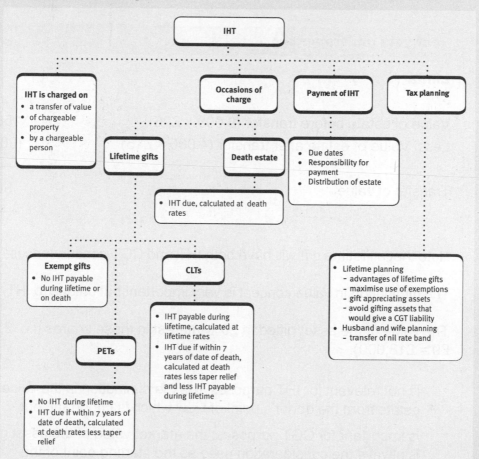

Test your understanding answers

Test your understanding 1

Linda

	£
Value of estate before transfer (6,000 × £26)	156,000
Less: Value of estate after transfer (4,000 × £15)	(60,000)
Transfer of value	96,000

Note that a lifetime gift will have both IHT and CGT consequences.

The diminution in value concept is very important but unique to IHT.

The value of the asset gifted; a 20% interest in these shares (i.e. 2,000 × £9 = £18,000):

- is not relevant for IHT purposes; it is the diminution in the value of the estate from the donor's point of view which is important, but

- is important for CGT purposes; the market value of the asset gifted is always the consideration used as the starting point of the chargeable gain computation.

KAPLAN PUBLISHING

Test your understanding 2

Julie

Chargeable amounts

	PET 31.8.10 2010/11 £	CLT 31.10.10 2010/11 £	CLT 31.5.11 2011/12 £	CLT 30.11.11 2011/12 £	PET 30.4.12 2012/13 £
Tax year of gift					
Transfer of value	600	800	2,100	1,100	5,000
Less: Annual exemption					
2010/11	(600)	(800)			
2009/10 b/f (£3,000 avail)	(–)	(–)			
(all lost as not used and can only c/f for one year)					
2011/12			(2,100)	(900)	
2010/11 b/f (£1,600 avail)			(–)	(200)	
(remaining £1,400 lost as not used)					
2012/13					(3,000)
2011/12 b/f (none available– already used)					(Nil)
Chargeable amount	Nil	Nil	Nil	Nil	2,000

Test your understanding 3

Maggie

Chargeable amounts

1.6.2012   Gift to husband = exempt inter-spouse transfer
4.11.2012 Gift to friend = small gift exemption applies as the gift is less than £250

	PET	PET	CLT
Tax year of gift	6.7.2012	27.9.2012	24.12.2012
	2012/13	2012/13	2012/13
	£	£	£
Transfer of value	15,000	20,000	270,000
Less: Marriage exemption	(5,000)		
Less: Annual exemption			
2012/13	(3,000)	(Nil)	(Nil)
2011/12 b/f	(3,000)	(Nil)	(Nil)
Chargeable amount	4,000	20,000	270,000

The gifts to the son and nephew are PETs – therefore no tax is payable unless Maggie dies within 7 years.

The gift into trust is a CLT and is chargeable during Maggie's lifetime. However, as she has no chargeable gifts in the preceding seven years, there will be no IHT to pay as the gift is covered by the NRB of £325,000 (see later).

Test your understanding 4

Charlotte

(a) Trustees to pay IHT

		CLT 13.6.2012
		£
Transfer of value		366,000
Annual exemption		
– Current year	2012/13	(3,000)
– Previous year	2011/12 b/f	(3,000)
Chargeable amount	Gross	360,000
NRB @ date of gift	2012/13	(325,000)
Taxable amount		35,000
IHT payable	@ 20%	7,000
Paid by		Trustees
Due date		30.4.2013
Gross chargeable amount c/f		360,000

(b) Charlotte to pay IHT

		CLT 13.6.2012
		£
		366,000
	2012/13	(3,000)
	2011/12 b/f	(3,000)
	Net	360,000
	2012/13	(325,000)
		35,000
	@ 25%	8,750
		Charlotte
		30.4.2013
	(£360,000 net + £8,750 tax)	368,750

Alex

	CLT 30.6.2003	PET 12.6.2007	CLT 30.6.2008	CLT 15.12.2012
	£	£	£	£
Transfer of value	170,000	150,000	191,000	256,000
Annual exemption				
– Current year	2003/04 (3,000)	2007/08 (3,000)	2008/09 (3,000)	2012/13 (3,000)
– Previous year	2002/03 b/f (3,000)	2006/07 b/f (3,000)	2007/08 b/f (Nil)	2011/12 b/f (3,000)
Chargeable amount	164,000	144,000	Gross 188,000	Net 250,000
			£	£
NRB @ date of gift	Gross		312,000	325,000
– 2003/04	£			
– 2008/09	255,000			
– 2012/13				
Less: GCTs < 7 years before gift	(Nil)		(164,000)	(188,000) *150,000*
(30.6.1996 – 30.6.2003)				
(30.6.2001 – 30.6.2008) (ignore PET)				
(15.12.2005 – 15.12.2012)				
(ignore PET and gift on 30.6.2003 drops out as too old)				
NRB available	(255,000)		(148,000)	(137,000)
Taxable amount	Nil	Nil	40,000	113,000
IHT payable	Nil	Nil	@ 20% 8,000	@ 25% 28,250
Paid by			Trustees	Alex
Due date of payment			30.4.2009	30.6.2013
Gross chargeable amount c/f	164,000	144,000	188,000	(£250,000 net + £28,250 tax) 278,250

Test your understanding 6

Sidney

	CLT 21.4.2002	PET 15.4.2007	CLT 19.3.2008	CLT 9.5.2012
	Gross £	£	Net £	Gross £
Transfer of value	98,000	140,000	221,000	395,000
Annual exemption				
– Current year	(3,000) 2002/03	(3,000) 2007/08	(Nil) 2007/08	(3,000) 2012/13
– Previous year	(3,000) 2001/02 b/f	(3,000) 2006/07 b/f	(Nil) 2006/07 b/f	(3,000) 2011/12 b/f
Chargeable amount	92,000	134,000	221,000	389,000
NRB @ date of gift	£		£	£
– 2002/03	250,000			
– 2007/08			300,000	
– 2012/13				325,000
Less: GCTs ‹ 7 years before gift				
(21.4.1995 – 21.4.2002)	(Nil)			
(19.3.2001 – 19.3.2008) (ignore PET)			(92,000)	
(9.5.2005 – 9.5.2012)				(224,250)
(ignore PET and gift on 21.4.2002 drops out as too old)				
NRB available	(250,000)		(208,000)	(100,750)
Taxable amount	Nil	Nil	13,000	288,250
IHT payable	Nil	Nil	3,250 @ 25%	57,650 @ 20%
Paid by			Sidney	Trustees
Due date of payment			30.9.2008	30.4.2013
Gross chargeable amount	92,000	134,000	224,250 (£221,000 net + £3,250 tax)	389,000

Test your understanding 7

Answer to example 1

IHT payable during lifetime

	PET 31.7.2003		PET 30.11.2006		PET 30.4.2007	
		£		£		£
Transfer of value		80,000		110,000		235,000
Annual exemption						
– Current year	2003/04	(3,000)	2006/07	(3,000)	2007/08	(3,000)
– Previous year	2002/03 b/f	(3,000)	2005/06 b/f	(3,000)	2006/07 b/f	(Nil)
Chargeable amount		74,000		104,000		232,000
IHT payable (as all PETs)		Nil		Nil		Nil
Gross chargeable amount c/f		74,000		104,000		232,000

All gifts are PETs, therefore there is no lifetime tax to pay. However the gross chargeable amount of the PETs must be established at the time of the gift.

Note: The earlier NRBs given in the question are not required, as they are only required if there is lifetime tax to pay.

(b) IHT payable on death

Date of death: 14 February 2013
7 years before: 14 February 2006

CLT on 1.5.2004 and PET on 30.6.2005 are more than 7 years before death – therefore no IHT payable on death

	PET 11.6.2006 £	CLT 11.11.2008 £
Gross chargeable amount b/f (as above)	165,000	140,000
NRB @ date of death – 2012/13	325,000	325,000
Less: GCTs ‹ 7 years before gift		
(11.6.1999 – 11.6.2006)		
(exclude PET on 30.6.2005 as it became completely exempt)	(176,000)	
(11.11.2001 – 11.11.2008) (£176,000 + £165,000)		
(exclude PET on 30.6.2005 as it became completely exempt, but include 11.6.2006 PET as it became chargeable)		(341,000)
NRB available	Nil	(Nil)
Taxable amount	16,000	140,000
IHT payable @ 40%	6,400	56,000
Less: Taper relief		
(11.6.2006 – 14.2.2013) (6 – 7 years before death)	(80%) (5,120)	
(11.11.2008 – 14.2.2013) (4 – 5 years before death)		(40%) (22,400)
Less: IHT paid in lifetime	(Nil)	(800)
IHT payable on death	1,280	32,800
Paid by (always the donee)	Nephew	Trustees
Due date of payment	31.8.2013	31.8.2013

(c) Nil rate band left to set against the death estate

	£
NRB at death	325,000
Less: GCTs in 7 yrs pre-death	
(14.2.06 to 14.2.13) (£165,000 + £140,000)	
(first two gifts = too old, include PET on 11.6.06 as became chargeable on death)	(305,000)
NRB available against death estate	20,000

Test your understanding 8

Timothy

IHT payable during lifetime

	CLT 1.6.2002		PET 16.3.2007	
		£		£
Transfer of value		180,000		228,000
Less: Annual exemption				
Current year	2002/03	(3,000)	2006/07	(3,000)
Previous year	2001/02 b/f	(3,000)	2005/06 b/f	(3,000)
Chargeable amount	Net	174,000		222,000
		£		
NRB @ date of gift – 2002/03		250,000		
Less: GCTs < 7 years before gift (1.6.1995 – 1.6.2002)		(Nil)		
NRB available		(250,000)		Nil
Taxable amount		Nil		Nil
IHT payable		Nil		Nil
Gross chargeable amount c/f		174,000		222,000

Note: The NRB given in the question for 2006/07 is not required, as the gift is a PET and there is no lifetime tax to pay on PETs

IHT payable on death

Date of death: 23 April 2012
7 years before: 23 April 2005

CLT on 1.6.2002 is more than 7 years before death – therefore no IHT payable on death

	PET 16.3.2007		Estate value 23.4.2012	
	£	£	£	£
Gross chargeable amount		222,000		627,560
NRB @ date of death – 2012/13	325,000		325,000	
Less: GCTs < 7 years before gift (16.3.2000 – 16.3.2007)	(174,000)			
Less: GCTs < 7 years before death (23.4.2005 – 23.4.2012) (earliest CLT on 1.6.2002 drops out)	—		(222,000)	
NRB available		(151,000)		(103,000)
Taxable amount		71,000		524,560
IHT payable @ 40%		28,400		209,824
Less: Taper relief (16.3.2007 – 23.4.2012) (5 – 6 years before death) (60%)		(17,040)		
Less: IHT paid in lifetime		(Nil)		
IHT payable on death		11,360		
Paid by		Cousin		Executors
Due date of payment		31.10.2012		31.10.2012

Test your understanding 9

Tom
Death estate – date of death 30 June 2012

		£	£
House			200,000
Cottage			250,000
Bank account			75,000
Quoted shares			100,000
Car			15,000
Allowable expenses	– Credit card		(2,000)
	– Income tax and CGT		(3,000)
			635,000
Exempt legacy to wife	– house		(200,000)
	– quoted shares		(100,000)
Gross chargeable estate			335,000
NRB at death (Note)		325,000	
Less: GCTs in 7 yrs pre-death (30.6.05 – 30.6.12) (W)		(109,000)	
NRB available			(216,000)
Taxable amount			119,000
IHT on chargeable estate (£119,000 × 40%)			47,600

Working: Lifetime gift to son

	£
Transfer of value	115,000
Less: AE – 2008/09	(3,000)
– 2007/08 b/f	(3,000)
Chargeable amount	109,000

Notes:

(1) No lifetime tax was payable on this gift as it was a PET.

(2) At death, the current NRB of £325,000 is applied to the gift. The NRB in 2008/09 given in the question is therefore not relevant.

KAPLAN PUBLISHING

Test your understanding 10

Wilma
Death estate – date of death 4 October 2012

	£	£
Main residence		243,000
Flat (Note 1)		150,000
Shops		231,250
Holiday cottage		20,000
Shares in ZAM plc (20,000 @ 200p)		40,000
Units in CBA trust (8,000 @ 130p)		10,400
Bank balances		57,850
Life insurance policy proceeds		260,000
		1,012,500
Less: Income tax due	(7,500)	
Funeral expenses	(2,000)	
		(9,500)
		1,003,000
Less: Exempt legacies – Husband		(170,000)
Gross chargeable estate		833,000
NRB at death	325,000	
Less: GCTs in 7 yrs pre-death (4.10.05 to 4.10.12)	(Nil)	
		(325,000)
Taxable amount		508,000
IHT due on Wilma's death (£508,000 × 40%)		203,200

Allocation of the IHT liability on the estate

The executors will pay the IHT out of the estate.

The tax is suffered by Wilma's son, Joe (the residual legatee).

Distribution of the estate

	£
Wilma's husband	170,000
Joe (residual legatee) (Note 2)	629,800
HMRC	203,200
Total estate to distribute	1,003,000

Notes:

(1) Since the endowment mortgage would have been repaid upon Wilma's death, it is not deducted from the value of the flat.

(2) Residual legacy

Joe will receive the residue of the estate calculated as follows:

	£
Value of estate (before specific legacies)	1,003,000
Less: Legacy to husband	(170,000)
IHT to HMRC	(203,200)
Residue of estate	629,800

KAPLAN PUBLISHING

Test your understanding 11

(a) **Neil made no lifetime transfers**

On Neil's death:

– no lifetime gifts, so all NRB available for his death estate

– the transfer of his estate to Joan is an exempt legacy

– so, no IHT was due on his estate, and

– therefore none of his NRB was utilised (i.e. 100% unutilised).

Joan – Death estate

	£
Gross chargeable estate	1,000,000
Less: NRB at date of Joan's death	(325,000)
Less: NRB transferred from Neil (Note)	
(£325,000 x 100%)	(325,000)
	————
Taxable amount	350,000
	————
IHT payable on death (£350,000 × 40%)	140,000
	————

This IHT is paid by executors, borne by Joan's children.

Note:

– Although the NRB available on Neil's death was only £263,000, the amount unused was 100% of the NRB. This percentage is applied to the current NRB of £325,000 to calculate the amount that can be transferred.

– Joan's executors must claim the transferred NRB on the submission of her IHT return within 2 years from her death, or 3 months after the executors start to act.

(b) **Neil made a lifetime gift to his son**

On Neil's death:

– Lifetime gift to son is a PET; therefore no lifetime IHT is due but the gift becomes chargeable on his death

– The PET is covered by the nil rate band available at death, therefore no death IHT is due

– However, the PET utilises £170,950 (£176,950 – (£3,000 x 2) AEs) of his nil rate band available at death

– The transfer of his estate to Joan is an exempt legacy

- – Therefore, after taking account of his lifetime gifts and death estate, £92,050 (£263,000 – £170,950) of his nil rate band is unutilised

- – The unutilised proportion is 35% ((£92,050 / £263,000) x 100)

On Joan's death:

	£
Gross chargeable estate	1,000,000
Less: NRB at date of Joan's death	(325,000)
Less: NRB transferred from Neil (£325,000 x 35%)	(113,750)
Taxable amount	561,250
IHT payable on death (£561, 250 x 40%)	224,500

Introduction to corporation tax

Chapter learning objectives

Upon completion of this chapter you will be able to:

- define the terms 'period of account', 'accounting period', and 'financial year'

- explain the rules for determining when an accounting period starts and ends

- identify the correct accounting period for corporation tax from information supplied

- define the rules of residence for a company and determine a company's residence using those rules

- identify the different taxable profits for a company and the basis of assessment

- explain the implications of receiving franked investment income

- compute the corporation tax liability for a single company.

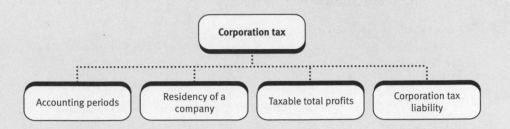

Introduction

UK resident companies are assessed to corporation tax on their worldwide income and chargeable gains arising in an accounting period.

This and the following five chapters deal with the way in which companies are assessed to corporation tax.

Corporation tax is an important topic as it will be the focus of question two in the examination, which will be either **25** or **30 marks**.

This first introductory chapter sets out the basis upon which companies are assessed to corporation tax and explains how a company's corporation tax liability is calculated.

1 Basis of assessment

- Corporation tax is assessed on a company's income and chargeable gains arising in a chargeable accounting period.

- The chargeable accounting period is not necessarily the same period as the company's set of accounts (period of account).

It is important when dealing with corporation tax to understand the terms 'period of account' and 'chargeable accounting period'.

Period of account

A period of account is any period for which a company prepares accounts. It is usually 12 months in length, but may be shorter or longer than this.

Chargeable accounting period

A chargeable accounting period (CAP) is the period for which a charge to corporation tax is made. It may **never** be **longer than 12 months**.

2 Chargeable accounting periods

When does a CAP start?

A CAP starts:

- when a company starts to trade (or receives income chargeable to corporation tax), and
- when the previous accounting period ends.

When does a CAP end?

The main situations where a CAP ends are:

- twelve months after the beginning of the accounting period
- the end of the company's period of account, and
- the date the company begins or ceases to trade.

Long periods of account

For corporation tax purposes, a CAP can never exceed 12 months.

Therefore, if a company prepares accounts for a period of more than 12 months, there must be two accounting periods for tax purposes.

The long period of account is divided into CAPs as follows:

- First CAP: first 12 months of long period
- Second CAP the balance of the long period.

Illustration – Accounting periods

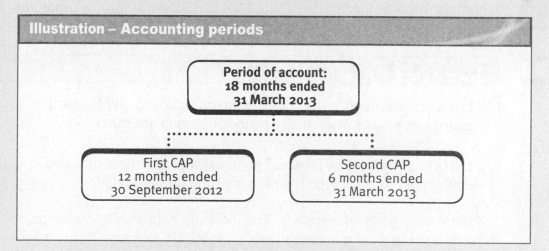

A corporation tax computation is prepared for each CAP. See Chapter 19 for the method of allocating the accounting profits between the two CAPs.

3 The tax residence of a company

Companies **resident** in the UK are chargeable to corporation tax on:

*   all profits and chargeable gains **wherever they arise**
    (i.e. on worldwide profits and gains).

It is therefore important to correctly determine where a company is resident.

Determining residence

A company is UK resident if it is:

*   **incorporated** in the UK, or

*   incorporated elsewhere, but is **centrally managed and controlled** in the UK.

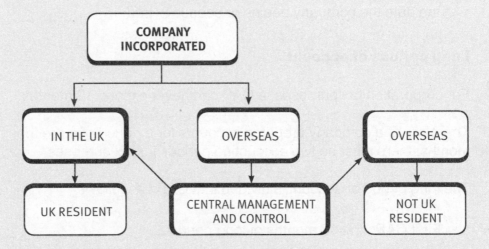

 A company that is incorporated in the UK is resident in the UK regardless of where it is centrally managed and controlled.

Example 1 – The tax residence of a company

X Ltd is incorporated in the UK. The directors hold monthly board meetings overseas when major policy decisions are made.

Y Ltd is incorporated overseas. The directors hold frequent board meetings in the UK, which is where the directors are based.

Z Ltd is incorporated overseas. The directors hold weekly meetings overseas, but have quarterly meetings in the UK because this is where the non-executive directors are based.

State which of the companies will be treated as UK resident.

Answer to example 1

- X Ltd is resident in the UK. If a company is incorporated in the UK it is irrelevant where meetings are held and decisions are made.

- Y Ltd would probably be treated as resident in the UK for corporation tax purposes. Although not incorporated in the UK, it would appear that the company is centrally managed and controlled from the UK.

- Z Ltd would probably not be treated as resident in the UK. The company is not incorporated in the UK, and it appears to be centrally managed and controlled from overseas.

Test your understanding 1

Matthew Ltd is incorporated in France but holds all its board meetings in Germany. Its directors live in the UK most of the year.

Mark Ltd is incorporated in Italy but holds its monthly board meetings in London. Other interim board meetings are held in Italy, where some of the directors are based. Most of the directors are based in the UK.

Luke Ltd is incorporated in the UK. Board meetings are held in France.

State which of the above companies will be treated as resident in the UK for corporation tax purposes.

4 Taxable total profits

- A company's corporation tax liability for an accounting period is calculated by computing taxable profits from all sources, and deducting qualifying charitable donations (QCDs).

- Included in the computation of a company's taxable profits are:
    - world-wide income (excluding dividends) **and**
    - net chargeable gains.
    - The resultant figure is known as **taxable total profits (TTP)**.

Layout of a corporation tax computation

Company name
Corporation tax computation for the year ended 31 March 2013

	£
Tax adjusted trading profit	X
Interest income	X
Property business profit	X
Chargeable gains	X
Total profits	X
Less: Qualifying charitable donation (QCD) relief	(X)
Taxable total profits (TTP)	X

Tax adjusted trading profit

- Assesses all trading income net of trading expenditure.

- See Chapter 19 for detail.

Interest income

- Assesses all interest receivable net of some interest payable.

- See Chapter 19 for detail.

Property business profit

- Assesses the profit (or loss) from letting furnished or unfurnished property and is calculated on the accruals basis.

- See Chapter 19 for more detail.

Dividends

- Dividends received from UK and overseas companies are exempt from corporation tax and are therefore **excluded** in the TTP computation.

- However, although exempt from corporation tax, dividends received have an impact on the rate of corporation tax that is applicable (see section 5).

Chargeable gains/losses

- Corporation tax is also charged on any chargeable gains that arise on disposals made by the company during an accounting period.

- Chargeable gains for companies are covered in detail in Chapter 20.

It is essential to understand that companies pay **corporation tax** on their chargeable gains, not capital gains tax.

Qualifying charitable donations

- All donations to charity by a company (except those allowed as a trading expense) are an allowable deduction in a corporation tax computation.

- The relief is referred to as 'qualifying charitable donations (QCD) relief' and applies whether or not a donation is made under Gift Aid.

- All charitable donations by a company are paid gross.

- Note that the tax treatment of Gift Aid payments made by a company is different from that applied to payments made by an individual (see Chapter 19 for more detail).

Example 2 – Taxable total profits

Westmorland Ltd has the following income and outgoings for the year ending 31 March 2013.

	£
Tax adjusted trading profit	1,456,500
Property business profit	25,000
Interest receivable	10,000
Chargeable gains	35,000
Dividends from UK companies	14,400
Charitable donation (gross)	(10,000)

Compute the taxable total profits for the y/e 31 March 2013.

Answer to example 2

Taxable total profits – y/e 31 March 2013

	£
Tax adjusted trading profits	1,456,500
Property business profit	25,000
Interest receivable	10,000
Chargeable gains	35,000
	1,526,500
Less: QCD relief	(10,000)
TTP	1,516,500

Notes:

(1) Dividends received are ignored when calculating taxable total profits as they are exempt from corporation tax.

(2) All charitable donations, whether paid under the Gift Aid scheme or not, are allowable deductions and are paid gross.

Test your understanding 2

Cumberland Ltd has the following income and outgoings for the year ended 30 September 2012.

	£
Tax adjusted trading profit	81,500
Property business profit	1,300
Non-trading loan interest receivable	2,200
Chargeable gains	3,000
Dividends from overseas companies	3,500
Dividends from UK companies	900
Charitable donation (gross)	1,000

Compute the taxable total profits for the y/e 30 September 2012.

5 The corporation tax liability

The company's corporation tax liability is calculated by applying the appropriate rate of corporation tax to the company's taxable total profits.

Rate of corporation tax

The rate of corporation tax is determined by the:

(1) financial year (FY), and

(2) augmented profits (A) of the company.

Financial year

- The rate of corporation tax is fixed by reference to financial years.

- A financial year runs from 1 April to the following 31 March and is identified by the calendar year in which it begins.

- The year commencing 1 April 2012 is the financial year 2012 (FY 2012).

  Financial years should not be confused with the tax years for income tax, which run from 6 April to the following 5 April.

- FY2012 is therefore the year ended 31 March 2013.

- The following rates apply to FY2012:

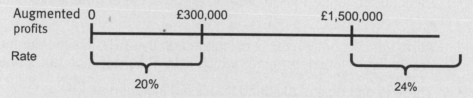

These rates and limits often change each financial year. They are given in the tax tables in the examination.

The upper and lower limits for augmented profits are fixed for each financial year, but have not changed for many years.

However, the rates of corporation tax have changed in FY2012.

- If A < lower limit (i.e. the augmented profits are below £300,000) TTP is charged at the small profits rate (20% in FY2012).

- If A > upper limit (i.e. the augmented profits exceed £1,500,000) TTP is charged at the main rate (24% in FY2012)

- Where A falls in between the limits of £300,000 and £1,500,000; special marginal relief applies.

Augmented profits

To determine the rate of corporation tax, a special definition of augmented profits applies as follows:

	£
Taxable total profits (TTP)	X
Plus: Franked investment income (FII)	X
	—
Augmented profits (A)	X
	—

The augmented profits figure is compared to the profits limits for the relevant financial year to determine the rate of corporation tax applicable.

The appropriate rate of tax is then applied to the company's TTP.

Franked investment income

Although dividends received from UK and overseas companies are exempt from corporation tax, they can have an impact on the rate of corporation tax that is applicable.

- Dividends received plus the associated 10% tax credit are known as franked investment income (FII).

- To calculate FII, take dividends received and multiply by 100/90.

- FII is added to the TTP in order to arrive at the augmented profits figure.

- Although corporation tax is calculated on the TTP, it is the augmented profits figure that determines which **rate** of corporation tax is applicable.

- There is one type of dividend that is not included as FII:
  - a dividend received from a 51% group company (see Chapter 22).

Test your understanding 3

Zachary Ltd has taxable total profits of £148,000 in the y/e 31 March 2013, and dividends received from other UK companies of £4,500.

Calculate Zachary Ltd's corporation tax liability for the y/e 31 March 2013.

Test your understanding 4

Argo Ltd has taxable total profits of £1,450,000 in the year ended 31 March 2013, and UK dividends received of £72,000.

Calculate Argo Ltd's corporation tax liability for the y/e 31 March 2013.

Marginal relief

If augmented profits fall between the 'lower and upper limits' of £300,000 and £1,500,000:

- the company is 'marginal' and its TTP is taxed as follows:

	£
TTP @ main rate	X
Less: Marginal relief	
Standard fraction × (U – A) × N/A	(X)
Corporation tax liability	X

where:
U = Relevant augmented profits upper limit (£1,500,000 for FY2012)
A = Augmented profits
N = Taxable total profits
Standard fraction = given in the tax tables (1/100 for FY2012)

Example 3 – The corporation tax liability

Small Ltd's taxable total profits for the y/e 31 March 2013 are:

	£
Trading profit	260,000
Property business profit	40,000
	300,000
Less: QCD relief	(10,000)
TTP	290,000

Calculate the company's corporation tax liability if:

(a) **no dividends are received.**

(b) **£9,000 of dividends are received.**

(c) **£45,000 of dividends are received.**

Answer to example 3

(a) **No dividends received**

TTP = Augmented profits (A) (as there is no FII)	£290,000

'A' is below the lower limit of £300,000 therefore the small profits rate applies:

Corporation tax liability = (£290,000 × 20%) = £58,000

(b) **Dividends received = £9,000**

	£
TTP	290,000
Plus: FII (£9,000 × 100/90)	10,000
Augmented profits (A)	300,000

'A' is equal to the lower limit and therefore the small profits rate applies:

Corporation tax liability = (£290,000 × 20%) = £58,000, as before.

The augmented profits level has not altered the decision.

(c) **Dividends received = £45,000**

	£
TTP	290,000
Plus: FII (£45,000 × 100/90)	50,000
Augmented profits (A)	340,000

KAPLAN PUBLISHING

'A' is above £300,000 but below £1,500,000; therefore marginal relief applies:

	£
Corporation tax (£290,000 × 24%)	69,600
Less: Marginal relief	
1/100 × (£1,500,000 – £340,000) × £290,000/£340,000	(9,894)
Corporation tax liability	59,706

Test your understanding 5

Sycamore Ltd has the following results for the y/e 31 March 2013:

Tax adjusted trading profit	£320,000
Chargeable gain	£10,000
Dividends received	£18,000

Calculate Sycamore Ltd's corporation tax liability for the year ended 31 March 2013.

Short accounting periods

- The upper and lower augmented profits limits of £1,500,000 and £300,000 apply for accounting periods of 12 months.

- If an accounting period is for less than 12 months, the limits must be reduced proportionately.

Example 4 – The corporation tax liability

Minnow Ltd has the following results for the three-month accounting period ended 31 March 2013:

	£
Tax adjusted trading profit	250,000
Dividends from UK companies	18,000

Compute the company's corporation tax liability for the period ended 31 March 2013.

Answer to example 4

Corporation tax computation – 3 m/e 31 March 2013

	£
TTP	250,000
Plus: FII (£18,000 × 100/90)	20,000
Augmented profits	270,000
Corporation tax (£250,000 × 24%)	60,000
Less: Marginal relief	
1/100 × (£375,000 – £270,000) × £250,000/£270,000	(972)
Corporation tax liability	59,028

Note: As the accounting period is only three months long, the limits are reduced to:

	£
Lower limit (£300,000 x 3/12)	75,000
Upper limit (£1,500,000 x 3/12)	375,000

As 'A' falls between these reduced limits, marginal relief applies.

Note that the reduced upper limit of £375,000 is used in the marginal relief calculation.

Test your understanding 6

Petal Ltd has the following results for the 9 m/e 31 December 2012:

Tax adjusted trading profit	£1,100,000
Chargeable gain	£60,000
Dividends from UK companies	£45,000

Calculate the company's corporation tax liability for the 9 m/e 31 December 2012.

Accounting periods straddling 31 March

Where a company's accounting period falls into two financial years then the corporation tax liability must be calculated for each financial year if either:

- the corporation tax rates, or
- the augmented profits limits have changed.

The rates of corporation tax changed on 1 April 2011 and 1 April 2012. Therefore, a two-part computation is required for a CAP straddling 31 March 2011 or 31 March 2012.

The corporation tax liability must be calculated for each financial year separately; applying the appropriate rates of tax to each.

The following table will be provided to you in the tax rates and allowances section of the exam:

Financial year:	2010	2011	2012
Small profits rate	21%	20%	20%
Main rate	28%	26%	24%
Lower limit	£300,000	£300,000	£300,000
Upper limit	£1,500,000	£1,500,000	£1,500,000
Standard fraction	7/400	3/200	1/100

Example 5 – Accounting periods straddling 31 March

Flute Ltd had taxable total profits of £400,000 and received dividends from UK companies of £45,000 in the year ended 30 September 2012.

Calculate Flute Ltd's corporation tax liability for the y/e 30 September 2012.

Answer to example 5

Corporation tax liability – y/e 30 September 2012

	£
TTP	400,000
Plus: FII (£45,000 x 100/90)	50,000
Augmented profits	450,000

As augmented profits are between the small profits lower limit of £300,000 and the upper limit of £1,500,000, marginal relief applies.

The company's CAP straddles 31 March 2012. The first six months (1.10.11 to 31.3.12) fall into FY2011 and the second six months (1.4.12 to 30.9.12) fall into FY 2012.

The rates of tax changed on 1 April 2012; therefore a two-part computation of the corporation tax liability is required as follows:

	£	£
FY2011		
(£400,000 x 26% x 6/12)	52,000	
Less: Marginal relief		
3/200 x (£1,500,000–£450,000) x £400,000/£450,000 x 6/12	(7,000)	
		45,000
FY2012		
(£400,000 x 24% x 6/12)	48,000	
Less: Marginal relief		
1/100 x (£1,500,000–£450,000) x £400,000/£450,000 x 6/12	(4,667)	
		43,333
Corporation tax liability		88,333

Test your understanding 7

Oboe Ltd had taxable total profits of £100,000 and franked investment income of £20,000 for the year ended 31 December 2012.

(a) **Calculate Oboe Ltd's corporation tax liability for the y/e 31 December 2012.**

(b) **Recalculate the liability assuming the y/e 31 December 2011.**

Test your understanding 8

Bassoon Ltd had taxable total profits of £850,000 and received dividends from UK companies of £16,200 in the y/e 30 June 2012.

Calculate Bassoon Ltd's corporation tax liability for the y/e 30 June 2012.

6 Chapter summary

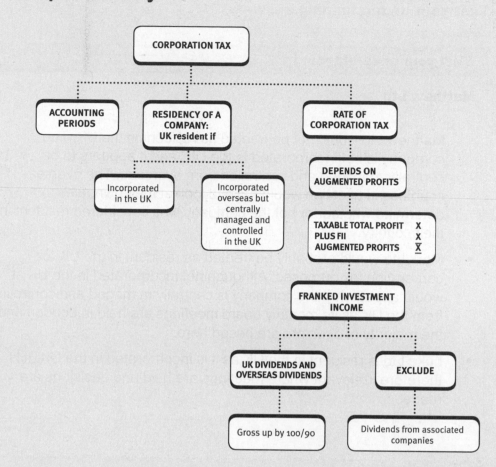

Test your understanding answers

Test your understanding 1

Matthew Ltd

- Matthew Ltd would not be treated as resident in the UK. The company is not incorporated in the UK, and it appears to be centrally managed and controlled from overseas. The overseas countries in question would have to look at their own rules to determine whether or not the company was considered resident in their country.

- Mark Ltd would probably be treated as resident in the UK for corporation tax purposes. Although not incorporated in the UK, it would appear that the company is centrally managed and controlled from the UK as its monthly board meetings are held in London and the majority of directors are based here.

- Luke Ltd is resident in the UK as it is incorporated in the UK. It is therefore irrelevant where meetings are held and decisions are made.

Test your understanding 2

Cumberland Ltd

Taxable total profits – y/e 30 September 2012

	£
Tax adjusted trading profits	81,500
Property business profit	1,300
Interest receivable	2,200
Chargeable gains	3,000
	88,000
Less: QCD relief	(1,000)
TTP	87,000

Note: Both UK and overseas dividends are exempt from UK corporation tax.

Test your understanding 3

Zachary Ltd

Step 1: Calculate augmented profits:

	£
Taxable total profits (TTP)	148,000
Plus: FII (£4,500 × 100/90)	5,000
Augmented profits	153,000

Step 2: From augmented profits determine the rate of corporation tax:

As augmented profits are less than the lower limit of £300,000; taxable total profits are taxed at the small profits rate.

Step 3: Determine the appropriate small profits rate for the financial year

y/e 31 March 2013 = FY2012 = 20%.

Step 4: Apply rate to taxable total profits:

Corporation tax liability (£148,000 × 20%) = £29,600.

Test your understanding 4

Argo Ltd

	£
Taxable total profits (TTP)	1,450,000
Plus: FII (£72,000 × 100/90)	80,000
Augmented profits	1,530,000

As augmented profits are more than £1,500,000; taxable total profits are taxed at the main rate.

y/e 31 March 2013 = FY2012 = 24%

Corporation tax liability (£1,450,000 × 24%) = £348,000.

Note: The fact that TTP are below the limit of £1,500,000 is irrelevant. Augmented profits determine the tax rate.

Test your understanding 5

Sycamore Ltd

Corporation tax computation – y/e 31 March 2013

	£
Tax adjusted trading profit	320,000
Chargeable gain	10,000
TTP	330,000
Plus: FII (£18,000 × 100/90)	20,000
Augmented profits (A)	350,000

'A' is between £300,000 and £1,500,000 and therefore marginal relief applies.

	£
Corporation tax (£330,000 x 24%)	79,200
Less: Marginal relief	
1/100 × (£1,500,000 – £350,000) × £330,000/£350,000	(10,843)
Corporation tax liability	68,357

Test your understanding 6

Petal Ltd

Corporation tax computation – 9 m/e 31 December 2012

	£
Tax adjusted trading profit	1,100,000
Chargeable gain	60,000
TTP	1,160,000
Plus: FII (£45,000 × 100/90)	50,000
Augmented profits	1,210,000
Corporation tax liability (£1,160,000 at 24%) (Note)	278,400

Note: As the CAP is only nine months , the small profits rate lower limit is reduced to £225,000 (£300,000 × 9/12) and the upper limit is reduced to £1,125,000 (£1,500,000 × 9/12).

As 'A' falls above the upper limit of £1,125,000; the main corporation tax rate applies. The 9 months ending 31 December all falls within FY2012, therefore the appropriate main rate is 24%.

Test your understanding 7

Oboe Ltd

(a) **Corporation tax computation – y/e 31 December 2012**

	£
TTP	100,000
Plus: FII	20,000
Augmented profits	120,000

As augmented profits are below the lower limit of £300,000 the small profits rate applies.

The company's CAP straddles 31 March 2012. The first three months (1 January 2012 to 31 March 2012) fall into FY 2011 and the second nine months (1 April 2012 to 31 December 2012) fall into FY 2012.

However, as there is no change in rate on 1 April 2012; the liability can be calculated for the whole CAP as follows:

(£100,000 x 20%)	£20,000

(b) **Corporation tax computation – y/e 31 December 2011**

The TTP and augmented profits are identical, and the small profits rate applies.

The company's CAP straddles 31 March 2011. The first three months (1.1.10 to 31.3.11) fall into FY2010 and second nine months (1.4.11 to 31.12.11) fall into FY2011.

The rates of tax changed on 1 April 2011; therefore a two-part computation of the corporation tax liability is required as follows:

	£
FY 2010: (£100,000 x 3/12 x 21%)	5,250
FY 2011: (£100,000 x 9/12 x 20%)	15,000
	———
Corporation tax liability	20,250
	———

Test your understanding 8

Bassoon Ltd

Corporation tax computation – y/e 30 June 2012

	£
TTP	850,000
Plus: FII (£16,200 × 100/90)	18,000
	———
Augmented profits	868,000
	———

As augmented profits are between the small profits lower limit of £300,000 and the upper limit of £1,500,000; marginal relief applies.

The CAP straddles 31 March 2012. The first nine months (1.7.11 to 31.3.12) fall into FY 2011 and the second three months (1.4.12 to 30.6.12) fall into FY 2012.

The rates of tax changed on 1 April 2012; therefore a two-part computation of the corporation tax liability is required as follows:

	£	£
FY2011		
(£850,000 x 26% x 9/12)	165,750	
Less: Marginal relief		
3/200 x (£1,500,000–£868,000) x £850,000/£868,000 x 9/12	(6,963)	
		158,787
FY2012		
(£850,000 x 24% x 3/12)	51,000	
Less: Marginal relief		
1/100 x (£1,500,000–£868,000) x £850,000/£868,000 x 3/12	(1,547)	49,453
Corporation tax liability		208,240

Introduction to corporation tax

Taxable total profits

Chapter learning objectives

Upon completion of this chapter you will be able to:

- identify the different taxable profits for a company and the basis of assessment

- calculate the tax adjusted trading profit or loss for a company

- explain how relief can be obtained for pre-trading expenditure

- compute capital allowances on plant and machinery

- compute property business profits

- distinguish between trading and non-trading loans and deposits

- identify the tax treatment of trade and non-trade interest and associated costs

- show the treatment of charitable donations made by a company

- prepare a computation of taxable total profits for an accounting period

- calculate taxable total profits for a long period of account.

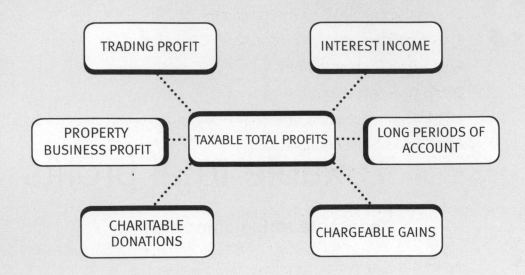

1 Taxable total profits

Companies pay corporation tax on their taxable total profits for a chargeable accounting period.

As illustrated in Chapter 18, taxable total profits is calculated as follows:

	£
Tax adjusted trading profit (section 2)	X
Interest income (section 3)	X
Property business profit (section 4)	X
Chargeable gains (Chapter 20)	X
	——
Total profits	X
Less: Qualifying charitable donations (QCD) relief (section 5)	(X)
	——
Taxable total profits	X
	——

This and the following chapters show in detail how each item within taxable total profits is calculated.

2 Trading profit

In Chapter 5 we studied how to adjust a sole trader's trading profit for tax purposes. The rules for companies are very similar.

For reference, a summary of the main adjustments is given below:

- Disallow expenditure which is not wholly and exclusively for the purposes of the trade

- Disallow entertaining (except entertaining staff)

- Disallow expenditure on capital items
- Adjust for leased high emission cars (CO_2 > 160 g/km)
- Adjust for gifts to customers
- Disallow depreciation
- Adjust for profits/losses on disposal of capital items
- Add back Gift Aid donations
- Adjust for non-trading income.

All the above rules apply for companies.

There are, however, a number of key differences which apply when computing the taxable trading profits for a company.

Differences relating to companies

The main differences are in relation to:

- private use adjustments
- interest payable/receivable
- dividends payable
- capital allowances.

Key differences

Private use adjustments – there are no private use restrictions for companies:

- Any private expenses of a director or employee of a company are fully allowable, when calculating the tax adjusted trading profit.
- Any private use of assets by a director or employee of the company is ignored in the capital allowances calculation. There is no restriction for private usage.

The director or employee may however suffer income tax on the private use as an employment benefit received (Chapter 4).

Interest payable/receivable – Companies have special rules which cover interest payments and interest income. These are known as the loan relationship rules.

The detail of the rules is covered in section 3, however, when adjusting trading profits the following rules apply:

- Any interest payable relating to trading activities is allowable as a deduction against trading profits, therefore no adjustment is required.

- Any interest payable in relation to non-trading activities must be added back to trading profit.

- Any interest receivable must be deducted from trading profit.

Dividends payable – Dividends payable by a company are an appropriation of profit and are not allowable as a trading expense.

Example 1 – Trading profit

The statement of profit or loss of Helen Ltd shows the following for the year ended 31 December 2012:

	£	£
Gross profit from trading		280,000
Interest receivable	6,320	
Rental income	2,850	
	———	9,170
		———
		289,170
Less: Expenses:		
Rent and rates	10,950	
Depreciation	6,730	
Interest payable (Note 1)	3,560	
Entertaining and gifts (Note 2)	7,420	
Delivery costs	2,890	
Motor expenses (Note 3)	5,480	
Miscellaneous (Note 4)	12,000	
	———	(49,030)
		———
Profit before tax		240,140
		———

Notes:

(1) Interest payable was in respect of a loan to acquire the rental property (non-trading interest).

(2) Entertaining and gifts comprise:

	£
Gifts to customers	1,500
(Christmas champagne: cost £25 per customer)	
Staff Christmas party	3,430
Client Christmas party	2,490

(3) Motor expenses represent costs for the director's car. He uses the car 60% for private use.

(4) Miscellaneous includes a £3,500 qualifying charitable donation under the Gift Aid scheme.

Calculate the tax adjusted trading profit before capital allowances for Helen Ltd, for the y/e 31 December 2012.

Your computation should commence with the profit before tax figure of £240,140 and should list all the items referred to in notes 1 to 4, indicating by the use of a zero (0) any items that do not require adjustment.

Answer to example 1

Adjustment of profits – y/e 31 December 2012

	£	£
Profits per accounts	240,140	
Interest receivable		6,320
Rental income		2,850
Rent and rates	0	
Depreciation	6,730	
Non-trading interest payable	3,560	
Gifts to customers: Drink (Note 1)	1,500	
Staff Christmas party	0	
Client entertaining	2,490	
Delivery costs	0	
Motor expenses (Note 2)	0	
Charitable donation (Note 3)	3,500	
	257,920	9,170
	(9,170)	
Adjusted trading profit (before capital allowances)	248,750	

Notes:

(1) Gifts to customers are disallowed unless they amount to £50 or less per customer during the year and display a conspicuous advert for the business. Gifts of food or drink or tobacco are disallowed irrespective of their cost.

(2) No adjustment is required for the private use motor expenses of the director. These are fully deductible when calculating company tax adjusted trading profits. The director will be taxed on the benefit of private use as an employment benefit.

(3) As for a sole trader, donations to charity under Gift Aid are disallowable as trading expenditure. However, for companies, whether under the Gift Aid scheme or not, the charitable donation is deductible when calculating TTP.

It is important to present the adjustment of profits as shown above in order to obtain the maximum marks (as shown in Chapter 5).

The notes above would not be required in the examination unless specifically asked for. They are therefore provided here for tutorial purposes only.

Test your understanding 1

Cornelius Ltd runs a small printing business and the managing director wishes to know the amount of the company's tax adjusted trading profit for the year ended 31 December 2012.

You are presented with the following statement of profit or loss for Cornelius Ltd, for the year to 31 December 2012.

	£	£
Gross profit from trading		21,270
Interest receivable		4,350
Profit on sale of business premises (Note 1)		1,750
		27,370
Advertising	642	
Impaired debts (Note 2)	80	
Depreciation	2,381	
Light and heat	372	
Miscellaneous expenses (Note 3)	342	
Motor car expenses (Note 4)	555	
Rates	1,057	
Repairs and renewals (Note 5)	2,598	
Staff wages (Note 6)	12,124	
Telephone	351	
		(20,502)
Profit before tax		6,868

Notes:

(1) The profit on the sale of premises relates to the sale of a small freehold industrial unit in which the company stored paper, before building the extension (see Note 5).

(2) The charge for impaired debts is made up as follows:

	£
Write-off of loan to customer	55
Write-off of trade debts	32
Increase in specific allowance against debts	10
Recovery of trade debts previously written off	(17)
Charge to the statement of profit or loss	80

(3) Miscellaneous expenses is made up as follows:

	£
Subscription to Printers' association	40
Contribution to a national charity	45
Gifts to customers:	
• Calendars costing £7.50 each and bearing the company's name	75
• Two food hampers bearing the company's name	95
Other allowable expenses	87
	342

(4) A director uses the motor car 75% for business purposes and 25% for private purposes.

(5) Repairs and renewals comprise the following expenditure:

	£
Redecorating administration offices	951
Building extension to enlarge paper store	1,647
	2,598

(6) Staff wages included an amount of £182 for a staff Christmas lunch.

Calculate Cornelius Ltd's tax adjusted trading profit before capital allowances for the y/e 31 December 2012.

Your computation should commence with the profit before tax figure of £6,868 and should list all the items referred to in notes 1 to 6, indicating by the use of a zero (0) any items that do not require adjustment.

Capital allowances

Chapter 6 covered the main principles of calculating capital allowances for sole traders.

The same rules apply for companies, but in addition, the following points should be noted when calculating capital allowances for companies:

Short accounting period

• Allowances are given for **accounting periods** by reference to acquisitions and disposals in that accounting period.

- As for sole traders, if the accounting period is less than 12 months:
  - the AIA and the WDA is proportionately reduced.
  - but FYAs are always given in full. They are never reduced for a short accounting period.

Long accounting period

- Unlike sole traders, where a company has a long period of account:
  - there will be two chargeable accounting periods (CAPs) for corporation tax purposes
  - two capital allowances computations will be required; one for each of these CAPs
  - the first CAP will be 12 months in length
  - the second CAP will be a short accounting period, therefore the rules above should be followed when calculating the capital allowances for this period.

Private use adjustments

- There are no private use adjustments where company assets are used by directors or employees in a company's capital allowances computation.

Example 2 – Trading profit

Bill Ltd prepares accounts to 31 March. The company's tax written down value at 1 April 2012 on the general pool was £23,500.

In the two years ended 31 March 2014, the following capital transactions took place:

Year ended 31 March 2013

| 1 November 2012 | Purchased plant costing £13,260. |
| 10 November 2012 | Sold two lorries (purchased for £8,450 each) for £2,500 each. Purchased two replacement lorries for £5,250 each. |

Year ended 31 March 2014

| 1 November 2013 | Purchased a motor car with CO_2 emissions of 149 g/km for £7,500. The car will be used by the MD 25% of the time for private purposes. |
| 1 December 2013 | Sold a machine for £12,000 (cost £18,600). |

Compute the capital allowances available to Bill Ltd for the years ended 31 March 2013 and 31 March 2014.

Assume the FY 2012 rules apply throughout.

Answer to example 2

		General pool	Allowance
y/e 31 March 2013	£	£	£
TWDV b/f		23,500	
Qualifying for AIA:			
Plant and machinery	13,260		
Lorries (£5,250 × 2)	10,500		
	23,760		
Less: AIA	(23,760)		23,760
		Nil	
Disposal proceeds		(5,000)	
		18,500	
Less: WDA (18%)		(3,330)	3,330
TWDV c/f		15,170	
Total allowances			27,090
y/e 31 March 2014			
Not qualifying for AIA or FYA:			
Cars (Note)		7,500	
Disposal proceeds		(12,000)	
		10,670	
Less: WDA (18%)		(1,921)	1,921
TWDV c/f		8,749	
Total allowances			1,921

Note: Private use of car by MD is not relevant for companies. Full capital allowances are available.

Test your understanding 2

Ellingham Ltd is a UK resident company that manufactures aeroplane components. The company has always prepared accounts to 31 March in each year and has now decided to change its accounts preparation date to 30 June, after having prepared accounts to 31 March 2012.

On 1 April 2012, the TWDVs of plant and machinery were as follows:

	£
General pool	149,280
Short-life asset (acquired May 2010)	13,440

The following assets were purchased during the 15 m/e 30 June 2013.

		£
11 April 2012	Heating system	12,800
5 June 2012	Equipment	25,800
22 September 2012	Motor car (CO_2 emissions 139 g/km)	11,760
18 November 2012	Van	7,200
11 December 2012	New motor car (CO_2 emissions 104 g/km)	12,200
14 May 2013	Plant and machinery	23,000

Ellingham Ltd made the following sales:

15 January 2013	Lorry	(14,160)
12 March 2013	Short-life asset	(5,520)

The lorry sold on 15 January 2013 for £14,160 originally cost £21,600.

Compute the capital allowances for the 15 m/e 30 June 2013.

Pre-trading expenditure

The rules for pre-trading expenditure are the same for companies and sole traders (see Chapter 5) and are as follows:

- Any revenue expenditure incurred in the **seven years** before a company commences to trade is treated as an expense, on the day that the company starts trading.

- Any capital expenditure is treated as if bought on the first day, when the trade commences. Any capital allowances will be claimed in the first capital allowances computation.

3 Interest income – loan relationship rules

All interest paid or received by a company is dealt with under the loan relationship rules.

The rules apply to:

- Payments in connection with borrowing money, for example:
    - interest paid on overdrafts, bank loans, corporate debt (i.e. company loan notes and loan stock), and
    - other costs such as arrangement fees, and other incidental costs incurred in raising loan finance.

- Income received from the lending of money, for example:
    - interest income
    - this includes interest from deposits, loans, government stocks and corporate bonds.

- In order to apply the loan relationship rules correctly, all interest paid/received must first be distinguished as either 'trading' or 'non-trading'.

Trade v non-trade purposes

- Generally, all interest receivable by a company is non-trade interest, unless it is the company's trade to lend money (e.g. a bank).

- Examples would be:
    - interest receivable on investments such as gilts, loan notes, loan stock and bonds.

- Examples of trading interest payable would be:
    - Interest on a loan taken out to purchase plant and machinery for the business.
    - Loan or overdraft to fund the daily operations (i.e. working capital).
    - Issue of loan notes to fund trading operations.

- Examples of non-trading interest payable would be:
    - interest payable on a loan to purchase a commercially let property (where the rent would be taxable as property business income, see section 4).
    - Interest payable on a loan to acquire the shares of another company.

Interest income

- All interest receivable by a company is normally assessable as non-trading interest income.

- Interest receivable should be deducted when calculating adjusted trading profits and included in the corporation tax computation as interest income.

- Interest received and receivable is usually credited in the company accounts on an 'accruals' basis. As interest receivable is taxed on an accruals basis, the figure included in the accounts is the figure which is taxed as interest income.

- Interest income is received **gross** by companies. No grossing up calculations are therefore required in the corporation tax computation.

Interest paid

- Interest paid and payable on borrowings for a trading purpose is deductible as a trading expense.

- Interest payable on borrowings for a non-trading purpose is:
  - added back to trading profit
  - deducted from interest income.

Assessment in taxable total profits

- All interest paid by a company is deductible on the accruals basis.

- As the company accounts are also prepared on the accruals basis, the figure included in the accounts is also the figure used for tax purposes.

- If only cash payments are provided, these would have to be adjusted for opening and closing accruals of interest payable/receivable.

- Where interest income exceeds interest payable
  - the net profit is assessed as interest income in taxable total profits.
  - the situation where interest payable exceeds interest income is not examinable.

Example 3 – Interest income – loan relationship rules

Trinity Ltd, a clothing manufacturer, received bank interest of £2,800, on 14 December 2012 and paid loan note interest of £19,500, on 26 September 2012.

The loan note were issued in January 2012, to raise finance for the purchase of a new packing machine.

The company prepares accounts to 31 December each year. Accrued loan note interest payable at 31 December 2012 was £9,000. There was no interest receivable at either 31 December 2011 or 31 December 2012.

Explain how the bank and loan note interest will be treated in the corporation tax computation for the year to 31 December 2012.

Answer to example 3

Bank interest receivable

The bank interest receivable in the period will be taxable as non-trading interest income.

As there was no interest receivable at the beginning or end of the year, the taxable interest income will be the amount received of £2,800.

Loan note interest payable

The loan note interest paid relates to finance issued for the purposes of the trade (i.e. to purchase new machinery). It is therefore allowed as a trading expense.

The interest will be recorded in the accounts on the accruals basis (i.e. interest payable of £28,500) (£19,500 paid + £9,000 accrued). No adjustment will therefore be required for tax purposes.

Note: The interest on the loan notes is paid gross and the interest income is received gross.

Example 4 – Interest income – loan relationship rules

PQR Ltd prepares its accounts to 31 December.

The company issued £100,000 of 12% loan notes on 1 May 2012. The proceeds of the issue were used to purchase a new factory.

Explain how the interest on the loan notes is treated for tax purposes for the year ended 31 December 2012.

Answer to example 4

The loan note interest paid relates to financing for the purposes of the trade (i.e. to purchase a new factory). It is therefore allowed as a trading expense.

For the year ended 31 December 2012, PQR Ltd will be entitled to a deduction against trading profits of £8,000 (£100,000 at 12% × 8/12).

Provided this amount is included in the accounts, no adjustment will be necessary when calculating the tax adjusted trading profit.

The amount of loan note interest actually paid is irrelevant as interest payable is deductible on the accruals basis.

Test your understanding 3

The profit before tax of Simon Ltd per the statement of profit or loss for the year ended 31 December 2012, is £105,940, which includes:

	£
Depreciation	9,750
Loan note interest payable (on loan to purchase machinery)	12,760
Bank interest payable (on loan to purchase an investment property)	6,590
Bank interest receivable	15,860

Notes:

(1) Bank interest receivable includes an accrual of £2,340 as at 31 December 2012 and £1,210, as at 31 December 2011. There were no accruals in respect of the loan note or bank interest payable at either the beginning or the end of the year.

(2) The company's capital allowances for the year are £11,800.

Calculate Simon Ltd's TTP for the y/e 31 December 2012.

Summary – interest payable/receivable

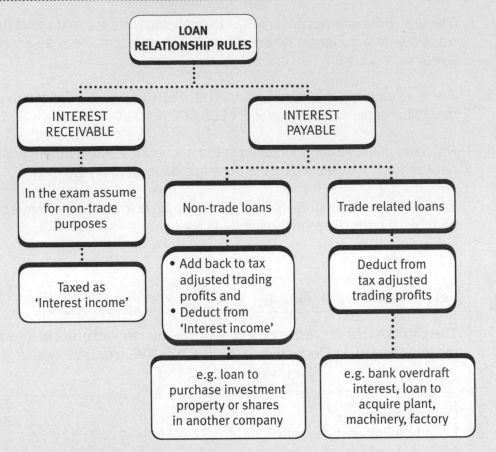

4 Property business profits

A trading company may hold property for investment purposes or have premises which are rented out, as they are surplus to the company's current trading requirements.

Treatment for companies

The income from these properties is assessed as property business income, calculated basically in the same way as for sole traders:

- Property business profits are taxed on the accruals basis.

- Allowable expenses are those associated with the normal running and upkeep of the property (generally revenue expenses, like property maintenance, repairs, insurance and irrecoverable debts).

KAPLAN PUBLISHING

There are, however, a few differences in the way that companies are assessed on their property business profits as follows:

- The company is assessed on the property business profit arising in the accounting period (not the tax year as for individuals).

- The treatment of interest payable.

- The treatment of property losses.

Interest on loan to buy a property

- Interest payable on a loan to acquire or improve an investment property, is not allowed as a deduction from property business income. Instead, it is taxed under the 'Loan Relationship' rules and is therefore deducted from interest income (see section 3).

Property business losses

- Profits and losses on properties are 'pooled' together to obtain an overall 'property business profit or loss' for an accounting period.

- A property business loss is:
  - first set off against total profits (before QCDs) of the same accounting period
  - then carried forward to be set against total profits (before QCDs) in the future.
  - also available for 'group relief' (Chapter 22).

Lease premiums

Where a company receives a premium for the grant of a lease, an element of the premium is taxed as property business income in the same way as for sole traders (see Chapter 3).

Example 5 – Property business profits

Speed Ltd prepares accounts for the y/e 31 March 2013 and during the year received a premium of £12,000 on the grant of a seven-year lease.

The building was rented out from 1 September 2012, for £6,000 p.a. It lay empty until this date. Rent is received quarterly in advance.

Calculate the property business income for the y/e 31 March 2013.

Answer to example 5

	£
Premium (W)	10,560
Rent (£6,000 × 7/12)	3,500
Total property business profit	14,060

Working: Assessment of premium

	£
Premium	12,000
Less: 2% × (7 − 1) × £12,000	(1,440)
	10,560

Alternative calculation: £12,000 × (51 − 7) / 50 = £10,560

Test your understanding 4

Tasman Ltd is a UK resident company that manufactures components for washing machines. Tasman Ltd lets out two warehouses that are surplus to requirements.

The company's results regarding income from property for the year ended 31 March 2013, are as follows:

- The first warehouse was empty from 1 April to 31 August 2012, but was let from 1 September 2012. On that date the company received a premium of £47,000, for the grant of a seven-year lease, and the annual rent of £10,500, which is payable in advance.

- The second warehouse was let until 31 January 2013, at an annual rent of £11,200. On that date the tenant left owing three months' rent, which the company is not able to recover. The roof of the warehouse was repaired at a cost of £7,200, during March 2013.

Calculate the property business profit for the y/e 31 March 2013.

5 Charitable donations

The tax treatment of charitable donations is different for companies and individuals.

For **individuals:**

- Donations to charity are only allowable if:
    - a small local donation; as a trading expense, or
    - made under the Gift Aid system.
- Gift Aid payments are paid net of basic rate tax.
- Tax relief is given by extending the basic and higher rate tax bands by the gross amount of the Gift Aid paid in the tax year.

For **companies:**

- All donations to charity by companies are allowable:
    - if a small local donation; as a trading expense
    - all other donations (whether under Gift Aid or not); as an allowable deduction from total profits.
- All charitable donations made by companies are paid gross.
- The amount **paid** in the accounting period is therefore allowable.
- If the QCDs paid exceed the total profits of the company:
    - no relief for the excess is given
      (i.e. it cannot be carried forward or carried back)
    - unless the company is part of a 75% group, in which case, group relief may be available (see Chapter 22).

6 Comprehensive examples

Test your understanding 5

Geronimo Ltd is a UK resident company that manufactures motorcycles. The company's summarised statement of profit or loss for the year ended 31 March 2013 is as follows:

	£	£
Gross profit		921,540
Operating expenses:		
Impaired debts (Note 1)	22,360	
Depreciation	83,320	
Gifts and donations (Note 2)	2,850	
Professional fees (Note 3)	14,900	
Staff party (Note 4)	7,200	
Repairs and renewals (Note 5)	42,310	
Other expenses (all allowable)	111,820	
		(284,760)
Operating profit		636,780
Income from investments		
Bank interest (Note 6)	2,800	
Loan interest (Note 7)	22,000	
Dividends (Note 8)	36,000	
		60,800
		697,580
Interest payable (Note 9)		(45,000)
Profit before taxation		652,580

KAPLAN PUBLISHING

Notes:

(1) Impaired debts

	£
Trade debts written off	19,890
Loan to customer written off	600
Increase in allowance for trade debtors	1,870
	22,360

(2) Gifts and donations

	£
Donation to a national charity	1,800
Donation to local charity (Geronimo Ltd received free advertising in the charity's magazine)	50
Gifts to customers (food hampers costing £40 each)	1,000
	2,850

(3) Professional fees

	£
Accountancy and audit fee	4,100
Legal fees re – the renewal of a 20-year property lease	2,400
Legal fees in connection with the issue of loan notes (see Note 10)	8,400
	14,900

(4) Staff party

The staff party, for employees only, cost £200 a head.

(5) Repairs and renewals

The figure of £42,310 for repairs includes £6,200 for replacing part of a wall that was knocked down by a lorry, and £12,200 for initial repairs to an office building that was acquired during the year ended 31 March 2013.

The office building was not usable until the repairs were carried out, and this fact was represented by a reduced purchase price.

(6) Bank interest received

The bank interest was received on 31 March 2013. The bank deposits are held for non-trading purposes.

(7) Loan interest received

The figure for loan interest received is calculated as follows:

	£
Accrued at 1 April 2012	(5,500)
Received 30 June 2012	11,000
Received 31 December 2012	11,000
Accrued at 31 March 2013	5,500
	────
	22,000
	────

The above figures are all gross. The loan was made for non-trading purposes.

(8) Dividends received

The dividends were received from other UK companies. The figure of £36,000 is the actual amount received.

(9) Interest payable

Geronimo Ltd raised funding through loan notes on 1 May 2012. The loan was used for trading purposes. Interest of £30,000 was paid on 31 October 2012, and £15,000 was accrued at 31 March 2013.

(10) Plant and machinery

On 1 April 2012 the tax written down value of the general pool of plant and machinery was £66,000. There were no purchases or sales of plant and machinery during the year ended 31 March 2013.

(11) Other information

Geronimo Ltd has no associated companies.

(a) **Calculate Geronimo Ltd's tax adjusted trading profit for the y/e 31 March 2013.**

Your computation should commence with the profit before taxation figure of £652,580 and should list all the items referred to in Notes 1 to 10, indicating by the use of a zero (0) any items that do not require adjustment.

(b) **Calculate the corporation tax payable by Geronimo Ltd for the y/e 31 March 2013.**

7 Long periods of account

Where a company has a period of account of more than 12 months, it must be split into two chargeable accounting periods (CAPs) as follows:

- First 12 months.
- Remainder of the period of account.

There are rules to determine how to allocate taxable income between these two accounting periods.

Allocation of taxable income

Income	Method of allocation
Trading profits before capital allowances	Adjust profit for period of account for tax purposes and then apportion on a time basis.
Capital allowances	Separate calculation for each accounting period. AIA and WDAs will be restricted if accounting period is less than 12 months.
Property income Interest income Other income	Calculate accrued amount for each CAP separately. If the information to apply the strict accruals basis is not available; time apportion.
Chargeable gains	Taxed in the accounting period in which disposal takes place.

Qualifying charitable donations (QCDs)	Deducted from profits of the accounting period in which donations are paid.
Franked investment income	Allocate to the accounting period in which it is received.

Having allocated profits and QCDs to the two separate CAPs:

- two separate corporation tax computations are prepared
- with two separate pay dates.

Example 6 – Long periods of account

Oak Ltd prepared accounts for the 15 months period to 30 June 2013, with the following results:

	£
Trading profit (adjusted for tax purposes before capital allowances)	289,205
Bank interest (received 30 September 2012)	22,000
Property business profit	10,000
Chargeable gain (asset disposed of 1 June 2013)	16,000
Charitable donation (1 January 2013)	24,000

Bank interest (income) accrued was as follows:

At 1 April 2012	5,200
At 31 March 2013	4,100
At 30 June 2013	9,780

The company bought plant costing £45,000 for use in its trade on 28 August 2012. The TWDV on the general pool on 1 April 2012 is £17,000.

Calculate Oak Ltd's taxable trading profits for the 15 m/e 30 June 2013.

Assume the FY2012 rates and allowance apply throughout.

Answer to example 6

Oak Ltd – Taxable total profits

	y/e 31.3.2013 £	3 m/e 30.6.2013 £
Trading profit (12:3)	231,364	57,841
Less: Capital allowances (W)	(31,660)	(1,365)
Tax adjusted trading profit	199,704	56,476
Interest income		
(£22,000 – £5,200 + £4,100)	20,900	
(£9,780 – £4,100)		5,680
Property income (12:3)	8,000	2,000
Chargeable gain	Nil	16,000
	228,604	80,156
Less: QCD relief	(24,000)	
TTP	204,604	80,156

Working: Capital allowances computation

	General pool £	Total allowances £
y/e 31 March 2013		
TWDV b/f	17,000	
Plant and machinery	45,000	
Less: AIA (max)	(25,000)	25,000
	20,000	
	37,000	
Less: WDA (18%)	(6,660)	6,660
TWDV c/f	30,340	
Total allowances		31,660

3 m/e 30 June 2013

	General pool £	Total allowances £
TWDV b/f	30,340	
Less: WDA (18% x 3/12)	(1,365)	1,365
TWDV c/f	28,975	
Total allowances		1,365

Test your understanding 6

Ash Ltd prepared accounts for the 17 month period to 31 August 2013, with results as follows:

	£
Trading profit (adjusted for tax purposes but before capital allowances)	376,699
Bank interest (received 30 November 2012)	11,540
Property business profit	25,500
Chargeable gain (asset disposed of 1 February 2013)	12,995
Charitable donations (1 January 2013)	16,500

Bank interest (income) accrued was as follows:

At 1 April 2012	7,400
At 1 April 2013	5,600
At 31 August 2013	10,540

The company bought plant costing £65,000, for use in its trade on 1 December 2012. The tax written down value on the general pool on 1 April 2012 is £45,000.

Calculate Ash Ltd's taxable total profits for the 17 month period.

8 Chapter summary

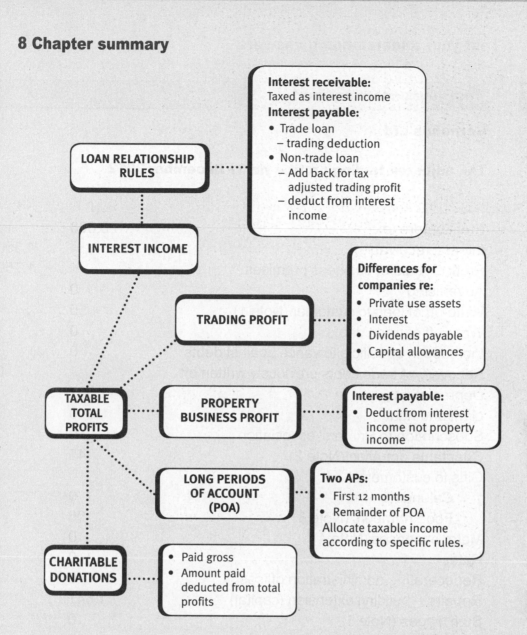

LOAN RELATIONSHIP RULES

Interest receivable:
Taxed as interest income
Interest payable:
- Trade loan
  – trading deduction
- Non-trade loan
  – Add back for tax adjusted trading profit
  – deduct from interest income

INTEREST INCOME

TRADING PROFIT

Differences for companies re:
- Private use assets
- Interest
- Dividends payable
- Capital allowances

TAXABLE TOTAL PROFITS

PROPERTY BUSINESS PROFIT

Interest payable:
- Deduct from interest income not property income

LONG PERIODS OF ACCOUNT (POA)

Two APs:
- First 12 months
- Remainder of POA
Allocate taxable income according to specific rules.

CHARITABLE DONATIONS
- Paid gross
- Amount paid deducted from total profits

Test your understanding answers

Test your understanding 1

Cornelius Ltd

Tax adjusted trading profit – y/e 31 December 2012

	£	£
Profit before tax	6,868	
Interest receivable		4,350
Profit on sale of business premises		1,750
Advertising	0	
Write-off of loan to customer (Note 1)	55	
Write-off of trade debts	0	
Increase in specific allowance against debts	0	
Recovery of trade debts previously written off		0
Depreciation	2,381	
Light and heat	0	
Subscription to Printers' association	0	
Charitable donation (Note 2)	45	
Gifts to customers:		
Calendars	0	
Food hampers (Note 3)	95	
Motor expenses (Note 4)	0	
Rates	0	
Redecorating administration offices	0	
Repairs – building extension (capital)	1,647	
Staff wages (Note 5)	0	
Telephone	0	
	11,091	6,100
	(6,100)	
Adjusted trading profit (before capital allowances)	4,991	

Notes:

(1) The write-off of a non-trade debt (e.g. loan to a customer) is not an allowable trading deduction.

(2) Charitable donations to a national charity made by a company are disallowable as trading expenditure but will be deductible when calculating TTP.

(3) Gifts to customers are disallowed, unless they amount to £50 or less per customer during the year and display a conspicuous advert for the business. Gifts of food or drink or tobacco are disallowed irrespective of their cost.

(4) Motor car expenses are all allowable for the company, although the director will be taxed as an employee on the private use of the car.

(5) The expenditure on the Christmas lunch is an allowable deduction for the employer.

It is important to present the adjustment of profits computation as shown above in order to obtain maximum marks (as shown in Chapter 5). The notes above would not normally be required in the examination and are for tutorial purposes.

Test your understanding 2

Ellingham Ltd

The 15 month period is split into two chargeable accounting periods:

(1) First 12 months: 12 m/e 31 March 2013

(2) Balance period: 3 m/e 30 June 2013

Capital allowances computation

	General pool £	Short life asset £	Special rate pool £	Allowances £
y/e 31 March 2013				
TWDV b/f	149,280	13,440		
Additions:				
Not qualifying for AIA or FYA:				
Car	11,760			
Qualifying for AIA (special rate pool):				
Heating system	12,800			
Less: AIA	(12,800)			12,800
	———		Nil	
Qualifying for AIA (general pool):				
Equipment	25,800			
Van	7,200			
	———			
	33,000			
Less: AIA (Note)	(12,200)			12,200
	———			
	20,800			
Disposal proceeds	(14,160)	(5,520)		
	———	———		
	167,680	7,920	Nil	
Balancing allowance		(7,920)		7,920
		———		
Less: WDA (18%)	(30,182)			30,182
Less: WDA (8%)			(Nil)	
Low emission car	12,200			
Less: FYA (100%)	(12,200)			12,200
	———	Nil		
	———			
TWDV c/f	137,498		Nil	
	———		———	
Total allowances				75,302
				———

Note: The AIA is allocated to the additions in the 'special rate pool' (WDA 8%) in priority to the addition in the general pool (WDA 18%).

KAPLAN PUBLISHING

	General pool	Allowances
	£	£	£
TWDV b/f		137,498	

3 m/e 30 June 2013

Additions:

Qualifying for AIA:

Plant	23,000		
Less: AIA (max £25,000 x 3/12)	(6,250)		6,250
		16,750	
		154,248	
Less: WDA (18% x 3/12)		(6,941)	6,941
TWDV c/f		147,307	
Total allowances			13,191

Test your understanding 3

Simon Ltd

Taxable total profits – y/e 31 December 2012

	£	£	£
Profit per accounts		105,940	
Non-trading interest payable		6,590	
Depreciation		9,750	
Non-trading interest receivable			15,860
Capital allowances			11,800
		122,280	27,660
		(27,660)	
Tax adjusted trading profit		94,620	
Interest income:			
Non-trading interest receivable	15,860		
Non-trading interest payable	(6,590)		
		9,270	
TTP		103,890	

Test your understanding 4

Tasman Ltd

Property business profit – y/e 31 March 2013

	£	£
Rent receivable		
(7/12 × £10,500)		6,125
(10/12 × £11,200)		9,333
Premium	47,000	
Less: 2% × (7 – 1) × £47,000	(5,640)	
	——	41,360
		——
		56,818
Less: Allowable expenses		
Irrecoverable debt (3/12 × £11,200)		(2,800)
Roof repairs		(7,200)
		——
Property business profits		46,818
		——

Note: There is no need to calculate individual profits or losses for each property. Profit and losses are pooled to obtain an overall property business profit.

Alternative calculation for assessment on the premium:

£47,000 × (51 – 7) / 50 = £41,360

Test your understanding 5

Geronimo Ltd

(a) **Tax adjusted trading profit – y/e 31 March 2013**

	£	£
Profit before tax	652,580	
Trade debts written off	0	
Loan to customer (Note 1)	600	
Increase in allowance for trade debtors	0	
Depreciation	83,320	
Donation to national charity (Note 2)	1,800	
Donation to local charity	0	
Gifts to customers	1,000	
Accountancy and audit fees	0	
Legal fees re renewal of short lease (Note 3)	0	
Legal fees re issue of loan notes (Note 4)	0	
Staff party (Note 5)	0	
Replacing part of a wall (Note 6)	0	
Initial repairs to office building	12,200	
Bank interest		2,800
Loan interest (Note 7)		22,000
Dividends		36,000
Interest payable	0	
Capital allowances (£66,000 @ 18%)		11,880
	751,500	72,680
	(72,680)	
Tax adjusted trading profit	678,820	

Notes:

(1) The loan to a customer is for non-trade purposes (money lending is not the company's trade). The write off of the loan is therefore not an allowable deduction in calculating taxable trading profits. The write off is allowable against interest income under the loan relationship rules.

(2) The donation to the national charity is deducted in the corporation tax computation from total profits and is therefore added back in calculating trading profits.

(3) Costs of renewing a short lease (< 50 years) are allowable.

(4) The legal fees in connection with the issue of the loan notes are incurred in respect of a trading loan relationship and are therefore deductible as a trading expense.

(5) The individual employees will be assessed to income tax on the excess cost of the party over £150 per head as a benefit of employment. However, all of the costs of providing the staff party are allowable for the company for corporation tax purposes.

(6) The replacement of the wall is allowable since the whole structure is not being replaced. The repairs to the office building are not allowable, being capital in nature, as the building was not in a usable state when purchased and this was reflected in the purchase price.

(7) Interest on the loan notes used for trading purposes is deductible in calculating the taxable trading profit on an accruals basis.

(b) **Geronimo Ltd**
Corporation tax computation – y/e 31 March 2013

	£	£
Trading profit		678,820
Interest income – Bank interest	2,800	
– Loan interest	22,000	
– Customer loan written off	(600)	
		24,200
Total profits		703,020
Less: QCD relief		(1,800)
TTP		701,220

Corporation tax liability (W)

	£	£
FY2012		
(£701,220 x 24%)		168,293
Less: Marginal relief		
1/100 × (£1,500,000–£741,220) × £701,220/£741,220		(7,178)
Corporation tax payable		161,115

Working: Corporation tax rate

	£
TTP	701,220
Plus: FII (£36,000 x 100/90)	40,000
Augmented profits	741,220
Upper limit	1,500,000
Lower limit	300,000
Therefore, marginal relief applies	

The year ended 31 March 2013 = FY2012, and the company is a marginal relief company.

Test your understanding 6

Ash Ltd

Taxable total profits

	y/e 31.3.13	5 m/e 31.8.13
	£	£
Trading profit (12:5)	265,905	110,794
Less: Capital allowances (W)	(40,300)	(5,228)
Trading income	225,605	105,566
Interest income		
(£11,540 – £7,400 + £5,600)	9,740	
(£10,540 – £5,600)		4,940
Property income (12:5)	18,000	7,500
Chargeable gain	12,995	Nil
	266,340	118,006
Less: QCD relief	(16,500)	Nil
TTP	249,840	118,006

Working: Capital allowances computation

	General pool	Allowances
	£	£	£
y/e 31 March 2013			
TWDV b/f		45,000	
Additions:			
Qualifying for AIA:			
Plant and machinery	65,000		
Less: AIA (max)	(25,000)		25,000
	——————	40,000	
		——————	
		85,000	
Less: WDA (18%)		(15,300)	15,300
		——————	
TWDV (c/f)		69,700	
		——————	
Total allowances			40,300
			——————
5 m/e 31 August 2013			
Less: WDA (18% x 5/12)		(5,228)	5,228
		——————	
TWDV c/f		64,472	
		——————	
Total allowances			5,228
			——————

Chargeable gains for companies

Chapter learning objectives

Upon completion of this chapter you will be able to:

- understand how to calculate the gain on the disposal of an asset by a company

- recognise when indexation is available for a company and calculate the indexation allowance

- calculate the indexed gain on the disposal of an asset for a company

- demonstrate how capital losses can be relieved against gains

- apply the correct matching rules for a company disposal of shares and securities

- calculate the gain on the disposal of shares by a company

- explain the treatment of a bonus issue

- explain the treatment of a rights issue

- explain the tax treatment on a takeover or reorganisation of a shareholding in exchange for other shares

- explain the treatment on a takeover where there is cash and shares consideration

- calculate the chargeable gain on the cash element

- explain and apply roll-over relief as it applies to companies.

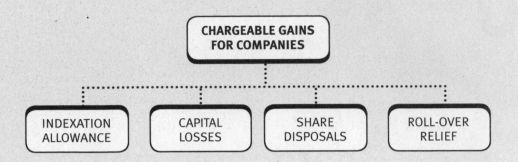

1 Introduction

The main principles of calculating chargeable gains for individuals were set out in Chapters 13 – 16.

Some of the content is applicable to companies, but there are some notable differences in the calculation of chargeable gains for companies.

Chargeable gains for a company

- The total net chargeable gains that a company makes during a **chargeable accounting period** (CAP) are included in the taxable total profits computation.

- It is important to remember that companies pay **corporation tax** on their chargeable gains, not capital gains tax.

Calculation of total net chargeable gains for a company

The following steps should be completed:

(1) Calculate the chargeable gains/allowable loss arising on the disposal of each chargeable asset separately

(2) Calculate the net chargeable gains arising in the CAP
= (chargeable gains less allowable losses)

(3) Deduct capital losses brought forward = total net chargeable gains

(4) Include in taxable total profits computation.

Note that there is no annual exempt amount available to companies. The total net chargeable gains is therefore simply included in the company's taxable total profits computation.

Pro forma – companies

	£
Disposal proceeds	X
Less: Incidental disposal costs	(X)
	—
Net proceeds	X
Less: Allowable expenditure (as for individuals)	(X)
	—
Unindexed gain	X
Less: Indexation allowance (section 2)	(X)
	—
Chargeable gain/(allowable loss)	X
	—

Note that:

- The calculation of capital gains is the same as for individuals except that companies are entitled to an indexation allowance (see section 2).

- There are a few other key differences when dealing with the disposal of assets by companies. These include
  - the treatment of capital losses (section 3)
  - the treatment of shares and securities (section 4), and
  - the availability of reliefs (section 7).

2 Indexation allowance

The indexation allowance (IA) gives a company some allowance for the effects of inflation in calculating a gain.

The aim is to ensure that the gains subject to tax represent the true increase in capital value of the asset in real terms.

The rules for the IA are as follows:

- the IA is based on the cost of the asset and the movement in the retail price index (RPI)

- it is available:
  - **from** the month of purchase
  - **to** the month of disposal

- the IA is calculated separately for each item of expenditure (e.g. calculate a different IA for the original acquisition cost and any subsequent enhancement expenditure because they have different purchase dates).

- the IA cannot create or increase a capital loss.

Calculation of the indexation allowance

The IA is calculated as follows:

IA = (indexation factor x allowable cost)

The indexation factor is calculated as follows:

$$\frac{\text{RPI in month of disposal} - \text{RPI in month of expenditure}}{\text{RPI in month of expenditure}}$$

 Note that the indexation factor must be rounded to three decimal places.

Example 1 – Indexation allowance

Kane Ltd sold a chargeable asset in June 2012, which it had bought in February 1987.

The RPI for February 1987 is 100.4 and for June 2012 it is 243.8.

Calculate the indexation factor to be used.

Answer to example 1

Indexation factor is:
(243.8 – 100.4)/100.4 = 1.428 (rounded to three decimal places).

Example 2 – Indexation allowance

Pye Ltd bought a factory for £250,000, on 1 April 1993. On 15 July 1996, the company spent £70,000 on an extension to the factory. The factory was sold on 30 September 2012, for £950,000.

Assume the relevant RPIs are as follows:

April 1993	140.6
July 1996	152.4
September 2012	246.7

Calculate Pye Ltd's chargeable gain.

Answer to example 2

	£
Sale proceeds	950,000
Less: Cost	(250,000)
Enhancement expenditure	(70,000)
Unindexed gain	630,000
Less: Indexation allowance (W)	
Cost (£250,000 × 0.755)	(188,750)
Enhancement expenditure (£70,000 × 0.619)	(43,330)
Chargeable gain	397,920

Working: Indexation factors

The indexation factor from April 1993 to September 2012 is:
(246.7 − 140.6)/140.6 = 0.755 (rounded to three decimal places)

The indexation factor from July 1996 to September 2012 is:
(246.7 − 152.4)/152.4 = 0.619 (rounded to three decimal places)

Test your understanding 1

Hobbit Ltd bought a factory for £175,000 on 1 June 1995. On 15 September 2001, the company spent £62,000 on an extension to the factory. The factory was sold on 31 August 2012, for £680,000.

Assume the relevant RPIs are as follows:

June 1995	149.8
September 2001	174.6
August 2012	244.9

Calculate Hobbit Ltd's chargeable gain.

- If there is a fall in the RPI between the month of purchase and the month of disposal; the IA is £Nil.

3 Capital losses

- A capital loss arises if the proceeds received for an asset are lower than the allowable expenditure.

- Remember that indexation cannot create or increase a capital loss.

Test your understanding 2

JNN Ltd is considering selling a field at auction in July 2012. It acquired the field in August 1987, for £10,000 and the sale proceeds are likely to be one of three figures:

(a) £25,000

(b) £12,000

(c) £8,000

Calculate the chargeable gain or loss under each alternative.

Assume the indexation factor from August 1987 to July 2012 is 1.385.

Utilisation of a capital loss

- Where allowable losses arise, they are set off against chargeable gains arising in the same accounting period.

- Any loss remaining, is carried forward against **chargeable gains** of future accounting periods, as soon as they arise.

- Capital losses **cannot** be:
    - set off against any other income of a company, nor
    - carried back against gains in previous accounting periods.

Example 3 – Capital losses

For the year ended 31 March 2013, Jump Ltd has a tax adjusted trading profit of £65,000, and a chargeable gain of £3,600.

At 1 April 2012, it had unused capital losses brought forward of £6,000.

Calculate Jump Ltd's corporation tax liability for the year ended 31 March 2013.

Answer to example 3

Corporation tax liability – y/e 31 March 2013

	£
Tax adjusted trading profit	65,000
Net chargeable gain (W)	Nil
Taxable total profits	65,000
Corporation tax (20% × £65,000) (Note)	13,000

Working: Net chargeable gain

	£
Chargeable gain	3,600
Less: Capital loss b/f	(6,000)
Capital loss c/f	(2,400)

Net chargeable gain in the accounting period is therefore £Nil.

The remaining capital losses cannot be set against the tax adjusted trading profit of the company in the year, they can only be carried forward and set against future capital gains.

Note: TTP = Augmented profits, which are below £300,000.
The year ended 31 March 2013 falls entirely within FY2012.
Therefore, the small profits rate of 20% is applied.

Test your understanding 3

For the year ended 31 December 2012, High Ltd has a tax adjusted trading profit of £400,000, and a chargeable gain of £17,000.

At 1 January 2012, it had unused capital losses brought forward of £23,000.

Calculate High Ltd's corporation tax liability for the year ended 31 December 2012.

4 Shares and securities

The issues regarding the disposal of shares by a company are similar to those set out in Chapter 15 for disposals by individuals.

Remember that:

- Shares and securities present a particular problem for capital gains computations, because any two shares in a company (of a particular class) are indistinguishable.

- Matching rules are therefore needed, to solve the problem of identifying acquisitions with disposals. They apply when there has been more than one purchase of shares or securities, of the same class, in the same company.

Matching rules

The matching rules for shares disposed of by companies are different from those for an individual.

For a company, disposals are matched against acquisitions as follows:

- shares acquired on the same day (as the sale)

- shares acquired during the nine days before the sale (FIFO basis)

- shares in the share pool (also known as the s104 pool or the 1985 pool).

Example 4 – Disposal of shares and securities

Minnie Ltd sold 3,000 shares in Mickey plc for £15,000, on 15 February 2013. The shares in Mickey plc were purchased as follows:

Date	Number	Cost £
1 July 2001	1,000	2,000
1 September 2005	1,000	2,500
8 February 2013	500	1,200
15 February 2013	1,500	6,000

Explain which shares Minnie Ltd is deemed to have sold.

Answer to example 4

Using the matching rules, the 3,000 shares sold are as follows:

	Number
(1) Same day purchases: 15 February 2013	1,500
(2) Previous 9 days purchases: 8 February 2013	500
	2,000

(3) Share pool:

All other shares were purchased more than 9 days ago, therefore they must be in the share pool.

1 July 2001	1,000	
1 September 2005	1,000	
Total number of shares in pool	2,000	
Disposal from the pool	(1,000)	1,000
Left in share pool	1,000	
Shares disposed of		3,000

Calculation of gains on same day and previous 9 day purchases

There is no IA on either of these calculations, even if the dates of acquisition and disposal straddle a month.

Hence, the gain is calculated as:

	£
Sale proceeds	X
Less: Allowable cost	(X)
Chargeable gain	X

Example 5 – Disposal of shares and securities

From the above example (Minnie Ltd), calculate the gains on the shares purchased:

(1) **on the same day**

(2) **in the previous 9 days.**

Answer to example 5

Calculate sale proceeds per share:

3,000 shares are sold for £15,000, therefore 1 share is sold for £5.00 (£15,000/3,000).

Gain on same day purchases (1,500 shares):

	£
Sale proceeds (£5 × 1,500)	7,500
Less: Allowable cost	(6,000)
Chargeable gain	1,500

Gain on previous 9 days purchases (500 shares):

	£
Sale proceeds (£5 × 500)	2,500
Less: Allowable cost	(1,200)
Chargeable gain	1,300

The share pool for companies is different to the share pool for individuals:

- It contains shares in the same company, of the same class, purchased **up to 9 days before** the date of disposal.

- The pool keeps a record of the:
    - number of shares acquired and sold
    - cost of the shares, and
    - indexed cost of the shares (i.e. cost plus IA)

- Each purchase and sale is recorded in the pool, but the indexed cost must be updated **before** recording the "operative event".

- When calculating the IA in the share pool, the indexation factor is **not** rounded to three decimal places.

  Note that this is the only situation where a non-rounded factor is used.

- When shares are disposed of out of the share pool, the appropriate proportion of the cost and indexed cost which relates to the shares disposed of is calculated on an average cost basis (as for individuals).

Pro forma for a company's share pool

	Number	Cost	Indexed cost
		£	£
Purchase	X	X ⟶	X
IA to next operative event			X
Purchase	X	X ⟶	X
	X̄	X̄	X̄
IA to next operative event			X
	X̄	X̄	X̄
Disposal	(X)	(X)	(X)
		W1	W2
Pool carried forward	X̲	X̲	X̲

Note:

(W1) Calculates the average pool cost of shares disposed of
(W2) Calculates the average indexed cost of shares disposed of

Calculation of the gain on shares in the share pool

Workings 1 and 2 feed into a normal gain computation, as follows:

	£
Sale proceeds	X
Less: Cost (W1)	(X)
	—
Unindexed gain	X
Less: Indexation allowance (W2 – W1)	(X)
	—
Chargeable gain	X
	—

It is important to show the cost (W1) and the indexation allowance (W2 – W1) separately in the gain computation, rather than simply deducting the indexed cost (W2) from sale proceeds, to ensure that the indexation allowance does not create / increase a loss.

Example 6 – Disposal of shares and securities

Continuing the example of Minnie Ltd (above), calculate the chargeable gain on the disposal from the share pool.

Assume the RPIs are as follows:

July 2001	173.3
September 2005	193.1
February 2013	248.7

Answer to example 6

	£
Sale proceeds (£5 × 1,000)	5,000
Less: Allowable cost (W)	(2,250)
	2,750
Less: Indexation allowance (£3,046 – £2,250) (W)	(796)
Chargeable gain	1,954

Working: Share pool	Number	Cost	Indexed cost
		£	£
July 2001 purchase	1,000	2,000	2,000
IA to next operative event: (July 2001 to September 2005) (193.1 – 173.3)/173.3 × £2,000			229
September 2005 purchase	1,000	2,500	2,500
	2,000	4,500	4,729
IA to next operative event (September 2005 to February 2013) (248.7 – 193.1)/193.1 × £4,729			1,362
	2,000	4,500	6,091
February 2013 sale (1,000 out of 2,000) (Note)	(1,000)	(2,250)	(3,046)
Pool carried forward	1,000	2,250	3,045

Note: Half of the shares sold, therefore take out half of the cost and indexed cost.

Braganza Ltd sold 10,000 ordinary shares in the FRP Co plc, a quoted company, on 20 December 2012, for £70,000.

The company had bought the ordinary shares on the following dates:

	Number of shares	Cost
		£
1 April 1998	8,000	25,250
22 December 2000	4,000	7,500

Calculate the chargeable gain arising on the disposal.

Assume retail price indices are:

April 1998	162.6
December 2000	172.2
December 2012	248.2

5 Bonus and rights issues

The key points to remember are as follows:

- A bonus issue is the distribution of free shares to shareholders, based on existing shareholdings.

- A rights issue involves shareholders paying for new shares, usually at a rate below market price and in proportion to their existing shareholdings.

- In both cases, therefore, the shareholder is making a new acquisition of shares.

- However, for matching purposes, such acquisitions arise out of the original holdings. They are not treated as a separate holding of shares.

- Bonus and rights issues therefore, attach to the original shareholdings, for the purposes of the identification rules.

Bonus issues

- As a bonus issue is free shares (i.e. no cost is involved), there is no indexation to be calculated.

- A bonus issue is not an operative event in the share pool.

- Simply, add the bonus issue shares to the share pool. When the next operative event occurs (e.g. next sale or purchase), index from the operative event before the date of the bonus issue.

Rights issue

- A rights issue is simply a purchase of shares (usually at a price below the market rate).

- Hence, it should be treated as an operative event, in the same way as a normal purchase in the share pool:

  - Index up to the date of the rights issue; then

  - Add in the number of shares and their cost.

Example 7 – Bonus issue

Alma Ltd acquired shares in S plc, a quoted company, as follows:

2,000 shares acquired in June 1997, for £11,500.

In October 2010, there was a 1 for 2 bonus issue.

Set up the share pool and deal with the events up to and including the bonus issue.

Answer to example 7

Share pool	Number	Cost £	Indexed cost £
Purchase (June 1997)	2,000	11,500	11,500
Bonus issue (October 2010) (1 for 2) 1/2 × £2,000	1,000	Nil	Nil
	3,000	11,500	11,500

Note: Do **not** index up to the date of the bonus issue as no cost is involved. The next time there is an operative event, IA will be calculated from June 1997 (the last operative event).

Test your understanding 5

Michael Ltd sold 2,000 ordinary shares out of a holding of 5,000 shares in Ryan Ltd, on 30 September 2012, for £15,400.

Michael Ltd prepares accounts every year to 31 March. The holding of shares in Ryan Ltd had been built up as follows:

Date acquired	Number of shares	Cost £
May 1995	4,000	7,000
March 2006 – Bonus issue 1 for 4	1,000	Nil

Compute the chargeable gain arising on the sale of shares, in the y/e 31 March 2013.

Assume the retail price indices are:

May 1995	149.6
March 2006	195.0
September 2012	246.7

Example 8 – Rights issue

Amber Ltd sold 2,600 shares in Pearl Ltd in December 2012 for £30,000.

Amber Ltd originally acquired 3,000 shares in Pearl Ltd in June 1997 for £11,500. In December 2004 Amber Ltd took up its entitlement to a 1 for 4 rights issue at £3 per share.

Calculate the chargeable gain arising on disposal of the shares, in December 2012.

Assume the following RPIs apply:

June 1997	157.5
December 2004	189.9
December 2012	248.2

Answer to example 8

Chargeable gain

	£
Sale proceeds	30,000
Less: Cost (W)	(9,533)
Unindexed gain	20,467
Less: Indexation (£14,604 – £9,533) (W)	(5,071)
Chargeable gain	15,396

Working: share pool	Number	Cost	Indexed cost
		£	£
Purchase – June 1997	3,000	11,500	11,500
IA to December 2004			
(189.9 – 157.5)/157.5 × £11,500			2,366
	3,000	11,500	13,866
December 2004			
– Rights issue (1 for 4) at £3	750	2,250	2,250
	3,750	13,750	16,116
IA to December 2012			
(248.2 – 189.9)/189.9 × £16,116			4,948
	3,750	13,750	21,064
Disposal – December 2012			
(2,600/3,750) × £13,750/£21,064	(2,600)	(9,533)	(14,604)
Balance to c/f	1,150	4,217	6,460

Note: The indexed cost is updated prior to the rights issue, because there is a purchase which involves additional cost (i.e. it is an operative event).

Following the disposal, there are 1,150 shares in the pool, with a cost of £4,217 and an indexed cost of £6,460.

This will be used as the starting point, when dealing with the next operative event.

KAPLAN PUBLISHING

6 Takeovers/reorganisations

Consideration: shares for shares

Where the consideration for the reorganisation or takeover only involves the issue of shares in the acquiring company, the tax consequences are:

- No chargeable gain arises at the time of the reorganisation or takeover.

- The cost of the original shares becomes the cost of the new shares.

- Where the shareholder receives more than one type of share, in exchange for the original shares:
  - the cost of the original shares is allocated to the new shares
  - by reference to the market values of the various new shares
  - on the first day of dealing in them.

Mixed consideration

When both cash and shares are received on a takeover:

- There is a part disposal of the original shares.

- A chargeable gain arises on the cash element of the consideration.

- The calculation of the chargeable gain is the same as for individuals (see Chapter 15) except that indexation allowance must be taken into account.

Example 9 – Takeovers/reorganisations

In June 1997, Major Ltd purchased 2,000 ordinary shares in Blue plc, for £5,000.

In July 2012, Blue plc was taken over by Red plc, and Major Ltd received 2 ordinary shares and 1 preference share in Red plc, for each ordinary share in Blue plc.

Immediately after the takeover, the ordinary shares in Red plc, were quoted at £2 and the preference shares in Red plc, were quoted at £1.

In December 2012, Major Ltd sold all of its holding of ordinary shares in Red plc, for £8,000.

Calculate the chargeable gain arising in December 2012.

Indexation factors:
June 1997 to July 2012	0.546
July 2012 to December 2012	0.019
June 1997 to December 2012	0.576

Answer to example 9

	£
Sale proceeds	8,000
Less: Cost (W3)	(4,000)
Unindexed gain	4,000
Less: Indexation allowance (£6,301 − £4,000) (Note)	(2,301)
Chargeable gain	1,699

Workings:

(W1) Share pool – Blue plc

	No.	Cost £	Indexed cost £
June 1997 – purchase	2,000	5,000	5,000
IA to takeover – July 2012 (0.546 x £5,000)			2,730
Balance at takeover	2,000	5,000	7,730

(W2) Allocation of cost of shares in Blue plc

Major Ltd received:	MV £	Cost £	Indexed cost £
4,000 ordinary shares (valued at £2)	8,000	4,000	6,184
2,000 preference shares (valued at £1)	2,000	1,000	1,546
	10,000	5,000	7,730

The cost and indexed cost attributable to the ordinary shares is calculated as: (8,000/10,000) x £5,000/£7,730

New share pools are then established for the new ordinary and preference shares received in Red plc.

(W3) **Share pool in Red plc – ordinary shares**

	No.	Cost £	Indexed cost £
July 2012	4,000	4,000	6,184
IA to December 2012			
(£6,184 x 0.019)			117
December 2012	4,000	4,000	6,301
Disposal	(4,000)	(4,000)	(6,301)

Tutorial note:

Technically IA should be calculated up to the date of the takeover (i.e. from June 1997 to July 2012) on the original shares in the share pool. The new shares then inherit the indexed cost at the date of the takeover. On the disposal of the new shares, this indexed cost is indexed from July 2012 to December 2012 as shown above.

However, performing just one IA calculation from June 1997 to December 2012 will not give a materially different answer. This approach is therefore an acceptable short cut in the examination.

	£
Sale proceeds	8,000
Less: Cost	(4,000)
Unindexed gain	4,000
Less: IA from June 1997 to December 2012	
(£4,000 x 0.576)	(2,304)
Chargeable gain	1,696

Test your understanding 6

In July 2012, during its year ended 31 December 2012, Concert Ltd sold its entire holding of ordinary shares in Corus plc, for £75,000.

Concert Ltd had originally purchased 20,000 £1 ordinary shares in BNB plc, at a cost of £20,000, in April 2002.

In July 2008, BNB plc was taken over by Corus plc. Concert Ltd received one ordinary 50p share and one 50p 6% preference share in Corus plc, for each ordinary share it held in BNB plc.

Immediately after the takeover, the values of these new shares were:

50p ordinary share	£1.80 each
50p preference shares	£0.80 each

(a) **Compute the chargeable gain arising in the y/e 31 December 2012.**
The relevant indexation factor to be used is 0.386.

(b) **Explain the consequences had Concert Ltd received cash of £16,000 rather than preference shares in July 2008.**

7 Reliefs available to companies

The **only** capital gains relief available to companies is roll-over relief. The other reliefs covered in Chapter 16 are not applicable to companies.

Roll-over relief for companies

There are generally no differences in the application of roll-over relief (ROR) for companies. The rules are summarised in expandable text.

Summary of roll-over relief

- ROR exists to allow a company to replace assets used in its trade, without incurring a corporation tax liability on the related chargeable gains.

- The gain arising on the disposal of the business asset, is deducted from (rolled over against), the acquisition cost of the new asset.

- Provided the proceeds are fully reinvested, no tax is payable at the time of the disposal.

- Common assets which qualify for ROR in the exam are:
  - Land and buildings that are both occupied and used for trading purposes.
  - Fixed plant and machinery ('fixed' means immovable).
- The acquisition of the replacement asset, must occur during a period that begins **one year before** the sale of the old asset and ends **three years after** the sale.
- Where disposal proceeds of the old asset are not fully reinvested, the surplus retained, reduces the amount of chargeable gain that can be rolled over.
- When an asset has not been used entirely for business purposes throughout the company's period of ownership, ROR is scaled down in proportion to the non-business use.
- If reinvestment is in a depreciating asset, the capital gain is deferred until the earliest of:
  - disposal of the depreciating asset
  - depreciating asset ceases to be used for trading purposes
  - 10 years since the asset was acquired.
- Any asset with a predictable life of not more than 60 years, is a depreciating asset.
- If a new non-depreciating asset is acquired before the deferred gain becomes chargeable, ROR can be reinstated.

The key differences in the rules for companies are as follows:

- **goodwill is not a qualifying asset** for companies
- the gain deferred is the 'indexed gain' (i.e. the gain **after** IA)
- claim must be made within four years of the **later of** the end of the accounting period in which the asset is
  - sold, and
  - replaced.

Test your understanding 7

Medway Ltd has been offered £160,000 for a freehold factory that it owns, and is considering disposing of the factory in January 2013.

The company acquired the factory on 15 March 2004, for £45,000. The factory has always been used by Medway Ltd for business purposes.

Explain the capital gains implications of each of the following alternative courses of action that Medway Ltd is considering taking:

(a) **Acquiring a larger freehold factory in April 2013, for £170,000.**

(b) **Acquiring a smaller freehold factory in April 2013, for £155,000 and using the remainder of the proceeds as working capital.**

(c) **Using the proceeds to pay a premium of £180,000 in April 2013, for a 40-year lease of a new factory (it is possible that a freehold warehouse will be bought in the next two or three years for an estimated cost of £200,000).**

Assume the following RPIs apply:

March 2004	184.6
January 2013	246.8

8 Chapter summary

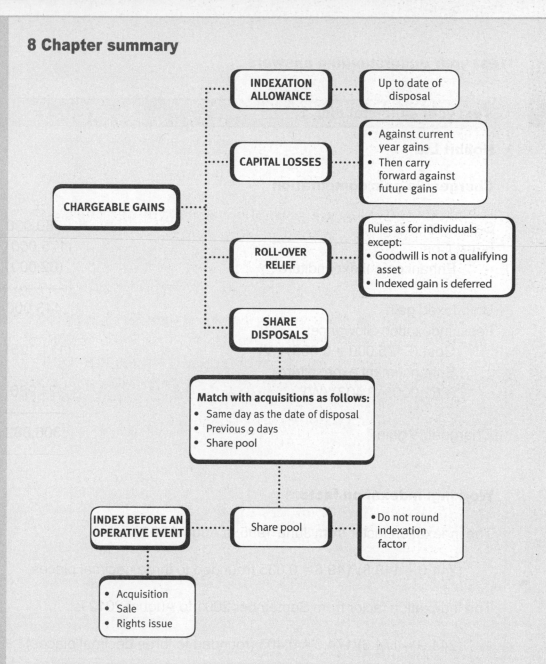

CHARGEABLE GAINS

INDEXATION ALLOWANCE → Up to date of disposal

CAPITAL LOSSES →
- Against current year gains
- Then carry forward against future gains

ROLL-OVER RELIEF →
Rules as for individuals except:
- Goodwill is not a qualifying asset
- Indexed gain is deferred

SHARE DISPOSALS

Match with acquisitions as follows:
- Same day as the date of disposal
- Previous 9 days
- Share pool

INDEX BEFORE AN OPERATIVE EVENT → Share pool →
- Do not round indexation factor

- Acquisition
- Sale
- Rights issue

Test your understanding answers

Test your understanding 1

Hobbit Ltd

Chargeable gain computation

	£
Sale proceeds	680,000
Less: Cost	(175,000)
Enhancement expenditure	(62,000)
Unindexed gain	443,000
Less: Indexation allowance:	
Cost (£175,000 × 0.635) (W)	(111,125)
Enhancement expenditure	
(£62,000 × 0.403) (W)	(24,986)
Chargeable gain	306,889

Working: indexation factors

The indexation factor from June 1995 to August 2012 is:

$(244.9 − 149.8)/149.8 = 0.635$ (rounded to three decimal places)

The indexation factor from September 2001 to August 2012 is:

$(244.9 − 174.6)/174.6 = 0.403$ (rounded to three decimal places)

Test your understanding 2

JNN Ltd

	(a) £	(b) £	(c) £
Sale proceeds	25,000	12,000	8,000
Less: Cost	(10,000)	(10,000)	(10,000)
Unindexed gain/(loss)	15,000	2,000	(2,000)
Less: Indexation allowance			
£10,000 × 1.385	(13,850)		
Restricted (see note)		(2,000)	Nil
Chargeable gain/(allowable loss)	1,150	Nil	(2,000)

Note: Part (b): IA is restricted as indexation cannot create a loss.

Part (c): no IA as indexation cannot increase a loss.

Test your understanding 3

High Ltd

Corporation tax liability – y/e 31 December 2012

	£
Tax adjusted trading profit	400,000
Net chargeable gain	Nil
	————
Taxable total profits	400,000
	————
Corporation tax (Note)	
FY2011 (£400,000 x 26% x 3/12)	26,000
Less: Marginal relief	
3/200 x (£1,500,000 – £400,000) x 3/12	(4,125)
FY2012 (£400,000 x 24% x 9/12)	72,000
Less: Marginal relief	
1/100 x (£1,500,000 – £400,000) x 9/12	(8,250)
	————
Corporation tax liability	85,625
	————

Working: Net chargeable gain

	£
Chargeable gain	17,000
Less: Capital loss b/f	(23,000)
	————
Capital loss c/f	(6,000)
	————

Therefore the net chargeable gain is Nil.

Note: TTP = Augmented profits, which are between £300,000 and £1,500,000.
Therefore, the marginal relief is applied.

However, a two part calculation is required as the year ended 31 December 2012 straddles 31 March 2012:
FY2011: 3 months (1.1.12 to 31.3.12)
FY2012: 9 months (1.4.12 to 31.12.12)

KAPLAN PUBLISHING

Test your understanding 4

Braganza Ltd

Chargeable gain computation

	£
Sale proceeds	70,000
Less: Acquisition cost (W)	(27,292)
Unindexed gain	42,708
Less: Indexation allowance (£41,128 – £27,292) (W)	(13,836)
Chargeable gain	28,872

Working: share pool	Number	Cost	Indexed cost
		£	£
1.4.98 acquisition	8,000	25,250	25,250
IA to December 2000 (172.2 – 162.6)/162.6 × £25,250			1,491
December 2000 acquisition	4,000	7,500	7,500
	12,000	32,750	34,241
IA to December 2012 (248.2 – 172.2)/172.2 × £34,241			15,112
	12,000	32,750	49,353
Disposal – December 2012	(10,000)	(27,292)	(41,128)
Balance c/f	2,000	5,458	8,225

Proportion of cost and indexed cost relating to the disposal:

Cost: (10,000/12,000) × £32,750 = £27,292
Indexed cost: (10,000/12,000) × £49,353 = £41,128

Test your understanding 5

Michael Ltd

Chargeable gain computation – y/e 31 March 2013

	£
Sale proceeds	15,400
Less: Acquisition cost (W)	(2,800)
Unindexed gain	12,600
Less: Indexation allowance (£4,617 – £2,800) (W)	(1,817)
Chargeable gain	10,783

Working: Share pool	Number	Cost	Indexed cost
		£	£
May 1995	4,000	7,000	7,000
March 2006 – bonus issue	1,000	Nil	Nil
	5,000	7,000	7,000
Index to September 2012 from May 1995			
(246.7 – 149.6)/149.6 × £7,000			4,543
	5,000	7,000	11,543
Disposal (Note)	(2,000)	(2,800)	(4,617)
Balance c/f	3,000	4,200	6,926

Note: The proportion of cost and indexed cost relating to the disposal is calculated as: (2,000/5,000) × £7,000 and £11,543 respectively.

Test your understanding 5

Test your understanding 6

Concert Ltd

(a) **Chargeable gain computation – y/e 31 December 2012**

	£
Sales proceeds	75,000
Less: Deemed acquisition cost (W)	(13,846)
Unindexed gain	61,154
Less: Indexation allowance (£13,846 × 0.386) (Note)	(5,345)
Chargeable gain	55,809

Working: Deemed acquisition cost

Following the takeover in July 2008 of BNB plc by Corus plc, Concert Ltd now owns shares in Corus plc as per the terms of the takeover.

	Total M.V. £	Original cost £
20,000 50p ordinary shares @ £1.80	36,000	13,846
20,000 50p preference shares @ £0.80	16,000	6,154
	52,000	20,000

Allocation of original cost incurred in April 2002, to the shares now owned in July 2008, using the average cost method.

To ordinary shares: (£36,000/£52,000) × £20,000 = £13,846
To preference shares (£16,000/£52,000) × £20,000 = £6,154

Note: Technically IA should be calculated up to the date of the takeover (i.e. from April 2002 to July 2008) on the original shares in the share pool. The new shares then inherit the indexed cost at the date of the takeover. On the disposal of the new shares, this indexed cost is indexed from July 2008 to July 2012.

However, performing just one IA calculation from April 2002 to July 2012 will not give a materially different answer. This approach is therefore an acceptable short cut in the examination.

(b) Mixed consideration on the takeover

If Concert Ltd had received cash in July 2008, a chargeable gain would have arisen in the year ended 31 December 2008 calculated as follows:

	£
Cash received	X
Less: Cost	(X)
	X
Less: IA from April 2002 to July 2008	X
Chargeable gain	X

Test your understanding 7

Medway Ltd

Chargeable gain

	£
Sales proceeds	160,000
Less: Cost	(45,000)
Unindexed gain	115,000
Less: Indexation allowance (246.8 – 184.6) / 184.6	
$\quad$ = (0.337 × £45,000)	(15,165)
Chargeable gain	99,835

(a) **Larger freehold factory**

As all the proceeds are reinvested, there will be no chargeable gain arising now and the gain will be rolled over against the base cost of the new factory.

	£
Cost of factory	170,000
Less: Rollover relief (deferred gain)	(99,835)
Base cost of new factory	70,165

(b) **Smaller freehold factory**

As only part of the proceeds are reinvested, the capital gain element that cannot be rolled over will be £5,000 (£160,000 – £155,000). This will be immediately chargeable to corporation tax.

The balance of the gain will be rolled over as above:

	£
Cost of factory	155,000
Less: Rollover relief (£99,835 – £5,000)	(94,835)
Base cost of new factory	60,165

(c) Lease

All of the proceeds are being used to acquire a depreciating asset (i.e. one with an expected life of less than 60 years). The chargeable gain is therefore not rolled over, but is instead 'frozen'.

It will become chargeable to corporation tax on the earlier of:

- the date that the lease is sold
- the date the lease ceases to be used in the trade
- the expiry of ten years from April 2013.

Therefore, the base cost of the lease remains at £180,000.

If, before the 'frozen' gain becomes chargeable, a non-depreciating asset is acquired, the gain can be rolled over in the usual way.

In this question, if the freehold warehouse is acquired in the next 2 to 3 years, all the proceeds will be reinvested and so the roll-over claim could be switched to the freehold warehouse.

The base cost of the freehold warehouse would be reduced to £100,165 (£200,000 – £99,835).

KAPLAN PUBLISHING

Losses for companies

Chapter learning objectives

Upon completion of this chapter you will be able to:

- determine a trading loss and explain the various ways of giving relief in a single company

- demonstrate the application of the trading loss reliefs in a corporation tax computation

- show how a trading loss is relieved on cessation of a trade

- identify the factors that influence the choice of a loss relief claim

- explain how relief for a property business loss is given

- demonstrate how capital losses can be relieved against gains.

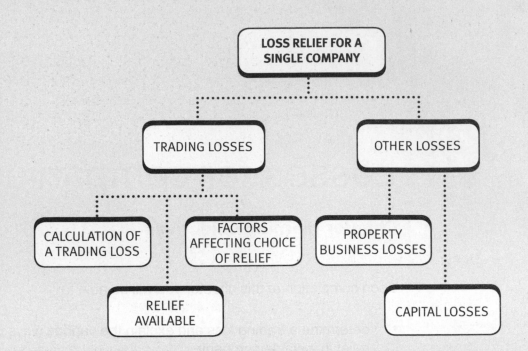

Introduction

This chapter covers the rules for loss reliefs available to a single company. The following losses are dealt with:

- Trading losses (section 1).

- Property business losses (section 4).

- Capital losses (section 5).

1 Trading losses

Calculation of a trading loss

- Trading losses are computed in the same way as tax adjusted trading profits:

	£
Tax adjusted net profit/(loss)	X/(X)
Less: Plant and machinery capital allowances	(X)
Adjusted trading loss	(X)

- If a company has made an adjusted trading loss, the tax adjusted trading profit for that period is £Nil.

Example 1 – Trading losses

Carlos Ltd had the following results for its year ended 31 August 2012:

	£	£
Gross profit		30,000
Less: Expenditure		
Depreciation	5,000	
Allowable costs	12,000	
		(17,000)
Net profit per accounts		13,000

The capital allowances for the year amount to £21,000.

(a) **Calculate the tax adjusted trading loss for the y/e 31 August 2012.**

(b) **Calculate the tax adjusted trading loss for the y/e 31 August 2012 assuming the facts are the same except that the company made a net loss per the accounts of £10,000.**

Answer to example 1

(a) **Tax adjusted trading loss – y/e 31 August 2012**

	£
Net profit per accounts	13,000
Add: Depreciation	5,000
	18,000
Less: Capital allowances	(21,000)
Tax adjusted trading loss	(3,000)
Tax adjusted trading profit included in TTP	Nil

(b) **Tax adjusted trading loss**

	£
Net loss per accounts	(10,000)
Add: Depreciation	5,000
	(5,000)
Less: Capital allowances	(21,000)
Tax adjusted trading loss	(26,000)
Tax adjusted trading profit included in TTP	Nil

Relief for trading losses

There are four ways in which a company can offset trading losses:

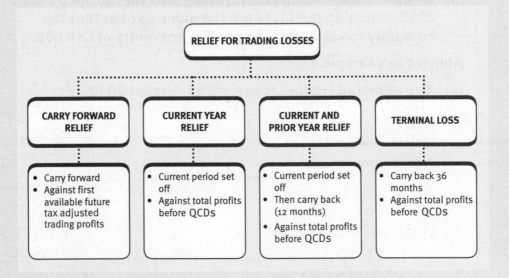

Carry forward loss relief

The key features of this relief are:

- The loss is carried forward for offset in future accounting periods.

- The loss is set against the **first available** tax adjusted trading profits from the **same trade**.

- The relief is automatic (i.e. no claim is required).

- The loss can be carried forward indefinitely.

- There is no need to make a current year or a prior year claim first.

KAPLAN PUBLISHING

Carry forward loss relief

- The loss can be carried forward indefinitely, but it must be set-off against the **first available** trading profits from the **same trade**.

- Therefore if the company changes their trading activity, any remaining losses are forfeited.

- Losses can be carried forward:
  - After a current year claim only.
  - After a current year and prior year claim.
  - If no claims are made.

- A claim to establish the amount of the loss available to carry forward should be made within four years of the end of the loss-making accounting period.

- The carry forward relief applies automatically against future trading profits as soon as they arise. They cannot be relieved against any other profits.

Example 2 – Trading losses

Poppy Ltd has a current year tax adjusted trading loss of £25,000, for the year ended 31 October 2012.

The company's projected tax adjusted trading profits are as follows:

	£
Year ended 31 October 2013	14,000
Year ended 31 October 2014	6,500
Year ended 31 October 2015	15,600

Poppy Ltd also receives property business income of £5,000 each year.

Calculate Poppy Ltd's taxable total profits for the four years ended 31 October 2015, assuming that the loss for the year ended 31 October 2012 is carried forward.

Answer to example 2

Year ended 31 October	2012	2013	2014	2015
	£	£	£	£
Tax adjusted trading profit	Nil	14,000	6,500	15,600
Less: Loss relief b/f	–	(14,000)	(6,500)	(4,500)
	Nil	Nil	Nil	11,100
Property income	5,000	5,000	5,000	5,000
TTP	5,000	5,000	5,000	16,100

Working – loss memorandum

Loss – y/e 31.10.2012	25,000
Used in – y/e 31.10.2013	(14,000)
y/e 31.10.2014	(6,500)
y/e 31.10.2015	(4,500)
Carry forward to y/e 31.10.2016	Nil

Current year relief

If a current year loss relief claim is made, trading losses are set off against:

- total profits before deduction of qualifying charitable donations (QCDs)
- of the same accounting period.

A current year claim must be made:

- for the whole loss; a partial claim is not allowed
- within two years of the end of the loss-making accounting period.

KAPLAN PUBLISHING

Example 3 – Trading losses

Sage Ltd had the following results for the y/e 31 March 2013.

	£
Tax adjusted trading loss	(40,000)
Property business income	10,000
Chargeable gain	50,000
Charitable donation	10,000

(a) **Show how the trading loss could be relieved with a current period claim.**

(b) **Show how your answer would be different if the tax adjusted trading loss was £60,000.**

Answer to example 3

(a) **Taxable total profits computation – y/e 31 March 2013**

	£
Tax adjusted trading profit	Nil
Property income	10,000
Chargeable gain	50,000
Total profits	60,000
Less: Loss relief – current year	(40,000)
	20,000
Less: QCD relief	(10,000)
TTP	10,000

Loss memorandum

	£
Year ended 31 March 2013	40,000
Less: Used in current period	(40,000)
	Nil

(b) **Taxable total profits computation – y/e 31 March 2013**

	£
Total profits (as before)	60,000
Less: Loss relief – current year	(60,000)
TTP	Nil
QCD wasted	(10,000)

As the loss is set off before the deduction of QCDs, the QCD payments have become excess (i.e. not used), as there are insufficient profits. It is an important principle that, where there is an available loss, no restriction in set off is permitted.

This means that it would **not** have been possible to restrict the loss relief to (£50,000), so as to then relieve the QCD of (£10,000), and find an alternative use for the remaining (£10,000) loss.

Excess QCDs cannot be carried forward or back and are therefore wasted unless the company is a member of a group (Chapter 22).

Carry back relief

Any trading loss remaining after a current year claim can be carried back.

Under carry back loss relief, trading losses are set off against:

- total profits (before deduction of QCDs)
- of the previous 12 months
- on a LIFO (last in first out) basis.

A carry back claim can only be made if a claim for current year loss relief has been made first.

The carry back claim:

- is optional
- must be made within two years of the end of the loss-making accounting period.

Trading losses – pro forma computation

Assume the loss arises in 2012	2011	2012	2013
	£	£	£
Tax adjusted trading profit	X	Nil	X
Less: Loss relief b/f			(X)
			–––––
			X
Other income	X	X	X
Chargeable gains	X	X	X
	–––––	–––––	–––––
Total profits	X	X	X
Less: Loss relief			
– Current year		(X)	
– 12 month carry back	(X)		
	–––––	–––––	–––––
	Nil	Nil	X
Less: QCD relief	Wasted	Wasted	(X)
	–––––	–––––	–––––
Taxable total profits	Nil	Nil	X
	–––––	–––––	–––––

Example 4 – Trading losses

Marjoram Ltd has the following results:

Year ended 31 March	2011	2012	2013
	£	£	£
Tax adjusted trading profits/(loss)	11,000	9,000	(45,000)
Building society interest	500	500	500
Chargeable gains	–	–	4,000
Charitable donation	250	250	250

Calculate the taxable total profits for all periods affected, assuming that loss relief is taken as soon as possible.

Answer to example 4

Marjoram Ltd – Corporation tax computations

Year ended 31 March	2011 £	2012 £	2013 £
Tax adjusted trading profit	11,000	9,000	Nil
Interest income	500	500	500
Chargeable gain	–	–	4,000
Total profits	11,500	9,500	4,500
Less: Loss relief (W)			
– Current year			(4,500)
– 12 month carry back		(9,500)	
	11,500	Nil	Nil
Less: QCD relief	(250)	Wasted	Wasted
TTP	11,250	Nil	Nil

Working – loss memorandum

	£
Loss for the y/e 31 March 2013	45,000
Less: Used in current year – y/e 31.3.13	(4,500)
Less: Used in 12 month carry back – y/e 31.3.12	(9,500)
Loss carried forward	31,000

Note: The y/e 31 March 2011 is not affected, as the loss cannot be carried back that far.

The QCDs in the years ended 31 March 2012 and 2013 are wasted.

Loss-making period of less than 12 months

The length of the loss-making period is not important:

- Full relief is given against the current period total profits.
- The remaining loss can be carried back in full in the normal way.

Test your understanding 1

Mint Ltd has the following results:

	y/e 31.3.11 £	y/e 31.3.12 £	9 m/e 31.12.12 £	y/e 31.12.13 £
Tax adjusted trading profit/(loss)	30,000	15,000	(100,000)	40,000
Interest income	3,000	5,000	10,000	10,000
Chargeable gain	10,000	–	40,000	–

Calculate the taxable total profits, for all of the accounting periods shown above, clearly indicating how you would deal with the trading loss, to obtain relief as soon as possible.

Short accounting periods prior to year of loss

If the accounting period preceding the period of the loss is less than 12 months:

- The profits of the accounting period that falls partly into the 12 month carry back period must be time apportioned.
- The loss can only be offset against those profits which fall within the 12 month carry back period.
- Remember, the loss is offset on a LIFO basis (i.e. against the later accounting period first).

Example 5 – Trading losses

Starbuck plc's recent results are as follows:

	y/e 31.12.10 £	5 m/e 31.5.11 £	y/e 31.5.12 £
Tax adjusted trading profit/(loss)	24,000	10,000	(50,000)
Interest income	3,500	2,000	6,000

Calculate the taxable total profits for all periods assuming the trading loss is relieved as early as possible.

Answer to example 5

	y/e 31.12.10 £	5 m/e 31.5.11 £	y/e 31.5.12 £
Tax adjusted trading profit/(loss)	24,000	10,000	Nil
Interest income	3,500	2,000	6,000
Total profits	27,500	12,000	6,000
Less: Loss relief			
– Current year			(6,000)
– 12 month carry back	(16,042)	(12,000)	
TTP	11,458	Nil	Nil

Loss Memorandum

	£
Trading loss y/e 31.5.12	50,000
Less: Used in current year claim – y/e 31.5.12	(6,000)
	44,000
Less: Used in 12 month carry back	
– 5 m/e 31.5.11	(12,000)
	32,000

  – y/e 31.12.10
  Lower of:
  (i) Total profits × 7/12 = (7/12 × £27,500) = £16,042
  (ii) Remaining loss = £32,000

	£
	(16,042)
Loss remaining to carry forward	15,958

KAPLAN PUBLISHING

Test your understanding 2

Catalyst Ltd has been trading for many years with the following results:

	y/e 31.3.11 £	9 m/e 31.12.11 £	y/e 31.12.12 £	y/e 31.12.13 £
Tax adjusted trading profit/(loss) before capital allowances	33,000	16,500	(75,000)	25,000
Capital allowances	5,400	4,050	6,550	5,000
Interest income	1,200	1,300	1,400	1,600
Chargeable gain/(loss)	Nil	(6,000)	Nil	12,000
Charitable donations	Nil	3,000	3,000	8,000

Assuming that Catalyst Ltd claims relief for its trading loss as early as possible, calculate the company's taxable total profits for the accounting periods ended 31 December 2013.

Your answer should show the amount of unrelieved losses as at 31 December 2013.

2 Terminal loss relief

When a company incurs a trading loss during the **final 12 months of trading**, then it is possible to make a carry back claim:

- set against **total profits** (before QCDs)
- of the **three years** preceding the loss-making period (not 12 months)
- on a **LIFO basis.**

However, the company must first claim to set the trading loss against total profits (before QCDs) of the accounting period of the loss.

Where the company has prepared accounts for a period other than 12 months during the three years preceding the loss making period:

- apportionment will be necessary in the same way as for a normal carry back claim
- so that losses are only carried back against the proportion of profits falling within the three year period.

Test your understanding 3

Brown Ltd has been trading for many years. The company prepared its annual accounts to 31 March, each year, but changed its accounting date to 31 December in 2011. The company ceased trading on 31 December 2012.

Period ended:	y/e 31.3.09	y/e 31.3.10	y/e 31.3.11	9 m/e 31.12.11	y/e 31.12.12
	£	£	£	£	£
Tax adjusted trading profit	450,000	87,000	240,000	45,000	Nil
Bank interest	9,000	3,000	6,000	1,500	1,500
Chargeable gain	7,500	–	–	–	–
Charity donation	30,000	30,000	30,000	30,000	30,000

In the year ended 31 December 2012, Brown Ltd made a tax adjusted trading loss of £525,000.

Calculate Brown Ltd's taxable total profits, for all of the above accounting periods, assuming terminal loss relief is claimed for the trading loss in the year ended 31 December 2012.

3 Choice of loss relief

Factors that influence choice of loss relief

Where there is a choice of loss reliefs available, the following factors will influence the loss relief chosen:

- Tax saving
- Cash flow
- Wastage of relief for QCDs.

In examination questions, it is usually the option that gives the most beneficial tax saving that is recommended.

Tax saving

The company will want to save (or obtain a refund at) the highest possible rate of tax.

- The effective rate of tax for profits in the margin is used to work out the tax saving.

- The effective rate of tax in the margin describes the rate of tax saved for each £1 of loss utilised.

The preferred order to claim relief to achieve the highest tax saving is against:

		Effective rate of tax saving:		
Profits subject to tax at:		**FY2010**	**FY2011**	**FY2012**
1	Main rate less marginal relief (Note)	29.75%	27.5%	25%
2	Main rate	28%	26%	24%
3	Small profits rate	21%	20%	20%

Note: The effective rates of tax in the margin (or marginal rate) are not provided in the exam. You need to learn the marginal rates for FY2010 to FY2012.

Marginal rate of tax

The marginal rate of tax of 29.75%, 27.5% and 25% is only accurate when a company does not receive any FII.

For an explanation of the effective rate of tax in the margin; see example 6 below.

Example 6 – Marginal rate of tax

The example below demonstrates how a company in the 'marginal' band between the small profits rate and the main rate, pays tax of 25% in FY2012 on each extra £1 it earns above the lower limit.

A Ltd has taxable total profits of £300,000, for the year ended 31 March 2013. B Ltd has taxable total profits of £310,000, for the year ended 31 March 2013. Neither company received any dividends in the year.

Calculate the corporation tax liability payable by each company and the marginal rate of tax on the additional profits of £10,000 earned by B Ltd.

Answer to example 6

Year ended 31 March 2013	A Ltd £	B Ltd £
TTP = Augmented profits	300,000	310,000
Corporation tax:		
£300,000 @ 20%	60,000	
£310,000 @ 24%		74,400
Less: Marginal relief		
1/100 × (£1,500,000 – £310,000)		(11,900)
		62,500

Additional tax paid by B Ltd = (£62,500 – £60,000) = £2,500

Additional taxable total profits earned by B Ltd = £10,000

Effective rate of tax on extra £10,000 profits over £300,000
= (£2,500/£10,000 × 100) = **25%**

Choice of loss relief

Cash flow

A company's cash flow position may affect its choice of loss relief.

A company may be prepared to accept loss relief at a lower marginal rate, if it results in an earlier receipt of cash.

Note that when a loss is carried back, it will probably result in a repayment of corporation tax, whereas carrying losses forward will only result in a reduction of a future tax liability.

Loss of relief for QCDs

Unrelieved QCDs cannot be carried forward and relieved against future tax adjusted trading profits. Therefore, certain claims for loss relief may lead to relief for QCDs being lost.

KAPLAN PUBLISHING

Disclaim capital allowances

If part of the loss is due to capital allowances, it may be advantageous for the company to consider not claiming the maximum capital allowances available in that period. This may be the case if there is insufficient other income in the year of the loss and in the previous 12 months against which to offset the loss.

As a result, the loss arising in the current period (which could only be set against future tax adjusted trading profits), can be reduced and the TWDV to carry forward to the following period for capital allowance purposes will be correspondingly higher.

This means that higher capital allowances (WDAs) will be available in the following years rather than creating a loss now. A further consequence could be that a higher tax adjusted trading loss arises in the future, which can be used against total profits.

Approach to questions

Loss questions will often give you taxable total profits information for a company for a number of years. This may initially appear daunting.

However, the following step by step approach will provide you with a logical way to attempt the question and ensure that you offset the losses correctly.

Step 1: Write out the skeleton TTP pro forma remembering to leave space for loss relief claims, lay out the years side by side.

Step 2: Fill in the pro forma with the TTP information provided, ignoring loss relief. In the year of the loss, the tax adjusted trading profit is £Nil.

Step 3: Keep a separate working for the 'trading loss'. Update the workings as the loss is relieved.

Step 4: Consider the loss relief options available.

- Where there is more than one loss to offset:
  - Deal with the earliest loss first
  - Losses brought forward are offset in priority to current year and carry back claims.

- If a question states 'relief is to be obtained as early as possible', the order of set-off is:
  - Current year claim followed by a carry back claim to the previous 12 months (or 36 months for a terminal loss).
  - Carry forward any remaining loss and offset against future trading profits.

- If a question asks you to identify the option that will save the most tax, consider in turn the three options:
  - Carry forward only
  - Current year claim and then carry forward any excess
  - Current year claim, followed by a carry back claim and then carry forward any excess

- Identify the amount of tax saving and loss of relief for QCDs under each option and conclude as to which option saves the most tax.

Step 5: Work out the revised TTP after the appropriate loss reliefs.

Example 7 – Choice of loss relief

Loser Ltd prepared its accounts to 31 March 2011 but has since changed to a 30 September accounting date and prepared a set of accounts to 30 September 2011.

The company forecasts a substantial tax adjusted trading loss for the y/e 30 September 2012. A small trading profit is forecast for the following year with steadily increasing profits thereafter.

Loser Ltd's tax adjusted trading profits for recent years have been:

	£
Year ended 31 March 2011	550,000
Period ended 30 September 2011	70,000

Advise Loser Ltd as to which loss relief claims would save the most tax.

Answer to example 7

Loser Ltd has the following options regarding the trading loss arising in the year to 30 September 2012:

(1) Carry the loss forward to off-set against the first available future trading profits.

As the trading profits in the year to 30 September 2013, are expected to be small, relief for the loss is likely to be at 20% (assuming the small profits rate is unchanged in the future).

(2) Current year off-set against the total profits of the year ended 30 September 2012 and balance carried forward.

Assuming that the non-trading income of the company in the current year is small, relief for the loss will be at the small profits rate of 20%.

(3) Current year off-set followed by a carry back claim

The carry back will be initially to the 6 month period ended 30 September 2011 and then the year ended 31 March 2011 (restricted to 6 months of the profits).

Relief in the current year and the period ended 30 September 2011, will be at the small profits rate of 20%.

The level of profits in the year ended 31 March 2011 (FY2010), will mean that relief for the loss in this year will be at the marginal rate of 29.75%.

Conclusion

Option 3 will therefore save the most tax.

Summary of trading loss reliefs

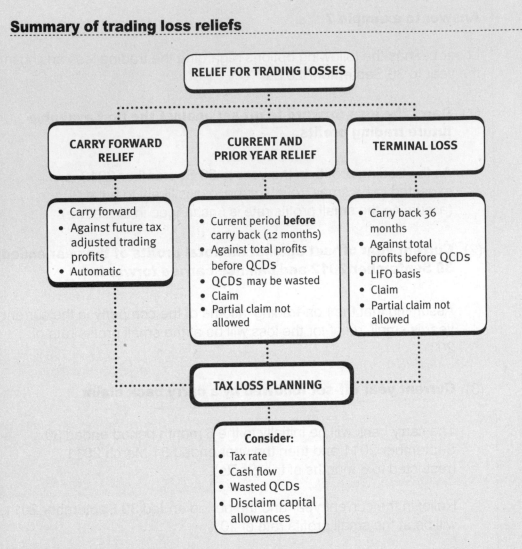

RELIEF FOR TRADING LOSSES

CARRY FORWARD RELIEF

- Carry forward
- Against future tax adjusted trading profits
- Automatic

CURRENT AND PRIOR YEAR RELIEF

- Current period **before** carry back (12 months)
- Against total profits before QCDs
- QCDs may be wasted
- Claim
- Partial claim not allowed

TERMINAL LOSS

- Carry back 36 months
- Against total profits before QCDs
- LIFO basis
- Claim
- Partial claim not allowed

TAX LOSS PLANNING

Consider:
- Tax rate
- Cash flow
- Wasted QCDs
- Disclaim capital allowances

4 Property business losses

Property business losses are:

- off-set against **total profits (before QCDs)** for the current period.

- any excess is carried forward and off-set against the **first available** future **total profits** (before QCDs) of the company.

Note that:

- Relief is automatic – no claim is required.

- There is no carry back facility for property business losses.

- Partial loss claims are not allowed.

- If applicable, property business losses are set off before trading losses.

Example 8 – Property business losses

Reas Ltd has the following results:

Year ended 31 January:	2012 £	2013 £
Tax adjusted trading profit	12,000	7,000
Property business profit/(loss)	(22,600)	800
Interest income	500	1,400
Charitable donation	(500)	(500)

Calculate taxable total profits for both years assuming all reliefs are claimed at the earliest opportunity.

Answer to example 8

Year ended 31 January:	2012 £	2013 £
Tax adjusted trading profit	12,000	7,000
Property business income	Nil	800
Interest income	500	1,400
	⎯⎯⎯	⎯⎯⎯
Total profits	12,500	9,200
Less: Property business loss (W)	(12,500)	(9,200)
	⎯⎯⎯	⎯⎯⎯
	Nil	Nil
Less: QCD relief	Wasted	Wasted
	⎯⎯⎯	⎯⎯⎯
TTP	Nil	Nil
	⎯⎯⎯	⎯⎯⎯

Working: Property business loss

	£
Loss in y/e 31 January 2012	22,600
Less: Used in current period – y/e 31 January 2012	(12,500)
	⎯⎯⎯
	10,100
Less: Used in carry forward – y/e 31 January 2013	(9,200)
	⎯⎯⎯
Unrelieved loss carried forward	900
	⎯⎯⎯

Comfy Ltd has the following results:

Year ended 31 December:	2010	2011	2012
	£	£	£
Tax adjusted trading profit/(loss)	12,450	(14,500)	4,000
Property business profit/(loss)	2,000	1,800	(500)
Interest income	1,000	600	1,000
Charitable donation	(400)	(400)	(400)

Calculate taxable total profits for all three years assuming all reliefs are claimed at the earliest opportunity.

5 Capital losses

A capital loss incurred in an accounting period is:

- relieved against any chargeable gains arising in the same accounting period.

- Any excess losses are then carried forward for relief against gains arising in future accounting periods.

Note that:

- Relief is automatic – no claim is required.

- A capital loss may never be carried back and relieved against chargeable gains for earlier periods.

- Capital losses can only be set against gains, they may not be set against the company's income.

- Partial claims are not allowed.

Example 9 – Capital losses

Rose Ltd has the following results:

Year ended 31 March:	2012	2013
	£	£
Tax adjusted trading profit/(loss)	(20,000)	18,000
Interest income	6,000	9,000
Capital loss	(2,000)	
Chargeable gains		7,000

Calculate the taxable total profits for the two accounting periods assuming that the trading loss is carried forward.

Show any unrelieved losses carried forward at 1 April 2013.

Answer to example 9

Trading losses carried forward are relieved against the first available tax adjusted trading profits.

Capital losses can only be set against current or future chargeable gains.

Rose Ltd

Taxable total profit computations

Year ended 31 March	2012	2013
	£	£
Tax adjusted trading profits	Nil	18,000
Less: Loss relief b/f	–	(18,000)
	Nil	Nil
Interest income	6,000	9,000
Chargeable gains (£7,000 – £2,000)	Nil	5,000
TTP	6,000	14,000
Trading loss carried forward at 31 March 2013 (£20,000 – £18,000)		2,000

Coriander Ltd started to trade on 1 January 2010 and has the following results:

Year ended 31 December:	2010	2011	2012
	£	£	£
Tax adjusted trading profit/(loss)	37,450	(81,550)	20,000
Interest income	1,300	1,400	1,600
Capital gain/(loss)	(6,000)	Nil	13,000
Charitable donations	3,000	3,000	3,000

Calculate taxable total profits for all relevant periods assuming loss relief is given as early as possible.

6 Comprehensive example

Test your understanding 6

Eagle Ltd is a UK resident company that manufactures components. The company's results for the y/e 31 March 2013 are:

	£
Trading loss (as adjusted for taxation but before taking account of capital allowances) (Note 1)	(279,873)
Income from property (Note 2)	56,950
Profit on disposal of shares (Note 3)	144,450
Donation to charity (Note 4)	(3,000)

Notes:

(1) **Plant and machinery**

On 1 April 2012 the TWDV on the general pool was £64,700. Some machinery was sold on 15 February 2013 for £12,400 (original cost £18,000).

The following assets were purchased during the year:

20 October 2012	Lorry	£32,400
15 December 2012	Equipment	£13,040
18 March 2013	Motor car (CO$_2$ emissions 136 g/km)	£11,300

(2) Income from property

Eagle Ltd lets out two warehouses that are surplus to requirements.

The first warehouse was empty from 1 April to 30 June 2012, but was let from 1 July 2012. On that date the company received a premium of £50,000 for the grant of an eight-year lease, and the annual rent of £12,600 which is payable in advance.

The second warehouse was let until 31 December 2012 at an annual rent of £8,400. On that date the tenant left owing three months rent which the company is not able to recover. The roof was repaired at a cost of £6,700 during February 2013.

(3) Profit on disposal of shares

The profit on disposal of shares relates to a 1% shareholding in a UK company that was sold on 22 December 2012 for £257,250.

The shareholding was purchased on 5 April 2001 for £112,800. Assume that the indexation allowance from April 2001 to December 2012 is £48,955.

(4) Donation to charity

The donation to charity was made under the Gift Aid scheme.

(5) Other information

Eagle Ltd has no associated companies. Its results for the year ended 30 September 2011 and the six-month period ended 31 March 2012 were as follows:

	y/e 30.9.11	p/e 31.3.12
	£	£
Tax adjusted trading profit	137,900	52,000
Property business profit/(loss)	(4,600)	18,700
Chargeable gain/(allowable loss)	(8,900)	18,200
Donation to charity	(2,300)	(2,600)

(a) Calculate Eagle Ltd's tax adjusted trading loss for the y/e 31 March 2013.

You should assume that the company claims the maximum available capital allowances.

(b) **Assuming that Eagle Ltd claims relief for its trading loss as early as possible, calculate the company's taxable total profits for the three accounting periods ended 31 March 2013.**

Your answer should show the amount of unrelieved trading losses as at 31 March 2013.

(c) **Describe the alternative ways in which Eagle Ltd could have relieved the trading loss for the y/e 31 March 2013.**

7 Chapter summary

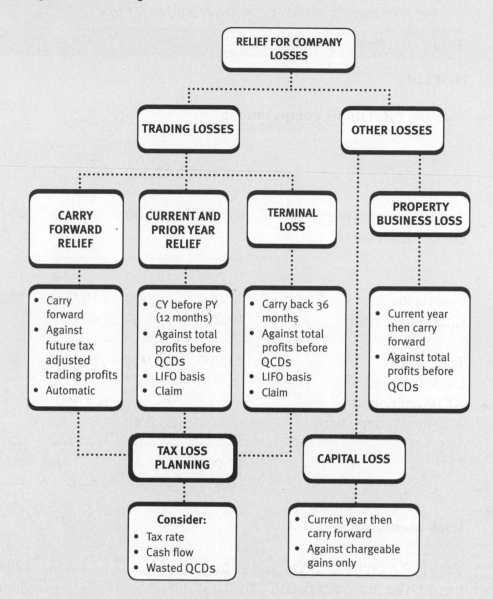

RELIEF FOR COMPANY LOSSES

TRADING LOSSES

OTHER LOSSES

CARRY FORWARD RELIEF
- Carry forward
- Against future tax adjusted trading profits
- Automatic

CURRENT AND PRIOR YEAR RELIEF
- CY before PY (12 months)
- Against total profits before QCDs
- LIFO basis
- Claim

TERMINAL LOSS
- Carry back 36 months
- Against total profits before QCDs
- LIFO basis
- Claim

PROPERTY BUSINESS LOSS
- Current year then carry forward
- Against total profits before QCDs

TAX LOSS PLANNING

Consider:
- Tax rate
- Cash flow
- Wasted QCDs

CAPITAL LOSS
- Current year then carry forward
- Against chargeable gains only

Test your understanding answers

Test your understanding 1

Mint Ltd

Taxable total profit computations

	y/e 31.3.11 £	y/e 31.3.12 £	p/e 31.12.12 £	y/e 31.12.13 £
Tax adjusted trading profit	30,000	15,000	Nil	40,000
Less: Loss relief b/f	–	–	–	(30,000)
	30,000	15,000	Nil	10,000
Interest income	3,000	5,000	10,000	10,000
Chargeable gain	10,000	–	40,000	–
Total profits	43,000	20,000	50,000	20,000
Less: Loss relief				
– Current period			(50,000)	
– 12 month carry back		(20,000)		
TTP	43,000	Nil	Nil	20,000

Loss memorandum

	£
Loss in 9 months to 31 December 2012	100,000
Less: Used in current period – 9 m/e 31.12.12	(50,000)
Used in 12 month carry back – y/e 31.3.12	(20,000)
Carried forward	30,000
Used in y/e 31.12.13	(30,000)
	Nil

Note: The length of the loss-making period is not important. The current period and 12 month carry back is unrestricted in amount.

Losses cannot be carried back to the y/e 31 March 2011.

Test your understanding 2

Catalyst Ltd

Taxable total profit computations

	12 m/e 31.3.11 £	9 m/e 31.12.11 £	12 m/e 31.12.12 £	12 m/e 31.12.13 £
Adjusted profits	33,000	16,500	Nil	25,000
Less: CAs	(5,400)	(4,050)	Nil	(5,000)
Tax adjusted trading profit	27,600	12,450	Nil	20,000
Less: Loss relief b/f				(20,000)
				Nil
Interest income	1,200	1,300	1,400	1,600
Chargeable gain (W1)		Nil		6,000
Total profits	28,800	13,750	1,400	7,600
Less: Loss relief				
– Current year			(1,400)	
– 12 month carry back	(7,200)	(13,750)		
	21,600	Nil	Nil	7,600
Less: QCD relief	Nil	–	–	(7,600)
		wasted	wasted	part wasted
TTP	21,600	Nil	Nil	Nil

Note: Unrelieved trading loss available to carry forward at 31 December 2013 is £39,200 (W2).

Working

(W1) Chargeable gain/capital loss

	£
p/e 31.12.11 (loss)	(6,000)
y/e 31.12.13 gain	12,000
Net gain – y/e 31.12.13	6,000

Note that as for individuals, for companies, the capital loss can only be offset against future chargeable gains.

(W2) Tax adjusted trading loss available and its utilisation

	£
Adjusted loss – y/e 31.12.12	75,000
Plus: Capital allowances	6,550
Tax adjusted trading loss available	81,550
Less: Used in current year claim – y/e 31.12.12	(1,400)
	80,150
Less: Used in 12 month carry back	
– 9 months (p/e 31.12.11)	(13,750)
	66,400
– Three months only (y/e 31.3.11)	
Maximum (3/12 × £28,800)	(7,200)
Available to carry forward	59,200
Less: Used against first available future	(20,000)
tax adjusted trading profit (y/e 31.12.13)	
Loss carried forward at 31.12.13	39,200

Test your understanding 3

Brown Ltd

Taxable total profit computations

	y/e 31.3.09	y/e 31.3.10	y/e 31.3.11	9 m/e 31.12.11	y/e 31.12.12
	£	£	£	£	£
Tax adjusted trading profit	450,000	87,000	240,000	45,000	Nil
Interest income	9,000	3,000	6,000	1,500	1,500
Chargeable gain	7,500	–	–	–	–
Total profits	466,500	90,000	246,000	46,500	1,500
Less: Loss relief					
– Current year					(1,500)
– Terminal loss	(116,625)	(90,000)	(246,000)	(46,500)	
	349,875	Nil	Nil	Nil	Nil
Less: QCD relief	(30,000)	Wasted	Wasted	Wasted	Wasted
TTP	319,875	Nil	Nil	Nil	Nil

Loss memorandum

	£
Tax adjusted trading loss of final 12 months of trading	525,000
Less: Used in current year – y/e 31.12.12	(1,500)
	523,500
Less: Used in Terminal loss carry back (LIFO):	
9 months to 31.12.11	(46,500)
12 months to 31.3.11	(246,000)
12 months to 31.3.10	(90,000)
3 months of y/e 31.3.09 (3/12 × £466,500)	(116,625)
Balance of loss = lost	24,375

Test your understanding 4

Comfy Ltd

Taxable total profit computations

Year ended 31 December:	2010 £	2011 £	2012 £
Tax adjusted trading profit	12,450	Nil	4,000
Less: Loss relief b/f	–	–	(Nil)
	12,450	Nil	4,000
Property income	2,000	1,800	–
Interest income	1,000	600	1,000
Total profits	15,450	2,400	5,000
Less: Property business loss (W2)			(500)
Less: Loss relief			
– Current year (W1)		(2,400)	
– 12 month carry back	(12,100)		
	3,350	Nil	4,500
Less: QCD relief	(400)	Wasted	(400)
TTP	2,950	Nil	4,100

Workings

(W1) Trading loss

	£
Trading loss – y/e 31.12.11	14,500
Less: Used in current year – y/e 31.12.11	(2,400)
Used in 12 month carry back – 31.12.10	(12,100)
Carry forward at 31 December 2011	Nil

(W2) Property business loss

	£
Loss in y/e 31 December 2012	500
Less: Used in current year – y/e 31 December 2012	(500)
Carry forward at 31 December 2012	Nil

Test your understanding 5

Coriander Ltd

Taxable total profit computations

Year ended 31 December:	2010 £	2011 £	2012 £
Tax adjusted trading profit	37,450	Nil	20,000
Less: Loss relief b/f	–	–	(20,000)
	37,450	Nil	Nil
Interest income	1,300	1,400	1,600
Chargeable gains (£13,000 – £6,000 b/f)	Nil	Nil	7,000
Total profits	38,750	1,400	8,600
Less: Loss relief			
– Current year		(1,400)	
– 12 month carry back	(38,750)		
	Nil	Nil	8,600
Less: QCD relief	Wasted	Wasted	(3,000)
TTP	Nil	Nil	5,600
Gift Aid = unrelieved	3,000	3,000	

Loss memorandum

	£
Loss in y/e 31 December 2011	81,550
Less: Used in current period	(1,400)
Less: Used in 12 month carry back – y/e 31 December 2010	(38,750)
Loss relief to carry forward	41,400
Less: Used in y/e 31 December 2012	(20,000)
Carry forward at 31 December 2012	21,400

Test your understanding 6

Eagle Ltd

(a) **Tax adjusted trading loss for the y/e 31 March 2013**

	£
Trading loss before capital allowances	(279,873)
Capital allowances	
– Plant and machinery (W1)	(40,127)
Tax adjusted trading loss	(320,000)

Working: Capital allowances computation

	£	General pool £	Allowances £
TWDV b/f		64,700	
Additions:			
No AIA or FYA:			
Car		11,300	
With AIA:			
Lorry	32,400		
Equipment	13,040		
	45,440		
Less: AIA (Maximum)	(25,000)		25,000
		20,440	
Disposal		(12,400)	
		84,040	
Less: WDA (18%)		(15,127)	15,127
TWDV c/f		68,913	
Total allowances			40,127

(b) **Corporation tax computations**

Period ended:	30.9.11	31.3.12	31.3.13
	£	£	£
Tax adjusted trading profit	137,900	52,000	Nil
Property income (W1)	–	18,700	49,950
Chargeable gains (W3)	–	9,300	95,495
Total profits	137,900	80,000	145,445
Less: Property loss (W2) (Note 1)	(4,600)	–	–
	133,300	80,000	145,445
Less: Loss relief			
– Current year (W4)			(145,445)
– 12 month carry back (W4)	(66,650)	(80,000)	
	66,650	Nil	Nil
Less: QCD relief (Note 2)	(2,300)	Wasted	Wasted
TTP	64,350	Nil	Nil

Notes:

(1) A property business loss is set off automatically against total profits of the same period and takes priority over relief for trading losses.

(2) All charitable donations made by a company, whether under the Gift Aid scheme or not, are tax allowable.

Workings:

(W1) The property business profit for the y/e 31 March 2013:

	£
Premium received	50,000
Less: £50,000 × 2% × (8 – 1)	(7,000)
(see alternative calculation)	43,000
Rent receivable	
– Warehouse 1 (£12,600 × 9/12)	9,450
– Warehouse 2 (£8,400 × 9/12)	6,300
– Irrecoverable debt (£8,400 × 3/12)	(2,100)
	56,650
Repairs to roof	(6,700)
Property income	49,950

Alternative calculation of assessment on premium received
= P x (51 – n) / 50 = £50,000 × (51 – 8) / 50 = £43,000

(W2) **Property loss**

The property business loss in the year ended 30 September 2011 is set off against total income of that period in priority to utilising the trading loss.

(W3) **Chargeable gains**

The capital loss of the year ended 30 September 2011 is carried forward and set against the chargeable gain in the following period.

Chargeable gain in p/e 31 March 2012
= (£18,200 – £8,900) = £9,300

The chargeable gain in y/e 31 March 2013 is calculated as follows:

	£
Sale proceeds	257,250
Less: Cost	(112,800)
Unindexed gain	144,450
Less: Indexation allowance	(48,955)
Chargeable gain	95,495

(W4) Loss relief

	£
Loss in y/e 31.3.13	320,000
Less: Used in current year	(145,445)
Used in 12 month carry back – p/e 31.3.12	(80,000)
	94,555
y/e 30.9.11 (restricted) Max (£133,300 × 6/12)	(66,650)
Loss available to carry forward	27,905

Note: The QCDs paid in the periods ending 31 March 2012 and 2013 are unrelieved.

(c) Alternative ways to relieve loss

The claim against total profits need not be made. The total loss can be carried forward against future trading profits of the same trade.

The claim against total profits could be restricted to just a current year claim in the year ended 31 March 2013 and no carry back. The balance of the loss can be carried forward.

Groups of companies

Chapter learning objectives

Upon completion of this chapter you will be able to:

- define an associated company

- identify associated companies from information provided

- determine the effect of associated companies for corporation tax

- define a 75% group for group loss relief

- identify the members of a 75% group relief group from information provided

- explain and apply the rules for allowing surrender of losses between 75% group relief companies

- identify the key factors in using group losses to minimise corporation tax liabilities for the group

- define a 75% group for capital gains purposes

- identify a capital gains group from information provided

- explain and apply the reliefs available on capital transactions in a 75% capital gains group to minimise corporation tax liabilities.

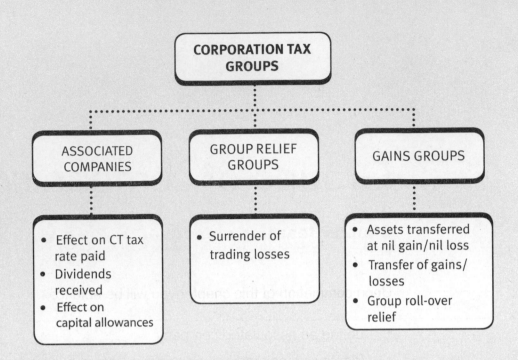

Introduction

This chapter deals with the tax position of groups of companies (i.e. where a company controls another company).

For corporation tax purposes, each company within the group is treated as a separate entity and is required to submit its own tax return, based on its individual results.

Being a member of a group however, has further corporation tax implications.

This chapter sets out the corporation tax implications of:

* associated companies

* groups for group relief purposes

* capital gains groups.

Groups may be examined as part of Question 2, or they could be examined in Question 4 or 5.

1 Associated companies

Definition

Two companies are 'associated' with each other if either:

- one of the companies is under the 'control' of the other; or
- they are both under the 'control' of the same person or persons (which can be a company, an individual or a partnership).

'Control' broadly means ownership of more than 50% of the company's issued ordinary share capital.

Control
For tax purposes 'control' means: - ownership of over 50% of issued share capital, or   - holding over 50% of the voting rights, or   - entitlement to over 50% of the company's distributable income, or   - entitlement to over 50% of the company's net assets, if the company were to wind up.

Points to note:

- Remember to include the parent company in the number of associated companies in the group
- Companies that are associated for only part of an accounting period are deemed to be associated for the whole of the accounting period.
- Both UK resident and overseas resident companies are included.
- Dormant companies are excluded.

Questions in the exam may require you to:

- identify the number of associated companies in a group, or
- could give the number of associated companies and ask you to justify the number.

Answers must explain why companies are included and excluded.

Example 1 – Associated companies

A Ltd is the holding company for a group of four companies. The relationships between the companies in the group, are shown below:

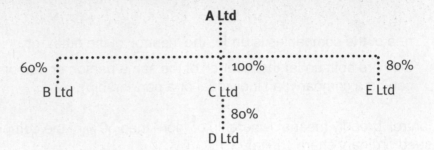

All of the companies are UK resident except for E Ltd, which is resident outside the UK and all its trading activities are conducted outside the UK. All of the companies have 31 December year ends.

B Ltd is a dormant company. D Ltd was bought by C Ltd on 1 July 2012.

State how many companies are associated for tax purposes in the y/e 31 December 2012.

Answer to example 1

A Ltd is associated with:

- C Ltd (owns more than 50%).

- D Ltd (bought by C Ltd in the year, associated for the whole year).

- E Ltd (even though it is resident overseas).

A Ltd is not associated with B Ltd, as it is a dormant company.

Therefore, there are four associated companies in the y/e 31 December 2012.

KAPLAN PUBLISHING

Test your understanding 1

W Ltd group has the following structure:

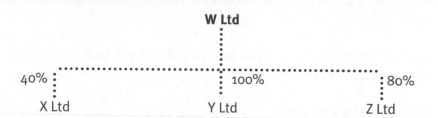

All of the companies are UK resident except for Y Ltd, which is resident outside the UK and all its trading activities are conducted outside the UK. All the companies have 31 December year ends.

Z Ltd is a dormant company. X Ltd was bought on 1 December 2012.

State how many companies are associated for tax purposes, in the y/e 31 December 2012.

Implications of being associated

The tax implications of being associated are:

- The upper and lower limits, used to determine the rate of corporation tax, are divided by the number of associated companies.

- Intra-group dividends (both UK and overseas) are not treated as franked investment income, for the purposes of calculating the company's augmented profits.

- Only one annual investment allowance (maximum £25,000 p.a.) is available for the group.

Tax rate

The identification of the number of associated companies, is the starting point for every 'group question', as this establishes:

- the applicable lower and upper limit for each company, and therefore

- the rate of corporation tax applicable to each company.

Note that if marginal relief applies; use the revised upper limit in the marginal relief calculation.

Example 2 – Associated companies

A Ltd, in Example 1, has tax adjusted trading profits for the y/e 31 December 2012 of £750,000. A Ltd had no dividend income during the year.

Calculate the corporation tax payable by A Ltd, for the y/e 31 December 2012.

Answer to example 2

There are four associated companies in the group.

Therefore, the corporation tax rate limits are as follows:

Upper limit: £1,500,000 ÷ 4 = £375,000.
Lower Limit: £300,000 ÷ 4 = £75,000.

A Ltd's augmented profits exceed the revised upper limit and therefore, it will pay corporation tax at the main rate.

A Ltd has a 31 December 2012 year end which straddles 31 March 2012. Therefore a two-part calculation of the corporation tax liability is required.

Corporation tax	£
FY2011 (£750,000 x 26% x 3/12)	48,750
FY2012 (£750,000 x 24% x 9/12)	135,000
	183,750

Test your understanding 2

Cob Ltd prepares accounts for the y/e 31 January 2013. On 1 February 2012, the company acquired 60% of the shares of a company, that is resident overseas. On 1 May 2012, it acquired 75% of the shares of a company, that is resident in the UK. Cob Ltd has held 10% of the shares in Bun Ltd for two years.

Cob Ltd has taxable total profits of £140,000, for the y/e 31 January 2013, and also received franked investment income of £10,000 from Bun Ltd during the year.

Calculate Cob Ltd's corporation tax payable for the y/e 31 January 2013.

Dividends

- Dividends received by UK companies from other companies (UK or overseas) are not taxable.

- Normally they are grossed up by 100/90 and included as franked investment income (FII), when calculating the company's augmented profits. The company's augmented profits then determine the rate of corporation tax payable.

- Dividends received from associated companies however, do not form part of FII.

Example 3 – Associated companies

Holly Ltd is the parent company of two wholly owned subsidiaries, Berry Ltd and Sprig Ltd. It also owns shares (< 5% shareholdings) in a number of other companies.

Holly Ltd had the following income for the y/e 30 November 2012:

	£
Tax adjusted trading profit	300,000
Interest income	50,000
Dividends received from Berry Ltd	60,000
Dividends received from Sprig Ltd	34,000
Dividends received from other UK companies	45,000

Calculate the corporation tax payable by Holly Ltd, for the y/e 30 November 2012.

Answer to example 3

Corporation tax computation – y/e 30 November 2012

	£
Tax adjusted trading income	300,000
Interest income	50,000
TTP	350,000

Corporation tax liability

	£	£
FY2011		
(£350,000 x 26% x 4/12)	30,333	
Less: Marginal relief		
3/200 x (£500,000 – £400,000) x £350,000/£400,000 x 4/12	(437)	
		29,896
FY2012		
(£350,000 x 24% x 8/12)	56,000	
Less: Marginal relief		
1/100 x (£500,000 – £400,000) x £350,000/£400,000 x 8/12	(583)	
		55,417
Corporation tax payable		85,313

Workings: Rate of tax

Holly Ltd has 2 associates and therefore, the limits for determining the corporation tax rate must be divided by 3, as follows:

Upper limit: £1,500,000 ÷ 3 = £500,000
Lower limit: £300,000 ÷ 3 = £100,000

	£
TTP	350,000
Plus: FII (£45,000 × 100/90) (Note)	50,000
Augmented profits	400,000

Therefore, Holly Ltd is a marginal relief company.

KAPLAN PUBLISHING

> **Note**
>
> - Dividends received are not taxable; therefore not included in TTP.
>
> - Only dividends received from non-associated companies, are included as FII.
>
> - As the y/e 30 November 2012 falls into FY2011 (4 months) and into FY2012 (8 months); a two-part calculation for corporation tax payable is required.

Test your understanding 3

Bill Ltd is the parent company of one wholly owned subsidiary, Ben Ltd. It also owns small shareholdings in other UK companies, each being an interest of 1% or less.

Bill Ltd had the following income for the y/e 31 August 2012:

	£
Tax adjusted trading profit	380,000
Interest income	25,000
Dividends from Ben Ltd	60,000
Dividends from other UK companies	76,500

Calculate the corporation tax payable by Bill Ltd, for the y/e 31 August 2012.

The annual investment allowance

For capital allowance purposes, only one AIA is available to a group of companies, therefore if there are associated companies, the allocation of the AIA between the group members will need to be considered.

When allocating the AIA, the group members can allocate the maximum £25,000 AIA in any way across the group.

It does not have to be divided equally between them.

2 Group relief group

Group loss relief is available to members of a 75% group relief group.

Losses of one member of the group can be surrendered to other group companies, to utilise against their own taxable total profits.

Definition of a 75% group relief group

- Two companies are members of a 75% group relief group where:
    - one company is the 75% subsidiary of the other, or
    - both companies are 75% subsidiaries of a third company.

- One company is a 75% subsidiary of another if:
    - at least 75% of its ordinary share capital is owned directly or indirectly by the other company, and
    - it has the right to 75% or more of distributable profits, and
    - it has the right to 75% or more of net assets on a winding up.

- For sub-subsidiaries to be in a group, the holding company must have an effective interest in the sub-subsidiary of at least 75%.

- Groups can be created through companies resident overseas.

- However, the companies actually claiming/ surrendering group relief must be resident in the UK.

Example 4 – 75% group relief group

The following information relates to the Holding Ltd group:

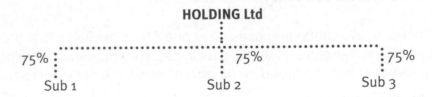

State which companies form a group for group relief purposes.

Answer to example 4

Holding Ltd has a 75% direct holding in Sub 1, Sub 2 and Sub 3 and therefore, all four companies are part of a 75% group for group relief purposes.

Example 5 – 75% group relief group

Beef Ltd owns 75% of Lamb Ltd. Lamb Ltd owns 75% of Bacon Ltd.

State which companies form a group for group relief purposes.

Answer to example 5

Beef Ltd and Lamb Ltd form a group as Beef Ltd directly owns 75% of Lamb Ltd.

Bacon Ltd does not belong to the same group relief group as Beef Ltd, as Beef Ltd only indirectly owns (75% × 75%) = 56.25%.

However, as Lamb Ltd directly owns 75% of Bacon Ltd, they will form a separate group relief group.

Therefore, there will be two group relief groups:

- Beef Ltd and Lamb Ltd.
- Lamb Ltd and Bacon Ltd.

Test your understanding 4

Toast Ltd owns:
- 75% of Honey Ltd.
- 100% of Marmalade Ltd.
- 65% of Jam Ltd.

Honey Ltd owns 75% of Butter Ltd.
Marmalade Ltd owns 75% of Crumpet Ltd.

State which companies form a group for group relief purposes.

Implications of being in a group relief group

Where a group of companies form a group relief group:

- Losses of one group company may be surrendered to other companies in the group.

- The recipient company can then relieve the losses against its own taxable total profits.

A loss may be surrendered by any member company to any other member of the same group, provided they are UK resident.

Example 6 – 75% group relief group

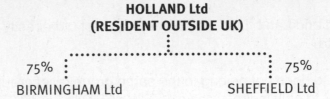

HOLLAND Ltd
(RESIDENT OUTSIDE UK)

75%   75%

BIRMINGHAM Ltd   SHEFFIELD Ltd

Birmingham Ltd and Sheffield Ltd are both UK resident companies.

State which companies form a group for group relief purposes and between which companies losses can be transferred.

Answer to example 6

Birmingham Ltd and Sheffield Ltd are within a 75% group, as both companies are 75% subsidiaries of Holland Ltd. Remember, that non-UK resident companies can be used to establish a group relief group.

Birmingham Ltd and Sheffield Ltd can therefore transfer losses between each other (i.e. Birmingham Ltd to Sheffield Ltd or vice versa).

Losses cannot be transferred to or from Holland Ltd, as the company is resident outside of the UK.

Test your understanding 5

GROUP 1	GROUP 2
HOLDING Ltd	HOLDING Ltd
90% ⋮	80% ⋮
Sub 1 Ltd	Sub 1 Ltd
90% ⋮	80% ⋮
Sub 2 Ltd	Sub 2 Ltd

From the above structures, identify which companies form a group for group relief purposes and between which companies losses can be transferred, assuming they are all UK resident.

Mechanics of group relief

- Companies which form part of the same group relief group can transfer losses between each other.

- The surrendering company is the company that surrenders its loss.

- The claimant company is the company to which the loss is surrendered.

- The losses which may be surrendered are:
  - trading losses
  - **unrelieved** QCDs
  - **unrelieved** property business losses.

- Only **current period** losses are available for group relief.

- Unrelieved QCDs should be surrendered before unrelieved property business losses.

- Capital losses cannot be surrendered to group companies under these rules (i.e. cannot be 'group relieved'). See section 3 for the transfer of capital losses.

The surrendering company

- The surrendering company may surrender **any amount** of its current period losses.

- There is no requirement for the surrendering company to relieve the loss against its own profits first.

The claimant company

- Offsets the loss against taxable total profits of its corresponding accounting period.

- The surrendering company may surrender any amount of its eligible loss. However, the maximum group loss relief that can be accepted by the claimant company is:

	£
Total profits per corporation tax computation	X
Less: Current year losses	(X)
Less: QCD relief	(X)
Maximum group loss relief that can be accepted	X

- Note that the maximum group loss relief that can be accepted by the claimant company is its total profits (after QCDs), assuming that losses brought forward and current year losses are offset first.

  This is usually the TTP of the claimant company, as brought forward trading losses must be offset as much as possible against trading profits in the year and a current year loss claim is often claimed.

  However, the current year loss claim is optional. Therefore, even if the current year loss claim is not made, an assumed claim must still be deducted to calculate the maximum group loss relief that the claimant company can accept.

- Group relief is deducted from TTP (i.e. **after** QCDs) in the claimant company's corporation tax computation.

Claim for group relief

The claim for group relief:

- is made by the claimant company on their corporation tax return

- within two years of the end of their CAP

- but requires a notice of consent from the surrendering company.

Test your understanding 6

Red Ltd has trading losses for the year to 31 December 2012, of £65,000. It has brought forward trading losses of £12,000.

Red Ltd owns 85% of Pink Ltd.

Pink Ltd has tax adjusted trading profits of £85,000, for the year to 31 December 2012. It has brought forward trading losses of £35,000 and brought forward capital losses of £5,000.

Show the maximum amount of group relief available in the year to 31 December 2012 and state the amount of any unrelieved losses.

Corresponding accounting periods

Losses surrendered by group relief, must be set against the claimant company's profits of a 'corresponding' accounting period as follows:

- A corresponding accounting period is any accounting period falling wholly or partly within the surrendering company's accounting period.

- Where the companies do not have coterminous (same) year ends, the available profits and losses must be time apportioned, to find the relevant amounts falling within the corresponding accounting period.

- In this situation, the maximum 'loss' that can be surrendered = lower of:

	£
(a) 'loss' in the surrendering (loss making) company for the corresponding accounting period, and	X
(b) 'taxable total profits' in the claimant company for the corresponding accounting period	X

Example 7 – 75% group relief group

Sugar Ltd incurs a trading loss of £27,000, in its nine months accounting period to 31 March 2013.

The taxable total profits of Cup Ltd are £24,000 and £38,000 for the 12 months accounting periods to 30 September 2012 and 2013 respectively.

State the maximum amount of group relief which Cup Ltd can claim from Sugar Ltd, for the two accounting periods to 30 September 2013.

Answer to example 7

As the companies have non-coterminous year ends, firstly identify the corresponding accounting periods:

- 9 m/e 31.3.13 and y/e 30.9.12:

  The corresponding accounting period is 1 July 2012 to 30 September 2012 (i.e. three months).

- 9 m/e 31.3.13 and y/e 30.9.13:

  The corresponding accounting period is 1 October 2012 to 31 March 2013 (i.e. six months).

Cup Ltd can therefore claim the following group relief:

CAP to 30.9.12

			£
Sugar Ltd	can surrender	3/9 × £27,000 loss	9,000
Cup Ltd	can claim	3/12 × £24,000	6,000

Therefore maximum loss claim is £6,000.

CAP to 30.9.13

			£
Sugar Ltd	can surrender	6/9 × £27,000 loss	18,000
Cup Ltd	can claim	6/12 × £38,000	19,000

Therefore maximum loss claim is £18,000.

Test your understanding 7

White Ltd and Black Ltd are in a group relief group and had the following recent results:

	£
White Ltd – trading loss for the y/e 30 June 2013	(24,000)
Black Ltd – taxable total profits:	
Y/e 30 September 2012	36,000
Y/e 30 September 2013	20,000

Explain the amount of group relief Black Ltd can claim from White Ltd, for the two accounting periods ended September 2013.

Companies joining / leaving the 75% group

If a company joins or leaves a group, group relief is only available for the 'corresponding accounting period' (i.e. when both companies have been a member of the same group).

The profits and losses are therefore time apportioned (as above) to calculate the maximum group relief available.

However, an alternative method of allocating the loss can be used, with agreement of HMRC, where it would be unjust or unreasonable to use time apportionment.

Always use time apportionment in the exam unless the question refers to an alternative method to be used.

Payment for group relief

If the claimant company pays the surrendering company for the group relief, the payment is ignored for corporation tax purposes:

* it is not tax allowable in the claimant company's computation, and
* it is not taxable income in the surrendering company's computation.

Tax loss planning

The following points should be considered, when deciding how to offset a trading loss which arises within a 75% group relief group company:

* Whether the loss should be surrendered.
* Order of surrender.

Choosing whether to surrender

A group member with a loss has the choice of:

* making a claim against its own profits, and / or
* surrendering some / all of the loss to another group member, and / or
* not claiming the maximum capital allowances to restrict the loss arising in the current period.

Remember that:

* Unlike utilising your own losses (which is **"all or nothing"**), group relief is very flexible.
* It is possible to specify the amount of loss to be surrendered within a group – which can be **any amount up to the maximum amount**
* The surrendering company may however claim both group relief and utilise some of its own losses, as it can restrict the group relief claim to ensure that it retains sufficient losses itself in order to bring its own augmented profits down to the small profits rate lower limit

In choosing the best option for losses, consideration should be given to:

- the rate of tax saved

- the cash flow position (a claim to carry back the loss could lead to a repayment of tax)

- not claiming the maximum capital allowances available.

Order of surrender

Losses should be surrendered in the following order, in order to save the maximum amount of tax:

(1) To companies that are subject to a marginal tax rate of 25% in FY2012, 27.5% in FY2011 and 29.75% in FY2010 (see Chapter 21), to bring their profits down to the 'small profits rate limit'

(2) To companies that are subject to the main tax rate of 24% in FY2012, 26% in FY2011 and 28% in FY2010, to bring their profits down to the small profits rate limit.

(3) To companies that are subject to tax at the small profits rate of 20% in FY2012 and FY2011, and 21% in FY2010.

Remember, that the upper and lower limits that determine the rate of tax, will be adjusted for the number of associated companies.

Example 8 – 75% group relief group

A Ltd has four wholly owned subsidiaries, B Ltd, C Ltd, D Ltd and E Ltd.

The group companies had the following tax adjusted trading results for the year ended 31 March 2013.

		£
A Ltd	Loss	(100,000)
B Ltd	Profit	20,000
C Ltd	Profit	83,000
D Ltd	Profit	96,000
E Ltd	Profit	375,000

None of the companies received any dividends in the year or had any other income or gains.

Calculate the corporation tax payable by each of the companies:

(a) **if no election for group relief is made**

(b) **if an election for group relief is made, on the assumption that the loss is allocated in such a manner as to save the maximum amount of tax.**

Answer to example 8

(a) **If no group relief**

Calculate the upper and lower limits and calculate the tax payable by each company, assuming no election for group relief is made.

Upper limit £1,500,000 ÷ 5 = £300,000
Lower limit £300,000 ÷ 5 = £60,000

	A Ltd	B Ltd	C Ltd	D Ltd	E Ltd
	£	£	£	£	£
Taxable total profits	Nil	20,000	83,000	96,000	375,000
Corporation tax					
at 20%		4,000			
at 24%			19,920	23,040	90,000
Less: Marginal relief					
1/100 × (£300,000 – £83,000)			(2,170)		
1/100 × (£300,000 – £96,000)				(2,040)	
Corporation tax liability	Nil	4,000	17,750	21,000	90,000

(b) **With group relief**

In order to save the maximum amount of tax, the loss of A Ltd, should be allocated as follows:

– First to companies paying tax at the marginal rate of 25%, so as to bring their profits down to the lower limit (i.e. to those companies with profits in the marginal rate relief band).

– Then surrender to companies paying tax at 24%.

– Any remaining loss should be surrendered to companies paying tax at the small profits rate of 20%.

– Remember the upper and lower limits have been revised for the number of associated companies.

Accordingly, the loss is first surrendered to C Ltd and D Ltd to bring their profits down to £60,000 (revised lower limit), the balance of the loss is surrendered to E Ltd.

	A Ltd £	B Ltd £	C Ltd £	D Ltd £	E Ltd £
TTP	Nil	20,000	83,000	96,000	375,000
Less: Group relief			(23,000)	(36,000)	(41,000)
TTP after group relief	Nil	20,000	60,000	60,000	334,000
Corporation tax @Nil/20%/20%/20%/24%	Nil	4,000	12,000	12,000	80,160

Test your understanding 8

A Ltd is the holding company for a group of four companies. The relationships between the companies in the group, are shown in the diagram below:

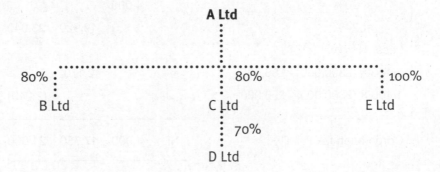

All of the companies are UK resident except for E Ltd, which is resident overseas and all its trading activities are conducted outside the UK.

All of the companies have an accounting year ended 31 March 2013 and their income/(losses) for this year, were as follows:

	Tax adjusted trading profit/(loss) £	Bank interest (non-trade) £
A Ltd	100,000	–
B Ltd	110,000	15,000
C Ltd	(110,000)	12,000
D Ltd	(25,000)	–
E Ltd	15,000	–

On the assumption that the most efficient use is made by the group of any trading losses, compute the corporation tax payable by each UK resident company.

3 75% capital gains group

Special capital gains advantages are available to members of a capital gains group. They enable:

- assets to be transferred tax efficiently around the group

- the efficient use of capital losses within the group

- the advantages of roll-over relief to be maximised.

Definition of a 75% capital gains group

- A capital gains group comprises of the parent company and its 75% (direct or indirect) subsidiaries and also, the 75% subsidiaries of the first subsidiaries and so on.

- The parent company must have an effective interest of over 50%, in ALL companies.

- A company which is a 75% subsidiary, cannot itself be a 'parent company' and form a separate gains group.

- While applying the 75% test, the shares held by overseas companies can be taken into account. Non-UK resident companies, however, cannot take advantage of the special reliefs available to UK resident members.

- The 75% requirement only applies to the ordinary share capital.

It is important to note that the definition of a gains group is different from that for a group relief group. It is essential to learn the different definitions.

Test your understanding 9

The A Ltd group consists of the following companies:

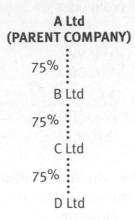

**A Ltd
(PARENT COMPANY)**

75%

B Ltd

75%

C Ltd

75%

D Ltd

(a) **State which companies form a capital gains group.**

(b) **State which companies form a group relief group.**

Implications of being in a 75% capital gains group

The reliefs that are available to members of a 75% capital gains group are:

(1) Assets are transferred at nil gain/nil loss.

(2) Capital gains and capital losses can be transferred around the group.

(3) Roll-over relief is available on a group basis.

Transfer of assets within a group

- Assets transferred within a gains group are automatically transferred at nil gain / nil loss (i.e. without a chargeable gain or allowable loss arising).

- The transfer is deemed to take place at a price that does not give rise to a gain or a loss (i.e. original cost plus indexation allowance to the date of the transfer).

- The transferor's deemed proceeds figure is also the deemed cost of the acquiring company.

- No claim is made – the treatment is automatic and mandatory.

- When the acquiring company sells the asset outside of the gains group, a chargeable gain/loss arises on the disposal in the normal way.

Example 9 – Inter group transfer then sale outside group

Green Ltd acquired an asset on 1 April 1993, for £100,000. The asset was transferred to Jade Ltd, a wholly owned subsidiary, on 1 October 2003, for £120,000, when the asset was worth £180,000.

On 1 December 2012, Jade Ltd sold the asset outside of the group for £350,000.

Calculate the chargeable gain, if any, arising on the transfer of the asset in October 2003 and the sale of the asset in December 2012.

Assume the RPIs as follows:

April 1993	140.6
October 2003	182.6
December 2012	248.2

Answer to example 9

Transfer of asset – October 2003

The transfer from Green Ltd to Jade Ltd, takes place at such a price that gives Green Ltd, no gain and no loss as follows:

	£
Cost	100,000
Plus: IA (April 1993 to October 2003)	
(182.6 – 140.6)/140.6 = 0.299 × £100,000	29,900
	———
Deemed proceeds	129,900
	———

Sale of asset – December 2012

When Jade Ltd sells the asset outside the group, its cost is deemed to be £129,900:

	£
Sale proceeds	350,000
Less: Deemed cost	(129,900)
	———
Unindexed gain	220,100
Less: IA (Oct 2003 to Dec 2012)	
(248.2 – 182.6)/182.6 = 0.359 × £129,900	(46,634)
	———
Chargeable gain	173,466
	———

The gain is chargeable on Jade Ltd; the company selling the asset.

Example 10 – Inter group transfer and sale outside group

Orange Ltd acquired an asset on 1 June 1995, for £80,000. The asset was transferred to Amber Ltd, a wholly owned subsidiary, on 1 September 2007, for £115,000, when the asset was worth £160,000.

On 21 November 2012, Amber Ltd sold the asset outside the group for £385,000.

Calculate the chargeable gain, if any, arising in September 2007 and November 2012.

Assume the following RPIs:

June 1995	149.8
September 2007	208.0
November 2012	247.3

Answer to example 10

Transfer of asset – September 2007

The transfer from Orange Ltd to Amber Ltd, takes place at such a price as gives Orange Ltd no gain and no loss as follows:

	£
Cost	80,000
Plus: IA (June 1995 to September 2007)	
(208.0 – 149.8)/149.8 = 0.389 x £80,000	31,120
	———
Deemed proceeds	111,120
	———

Sale of asset – November 2012

When Amber Ltd sells the asset outside the group, its cost is deemed to be £111,120:

	£
Sale proceeds	385,000
Less: Deemed cost	(111,120)
Unindexed gain	273,880
Less: IA (Sept 2007 to Nov 2012)	
(247.3 – 208.0)/208.0 = 0.189 x £111,120	(21,002)
Chargeable gain	252,878

The gain is chargeable in Amber Ltd; the company selling the asset.

Transfer of capital gains and losses

As shown above, assets can be transferred around a capital gains group with no tax cost (i.e. assets are transferred at nil gain/nil loss).

A company will typically transfer an asset in this way if the other group company wants to use the asset in its business.

However, it is also possible to elect to transfer capital gains / losses within a group without physically transferring the asset.

Election to transfer capital gains and losses

Members of capital gains groups can make a **joint election** to transfer capital gains or losses to any other company in the group.

As a result, a group can:

- plan to maximise the use of its capital losses as early as possible by matching chargeable gains with capital losses, and

- ensure gains crystallise in the company paying the lowest rate of tax,

- without having to make an actual transfer of an asset.

The joint election:

- is available provided both companies are members of the gains group at the time the gain or loss arose

- must be made within 2 years of the end of the accounting period, in which the asset is disposed of outside of the group

- must specify which company in the group is to be treated for tax purposes, as having disposed of the asset.

Note, however, that only **current year** capital gains or losses can be transferred, not brought forward losses.

Benefits of the joint transfer election

- As no actual transfer of assets is taking place within the gains group, there will be savings in legal and administrative costs.

- The two-year time limit for making the election, means that tax planning can be undertaken retrospectively.

- An election can apply to a specified portion of a disposal (i.e. effectively, part of a gain or loss can be transferred). This gives increased flexibility with tax planning.

Example 11 – 75% capital gains group

Red Ltd has brought forward capital losses of £60,000.

Its 100% subsidiary Blue Ltd, disposed of an asset on 15 June 2012, that resulted in a chargeable gain of £55,000.

Both companies prepare accounts to 31 March.

Explain how Red Ltd and Blue Ltd can make an election to minimise the tax payable for the y/e 31 March 2013.

KAPLAN PUBLISHING

Answer to example 11

The two companies can make a joint election to transfer Blue Ltd's gain to Red Ltd.

The election must be made by 31 March 2015 (i.e. two years after the year ended 31 March 2013). There is no need for the asset to actually be transferred from Blue Ltd to Red Ltd.

Red Ltd can then set off its capital losses brought forward against the chargeable gain arising on the disposal outside of the group.

Note that Red Ltd cannot transfer its capital losses to Blue Ltd as capital losses brought forward cannot be transferred around the group.

Test your understanding 10

In the accounting period to 31 March 2013, Alpha Ltd disposed of a chargeable asset which will result in a chargeable gain of £90,000.

Alpha Ltd also has a 80% subsidiary, Beta Ltd.

In the accounting period to 31 March 2013, Beta Ltd disposed of a chargeable asset, which resulted in a capital loss of £65,000.

Alpha Ltd and Beta Ltd are both UK resident companies.

Show how the tax liabilities of the Alpha Ltd group may be minimised.

Explain whether your advice would change if Beta Ltd also had £20,000 capital losses brought forward.

Group roll-over relief

Roll-over relief (ROR) is covered in detail in Chapters 16 and 20.

- Companies within a 75% gains group, are treated as if they form a single trade, for the purposes of roll-over relief.
- Roll-over relief can therefore be claimed, where:
  - one company within a gains group, disposes of an eligible asset and makes a gain, and
  - another company within the same gains group, acquires a replacement eligible asset.

Example 12 – 75% capital gains group

Cheese Ltd sold a factory for £600,000, in the year ended 31 December 2012. The original cost of the factory was £200,000 and indexation to the date of sale was £65,000.

Cheese Ltd owns 75% of Ham Ltd.

Ham Ltd bought a warehouse costing £750,000, in the year ended 31 December 2013.

(a) **Calculate the chargeable gain arising on the sale of the factory assuming all available reliefs are taken.**

(b) **Calculate the base cost of the warehouse.**

Answer to example 12

Gain on sale of factory for Cheese Ltd

	£
Proceeds	600,000
Less: Cost	(200,000)
Unindexed gain	400,000
Less: IA	(65,000)
Indexed gain	335,000
Less: ROR	(335,000)
Chargeable gain	Nil

Note: Full ROR is available, as all proceeds were reinvested by a member of the gains group, within the required time limit.

Base cost of the warehouse for Ham Ltd

	£
Original cost	750,000
Less: ROR	(335,000)
Base cost	415,000

KAPLAN PUBLISHING

4 Chapter summary

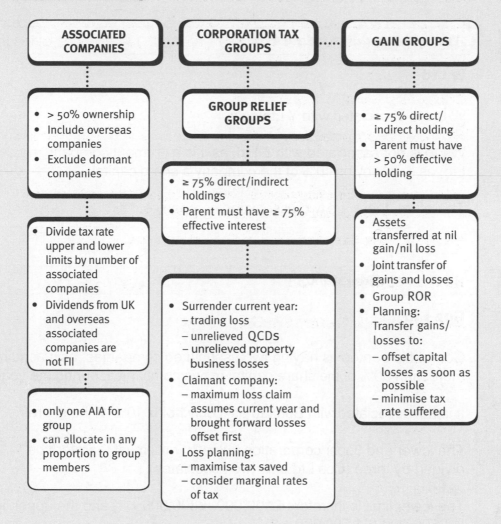

ASSOCIATED COMPANIES

- \> 50% ownership
- Include overseas companies
- Exclude dormant companies

- Divide tax rate upper and lower limits by number of associated companies
- Dividends from UK and overseas associated companies are not FII

- only one AIA for group
- can allocate in any proportion to group members

CORPORATION TAX GROUPS

GROUP RELIEF GROUPS

- ≥ 75% direct/indirect holdings
- Parent must have ≥ 75% effective interest

- Surrender current year:
  - trading loss
  - unrelieved QCDs
  - unrelieved property business losses
- Claimant company:
  - maximum loss claim assumes current year and brought forward losses offset first
- Loss planning:
  - maximise tax saved
  - consider marginal rates of tax

GAIN GROUPS

- ≥ 75% direct/ indirect holding
- Parent must have \> 50% effective holding

- Assets transferred at nil gain/nil loss
- Joint transfer of gains and losses
- Group ROR
- Planning: Transfer gains/ losses to:
  - offset capital losses as soon as possible
  - minimise tax rate suffered

Test your understanding answers

Test your understanding 1

W Ltd

W Ltd is associated with Y Ltd only.

W Ltd is not associated with Z Ltd, as it is a dormant company, nor X Ltd, as it only owns 40% of the company's share capital.

Therefore, there are two associated companies.

Test your understanding 2

Cob Ltd

Cob Ltd is treated as having two associated companies, as it acquired more than 50% of the share capital of two companies, during the year.

It is not associated with Bun Ltd as it only holds 10% of the shares.

The lower and upper corporation tax rate limits must therefore be divided by three (Cob Ltd plus two associates).

The lower limit is therefore £100,000 (£300,000 ÷ 3) and the upper limit is £500,000 (£1,500,000 ÷ 3).

Cob Ltd – year ended 31 January 2013

	£
TTP	140,000
Plus: FII	10,000
Augmented profits	150,000

The augmented profits of £150,000 lie between £100,000 and £500,000, so marginal relief applies.

As the year ended 31 January 2013 straddles 31 March 2012, a two-part corporation tax liability computation is required.

Corporation tax liability

	£	£
FY2011		
(£140,000 x 26% x 2/12)	6,067	
Less: Marginal relief		
3/200 × (£500,000 – £150,000) × £140,000/£150,000 x 2/12	(817)	
	———	
		5,250
FY2012		
(£140,000 x 24% x 10/12)	28,000	
Less: Marginal relief		
1/100 × (£500,000 – £150,000) × £140,000/£150,000 x 10/12	(2,722)	
	———	25,278
		———
Corporation tax payable		30,528
		———

Note: The revised upper limit is used in the marginal relief calculation.

Test your understanding 3

Bill Ltd

Corporation tax computation – y/e 31 August 2012

	£
Tax adjusted trading profits	380,000
Interest income	25,000
TTP	405,000

Corporation tax liability

	£	£
FY2011		
(£405,000 x 26% x 7/12)	61,425	
Less: Marginal relief		
3/200 × (£750,000 – £490,000) × £405,000/£490,000 × 7/12	(1,880)	
		59,545
FY2012		
(£405,000 x 24% x 5/12)	40,500	
Less: Marginal relief		
1/100 × (£750,000 – £490,000) × £405,000/£490,000 × 5/12	(895)	
		39,605
Corporation tax payable		99,150

Working: Rate of tax

Bill Ltd has one associated company and therefore the limits for determining the corporation tax rate must be divided by 2:

Upper limit: £1,500,000 ÷ 2 = £750,000
Lower limit: £300,000 ÷ 2 = £150,000

Test your understanding 3

KAPLAN PUBLISHING

	£
TTP	405,000
Plus: FII (£76,500 × 100/90)	85,000
Augmented profits	490,000

Therefore, Bill Ltd is a marginal relief company.

Note that the year ended 31 August 2012 straddles 31 March 2012, therefore a two-part calculation of corporation tax payable required.

Test your understanding 4

Toast Ltd

Toast Ltd and all its direct 75% holdings:

- Honey Ltd.
- Marmalade Ltd.

Toast Ltd only own 65% of Jam Ltd, therefore, it does not form part of the group.

Also include any 75% indirect holdings of Toast Ltd:

- Crumpet Ltd
  (Toast Ltd indirectly holds (100% × 75%) = 75% of Crumpet Ltd).

Note: Butter Ltd is not included, as Toast Ltd only indirectly holds
(75% × 75% = 56.25%)

Honey Ltd owns 75% of Butter Ltd, so they will form a second group relief group.

Therefore, there are two groups:

- Toast Ltd, Honey Ltd, Marmalade Ltd and Crumpet Ltd.
- Honey Ltd and Butter Ltd.

Test your understanding 5

Group 1

Holding Ltd (H), Sub 1 (S1) and Sub 2 (S2) are within a 75 % group.

The direct shareholding links between the group are all 75% and over.

In addition, Holding Ltd has an indirect shareholding in Sub 2 Ltd, of over 75% (90% × 90% = 81%).

Losses can be transferred from:

H to S1 and S2

S2 to S1 and H

S1 to H and S2.

Group 2

Holding Ltd (H) and Sub 1 are within a 75% group; Sub 1 and Sub 2 are within another 75% group.

Holding Ltd and Sub 2 are **not** within a 75% group **because** H's effective holding in Sub 2, is only 64% (80% × 80%).

Losses can be transferred between:

H to S1 or S1 to H,

S1 to S2 or S2 to S1

but not from H to S2 **or** S2 to H.

Test your understanding 6

Red Ltd

Maximum group relief, the lower of:

• Loss of Red Ltd	£65,000
• Maximum claim by Pink Ltd (W)	£50,000

Therefore, Red Ltd can group relieve £50,000 of its current year trading losses, to Pink Ltd.

Working: Maximum loss that can be accepted

	£
Tax adjusted trading profits	85,000
Less: Trading losses b/f	(35,000)
Maximum claim by Pink Ltd	50,000

Unrelieved losses

Red Ltd:

Assuming maximum group relief is claimed:

Red Ltd will have £15,000 of current year trading losses unrelieved. A current year or prior year claim, can be made to relieve these losses against total profits.

Alternatively, they will be carried forward against the first available future tax adjusted trading profits.

Red Ltd's trading losses b/f of £12,000, will continue to be carried forward and set against the first available tax adjusted trading profits.

Pink Ltd:

Pink Ltd's brought forward trading losses of £35,000, will be utilised in the year to 31 December 2012.

The company's capital losses b/f, will be carried forward and used against the first chargeable gains of the company.

Test your understanding 7

White Ltd and Black Ltd

Firstly, identify the corresponding accounting period:

- Y/e 30.9.12 and y/e 30.6.13:

    The corresponding accounting period is 1 July 2012 to 30 September 2012 (i.e. three months).

- Y/e 30.9.13 and y/e 30.6.13

    The corresponding accounting period is 1 October 2012 to 30 June 2013 (i.e. nine months).

Black Ltd can therefore claim the following group relief:

y/e 30 September 2012

			£
Black Ltd	can claim	(£36,000 × 3/12)	9,000
White Ltd	can surrender	(£24,000 × 3/12)	(6,000)

Black Ltd can claim group relief of £6,000 against its profits, for the y/e 30 September 2012.

y/e 30 September 2013

			£
Black Ltd	can claim	(£20,000 × 9/12)	15,000
White Ltd	can surrender	(£24,000 × 9/12)	(18,000)

Black Ltd can claim group relief of £15,000, against its profits for the y/e 30 September 2013.

Test your understanding 8

A Ltd

Associated companies

A Ltd controls more than 50% of B Ltd, C Ltd, D Ltd as well as E Ltd.

Therefore, including A Ltd, there are 5 associated companies in the group.

Note: Non-UK resident companies (i.e. E Ltd) are treated as associated companies.

Group relief group

A Ltd, B Ltd and C Ltd form a group of companies for group relief purposes.

D Ltd is not a group member, as it is not a 75% subsidiary.

E Ltd is non-UK resident and therefore, cannot participate in a group relief claim.

Corporation tax computations – y/e 31 March 2013

	A Ltd £	B Ltd £	C Ltd £	D Ltd £
Tax adjusted trading profit	100,000	110,000	Nil	Nil
Interest income	Nil	15,000	12,000	
Total profits	100,000	125,000	12,000	Nil
Less: Loss relief				
– Current year claim (W2)			(5,000)	
– Group relief (W2)	(40,000)	(65,000)		
TTP	60,000	60,000	7,000	Nil
CT @ 20%	12,000	12,000	1,400	Nil

Note: The trading loss of D Ltd (£25,000), can only be carried forward in D Ltd for set-off against its first available future tax adjusted trading profits as it is not a member of the group relief group.

Workings

(W1) Associated companies

There are five associated companies; therefore, the upper and lower limits applicable to each company are:

£1,500,000 ÷ 5 = £300,000 and £300,000 ÷ 5 = £60,000

The following would not be not required in the examination but is provided for you to understand the implications of the relevant limits applicable to each company.

When 'profits' are:	TTP charged
≤ £60,000	Small profits rate (20%)
> £60,000 and ≤ £300,000	Main rate less MR (25%)
> £300,000	Main rate (24%)

The loss of C Ltd, is utilised most efficiently by surrendering sufficient of the loss to A Ltd and B Ltd to reduce their profits to the lower limit of £60,000.

Relief for the loss will be at 25%. Any remaining loss can be relieved against C Ltd's other profits, where relief is obtained at 20%.

Note: Further loss relief to A Ltd or B Ltd would also save tax at 20%.

(W2) Utilisation of loss

Trading loss available in C Ltd and its efficient utilisation:

	£
Available loss in C Ltd	110,000
Utilisation: to A Ltd (Note)	(40,000)
to B Ltd (Note)	(65,000)
	5,000
in C Ltd	(5,000)
	Nil

Note: Loss given to bring the profits down to £60,000.

You could have surrendered to B Ltd first and then A Ltd. However, in total you want to surrender £105,000 of the loss, from C Ltd to A Ltd and B Ltd.

The following would not be required in the examination but is provided to aid your understanding

If C Ltd had used its own loss and not transferred any loss under group relief to A Ltd and B Ltd, then it would not have any TTP and the loss available to carry forward would have been £98,000 (£110,000 – £12,000).

	A Ltd £	B Ltd £	C Ltd £	D Ltd £
Tax adjusted trading profit	100,000	110,000	Nil	Nil
Interest income	Nil	15,000	12,000	
Total profits	100,000	125,000	12,000	
Less: Current year claim			(12,000)	
TTP	100,000	125,000	Nil	Nil

Note: TTP = Augmented profits

	A Ltd £	B Ltd £	C Ltd £	D Ltd £
Corporation tax				
£100,000/£125,000 @ 24%	24,000	30,000		
Less: MR				
1/100 × (£300,000 – £100,000)	(2,000)			
1/100 × (£300,000 – £125,000)		(1,750)		
Corporation tax payable	22,000	28,250	Nil	Nil

From the 'group' viewpoint, the total corporation tax (CT) payable, **without** making any claim for group loss relief, is **£50,250** (£22,000 + £28,250).

In our answer with group relief, the total CT payable was **£25,400** (£12,000 + £12,000 + £1,400).

We have allocated group relief as follows:

To A Ltd: £40,000 (to bring the TTP down to £60,000)

	£
CT of A Ltd (without group relief)	22,000
CT of A Ltd (with group relief)	(12,000)
Difference	10,000

This means that we have relieved the loss of £40,000 at an effective rate of 25% ((£10,000/£40,000) x 100).

To B Ltd: £65,000 (to bring the TTP down to £60,000)

	£
CT of B Ltd (without group relief)	28,250
CT of B Ltd (with group relief)	(12,000)
Difference	16,250

This means that we have relieved the loss of £65,000 at an effective rate of 25% ((£16,250/£65,000) x 100).

Note: In this question TTP = augmented profits, therefore the aim is to bring TTP down to the lower limit.

However, remember that if there is FII, the aim should be to bring the augmented profits (not TTP) down to the lower limit.

Test your understanding 9

A Ltd group

Gains group

- A Ltd, B Ltd and C Ltd are in a gains group, as there is 75% ownership at each level and A Ltd (the parent) owns more than 50% (75% × 75% = 56.25%) in C Ltd.

- A Ltd does not own more than 50% of D Ltd (75% × 75% × 75% = 42.19%) and therefore D Ltd does not form part of the gains group.

- C Ltd and D Ltd, cannot form a separate gains group, as C Ltd is part of the A Ltd gains group and cannot therefore, be itself a 'parent' company and form a separate gains group.

Group relief group

There are three group relief groups:

- A Ltd and B Ltd.
- B Ltd and C Ltd.
- C Ltd and D Ltd.

Remember that for a group relief group the parent company (A Ltd) must have an effective interest in all companies of at least 75%.

Test your understanding 10

Alpha Ltd

As the two companies satisfy the criteria of a gains group, they can make a joint election to either:

* transfer Beta Ltd's capital loss of £65,000 to Alpha Ltd, or
* transfer Alpha Ltd's capital gain of £90,000 to Beta Ltd.

In both instances, the capital loss will be set off against the chargeable gain, resulting in a net chargeable gain of £25,000, chargeable to corporation tax.

It is therefore possible to ensure that the gain of £25,000 is taxed in the company that is subject to the lower rate of corporation tax.

The time limit for making the election is 31 March 2015 (i.e. within two years from 31 March 2013).

If Beta Ltd also had £20,000 capital losses brought forward

* The advice concerning the transfer of the capital gain or loss above is still valid

* However, as the brought forward capital loss cannot be transferred, it would be preferable to ensure that at least net gains of £20,000 out of the £25,000 arises in Beta Ltd so that the capital losses brought forward can be utilised

* It is then possible to ensure that the remaining £5,000 (£25,000 − £20,000) gain should arise in the company paying the lower rate of tax.

Overseas issues for companies

Chapter learning objectives

Upon completion of this chapter you will be able to:

- explain the basis for charging overseas profits to UK corporation tax

- determine the amount of overseas chargeable profits

- explain the treatment of overseas dividends

- explain how relief is given for overseas tax suffered

- calculate double tax relief when withholding tax is suffered

- explain the purpose of the transfer pricing rules as they apply to transactions between a UK and an overseas company.

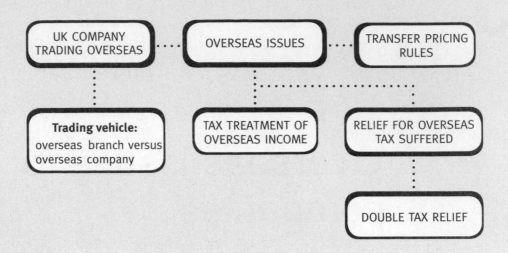

Introduction

Overseas aspects of corporation tax may be examined as part of Question 2, or it could be examined in Question 4 or 5 for 15 marks.

1 Overseas operations

Companies **resident** in the UK are chargeable to corporation tax on:

* all profits and chargeable gains
* wherever they arise (i.e. worldwide profits including gains).

Definition – residency

A company is resident in the UK if:

* it is incorporated in the UK, or
* it is 'centrally managed and controlled in the UK'.

A company which is incorporated in the UK or an overseas company which is centrally managed and controlled in the UK, will therefore be chargeable to UK corporation tax on their worldwide profits.

Overseas operations of a UK company

A UK resident company considering whether or not to set up an operation overseas must consider whether to operate through an overseas resident company or an overseas branch. Each set up has different tax implications.

Overseas resident company

To operate through an overseas resident company, the UK company must set up a separate legal entity abroad; separate from the UK company.

Accordingly, the tax implications of operating through an overseas resident company, are as follows:

- Profits of the overseas company are not taxed in the UK.
- Dividends paid to the UK parent company are exempt from UK corporation tax.
- If the overseas company is controlled (> 50% ownership) by the UK company:
    - it will be classed as an associated company, for the purposes of determining the rate of UK corporation tax payable by the UK company.
    - dividends received are not included as FII.
- If the overseas company is not controlled by the UK company (≤ 50% ownership):
    - dividends **received** are treated in the same way as UK dividends (i.e. grossed up at 100/90 and treated as FII).
    - note that if overseas tax has been suffered at source:
        - the dividend is **not** grossed up for overseas tax, and
        - there is no double taxation relief (DTR) (see section 2) as the dividends are exempt in the UK and therefore not taxed twice.

Note also that the following benefits are not available:

- No UK capital allowances on the overseas company's assets.
- No relief in the UK for losses incurred by the overseas company.

Overseas branch of a UK resident company

An overseas branch of a UK company is effectively an extension of the UK trade.

Accordingly, the tax implications of operating through an overseas branch, are as follows:

- 100% of the branch profits will be assessed to UK corporation tax. Whether profits are remitted to the UK is irrelevant.
- The branch profits will normally be taxed as UK trading profits.
- UK capital allowances are available on the branch's assets.

- Branch trading losses are eligible for UK loss relief, including group relief.

- UK trading losses can be offset against overseas branch profits.

Election to exempt profits of overseas branches

It is possible for a UK company to make an irrevocable election to exempt profits of its overseas permanent establishments (e.g. branches) from UK corporation tax.

If this exemption election is made, the tax treatment of overseas branches will be as follows:

- The profits of an overseas branch will be exempt in the UK.

- There will be no relief for branch losses in the UK.

- There will be no UK capital allowances available for plant and machinery used by the overseas branch.

- Capital gains arising in the overseas branch will not be subject to UK corporation tax.

- The overseas branch will still not affect the upper and lower limits for small profits rate purposes.

The exemption election:

- can be made at any time

- is effective from the start of the accounting period following that in which the election is made, and

- once made, applies to all overseas branches of that company.

It may therefore not be beneficial to make such an election where:

- the company has a loss-making branch, or anticipates that it may have losses in a branch overseas in the foreseeable future, and/or

- double taxation relief means that there is little or no corporation tax payable.

Overseas chargeable profits

- Profits from an overseas branch are normally taxed as UK trading profits, unless the exemption election is made.

- Dividends received from an overseas company are exempt, but will be FII if received from a non-associated company.

- Overseas rental income is assessed as property income and overseas interest as interest income.

Example 1 – Overseas operations

Probe plc, a UK resident company, has a tax adjusted trading profit of £1,400,000, for the y/e 31 March 2013.

The company has a 5% shareholding in Deep Inc, an overseas resident company. During the y/e 31 March 2013, Deep Inc paid a dividend of £360,000. This is after the deduction of overseas tax at the rate of 3%.

Calculate the augmented profits used to determine the rate of corporation tax paid by Probe plc for the y/e 31 March 2013.

Answer to example 1

Augmented profits computation – y/e 31 March 2013

	£
Tax adjusted trading profit = TTP	1,400,000
Plus: FII – Dividend from overseas company (£360,000 × 5% × 100/90) (Note)	20,000
Augmented profits to determine rate of tax	1,420,000

Note: Overseas dividends are not grossed up for any overseas tax suffered. The dividend **received** is grossed up by 100/90.

Test your understanding 1

Happy Ltd, a UK resident company, has tax adjusted trading profits of £1,650,000, for the y/e 31 December 2012.

The company has an 8% shareholding in Jolly Inc, an overseas resident company. During the year Jolly Inc paid a dividend to Happy Ltd of £31,500 (after the deduction of 22% overseas tax).

Calculate the augmented profits used to determine the rate of tax of Happy Ltd, for the y/e 31 December 2012.

2 Double tax relief (DTR)

- Overseas dividend income and, where the exemption election has been made, overseas branch profits, are exempt from UK corporation tax.

- However, overseas branch profits where the exemption election has not been made, rental income from abroad and foreign interest are all chargeable and may be subject to both overseas tax and UK corporation tax.

- In practice, relief for double taxation is usually given in accordance with formal double taxation treaties the UK has with most countries in the world.

- However, where no treaty agreement exists, relief for double taxation is given as a 'tax credit' to the UK resident company (known as 'unilateral relief').

- Many actual treaties the UK has with other countries also require relief to be given in this way.

- In the F6 examination, only 'unilateral relief' is examinable.

Relief for overseas tax suffered

Relief for overseas tax suffered is given as follows:

- The chargeable overseas income is included in the TTP computation **gross of overseas tax**.

- Double tax relief (DTR) is given for the overseas tax suffered by way of credit against the corporation tax liability.

- The amount of DTR is limited to the **lower** of:
  - the amount of overseas tax on the overseas income
  - the UK corporation tax payable on that overseas income.

Operation of DTR

DTR must be calculated on a 'source by source' basis, not a global basis.

Therefore, each source of overseas income, and its related overseas and UK tax liability, must be dealt with separately (i.e. if a company has chargeable overseas branch profits and overseas rental income, separate DTR calculations are needed).

Approach a question with different sources of overseas income as follows:

- Include overseas income inclusive of overseas taxes as part of TTP. Use a columnar layout to recognise each different overseas source of income.

- The overseas income is included as TTP and therefore, taxed at the appropriate UK rate.
- Deduct from the UK corporation tax liability, the **lower** of:
  - attributable UK corporation tax on overseas profits; and
  - overseas tax suffered.

Example 2 – Double tax relief

A Ltd, a UK resident company, has tax adjusted trading profits of £500,000, during the y/e 31 March 2013. Due to the number of associated companies in the A Ltd group, the company pays tax at the rate of 24%.

The company also had the following overseas income during the year:

- a dividend of £10,000 (gross) from ABC Inc. This has been taxed overseas at the rate of 20%. A Ltd has a 60% interest in ABC Inc.

- overseas branch profits of £10,000 (gross). These profits have been taxed overseas at the rate of 66%.

- overseas rental income of £7,000 (gross). This income was taxed overseas at the rate of 23%.

Calculate A Ltd's UK corporation tax liability, after double tax relief for the y/e 31 March 2013 assuming the exemption election for overseas branches

(a) **has not been made**

(b) **has been made.**

Answer to example 2

(a) **Assuming the exemption election has not been made**

	Total £	UK income £	Branch profits £	Rental income £
TTP	517,000	500,000	10,000	7,000
UK CT at 24% (Note)	124,080	120,000	2,400	1,680
Less: DTR – lower of				
(i) Branch profit:				
UK CT: £2,400 (above)	(2,400)		(2,400)	
Overseas tax (66% × £10,000) = £6,600				
(ii) Rental income				
UK CT: £1,680 (above)				
Overseas tax: (23% × £7,000) = £1,610	(1,610)			(1,610)
UK CT liability	120,070	120,000	Nil	70

Note: The overseas dividends are exempt from UK corporation tax. As A Ltd owns a controlling interest in AB Inc, the dividends are group income and not treated as FII.

(b) **Assuming the exemption election has been made**

	Total £	UK income £	Rental income £
TTP	507,000	500,000	7,000
UK CT at 24% (Note)	121,680	120,000	1,680
Less: DTR – lower of			
UK CT: £1,680 (above)			
Overseas tax: (23% × £7,000) = £1,610	(1,610)		(1,610)
UK CT liability	120,070	120,000	70

KAPLAN PUBLISHING

Note: In this case as the UK tax on the branch profits is fully offset by DTR, such that no UK tax is payable, the UK tax position is the same as if the branch exemption election had been made.

Overseas tax suffered

Overseas tax suffered on overseas income is called withholding tax (WHT).

WHT is any direct tax imposed at source by the overseas country.

Note that WHT can apply to any source of overseas income.

Example 3 – Double tax relief

Maxwell Ltd, a UK resident trading company, owns an overseas branch in Malawi. In addition it received rental income from renting a property in Spain and owns 8% of the share capital of Zulu Inc, an overseas resident company.

Maxwell Ltd also has a controlling interest in two other UK resident companies.

The following information relates to Maxwell Ltd's y/e 31 March 2013:

	£
Tax adjusted trading profits	490,000
Overseas income:	
Branch profits	
– after deduction of withholding tax of 30%	35,000
Rental income	
– after deduction of withholding tax of 5%	38,000
Dividend from Zulu Inc	
– after deduction of withholding tax of 19%	18,000

The exemption election has not been made in respect of the overseas branch profits.

Calculate the UK corporation tax payable for the above period by Maxwell Ltd, showing clearly your treatment of double taxation.

Answer to example 3

Corporation tax computation – y/e 31 March 2013

	Total £	UK income £	Branch profits £	Rental income £
Tax adjusted trading profit	490,000	490,000		
Overseas income (W1)	90,000		50,000	40,000
Total profits = TTP	580,000	490,000	50,000	40,000
Corporation tax				
(£580,000 @ 24%) (W2)	139,200	117,600	12,000	9,600
Less: DTR (W3)	(14,000)		(12,000)	(2,000)
CT payable	125,200	117,600	Nil	7,600

Note: Overseas dividends from Zulu Inc are exempt from UK corporation tax but are treated as FII.

Workings

(W1) Grossing up the overseas income

	Branch profits £	Rental income £
Income received	35,000	38,000
Add: WHT (30/70)/(5/95)	15,000	2,000
	50,000	40,000

KAPLAN PUBLISHING

(W2) Associated companies

There are 3 companies under common control, as Maxwell Ltd has a controlling interest in 2 other UK resident companies.

Zulu Inc is not an 'associated' company as Maxwell Ltd only has an 8% interest.

Limits for determining the tax rate:

£1,500,000 ÷ 3 = £500,000
£300,000 ÷ 3 = £100,000

	£
TTP	580,000
Plus: FII (£18,000 × 100/90) (Note)	20,000
Augmented profits	600,000

Therefore with augmented profits of £600,000, the main rate of 24% applies.

Note: Do not gross up the dividend received for overseas tax.

(W3) DTR relief

	Branch profits £	Rental income £
Lower of:		
(i) UK CT liability on overseas profits	12,000	9,600
(ii) Overseas taxes suffered	15,000	2,000
Lower amount	12,000	2,000

Test your understanding 2

London Ltd, a UK resident trading company, owns two overseas branches, one in Paris and one in Rome.

It also owns 4% of the share capital of Berlin GmbH, an overseas company and owns an overseas property from which it receives rental income.

London Ltd also has a controlling interest in three other UK resident companies.

The following information relates to London Ltd's y/e 31 March 2013:

	£
Tax adjusted trading profits	380,000
Overseas income:	
Paris branch profits	
– after deduction of withholding tax of 40%	54,000
Rome branch loss	(12,000)
Rental income	
– after deduction of withholding tax of 15%	43,435
Dividend from Berlin GmbH	
– After deduction of withholding tax of 27%	2,700

Compute London Ltd's UK corporation tax payable for the y/e 31 March 2013 assuming the overseas branch exemption election:

(a) **has not been made**

(b) **has been made.**

Summary

- Overseas income (excluding dividends and overseas branch profits where the exemption election has been made) is included gross of overseas tax in the corporation tax computation.

- The amount of DTR is limited to the lower of:
    - the amount of overseas tax on the overseas income
    - the UK corporation tax payable on that overseas income.

- DTR is calculated on a 'source by source' basis.

3 Transfer pricing

If a UK resident company has a 'controlling' interest in an overseas resident subsidiary, it might try to:

- sell goods to the subsidiary at an undervalue or overvalue, or
- buy goods from it at an overvalue or undervalue
- in order to manipulate where the profits should arise (i.e. in the UK or overseas).

The aim of these arrangements would be to move the profits to the country with the lowest corporation tax rate.

However, the transfer pricing rules prevent UK companies from charging artificial prices for goods and services in order to gain a tax advantage.

Transfer pricing – rules

- The basic rule for transfer pricing is that transactions between group members should be charged on an arms-length basis.
- An 'arms-length' price is what it could have been sold for to an independent third party dealing on commercial terms (e.g. market prices).
- For example, where sales are made to an overseas resident group company at an undervalue, then its true market price should be substituted for the transfer price.
- Under self-assessment rules, if transactions are not made on an arms-length basis, an adjustment to substitute arms-length prices should be made by the UK resident company in its corporation tax return.
- There are detailed rules for establishing which companies are within the scope of the transfer pricing rules, but the basic test is one of control.
- Arrangements are available to enable a company to agree in advance with HMRC that its 'transfer pricing policy' is acceptable.
- The transfer pricing rules can also apply between two UK resident companies. However, the examiner has stated that any question on transfer pricing will involve an overseas company.

Example 4 – Transfer pricing

Focus plc, a UK resident company, is to export cameras that it manufactures, to its 100% overseas subsidiary, at a discount of 30% to their normal trade selling price.

The company wishes to maximise the subsidiary's profits, as these are only subject to corporation tax overseas at the rate of 15%.

Discuss the tax implications of the above arrangement.

Answer to example 4

- The invoicing of cameras by Focus plc at a discount of 30% to the normal trade selling price, will have the effect of reducing its taxable trading profits, and hence UK corporation tax.

- The sales are at an under-valuation to an overseas company which it controls. Therefore a market price must be substituted for the transfer price when calculating Focus plc's taxable total profits.

- The market price will be an 'arm's length' one that would be charged if the parties to the transaction were independent of each other.

- Under self-assessment, transfer pricing adjustments are not made by HMRC, but should be made by the company concerned, in this case, Focus plc.

4 Chapter summary

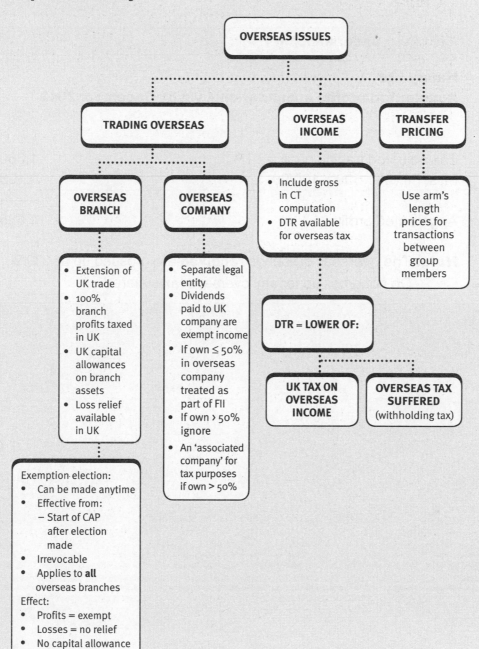

OVERSEAS ISSUES

TRADING OVERSEAS

OVERSEAS INCOME
- Include gross in CT computation
- DTR available for overseas tax

TRANSFER PRICING

Use arm's length prices for transactions between group members

OVERSEAS BRANCH

OVERSEAS COMPANY

OVERSEAS BRANCH
- Extension of UK trade
- 100% branch profits taxed in UK
- UK capital allowances on branch assets
- Loss relief available in UK

OVERSEAS COMPANY
- Separate legal entity
- Dividends paid to UK company are exempt income
- If own ≤ 50% in overseas company treated as part of FII
- If own > 50% ignore
- An 'associated company' for tax purposes if own > 50%

DTR = LOWER OF:

UK TAX ON OVERSEAS INCOME

OVERSEAS TAX SUFFERED (withholding tax)

Exemption election:
- Can be made anytime
- Effective from:
  – Start of CAP after election made
- Irrevocable
- Applies to **all** overseas branches

Effect:
- Profits = exempt
- Losses = no relief
- No capital allowance

Test your understanding answers

Test your understanding 1

Happy Ltd
Augmented profits computation – y/e 31 December 2012

	£
Tax adjusted trading profit = TTP	1,650,000
Plus: FII (£31,500 × 100/90)	35,000
Augmented profits	1,685,000

Note: The overseas dividends **received** are grossed up at 100/90.
Do not gross up for any overseas tax suffered.

Test your understanding 2

London Ltd

(a) **Overseas branch exemption election has not been made**
Corporation tax computation – y/e 31 March 2013

	Total	UK income	Paris profits	Rental Income
	£	£	£	£
Trading profit	380,000	380,000		
Overseas income (W1)	141,100		90,000	51,100
Overseas branch loss (Note)	(12,000)	(12,000)		
Total profits = TTP	509,100	368,000	90,000	51,100
Corporation tax				
£509,100@ 24% (W2)	122,184	88,320	21,600	12,264
Less: DTR (W3)	(29,265)		(21,600)	(7,665)
CT payable	92,919	88,320	Nil	4,599

Notes:

(1) The overseas branch loss is offset against the UK income, rather than the overseas sources of income, in order to maximise the available DTR.
The examiner gives a similar example in his Finance Act 2012 article, however, he says that you do not need to know the importance of the order of set off of losses in the real examination.

(2) The overseas dividend from Berlin GmbH is exempt but is treated as FII.

(b) **Overseas branch exemption election has been made.**

Corporation tax computation – y/e 31 March 2013

	Total	UK income	Rental income
	£	£	£
Tax adjusted trading profit	380,000	380,000	
Overseas income (W1)	51,100		51,100
Total profits = TTP	431,100	380,000	51,100
Corporation tax			
£431,100 @ 24% (W4)	103,464	91,200	12,264
Less: DTR (W3)	(7,665)		(7,665)
CT payable	95,799	91,200	4,599

The exemption election should not be made as:

- relief for the overseas branch loss is not available, and

- the corporation tax liability is correspondingly £2,880 higher (£95,799 – £92,919).

Alternative calculation of the difference
= (£12,000 branch loss lost x 24%) = £2,880.

Workings

(W1) Grossing up the overseas income

	Branch Paris	Rental income
	£	£
Income received	54,000	43,435
Add: WHT (40/60)/(15/85)	36,000	7,665
	90,000	51,100

(W2) Associated companies

There are three companies under common control, as London Ltd has a controlling interest in three other UK resident companies. Berlin GmbH is not an 'associated' company.

Therefore, the applicable limits for determining the tax rate for each company are:

£1,500,000 ÷ 4 = £375,000
£300,000 ÷ 4 = £75,000

	£
TTP	509,100
Plus: FII (£2,700 × 100/90)	3,000
Augmented profits	512,100

Therefore, with augmented profits of £512,100, the main rate applies.

(W3) DTR relief

	Branch	Rental
Lower of:	£	£
UK CT on overseas profits	21,600	12,264
Overseas taxes suffered	36,000	7,665
Lower amount	21,600	7,665

(W4) Tax rate – branch exemption election

The company still has three associated companies, so the profit limits are £75,000 and £375,000.

	£
TTP	431,100
Plus: FII (W2)	3,000
Augmented profits	434,100

Therefore, the main rate applies.

Tax administration for a company

Chapter learning objectives

Upon completion of this chapter you will be able to:

- explain and apply the self-assessment system as it applies to companies

- state the time limits for filing a tax return

- list the information and records that the company needs to retain for tax purposes together with the retention period.

- state when corporation tax is due for companies which are not large

- state the time limits for key claims

- define a large company and explain how they are required to pay corporation tax on a quarterly basis

- calculate late payment interest

- state the penalties for late submission of tax returns/notification of liability

- explain the circumstances in which HM Revenue and Customs can enquire into a tax return

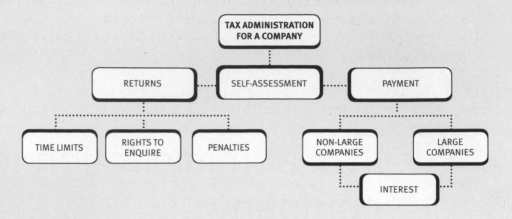

1 The self-assessment system for companies

As with individuals, self-assessment exists for corporate taxpayers. Responsibility rests with the company to:

- calculate their own corporation tax liability for each accounting period

- submit a self-assessment corporation tax return **within 12 months** after the end of the period of account

- pay any corporation tax due **within nine months and one day** after the end of the accounting period.

Given the timing of the due date for payment of tax, in practice, many companies will aim to complete the self-assessment tax return prior to the nine-month deadline for paying the corporation tax.

The self-assessment tax return

The self-assessment tax return (CT600 return) must be submitted either:

- **within 12 months** after the end of the period of account; or

- **three months** after the issue of the notice to file a return (if this is later than the normal submission date).

The return must:

- contain all information required to calculate the company's taxable total profits.

- include a self-assessment of the amount of corporation tax payable for that accounting period.

- be submitted online.

A company has to submit a copy of its financial accounts together with the self-assessment tax return.

All companies must file self assessment returns and copies of accounts electronically using 'Inline eXtensible Business Reporting Language' (iXBRL). iXBRL is the global standard for exchanging business information in an electronic format.

HMRC provide free online filing software applications for companies with straightforward tax affairs. The software automatically produces and submits a CT600 with PDF accounts and computations in the required iXBRL format.

For other companies, commercial software applications and services enable the submission of the return in one of three ways:

(1) Integrated software applications – automatically inserts iXBRL tags to data and produces iXBRL accounts and/or computations.

(2) Managed tagging services – a service provided by agents whereby the company outsources the process of applying the appropriate iXBRL tag to each item of data, which then converts non-iXBRL accounts and computations into the required format.

(3) Conversion software applications – allows the company to apply the appropriate iXBRL tag to each item of data itself to convert the accounts and computations into the required format.

The items to be tagged are those which appear in 'taxonomies' (i.e. classifications according to a pre-determined, pre-ordered layout).

HMRC has published minimum tagging lists for UK GAAP, UK IFRS and corporation tax computation taxonomies.

They intend to extend the requirement to full comprehensive tagging for accounts, however they have announced that the current reduced 'minimum' tagging for corporation tax computations will remain indefinitely.

Making claims

Any claims must be included in the self-assessment tax return.

A claim for a relief, allowance or repayment must be quantified at the time that the claim is made. For example, if loss relief is claimed, then the amount of the loss must be stated.

Notification of chargeability

A company coming within the scope of corporation tax for the first time must notify HMRC when its first accounting period begins, **within three months** of the start of its first accounting period.

Companies that do not receive a tax return are required to notify HMRC if they have income or chargeable gains on which tax is due.

The time limit for notifying HMRC of chargeability is **12 months** from the end of the accounting period in which the liability arises.

A standard penalty may be imposed for failure to notify HMRC of chargeability (see section 6).

Penalties for failure to submit a return

HMRC can impose fixed penalties and tax-geared penalties for the failure to submit a return, depending on the length of the delay in submitting the return.

See section 6 for details of the penalties that can be imposed.

Determination assessments

To prevent companies deliberately delaying the submission of the return, HMRC have the following actions available:

- HMRC may determine the amount of corporation tax due by issuing a determination assessment.

- The determination assessment is treated as a self-assessment by the company, and will be replaced by the actual self-assessment when it is submitted by the company.

- There is no appeal against a determination assessment. Instead, the company must displace it with the actual self-assessment return.

- A determination assessment can be raised at any time **within three years** of the filing date (i.e. four years from the end of the financial accounting period).

Records

Companies are required to keep and preserve records necessary to make a correct and complete return.

The records that must be kept include records of:

- all receipts and expenses

- all goods purchased and sold

- all supporting documents relating to the transactions of the business, such as accounts, books, contracts, vouchers and receipts.

The records must be retained for **six years** after the end of the accounting period to which they relate.

A penalty may be charged for failure to keep or retain adequate records.

The maximum penalty is only likely to be imposed in the most serious cases, such as, where a company deliberately destroys its records in order to obstruct a HMRC enquiry.

See section 6 for the detail of penalties that can be imposed.

2 Tax returns – amendments and errors

Either the company or HMRC may make amendments to a return:

- HMRC may correct any obvious errors or mistakes **within nine months** of the date that the return is filed with them. For example, they will correct arithmetical errors or errors of principle. This type of repair does not mean that HMRC has accepted the return as accurate.

- A company can amend the return **within 12 months** of the filing date. For a CAP ending on 31 March 2013, the filing date is 31 March 2014, and the company has until 31 March 2015 to make any amendments.

- If an error is discovered at a later date, then the company can make a claim for overpayment relief to recover any corporation tax overpaid.

Claims for overpayment relief

Where an assessment is excessive due to an error or mistake in a return, the company can claim relief. A claim can be made in respect of errors made, and mistakes arising from not understanding the law.

The claim must be made **within four years** of the accounting period to which it relates.

3 Due dates for payment

The payment date for corporation tax depends on the size of the company:

- For companies which are not 'large'
  - the due date is **nine months and one day** after the year end.

- For 'large' companies
  - the liability is settled under the **quarterly instalment scheme.**

All companies must pay their corporation tax electronically.

4 Quarterly instalment payments for large companies

HMRC does not provide large companies with the same delayed payment date for their corporation tax liability. Instead, a specific scheme is in place requiring such companies to settle their liability on an ongoing basis.

Definition of a large company

The key points here are:

- A large company pays the main rate of corporation tax (i.e. 24%).

- By definition, all other companies are not large (i.e. those paying the small profits and marginal relief rates of corporation tax) and are therefore not required to pay corporation tax by instalments.

A company without any associated companies, will therefore pay tax by instalments, if its augmented profits are at least £1.5 million.

This limit is reduced where a company has associated companies. However, instalments are never due if a company's corporation tax liability is below £10,000.

Companies that become large during an accounting period do not have to make instalment payments provided:

- their augmented profits for the accounting period do not exceed £10 million (reduced accordingly if there are associated companies), and

- they were not a large company for the previous accounting period.

Instalment dates

Four quarterly instalments are due

- by the 14th day
- in months 7, 10, 13 and 16 following the **start** of the accounting period.

Note that the first two instalments are therefore paid **during** the CAP.

Basis of payment

Instalments are based on the expected corporation tax liability for the **current** accounting period. It is, therefore, necessary for companies to produce an accurate forecast of their current period tax liability.

Companies will normally be able to obtain a refund, if they subsequently find that instalments have been overpaid.

Example 1 – Quarterly instalment payments for large companies

ABC plc estimates that its corporation tax liability for the y/e 31 December 2012 will be £800,000. ABC plc is a large company, paying tax at 24%.

Show when ABC plc's corporation tax liability will be due.

Answer to example 1

ABC plc's corporation tax liability is due by instalments:
£200,000 on 14 July 2012
£200,000 on 14 October 2012
£200,000 on 14 January 2013
£200,000 on 14 April 2013

Test your understanding 1

XYZ Ltd has an expected corporation tax liability of £2,000,000 for the y/e 31 March 2013. XYZ Ltd has been a large company for corporation tax purposes for a number of years.

State when XYZ Ltd's corporation tax liability for the y/e 31 March 2013 will be due.

Special rules apply where the accounting period is less than 12 months.

Short accounting periods

Where the accounting period is less than 12 months:

- First instalment due by:
  14th day of 7th month after the start of the CAP (as normal)

- Subsequent instalments are due at 3 monthly intervals thereafter
  - except for the last instalment where the remaining period of account is less than 3 months
  - in which case, the instalment is due by:
    14th day of the next month (if one month remaining) or
    14th day of the second month following the previous instalment (if 2 months remaining)

- The amount of each instalment:
= (estimated CT liability for CAP) x (n / length of CAP)

  Where n = 3 months for a full quarterly instalment
  But n = 2 or 1 for the last instalment if the remaining period is less than 3 months

- The amount of each instalment:
= (estimated CT liability for CAP) x (n / length of CAP)

  Where n = 3 months for a full quarterly instalment
  But n = 2 or 1 for the last instalment if the remaining period is less than 3 months

Example 2 – Short accounting periods

Assume ABC plc in example 1 prepared accounts for the 8 months ended 31 December 2012 and that its corporation tax liability is £800,000.

Show when ABC plc's corporation tax liability will be due.

Answer to example 2

ABC plc's corporation tax liability will be due by instalments as follows:

Due date		Paying	Amount £
14.11.12	(14th day of 7th month after start of CAP)	3/8 x £800,000	300,000
14.2.13	(three months later)	3/8 x £800,000	300,000
14.4.13	(two months later)	2/8 x £800,000	200,000
		8 months	800,000

5 Interest

There are two key types of interest:

- Late payment interest
  - calculated at 3% p.a.
- Repayment interest
  - calculated at 0.5% p.a.

The interest rates will be provided in the tax rates and allowances section of the exam.

Late payment interest

Interest is automatically charged if corporation tax is paid late.

Interest runs:

- **from:** the normal due date
- **to:** the date of payment.

Interest paid to HMRC on corporation tax paid late is a deductible expense from interest income.

> ### Test your understanding 2
>
> Able Ltd prepares accounts to 31 March.
>
> The company has a corporation tax liability of £75,000, for the y/e 31 March 2013. Able Ltd paid £25,000 of its corporation tax liability on 1 January 2014, but did not pay the balance of £50,000 until 15 March 2014.
>
> **Explain how interest is calculated on the late payment of corporation tax. Assume A Ltd is not a large company.**

Repayment interest

Interest is paid by HMRC on any overpayment of corporation tax.

Where interest is due, the interest runs:

- **from:** the later of:
    - the due date
    - the date of actual payment
- **to:** the date of repayment.

Interest paid by HMRC on overpayments of corporation tax is taxable interest income.

6 Penalties

In addition to interest on the late payment of tax, HMRC can impose penalties.

Standard penalty

HMRC has standardised penalties across taxes for the submission of incorrect returns and failure to notify liability to tax. The rules are explained in Chapter 12 section 7.

The penalty is calculated as a percentage of 'potential lost revenue' which is generally the tax unpaid, but can be reduced where the taxpayer makes a disclosure and co-operates with HMRC to establish the amount of tax unpaid.

Other penalties

Offence	Penalty
Late filing of corporation tax return: • within 3 months of filing date • more than 3 months after filing date	 • Fixed penalty = £100 (Note) • Fixed penalty increased to £200 (Note)
Additional penalties: • 6 – 12 months after filing date • More than 12 months after filing date	 • Additional 10% of tax outstanding 6 months after filing date • Additional penalty increased to 20% **Note:** Fixed penalties rise to £500 and £1,000 if persistently filed late (i.e. return for 2 preceding periods also late)
Failure to keep and retain required records	Up to £3,000 per accounting period

Example 3 – Self-assessment for companies

Late Ltd submits its self-assessment return for the y/e 31 March 2013, on 30 November 2014. The corporation tax due of £50,000 was paid on the same day. Late Ltd has submitted its previous tax returns on time.

State the penalties that are due as a result of the late submission of the tax return.

Answer to example 3

The tax return should have been submitted by 31 March 2014, and so it is eight months late.

The fixed penalty is therefore £200, and the tax geared penalty is £5,000 (£50,000 at 10%).

Test your understanding 3

Everlate Ltd submits its corporation tax return for the y/e 28 February 2013, on 30 September 2014. This is the fifth consecutive occasion the company has submitted its return late.

The corporation tax liability for the year was £100,000; this was paid when the return was submitted.

State the penalties that are due as a result of the late submission of the tax return.

7 Compliance checks into returns

HMRC have the right to enquire into the completeness and accuracy of any self-assessment tax return and issue discovery assessments under their compliance check powers. The procedures and rules are similar to those for individuals.

Enquiries into returns

The enquiry may be made as a result of any of the following:

- suspicion that income is undeclared
- suspicion that deductions are being incorrectly claimed
- other information in HMRC's possession
- being part of a random review process.

Additional points:

- HMRC do not have to state a reason for the enquiry and are unlikely to do so.
- HMRC must give **written notice** before commencing an enquiry by the following dates:

If return filed:	Notice must be issued within 12 months of:
On time	the actual delivery of the tax return to HMRC
Late	the 31 January, 30 April, 31 July or 31 October next following the actual date of delivery of the tax return to HMRC

- Once this deadline is passed, the company can normally consider the self-assessment for that accounting period as final.

Enquiry procedure

HMRC can demand that the company produce any or all of the following:

- documents
- accounts
- other written particulars
- full answers to specific questions.

The information requested should be limited to that connected with the return.

- The company has 30 days to comply with the request. An appeal can be made against the request.
- The enquiry ends when HMRC give written notice that it has been completed.
- The notice will state the outcome of the enquiry and HMRC's amendments to the self assessment.
- Refer to Chapter 12 for details about appeal procedures.
- The company then has 30 days to appeal, in writing, against HMRC's amendment.

Discovery assessments

HMRC has the capacity to raise additional assessments, referred to as discovery assessments. The key points are:

- The use of a discovery assessment is restricted where a self-assessment return has already been made. However, although enquiries must normally begin **within 12 months** of the actual submission date, a discovery assessment can be raised at a later date to prevent the loss of corporation tax.
- Unless the loss of corporation tax was brought about carelessly or deliberately by the company, a discovery assessment cannot be raised where full disclosure was made in the return, even if this is found to be incorrect.
- HMRC will only accept that full disclosure has been made if any contentious items have been clearly brought to their attention – perhaps in a covering letter.
- Only a company that makes full disclosure in the self-assessment tax return, therefore, has absolute finality 12 months after the actual submission date.

- The time limit for making a discovery assessment is:

	Time from the end of the CAP
Basic time limit	four years
Careless error	six years
Deliberate error	twenty years

- A discovery assessment may be appealed against.

8 Chapter summary

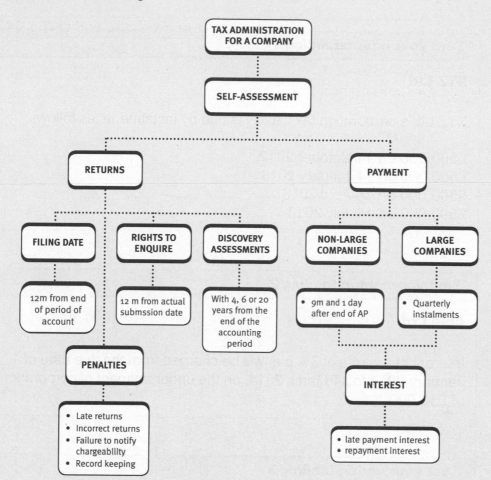

TAX ADMINISTRATION
FOR A COMPANY

SELF-ASSESSMENT

RETURNS

PAYMENT

FILING DATE

RIGHTS TO
ENQUIRE

DISCOVERY
ASSESSMENTS

NON-LARGE
COMPANIES

LARGE
COMPANIES

12m from end
of period of
account

12 m from actual
submssion date

With 4, 6 or 20
years from the
end of the
accounting
period

• 9m and 1 day
after end of AP

• Quarterly
instalments

PENALTIES

INTEREST

• Late returns
• Incorrect returns
• Failure to notify
chargeabllity
• Record keeping

• late payment interest
• repayment interest

Test your understanding answers

Test your understanding 1

XYZ Ltd

XYZ Ltd's corporation tax liability is due by instalments as follows:

£500,000 on 14 October 2012
£500,000 on 14 January 2013
£500,000 on 14 April 2013
£500,000 on 14 July 2013

Test your understanding 2

Able Ltd

Interest at the rate of 3% p.a. will be charged from the due date of 1 January 2014 to 14 March 2014, on the underpayment of corporation tax of £50,000.

Test your understanding 3

Everlate Ltd

The tax return should have been submitted by 28 February 2014, and so it is seven months late.

The fixed penalty is therefore £1,000 (as the return is more than three months late and Everlate is a persistent offender).

The tax geared penalty is £10,000 (£100,000 at 10%).

VAT: Outline

Chapter learning objectives

Upon completion of this chapter you will be able to:

- state the scope and nature of VAT

- explain the significance of the different types of supply for VAT

- list the principal zero-rated and exempt supplies

- identify the two key situations which require compulsory VAT registration

- discuss the advantages and disadvantages of voluntary registration

- define the relationship required for group VAT registration

- explain the effects and outline any advantages or disadvantages of group VAT registration

- identify when pre-registration input VAT can be recovered

- explain when a person must compulsorily/may voluntarily deregister for VAT

- outline the alternative VAT treatments on the sale of a business

- determine the date when goods and services are supplied

- identify the value of a supply and calculate the relevant VAT

- identify recoverable input VAT on key purchases and expenses

- compute the relief that is available for impaired trade debts.

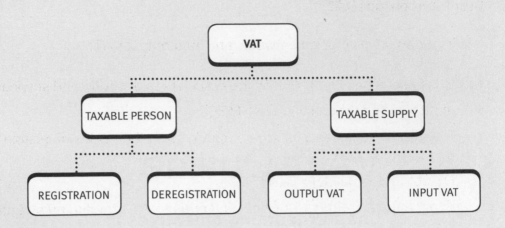

1 Introduction

Value added tax (VAT) is:

- an indirect tax
- charged on most goods and services, supplied within the UK, and
- is borne by the final consumer.

VAT is an important tax for the examination. There will always be a minimum of 10 marks on VAT.

VAT will normally be included within question one or question two, although there might be a separate question on VAT.

2 The scope and nature of VAT

There are three essentials needed before VAT can be charged

- A taxable person is one who is or should be registered for VAT, because they make taxable supplies (see registration section 4).

  A person can be an individual or a legal person, such as a company.

- A taxable supply is everything which is not exempt or outside the scope of VAT. It includes sales and purchases of most goods or services.
- For VAT to apply the taxable supply must be made in the course or furtherance of a business carried on by a taxable person.

Input and output VAT

It is important to distinguish between input and output VAT:

- Businesses pay input VAT on their purchases of goods and services.
- Input VAT is reclaimable from HMRC.
- Registered businesses charge output VAT on their sales of taxable goods and services.
- Output VAT is payable to HMRC.
- Every month or quarter the input and output VAT is netted off and paid to or recovered from HMRC.

Test your understanding 1

Which of the following statements are correct?

(1) VAT is an indirect tax.

(2) Lucy is an accountancy student. She sells some of her spare CDs to a friend. She should charge the friend VAT on the sale.

(3) Businesses may keep all the output VAT they charge to customers.

3 Types of supply

Supplies can be taxable, exempt or outside the scope of VAT.

Taxable supplies

- VAT is charged on taxable supplies but not on exempt supplies or supplies which are outside the scope of VAT.

  It is therefore important to be able to correctly classify supplies in order to determine whether VAT should be charged.

- It is also important to correctly classify supplies because:
  - only taxable supplies are taken into account in determining whether a trader needs to register for VAT
  - input VAT related to exempt supplies is not recoverable.

- Taxable supplies are charged to VAT at one of three rates:

    - **zero rate:** This is a tax rate of nil.

        No VAT is charged but it is classed as a taxable supply. It is therefore taken into account in determining whether a trader should register for VAT and whether input VAT is recoverable.

    - **reduced rate:** Some supplies, mainly for domestic or charitable use are charged at the reduced rate.

        Note that the reduced rate is not important for the examinations.

    - **standard rate:** Any taxable supply which is not charged at the zero or reduced rates is charged at the standard rate of 20%.

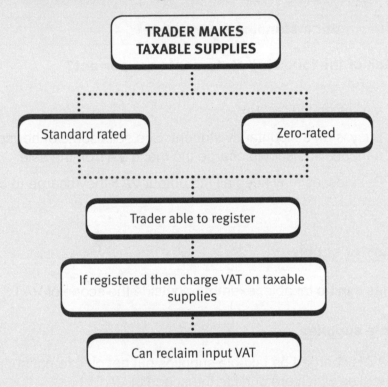

Zero-rated and exempt supplies

You must be careful to distinguish between zero-rated and exempt supplies.

Trader making:	Exempt Supplies	Zero-rated supplies
• Can charge VAT?	X	√ at 0%
• Can reclaim input VAT?	X	√
• Can register for VAT?	X	√

KAPLAN PUBLISHING

Test your understanding 2

Fill in the blanks in the following statements:

(1) Traders making wholly exempt supplies .... register for VAT.

(2) The standard rate of VAT is ....

(3) Traders who are registered for VAT must charge VAT on all their taxable ....

(4) The difference between zero-rated and exempt traders is that zero-rated traders .... recover input VAT, whereas exempt traders ....

You do not need to remember the rates of VAT which apply to different goods and services. However, it is useful to know the treatment of some of the more common types of supply.

For example, items such as wages and dividends are outside the scope of VAT.

Remember that taxable supplies, which are not zero-rated or chargeable at the reduced rate, are standard rated.

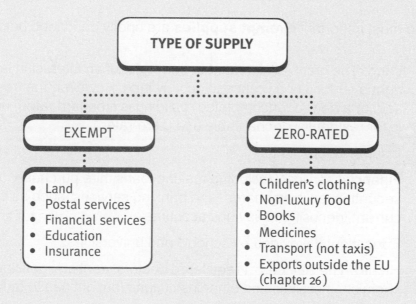

Zero-rated and exempt supplies

The most important **zero-rated items** are briefly described below.

- Food: Food of a kind used for human consumption unless it is either a supply in the course of catering (e.g. in a restaurant) or is classed as a luxury item, such as alcohol or confectionery.

- Books and other printed matter: This includes a wide range of printed material (e.g. newspapers, books, maps and sheet music).

- Construction of dwellings, etc: This includes new buildings for residential or charitable use. However, it does not cover the situation where an existing building is reconstructed, altered or enlarged.

- Transport: Transporting passengers by road, rail, sea or air, provided the vehicle or ship is designed to carry more than 11 passengers (e.g. not taxis).

- Drugs, medicines and appliances: Drugs supplied on prescription by a chemist and certain appliances and equipment supplied to the disabled.

- Charities: Gifts to charities are zero-rated.

- Clothing and footwear: Young children's clothing and footwear, provided they are unsuitable for older persons.

The most important **exempt supplies** are briefly described below.

- Land: The grant, assignment or surrender of an interest in land, a right over land or a licence to occupy land. However, the freehold sale of a new (or uncompleted) building is standard rated, unless it is for residential or charitable use (zero-rated).

- Insurance: premiums.

- Financial services, including making loans, hire purchase, dealing in securities, such as shares, and banking services, such as providing current, deposit and savings accounts.

- Education: If provided by schools and universities.

- Health: The services of registered doctors, dentists, opticians, chemists, hospitals and other institutions (but not health farms).

- Sports: Entry fees to sports competitions used to provide prizes or charged by non-profit making sporting bodies.

Test your understanding 3

Fill in the following table by ticking the relevant column to indicate whether the item is zero-rated or exempt.

Item	Zero-rated	Exempt
Bread sold in a supermarket		
Children's shoes		
Sale of motor insurance policy		
Newspapers		
Sale of shares		
Train ticket		

4 VAT registration – compulsory

Registration limits

If a person's taxable supplies (excluding sales of capital assets) exceed the registration limits, then registration is compulsory.
There are two separate tests for compulsory registration:

- Historic turnover test

- Future prospects test

Historic turnover test

At the end of each month, the trader must look at the cumulative total of taxable supplies for the last 12 months, or since commencing trade, whichever is the shorter.

If the total exceeds the registration limit, currently £77,000, then the trader must register as follows:

- Notify HMRC **within 30 days** of the end of the month in which the turnover limit is exceeded, by completing form VAT1.

- Registration is effective from the **end of the month** following the month in which turnover exceeded the limit, or an earlier agreed date.

- A trader need not register if his taxable supplies for the next 12 months are expected to be less than the deregistration limit (see below) currently £75,000.

The registration and deregistration limits are provided in the tax rates and allowances in the examination.

Example 1 – VAT registration – compulsory

Hill Ltd commenced trading on 1 January 2011. Its monthly taxable supplies are as follows:

	2011 £	2012 £
January	3,300	4,890
February	3,400	4,960
March	3,500	5,580
April	3,600	5,650
May	3,640	5,770
June	3,710	6,240
July	3,780	6,560
August	3,850	7,030
September	3,920	7,900
October	4,290	8,800
November	4,350	9,550
December	4,430	9,850

In addition, in May 2012 the company sold surplus plant for £3,450.

State from what date Hill Ltd is liable to register for VAT.

Answer to example 1

At the end of November 2012, Hill Ltd's taxable turnover for the previous 12 months is:

	£
Value of supplies for registration purposes:	
Supplies to customers	77,360
Supply of plant (disregarded)	Nil
	———
	77,360
	———

Hill Ltd is therefore liable to register, and must notify HMRC by 30 December 2012.

The company will be registered from 1 January 2013, or such earlier date as may jointly be agreed.

Test your understanding 4

Jay owns a shop selling newspapers (zero-rated) and stationery (standard-rated). In his first year of trading to 30 September 2011, his sales of newspapers were £2,950 per month and of stationery £2,150 per month. In his second year of trading, these figures increased to £4,100 and £2,780, respectively.

State from what date Jay is liable to register for VAT.

Future prospects test

This test is considered at any time, when taxable supplies in the next 30 days in isolation are expected to exceed £77,000.

- HMRC must be notified before the end of the 30 days, by completing form VAT1.
- Registration will be effective from the beginning of the 30-day period.

Example 2 – VAT registration – compulsory

Cat Ltd signs a lease for new business premises on 1 May 2012 and opens for business on 20 July 2012. The company estimates, from the outset, that taxable supplies will be in the region of £80,500 per month.

State when, if at all, Cat Ltd is liable to register.

Answer to example 2

Cat Ltd is liable to registration because supplies for the 30 days to 18 August 2012, are expected to exceed £77,000.

The company must notify HMRC of its liability to registration by 18 August 2012 and is registered with effect from 20 July 2012.

Note: Cat Ltd does not make any taxable supplies during the period 1 May 2012 to 19 July 2012, so the liability to register under the future prospects test cannot arise during that period.

Test your understanding 5

State which of the following unregistered traders are liable to register for VAT and the effective date of registration.

Name	Supplies	Details
Majid	Accountancy services	Started in business 1 November 2012. Estimated fees £15,700 per month.
Jane	Baby wear	Established the business 1 March 2013 when Jane signed a contract to supply a local nursery. Sales for March 2013 are expected to be £79,000.
Sayso Ltd	Insurance	Commenced trading 2 January 2013. Sales are £100,000 per month.

Consequences of registration

Once registered, a certificate of registration is issued and the taxable person must start accounting for VAT:

- Output tax must be charged on taxable supplies.

- Each registered trader is allocated a VAT registration number, which must be quoted on all invoices.

- Each registered trader is allocated a tax period for filing returns, which is normally every three months.

- Input tax (subject to some restriction) is recoverable on business purchases and expenses.

- Appropriate VAT records must be maintained.

There are penalties for late registration. In addition, the trader can be asked to pay over the VAT they should have collected in the period that they should have been registered.

Number of registrations

A person is registered for VAT, not the business.

A person can be registered only once, and this registration includes all the businesses that the person carries on. Therefore a sole trader with several unincorporated businesses will only have one VAT registration.

A partnership is however treated as a separate person for VAT registration purposes. Therefore a sole trader would have a separate registration from a partnership in which he is a partner. However, separate businesses carried on by the same partners, will have a single registration.

A company is also treated as a separate person for VAT registration purposes.

5 Voluntary registration

Actual or intending traders

Even if not required to register, a person may register voluntarily provided he is making, or intending to make, taxable supplies.

HMRC will register the trader from the date of the request for voluntary registration, or a mutually agreed earlier date.

Advantages and disadvantages of voluntary registration

Advantages	Disadvantages
• Avoids penalties for late registration. • Can recover input VAT on purchases. • Can disguise the small size of the business.	• Business will suffer the burden of compliance with all VAT administration rules. • Business must charge VAT. This makes their goods comparatively more expensive than an unregistered business, for customers who cannot recover the VAT (i.e. final consumers).

Voluntary registration is therefore beneficial where the business is making:

*   zero-rated supplies and has input VAT that it can recover, or
*   supplies to VAT registered customers

but is probably not beneficial where the business is making:

*   supplies to non-VAT registered customers (i.e. the general public).

Example 3 – Voluntary registration

Alfred sells goods, which would be standard-rated if he were registered for VAT. All of his sales are to members of the public. His current annual turnover is £40,000. He incurs input VAT of £5,000 on purchases each year.

Assuming that, due to the competitive nature of his business, Alfred is unable to increase his prices to the public advise him whether it would be beneficial to register voluntarily for VAT.

Answer to example 3

If Alfred registered for VAT he would be required to charge his customers output VAT. As he is unable to increase his prices his VAT inclusive turnover would be £40,000 and he would have to account for output VAT to HMRC of £6,667 (£40,000 × 20/120). His profits would therefore decrease by £6,667.

He would however be able to reclaim input VAT of £5,000 p.a. The net cost to Alfred of registering for VAT would be £1,667 (£6,667 – £5,000) and it is therefore not beneficial for him to register voluntarily.

If Alfred's sales were to other VAT registered businesses, he would be able to charge VAT in addition to his normal selling price, as his customers would be able to recover the VAT charged.

In this situation it would be beneficial for Alfred to register for VAT voluntarily. He would be able to recover the input tax, on his purchases and, as a result his profits would increase by £5,000.

Accepting additional new business

Accepting additional new work may increase the taxable supplies of the business above the compulsory registration threshold.

The VAT status of the customers of the business is therefore very important in deciding whether or not taking on the new business is beneficial.

- If customers are VAT registered:
    - they can recover the output VAT charged, and
    - it will be advantageous to accept the new work.

- If customers are not VAT registered:
    - they cannot recover the output VAT charged, and
    - if the selling price cannot be increased, the output VAT will become an additional cost to the business

    This may make the additional new work unattractive:

    - it may be beneficial to decide to not accept the work, and
    - maintain taxable supplies below the VAT registration threshold.

6 VAT Groups

Companies that are under common control can elect for a group VAT registration, provided that all the companies are UK resident.

A VAT group is treated as if it is a single company for the purposes of VAT. Group registration is optional; not all members of the group have to join the VAT group.

The effect of a group VAT registration is as follows:

- Goods and services supplied by one group company to another within the group are outside the scope of VAT. Therefore there is no need to account for VAT on intra-group supplies.

- The VAT group appoints a representative member who is responsible for accounting for all input and output VAT for the group.

- The representative member submits a single VAT return covering all group members, but all companies are jointly and severally liable for the VAT payable.

- The normal time limits apply for submission of VAT returns.

- An application for group VAT registration has immediate effect, although HMRC has 90 days during which they can refuse the application.

Advantages and disadvantages of group VAT registration

Advantages	Disadvantages
• VAT on intra-group supplies eliminated	• All members remain jointly and severally liable
• Only one VAT return required, which should save administration costs	• A single return may cause administrative difficulties collecting and collating information
	• Limits for joining the cash accounting scheme (see Chapter 26) are applied to the whole group, rather than the individual companies. The other VAT schemes for small businesses are not available to companies registered as a group.

7 Recovery of pre-registration input VAT

Normally, VAT incurred before registration cannot be accounted for as input VAT. If the conditions below are satisfied, however, then it can be treated as input tax and reclaimed accordingly.

Goods	Services
• The goods must be acquired for business purposes and should not be sold or consumed prior to registration (i.e. should still be in inventory). • The goods have not been acquired more than **four years** prior to registration.	• The services must be supplied for business purposes. • The services should not have been supplied more than **six months** prior to registration.

Test your understanding 6

X Ltd registered for VAT with effect from 1 January 2013. The company incurred the following expenditure prior to registration:

(1) 12.2.12   Paid their accountants £500 plus VAT for preparing cash flow forecasts.

(2) 14.8.12   Paid rent of £1,500, to a landlord who is an exempt trader hence no VAT paid.

(3) 15.10.12   Bought headed stationery, paying £1,150 including VAT.

(4) 1.11.12   Bought inventory intended for resale, costing £5,000 plus VAT.

(5) 14.11.12   Bought machinery, costing £6,500 plus VAT.

At the date of registration, 60% of the inventory intended for resale had already been sold. The stationery was unused and the company still owned the machine.

State the amounts of pre-registration input VAT that can be claimed.

8 Deregistration

Compulsory deregistration

A person must deregister when he ceases to make taxable supplies.

- HMRC should be notified **within 30 days** of ceasing to make taxable supplies.

- VAT registration is cancelled from the date of cessation or a mutually agreed later date.

Voluntary deregistration

A person may voluntarily deregister, even if the business continues, if there is evidence that taxable supplies in the next 12 months, will not exceed £75,000.

- The 12-month period is measured starting at any time.

- The onus is on the trader to satisfy HMRC that they qualify.

- VAT registration is cancelled from the date of request or an agreed later date.

Effect of deregistration

On deregistration, VAT output tax must be accounted for on the value of non-current assets and inventory held at the date of deregistration, on which a deduction for input tax has been claimed.

However, this final tax liability is waived if it is £1,000 or less.

Test your understanding 7

(1) Jig Ltd closes down its business on 10 January 2013.

(2) At 1 January 2013, Elk Ltd thinks that taxable turnover for the year to 31 December 2013, will be £40,000. He immediately decides to apply for deregistration.

State when Jig Ltd should notify HMRC of his business cessation and from when he will be deregistered.

State when Elk Ltd will be deregistered.

9 VAT on sale of a business

Alternative treatments

Compulsory deregistration applies where a business is sold or otherwise transferred as a going concern to new owners.

The sale may be treated in one of two ways:

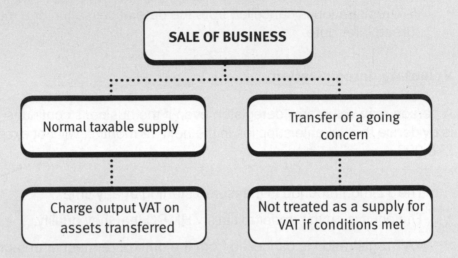

Conditions for transfer of business as a going concern

If the following conditions are satisfied, then the sale/transfer:

- will not be treated as a taxable supply

- no output tax will therefore be charged on the assets transferred by the seller, and

- no input tax is recoverable by the purchaser.

Conditions:

- The business is transferred as a going concern.

- There is no significant break in the trading.

- The same type of trade is carried on after the transfer.

- The new owner is or will be registered for VAT, immediately after the transfer.

Note that **all** these conditions **must** be met.

KAPLAN PUBLISHING

Transfer of registration

On the sale of a business it is normally compulsory to deregister. However, instead of doing so, both the transferor and the transferee may make a joint election, for the transferor's registration to be transferred to the transferee.

Where this is done, the transferee assumes all rights and obligations in respect of the registration, including the liability to pay any outstanding VAT. Therefore, this may not be a good commercial decision.

10 The time of supply (the tax point)

Importance of tax point

VAT is normally accounted for on a quarterly basis, so it is important to know the time of a supply, to identify the quarter in which it falls.

Also, if the standard rate of VAT were to change or if the classification of a supply altered (e.g. a zero-rated supply became standard-rated), it would be necessary to know whether a supply had been made before or after the date of change.

Basic tax point

The rules are different for goods and for services:

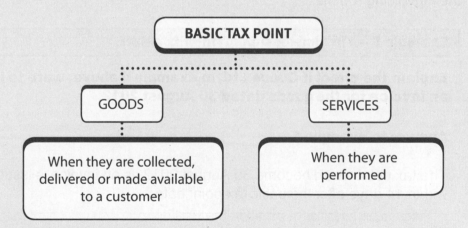

Example 4 – The time of supply (the tax point)

Queue Ltd received an order for goods from a customer on 14 August 2012. The goods were despatched on 18 August 2012 and the customer paid on 15 September 2012 when they received their invoice, which was dated 13 September 2012.

State what is the basic tax point date.

Answer to example 4

The basic tax point date is 18 August 2012 (i.e. the date of despatch).

Actual tax point

The basic tax point (BTP) is amended in two situations:

ACTUAL TAX POINT (ATP)

(1) EARLIER

- A tax invoice is issued or a payment is received before the basic tax point.
- In these circumstances the date of invoice or date of payment is the time when the supply is treated as taking place.

(2) LATER

- A tax invoice is issued with 14 days after the BTP
- In these circumstances the date of issue of the invoice is the time when the supply is treated as taking place provided an ATP has not arisen under (1)

Note that traders can agree a different tax point with HMRC, to fit in with their invoicing routines.

Example 5 – The time of supply (the tax point)

Explain the effect if Queue Ltd, in example 4 above, were to issue an invoice for the goods dated 30 August 2012.

Answer to example 5

The tax point would become 30 August 2012 as an invoice is issued within 14 days after the basic tax point date.

Tax point – special rules

Certain supplies of goods do not fit naturally into the above scheme:

- **Goods on sale or return**:
  The time of supply is the **earlier of**:
  - the date when the goods are adopted by the customer, or
  - 12 months after the dispatch of the goods.

- **Continuous supplies**:
  Supplies such as electricity (goods) and tax advice (services) do not have a basic tax point.

  The time of supply is the **earlier of**:
  - a tax invoice being issued, and
  - a payment received.

  The supplier may issue a tax invoice once a year in advance, showing the periodical payments and their due dates. In this case, there is a separate tax point for every amount due, being the earlier of the due date and the date on which payment is received.

- **Sales under hire purchase**. The goods are taxed as normal at the standard or zero-rate. The interest charge is an exempt supply, provided it is disclosed as a separate amount.

  The time of supply for the full value of the goods follows the normal rules (i.e. the time that the goods are collected, delivered or made available).

Test your understanding 8

On 30 April 2012, Oak Ltd ordered a new felling machine, and on 16 May 2012, paid a deposit of £25,000. The machine was despatched to Oak Ltd, on 31 May 2012. On 12 June 2012, an invoice was issued to Oak Ltd for the balance due of £75,000. This was paid on 20 June 2012.

State the tax point for:

(a) the £25,000 deposit?
(b) the balance of £75,000?

11 The value of a supply

Basic rule

The value of a taxable supply is the amount on which the VAT charge is based. This is normally the price (before VAT) charged by the supplier.

VAT fraction for standard-rated goods

The price of goods before VAT is the **VAT exclusive amount**. If the price includes VAT, then this is the **VAT inclusive amount**.

- VAT is 20% of the VAT exclusive amount.
  If a standard-rated supply is made at a price of (£2,000 + VAT), then the value of the supply is £2,000 and the total consideration given for the supply is £2,400.

- If the VAT inclusive amount is given, then the VAT element is (20/120) of the gross amount. The fraction of (1/6) gives the same result and is more commonly used.

Discounts

If a cash discount is offered, then VAT must be calculated as if the maximum discount available was taken.

Example 6 – The value of a supply

Gurminder sells standard-rated goods for £4,000, excluding VAT. A cash discount of 5% is allowed if the customer pays within seven days. Gurminder does not receive payment from the customer until a month after issuing the invoice.

Calculate the amount of VAT that should be charged on the sale assuming the standard rate of VAT is 20%.

Answer to example 6

VAT must be charged when the invoice is issued, based on the discounted amount, assuming the customer will comply with the discount terms even though the customer does not actually pay the invoice within the terms of the discount.

VAT = (20% × 95% × £4,000) = £760

Goods for own use

Where the trader withdraws goods from the business for own use, output VAT must be accounted for on the **replacement** value of the supplies.

Gifts

Gifts of inventory or non-current assets are treated as taxable supplies at replacement value, except gifts of:

- goods to the same person which cost the trader £50 or less in a 12-month period

- business samples, regardless of the number of same samples given to the recipient.

Gifts of services, whether to employees or customers, are not taxable supplies.

Test your understanding 9

State the amount of VAT due in each of the following cases:

Description	Output VAT
Sale of standard-rated goods for £500, excluding VAT. A cash discount of 3% is offered.	
Sales of standard-rated goods for £5,500, including VAT.	
Gifts of 10 calendars costing £5 each, including VAT.	
Drawings of standard-rated goods by the owner. The goods cost £20 and would cost £22 to replace, both figures exclude VAT.	

Assume that all transactions are in the quarter to 30 June 2012.

12 Recovery of input VAT

Conditions for obtaining input VAT relief

Input VAT is recoverable by taxable persons on goods and services which are supplied to them for business purposes.

A VAT invoice (see below) is needed to support the claim.

Capital vs revenue expenditure

Unlike other taxes, there is **no distinction** between capital and revenue expenditure for VAT.

Provided the assets are used for the purposes of the trade, the related input VAT is recoverable on both capital assets (i.e. purchase of plant and machinery, delivery vans, equipment, etc.) and revenue expenditure.

If capital assets are subsequently sold, output VAT must be charged as a taxable supply of goods.

However, the exception to this rule is the purchase of motor cars (see below).

Irrecoverable input VAT

Input VAT on the following goods and services cannot be recovered:

- Business entertaining (e.g. entertaining suppliers and **U.K.** customers)
    - although VAT incurred on staff entertaining and entertaining overseas customers is recoverable.

- Motor cars, unless they are:
    - used 100% for business purposes (e.g. driving school cars), in which case 100% recovery available, or
    - leased, in which case 50% of input VAT is recoverable where the car has some private use.

Note that where input VAT cannot be recovered on the purchase of a motor car, no output VAT will be due on its disposal.

KAPLAN PUBLISHING

Example 7 – Recovery of input VAT

Riker plc sells standard-rated supplies and is registered for VAT. It incurs the following costs during 2012.

(1) £5,400 on business entertaining (UK customers) and £2,400 on staff entertaining.

(2) £30,000 on a new car for the managing director and £72,000 on new delivery lorries.

The managing director's car is used partly for private purposes.

All figures are VAT exclusive.

State the amount of input tax relief the business can claim and the figures that should be included in the financial statements in respect of these items.

Answer to example 7

(1) **Entertaining UK customers**

No VAT recoverable on business entertaining of UK customers. The VAT inclusive figure of (£5,400 + 20%) = £6,480, charged against profit will be a disallowed expense for the purpose of the tax-adjusted profit computation.

VAT of £480 (20% × £2,400), will be recoverable on staff entertaining. The VAT exclusive amount of £2,400 will be charged against profits and is an allowable expense for tax purposes.

(2) **Car and lorries**

No VAT recoverable on cars with private use. The VAT inclusive figure of (£30,000 + 20%) = £36,000, will be capitalised in the accounts and will be eligible for capital allowances.

VAT of £14,400 (20% × £72,000) is recoverable on the lorries. The VAT exclusive £72,000 will be capitalised in the accounts and will be eligible for capital allowances.

Private use

Input VAT cannot be claimed for goods or services that are not used for business purposes.

Where goods or services are used partly for private and partly for business purposes (e.g. use of telephone / mobile phone), an appropriate apportionment is made to calculate the recoverable input VAT.

The exception to this rule is however the recoverability of input VAT on motor expenses (see below).

Motor expenses

A business can recover **all** input VAT incurred on the running costs of a car, such as fuel and repairs, even when there is some private use.

Note that VAT is not charged on the insurance and road fund licence.

When a business pays for fuel costs for an employee, sole trader or partner and there is some private use of the vehicle, a VAT charge will be payable:

- output VAT is payable on the cost of fuel reimbursed by the employee
- if the employee does not reimburse the employer, output VAT is due based on a prescribed scale charge.

The scale charge depends on the CO_2 emissions of the car. The scale charges will be provided in the examination if necessary.

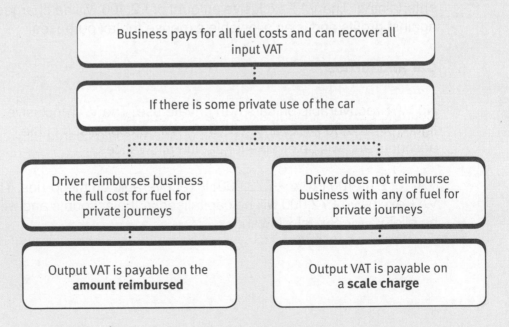

Note that for the 2013 examinations, partial reimbursement of fuel costs is not examinable.

Example 8 – Recovery of input VAT

Forge Ltd provides a company car with CO_2 emissions of 205 g/km for the managing director for business and private use. The company pays for all running costs including petrol, with no reimbursement by the employee. The relevant VAT fuel scale charge is £517.

State the value of the output and output tax in respect of the running costs for this car for the quarter to 31 December 2012.

Answer to example 8

The scale charge for a petrol car with CO_2 emissions of 205 g/km is £517. This means that £517 is the value of the VAT inclusive output.

The output VAT charge is £86 (£517 × 1/6).

Note the scale charge will be given in the question in the examination.

Test your understanding 10

State which of the following statements are true or false. Assume all the businesses in the question are VAT registered traders and the transactions occur in the quarter to 30 September 2012.

(1) VAT incurred by a business on entertaining overseas customers is recoverable.

(2) Firmin plc can recover £3,000 on the purchase of an item of plant and machinery costing £15,000, including VAT.

(3) A business can never recover the VAT incurred on buying a car.

(4) A business supplies a company car with CO_2 emissions of 200 g/km to Albert. The company pays all the running costs of the car, incurring £2,100 of input tax for the VAT quarter. Albert does not reimburse any of the fuel costs. The quarterly scale charge for a car with CO_2 emissions of 200 g/km is £500 (VAT inclusive). The net input tax recoverable in respect of motor expenses is £2,017.

13 Relief for impaired debts

Normally, VAT output tax is accounted for when an invoice is issued. If the debt becomes irrecoverable, the seller has paid VAT to HMRC and never recovers this from the customer. This position is addressed by the seller being able to claim VAT relief for impairment losses.

The following conditions apply:

- At least **six months** must have elapsed from the time that payment was due (or the date of supply if later).

- The debt must have been written off in the seller's VAT account.

- Relief is obtained by adding the VAT element of the impaired debt to the input tax claimed.

- Claims for relief for impaired debts are subject to a three-year time limit.

Example 9 – Relief for impaired debts

Fox Ltd made sales to X Ltd as follows: £3,500 due for payment on 1 August 2012 and £2,260 due for payment on 1 September 2012. Fox Ltd wrote off the debts in January 2013.

State the amount of relief for impaired debts available to Fox Ltd, in the quarter to 31 March 2013.

Answer to example 9

At 31 March, both invoices are unpaid more than 6 months from the due date of payment.

The total debt to be written off is £5,760, including VAT. A claim for relief can be made for the VAT element of £960 (£5,760 × 1/6).

This claim can be made by adding £960 to the input tax claimed for the quarter.

Note that VAT is recovered at the rate at which it was originally charged, not at the rate at the time of the VAT recovery.

Test your understanding 11

On 1 December 2012, Berry Ltd wrote off two debts. The first was a debt of £2,456, due for payment on 1 May 2012 and the second a debt of £3,100, due for payment on 31 August 2012.

State the amount of relief for impaired debts available to the company in the return for the quarter ended 31 December 2012.

14 Comprehensive example

Test your understanding 12

Dynamo Ltd commenced trading as a wholesaler on 1 November 2011. Its sales have been as follows:

		£			£
2011	November	3,950	2012 June		5,350
	December	4,550	July		5,150
2012	January	5,050	August		5,950
	February	4,850	September		6,450
	March	4,250	October		9,350
	April	4,450	November		10,650
	May	4,650	December		11,650

The company's sales are all standard-rated, and the above figures are exclusive of VAT.

(a) Explain from what date Dynamo Ltd will be required to compulsorily register for VAT, and what action the company must then take.

(b) Explain the circumstances in which Dynamo Ltd will be allowed to recover input VAT incurred on goods purchased and services incurred prior to the date of VAT registration.

(c) Advise Dynamo Ltd of the VAT rules that determine the tax point in respect of a supply of goods.

15 Chapter summary

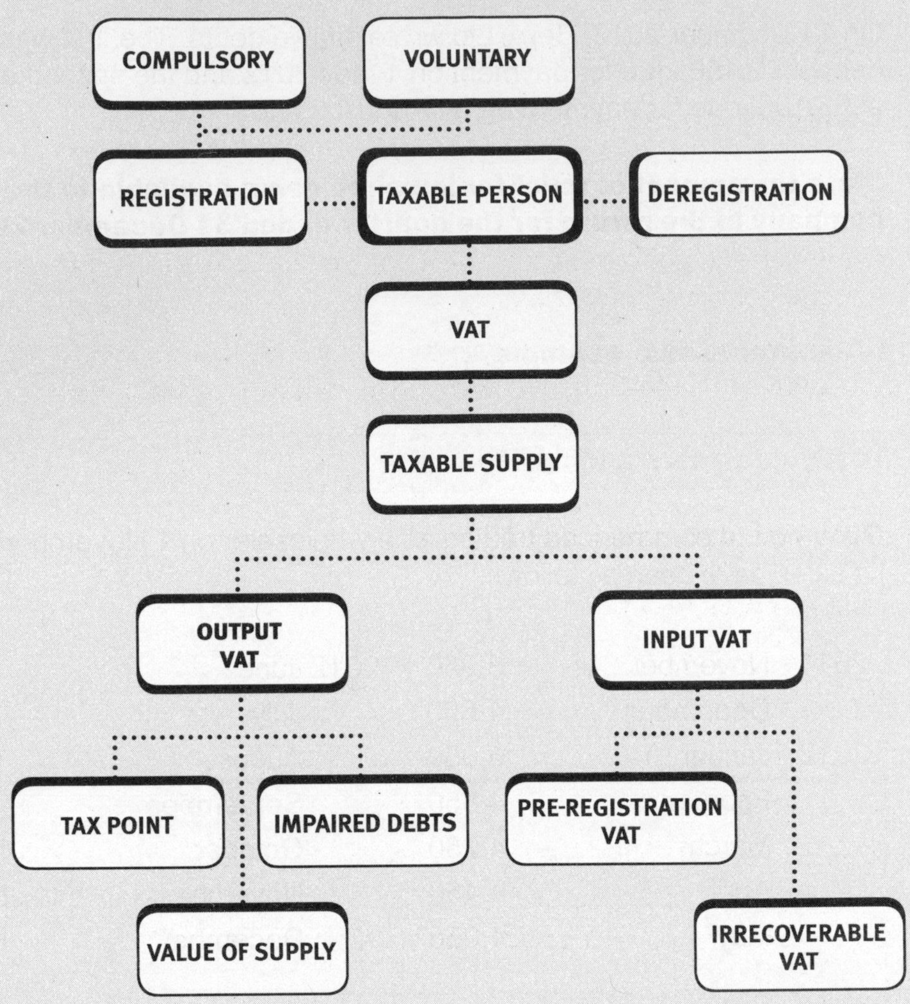

Test your understanding answers

Test your understanding 1

Correct or incorrect

(1) Correct.

(2) Incorrect. Lucy is not a taxable person and is not making a supply in the course of a business.

(3) Incorrect. Businesses must pay output VAT over to HMRC after deducting any input VAT they have suffered for the period.

Test your understanding 2

Missing words

(1) cannot

(2) 20%

(3) supplies

(4) can, cannot

Test your understanding 3

Zero-rated or exempt

Item	Zero rated	Exempt
Bread sold in a supermarket	√	
Children's shoes	√	
Sale of motor insurance policy		√
Newspapers	√	
Sale of shares		√
Train ticket	√	

Test your understanding 4

Jay

Both newspapers and stationery are taxable supplies, so Jay must register when his sales for the previous 12 months exceed the registration limit of £77,000.

In his first year, sales are £5,100 per month, so his turnover for the year ended 30 September 2011, is £61,200. Thereafter, his sales are £6,880 per month, so each month he sells £1,780 more than one year ago.

His cumulative turnover for the previous 12 months at each month end thereafter is as follows:

Month end	£
31 October 2011	62,980
30 November 2011	64,760
31 December 2011	66,540
31 January 2012	68,320
28 February 2012	70,100
31 March 2012	71,880
30 April 2012	73,660
31 May 2012	75,440
30 June 2012	77,220

He must notify HMRC by 30 July 2012 and will be registered with effect from 1 August 2012, or an earlier date agreed with HMRC.

Test your understanding 4

Test your understanding 5

Name	Supplies	Details
Majid	Accountancy services	Taxable turnover will exceed £77,000 at the end of March 2013. Notify HMRC by 30 April 2013 and register with effect from 1 May 2013.
Jane	Baby wear	Sales for the next 30 days will exceed £77,000, so Jane must notify HMRC by the end of the 30 days on 30 March 2013 and will be registered with effect from 1 March 2013. Note that Jane could apply for exemption from registration as she is making wholly zero-rated supplies, but she would not be able to reclaim any input tax. Jane must complete a VAT registration form in accordance with the compulsory registration rules. However she can claim exemption from registration on that form.
Sayso Ltd	Insurance	Making wholly exempt supplies so cannot register.

Test your understanding 6

X Ltd

(1) Accountancy is a service. It is supplied more than six months prior to registration, hence, no input VAT can be reclaimed.

(2) Rent is exempt so no VAT paid and no VAT reclaimable.

(3) VAT of £192 (£1,150 × 20/120) is included in the cost of stationery. This can be recovered as the stationery had not been used prior to registration.

(4) 40% of the inventory is unsold at registration, so 40% of the VAT on the goods can be recovered. This is £400 (40% × 20% × £5,000).

(5) The machinery is still owned by the company, so the VAT of £1,300 (£6,500 × 20%) can be recovered.

Test your understanding 7

Jig Ltd and Elk Ltd

If Jig Ltd closes down its business on 10 January 2013, the company must notify HMRC on or before 9 February 2013 and is then deregistered from 10 January 2013, or an agreed later date.

If Elk Ltd thinks that taxable turnover for the year to 31 December 2013 will be £40,000, and applies for deregistration on 1 January 2013, the company can be deregistered with effect from 1 January 2013 or an agreed later date.

Test your understanding 8

(a) **£25,000 deposit**

The basic tax point is the date of despatch, 31 May 2012.

As the deposit was paid before the date of despatch, this is the actual tax point (i.e. 16 May 2012).

(b) **The balance of £75,000**

As an invoice was issued within 14 days of the basic tax point; the date of the invoice is the actual tax point (i.e. 12 June 2012).

Test your understanding 9

Description	Output VAT
Sale of standard-rated goods for £500, excluding VAT. A cash discount of 3% is offered.	(20% × £500 × 97%) = £97
Sales of standard-rated goods for £5,500, including VAT.	(1/6 × £5,500) = £917
Gifts of 10 calendars costing £5 each, including VAT.	As less than £50 each, no output VAT
Drawings of standard-rated goods by the owner. The goods cost £20 and would cost £22 to replace, both figures excluding VAT.	(20% × £22) = £4

Note that calculations in the examination are to the nearest £.

Test your understanding 10

True or false

(1) True

(2) False. (1/6 of £15,000) = £2,500.

(3) False. Input VAT can be recovered for cars with 100% business use.

(4) True. The business can recover £2,100 input tax but must account for £83 (£500 × 1/6) of output tax on the fuel scale charge. The net input tax recoverable is £2,017 (£2,100 – £83).

Test your understanding 11

Berry Ltd

The second debt is less than six months old, so no relief is available yet.

On the first debt the VAT included of (1/6 × £2,456) = £409, can be recovered.

Test your understanding 12

Dynamo Ltd

(a) **Compulsory registration**

- Dynamo Ltd will become liable to compulsory VAT registration when its taxable supplies during any 12-month period exceed £77,000.

- This will happen on 31 December 2012 when taxable supplies will amount to £77,800 (£5,050 + £4,850 + £4,250 + £4,450 + £4,650 + £5,350 + £5,150 + £5,950 + £6,450 + £9,350 + £10,650 + £11,650).

- Dynamo Ltd will have to notify HMRC by 30 January 2013, being 30 days after the end of the period.

- The company will be registered from 1 February 2013 or from an agreed earlier date.

(b) **Recovery of input VAT on goods and services purchased prior to registration**

- The goods must be acquired for business purposes, and not be sold or consumed prior to registration.

- The goods were not acquired more than four years prior to registration.

- The services must be supplied for business purposes.

- The services were not supplied more than six months prior to registration.

(c) **The supply of goods**

- The basic tax point is the date goods are made available to the customer.

- If an invoice is issued or payment received before the basic tax point, then this becomes the actual tax point.

- If an invoice is issued within 14 days of the basic tax point, the invoice date will replace the basic tax point date provided an actual tax point has not already arisen as above.

26

VAT: Administration and overseas aspects

Chapter learning objectives

Upon completion of this chapter you will be able to:

- prepare the computation of VAT payable/repayable for a return period

- explain the VAT return and payment procedures for different types of traders

- list the business records which must be retained for VAT

- list the information required on a normal VAT invoice

- explain when a less detailed VAT invoice can be issued and list the content

- identify how a default surcharge penalty arises and calculate it

- explain the procedure and effect when errors on earlier VAT returns are identified

- describe when a default interest charge will arise and calculate it

- list the conditions for the cash accounting, annual accounting and flat rate schemes

- understand the primary purpose of the cash accounting scheme and when it would be advantageous to use the scheme

- understand the primary purpose of the annual accounting scheme, when it would be advantageous to use and how it operates

- demonstrate how a flat rate scheme operates and state when this will be advantageous

- advise on the VAT implications of imports and exports

- advise on the VAT implications of acquisitions and supplies within the EU.

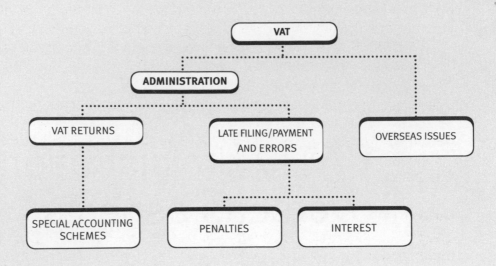

1 VAT computation

All registered traders have to:

- complete a VAT return every return period (see below), and
- pay net VAT due to HMRC or reclaim net VAT repayable from HMRC.

Details of output and input VAT must be included, together with claims for relief for impaired debts and any errors made on earlier returns below a de minimis limit (see section 7).

Example 1 – VAT computation

Cart Ltd is registered for VAT, and its sales are all standard rated.

The following information relates to the company's VAT return for the quarter ended 31 December 2012:

(1) Standard-rated sales amounted to £240,000. Cart Ltd offers its customers a 5% discount for prompt payment, and this discount is taken by half of the customers.

(2) Standard-rated purchases and expenses amounted to £71,280. This figure includes £960 for entertaining UK customers.

(3) On 15 December 2012, the company wrote off irrecoverable debts of £4,000 and £1,680, in respect of invoices due for payment on 10 May and 5 August 2012, respectively. The amounts represent the discounted amount.

(4) On 30 December 2012, the company purchased a motor car at a cost of £32,900, for the use of a director, and machinery at a cost of £42,300. Both these figures are inclusive of VAT. The motor car is used for both business and private mileage.

Unless stated otherwise, all of the above figures are exclusive of VAT.

Calculate the amount of VAT payable by Cart Ltd for the quarter.

Answer to example 1

	£	£
Output VAT		
Sales (£240,000 × 95% × 20%)		45,600
Input VAT		
Purchases and expenses		
(£71,280 – £960) = £70,320 × 20%)	14,064	
Relief for impaired debts (£4,000 × 20%)	800	
Machinery (£42,300 × 1/6)	7,050	
		(21,914)
VAT payable		23,686

Notes:

(1) The calculation of output VAT must take into account the discount for prompt payment, even if customers do not take it.

(2) Input VAT on business entertaining (for UK customers) cannot be reclaimed.

(3) Relief for an impaired debt is not given until six months from the time that payment is due. Relief is given on the discounted amount.

(4) Input VAT on motor cars not used wholly for business purposes cannot be reclaimed.

Test your understanding 1

Hairby Ltd has provided the following information for the quarter to 31 March 2013.

(1) Sales consisted of £45,000 of standard-rated sales and £15,000 of zero-rated sales.

(2) Purchases for resale were all standard rated and totalled £31,000.

(3) Standard-rated expenses were £7,600, including £350 for entertaining UK customers.

(4) One gift to a customer out of inventory costing £250 was made. The replacement cost of the goods was £300.

(5) A photocopier costing £6,400 was purchased.

All figures exclude VAT.

Calculate the amount of VAT payable by Hairby Ltd for the quarter ended 31 March 2013.

2 VAT return and payment procedures

Normal VAT accounting

VAT return periods are normally three months long, but traders who regularly receive repayments, can opt to have monthly return periods to receive their repayments earlier.

- VAT returns show total output VAT and total input VAT for the period.

- All businesses must file their VAT return and pay VAT electronically.

- The deadline for filing and payment online is:
    - **One month and seven days** after the end of the quarter.

VAT refunds

- VAT refunds are normally made within 28 days.

- Where it is discovered that VAT has been overpaid in the past, the time limit for claiming a refund is four years from the accounting period end.

> ### Substantial traders
>
> Substantial traders are those with a VAT liability exceeding £2.3 million p.a.
>
> - Monthly payments on account are required.
> - Payments at the end of months 2 and 3 in every quarter are 1/24th of the annual liability for the previous year.
> - Any additional amounts are paid with the normal VAT return.
>
> Other methods can be agreed with HMRC for calculating the payments on account.

3 VAT records

Records must be kept of all goods and services received and supplied in the course of a business. No particular form is specified, but they must be sufficient to allow the VAT return to be completed and to allow HMRC to check the return.

Records must be kept up-to-date and must be preserved for **six years**.

In practice, the main records that must be kept are as follows:

- Copies of all VAT invoices issued.
- A record of all outputs (e.g. a sales day book).
- Evidence supporting claims for the recovery of input VAT (e.g. invoices).
- A record of all inputs (e.g. purchase day book).
- VAT account.

4 Normal VAT invoices

A VAT invoice must be issued when a standard-rated supply is made to a VAT registered business. No invoice is required if the supply is exempt, zero-rated or to a non-VAT registered customer (however, see below regarding invoices issued by retailers).

A VAT invoice should be issued within 30 days of the date that the taxable supply is treated as being made.

The original VAT invoice is sent to the customer and forms their evidence for reclaiming input VAT, and a copy must be kept by the supplier to support the calculation of output VAT.

A VAT invoice must contain the following particulars:

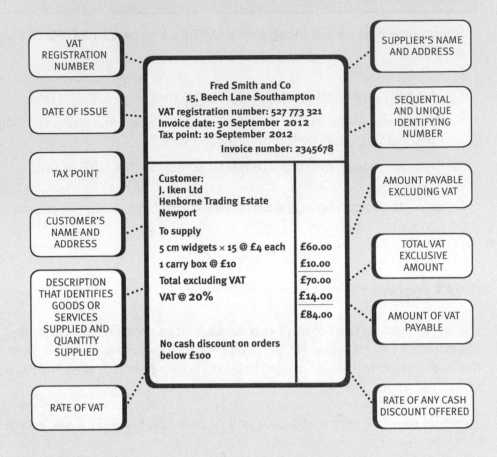

5 Less detailed VAT invoices issued by retailers

In broad terms, a retailer is someone who supplies goods and services to the general public, rather than to other traders. They are not necessarily retail shops, so a hairdresser is just as much a retailer as a newsagent or garage proprietor.

Retailers only have to provide a VAT invoice if a customer requests it. Such an invoice can be less detailed than normal, if the consideration for the supply is £250 or less.

This less detailed invoice must show the following information:

- The retailer's name, address and VAT registration number.
- The date of supply.
- A description of the goods or services supplied.
- The consideration for the supply.
- The rate of VAT in force at the time of supply.

KAPLAN PUBLISHING

Test your understanding 2

State which of the following statements are true or false:

(1) All VAT invoices must show the rate of VAT on the supply.

(2) A VAT invoice should show the customer's VAT registration number.

(3) Retailers must always supply a full VAT invoice to their customers when requested.

(4) Where the value of a supply is more than £250, a retailer should always issue a detailed VAT invoice.

6 The default surcharge

A default occurs if a VAT return is not submitted on time or a payment of VAT is made late. The sequence is as follows:

- On the first default, HMRC will serve a surcharge liability notice on the trader.

- The notice specifies a surcharge period, starting on the date of the notice and ending on the 12-month anniversary of the end of the VAT period to which the default relates.

- If the trader has a further default during the surcharge period, there are two consequences:
  - The surcharge period is extended to the 12-month anniversary of the VAT period to which the new default relates.

  - If the default involves the late payment of VAT, then the trader will be subject to a surcharge penalty.

- There is no surcharge penalty where a late VAT return involves the repayment of VAT, or if the VAT payable is £Nil.

Calculating the surcharge penalty

The rate of surcharge penalty depends on the number of defaults in the surcharge period:

Default in the surcharge period	Surcharge as a percentage of the unpaid VAT due
First	2%
Second	5%
Third	10%
Fourth	15%

- Surcharge penalties at the rates of 2% and 5% are not made for amounts less than £400.

- Where the rate of surcharge is 10% or 15%, a surcharge penalty is the higher of:

  (i)   £30, or

  (ii) the actual amount of the calculated surcharge.

- The surcharge liability period will only end when a trader submits four consecutive quarterly VAT returns on time, and also pays any VAT due on time.

Example 2 – The default surcharge

Mole Ltd's VAT return for the quarter ended 30 June 2012, was submitted late, and the VAT due of £14,500 was not paid until 16 August 2012.

The company's VAT return for the following quarter to 30 September 2012, was also submitted late and the VAT due of £26,200, was not paid until 9 November 2012.

State the consequences for Mole Ltd.

Answer to example 2

VAT return period for the quarter ended 30 June 2012	VAT return period for the quarter ended 30 September 2012
• First default	• First default within the surcharge period
• Surcharge liability notice issued	• Surcharge penalty 2% of £26,200 = £524
• Surcharge period ends 30 June 2013	• Surcharge period extended to 30 September 2013

Test your understanding 3

Fill in the missing blanks in the following statements:

(1) If a business submits its VAT return late then HMRC will issue a . . . .
. . . . (3 words).

(2) The . . . . default within a surcharge period will attract a penalty of 5%.

(3) In order to avoid further surcharges, a business must submit all VAT returns and pay all VAT due, on time for a period of . . . . months.

(4) If a trader's first default produces a penalty of £300, then HMRC . . . .
. . . . collect it.

7 Errors on VAT returns

Self-assessment

VAT is a self-assessed tax. The trader calculates their own liability or repayment.

- HMRC make occasional control visits to check that returns are correct.

- HMRC have the power to enter business premises, inspect documents, including income statements and statements of financial position, take samples, and inspect computers records. See Chapter 12 for HMRC information and inspection powers.

Errors found on earlier VAT returns

If a trader realises that there is an error, this may lead to a standard penalty as there has been a submission of an incorrect VAT return.

The calculation of the standard penalty is covered in Chapter 12, section 7.

However, if the error is below the de minimis level and voluntarily disclosed, no default interest will be charged.

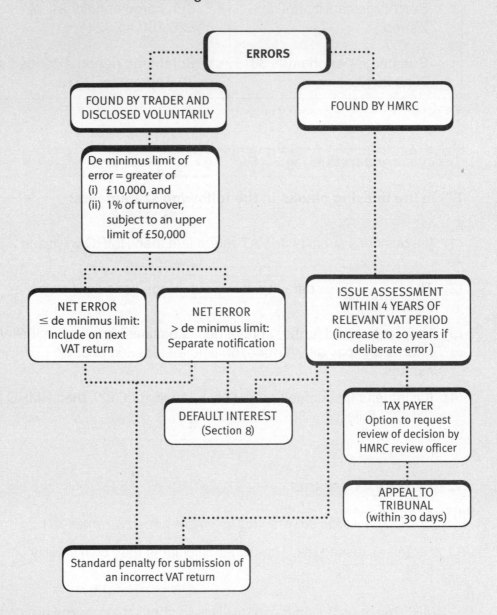

Example 3 – Errors on VAT returns

Bishop is a registered trader who prepares VAT returns quarterly. In his quarter to 30 June 2012, he has a turnover of £103,450 and he discovers the following errors in earlier returns:

(1) Bishop misread the total of output VAT for the previous quarter as £45,590, when it actually read £54,590. He entered £45,590 on his return.

(2) Input VAT on UK customer entertaining of £180, was wrongly reclaimed as input tax in the same quarter.

(3) No input tax was reclaimed on the purchase of a computer in September 2011, costing £1,680 plus VAT.

State the action Bishop should take to correct these errors.

Assume the rate of VAT has always been 20%.

Answer to example 3

		£
(1) Output VAT	(£54,590 – £45,590)	9,000
(2) UK customer entertaining		180
(3) Computer input VAT	(£1,680 x 20%)	(336)
		8,844

De minimis limit = greater of:

(i) £10,000

(ii) (1% x £103,450) = £1,034

As the net error of £8,844 < the de minimis limit of £10,000:

Bishop should include the amounts on his return to 30 June 2012.

This increases his VAT payable for the quarter ended 30 June 2012 by £8,844.

No default interest will be imposed by HMRC (but there may be a standard penalty for the submission of an incorrect VAT return).

HMRC assessments

- HMRC may find that a VAT return is incomplete or incorrect. If so, they can issue an assessment to collect the VAT that has been underpaid, if applicable, by the trader.

- An assessment must be made within four years of the relevant VAT period. The four-year time limit is increased to 20 years where VAT has been lost, due to fraud or dishonest conduct.

- Appeals in connection with VAT, are made to the two tier Tribunal system (see Chapter 12). The normal time limit for appealing is 30 days.

- Before an appeal the taxpayer has the option to request a review of a decision by a HMRC review officer.

8 Default interest

Interest is charged, if HMRC raise an assessment, or an error is voluntarily disclosed by the trader, and the net value of errors exceeds the de minimis limit.

Interest is charged from the date that the outstanding VAT should have been paid, to the actual date of payment.

Any interest charged by HMRC is limited to a maximum of three years, prior to the date of the assessment or voluntary disclosure.

Example 4 – Default interest

Hem Ltd discovers that in the quarter ended 31 May 2012, it made an error on its VAT return and output VAT of £12,800 was under declared. This was in excess of the de minimis limit.

The company voluntarily disclosed the amount to HMRC, paying the VAT due on 7 October 2012.

Assuming the rate of default interest is 3%, calculate the charge made on Hem Ltd.

Answer to example 4

The under declared VAT should have been paid on 7 July 2012.

Default interest will be charged from 7 July to 7 October 2012. This will be (£12,800 × 3% × 3/12) = £96.

Test your understanding 4

HMRC issue an assessment on 30 April 2013 showing £4,100 VAT payable, for the quarter ended 30 June 2012. Grab Ltd pays the outstanding sum on 7 May 2013.

Assume the rate of interest is 3%.

Calculate, to the nearest pence, the default interest charged on Grab Ltd.

9 The cash accounting scheme

Purpose of the scheme

Normally VAT is accounted for on the basis of invoices issued and received in a return period. Accordingly:

- output VAT is paid to HMRC by reference to the period in which the invoice is issued regardless of whether payment has been received from the customer.

- input VAT is reclaimed from HMRC by reference to the invoices received in the return period, even if payment has not been made to the supplier.

This can give cash flow and impaired debt problems, particularly in the case of smaller businesses. As a result:

- 'Smaller' businesses may optionally use the cash accounting scheme if the conditions, set out below, are met.

- Under the cash accounting scheme VAT is accounted for on the basis of cash receipts and payments, rather than on the basis of invoice dates, issued and received.

- The tax point becomes the time of receipt or payment.

Advantages	Disadvantages
• Businesses selling on credit do not have to pay output VAT to HMRC until they receive it from customers.	• Input tax cannot be claimed until the invoice is paid. This delays recovery of input VAT.
• This gives automatic relief for impaired debts.	• Not suitable for businesses with a lot of cash sales or zero-rated supplies which would simply suffer a delay in the recovery of input VAT.

Conditions

The scheme is aimed at smaller businesses, hence, there are a number of conditions:

- Trader's VAT returns must be up-to-date and they must have no convictions for VAT offences or penalties for dishonest conduct.

- Taxable turnover, including zero-rated sales, but excluding sales of capital assets, must not exceed £1,350,000 p.a.

- A trader must leave the scheme once their taxable turnover exceeds £1,600,000 p.a.

- The cash accounting scheme cannot be used for goods that are invoiced more than six months in advance of the payment date, or where an invoice is issued prior to the supply actually taking place.

Test your understanding 5

State which of the following businesses would benefit from joining the cash accounting scheme:

(1) JB Ltd, which operates a retail shop selling directly to the public. All sales are for cash.

(2) Amber and Co, which manufactures and sells computer printers to other businesses.

(3) John Smith, who manufactures children's shoes and sells them to retailers.

10 Annual accounting

Purpose of the scheme

Smaller businesses may find it costly or inconvenient to prepare (the normal) four quarterly VAT returns.

An 'annual' accounting scheme is available, whereby, a single VAT return is filed for a 12-month period (normally, the accounting period of the business). This helps relieve the burden of administration.

How the scheme works

Only one VAT return is submitted each year, but VAT payments must still be made regularly. The scheme works as follows:

- The annual return must be filed **within two months** of the end of the annual return period.

- Normally, nine payments on account of the VAT liability for the year, are made at the end of months 4 to 12 of the year. Each payment represents 10% of the VAT liability for the previous year.

- Regular payments aid budgeting and possibly cashflow if the VAT payable is increasing.

- A new business will base its payments on an estimate of the VAT liability for the year.

- A balancing payment (or repayment) is made when the return is filed.

- Businesses may apply to HMRC to agree quarterly payments on account instead of the normal nine monthly payments.

Conditions for the annual accounting scheme

As with cash accounting the scheme is aimed at smaller businesses:

- Businesses can join the scheme provided their taxable turnover (excluding the sale of capital assets) does not exceed £1,350,000 p.a.

- The business must be up-to-date with its VAT returns.

Test your understanding 6

Jump Ltd applies to use the annual accounting scheme from 1 January 2012. The company's net VAT liability for the y/e 31 December 2011, was £3,600. The actual net VAT liability for the y/e 31 December 2012, is £3,821.

Explain the returns and payments Jump Ltd must make for the y/e 31 December 2012.

11 The flat rate scheme

Operation of the scheme

The optional flat rate scheme is aimed at simplifying the way in which very small businesses calculate their VAT liability.

Under the flat rate scheme, a business calculates its VAT liability by simply applying a flat rate percentage to total turnover.

This removes the need to calculate and record output VAT and input VAT and can save the business money.

- The flat rate percentage is applied to the gross (VAT inclusive) total turnover figure (inclusive of zero-rated and exempt supplies); with no input VAT being recovered.

- The percentage varies according to the type of trade that the business is involved in, and will be given to you in the examination.

- A VAT invoice must still be issued to customers and VAT at the rate of 20% is still charged on standard-rated supplies.

- The flat rate scheme percentage is only used to calculate the VAT due to HMRC.

Conditions for the scheme

To join the scheme the expected taxable turnover (excluding VAT) for the next twelve months must not exceed £150,000.

A business has to leave the scheme if total turnover (including VAT) exceeds £230,000.

> **Test your understanding 7**
>
> In the y/e 31 December 2012, Apple Ltd has annual sales of £90,500, all of which are standard rated and to the general public. The company incurs standard-rated expenses of £4,500 p.a. These figures are inclusive of VAT.
>
> **Calculate Apple Ltd's VAT liability using:**
>
> (1) **The normal method.**
>
> (2) **The flat rate scheme.**
>
> Assume a relevant flat rate percentage for Apple Ltd's trade of 10%.

12 Overseas aspects of VAT

VAT is a tax levied within the European Union (EU) only. It is therefore necessary to distinguish imports and exports from outside the EU from transactions within the EU.

Imports from outside the EU

Goods

VAT is charged on goods imported from outside the EU as if it were a customs duty. It is normally collected direct from the importer at the place of importation, such as a port or airport.

- If the imported goods are immediately placed in a bonded warehouse or free zone, then VAT is postponed until the goods are removed from the warehouse or zone.

- Approved traders can pay all their VAT on imports through the Duty deferment system. This allows all VAT on imports to be paid on the 15th of the month following the month of importation. This assists the traders' cash flow and is more convenient than having to be paid at the point of import.

- VAT can then be reclaimed as input VAT on the VAT return for the period during which the goods were imported.

- The net effect of importing goods is therefore the same as if the goods were bought within the UK.

Services

The treatment of services purchased from outside the EU is generally the same as the treatment of services purchased from within the EU, and is discussed later in this section.

Exports outside the EU

Goods

The export of goods outside the EU is a zero-rated supply.

This is a favourable treatment for the exporter as it allows them to recover input tax. It also means the customer is not charged VAT.

Services

The supply of services outside the EU is outside the scope of VAT.

Transactions within the EU

Goods

The following table summarises the two situations which can occur when trading goods between EU countries.

	Transactions	Accounting for VAT
Supplier and customer registered (the destination system).	Zero-rated in country of origin. Chargeable at the appropriate rate in force in country of destination.	(a) Supplier does not account for output VAT – supply zero-rated. (b) Customer must account for output VAT on their VAT return at the rate in force in customer's country. (c) VAT suffered by customer may be reclaimed by them as input VAT in the appropriate quarter.
Supplier registered but not customer (the origin system).	Chargeable at the appropriate rate in force in the country of origin.	(a) Supplier accounts for output VAT. (b) No input VAT recoverable by the customer.

The output VAT on purchases from the EU must be accounted for by the customer in their VAT return for the date of acquisition.

The date of acquisition is the earlier of:

- The date of the VAT invoice

- The 15th day of the month following the month in which the goods came into the UK.

Both the output VAT and input VAT are therefore likely to be on the same VAT return and will cancel out.

Services

The rules governing VAT on the supply of services are complex. These notes just cover the basic principles needed for the F6 examination.

For services, VAT is generally charged in the place of supply.

The place of supply varies depending on whether the customer is a business or non-business customer.

Supply of service to	Place of supply
Business customer	Where the customer is established
Non-business customer	Where the supplier is established

These rules can be applied to a UK business as follows:

UK business		Accounting for VAT
Supplies services to	Overseas business customer	• Place of supply is overseas • Outside the scope of UK VAT
	Overseas non-business customer	• Place of supply is UK. • Output VAT charged at standard UK rate
Receives services from	Overseas business	• Place of supply is UK • Reverse charge procedure: UK business accounts for 'output VAT' at standard UK rate on VAT return. This VAT can then be reclaimed as input VAT.

Time of supply for cross border supplies of services

The rules are governed primarily by when a service is performed and a distinction is made between single and continuous supplies.

- For single supplies, the tax point will occur when the service is completed or when it is paid for if this is earlier.

- In the case of continuous supplies, the tax point will be the end of each billing or payment period.

Test your understanding 8

Overseas Ltd has been importing computers from Ruritania since 1 January 2013. Ruritania is not currently a member of the European Union but is expected to join in the near future. Overseas Ltd makes only taxable supplies. For the quarter ended 31 March 2013 imports of £100,000 have been made. This amount excludes any VAT or duties.

Explain how Overseas Ltd will have to account for VAT on the computers imported from Ruritania.

State how will this change if Ruritania becomes a member of the European Union and show the entries required on Overseas Ltd's VAT return in this case.

Test your understanding 9

Foreign Ltd, a UK resident company registered for VAT, has the following international transactions.

(a) Sale of children's toys to a customer in Germany, who is VAT registered.

(b) Sale of ladies' handbags to Venezuela.

(c) Sale of men's ties to an Italian customer, who is not VAT registered.

(d) Purchase of silk fabric from Hong Kong.

Outline the VAT treatment in each case for Foreign Ltd.

Note that Germany and Italy are EU countries.

13 Chapter summary

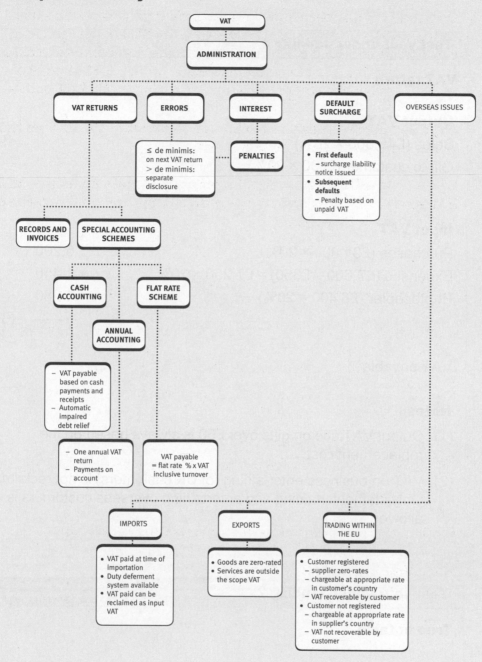

Test your understanding answers

Test your understanding 1

VAT return

Output VAT	£	£
Sales (£45,000 × 20%)		9,000
Gift to customer (£300 × 20%)		60
		9,060
Input VAT		
Purchases (£31,000 × 20%)	6,200	
Expenses (£7,600 – £350) = £7,250 × 20%	1,450	
Photocopier (£6,400 × 20%)	1,280	
		(8,930)
VAT payable		130

Notes

(1) Output VAT due on gifts over £50 is always based on the replacement cost.

(2) VAT on business entertaining (of UK customers) is not reclaimable. Only staff entertaining and entertaining overseas customers is allowed.

Test your understanding 2

True or false

(1) True

(2) False – it should show the **supplier's** VAT registration number.

(3) False – for supplies below £250 they need only issue a less detailed invoice.

(4) False – only if the customer requests.

KAPLAN PUBLISHING

Test your understanding 3

Missing words

(1) Surcharge liability notice

(2) Second

(3) Twelve

(4) Will not

Test your understanding 4

Grab Ltd

Interest runs from 7 July 2012 to 7 May 2013.

Default interest at 3% for 10 months will be charged:

(£4,100 × 3% × 10/12) = £102.50

Test your understanding 5

Cash accounting scheme

Amber and Co would benefit from joining the cash accounting scheme.

JB Ltd makes cash sales, and John Smith zero-rated sales, so neither of them have a problem with VAT on impaired debts.

Joining the scheme may also delay the recovery of input VAT on supplies.

They are therefore unlikely to benefit from joining the cash accounting scheme.

Test your understanding 6

Jump Ltd

Jump Ltd's annual VAT return must be submitted by 28 February 2013.

Payments of VAT will be made as follows:

	£
Monthly payments: April 2012 to December 2012	
9 at £360 (£3,600 × 10%)	3,240
Final payment due on 28 February 2013	
(£3,821 – £3,240)	581
	———
	3,821
	———

Test your understanding 7

Apple Ltd

(1) Using the normal method, Apple Ltd has a VAT liability as follows:

		£
Output VAT	(£90,500 × 1/6)	15,083
Input VAT	(£4,500 × 1/6)	(750)
		———
VAT payable		14,333
		———

(2) Using the flat rate method Apple Ltd, has the following VAT liability:

(£90,500 × 10%) = £9,050

By using the flat rate scheme:

- there is a VAT saving of £5,283 (£14,333 – £9,050).

- Administration is also simplified; Apple Ltd will not have to issue VAT invoices, as none of its customers are VAT-registered.

Overseas Ltd

(1) **Ruritania is not in the EU**

Overseas Ltd will have to account for VAT on the value of the computers (including any carriage and import charges) at the point of importation. This will amount to £20,000 (£100,000 × 20%). Overseas Ltd can then claim input tax relief of £20,000 on their next VAT return.

Overseas Ltd may be able to defer the payment of VAT on import under the duty deferment scheme and pay monthly on the 15th of the month following the month of importation.

(2) **Ruritania is in the EU**

The goods will be zero-rated supplies in Ruritania and Overseas Ltd will be responsible for paying over the output VAT on the computers at the rate in force in the UK. This is essentially the same as if Ruritania were not in the EU, except that the VAT does not have to be paid over immediately at the date of importation.

The output VAT will be due on the earliest of:

– The date the invoice is issued; or

– The 15th of the month following that in which the goods are removed.

As before, Overseas Ltd will be able to reclaim the VAT as input VAT on their next VAT return which will therefore include the following:

Output tax

     On acquisition from Ruritania   £20,000

Input tax

     On acquisition from Ruritania   £20,000

Test your understanding 9

Foreign Ltd

(a) Foreign Ltd will charge VAT at zero rate because it is an EU transaction, and the customer is VAT registered.

(b) The transaction is zero rated as an export outside EU.

(c) The transaction must be charged in the UK at the standard rate as the customer is not VAT registered.

(d) VAT will be paid at point of entry into UK. Foreign Ltd will then recover VAT through the quarterly system.

Questions & Answers

1 The UK tax system

There are no questions for this chapter.

2 Basic income tax computation

There are no questions for this chapter.

3 Property and investment income

Amos Groves

Question 1

Amos Groves owns four houses that he lets out to tenants. Details of the income and expenditure incurred in respect of the houses in the year to 5 April 2013 is as follows:

House 1

Amos purchased this house on 1 June 2012. He immediately undertook repair work to the leaking roof that cost £5,000 and redecorated the house at a cost of £800. The house was rented out, unfurnished, from 1 September 2012 on a six-year lease at an annual rental of £4,500, payable quarterly in advance. The incoming tenant was charged a premium of £2,500.

House 2

This house was let furnished throughout the year at a monthly rent of £650, payable monthly in advance. Amos incurred the following expenditure during the year; water rates £300, council tax £850, property insurance £500, purchase of new cooker £400. He also incurred loan interest of £2,500 on a loan taken out to purchase the property.

Amos claims the wear and tear allowance for this property.

House 3

The tenants left this unfurnished house on 30 November 2012, owing two month's rent totalling £1,000, which Amos was unable to recover. Decoration work was carried out in January 2013 at a cost of £2,500 and advertising costs of £450 were incurred in looking for new tenants. Other allowable costs for the year amounted to £550. The property was re-let on 1 April 2013, again unfurnished, at a monthly rent of £600, payable in advance.

House 4

This house was let out unfurnished to tenants throughout the year at a monthly rent of £450, payable in advance. Amos replaced a broken window at a cost of £100 during the year. The property was insured at a cost of £300 and £400 for the two years ended 30 June 2012 and 2013 respectively. Other allowable costs amounted to £200 for the year.

Other income

Amos received income from a part-time employment of £8,440 during the year to 5 April 2013 from which PAYE of £67 was deducted. In addition he received interest of £500 on a bank deposit account and dividends of £450 from UK quoted companies during the year.

Required:

(a) Calculate Amos' property income assessment for 2012/13.

(11 marks)

(b) Calculate the income tax payable by Amos for 2012/13.

(4 marks)
(Total: 15 marks)

4 Employment income

Mr Drake

Question 1

Mr Drake is employed as the sales director of Drakemain Ltd at a salary of £20,000 p.a.

Details of expenses paid by his employer for the year ended 5 April 2013, are as follows:

	£
Entertainment expenses reimbursed	683
Travelling and subsistence expenses (including £385 rail fares home to office)	826
Gross annual value of company house	650
Medical subscription	409
Home telephone (calls)	160

You are given the following further information.

(1) A petrol driven motor car and private fuel were provided throughout the year, (CO_2 emissions of 156 g/km, list price £21,800). £10 per month is deducted from Mr Drake's net salary to cover his private use of the motor car and £40 per month as rent for the house.

(2) Mr Drake paid the council tax on the company house in the year 2012/13 this amounted to £325.

(3) The telephone installed in the company house is used only 40% for business.

(4) Unless otherwise indicated, all expenses reimbursed to Mr Drake were incurred for business purposes.

(5) The company purchased a TV on 6 April 2011 and allowed Mr Drake the use of it for the whole of the years ended 5 April 2012 and 2013. The set was then given to him on 5 April 2013. The set cost £500 and was worth £150 in April 2013.

Calculate Mr Drake's taxable employment income for 2012/13.

5 Income from self-employment

Peter

Question 1

For the past five years Peter has run a business importing electrical goods from the Far East, which he then sells to wholesalers in the UK.

His statement of profit or loss for the y/e 31 December 2012 shows:

	£	£
Sales revenue		325,000
Less: Cost of goods sold		(172,500)
Gross profit		152,500
Rent received (Note 1)		9,500
		162,000
Wages and salaries	50,200	
Rent and rates (Note 1)	12,900	
Light and heat (Note 1)	5,250	
Depreciation of fixtures and fittings	1,500	
Insurance	3,550	
Travelling and entertaining (Note 2)	10,750	
Impaired debts (Note 3)	6,750	
Depreciation of vehicles	7,500	
Motor car expenses (Note 4)	4,500	
Sundry expenses (Note 5)	750	
Legal and professional charges (Note 6)	4,750	
Interest on bank overdraft	1,500	
Van expenses	9,300	
Telephone	3,350	
Repairs and renewals (Note 7)	3,500	
		(126,050)
Net profit		35,950

Notes:

(1) Rent received

Rent received is in respect of a flat above Peter's business premises that is rented out. Peter estimates that a tenth of the rent and rates, and a seventh of the light and heat expenses relate to the flat.

(2) Travelling and entertaining expenses:

	£
Peter's business travelling expenses	5,175
Christmas presents for staff	250
Entertaining overseas suppliers	2,750
Entertaining UK customers	2,300
Gifts to customers that carry the business name	
Boxes of chocolates costing £5.00 each	125
Calendars costing £1.50 each	150
	10,750

(3) Impaired debts

	£
Trading debts written off	3,750
Increase in allowance for receivables	1,750
Supplier loan written off	1,700
Trade debt recovered (written off last year)	(450)
	6,750

(4) Motor car expenses

	£
Peter's motor car expenses	3,300
Salesman's motor car expenses	1,200
	4,500

Peter's total mileage for the year was 12,000 miles. During the year he drove 2,000 miles on a touring holiday and estimates that the balance of his mileage is 20% private and 80% business.

(5) Sundry expenses

	£
Donation to national charity	50
Donation to local political party	100
Subscription to Chamber of Commerce	25
Wedding gift to a member of staff	45
Peter's squash club subscription	250
Advertising in trade press	280
	___
	750
	___

Peter often uses his squash club as a place to take customers since several of them are keen squash players.

(6) Legal and professional charges

	£
Cost of renewing a 21-year lease on business premises	250
Accountancy	3,050
Debt collection	300
Legal fees in connection with an action by an employee for unfair dismissal	1,150
	_____
	4,750
	_____

Included in Peter's accountancy fee is £950 for taxation services. Of this, £200 is for the normal taxation work involved in submitting accounts to HMRC. The balance is in respect of calculating Peter's capital gains tax liability following the disposal of some shares that he had owned.

(7) Repairs and renewals

	£
Repairs to the office photocopier	175
New printer for the office computer	650
Installation of new central heating for the office	2,200
Decorating the office	475
	_____
	3,500
	_____

(8) During the year ended 31 December 2012 Peter took various electrical goods out of inventory for his own and his family's use without paying for them. These goods cost £450 and would have normally been sold at a mark up of 30%. No adjustments have been recorded in Peter's statement of profit or loss to reflect this.

(9) Peter has a room in his private house that he uses as an office as he often works at home. The allowable amount for the use of the office is £250 and appears to be a fair estimate. Also, Peter makes business calls from his private telephone and he estimates the business use as two fifths. The total of his private telephone calls for the year was £450.

Required:

Calculate Peter's adjusted trading profit (before capital allowances) for the year ended 31 December 2012.

(Total: 15 marks)

6 Capital allowances – plant and machinery

Austin Scuba

Question 1

Austin Scuba commenced business as a self-employed decorator on 1 June 2012.

His tax adjusted trading profits before capital allowances, have been:

Period ended 31 March 2013	£91,000
Year ended 31 March 2014	£115,600

The following capital transactions took place:

		£
15 May 2012	Purchased equipment	9,760
1 June 2012	Purchased a short-life asset	2,400
1 June 2012	Purchased a van	16,500
15 June 2012	Purchased a motor car	15,600
1 May 2013	Sold equipment (original cost £600)	500
12 May 2013	Purchased equipment	20,200
20 August 2013	Purchased furniture	8,020
18 January 2014	Sold the short-life asset	550

KAPLAN PUBLISHING

The motor car purchased on 15 June 2012 is used by Austin, and 15% of the mileage is for business purposes. The car has CO_2 emissions of 138 g/km.

Required:

Compute the adjusted trading profits (after capital allowances) for the two periods of account ended 31 March 2014.

Assume the 2012/13 rules apply throughout.

(Total: 12 marks)

7 Sole traders: Basis of assessment

Rachel

Question 1

Rachel commenced in business as a fashion designer on 1 July 2011, and prepared her first accounts to 30 April 2013. Her profit for the period, adjusted for taxation, was £33,000.

Required:

(a) Calculate the tax adjusted trading profits assessable on Rachel for the first three years of assessment, and the amount of 'overlap profits'.

(7 marks)

(b) State one disadvantage of having 'overlap profits'.

(1 mark)

(c) State how Rachel could have avoided the creation of 'overlap profits', supporting your statement with a relevant example.

(3 marks)
(Total: 11 marks)

Maggie Smith

Question 2

Maggie Smith commenced in business on 1 November 2009 manufacturing ladies clothing. Her tax adjusted trading profits were:

	£
Period to 31 December 2010	32,000
Year ended 31 December 2011	38,000
Year ended 31 December 2012	45,000

Capital allowances were as follows:

	£
Period to 31 December 2010	18,000
Year ended 31 December 2011	15,675
Year ended 31 December 2012	17,550

Required:

Calculate the trading profits assessable on Maggie for the years 2009/10 to 2012/13 inclusive and the amount of any overlap profits.

(Total: 14 marks)

8 Partnerships

Roger, Brigitte and Xavier

Question 1

Roger and Brigitte commenced in business on 1 October 2009 as hotel proprietors, sharing profits equally.

On 1 October 2011 their son Xavier joined the partnership and from that date each of the partners, was entitled to one third, of the profits.

The profits of the partnership adjusted for income tax are:

		£
Period ended	30 June 2010	30,000
Year ended	30 June 2011	45,000
Year ended	30 June 2012	50,000
Year ended	30 June 2013	60,000

Required:

(a) Calculate the assessable profits on each of the partners for all relevant years from 2009/10 to 2013/14.

(7 marks)

(b) State the amount of the overlap profits for each of the partners.

(4 marks)

(Total: 11 marks)

9 Tax adjusted trading losses for individuals

Lucifer

Question 1

Lucifer commenced trading as a second-hand car dealer on 6 April 2010. He had no taxable income prior to 2010/11.

Trading results, adjusted for income tax and capital allowances, were:

		£
Period ended	30 September 2010	(20,000) loss
Year ended	30 September 2011	(10,000) loss
Year ended	30 September 2012	11,000 profit

He received dividend income as follows:

	£
2010/11	3,375 net
2011/12	2,500 net
2012/13	1,800 net

In 2010/11 he had also realised a capital gain (before deducting the annual exempt amount) of £15,000 on the sale of quoted shares.

Required:

(a) State the ways in which the trading losses may be relieved.

(3 marks)

(b) Show how the trading losses can be utilised most effectively by Lucifer, giving your reasoning.

(8 marks)
(Total: 11 marks)

10 Pensions

There are no questions for this chapter.

11 National Insurance

There are no questions for this chapter.

KAPLAN PUBLISHING

12 Tax administration for individuals

Tom Ching

Question 1

Tom has been a self-employed interior designer for a number of years, preparing his accounts to 30 April each year. His income for 2012/13 was as follows:

	£
Tax adjusted trading profit	56,250
Property business income	5,200
Building society interest (net)	2,100
Dividends received from UK companies	3,200

During 2012/13 Tom paid £12,000 into his registered personal pension.

Tom's payments on account for 2012/13 totalled £10,255. Tom has a capital gains tax liability for 2012/13 of £3,000.

Required:

(a) Calculate Tom's income tax and Class 4 NIC payable for 2012/13.

(8 marks)

(b) Calculate Tom's balancing payment for 2012/13 and his payments on account for 2013/14 and state the relevant payment dates.

(2 marks)

(c) State:

  (i) the consequences of Tom not paying the balancing payment for 2012/13 by the due date.

(2 marks)

  (ii) the due date by which Tom should file his tax return for 2012/13 assuming he wishes to file a paper return.

(1 mark)

  (iii) how long Tom should retain his accounting records for the year to 30 April 2012.

(2 marks)

(Total: 15 marks)

13 Computation of gains and tax payable

Lorraine Campbell

Question 1

Lorraine Campbell disposed of the following assets during 2012/13:

(1) On 30 June 2012, Lorraine sold a freehold warehouse for £140,000. The warehouse was purchased on 1 September 2005 for £95,000.

(2) On 30 November 2012, Lorraine sold a motor car for £25,000. The motor car was purchased in November 2006 for £23,500.

(3) On 15 February 2013, Lorraine sold a factory for £320,000. The factory had been purchased on 14 October 1996 for £194,000, and was extended at a cost of £58,000 during March 1999. During May 2001, the roof of the factory was replaced at a cost of £44,000 following a fire. The building was not insured.

Lorraine had incurred legal fees of £3,600 in connection with the purchase of the factory, and £6,200 in connection with the disposal.

Lorraine had always used the factory for business purposes in her trade since it was bought in 1996. The factory is a small insignificant part of her business which she continues to operate.

Lorraine incurred a capital loss of £17,100 during 2010/11 and made a chargeable gain of £11,500 during 2011/12.

Lorraine's taxable income for 2012/13 was £28,000.

Required:

Calculate Lorraine's CGT liability for 2012/13 and advise her by when this should be paid.

Assume that the AEA for 2012/13 applies throughout.

(Total: 15 marks)

14 Computation of gains: special rules

Mr and Mrs Steel

Question 1

Mr and Mrs Steel had the following capital transactions in 2012/13.

Mr Steel

(1) A house, which had been bought for £4,000 on 3 April 1994 and let to tenants thereafter, was sold on 1 July 2012. On 2 April 1995 an extension costing £2,000 was built, and on 12 June 2007 the loft was converted into a bedroom at a cost of £3,000. The net proceeds of sale were £63,250.

(2) Sold a piece of sculpture for £6,500 on 30 August 2012, which he had bought for £5,500 on 31 May 2005.

(3) Sold a one-tenth share in a racehorse on 31 August 2012 for £6,200. The interest had cost £1,340 in November 2002.

(4) Sold a vintage Alfa Romeo motor car for £76,500 on 19 December 2012. The car had cost £17,400 on 31 March 2004. During his period of ownership Steel had never used the car on the road.

Mr Steel's taxable income for 2012/13 was £42,000.

Mrs Steel

(1) Sold a rare Russian icon on 24 July 2012 for £5,600 which had cost £6,300 on 20 June 2005.

(2) Sold three acres out of a 12 acre plot of land on 14 December 2012 for £15,000. The whole plot had been purchased for £4,500 on 15 June 2005. On 14 December 2012 the unsold acres had an agreed market value of £25,000.

(3) Sold a piece of Chinese jade for £11,500 on 1 September 2012. This was purchased at auction in March 1998 for £6,500.

(4) Sold a plot of land for £12,000 on 1 October 2012. Mr Steel acquired the land for £2,000 in April 2005 and gave it to his wife in June 2008.

Mrs Steel has no taxable income in 2012/13.

Required:

Calculate the CGT liability of both Mr Steel and Mrs Steel for 2012/13.

(Total: 20 marks)

15 CGT: Shares and securities for individuals

Jasper

Question 1

Jasper had the following transactions during the year 2012/13:

(1) Sold 2,145 ordinary shares in Carrot plc on 19 November 2012 for net sale proceeds of £8,580.

His previous dealings in these shares were as follows:

July 2005   purchased 1,750 shares for £2,625
May 2006   purchased 200 shares for £640
June 2007   took up 1 for 10 rights issue at £3.40 per share

(2) Sold 400 £1 ordinary shares in Grasp plc for £3,600 on 31 March 2013. Jasper had acquired these Grasp plc shares as a result of a takeover bid by Grasp plc of Cawte plc on 5 December 2012.

Prior to the takeover Jasper had owned 12,000 £1 ordinary shares in Cawte plc, which he had acquired for £15,700 on 3 May 2006.

The terms of the takeover bid were:

– one £1 ordinary share in Grasp plc, plus
– two 10% preference shares in Grasp plc, plus
– 40p in cash

for every £1 ordinary share in Cawte plc.

The quoted prices for Grasp plc shares at 5 December 2012 were:

£1 ordinary shares	350p
10% preference shares	110p

Jasper has never worked for Carrot plc, Grasp plc or Cawte plc.

Required:

Calculate the total chargeable gains arising in 2012/13.

(Total: 10 marks)

16 CGT: Reliefs for individuals

Jack Chan

Question 1

Jack Chan, aged 45, has been in business as a sole trader since 1 May 1997. On 28 February 2013 he transferred the business to his daughter Jill, at which time the following assets were sold to her:

(1) Goodwill with a market value of £60,000. The goodwill has been built up since 1 May 1997, and has a nil cost. Jill paid Jack £50,000 for the goodwill.

(2) A freehold office building with a market value of £130,000. The office building was purchased on 1 July 2007 for £110,000, and has always been used by Jack for business purposes. Jill paid Jack £105,000 for the office building.

(3) A freehold warehouse with a market value of £140,000. The warehouse was purchased on 1 September 2005 for £95,000 and has never been used by Jack for business purposes. Jill paid Jack £135,000 for the warehouse.

(4) A motor car with a market value of £25,000. The car was purchased on 1 November 2007 for £23,500, and has always been used by Jack for business purposes. Jill paid Jack £20,000 for the car.

Jack and Jill have elected to hold over any gains possible.

Jack has unused capital losses of £6,400 brought forward from 2011/12.

Jack has taxable income in 2012/13 of £56,000.

Required:

Calculate Jack's capital gains tax liability for 2012/13, and advise him by when this should be paid.

Ignore Entrepreneurs' relief.   **(Total: 15 marks)**

Sophie

Question 2

During 2012/13 Sophie made the following disposal of assets:

(1) On 1 September 2012 Sophie incorporated her sole trader business that she had run since 2001. All of the assets of the business were transferred, as a going concern, to the new company, Sophie Ltd:

	M.V. at 1 Sept 2012	Cost
	£	£
Goodwill	50,000	Nil
Freehold premises	200,000	80,000
Car	12,000	18,000
Inventory and debtors	60,000	65,000
	322,000	

The goodwill had been built up since 2001. The freehold premises were purchased on 1 February 2001 and have always been used for business purposes. The car was purchased on 15 March 2005.

The consideration paid by Sophie Ltd for the assets transferred consisted of 200,000 £1 ordinary shares valued at £200,000 and £122,000 in cash.

(2) On 1 July 2012 Sophie sold a house for £450,000. Sophie had bought the house on 1 July 2001 for £120,000. She occupied the house as her main residence until 1 February 2004 when she went to live with her mother. The house was left unoccupied until she returned on 30 June 2005. She then lived in the house until 30 June 2006 when she purchased and moved into a new house. The house was left empty until its sale on 1 July 2012.

Sophie has made no other capital disposals during 2012/13.

Sophie's taxable income for 2012/13 was £50,000.

Required:

(a) Assuming that Sophie elects for incorporation relief not to apply, on the transfer of the business to Sophie Ltd, calculate her capital gains tax liability for 2012/13 on the above disposals.

(12 marks)

(b) State the conditions that must be met in order for incorporation relief to be available to Sophie on the transfer of her business.

(3 marks)

(c) Calculate the chargeable gains on the incorporation of Sophie's business if she had taken advantage of incorporation relief, and identify the base cost of the shares.

(5 marks)
(Total: 20 marks)

17 Inheritance tax

Gerry Generous

Question 1

Gerry Generous has made the following gifts during his lifetime. Gerry agreed that he would pay any inheritance tax arising on these gifts.

		Nil rate band
4 June 2004	£331,000 cash gift to a trust.	£263,000
4 March 2006	£10,000 cash as a wedding gift to his son Jack.	£275,000
4 June 2011	A further £100,000 cash gift to the trust.	£325,000

Required:

Explain the IHT implications arising from Gerry's lifetime gifts.

Your answer should include a calculation of any IHT payable, an explanation of any exemptions available and the date the tax is payable.

Martin

Question 2

Martin died on 31 July 2012. At the time of his death, Martin owned the following assets:

(1) 100,000 £1 ordinary shares in ABC plc, a quoted trading company with an issued share capital of 20,000,000 shares. ABC plc's shares were valued at 242.5p for that day.

(2) A holiday cottage valued at £120,000.

(3) Bank and cash balances of £150,000.

(4) Other assets valued for IHT purposes at £208,000.

(5) Martin had a life insurance policy, which provided proceeds of £88,000 to his estate on his death.

Under the terms of his will, Martin left £55,000 in cash to his wife, and the residue of his estate to his daughter.

Martin made no lifetime gifts.

Required:

Calculate the IHT liability arising as a result of Martin's death.

State who will pay the tax due, the due date and who suffers the burden of the tax.

(10 marks)

Jane Macbeth

Question 3

Jane Macbeth, aged 61, died on 20 November 2012. At the date of her death Jane owned the following assets:

(1) A main residence valued at £235,000. This had an outstanding repayment mortgage of £40,000.

(2) Building society deposits of £87,000.

(3) 10,000 £1 ordinary shares (a 4% shareholding) in Banquo plc. On 20 November 2012 the shares were valued at £9.48 per share.

(4) A life assurance policy on her own life. Immediately prior to the date of Jane's death, the policy had an open market value of £86,000. Proceeds of £104,000 were received following her death.

(5) A plot of land valued at £58,000.

Jane made the following gifts during her lifetime (any IHT arising was paid by Jane):

(1) On 28 November 2002 she made a cash gift of £65,000 into a trust.

(2) On 15 April 2006 she made a gift of 50,000 shares (a 2% shareholding) in Shakespeare plc, to her son as a wedding gift. The shares were valued at £71,000.

(3) On 10 March 2007 she made a cash gift of £268,000 into a trust.

Jane's husband Duncan is wealthy in his own right. Under the terms of her will Jane has therefore left a specific gift of £100,000 to her brother, with the residue of the estate being left to her children.

Required:

(a) Calculate the IHT that will be payable as a result of Jane's death.

The nil rate bands for earlier years are as follows:

2002/03	£250,000
2006/07	£285,000

(12 marks)

(b) State who is primarily liable for the tax, the due dates of the IHT liabilities, and the amount of inheritance that will be received by Jane's children.

(3 marks)
(Total: 15 marks)

18 Introduction to corporation tax

There are no questions for this chapter.

19 Taxable total profits

There are no questions for this chapter.

20 Chargeable gains for companies

Earth Ltd

Question 1

Earth Ltd sold the following shareholdings during the year ended 31 March 2013:

(1) On 20 November 2012 Earth Ltd sold 25,000 £1 ordinary shares in Venus plc for £115,000. Earth Ltd had originally purchased 40,000 shares in Venus plc on 19 June 1996 for £34,000. On 11 October 2007 Venus plc made a 1 for 4 bonus issue.

Assume the retail price indices (RPIs) are as follows:

June 1996	153.0
October 2007	208.9
November 2012	247.3

(2) On 22 January 2013 Earth Ltd sold 30,000 £1 ordinary shares in Saturn plc for £52,500. Earth Ltd purchased 30,000 shares in Saturn plc on 9 February 2001 for £97,500. The indexed value of the share pool on 3 January 2013 was £139,901.

On 3 January 2013 Saturn plc made a 1 for 2 rights issue. Earth Ltd took up its allocation under the rights issue in full, paying £1.50 for each new share issued.

(3) On 28 March 2013 Earth Ltd sold its entire holding of £1 ordinary shares in Jupiter plc for £55,000. Earth Ltd had originally purchased 10,000 shares in Mercury plc on 5 May 2004 for £14,000. The indexed value of the share pool on 7 March 2013 was £18,684.

On 7 March 2013 Mercury plc was taken over by Jupiter plc. Earth Ltd received two £1 ordinary shares and one £1 preference share in Jupiter plc for each share held in Mercury plc. Immediately after the takeover £1 ordinary shares in Jupiter plc were quoted at £2.50 and £1 preference shares were quoted at £1.25.

Earth Ltd has never held more than a 1% shareholding in any of the above companies.

Required:

Calculate the chargeable gain or capital loss arising from each of Earth Ltd's disposals during the year ended 31 March 2013.

Each of the three sections of this question carries 5 marks.

(Total: 15 marks)

21 Losses for companies

Alfred Ball

Question 1

Alfred Ball Ltd has the following results:

Year ended 31 December:	2010	2011	2012	2013
	£	£	£	£
Tax adjusted trading profit/(loss)	42,000	19,000	(67,000)	16,000
Bank interest received	3,000	2,000	1,000	2,000
Chargeable gains	4,000	4,000	4,000	4,000
Charitable donations	10,000	10,000	–	2,500

Calculate the taxable total profits, for all of the accounting periods shown above, clearly indicating how you would deal with the trading loss, to obtain relief as soon as possible.

22 Groups of companies

Gold Ltd

Question 1

Gold Ltd owns 100% of the ordinary share capital of Silver Ltd. Gold Ltd has an accounting date of 31 December, whilst Silver Ltd has an accounting date of 30 June.

The results of Gold Ltd are as follows:

Year ended	31.12.11	31.12.12
	£	£
Tax adjusted trading profit	177,000	90,000
Property income	5,000	–
Chargeable gain	–	12,000
Donation to national charity	(2,000)	(2,000)

For the y/e 30 June 2011 Silver Ltd had taxable total profits of £260,000. The company made a tax adjusted trading loss of £140,000 for the y/e 30 June 2012. No information is available regarding the y/e 30 June 2013.

Gold Ltd has no other associated companies.

Required:

(a) Assuming that the maximum possible claim for group relief is made in respect of Silver Ltd's tax adjusted trading loss of £140,000, calculate Gold Ltd's corporation tax liabilities for the year ended 31 December 2011 and the year ended 31 December 2012.

(8 marks)

(b) Explain how loss relief should be allocated within a group of companies in order to maximise the potential benefit of the relief for the group as a whole.

(4 marks)

(c) Based on the information available, advise Silver Ltd of the most beneficial way of relieving its trading loss of £140,000.

(3 marks)
(Total: 15 marks)

Apple Group

Question 2

Apple Ltd owns 100% of the ordinary share capital of Banana Ltd and Cherry Ltd.

The results of each company for the year ended 31 March 2013 are:

	Apple Ltd £	Banana Ltd £	Cherry Ltd £
Tax adjusted trading profit/(loss)	(125,000)	650,000	130,000
Chargeable gain/(loss)	180,000	(8,000)	–

Apple Ltd's chargeable gain arose from the sale of a freehold warehouse on 15 April 2012 for £418,000. Cherry Ltd purchased a freehold office building for £290,000 on 10 January 2013.

Required:

(a) Explain the group relationship that must exist in order that group relief can be claimed.

(3 marks)

(b) Explain how group relief should be allocated between the respective claimant companies in order to maximise the potential benefit obtained from the relief.

(3 marks)

(c) Assuming that reliefs are claimed in the most favourable manner, calculate the corporation tax liabilities of Apple Ltd, Banana Ltd and Cherry Ltd for the y/e 31 March 2013.

(9 marks)
(Total: 15 marks)

23 Overseas issues for companies

There are no questions for this chapter.

24 Tax administration for a company

Ramble Ltd

Question 1

Ramble Ltd's taxable total profits for the two years to 31 March 2012 and 2013 were £2,150,000 and £2,660,667 respectively.

The company filed its tax return for the y/e 31 March 2012 on 15 October 2013 and on the same date made a payment of the tax outstanding.

Ramble Ltd made the following payments on account of its corporation tax liability for the y/e 31 March 2013:

	£
1 May 2013	434,000
1 January 2014	204,560

KAPLAN PUBLISHING

Required:

(a) State the date that the company's self assessment corporation tax return for the y/e 31 March 2012 was due and advise the company of the consequences of filing the return on 15 October 2013.

(3 marks)

(b) State the due date(s) for the payment of the company's corporation tax liability for the y/e 31 March 2013 and advise the company of any late payment interest that will be payable in respect of this year (interest calculations are not required).

Assume that the rates of tax FY2012 continue in the future.

(7 marks)
(Total: 10 marks)

25 VAT: outline

There are no questions for this chapter.

26 VAT: administration

Mary

Question 1

You are provided with the following information for the quarter ended 31 March 2013 relating to your client Mary who is registered for VAT.

Supplies (all VAT-exclusive):

	£
Standard-rated supplies	
– Sales invoices issued by Mary (offers a 2½% discount)	230,000
Zero-rated supplies	50,000
Purchases and expenses	
Standard-rated purchases (excluding VAT)	102,440
Standard-rated expenses (excluding VAT)	18,000
(includes £5,000 for entertaining UK customers)	
Exempt purchases	14,350
Cars (excluding VAT and bought on 1 February 2013)	16,200

Irrecoverable debts of £3,000 (exclusive of VAT) were written off in March 2013 in respect of three separate invoices, each of £1,000 for goods supplied on 1 May 2012, 1 August 2012 and 1 November 2012, payment for which was due on 1 June 2012, 1 September 2012 and 1 December 2012 respectively. These amounts are the discounted amounts.

The car bought on 1 February 2013 was used 60% for business and has CO_2 emissions of 210 g/km. Petrol for both private and business mileage was paid for by the business. The quarterly scale charge figure is £533 (inclusive of VAT).

Required:

Calculate the VAT payable for the quarter ended 31 March 2013 and state when this will be payable to HMRC.

(Total: 11 marks)

Test your understanding answers

Amos Groves

Answer 1 – Chapter 3

(a) **Property business income – y/e 5 April 2013**

	£	£
Rent accruing		
(£2,625 (W1) + £7,800 (W2) + £4,000 (W3) + £5,400 (W4))		19,825
Premium assessable (W1)		2,250
		22,075
Repairs and decorating (£800 + £2,500 + £100)	3,400	
Expenses (£1,650 + £1,000 + £575)	3,225	
Irrecoverable debt	1,000	
Loan interest	2,500	
Wear and tear allowance (W2)	665	
		(10,790)
Property business income		11,285

Workings

(W1) House 1

(i) Rent from 1 September 2012: (£4,500 × 7/12) = £2,625

(ii) Lease premium

	£
Premium	2,500
Less: (6 – 1) × 2% × £2,500	(250)
Assessable premium	2,250

(iii) Roof repairs are not allowable as they were making good a deficiency on purchase, and are therefore capital expenditure.

(W2) **House 2**

(i) Rent: (£650 × 12) = £7,800

(ii) Allowable expenses = (£300 + £850 + £500) = £1,650

(iii) The cooker is capital expenditure and is therefore disallowable

(iv) Wear and tear allowance
= (£7,800 − £300 − £850) × 10% = £665

(W3) **House 3**

(i) Rent from expired lease: (£500 × 8) = £4,000

(ii) Rent from new lease: £Nil

(iii) Taxable on an accruals basis (ignore 5 days in April 2013)

(iv) Allowable expenses = (£450 + £550) = £1,000

(W4) **House 4**

(i) Rent: (£450 × 12) = £5,400

(ii) Insurance for the year to 5 April 2013:
(£300 × 3/12 + £400 × 9/12) = £375

(iii) Allowable expenses = (£375 + £200) = £575

(b) **Amos Groves**
Income tax computation – 2012/13

	Total	Other income	Savings income	Dividend income
	£	£	£	£
Employment income	8,440	8,440		
Property income (part a)	11,285	11,285		
Interest income (£500 × 100/80)	625		625	
Dividend income (£450 × 100/90)	500			500
Total income	20,850	19,725	625	500
Less: PA	(8,105)	(8,105)		
Taxable income	12,745	11,620	625	500

Income tax:	£	£
On other income	11,620 x 20%	2,324
On savings income	625 x 20%	125
On dividend income	500 x 10%	50
	12,745	
Income tax liability		2,499
Less: Tax credits		
Dividend (£500 x 10%)		(50)
PAYE		(67)
Interest (£625 x 20%)		(125)
Income tax payable		2,257

Mr Drake

Answer – Chapter 4
Taxable employment income

	£	£
Salary		20,000
Expenses reimbursed:		
Entertainment expenses	683	
Travelling and subsistence expenses	826	
Telephone	160	
	1,669	
Less: Business element of expenses		
Entertaining	(683)	
Travelling, etc. (other than home to office)	(441)	
Telephone (£160 × 40%)	(64)	
		481
Benefits:		
Annual value of house	650	
Less: Employee contribution	(480)	
		170
Medical subscription		409
Company car (22% x 21,800) (W1)	4,796	
Less: Employee contribution	(120)	
		4,676
Private fuel (22% x £20,200)		4,444
Benefit for use of TV (20% x £500)		100
Benefit for gift of TV (£500 – £100 – £100) (Note)		300
Employment income assessment		30,580

Working

156 g/km	Basic %	11%
	Plus (155 – 100) × 1/5	11%
		22%

Note: Reimbursed entertaining costs are allowable from the viewpoint of Mr Drake. However, the costs will be disallowed in the employer's tax computation.

The council tax is the personal liability of Mr Drake. If his employer met the cost, it would be taxed on Mr Drake as a benefit.

The market value of the TV at the time of the gift is £150, therefore the £300 benefit calculation is used as it is higher.

Peter

Answer 1 – Chapter 5

Adjusted trading profit – y/e 31 December 2012

	£	£
Profit per accounts	35,950	
Rent received		9,500
Wages and salaries	0	
Rent and rates (£12,900 × 1/10)	1,290	
Light and heat (£5,250 × 1/7)	750	
Depreciation of fixtures and fittings	1,500	
Insurance	0	
Business travel expenses	0	
Christmas presents for staff	0	
Entertaining suppliers	2,750	
Entertaining customers	2,300	
Gifts of food	125	
Gifts of calendars	0	
Trading debts written off	0	
Increase in allowances for receivables	0	
Supplier loan written off	1,700	
Trade debt recovered		0
Depreciation of vehicles	7,500	
Private motor expenses (£3,300 × 4,000/12,000)	1,100	
Salesman's motor expense	0	
Donation to national charity	50	
Political donation	100	
Subscription to Chamber of Commerce	0	
Wedding gift to member of staff	0	
Squash club subscription	250	
Advertising in trade press	0	
Cost of renewing 21 year lease	0	
Taxation services re capital gains tax	750	
Debt collection	0	
Legal fees re unfair dismissal of employee	0	
Interest on bank overdraft	0	
Van expenses	0	
Telephone	0	
Repairs to office photocopier	0	
New printer – capital	650	
Central heating – capital	2,200	
Decorating the office	0	
Own consumption (£450 × 130/100)	585	
Use of office		250
Private telephone (£450 × 2/5)		180
	———	———
	59,550	9,930
	(9,930)	———
	———	
Adjusted trading profit (before capital allowances)	49,620	
	———	

Austin Scuba

Answer 1 – Chapter 6

Taxable trading profits

	Adjusted profit before CAs £	Capital allowances (W) £	Tax adjusted trading profits £
10 m/e 31.3.2013	91,000	(22,358)	68,642
y/e 31.3.2014	115,600	(28,168)	87,432

Working: Capital allowances computation

10 m/e 31 March 2013	£	General pool £	Short life asset £	Private use car £	B.U. %	Allowances £
Additions (no AIA or FYA):						
Private use car				15,600		
Additions (eligible for AIA):						
Equipment (Note 1)		9,760	2,400			
Van		16,500				
		26,260				
Less: AIA (Max) (Note 2)		(20,833)	(Nil)			20,833
			5,427			
		5,427	2,400	15,600		
Less: WDA (18% × 10/12)		(814)				814
WDA (18% × 10/12)				(2,340)	× 15%	351
WDA (18% × 10/12)			(360)			360
TWDV c/f		4,613	2,040	13,260		
Total allowances						22,358
y/e 31 March 2014						
Additions (eligible for AIA):						
Equipment		20,200				
Furniture		8,020				
		28,220				
Less: AIA		(25,000)				25,000
		3,220				
Less: Disposal		(500)	(550)			
		7,333	1,490	13,260		
Balancing allowance			(1,490)			1,490
Less: WDA (18%)		(1,320)				1,320
WDA (18%)				(2,387)	× 15%	358
TWDV c/f		6,013	Nil	10,873		
Total allowances						28,168

Notes:
1. Expenditure incurred pre-trading is treated as if incurred on the first day of trading.
2. Maximum AIA for a 10 month period is £20,833 (£25,000 x 10/12). This is allocated to general plant and machinery in preference to the short life asset.

Rachel

Answer 1 – Chapter 7

(a) **Assessable tax adjusted trading profits**

Tax year	Basis period		Assessable profits £
2011/12	(1 July 2011 – 5 April 2012)		
	Actual basis	9/22 × £33,000	13,500
2012/13	(6 April 2012 – 5 April 2013)		
	Actual basis	12/22 × £33,000	18,000
2013/14	(1 May 2012 – 30 April 2013)		
		12/22 × £33,000	18,000

Overlap profits

The profits assessed twice are those for the period 1 May 2012 to 5 April 2013 = (11/22 × £33,000) = £16,500

(b) **Disadvantage of overlap profits**

The disadvantage of overlap profits is that they can only be utilised in the future and will therefore lose value as no allowance is made for the effect of inflation.

(c) **Avoidance of overlap profits**

By choosing an accounting date co-terminous with the tax year it is possible to avoid the creation of 'overlap profits'.

If Rachel had chosen 5 April as her accounting date instead of 30 April the assessments for the first three years would have been based on the following basis periods with a consequent absence of 'overlap profits'.

Tax year	Basis period
2011/12	1.7.11 – 5.4.12
2012/13	6.4.12 – 5.4.13
2013/14	6.4.13 – 5.4.14

Tutorial note

Using a 5 April and not a 30 April year end may make a significant difference to assessable amounts in the year of cessation.

If Rachel ceases on 31 December 2018, for example, her 2018/19 basis period is nine months from 6 April 2018 in the first instance, but is 20 months from 1 May 2017 in the second instance, albeit with 11 months of overlap relief brought forward. In terms of 2018 values, the overlap relief created seven years earlier may not be sufficient to give a 'fair' nine months of assessable profits.

Maggie Smith

Answer 2 – Chapter 7

Tax adjusted trading profit assessments

Tax year	Basis period		Assessable profits £
2009/10	Actual		
	(01.11.09 – 05.04.10)	£14,000 (W) × 5/14	5,000
2010/11	Year ended 31.12.10	£14,000 (W) × 12/14	12,000
2011/12	Year ended 31.12.11	(W)	22,325
2012/13	Year ended 31.12.12	(W)	27,450

Overlap profits (01.01.10 – 05.04.10): (£14,000 × 3/14) = £3,000.

Working: Adjusted profit after capital allowances

	Adjusted profit £	CAs £	Tax adjusted trading profit £
14 m/e 31.12.10	32,000	(18,000)	14,000
Y/e 31.12.11	38,000	(15,675)	22,325
Y/e 31.12.12	45,000	(17,550)	27,450

Roger, Brigitte and Xavier

Answer 1 – Chapter 8

(a) **Assessable profits for each partner**

Profits will be allocated between the partners as follows:

	Total £	Roger £	Brigitte £	Xavier £
9 m/e 30 June 2010	30,000	15,000	15,000	
Y/e 30 June 2011	45,000	22,500	22,500	
Y/e 30 June 2012				
1.7.11 – 30.09.11				
£50,000 × 3/12 (1/2:1/2)	12,500	6,250	6,250	
1.10.11 – 30.6.12				
£50,000 × 9/12 (1/3:1/3:1/3)	37,500	12,500	12,500	12,500
Total	50,000	18,750	18,750	12,500
Y/e 30 June 2013	60,000	20,000	20,000	20,000

Roger and Brigitte will both be assessed on the opening year rules commencing in 2009/10:

Tax year	Basis period	Assessable profits £
2009/10	1.10.09 – 5.4.10: Actual (£15,000 × 6/9)	10,000
2010/11	1.10.09 – 30.9.10: 1st 12 months (£15,000 + (£22,500 × 3/12)	20,625
2011/12	Y/e 30.6.11: CYB	22,500
2012/13	Y/e 30.6.12: CYB	18,750
2013/14	Y/e 30.6.13: CYB	20,000

(iii) Where the loss exceeds the total income for the year, relief may be set off against chargeable gains of the year

Note that the special opening year loss relief option is not available as Lucifer has no taxable income prior to 2010/11.

(b) **Most effective utilisation of the trading loss**

(i) **Calculation of loss**

	£
2010/11 – Actual basis	
6.4.10 to 5.4.11	
Period ended 30.09.10	20,000
Year ended 30.09.11 (01.10.10 – 05.04.11)	
(6/12 × £10,000)	5,000
	25,000

	£
2011/12 – CYB	
Year ended 30.09.11	10,000
Less: Used in 2010/11	(5,000)
	5,000

(ii) **Income tax computations after loss relief**

	2010/11 £	2011/12 £		2012/13 £
Tax adjusted trading profit	Nil	Nil		11,000
Less: Loss relief b/f	–	–	(1)	(6,250)
	–	–	(2)	(4,750)
	Nil	Nil		Nil
Dividends (× 100/90)	3,750	2,778		2,000
Less: Loss relief				
– Current year	(3,750)			
Net income	Nil	2,778		2,000

(iii) **Chargeable gain computation – 2010/11**

	£
Chargeable gain	15,000
Less: Trading loss relief	(15,000)
	Nil

(iv) Explanation of optimum use of loss

Although the method of loss utilisation chosen entails a loss of PAs for 2010/11 it is considered the best of the several options available, as relief can be given against chargeable gains in that year.

There is rarely a guarantee of future profits and in view of the poor trading results it is thought the maximisation of cash flow and claiming relief as early as possible is the critical factor.

The dividend income in 2011/12 is covered by the PA. A claim against total income is not therefore made in this year.

(v) Loss memoranda

2010/11	£
Loss (part (b) (i))	25,000
Less: Used in 2010/11 – Total income	(3,750)
Used in 2010/11 – Chargeable gains	(15,000)
Loss to carry forward	6,250
Less: Used in 2012/13	(6,250)
Loss to carry forward	Nil

2011/12	£
Loss (part (b) (i))	5,000
Less: Used in 2012/13	(4,750)
Loss to carry forward to 2013/14	250

Key answer tips

Loss questions should be answered by following a few simple rules:

*   Firstly, identify the loss of the tax year, and
*   secondly, deal with each loss separately and in chronological order.

The choice is usually to relieve total income in the tax year of loss and/or the previous year.

If there is a chargeable gain, it may be worthwhile making a claim against it.

Any loss remaining must be carried forward.

Tom Ching

Answer 1 – Chapter 12

(a) **Income tax and NIC payable – 2012/13**

	£
Tax adjusted trading profit	56,250
Property business income	5,200
Building society interest (£2,100 × 100/80)	2,625
Dividend income (£3,200 × 100/90)	3,556
Total income	67,631
Less: PA	(8,105)
Taxable income	59,526

Income tax:	£		£
Other income – Basic rate (Note)	49,370	x 20%	9,874
Other income – Higher rate	3,975	x 40%	1,590
	53,345		
Savings income	2,625	x 40%	1,050
Dividends	3,556	x 32.5%	1,156
	59,526		

	£
Income tax liability	13,670
Tax suffered at source	
– Dividends (£3,556 × 10%)	(356)
– BSI (£2,625 × 20%)	(525)
Income tax payable	12,789

	£	
Class 4 NIC		
(£42,475 – £7,605) × 9%	3,138	
(£56,250 – £42,475) × 2%	275	3,413
Total income tax and NIC payable		16,202

Note: The basic rate band is extended by the gross amount of the personal pension contributions of £15,000 (£12,000 × 100/80). The extended basic rate band is therefore £49,370 (£34,370 + £15,000).

(b) Tax payments

(i) Balancing payment – 2012/13

	£
Total income tax and NIC payable	16,202
Capital gains tax liability	3,000
Total tax payable	19,202
Less: POAs	(10,255)
Balancing payment due 31 January 2014	8,947

(ii) Payments on account – 2013/14

POAs for 2013/14 are based on the total income tax and Class 4 NIC liability of the previous tax year:

Total income tax and NIC payable in 2012/13	16,202
POAs for 2013/14:	
– 31 January 2014 (50% × £16,202)	8,101
– 31 July 2014 (50% × £16,202)	8,101

Note that POAs are not required for CGT.

(c) (i) Paying tax late

If Tom does not pay the balancing payment for 2012/13 by the due date, interest will be charged from 31 January 2014 until the date of payment.

In addition, a 5% penalty of £447 (£8,948 at 5%) will be imposed if the balancing payment is not made within 30 days of the due date.

A further 5% penalty will be imposed if the payment has still not been made six months after the due date, and a further 5% if it has still not been made after 12 months.

(ii) **Filing date**

If Tom wishes to submit a paper return he should file his 2012/13 tax return by 31 October 2013.

(iii) **Retention of records**

The accounting records for the year to 30 April 2012 form the basis of the tax return for 2012/13.

Business records should be retained for five years after the normal filing date.

The accounting records for the year to 30 April 2012 should therefore be retained until 31 January 2019 (i.e. 5 years after 31 January 2014).

Lorraine Campbell

Answer 1 – Chapter 13

Capital gains computation – 2012/13

	£	£
Warehouse		
Sale proceeds	140,000	
Less: Cost	(95,000)	
Chargeable gain		45,000
Motor Car		Exempt

	£	
Factory		
Sale proceeds	320,000	
Less: Incidental costs of disposal	(6,200)	
Net sale proceeds	313,800	
Less: Cost	(194,000)	
Incidental costs of acquisition	(3,600)	
Enhancement expenditure	(58,000)	
Chargeable gain (Note)		58,200
Net chargeable gains for the year		103,200
Less: Capital loss b/f (W)		(16,200)
		87,000
Less: Annual exempt amount		(10,600)
Taxable gains		76,400

Capital gains tax

	£	£
Basic rate (£34,370 – £28,000)	6,370 × 18%	1,147
Higher rate	70,030 × 28%	19,608
	76,400	
Capital gains tax liability		20,755
Due date		31.1.2014

Note: The expenditure incurred in May 2001 for replacing the roof does not enhance the cost of the factory and is not an allowable deduction – as it is replacing a roof that was already there!

The factory is an insignificant part of Lorraine's business and the disposal is not associated with the disposal of the entire business. Therefore Entrepreneurs' relief is not applicable (see Chapter 16).

Working: Capital losses

In 2011/12, £900 (£11,500 – £10,600) of the capital loss brought forward is used to reduce that years gains to the level of the AEA.

The remaining capital loss of £16,200 (£17,100 – £900) is available to carry forward to 2012/13.

Mr and Mrs Steel

Answer 1 – Chapter 14

Mr Steel – Capital gains tax computation – 2012/13

House	£	£
Net sale proceeds	63,250	
Less: Cost	(4,000)	
Extension	(2,000)	
Loft	(3,000)	
Chargeable gain		54,250

Sculpture		
Sale proceeds	6,500	
Less: Cost	(5,500)	
Chargeable gain	1,000	
Gain cannot exceed (£6,500 – £6,000) × 5/3	833	833

One tenth interest in racehorse

Exempt as a chattel which is also a wasting asset	Nil

Alfa Romeo vintage car

Cars are exempt assets	Nil

Total chargeable gains	55,083
Less: AEA	(10,600)
Taxable gain	44,483
Capital gains tax (£44,483 x 28%)	12,455

Note: Mr Steel has no basic band remaining in 2012/13, therefore all his gains are taxed at 28%.

Mrs Steel – Capital gains tax computation – 2012/13

	£	£
Icon		
Deemed sale proceeds	6,000	
Less: Cost	(6,300)	
	———	
Allowable loss		(300)
Plot of land		
Sale proceeds (3 acres)	15,000	
Less: Cost (3 acres)		
£4,500 × £15,000/(£15,000 + £25,000)	(1,688)	
	———	
Chargeable gain		13,312
Jade		
Sale proceeds	11,500	
Less: Cost	(6,500)	
	———	
Chargeable gain		5,000
Land		
Disposal proceeds	12,000	
Less: Deemed acquisition cost	(2,000)	
	———	
Chargeable gain		10,000
		———
Net chargeable gains		28,012
Less: AEA		(10,600)
		———
Taxable gain		17,412
		———
Capital gains tax (£17,412 x 18%)		3,134
		———

Note: All of Mrs Steel's gains fall within her basic rate band and are therefore taxed at 18%.

Jasper

Answer 1 – Chapter 15

Total chargeable gains – 2012/13

	£	£
Shares in Carrot plc		
Net sale proceeds	8,580	
Less: Cost (W1)	(3,928)	
		4,652
Takeover		
Cash received (W2)	4,800	
Less: Cost (W2)	(1,030)	
		3,770
Shares in Grasp plc		
Sale proceeds	3,600	
Less: Cost (W2) £9,008 x 400/12,000	(300)	
		3,300
Total chargeable gains		11,722

Workings

(W1) Carrot plc

		Number	Cost £
July 2005	Purchase	1,750	2,625
May 2006	Purchase	200	640
		1,950	3,265
June 2007	Rights issue (1:10) @ £3.40	195	663
		2,145	3,928
November 2012	Sale	(2,145)	(3,928)

(W2) **Grasp plc**

Apportionment of cost of Cawte plc securities to new securities and cash acquired at date of takeover.

	Market value £	Cost allocation £
For 12,000 Cawte plc ord shares:		
12,000 Grasp £1 ord shares at 350p	42,000	9,008
24,000 Grasp 10% pref shares at 110p	26,400	5,662
Cash (12,000 × 40p)	4,800	1,030
	_____	_____
	73,200	15,700
	_____	_____

KAPLAN PUBLISHING

Jack Chan

Answer 1 – Chapter 16

CGT computation – 2012/13

	£	£
Goodwill		
Market value (Note 1)	60,000	
Less: Cost	(Nil)	
	60,000	
Less: Gift relief (£60,000 – £50,000) (Note 2)	(10,000)	
		50,000
Freehold office building		
Market value	130,000	
Less: Cost	(110,000)	
	20,000	
Less: Gift relief (Note 3)	(20,000)	
		Nil
Freehold warehouse (Note 4)		
Market value	140,000	
Less: Cost	(95,000)	
		45,000
Motor cars (Note 5)		Nil
Net chargeable gains for the tax year		95,000
Less: Capital loss brought forward		(6,400)
		88,600
Less: Annual exempt amount		(10,600)
Taxable gains		78,000
		£
Capital gains tax (£78,000 x 28%) (Note 6 and 7)		21,840
Due date for CGT liability		31 January 2014

Notes:

(1) Jack and Jill are connected persons, and therefore the market values of the assets sold are used.

(2) The consideration paid for the goodwill exceeds the original cost by £50,000 (£50,000 – Nil). This amount is immediately chargeable to CGT.

(3) The consideration paid for the office building does not exceed the original cost, so full gift relief is available. Gift relief is not restricted.

(4) The warehouse does not qualify for gift relief as it has never been used for business purposes.

(5) Motor cars are exempt from CGT.

(6) Jack does not have any basic rate band remaining, therefore all his gains are taxed at 28%.

(7) The gain on the goodwill left after gift relief would also qualify for Entrepreneurs' relief as the whole of the business is disposed of. Therefore £50,000 of the gain should be taxed at 10% and the remaining £28,000 relating to the warehouse is taxed at 28%. However, the question says that Entrepreneurs' relief should be ignored.

Sophie

Answer 2 – Chapter 16

(a) **Sophie – Capital gains computation – 2012/13**

	£	£
Not qualifying for Entrepreneurs' relief		
Sale of house (W1)	90,000	
Qualifying for Entrepreneurs' relief		
Sale of trading business:		
Freehold premises (£200,000 – £80,000)		120,000
Goodwill (£50,000 – £Nil)		50,000
	90,000	170,000
Less: Annual exempt amount (Note 3)	(10,600)	(Nil)
Taxable gains	79,400	170,000

Capital gains tax:		
Qualifying gains	(£170,000 x 10%)	17,000
Non-qualifying gains	(£79,400 x 28%)	22,232
		39,232

Note: The non-qualifying gains are taxed at 28% as Sophie is a higher rate taxpayer.

Workings

(W1) Sale of house

	£
Sale proceeds	450,000
Less: Acquisition cost	(120,000)
	330,000
Less: PPR exemption	
(£330,000 x (96/132)) (W2)	(240,000)
Chargeable gain	90,000

(W2) PPR relief

	Total	Exempt	Chargeable
1.7.01 – 31.1.04	31		
Actual occupation		31	
1.2.04 – 30.6.05	17		
Part of 3 years for any reason		17	
1.7.05 – 30.6.06	12		
Actual occupation		12	
1.7.06 – 30.6.12	72		
Last 3 years		36	
Rest of period – chargeable			36
Number of months	132	96	36

Notes:

(1) The period spent living with her mother is deemed occupation, being part of the three years absence for any reason, as Sophie lived in the property both before and after the period of absence.

(2) The last three years of ownership represents a deemed period of occupation, even if the owner has elected for another property to be treated as his PPR in the same period.

(3) The remaining 36 month period of absence does not qualify as deemed occupation as the property was not reoccupied after the period of absence.

(b) **Incorporation relief**

Incorporation relief is available where the following conditions apply:

– The unincorporated business is transferred as a going concern.

– All of the assets of the business (other than cash) are transferred.

– The consideration for the transfer of the business must be wholly or mainly shares in the company.

(c) Effect of incorporation relief

Incorporation relief operates such that the gains arising on the deemed disposal of the individual assets are rolled over against the acquisition cost of the shares in the new company.

However where part of the consideration for the transfer of the business is not shares (e.g. cash), the gain eligible for relief is:

$$\text{Net chargeable gains} \times \frac{\text{Value of shares issued}}{\text{Total consideration}}$$

Therefore if Sophie had taken advantage of incorporation relief part of the gain would have been rolled over against the base cost of the shares in Sophie Ltd and would not have been chargeable in 2012/13.

The chargeable gains on incorporation would be:

	£
Total capital gains on incorporation	170,000
Less: Incorporation relief	
£170,000 x (£200,000/£322,000)	(105,590)
Chargeable gain after incorporation relief	64,410

This gain would be taxed at 10% as it would also qualify for Entrepreneurs' relief.

	£
Base cost of shares:	
Market value	200,000
Less: Incorporation relief	(105,590)
	94,410

Gerry Generous

Answer 1 – Chapter 17

IHT payable during lifetime

	CLT 4.6.2004		PET 4.3.2006		CLT 4.6.2011	
	£		£		£	
Transfer of value		331,000		10,000		100,000
Less: Marriage exemption				(5,000)		
Less: Annual exemption						
Current year	2004/05 b/f	(3,000)	2005/06	(3,000)	2011/12	(3,000)
Previous year	2003/04 b/f	(3,000)	2004/05 b/f	(Nil)	2010/11 b/f	(3,000)
Chargeable amount		325,000		2,000		94,000
	Net	£	Net		Net	£
NRB @ date of gift						
– 2004/05		263,000				
– 2011/12						325,000
Less: GCTs < 7 years before gift						
(4.6.1997 – 4.6.2004)		(Nil)				
(4.6.2004 – 4.6.2011) (ignore PET)						(340,500)
NRB available		(263,000)		Nil		(Nil)
Taxable amount		62,000				94,000
IHT payable	@ 25%	15,500		Nil	@ 25%	23,500
Paid by		Gerry				Gerry
Due date of payment		30.4.2005				30.4.2012
Gross chargeable amount c/f	(£325,000 net + £15,500 tax)	340,500		2,000	(£94,000 net + £23,500 tax)	117,500

Notes:

1   No further IHT will be due in respect of the first CLT as Gerry will have survived the gift by more than 7 years.

2   The wedding gift to Jack is a PET. There is no IHT payable during Gerry's lifetime and providing Gerry survives until 4 March 2013, no IHT will arise in relation to this gift at all. However, if Gerry dies before 4 March 2013, the PET will become chargeable. The £2,000 chargeable amount will be liable at 40%, but taper relief will reduce the IHT by 20% per annum if Gerry survives for more than three years.

3   Should Gerry die before 4 June 2018, additional IHT at death rates of 40% may become payable on the last CLT. Taper relief may be available and the lifetime tax paid is an allowable deduction.

Martin

Answer 2 – Chapter 17

Estate computation – Death on 31 July 2012

	£	£
Shares in ABC plc (100,000 × 242.5p)		242,500
Insurance policy proceeds		88,000
Holiday cottage		120,000
Bank and cash balances		150,000
Other assets		208,000
		————
		808,500
Less: Exempt legacy – wife		(55,000)
		————
Gross chargeable estate		753,500
NRB at death	325,000	
Less: GCTs in 7 yrs pre-death (31.7.05 – 31.7.12)	(Nil)	
	————	
NRB available		(325,000)
		————
Taxable amount		428,500
		————
IHT due on death (£428,500 x 40%)		171,400
		————

The tax is payable by the executors of Martin's estate, and is due by 31 January 2013 or on submission of the estate accounts to HMRC if earlier.

The tax will be paid out of the estate and is therefore borne by Martin's daughter, who inherited the residue of the estate.

Jane Macbeth

Answer 3 – Chapter 17

Jane Macbeth

(a) IHT payable during lifetime

		CLT 28.11.2002 £	PET 15.4.2006 £	CLT 10.3.2007 £
Transfer of value		65,000	71,000	268,000
Less: Marriage exemption			(5,000)	
Less: Annual exemption				
Current year	2002/03 / 2006/07 / 2006/07	(3,000)	(3,000)	(Nil)
Previous year	2001/02 b/f / 2005/06 b/f / 2005/06 b/f	(3,000)	(3,000)	(Nil)
Chargeable amount		59,000	60,000	268,000
		£		£
NRB @ date of gift				
– 2002/03	Net	250,000		
– 2006/07	Net			285,000
Less: GCTs < 7 years before gift				
(28.11.1995 – 28.11.2002)		(Nil)		
(10.3.2000 – 10.3.2007) (ignore PET)				(59,000)
NRB available		(250,000)		(226,000)
Taxable amount		Nil	Nil	42,000
IHT payable		Nil	Nil	@ 25% 10,500
Paid by				Jane
Due date of payment				30.9.07
Gross chargeable amount		59,000	60,000	278,500
		(£59,000 net + £Nil tax)		(£268,000 net + £10,500 tax)

IHT payable on death

Date of death: 20 November 2012
7 years before: 20 November 2005

CLT on 28.11.2002 is more than 7 years before death – therefore no IHT payable on death

	PET 15.4.2006		CLT 10.3.2007	
	£	£	£	£
Gross chargeable amount b/f (as above)		60,000		278,500
NRB @ date of death – 2012/13	325,000		325,000	
Less: GCTs < 7 years before gift				
(15.4.1999 – 15.4.2006)	(59,000)			
(10.3.2000 – 10.3.2007) (£59,000 + £60,000)			(119,000)	
(include 15.4.2006 PET as it became chargeable)				
NRB available		(266,000)		(206,000)
Taxable amount		Nil		72,500
IHT payable @ 40%		Nil		29,000
Less: Taper relief				
(10.3.2007 – 20.11.2012) (5 –6 years before death)			(60%)	(17,400)
Less: IHT paid in lifetime		(Nil)		(10,500)
IHT payable on death		Nil		1,100
Paid by (always the donee)				Trustees
Due date of payment				31.5.2013

IHT on Estate at death – 20 November 2012

	£	£
Main residence		235,000
Mortgage		(40,000)
		―――――
		195,000
Building society deposits		87,000
Ordinary shares in Banquo plc (10,000 × £9.48)		94,800
Life assurance policy		104,000
Land		58,000
		―――――
Gross chargeable estate		538,800
NRB at death	325,000	
Less: GCTs in 7 yrs pre-death (20.11.05 – 20.11.12) (£60,000 + £278,500) (first gift is too old, Include PET as chargeable on death)	(338,500)	
	―――――	
NRB available		(Nil)
		―――――
Taxable amount		538,800
		―――――
IHT due on death (£538,800 x 40%)		215,520
		―――――

(b) **Payment of IHT liability**

The additional IHT in respect of the gift made on 10 March 2007 is payable by the trustees of the trust by 31 May 2013.

The IHT liability of the estate will (in practice) be payable by the executors of Jane's estate on the earlier of 31 May 2013 or the delivery of their account.

Inheritance received by Jane's children

Jane's children will inherit £223,280 (W).

Working:

Inheritance to children

	£
Chargeable estate	538,800
Less: Specific gift to brother	(100,000)
IHT payable on the estate (Note)	(215,520)
Estate value to be shared between the children	223,280

Note: The IHT payable on the whole estate comes out of the residue of the estate and is therefore borne by the residual legatees (i.e. the children). This is because specific gifts of UK property (e.g. £100,000 to the brother) do not normally carry their own tax.

Earth Ltd

Answer 1 – Chapter 20

(1) **Venus plc – sale of 25,000 shares**

	£
Sale proceeds	115,000
Less: Cost (W)	(17,000)
Unindexed gain	98,000
Less: IA (£27,478 – £17,000) (W)	(10,478)
Chargeable gain	87,522

Share pool	Number	Cost £	Indexed cost £
Purchase – June 1996	40,000	34,000	34,000
Bonus issue – October 2007			
(40,000 × ¼)	10,000	Nil	Nil
	50,000	34,000	34,000
Indexation to November 2012			
£34,000 × (247.3 – 153.0)/153.0			20,956
	50,000	34,000	54,956
Disposal – November 2012			
Cost/Indexed cost× (25,000/50,000)	(25,000)	(17,000)	(27,478)
Balance c/f	25,000	17,000	27,478

(2) **Saturn plc**

	£
Sale proceeds	52,500
Less: Cost (W)	(80,000)
Allowable capital loss	(27,500)

Share pool	Number	Cost £	Indexed cost £
3 January 2013	30,000	97,500	139,901
Rights issue (1 : 2) @ £1.50	15,000	22,500	22,500
	45,000	120,000	162,401
Disposal – 22 January 2013	(30,000)	(80,000)	(108,267)
Balance c/f	15,000	40,000	54,134

Note: Indexation cannot be used to increase a capital loss.

(3) Jupiter plc

	£
Sale proceeds	55,000
Less: Cost	(11,200)
Unindexed gain	43,800
Less: IA (£14,947 – £11,200)	(3,747)
Chargeable gain	40,053

Share pool	Number	Cost £	Indexed cost £
7 March 2013	10,000	14,000	18,684

Takeover consideration	Value £
20,000 Ordinary shares @ £2.50	50,000
10,000 Preference shares @ £1.25	12,500
	62,500

Allocation of cost and Indexed cost

	Cost £	Indexed cost £
Ordinary shares		
(50,000/62,500) × £14,000/£18,684	11,200	14,947
Preference shares		
(12,500/62,500) × £14,000/£18,684	2,800	3,737
	14,000	18,684

Alfred Ball

Answer 1 – Chapter 21

Alfred Ball Ltd

Year ended 31 December	2010 £	2011 £	2012 £	2013 £
Tax adjusted trading profit	42,000	19,000	Nil	16,000
Less: Trading loss b/f	–	–	–	(16,000)
				Nil
Interest income	3,000	2,000	1,000	2,000
Chargeable gains	4,000	4,000	4,000	4,000
Total profits	49,000	25,000	5,000	6,000
Less: Loss relief				
– Current year			(5,000)	
– 12 month carry back		(25,000)		
	49,000	Nil	Nil	6,000
Less: QCD relief (Note)	(10,000)	Wasted	–	(2,500)
Taxable total profits	39,000	Nil	Nil	3,500

Loss memorandum

	£
Loss in y/e 31 December 2012	67,000
Less: Used in current year – y/e 31.12.12	(5,000)
Used in 12 month carry back – y/e 31.12.11	(25,000)
Loss carried forward	37,000
Less: Used in y/e 31.12.13	(16,000)
Loss carried forward at 31.12.13	21,000

Notes:

(1) The QCD of £10,000 paid in the y/e 31 December 2011 is wasted. Note that the amount of the loss off-set cannot be restricted to leave sufficient profits to be covered by the QCD.

(2) The unrelieved loss of £37,000 as at 31 December 2012 is automatically carried forward for off-set against the first available future trading profits of the same trade. Therefore, £16,000 will be used against profits in the y/e 31 December 2013.

Gold Ltd

Answer 1 – Chapter 22

(a) Gold Ltd – Corporation tax liabilities

Year ended	31.12.11	31.12.12
	£	£
Tax adjusted trading profit	177,000	90,000
Property income	5,000	–
Chargeable gain	–	12,000
Total profits	182,000	102,000
Less: QCD relief	(2,000)	(2,000)
	180,000	100,000
Less: Group relief	(70,000)	(50,000)
TTP	110,000	50,000
Corporation tax liability		
FY2010 (£110,000 x 21% x 3/12)	5,775	
FY2011 (£110,000 x 20% x 9/12)	16,500	
FY2011/2012 (£50,000 x 20%)		10,000
	22,275	10,000

Notes:

(1) The CAPs are not coterminous, so both Gold Ltd's taxable total profits and Silver Ltd's tax adjusted trading loss must be time apportioned.

(2) For the y/e 31 December 2011 group relief is the lower of Gold Ltd's available profits of £90,000 (£180,000 × 6/12) and Silver Ltd's available loss of £70,000 (£140,000 × 6/12).

(3) For the y/e 31 December 2012 group relief is the lower of Gold Ltd's available profits of £50,000 (£100,000 × 6/12) and Silver Ltd's available loss of £70,000 (£140,000 × 6/12).

(4) Gold Ltd has one associated company so the small profits rate lower limit is £150,000 (£300,000 x 1/2).

(5) The y/e 31 December 2011 straddles 31 March 2011. Therefore, a two-part corporation tax liability computation is required.

The y/e 31 December 2012 straddles 31 March 2012. However, as there is no change of rate of tax, only one corporation tax liability computation is required.

(b) **Maximising benefit of group relief**

- Relief should initially be claimed against profits subject to corporation tax at the marginal rate of 27.5% or 25% and then profits subject to the main rate of 26% or 24%.

- Where group relief is concerned, the amount surrendered should be sufficient to bring the claimant company's profits down to the small profits rate lower limit.

- Any remaining loss should be claimed against profits subject to corporation tax at the small profits rate of 20%.

- Consideration should also be given to the timing of the relief obtained (an earlier loss relief claim is generally preferable), and the extent to which QCD relief will be lost if loss relief is carried back.

(c) **Most beneficial way to relieve Silver Ltd's trading loss**

- The group relief claim for the y/e 31 December 2011 should be restricted to £30,000 so that Gold Ltd's profits are reduced to exactly £150,000 (£180,000 – £30,000) and relief is obtained for the loss at the marginal rate.

- No group relief claim should be made for the y/e 31 December 2012 since Gold Ltd's profits are already below the small profits rate lower limit and the losses are therefore only being relieved at the small profits rate.

- The remaining £110,000 (£140,000 – £30,000) of the loss should be carried back to the y/e 30 June 2011 in order to reduce Silver Ltd's profits to £150,000 (£260,000 – £110,000), hence obtaining relief at the marginal rate.

Apple Group

Answer 2 – Chapter 22

(a) **Group relationship – Group relief**

One company must be a 75% subsidiary of the other, or both companies must be 75% subsidiaries of the holding company.

The holding company must have an effective interest of at least 75% of the subsidiary's ordinary share capital.

The holding company must have the right to receive at least 75% of the subsidiary's distributable profits and net assets (were it to be wound up).

(b) **Allocation of group relief**

Surrender should be made initially to companies subject to corporation tax at the small profits marginal rate of 25%.

Surrender should then be to those companies subject to the main rate of corporation tax of 24%.

The amount surrendered should be sufficient to bring the claimant company's taxable total profits down to the small profits rate limit.

(c) Corporation tax liabilities – y/e 31 March 2013

	Apple Ltd £	Banana Ltd £	Cherry Ltd £
Tax adjusted trading profit	–	650,000	130,000
Chargeable gain	120,000	–	–
Total profits	120,000	650,000	130,000
Less: Loss relief			
– Current year	(20,000)		
Less: Group relief		(75,000)	(30,000)
TTP	100,000	575,000	100,000
CT @ 20%/24%/20%	20,000	138,000	20,000

Apple Ltd has two associated companies, so the relevant lower and upper limits for corporation tax purposes are £100,000 (£300,000 x 1/3) and £500,000 (£1,500,000 x 1/3) respectively.

Some of Apple Ltd's chargeable gain can be rolled over against the reinvestment by Cherry Ltd. The proceeds not reinvested of £128,000 (£418,000 – £290,000) remain chargeable in the year ended 31 March 2013. The balance can be deferred.

Banana Ltd and Apple Ltd should make a joint election to transfer the capital loss realised by Banana Ltd to Apple Ltd to be set against Apple Ltd's gain.

Net chargeable gain = (£128,000 – £8,000) = £120,000.

Apple Ltd's tax adjusted trading loss is relieved so as to reduce both its own and Cherry Ltd's profits down to the small profits rate limit. The balance of the loss is surrendered to Banana Ltd.

The order of the claims to use the losses would be as follows:

(1) Group relief to Cherry Ltd of £30,000.

(2) Group relief to Banana Ltd of £75,000.

(3) Current year relief against total profits of Apple Ltd of £20,000.

Remember that a current year claim against total profits is an all or nothing claim. So, in order to just leave £20,000 of losses to be relieved in Apple Ltd in the current year, the group relief claims must be made first.

Ramble Ltd

Answer 1 – Chapter 24

(a) **Self-assessment tax return**

Ramble Ltd's self assessment corporation tax return for the y/e 31 March 2012 was due by 31 March 2013.

As the company did not submit the return until 15 October 2013 there will be a late filing penalty of £200 as the return was submitted more than three months late.

As a payment of tax was also made on 15 October 2013 there will also be a tax-geared penalty of 10% of the tax unpaid more than six months after the filing date.

(b) **Corporation tax payments**

Ramble Ltd's TTP for the y/e 31 March 2013 exceed £1,500,000. It will therefore pay corporation tax at the main rate and is a large company for the purposes of paying its corporation tax liability. The company is therefore required to pay by quarterly instalments as follows:

– 14 October 2012 (month 7) (£2,660,667 × 24% × 1/4) £159,640
– 14 January 2013   £159,640
– 14 April 2013   £159,640
– 14 July 2013   £159,640

Interest will be due on the late payment of corporation tax as follows:

– £159,640   – from 14 October 2012 to 30 April 2013
– £159,640   – from 14 January 2013 to 30 April 2013
– £114,720   – from 14 April 2013 to 30 April 2013
– £44,920 (W) – from 14 April 2013 to 31 December 2013
– £159,640   – from 14 July 2013 to 31 December 2013

Working: underpayment

	£
Outstanding payments (3 × £159,640)	478,920
Less: Payment on 1 May 2013	(434,000)
Underpayment	44,920

Mary

Answer 1 – Chapter 26

VAT return – quarter ended 31 March 2013

Output tax £

Standard-rated supplies (£230,000 x 97½%) = £224,250

(20% × £224,250) (net of discount sales)   44,850

Zero-rated sales (0% × £50,000)   Nil

Car fuel charge (2/3 × £533 × 1/6)   59

    ———

    44,909

Input tax

Standard-rated purchases (£102,440 @ 20%)   (20,488)

Standard-rated expenses (£18,000 – £5,000) @ 20%   (2,600)

Relief for impaired debts (£1,000 + £1,000) @ 20% (Note)   (400)

    ———

VAT payable   21,421

    ———

Due and payable date is 7 May 2013
(filed and paid electronically)

Notes:

The car was bought on 1 February 2013 – therefore, in this quarter there are only two months of private use. The scale rates are VAT inclusive amounts, therefore the VAT element is (20/120) or (1/6).

Relief for impaired debts is available for the sales invoice issued on 1 May 2012 and 1 August 2012 as:

- the payment for these invoices was due on 1 June 2012 and 1 September 2012

- the debts are written off, and

- more than six months overdue.

Relief is given on the discounted amounts. Relief for the VAT suffered on the debts will be given at the rate at which it was originally paid (i.e. 20% in this case). Relief for the invoice issued on 1 November 2012, the payment for which was due on 1 December 2012 is not available in this quarter as the debt is not over six months old.

Index

Index

Index

Index

Index

W

Z

Index